TEXT-SUPPORTING W[...]

SOUTH-WESTER[...] [...]E CENTER

A unique, rich, and robust online [...] r finance students, http://finance.swlearning.com provides customer service and product information, learning tips and tools, access to all of South-Western's text-supporting Web sites, and other cutting-edge educational resources such as our highly regarded NewsWire: Finance in the News, Finance Interactive, NewsEdge, Investment Analysis Calculator, FinanceLinks Online, and TextChoice: Finance Online Case Library.

MOYER / McGUIGAN / RAO SUPPORT WEB SITE

The Moyer / McGuigan / Rao Web site, http://moyer.swlearning.com, provides you with open access to online quizzes with immediate student feedback, the opportunity to communicate with us, direct links to all the Internet addresses and activities mentioned in the text, downloadable learning support tools, and much more.

DON'T THROW THIS CARD AWAY!
THIS MAY BE REQUIRED FOR YOUR COURSE!

6 MONTHS ACCESS FREE WITH THIS TEXT!

THOMSON ONE Business School Edition

Congratulations!

Your purchase of this NEW textbook includes complimentary access to Thomson ONE – Business School Edition for Finance. Thomson ONE – Business School Edition is a Web-based portal product that provides integrated access to Thomson Financial content for the purpose of financial analysis. This is an educational version of the same financial resources used by Wall Street analysts on a daily basis!

For hundreds of companies, this online resource provides seamless access to:

- **Current and Past Company Data:** Worldscope which includes company profiles, financials and accounting results, market per-share data, annual information, and monthly prices going back to 1980.

- **Financial Analyst Data and Forecasts:** I/B/E/S Consensus Estimates which provides consensus estimates, analyst-by-analyst earnings coverage, and analysts' forecasts.

- **SEC Disclosure Statements:** Disclosure SEC Database which includes company profiles, annual and quarterly company financials, pricing information, and earnings.

- **And More!**

THOMSON SOUTH-WESTERN

THOMSON ONE Business School Edition

SERIAL NUMBER

SC-0006M9MQ-TAFN

HOW TO REGISTER YOUR SERIAL NUMBER

1. Launch a web browser and go to **http://tobsefin.swlearning.com**

2. Click the "Register" button to enter your serial number.

3. Enter your serial number **exactly** as it appears here and create a unique User ID, or enter an existing User ID if you have previously registered for a different South-Western product via a serial number.

4. When prompted, create a password (or enter an existing password, if you have previously registered for a different product via a serial number). Submit the necessary information when prompted **Record your User ID and password in a secure location.**

5. Once registered, return to the URL above and select the "Enter" button; have your User ID and password handy.

Note: The duration of your access to the product begins when registration is complete.

For technical support, contact 1-800-423-0563 or email **tl.support@thomson.com**

CONTEMPORARY FINANCIAL MANAGEMENT FUNDAMENTALS

R. CHARLES MOYER
Wake Forest University

JAMES R. McGUIGAN
JRM Investments

Ramesh P. Rao
Oklahoma State University

THOMSON

SOUTH-WESTERN

Australia · Canada · Mexico · Singapore · Spain · United Kingdom · United States

Contemporary Financial Management Fundamentals, 1e

R. Charles Moyer, James R. McGuigan, and Ramesh P. Rao

VP/Editorial Director:
Jack W. Calhoun

VP/Editor-in-Chief:
Michael P. Roche

Executive Editor:
Mike Reynolds

Senior Developmental Editor:
Susanna C. Smart

Production Editor:
Chris Hudson

Media Technology Editor:
Vicky True

Media Developmental Editor:
John Barans

Media Production Editor:
Mark Sears

Manufacturing Coordinator:
Sandee Milewski

Production House:
Pre-Press Company, Inc.

Printer:
R.R. Donnelley
Willard, Ohio

Design Project Manager:
Tippy McIntosh

Cover and Internal Designer:
Tippy McIntosh

Cover Images:
Adobe Image Library

To Sally, Craig, and Laura
RCM

To the memory of my mother and father
JRM

To Uma, Anil, and Nikhil
RPR

ABOUT THE AUTHORS

R. Charles Moyer

R. Charles Moyer is Dean Emeritus, and holds the GMAC Insurance Chair in Finance, at the Babcock Graduate School of Management, Wake Forest University. He earned his B.A. in Economics from Howard University, and his M.B.A. and Ph.D. in Finance and Managerial Economics from the University of Pittsburgh. Professor Moyer is coauthor of *Contemporary Financial Management,* 9th edition (South-Western, 2003) and *Managerial Economics,* 10th edition (South-Western, 2005) and has been published in many leading journals—including *Financial Management, Journal of Financial and Quantitative Analysis, Journal of Finance, Strategic Management Journal,* and many others. He has considerable international teaching experience including in France, Germany, and Russia.

James R. McGuigan

James R. McGuigan owns and operates his own numismatic investment firm. Prior to this, he was Associate Professor of Finance and Business Economics in the School of Business Administration at Wayne State University. Professor McGuigan received his undergraduate degree from Carnegie-Mellon University, his M.B.A. from the Graduate School of Business at the University of Chicago, and his Ph.D. from the University of Pittsburgh. In addition to his interests in finance, he has also coauthored books including *Managerial Economics,* 10th edition (South-Western, 2005) and *Contemporary Financial Management*, 9th edition (South-Western, 2003).

Ramesh P. Rao

Ramesh P. Rao is a professor and Paul C. Wise Chair of Finance in Oklahoma State University's College of Business Administration, and earned his B.S. at the University of the Philippines, M.B.A. from the Asian Institute of Management, and Ph.D. from Texas Tech University. He was the recipient of the Merrick Foundation Teaching Award, MBA Outstanding Faculty Award, COBA research award, a college nominee for the Barney E. Rushing Faculty Distinguished Research Award, and a Visiting Fellow at Massey University in New Zealand. He has coauthored more than 40 journal articles in publications such as *Journal of Business, Journal of Finance, Financial Management, Journal of Empirical Finance, Journal of Financial Research, Managerial and Decision Economics,* and *Financial Review.*

BRIEF CONTENTS

CONTENTS

PART FIVE: FINANCIAL PLANNING, WORKING CAPITAL MANAGEMENT, AND INTERNATIONAL FINANCE   425

Contemporary Financial Management Fundamentals (CFM Fundamentals) was written with one goal in mind—making financial management concepts and techniques accessible to the undergraduate student whose only course in finance may be the one based on this book. Most instructors consider the task of teaching the undergraduate introductory course in finance to be a daunting one. In part this is because students come from varying backgrounds, and not all of them are or will become finance majors. With that as a backdrop, we have set out to write a book that conveys the essence of finance without being overbearing on the theoretical and quantitative aspects of the subject matter. We accomplish our goal in several ways.

Throughout the book we emphasize intuition over rigorous theory in explaining difficult concepts. For example, in developing the concept of portfolio risk we rely on an entirely intuitive approach using real data to introduce the notions of systematic and unsystematic risk. We forsake theoretical and quantitative rigor in favor of a more intuitive approach that students can easily relate to. However, where necessary we do emphasize the quantitative aspects of financial problem solving, such as in time value of money problems, securities valuation, and capital budgeting analysis. In developing the quantitative aspects of financial problem solving, we are careful to highlight the application aspects (as opposed to the derivation) of the models used in financial decision making.

To keep the student engaged, where possible we use real data to explain concepts and solve problems. For example, the chapters on statement analysis and ratio analysis (Chapters 3 and 4) are based on the financial statements of Furniture Brands International, a manufacturer of brand name household furniture including Broyhill, Lane, and Thomasville. From experience students tend to be much more motivated to learn if they can relate to the material, and one way to accomplish that is to illustrate concepts and applications based on companies they are familiar with. The use of real data also figures prominently in the chapters on risk and return, securities valuation, and cost of capital estimation (Chapters 6, 7, 8, and 11).

The topics covered and the limited number of chapters in the book (18) also reflect the target audience for the book. We have omitted chapters devoted to specialized topics such as mergers and acquisitions, options, bankruptcy, leasing, and investment banking. We feel that these topics are best left to more advanced courses in finance. Our objective was to develop a book for a course on basic principles in financial management that can be covered in one semester. This is in keeping with the core requirement of one financial management class in most undergraduate business programs.

While the book is written with the undergraduate student in mind, it is also suitable for an introductory graduate course in financial management for students who come from a non-business undergraduate program or who have not had a prior course in financial management. The book is also suitable for management development programs and as a reference aid to the professional or layperson with an interest in finance. The book is designed for use in a three-semester-hour course in financial management.

ORGANIZATION

CFM Fundamentals is organized into five major parts. Part I defines the finance function, examines the goals of the firm, considers the role of the financial manager, reviews the structure and functioning of the financial marketplace, and reviews financial statements fundamentals, including the analysis of financial performance. It also introduces the concept of return and acquaints the reader with the basics of interpreting financial markets data such as those appearing in *The Wall Street Journal*. The basic forms of business organizations and their salient features are also covered. Part II develops the theory of valuation, including a comprehensive treatment of time value of money concepts, the concepts of and relationship between risk and return, the valuation of fixed income securities, and the valuation of equity securities. Part III presents the capital investment decision with separate chapters emphasizing the cash flow estimation and evaluation aspects of capital budgeting analysis. A discussion of the role played by real options in the capital budgeting process is also presented. Part IV deals with the cost of capital, the determinants of an optimal capital structure, and dividend policy. Part V considers short-term and long-term financial planning and working capital management decisions in the areas of cash, marketable securities, accounts receivable, and inventories. It also includes coverage of current liabilities with an emphasis on the costs and sources of various short-term borrowings. It concludes with a discussion of several aspects of international finance that are relevant to the financial management of the firm.

Those instructors who wish to cover topics in an order other than that of the text will find it easy to make adjustments.

DISTINCTIVE FEATURES AND PEDAGOGICAL AIDS

CFM Fundamentals has been carefully designed to assist the student in learning and to stimulate student interest. Distinctive pedagogical features include:

1. **Extensive use of real firm data to illustrate financial concepts and problems.** Throughout the book we have illustrated financial management concepts and problems using real data where possible. For example, in Chapters 3 and 4 we use data from Furniture Brands International to review financial statements and analyze them. In Chapter 11 we implement a cost of capital exercise using data for Lilly (Eli) & Company. There are numerous other examples scattered throughout the book to illustrate other concepts such as bond and stock valuation, security risk measurement, working capital policy, and capital structure and dividend policies. By minimizing the number of hypothetical firm situations and using data and situations facing actual firms that the students will recognize and can relate to, *CFM Fundamentals* aims to further enhance the realism and excitement of learning.

2. **Early exposure to understanding security markets.** Students are exposed to financial markets data early in the textbook (Chapter 2) through illustration of how to interpret selected financial markets data from *The Wall Street Journal*. By doing so, students gain an early appreciation of the all-important concepts of security valuation, shareholder wealth maximization, and risk and return. Although formal treatment of these concepts occurs later, students gain an intuitive appreciation for them and begin to internalize the fact that business and financial decisions must be evaluated in light of their impact on risk, return, and valuation.

3. **Chapter Objectives.** Each chapter begins with an introduction that lists the chapter objectives. The objectives clearly identify the concepts and problem-solving tools that will be covered in the chapter. The objectives are designed to provide a "big picture" view of the chapter so that the student can relate the detailed exposition in the chapter to the overall objectives of the chapter.

4. **Calculator Solution Illustrations.** Many chapters have easy-to-follow, step-by-step calculator keystrokes to solve many of the time value of money examples developed in the text. These "Calculator Solution" sections are set up in a generic calculator format and can be used with virtually any financial calculator.

5. **Spreadsheet Strategies.** Many chapters have illustrative examples of how spreadsheet software (Microsoft Excel) may be used to solve finance problems, including time value of money problems, bond valuation, capital budgeting cash flow estimation and evaluation, and financial planning and forecasting.

6. **Comprehension Check Questions.** Scattered throughout the chapter are a series of Comprehension Check Questions designed to make the student pause and reflect on the material covered to that point. By doing so students are encouraged to pace themselves and test their understanding of the material just covered before proceeding to the next set of topics.

7. **Intuitive use of notation.** Notation in the text is simplified and intuitive to aid student learning. Inside the back cover we have provided a handy summary of the key notation used throughout the book.

8. **Finance & The Real World.** Scattered throughout various chapters are "Finance & The Real World" boxes to highlight a real world situation that is of relevance to the chapter. The boxes include financial decisions confronting a firm or made by a firm that have special significance to the chapter. The selections were carefully chosen to make the student reflect on how these real world situations were impacted or may be impacted by the concepts covered in the chapter.

9. **Internet applications.** There are numerous references throughout each chapter to interesting Internet applications that can be found on the World Wide Web. These Internet applications provide students with handy references that can be used to explore the Internet for additional information and data dealing with the topic of the chapter.

10. **Problem sets.** The end-of-chapter problem sets have been selected keeping in mind the introductory nature of the course. The problems are intended to test students' understanding of the basic concepts and their ability to apply problem solving techniques developed in the chapter, rather than to test their ability to manipulate mathematical formulas to arrive at an answer. In addition, the problems have been identified with *a difficulty rating* ranging from Basic, to Intermediate, to Challenging. Answers to selected problems can be found on the text Web site.

11. **Self-Test Problems.** Each chapter includes end-of-chapter Self-Test Problems, complete with detailed solutions, that students can use for further practice and enhanced understanding of the concepts developed in the chapter. Complete and detailed solutions are at the end of the text.

12. **Resource margin notes.** The following finance information resources are high-lighted throughout:

> **NewsWire: Finance in the News**—these notes remind students to check the NewsWire: Finance in the News resource on the South-Western Finance Resource Center for current article synopses related to chapter topics.

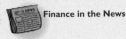

> **FinanceLinks Online**—sends students to this Web page accessed through the South-Western Finance Resource Center for Internet links that provide data and information.

13. **A detailed discussion of real options embedded in many capital investment projects.** Finance scholars and practitioners have increasingly focused attention on "embedded options" in capital investment projects, such as the option to abandon, the option to expand, and the option to defer investments. These options add value to an investment project, above that normally identified in a net present value calculation. Chapter 10 includes an intuitive discussion of real options in capital budgeting.

14. **Coverage of the newest financial analysis and performance appraisal concepts.** The increased attention given to the objective of shareholder wealth maximization has brought about the development of new performance appraisal models that can be used to judge a firm's performance and motivate managers to create value. The "Market Value Added" and "Economic Value Added" concepts, developed by Stern-Stewart, are covered in detail in Chapter 4. These are also emphasized again in Chapter 11 on cost of capital.

15. **Thomson ONE—Business School Edition.** Thomson ONE is a powerful tool that combines elements of a search engine with several sources of current corporate and financial markets data. We use this powerful tool to devise a set of exercises that requires students to use "real" data to examine concepts discussed in selected chapters.

ANCILLARY MATERIALS

> The **Study Guide,** created by Richard Gendreau of Bemidji State University, is available for students. It contains detailed chapter outlines, key chapter equations, and Internet exercises. Numerous self-test materials are also provided: multiple-choice questions, true/false questions, and numerical problems, all with answers and solutions.

> **Thomson ONE—Business School Edition.** Thomson ONE is an easy-to-use but powerful tool that combines elements of a search engine with several sources of current corporate and financial markets data. Thomson ONE combines a full range of fundamental financials, earnings estimates, and market data for hundreds of real world companies. This is an educational version of the same tools used by Wall Street analysts every day. Given the ease of use, instructors may find it beneficial to create their own set of exercises, in addition to those in the text, that require students to access "real" data to solve financial problems or examine financial concepts. Access to Thomson ONE—Business School Edition is provided by registering a unique serial number that comes with each new book.

> **Moyer Xtra!** The Moyer Xtra! Web site, available at http://moyerxtra.swlearning.com, provides students with a robust set of additional online learning tools. Instructors may have access to Moyer Xtra! bundled with the textbook via an access certificate, or students may purchase access at the Moyer Xtra! Web site. Here is a tour through some of the study features found in Moyer Xtra!:

> > **e-Lectures:** Difficult concepts from each chapter are explained and illustrated via streaming video and animated tutorials. These video clips and tutorials can

be extremely helpful review and clarification tools if you had trouble under-standing an in-class lecture or if you are a visual learner sometimes needing help with concepts as they are written in the text. Icons in the text margins highlight topics with associated e-Lectures.

➤ **Ask the Author Videos:** Frequently asked questions from each chapter are ex-plained and illustrated, allowing students to review key concepts on their own time and at their own pace.

➤ **CNN Video:** CNN Video segments bring the "real world" right to your desktop. The accompanying CNN video exercises help to illustrate how finance is an im-portant part of your daily life.

➤ **Xtra! Quizzing:** In addition to the open-access chapter-by-chapter quizzes found at the product support Web site, Moyer Xtra! offers an opportunity to practice for midterms and finals by taking online quizzes that span multiple chapters.

➤ **The Problem Bank: Practice Problems for Financial Management** has been re-vised to fit specifically with this text and contains over 400 multiple-choice finance problems with solutions, divided into seven major categories such as Time Value of Money, Capital Budgeting, Risk and Return, and so on. Solving these problems re-quires the use of a financial calculator and is intended to supplement the text's end-of-chapter problems, thereby providing additional practice for students in their preparation of homework assignments and for exams.

➤ A **PowerPoint™ Slide Presentation** package, also by Richard Gendreau of Bemidji State University, is offered to enhance lecture materials, and presents the key top-ics and figures in each chapter. The slides can be printed for student note-taking and for use as transparency masters. These are available on the text Web site.

➤ **Excel™ Templates.** Excel spreadsheets used in the text examples are available to instructors and students on the text Web site. Students can use them as a template to solve some of the end-of-chapter problems and instructors can use them in their lectures.

➤ **Product Support Web Site.** The text's Web site at http://moyer.swlearning.com con-tains student resources, instructor resources, Internet updates and links, spreadsheet software, PowerPoint slides, online quizzes, and other useful features. Students can go directly to the text Web site to link to the Internet addresses in the text margins.

➤ **South-Western Finance Resource Center** at http://finance.swlearning.com. The South-Western Finance Resource Center provides instructors and students with unique features such as "NewsWire: Finance in the News" and "FinanceLinks On-line." It also provides customer service information and links to book-related Web sites. Learn about valuable products and services to help with your finance studies, contact the finance editors, register for Thomson Financial Network, and more.

➤ **Web Tutor™ ToolBox.** Web Tutor™ ToolBox provides instructors with links to content from our book companion Web sites. It also provides rich communica-tion tools to instructors and students including a course calendar, chat, and e-mail. Access to Web Tutor™ ToolBox may be bundled with new texts.

➤ An **Instructor's Resource Manual (IRM)** is available to instructors. It contains de-tailed solutions to the end-of-chapter questions and problems. The solutions to text questions and problems have been thoroughly checked to assure their accu-racy. The IRM is also available to instructors on the text Web site.

➤ An extensive **Test Bank** by the text authors offers over 1,500 multiple-choice ques-tions and problems. This unique test bank is designed with the instructor in mind.

Approximately 60 percent of the questions are "fact" questions, taken directly from the discussion in the text. Approximately 20 percent of the questions are "elementary problem" questions that closely parallel problem examples developed in the chapter and easier problems at the end of the chapter. Approximately 20 percent of the questions are "challenging problems" that require the student to apply concepts developed in the chapter to new problem situations.

Following each "fact" question, the instructor is provided with (1) the correct answer and (2) an identification of the question topic (that is, a reference to the major heading and subheading in the text where the correct answer is found).

Following each "elementary problem" and "challenging problem," the instructor is provided with (1) the correct answer, (2) an identification of the question topic (that is, a reference to the major heading and subheading in the text where the procedure for calculating the correct answer is found), and (3) a detailed solution to the problem.

➤ **ExamView™ Testing Software.** This computerized testing program contains all of the questions in the printed test bank. **ExamView™ Testing Software** is an easy-to-use test creation software compatible with Microsoft Windows. Instructors can add or edit questions, instructions, and answers, and select questions by previewing them on the screen, selecting them randomly, or selecting them by number. Instructors can also create and administer quizzes online, whether over the Internet, a local area network (LAN), or a wide area network (WAN).

➤ A **Supplemental Problem Set** that can be assigned to students is available to instructors on the text Web site, and contains over 400 problems.

➤ A set of **Demonstration Problems** in transparency master format is available on the text Web site for instructors. The problems parallel the major examples developed in the text.

➤ An **Instructor's Resource CD-ROM** is available to instructors and contains all instructor supplements in electronic format, including the Instructor's Resource Manual and the Test Bank in Word files.

➤ **InfoTrac® College Edition** allows you to package an entire online library of articles from hundreds of journals such as *Fortune, Journal of Finance, Money,* and *U.S. News and World Report* with any new South-Western textbook at no additional cost to you or your students. It offers a database updated daily, full-length articles, and keyword searches that quickly and efficiently scan the entire database.

➤ The **Finance Online Case Library** allows you to easily and quickly create your own customized bound finance casebook and add your own material, such as a course syllabus, preface, or specific course information. Choose from more than 100 finance cases to create your course-specific casebook. Search by either course or topic for cases covering various finance issues. New cases are added each year! For more information, go to http://www.textchoice.com or contact your South-Western/Thomson Learning sales representative.

INFOTRAC®
COLLEGE EDITION
Exclusively from Gale Group and Thomson Learning

ACKNOWLEDGMENTS

The authors wish to acknowledge the helpful comments from reviewers of this first edition of the book. We are particularly grateful for the careful reviews and suggestions made by the following professors: Michael J. Alderson, St. Louis University; Sam Basu, CSU–Hayward; Laurence E. Blose, Grand Valley State University; Susan Coleman, University of Hartford; Thomas Eyssell, University of Missouri–St. Louis; David R. Fewings, Western Washington University; Larry C. Holland, University of Arkansas–Little Rock; Joel Jankowski, University of Tampa; Frederick Kelly, Roger Williams University; Peppi M. Kenny, Western Illinois University; Robert Kleiman, Oakland University; Morris Knapp, Miami-Dade Community College; Robert B. McElreath, Clemson University; John K. Mullen, Clarkson University; Vivian Nazar, Ferris State University; Jeffrey Phillips, SUNY–Morrisville; Russ Ray, University of Louisville; Rakesh Sah, Montana State University–Billings; Barry B. Schweig, Eureka College; John Stephens, Western Michigan University; and Daniel L. Tompkins, Niagara University.

The authors would also like to thank several graduate and undergraduate students who provided very diligent help with various aspects of the book. These students are: Sudip Bandyopadhyay, Vusal Najafov, and Moe Sann. Thanks are also due Nikhil P. Rao for his careful reading of the manuscript and valuable editorial suggestions.

We are also indebted to Oklahoma State University, Texas Tech University, and Wake Forest University for the considerable support they provided while this edition was being developed. We owe thanks, as well, to our deans and fellow faculty members at our universities for the encouragement and assistance they provided on a continuing basis during the preparation of the manuscript.

Finally, we wish to express our thanks to the Finance team members at South-Western/Thomson Learning. We are particularly appreciative of the support provided by our editors and marketing staff: Mike Reynolds, our executive editor; Susanna Smart, our senior developmental editor; our marketing team; Chris Hudson, our production editor; John Barans, our media development editor; and Tippy McIntosh, our text designer.

R. Charles Moyer

James R. McGuigan

Ramesh P. Rao

INTRODUCTION

PART ONE

This part includes several chapters that provide an overview of finance and background material to enhance the understanding of subsequent material. Chapter 2 reviews the major elements of the financial marketplace. It includes a discussion of the structure of the U.S. financial system and the role of stock exchanges. It also introduces the concept of return and acquaints the reader with the basics of interpreting security price quotes such as those that appear in *The Wall Street Journal*. Chapter 3 provides a review of financial statements while Chapter 4 shows how financial ratios can be used to evaluate firm performance.

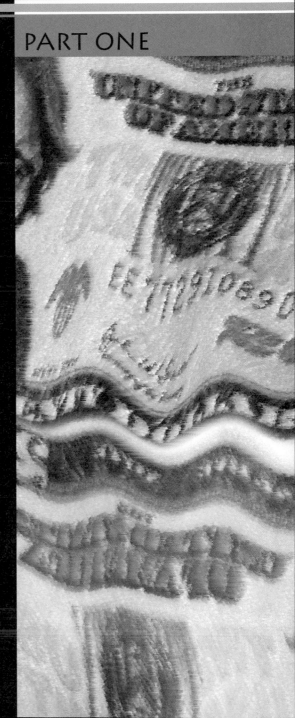

CHAPTER 1

The Role and Objective of Financial Management

Financial managers have the primary responsibility for acquiring funds (cash) needed by a firm and for directing those funds into activities that will maximize the value of the firm for its owners. Articles appear regularly in the major business periodicals, such as *The Wall Street Journal, Business Week, Fortune,* and *Forbes,* describing financial managers' involvement in important and daunting tasks. Consider the challenges facing airline executives in the aftermath of the September 11, 2001 terrorist attacks in New York City and Washington D.C. In the face of falling passenger-load factors, should service be cut—as was done by Delta, US Airways, United, American, and most other major airlines, or should this be viewed as an opportunity to expand and gain market share—as was done by the financially strong Southwest Airlines?

And what about the decision facing the management and shareholders of Hewlett-Packard and Compaq in early 2002 regarding whether or not to merge? Was this the right decision for the managers and owners of the two firms concerned? Was it in the interest of Hewlett-Packard shareholders to approve the merger between the two companies? What benefits could Compaq anticipate from the merger? Was the merger priced appropriately? In February 2000 Motorola announced a $1.5 billion telecommunications equipment order from Telsim, the second largest wireless phone operator in Turkey. As part of the deal, Motorola agreed to provide Telsim with a loan to finance the large purchase order. Barely 2 years later, in January 2002, Motorola sued Telsim for failing to make payments on the loan. Do you think it is a good idea for manufacturers to provide financing for their customers? How could Motorola have ensured that Telsim was a good credit risk before deciding to extend them a loan?

Any business has important financial concerns, and its success or failure depends in large part on the quality of its financial decisions. Every key decision made by a firm's managers has important financial implications. Managers daily face questions such as:

- ➤ Will a particular capital investment be successful? Where will the funds come from to finance the investment?
- ➤ Does the firm have adequate cash, or access to cash, through bank borrowing agreements, for example, to meet its daily operating needs?
- ➤ Which customers should be offered credit, and how much should they be offered?
- ➤ How much inventory should be held?
- ➤ Is a merger or acquisition advisable?
- ➤ How should cash flows be used or distributed? That is, what is the optimal dividend or stock repurchase policy?
- ➤ In trying to arrive at the best financial management decisions, how should risk and return be balanced?

The field of financial management is an exciting and challenging one, with a wide primary range of rewarding career opportunities. Corporate financial management, the focus of this text, emphasizes the management of a company's assets and the financing of those assets. And investment banking, investment analysis and portfolio management, commercial banking, real estate, insurance, and the public sector—to name only a few broad areas—offer other career opportunities to those with an interest in finance.

To provide you with the basics of financial management, this text presents an introduction to the theory, institutional background, and analytical tools essential for proper decision making in all these and other related areas. You will be introduced to the financial management process of typical firms. Learning how this process works is one of the key building blocks of a successful career in financial management. This chapter presents an overview of the business organization, its goal, and the role of the financial manager. We conclude the chapter by presenting an overview of the textbook.

Chapter Objectives

After reading this chapter, you should have an understanding of the following topics:

1. The primary goal of the firm
2. The determinants of the value of a firm
3. The meaning and implication of agency problems in a corporation
4. The importance of ethics in running a business organization
5. The major types of business organizations and their distinguishing features
6. The role and function of the financial manager
7. The relationship between finance and other business disciplines

PRIMARY GOAL OF THE FIRM: MAXIMIZING SHAREHOLDER WEALTH

Effective financial decision making requires an understanding of the goal of the firm. What objective *should* guide business decision making? That is, what should management try to achieve for the owners of the firm? Several objectives come to mind:

➤ Maximize sales or market share of the firm
➤ Maintain the highest quality product or service in the industry
➤ Maximize profits of the firm

While these objectives appear to be reasonable, we shall show they are not appropriate. *The most appropriate objective for a firm is to maximize* **shareholder wealth.** Shareholder wealth is measured by the **market value** of the shareholders' **common stock** holdings. Market value of a share is defined as the price at which the stock trades in the marketplace, such as on the New York Stock Exchange. Therefore, total shareholder wealth equals the number of shares outstanding times the market price per share.

Thus, shareholder wealth maximization implies that management should seek to maximize the stock price of the firm. After all, as a shareowner, you determine how well your investments are doing by their *value* in the marketplace, by what the shares will fetch in the stock exchange. As we will see, stock prices and, indeed the value of any asset, reflect the *amount, timing,* and *risk* of future **cash flows.** We will look more closely at these factors later in this chapter. Basically cash flows refer to the difference between the cash coming in to the firm (e.g., cash generated from sales) and the cash flowing out of the firm (cash expenses paid out for raw materials, labor, taxes etc.). This in turn affects the cash flow to shareholders. In general:

➤ The greater the amount of the cash flows, the higher the stock price.
➤ The more distant (timing) the cash flows, the lower the stock price.
➤ The greater the risk or uncertainty of the cash flows, the lower the stock price.

The Appropriateness of the Goal

The objective of shareholder wealth maximization has a number of distinct advantages. First, this objective explicitly considers the amount or magnitude, timing, and the risk of the cash flows expected to be received from stock ownership. Managers must consider the elements of magnitude, timing, and risk as they make important financial decisions, such as whether or not to invest in new capital equipment, inventories, and customer financing. In this way, managers can make decisions that will contribute to increasing shareholder wealth.

Second, it is conceptually possible to determine whether a particular financial decision is consistent with this objective. If a decision made by a firm has the effect of increasing the market price of the firm's stock, it is a good decision. If it appears that an action will not achieve this result, the action should not be taken (at least not voluntarily).

Third, shareholder wealth maximization is an impersonal objective. It is determined by the market as a whole and is not the result of a subjective judgment of an individual or a few individuals. In other words, the CEO or top management of a firm may want to pursue company size maximization as a goal for personal reasons, but shareholders may object to such a goal because it is not in their interest. However, it is unlikely that shareholders would ever object to a company that maximizes their stock price. Thus stock price maximization serves as an unbiased objective that should appeal to all shareholders.

Now let us examine why some of the other objectives listed on page 4 are inappropriate. Let's take the first, the objective of maximizing sales or market share. What is wrong with a firm wanting to increase market share, say, from 22 percent to 28 percent? There is nothing wrong with that, and indeed most firms, as part of their business plan, have target market shares in mind. However, if the increase in market share requires that the firm spend an inordinate amount of resources to achieve it, it may not be in the interest of shareholders. For example, is it a good objective if the increase in market share can only be achieved by doubling the advertising budget along with an associated decline in cash flow? Probably not. For similar reasons the second primary objective, of maintaining the highest product and service quality standards, may not be appropriate. A manufacturing entity such as an automobile firm can target a zero-defect policy, but doing so may require such a heavy investment in capital equipment and quality control that cash flows are drastically reduced. Most automobile manufacturers, for example, tolerate a certain number of defects per vehicle even though it is possible to develop a zero-defect policy; if firms were to adopt a manufacturing policy with a zero-defect policy they probably would not be able to maximize shareholder wealth.

The Problem with Profit Maximization

The third objective previously listed is the one most difficult to accept as being inappropriate (especially for those without prior finance background): the profit maximization objective. In part this is because of the prominence placed by media and financial analysts—and by management—on quarterly and annual earnings (net profit) disclosures. While it is natural to expect profit maximization to lead to shareholder wealth maximization, the profit maximization objective has too many shortcomings to provide consistent guidance to the practicing manager.

First, profit maximization lacks a time dimension: Should management maximize short-term profits or long-term profits? A drug company, for instance, can boost short-term profits by cutting back on research and development expenditures. Such an action would maximize profits in the short run but probably result in lower longer-term earnings. As a stockowner, would you support management acting in such a manner? Toward the end of 2001, Merck shares fell significantly even as reported earnings were in line with expectations. In part, the stock prices fell because of investors' concerns that Merck may not have enough new drugs in the pipeline to replace the ones coming off patent in the next few years. This illustrates that decisions made by management have both short-term and long-term impacts. A central concern of management is the trade-off between short-run and long-run profits. The profit maximization objective does not provide any clear guidance on these types of decisions.

The second limitation of the profit maximization objective has to do with the definition of *profit*. **Generally accepted accounting principles (GAAP)**, discussed in Chapter 3, result in literally hundreds of definitions of profit for a firm because of the latitude permitted in recognizing and accounting for costs and revenues. For example, in 1990, Carolina Power & Light Company (CPL) was forced to reduce its earnings by $81.6 million because of an unfavorable regulatory ruling regarding its Harris nuclear plant. To offset this impact on the firm's earnings, CPL "changed its method of accounting for revenues to accrue unbilled revenues as of the date service is rendered, rather than when billed. The net effect of this accounting change for 1990 is an increase in net income of $77 million, or $0.92 per share." (Carolina Power & Light Company, "Letter to Members of the Financial Community," January 25, 1991). This arbitrary accounting change has *no* impact on the cash flows or economic well-being of CPL and hence has no impact on its value.

Finance in the News

Click on this button at **http://finance.swlearning.com** *for synopses of articles on The Goals and Environment of Financial Management.*

Even if we could agree on the appropriate accounting definition of profit, it is not clear whether a firm should attempt to maximize total profit, the rate of profit, or earnings per share (EPS). Consider Columbia Beverages, Inc., a firm with 10 million shares outstanding that currently earns a profit of $10 million after tax. If the firm sells an additional 1 million shares of stock and invests the proceeds to earn $100,000 per year, the total profit of the firm will increase from $10 million to $10.1 million. However, are shareholders better off? Prior to the stock sale, earnings per share is $1 ($10 million profit divided by 10 million shares of stock). After the stock sale, earnings per share decline to $0.92 ($10.1 million in earnings divided by 11 million shares). Although total profit has increased, earnings per share has declined. Thus, stockholders are not better off from this action.

The preceding example might lead one to conclude that managers should seek to maximize earnings per share (for a given number of shares outstanding). This, too, can result in misleading actions as illustrated in Table 1.1. For example, say a firm has total assets of $10 million at the start of the year. The firm is financed entirely with stock (1 million shares outstanding) and has no debt. After-tax earnings are equal to $1 million, resulting in a return on stockholders' equity of 10 percent ($1 million in earnings divided by $10 million in stockholders' equity), and earnings per share of $1. The company decides to keep one-half of this year's earnings (increasing assets and equity to $10.5 million) and pay out the balance in stockholders' dividends. Next year the company's earnings total $1.02 million, resulting in earnings per share of $1.02. Are shareholders better off because of the decision by managers to reinvest $500,000 in the firm? In this example, a strong argument can be made that the position of shareholders has *deteriorated*. Although earnings per share have increased from $1 per share to $1.02 per share, the realized return on stockholders' equity actually has declined, from 10 percent to 9.7 percent ($1.02 million divided by $10.5 million of stockholders' equity). In essence, the company's managers have reinvested $500,000 of stockholders' money to earn a return of only 4 percent ($0.02 million of additional earnings divided by

Table 1.1 Illustration of Why Maximizing Earnings Per Share Can Be Misleading

	Current Year	Next Year (Assume $500,000 is retained from current year and the firm earns $1,020,000 after taxes)
Total assets (Beginning):	$10,000,000	$10,500,000
Stockholders' equity (Beginning):	$10,000,000	$10,500,000
Shares outstanding:	1,000,000	1,000,000
After-tax earnings:	$ 1,000,000	$ 1,020,000
Earnings per share:		
$= \dfrac{\text{After-tax earnings}}{\text{Shares outstanding}}$	$= \dfrac{\$1,000,000}{1,000,000}$ $= \$1.00$	$= \dfrac{\$1,020,000}{1,000,000}$ $= \$1.02$
Return on stockholders' equity:		
$= \dfrac{\text{After-tax earnings}}{\text{Stockholders' equity}}$	$= \dfrac{\$1,000,000}{\$10,000,000}$ $= .10 \text{ or } 10\%$	$= \dfrac{\$1,020,000}{\$10,500,000}$ $= .097 \text{ or } 9.7\%$

$0.5 million of additional investment). This type of investment is not likely to result in maximum shareholder wealth. Shareholders could do better by simply investing in risk-free government bonds yielding more than 4 percent.

The third major problem associated with the profit maximization objective is that it provides no direct way for financial managers to consider the risk associated with alternative decisions. For example, two projects generating identical future expected cash flows and requiring identical outlays may be vastly different with respect to the risk of the expected cash flows. Similarly, a firm can often increase its earnings per share by increasing the proportion of debt financing used in the firm's capital structure. However, leverage-induced increases in EPS (earnings per share) come at the cost of increased financial risk. The financial marketplace will recognize the increased risk of financial distress that accompanies increases in debt financing and will value the resulting EPS accordingly.

DETERMINANTS OF VALUE

By now you should be convinced that the appropriate objective of management is to maximize shareholder wealth or share value. Previously we mentioned that the three major factors that determine the market value of shares are: *the amount or magnitude of the cash flows expected to be generated for the benefit of stockholders; the timing of these cash flows; and the risk of the cash flows.* We now discuss in detail these three components of stock value. As we discuss these, it is important to keep in mind that these three components impact the value of any asset, not just common stocks.

Cash Flows. Throughout this book we stress the importance of cash flows in the practice of financial management. Cash flow relates to the actual cash generated by the firm. In simple terms cash flow refers to the difference between cash inflows, such as those resulting from collections on sales, and cash outflows including outflows for salaries, payment for raw material purchases, tax payments, and equipment purchases. In contrast, the accounting system focuses on earnings (or profits) that are based primarily on a matching over time of the historic, cost-based revenues and the expenses of a company. But accounting earnings often are misleading because they do not reflect the actual cash inflows and outflows of the firm. For example, an accountant records depreciation expense on an asset each period over the depreciable life of that asset. Depreciation is designed to reflect the decline in value of that asset over time. However, depreciation itself results in no cash outflow. The entire cash outflow occurred when the asset was purchased originally.

Timing. The market value of a share of stock is influenced not only by the amount of the cash flows it is expected to produce but also by the timing of those cash flows. If faced with the opportunity of receiving $100 today or $100 3 years from today, you would surely choose the $100 today because you could invest that $100 for 3 years and accumulate the interest. In other words, $100 to be *received* 3 years from now is worth less than $100 to be received today. Thus, financial managers must consider both the amount or magnitude of the cash flows they expect to generate and the timing of these cash flows, because investors will reflect these dimensions of return in their valuation of the enterprise.

Risk. Finally, the market value of a share of stock is influenced by the perceived risk of the cash flows it is expected to generate. The relationship between risk and required rate of return is an important concept in financial management and is discussed in detail in Chapter 6. In general, the greater the perceived risk associated with an expected cash flow, the greater the rate of return required by investors and managers. Investors consider risk in their valuation of the enterprise.

As you see, any decisions undertaken by managers should be evaluated in the light of their impact on the magnitude, timing, and risk of cash flows to shareholders, which together determine the impact of the decision on shareholder value.

DIVERGENT OBJECTIVES AND AGENCY PROBLEMS

The goal of shareholder wealth maximization specifies how financial decisions *should* be made. In practice, however, there often may be a divergence between the shareholder wealth maximization goal and the *actual* goals pursued by management. For example, the management consulting company of Stern Stewart & Co. has developed an index of managerial performance known as ***Economic Value Added (EVA®)*** that measures the success of managers in achieving a goal of shareholder wealth maximization (http://www.sternstewart.com). Based on this measure firms such as Microsoft, ExxonMobil, and Wal-Mart have consistently ranked high on improving shareholder wealth. Other firms such as Sears and Kmart have ranked poorly. The poor performances may be due, in part, to a lack of attention to stockholder interests and the pursuit of objectives more in line with managers' self-interests. As an illustration: A concern for job security may lead management to minimize (or limit) the amount of risk incurred by the firm, because unfavorable outcomes can lead to their dismissal or possible bankruptcy for the firm. Thus firms may diversify into businesses that reduce the risk of the firm even if such a move is not in the interest of shareholders. In another instance, if compensation is tied to the size of the organization, top management may pursue acquisitions to increase the size of the firm even if it does not add to shareholder value.

Consider the case of Sears, Roebuck & Co. In the 1970s and 1980s Sears decided to look for opportunities in areas other than their traditional business of retail department stores. In part this was because management felt their core retail area had little opportunity for future growth and the business itself was getting riskier as a result of competitive pressures from discount department chains such as Wal-Mart. Consequently Sears' management decided to invest huge sums in insurance (Allstate Insurance), financial services including credit cards (Discover brand credit card), stock brokerage and mutual funds (Dean Witter), and real estate (Coldwell Banker). While top management was busy pursuing these new businesses, the core retail segment suffered from ineffective management because top management's attention and resources focused on the non–department store–related businesses. Under pressure from shareholders, Sears finally divested itself of its noncore businesses in the early 1990s to return to a focus on its core department store business. Why had the management of Sears pursued these non–department store businesses? Was it because they wanted to safeguard their jobs by diversifying Sears out of the retail business that was becoming more and more competitive? Were they concerned about their professional reputations and the need to be identified with a high growth firm rather than with a firm that had peaked? While it would be impossible to know the true motivations of top management in pursuing various strategies, investors should not automatically assume that managerial actions are always aligned with shareholder interests. Can you think of other firms where you can question whether managerial actions were consistent with shareholder wealth maximization?

http://www.sternstewart.com

Agency Problems

The primary reason for the divergence of objectives between managers and shareholders has been attributed to separation of ownership (shareholders) and control (management) in corporations. This can lead to *agency problems*, also known as **principal–agent** conflicts. The principals are the shareholders, and the agents are the managers who are hired by shareholders to manage the business. In most publicly held corporations managers own a very small percentage of the shares. Consequently, the potential for agency problems can be severe. For example, Eastman Kodak Corporation has over 291 million shares outstanding, with outside shareholders owning more than 99.7 percent of the shares, as compared to insiders (shares held by management) who own about 0.3 percent of the stock. Because management does not own the entire firm there is a potential that managers may pursue goals consistent with their self-interests rather than in the interest of the owners of the firm (shareholder wealth).

One example of a principal–agent conflict or management–shareholder conflict involves job security. In order to reduce the chance of losing their jobs due to bankruptcy, managers may engage in diversifying acquisitions that reduce the earnings volatility of the firm. Another example of a principal–agent problem involves excessive perquisite (perks) consumption. Examples include having a luxurious office with expensive art, the use of corporate jets, having a larger staff than necessary to conduct business, executive club memberships, having the company buy raw materials from your brother-in-law's company at above market prices, etc. As one example, in 2002, Dennis Kozlowski, the former CEO of the conglomerate firm Tyco, was indicted for using company funds to purchase expensive art to grace the walls of his personal residence.

The financial management literature identifies several mechanisms designed to reduce managerial–shareholder conflicts. These include the following:

Managerial Compensation Properly designed compensation contracts can help to align shareholder–management conflicts. For example, providing part of the compensation in the form of stock or options to purchase stock can reduce agency conflicts. Stock options, especially, have become a significant part of managerial compensation. Stock options granted to managers entitle them to buy shares of the company at a particular price *(exercise price)*. Typically, the options are set at an exercise price greater than the price of the stock at the time options are granted and can be exercised only after a certain period of time has elapsed. These conditions are imposed so that managers won't be tempted to cash in their options immediately and leave the company. More important to stock value, this is an attempt to align their interests more closely with those of the shareholders: Firms, including Disney, Pepsico, and Anheuser-Busch, provide key managers with significant stock options that increase in value with improvements in the firm's performance.

Many firms today, such as Panhandle Eastern, International Multifoods, and Ford Motor Company, for example, expect top managers and directors to have a significant ownership stake in the firm. Panhandle Eastern's president has been paid entirely in the company's common shares, 25,000 per quarter—no severance, no retirement plan, just stock and medical benefits. Ford requires each of its top 80 officers to own common stock in the company at least equal to their annual salary. As the company's former chairman, Alex Trotman, explains "I want everyone thinking about the price of Ford stock when they go to work."

Monitoring by the Board of Directors Every publicly held corporation has a board of directors that is elected by the shareholders and has the fiduciary responsibility to act in the interest of shareholders. The board has ultimate authority to hire and fire top management. Thus, an *effective* board can ensure that conflicts between managerial and shareholder interests are minimized. Generally, for a board to be effective, a majority of the directors should be independent—that is, they must not be current or former officers of the company or have any business dealings with the company. Many of the large shareholders and regulatory bodies including the Securities and Exchange Commission and stock exchange authorities such as the New York Stock Exchange are now urging firms to maintain effective boards by including a significant number of independent board members.

Threat of Takeovers Takeovers also can serve as an important deterrent to shareholder–management conflicts. The argument goes as follows: If managers act in their self-interest then share values will be depressed, providing an incentive for someone to take over the company at a depressed level. The acquirer can then benefit from instituting policies that are consistent with shareholder wealth maximization, such as eliminating underperforming units and cutting overhead.

In addition to the above mechanisms we will learn in later chapters that certain corporate financial policies, such as dividends and capital structure, can also serve to control agency conflicts.

BUSINESS ETHICS AND FINANCIAL MANAGEMENT

The recent scandals at such leading companies as Enron, WorldCom, Tyco, and Citigroup have brought to sharp focus the role of business ethics in running an organization. The consequences to the organization and the people behind the organization can be severe. In the fall of 2001, Enron Corporation, a leading energy-generating and -trading company, was indicted by the SEC for improprieties involving the use of Special Purpose Entities (SPEs). The SPEs were partnerships created by Enron involving outside parties as well as some of the key top management figures. Among other things, it was alleged that Enron used these partnerships to hide the losses and debt it incurred in its energy-trading operations. While the existence of the SPEs was disclosed in the financial statements, investors were not fully aware of the nature of the SPEs and the exposure of Enron Corporation to these partnerships.

Following the SEC's investigation, Enron as a business completely unraveled to the point where most of its assets were liquidated. The key executives lost their jobs along with thousands of other employees. The stock, which was trading as high as $59.40 on March 19, 2001, was trading at only $0.21 on March 18, 2002. Arthur Andersen, Enron's auditor of many years, was also implicated in the scandal and it too paid the steep price of losing not just its reputation but also the firm's existence itself. Until the disclosure of the scandal, Enron was considered one of the most innovative companies in the energy sector and credited with developing the derivatives markets for many energy-related products. Citigroup, the well-known banking institution, was also the subject of front-page headline news involving questionable ethical practices. In 2002, the New York attorney general brought charges that Citigroup, in order to generate greater revenues for its investment banking unit, pressured a financial analyst working for its Salomon Smith Barney unit to provide a fa-

FINANCE & The Real World

Maximizing Shareholder Wealth by Downsizing?

Since the mid-1980s, companies have tried to cut costs by "downsizing"—laying off employees during times of weak sales. Managers reason that if you cut labor costs, profits will rise and investors will reward you with higher share prices.

But economists and consultants who studied the relationship between layoffs and corporate performance say that downsizing can damage customer relationships and have a demoralizing effect on surviving workers. According to Alan Blinder, former vice chairman of the Federal Reserve Board and now a Princeton University professor, there is little evidence that downsizing boosts corporate productivity. A study by Watson Wyatt Worldwide found that fewer than half of the companies surveyed met profit goals after downsizing. Mercer Management Consulting found that 68 percent of the downsized companies it studied didn't achieve profit growth for five years. And consultant Bain & Co. found that companies that announced mass layoffs did worse in the stock market over a three-year period. Even seemingly benign approaches like reducing payrolls through attrition can have unintended consequences, says management professor Kim Cameron of the University of Michigan, because the people who leave may not be the ones you want to leave. With employees gone, some companies find that they have to pay consultants or freelance contractors hefty fees to get needed work done.

Look what happened in the brokerage industry. Wall Street firms downsized during the 2000–2003 bear market only to have smaller brokerage firms hire their former talent. In early 2003, First Albany, an upstate New York brokerage firm, hired 60 traders, analysts, salespeople, and investment bankers, including people dismissed from giant J.P. Morgan Chase & Co. and others. Ranks of the New York-based Jefferies Group have swelled 35 percent since 2000, while staffing across Wall Street is down by nearly 10 percent. The result: Wall Street suffers a brain drain to shore up short-term profits, but boosts smaller firms' competitive positions in the process. To avoid this problem, Charles Schwab & Co., a San Francisco-based discount brokerage firm, cut costs by asking employees to take unpaid three-day weekends. A spokesman reasons: "You don't engender loyalty and a sense of shared mission by resorting to layoffs first."

It is apparent that the decision to downsize may have unintended consequences. Management should consider the potential impact of downsizing on short term vs. long term gains, on employee morale, and business ethics before engaging in such activity.

Sources: The Wall Street Journal, February 21, 2001, "Many Say Layoffs Hurt Companies More Than They Help"; *Business Week,* February 3, 2003, "The New Global Job Shift"; *The Wall Street Journal,* March 6, 2003, "Small Brokerages Are Hiring as Big Competitors Cut Back."

vorable stock report for AT&T Corporation, from whom it was soliciting investment banking business. While the scandal has affected Citigroup's reputation and resulted in loss in share value, Citigroup is still in business and is putting in place organizational changes so that such ethical lapses will not happen in the future. Both of these events illustrate the pressures firms face to engage in questionable business practices and the severity of the consequences of engaging in such behavior.

The concept of what constitutes ethical business practices is not precise. There is often a strong cultural dimension to the concept of ethical behavior. What may be viewed as unethical in the United States might be viewed quite differently in other cultures. For example, in some countries the practice of making "facilitating payments" to competitors or government officials might be widely accepted as a normal cost of doing business, whereas in the United States it might be called bribery. The distinctions are often not clear. *At a minimum, ethical business practices mandate that a company and its managers operate within the confines of what is legal. But generally, the concept of ethical business behavior is broader than that. Ethical management practices often incorporate concepts such as honesty and fairness when dealing with customers, employees, government, and suppliers of goods, services, and capital.* In addition, ethical management practices incorporate the concept of what is "good for society," by considering the environmental consequences and side costs and benefits of business actions. Finally, ethical business practices are those that preserve the good reputation of a company among its customers, suppliers, and employees.

Although the Enron and Citigroup incidents reflect instances of ethical lapses that gained widespread media coverage, ethical issues confront most businesses on a day-to-day basis. For example, as a new bank loan officer, should you recommend approval of a loan to a longtime friend, even though she does not quite meet the normal loan standards of the bank? As an account executive for a brokerage firm, should you recommend to your clients the securities of firms with poor environmental management records or that deal in products that are potentially harmful to one's health, such as alcohol and tobacco? Should you tell your father-in-law that your firm is likely to become a candidate for a takeover before this is publicly announced? As a division manager being evaluated in part on a return-on-assets calculation, should you lease assets to keep them out of the asset base for evaluation purposes and thereby enhance your apparent performance? Should your firm aggressively use allowable accounting practices to mask a fundamentally deteriorating level of performance? Should your firm move its plant from the Northeast to the Southeast in an attempt to break the union and save labor costs?

This brief sampling of the areas of business and financial-management decision making provides a feel for the breadth of ethical issues facing financial managers. In most cases, the answers to these questions are not clear-cut. Actual decision making is very complex and involves many trade-offs among parties with competing interests. However, explicitly recognizing the costs and benefits associated with each of these decisions and making the decision in an atmosphere of balanced objectivity and fairness can help financial managers avoid apparent or real breaches of their ethical trust.

An important concern for financial managers, who are entrusted with the resources of stockholders, is: How does a concern for ethics in the practice of financial management impact the goal of shareholder wealth maximization? Firms that expect employees to act according to a code of ethics in their business dealings can expect to have reduced litigation and damages expenses. A recent survey concluded that some 90 percent of the Fortune 500 companies have adopted a published code of conduct for their managers and other employees; high ethical standards are respected by customers and valued by investors. One could argue that ethical business dealings build long-term value for investors, whereas breaches of standards of business ethics may provide short-term gains at the expense of future returns.

Comprehension Check Questions

1. How is shareholder wealth measured?
2. What are some of the problems in using profit maximization as the primary objective of the firm?
3. Do managers always maximize shareholder wealth in practice? Why or why not?
4. What constitutes "good" ethical practice?

FORMS OF BUSINESS ORGANIZATION

Up until now we have discussed the goal of the firm and related issues without talking about the particular type of business organization. Clearly, the role of financial management will vary with the size and complexity of the company.

In this section we show why firms normally assume one of three basic forms of business organization. The simplest is the sole proprietorship, next comes the partnership, and then the corporation, which can be very complex. In starting a new business, one has to answer the basic question: What type of business organization is the most appropriate? In addition to the three basic organization types there are a number of additional forms of business organization that incorporate features from the three basic types.

Sole Proprietorship

A *sole proprietorship is a business owned by one person.* It is the simplest form of organization, requiring little more than putting up a sign and opening the doors for business. Typically, individuals wanting to set up a sole proprietorship first select a business name, which they register with the county treasurer for a nominal fee.

The sole proprietorship, although simple, has a number of limitations. The major disadvantage of a sole proprietorship is that the owner of the firm has *unlimited personal liability* for all debts and other obligations incurred by the firm. Let's suppose that you set up a lawn mowing business with $5,000 of your own money and borrow another $15,000 from a financial institution. In the event you are unable to pay the loan from the earnings of the business, the financial institution can legally force you to sell (liquidate) your business *and* personal assets to satisfy its claims. Suppose the liquidation of the business yields $5,000. This means that you may have to sell personal property (your home, for example) to realize another $10,000 to pay off the loan obligation. Thus, you have lost not only the equity you put into the business—the $5,000 you initially invested—but also $10,000 of your personal assets.

Another limitation of the sole proprietorship is that *it does not have any continuity*; it ceases to exist when the owner dies or gives up the business. Finally, with a sole proprietorship it is difficult to raise additional funds from the financial markets. Therefore, funding for growth has to come largely from reinvesting earnings from the business and any additional capital invested by the sole proprietor.

However, there are certain advantages to the sole proprietorship. Chief among them is that your earnings are *taxed only once*. No distinction is made between the earnings from the business and your other earnings; therefore you pay taxes only once. This is unlike the double taxation one faces in the corporate structure, where earnings from the corporation are subject to corporate taxes and the earnings distributed to the shareholders in the form of dividends are again subject to taxes at the individual level.

The sole proprietorship form of organization is best suited for businesses that are small and are owned and managed by an individual. Such businesses may include lawn mowing services, retail stores, restaurants, insurance agencies, legal or accounting practices, etc. It is also important to note that although many businesses start as a sole proprietorship, as they grow they may shift to a partnership or corporate structure. Many of today's large corporations can be traced to their origins as a sole proprietorship. Wal-Mart, for instance, had its origins as a sole proprietorship. Sam Walton, the legendary founder of Wal-Mart, started the business as a sole proprietor owner of a Ben Franklin variety store in Newport, Arkansas, in 1945. He later opened a number of other variety stores organized as partnerships between him and other family members and, in some instances, even store managers. In 1970 Sam Walton incorporated his business as Wal-Mart Stores, Inc. and went public. Other well-known firms that started out as sole proprietorships include Marriott Corporation, J.M. Smucker Company, and JCPenney.

Partnership

Partnerships are businesses formed by two or more co-owners (partners). Each partner provides a certain percentage of the capital necessary to start the business and shares accordingly in the profits or losses generated by the enterprise. Partnerships may be either general or limited.

In a *general partnership*, each partner has unlimited liability for all obligations of the business. Thus, general partnerships have the same major disadvantage as sole proprietorships.

A *limited partnership* involves at least one general partner and one or more limited partners. The general partner typically assumes the responsibility of managing the business and is subject to unlimited liability for all obligations of the business. The limited partner or partners, on the other hand, tend to assume a passive role in the firm, with their liability limited to only the capital they contributed to the partnership.

Regardless of the type of partnership, the responsibilities and share of profits of the business among the partners are spelled out in a *partnership agreement*. The partnership is dissolved if a general partner dies or wishes to leave the business. However, the remaining partners may form a new partnership to carry on the business.

As is the case with sole proprietorships, the partnership itself is *not taxed on its earnings*; instead, the share of profits from the partnership are added to the individual partner's other income in determining the taxes owed. The advantages and disadvantages of the partnership mirror those of the sole proprietorship, with the exception that partnerships have somewhat *greater access to capital* because of the plurality of owners. However, this financial flexibility is still very limited when compared to the corporate form of organization.

Partnerships appear to be common in certain lines of businesses including legal services, professional accounting services, real estate ventures, and investment banking.

Corporation

The corporate form of business organization is the most dominant in terms of its economic clout. Corporations account for nearly 90 percent of business revenues and approximately 70 percent of business profits.

Corporations are formed through articles of incorporation in a given state. These articles describe certain legal responsibilities of the firm and certain other aspects of the organization and structure of the firm. Most of the large corporations of today are incorporated in the state of Delaware because of its favorable legal climate for businesses. Ownership in a corporation is obtained by purchasing shares of the capital stock in the firm. Owners may be individuals or other business entities. However, as a legal entity in its own right, *the corporation exists independent of the shareowners*, i.e., a corporation can purchase and own assets, borrow money, sue, and be sued. Thus, *obligations of a corporation are distinct from the obligations of its shareowners*. This aspect defines one of the major benefits of the corporate setup—that being the *limited liability* feature. That is, if a corporation were to go bankrupt, the most a shareholder would lose is his or her investment in the firm. There is no recourse to the shareholder's personal property to make up any deficiency to a creditor such as a bank.

http:
Do you know who the 400 richest people in America are? Which are the 200 best-run small companies? The 500 largest private firms? Forbes *magazine can tell you.*
http://www.forbes.com

Because the corporation is a distinct legal entity, it has the element of *permanency* and continuity not associated with the sole proprietorship and many partnerships. Individual shareowners may buy, sell, or transfer shares without getting the firm involved in the transaction. As a consequence of this feature, there is greater **liquidity** (the ability to convert their shares into cash) for shareowners in a corporation. In the case of a sole proprietorship or a general partnership, the only way to convert your holdings into cash would be to sell the business itself; at which point the business ceases to exist as originally formed. The limited liability feature of corporations along with the liquidity of shares greatly enhances the ability of corporations to raise additional funds for growth. Corporations also have the advantage of cross-border mobility. Among organizational forms, corporations can more easily set up operations in a foreign country. Cross-border mobility is especially important given the trend toward increasing globalization of trade.

The corporate form is not without its disadvantages. The primary disadvantage of the corporate structure is the *double taxation* to which investors are subject. Because a corporation is an independent legal entity, it is obligated to pay taxes on earnings generated by the firm. However, the corporation's earnings that are disbursed to shareholders in the form of dividends are taxed again at the individual level, giving rise to the double taxation phenomenon. In the case of sole proprietorships and partnerships, taxes are paid only once at the individual level but not at the firm level.

Another disadvantage of the corporate firm is the potential for *agency problems* between managers and shareholders. This is especially true of the large, publicly held corporation where shareholders tend to be widely dispersed and the professional managers hired to run the company have a very small ownership stake in the firm. Because managers do not have a significant stake in the firm, there exists a potential for conflict of interest between managers and the owners of the firm. As we observed earlier, managers in these situations may pursue policies that are not necessarily in the best interests of the shareowners.

Other Types of Business Organizations

Though sole proprietorships, partnerships, and corporations are the three basic forms of business organization, there are other types of organizations that have features of each of these basic forms, sometimes referred to as *hybrid organizations*.

The *Subchapter S corporation* is one such example. The Internal Revenue Code permits companies with 75 or fewer domestic stockholders, and that meet certain other requirements, to register as an S corporation. With the S corporation, stockholders avoid the double taxation of earnings and pay taxes similar to partnerships. The S corporation, however, preserves the other benefits of the corporate setup, including limited liability. In recent years there has been an increase in the number of firms registering as S corporations for tax purposes.

An increasingly popular form of hybrid organization is the *limited liability company (LLC)*. Like the S corporation, the earnings of the LLC flow through to the owners (called members) and are taxed at the individual level. Also, like the corporation, the LLC members have the benefit of limited liability. The LLC has fewer restrictions than the S corporation in terms of who can qualify as owners and greater flexibility in terms of accounting requirements. For example, the members need not be domestic, and from an accounting perspective no annual reports need to be filed. An example of an LLC is Lazard LLC, a prestigious investment banking firm formerly known as Lazard Freres & Co.

The *limited liability partnership (LLP)* is another type of business organization where all partners have limited liability. LLPs are taxed like any other partnership; thus, they share the tax advantage of regular partnerships and sole proprietorships.

Table 1.2 Forms of Business Organization

Type of organization:	Sole Proprietorship	Partnership	Corporation
Ease of formation:	Easy. Little paperwork involved.	Moderate. Requires partnership agreement	Complex. Must be incorporated in a state.
Liability:	Unlimited. Liabilities of shareholder in the business are not distinguished from the liabilities of the individual.	Unlimited for the general partner—similar to the sole proprietor. For limited partners, liability is limited to funds invested in the partnership.	Limited. The most a shareholder in a corporation can lose is what he or she paid for the shares.
Continuity:	Business is terminated whenever the owner chooses to do so or upon owner's death.	Partnership ends when the partners decide to dissolve it or upon the death of one or more of the partners. The partnership agreement usually spells out the conditions for termination.	Unlimited lifetime. The corporation is a separate entity that exists apart from the owners. Owners are free to sell their shares in the corporation to another investor.
Raising capital:	Very difficult. Capital is usually limited to personal resources of the sole proprietor and to the earnings generated from the business. Very difficult and expensive to obtain loans.	Better than sole proprietorship as capital may be raised from several partners or more partners may be added. Difficult and expensive to obtain loans.	Easiest. Corporation can sell additional shares to raise more capital. Also banks and other creditors are more willing to lend to corporations and at lower cost.
Taxes:	No double taxation as business income and personal income of owner are lumped together.	No double taxation as partnership income and personal income are combined.	The corporation pays tax on the income it generates. Any profits disbursed to shareholders as dividends are taxed again at the personal level. Thus, investors in a corporation are subject to double taxation.
Liquidity:	Illiquid. To convert ownership stake to cash, the owner will have to find a buyer for the business.	Liquidity is slightly better than sole proprietorship. Partnership interest may be purchased by remaining partners, depending upon partnership agreement.	For large corporations a that are listed on an exchange, liquidity is very good.
Agency conflicts:	None. If the owner is also the manager then there is no agency conflict.	Minimal. If the partners are involved in managing the business then agency conflicts will be minimal.	High. Potential for agency conflicts are high since owners tend to be dispersed and not involved in actively managing the firm.

A form of LLP is the professional limited liability partnership (PLLP), which is a partnership formed to render specific professional services such as legal, accounting, or medical services. Examples of LLPs include Baker and Botts LLP (legal practice) and PriceWaterhouseCoopers LLP (accounting and other management services). Goldman Sachs, a well-known investment banking firm, used to be a limited partnership until May 1999, when it converted to the corporate form in order to have better access to capital to finance growth, enable broad employee ownership of the firm, and enable the firm to engage in strategic acquisitions.

Table 1.2 summarizes the main features of the three basic types of business organizations—sole proprietorships, partnerships, and corporations.

Comprehension Check Questions

1. What are the main advantages of the sole proprietorship, partnership, and corporate forms of business organization?
2. What are the disadvantages of the three basic organization forms?
3. How does ease of funding differ among the three business forms?
4. How is taxation different among the three forms of business organizations?

THE FINANCIAL MANAGEMENT FUNCTION

This section describes the role and responsibilities of the financial manager. A sample corporate organization chart emphasizing the finance function is shown in Figure 1.1. Many firms divide the decision-making responsibilities of management among several different officers, which often include those in manufacturing, marketing, finance, personnel, and engineering. The finance function is usually headed by a vice president of finance or *chief financial officer* (CFO), who reports to the president or the chief executive officer (CEO). In some corporations the CFO may also be a member of the board of directors. *In a nutshell, the CFO has the primary responsibility for acquiring funds (cash) needed by a firm and for directing those funds into activities that will maximize the value of the firm for its owners.* In addition to overseeing the accounting, treasury, tax, and audit functions, today's CFO often has responsibility for strategic planning, monitoring and trading foreign currencies, managing the risk from volatile interest rates, and monitoring production and inventory levels. CFOs also must be able to communicate effectively with the investment community concerning the financial performance of the company.

The chief financial officer often distributes the financial management responsibilities between the *controller* and the *treasurer*. The controller normally has responsibility for all accounting-related activities. These include such functions as:

1. **Financial Accounting.** This function involves the preparation of the financial statements for the firm, such as the balance sheet, income statement, and the statement of cash flows.
2. **Cost Accounting.** This department often has responsibility for preparing the firm's operating budgets and monitoring the performance of the departments and divisions within the firm.
3. **Taxes.** This unit prepares the reports that the company must file with the various government (local, state, and federal) agencies.
4. **Data Processing.** Given its responsibilities involving corporate accounting and payroll activities, the controller also may have management responsibility for the company's data processing operations.

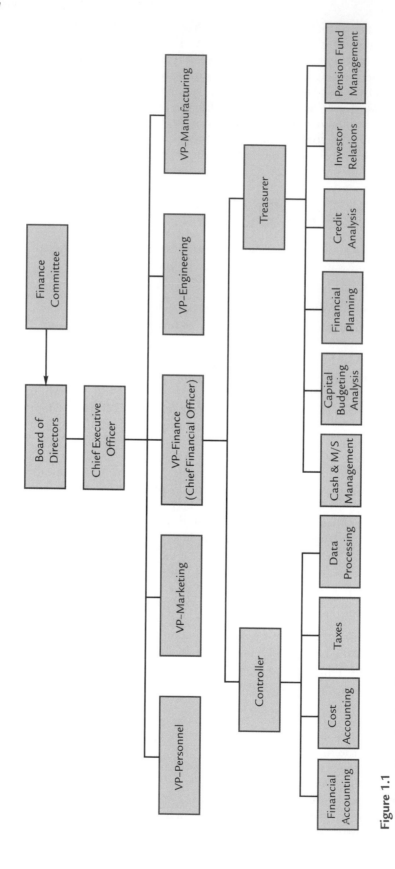

Figure 1.1
Corporate Organization Chart

The treasurer normally is concerned with the acquisition, custody, and expenditure of funds. These duties often include:

1. **Cash and Marketable Securities Management.** This group monitors the firm's short-term finances—forecasting its cash needs, obtaining funds from bankers and other sources when needed, and investing any excess funds in short-term interest-earning securities.

2. **Capital Budgeting Analysis.** This department is responsible for analyzing capital expenditures—that is, the purchase of long-term assets, such as new facilities and equipment.

3. **Financial Planning.** This department is responsible for analyzing the alternative sources of long-term funds, such as the issuance of bonds or common stock, that the firm will need to maintain and expand its operations.

4. **Credit Analysis.** Most companies have a department that is responsible for determining the amount of credit that the firm will extend to each of its customers. Although this group is responsible for performing financial analysis, it sometimes is located in the marketing area of the firm because of its close relationship to sales.

5. **Investor Relations.** Many large companies have a unit responsible for working with institutional investors (for example, mutual funds), bond rating agencies, stockholders, and the general financial community.

6. **Pension Fund Management.** The treasurer also may have responsibility for the investment of employee pension fund contributions. The investment analysis and portfolio management functions may be performed either within the firm or through outside investment advisors.

It should be emphasized that the specific functions of the controller and treasurer shown in Figure 1.1 are illustrative only and that the actual functions performed vary from company to company. For example, in some companies, the treasurer may have responsibility for tax matters. Also, as shown in Figure 1.1, the board of directors of the company may establish a finance committee, consisting of a number of directors and officers of the firm with substantial financial expertise, to make recommendations on broad financial policy issues.

FINANCIAL MANAGEMENT AND OTHER DISCIPLINES

As you pursue your study of financial management, you should keep in mind that financial management is not a totally independent area in business administration. Instead, it draws heavily on related disciplines and fields of study. The most important of these are *accounting* and *economics. Marketing, production, quantitative methods, information systems,* and *human resource management* also have an impact on the financial management field. Each of these related fields is discussed below, and Figure 1.2 depicts the relationship between financial management and its primary supportive disciplines.

Accounting

Financial executives manage a firm's financial and real assets and secure the funding needed to support these assets. Accountants are the scorekeepers. Financial managers often turn to accounting data to assist them in making decisions. Generally a company's accountants are responsible for developing financial reports and measures that assist its managers in assessing the past performance and future direction of the firm and in meeting certain legal obligations, such as the payment of taxes. The accountant's role includes the development of financial

**Figure 1.2
Impact of Other Disciplines on Financial Management**

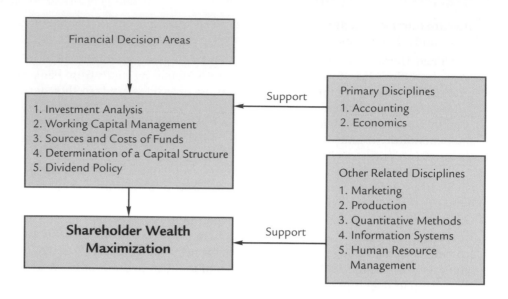

statements, such as the balance sheet, the income statement, and the statement of cash flows.

Financial managers are primarily concerned with a firm's cash flows, because they often determine the feasibility of certain investment and financing decisions. The financial manager refers to accounting data when making future resource allocation decisions concerning long-term investments, when managing current investments in working capital, and when making a number of other financial decisions (for example, determining the most appropriate capital structure and identifying the best and most timely sources of funds needed to support the firm's investment programs). In many small and medium-sized firms the accounting function and the financial management function may be handled by the same person or group of persons. In such cases, the distinctions just identified may become blurred.

Economics

The typical firm is heavily influenced by the overall performance of the economy and is dependent upon the money and capital markets for investment funds. Thus, financial managers should recognize and understand how monetary policies affect the cost of funds and the availability of credit. Financial managers should also be well versed in fiscal policy and how it affects the economy. What the economy can be expected to do in the future is a crucial factor in generating sales forecasts as well as other types of forecasts.

Marketing, Production, Quantitative Methods, Information Systems, and Human Resources

Marketing, production, quantitative methods, information systems and human resource management are indirectly related to the key day-to-day decisions made by financial managers. For example, financial managers should consider the impact of new product development and promotion plans made in the marketing area because these plans will require capital outlays and have an impact on the firm's projected cash flows. Similarly, changes in the production process may necessitate capital expenditures, which the firm's financial managers must evaluate and then finance. The tools of analysis developed in the quantitative methods area frequently are helpful in analyzing complex financial management problems. Since effective financial management relies on accurate and timely information gathering, information systems and technology management play a vital role in effective financial decision making. Finally, human resource management—including planning for an adequate workforce and the design of an appropriate compensation policy—has implications for financial planning and performance.

Comprehension Check Questions

1. For which decision areas is the financial manager responsible?
2. What are the functions of the controller and the treasurer?
3. What is the relationship between accounting and financial management?

CAREER OPPORTUNITIES IN FINANCE

The finance profession offers a number of exciting career opportunities. As illustrated in the organization chart in Figure 1.1, the corporate finance function encompasses a wide range of activities involved with acquisition and expenditure of the firm's resources. In addition to careers in corporate finance, opportunities are available in the financial services sector. The financial services sector includes such businesses as commercial banks, securities brokers, investment banks, mutual funds, pension funds, real estate companies, and insurance companies.

Detailed job responsibilities and duties are shown in Figure 1.3 for selected positions in the field of finance. Career opportunities span the spectrum from entry-level jobs to leadership roles in corporate finance and financial services. One should keep in mind that organizational structures differ significantly among various companies and that the specific responsibilities and duties for a given position may vary considerably among companies.

PROFESSIONAL FINANCE AFFILIATIONS

There are several professional organizations for practicing financial managers. These include the Financial Executives Institute, the Institute of Chartered Financial Analysts, and the Financial Management Association. These organizations provide an opportunity for professional interaction and lifelong learning.

FinanceLinks Online

Click on this button at **http://finance.swlearning.com** *for links to professional organizations.*

The Financial Management Association (FMA) serves as a bridge between the academic study of finance and the application of financial principles by financial managers. This is achieved through the sponsorship of several annual conferences and publication of a number of journals including *Financial Management* and *Journal of Applied Finance*. The FMA sponsors student chapters at many universities and sponsors the National Honor Society, the only national honorary organization for students of finance. The FMA also holds an annual meeting featuring the presentation of financial research, panel discussions led by leading academic and financial practitioners, and tutorials on new developments in finance. Additional membership information can be obtained from the Financial Management Association, College of Business Administration, University of South Florida, Tampa, Florida 33620, http://www.fma.org.

http://www.fma.org

ORGANIZATION OF THE TEXT

This text provides an introduction to both analytical tools and descriptive materials that are useful in corporate financial management. In keeping with the introductory

VICE PRESIDENT—FINANCE

Basic Function: Plan, direct, and execute long-term financing required to fund corporate capital requirements at the lowest cost.

Primary Responsibilities and Duties:

➢ Plan and execute the financings required to fund corporate capital requirements while maintaining a balanced capital structure

➢ Direct, support, and review the actions of the department in obtaining long-term financing and maintaining positive relations with lenders and rating agencies

➢ Provide a capital budgeting and financial projection system

➢ Integrate projections of capital requirements with the status of credit markets and the company's capital structure

➢ Coordinate the activities of underwriters, lawyers, and accountants in order to complete financing in timely manner

➢ Maintain contact with all company lenders and keep them informed of the company's goals and progress

➢ Provide financial support for various contractual arrangements

➢ Monitor pension fund assets and various special projects

DIRECTOR—INVESTOR RELATIONS

Basic Function: Primary work is in investor relations with additional responsibility for pension fund investments and corporate financings.

Primary Responsibilities and Duties:

➢ Keep informed regarding business conditions of all company operating subsidiaries, strategic planning directions, and financial developments at the corporate level

➢ Stay abreast of industry matters to help explain external influences on the company as well as to keep up with the operating and financial results of the company and its competitors

➢ Communicate on a daily basis with the investment community in order to accurately portray company results and general expectations within the guidelines of SEC policy

➢ Arrange meeting times and places of senior management presentations around the country with investment analyst groups

➢ Act as a host to analysts who visit company

➢ Establish plans and procedures when company hosts inspection trips or special seminars requiring special coordination among operating subsidiaries

➢ Select and set up personal meetings with institutional owners in order to develop greater support for our stock by the institution's portfolio managers

➢ Prepare monthly reports on investor relations matters, review policy and plans, and make recommendations for changes

➢ Monitor investment results of investment managers

➢ Prepare monthly and quarterly reports on results and outlook

➢ Work with actuary and consultants on long-term strategy, including asset allocation and manager selection.

ASSISTANT TREASURER—CASH CONTROL AND RISK MANAGEMENT

Basic Function: Responsible for operations of the Treasury Department involving cash management operations with specific attention to the effective direction and control of corporate funds internally and through the company's various bank accounts.

Primary Responsibilities and Duties:

➤ Manage, in conjunction with lockbox banks retained by company, the processing of over 120,000 customer payments daily
➤ Disbursement of all company funds, including payrolls, pensions, and vendor payments
➤ Direct the management staff to assure compliance with stated objectives and planning in order to assure the effectiveness of the organization
➤ Sign checks and review and approve various documents such as wire transfer confirmations and investment letters
➤ Meet with banks and their representatives
➤ Perform various assignments of senior management
➤ Also responsible for the risk management/insurance function

FINANCIAL ANALYST—CAPITAL BUDGETS

Basic Function: Review capital expenditure and lease requests that require finance concurrence, coordinate and compile data for the annual capital budget, and compile actual and projected capital cash flows for reports.

Primary Responsibilities and Duties:

➤ Check accuracy of financial and accounting treatment for capital and lease requests
➤ Check for compliance with corporate regulations
➤ Prepare executive summaries for major capital projects
➤ Travel to obtain further details on capital projects
➤ Provide analysis and control prior to authorization of the project
➤ Coordinate and compile data for annual capital budget
➤ Analyze all projects submitted for the budget
➤ Prepare executive summaries on projected authorization, expenditures, and variances from historical data
➤ Compile actual and projected capital cash flows for quarterly reports

Source: Jack S. Rader, Careers in Finance *(Tampa, FL: Financial Management Association International, College of Business Administration, University of South Florida (813-9743-2084, 1995). Reprinted with permission.*

---

nature of the book, it is not designed to present an exhaustive discussion of all aspects of corporate financial management. Instead it is intended to do the following:

➤ Acquaint the reader with the major types of decisions faced by financial managers
➤ Develop a framework for analyzing these decisions in a systematic manner
➤ Provide the reader with the background necessary to pursue more advanced readings and courses in financial management

For convenience we have divided the book into several parts. However, in reality and practice, the various topics and financial decisions are interrelated and should not be considered in isolation from one another.

Each chapter begins with a brief overview of the chapter and a listing of the learning objectives for the chapter. Dispersed throughout the chapter are a series of comprehension check questions. These questions are designed to encourage you to pause and reflect on your understanding of the material covered up to that point. At the end of each chapter are a point-by-point summary of the chapter and extensive sets of discussion questions and problems, including "Self-Test Problems" with detailed solutions that you can use to test your mastery over the material covered in the chapter. A glossary of key terms is provided at the end of the book. Most chapters include *Finance & The Real World* sections to highlight events or real situations that are closely related to the topic(s) covered in the chapter. We also highlight the interrelation between finance and other disciplines where appropriate. "Check" answers to selected problems appear at the end of the book. One of the unique aspects of the book is the integration of how to use financial calculators and Excel spreadsheet to solve a variety of financial problems. These are scattered throughout the various chapters as appropriate.

Parts of the Text

Part I: Introduction. This part includes several chapters that provide an overview of finance and background material to enhance the understanding of subsequent material. Chapter 2 reviews the major elements of the financial marketplace. It includes a discussion of the structure of the U.S. financial system and the role of stock exchanges. It also introduces the concept of return and acquaints the reader with the basics of interpreting security price quotes such as those that appear in *The Wall Street Journal.* Chapter 3 provides a review of financial statements, and Chapter 4 shows how financial ratios can be used to evaluate firm performance.

Part II: Determinants of Valuation. Valuation is the central theme of financial management and finance in general. Chapter 5 develops the concept of the time value of money. This concept is used in the valuation of securities and the evaluation of investment projects expected to provide benefits over a number of years. Chapter 6 provides a comprehensive introduction to the concept of risk in finance and the relationship between risk and required return. Chapter 7 discusses long-term debt, including the characteristics of long-term debt and the valuation of bonds. Chapter 8 deals with the valuation of common stocks and preferred stocks.

Part III: The Capital Investment Decision. This portion of the text focuses on capital expenditures—that is, investments in long-term assets. Chapter 9 deals with the measurement of the cash flows (benefits and costs) associated with long-term investment projects. Chapter 10 considers various decision-making criteria that can be used when choosing projects that will maximize the value of the firm.

Part IV: Capital Structure and Dividend Policy. This section of the book examines the cost of capital of the firm and how it is impacted by the capital structure of the firm. The dividend policy decision of the firm is also examined. Chapter 11 illustrates the principles of measuring a firm's cost of capital. The cost of funds to a firm is an important input in the capital budgeting process. Chapters 12 and 13 address the relationship of a firm's capital structure to its cost of capital. Chapter 14 discusses the factors that influence the choice of a dividend policy and the impact of various dividend policies on the value of a firm.

Part V: Financial Planning, Working Capital Management, and International Finance.
Chapter 15 deals with short-term and long-term financial planning. Chapter 16 begins with a discussion of working capital management including the risk-return trade-offs of alternative working capital policies. The chapter then focuses on effective management of the current assets of the firm including cash, marketable securities, accounts receivable, and inventory. Chapter 17 deals with management of current liabilities including a discussion of the sources and costs of various short-term sources of borrowing. Chapter 18, the final chapter of the text, discusses aspects of international finance relevant to financial management of the firm.

Summary

➤ The primary goal of financial management decision making is the maximization of shareholder wealth as measured by the value of the firm's stock.

➤ The primary reason for the divergence of objectives between managers and shareholders has been attributed to separation of ownership (shareholders) and control (management) in corporations. This divergence in objectives between managers and shareholders is known as agency conflict or principal–agent conflict.

➤ There exist several mechanisms to reduce agency conflicts between managers and shareholders. These include management compensation, monitoring by the board of directors, and the threat of takeovers.

➤ Effective financial management requires that due consideration be given to ethical behavior in the conduct of business decisions.

➤ The value of a firm, or of any asset, depends on the amount or magnitude, timing, and risk of the cash flows generated by the firm. These cash flows are determined, in part, by key financial management decisions, including investment decisions, dividend decisions, financing decisions, and ownership structure decisions. These decisions must be made in the context of factors in the broader economic environment.

➤ The three principal forms of business organization are the sole proprietorship, the partnership, and the corporation. Corporations have certain advantages and disadvantages compared to sole proprietorships and partnerships. Corporations are a legal entity by themselves and therefore have a continuity and permanency not associated with the other types of business organizations. Corporations can more easily raise additional funds for investment compared to sole proprietorships and partnerships. The main disadvantage of corporations is that shareholders are subject to double taxation.

➤ The finance function usually is headed by a vice president or chief financial officer. The financial management responsibilities often are divided between the controller and the treasurer. The controller normally has responsibility for all accounting related activities. The treasurer is normally concerned with the acquisition, custody, and expenditure of funds.

➤ Financial management is closely related to other areas of business decision making, particularly accounting and economics.

➤ The finance profession offers a number of exciting career opportunities both within the corporate finance function and in the financial services sector.

Questions and Topics for Discussion

1. Define shareholder wealth. Explain how it is measured.
2. Define the following terms or phrases:
   a. limited and unlimited liability
   b. double taxation
   c. separation of ownership and control
   d. hybrid organization
   e. principal–agent conflict

3. What are the differences between shareholder wealth maximization and profit maximization?

4. Which type of corporation is more likely to be a shareholder wealth maximizer—one with wide ownership and no owners directly involved in the firm's management or one that is closely held where the owners are actively involved in managing the firm?

5. Is the shareholder wealth maximization goal a short- or long-term goal? Explain your answer.

6. Is ethical behavior the same as operating within legal boundaries?

7. Explain why management may tend to pursue goals other than shareholder wealth maximization.

8. Give some examples of manager–shareholder conflicts.

9. What are some of the ways in which manager–shareholder conflicts may be controlled?

10. Explain the differences in the responsibilities of the treasurer and the controller in a large corporation.

11. Why is earnings per share not a consistently good measure of a firm's performance?

12. What are the major factors that determine the value of a firm's stock?

13. How can the adherence to high standards of ethical business practice contribute to the goal of shareholder wealth maximization?

CHAPTER

2 The Business Environment

This chapter provides a basic understanding of the environment in which a business operates. We highlight the role of the firm in the much larger economic system of which it is a part, with special emphasis on the interaction between the firm and the financial markets. In doing so, we present an overview of financial markets, including the stock market. The chapter also exposes the reader to information sources in popular business journals that are especially relevant to the financial manager. It concludes with an illustration of how to calculate the *rate of return* on investments, a concept that is fundamental to finance.

Chapter Objectives

Upon completion of the chapter, you should have a clear understanding of the following:

1. The interaction between a firm and its business environment

2. The role of financial markets and significant aspects of them

3. The meaning of market efficiency

4. Interpretation of basic stock and bond market data

5. Calculation of *holding period returns*

ASPECTS OF THE BUSINESS ENVIRONMENT

Businesses are formed to provide a valuable service or product and generate a satisfactory rate of return to its investors. In the course of conducting their normal business, firms are constantly interacting with a number of markets. This is a necessity; no organization can exist in a vacuum. Figure 2.1 illustrates this concept: Lines radiate from the focal point, the firm, to a number of different markets with which the firm interacts.

Every firm interacts with the *product market*, where the firm markets its products or services and competes with rival firms. For example, General Motors, Ford, Toyota, and BMW, among others, compete against each other for potential customers interested in buying a new automobile. Firms are also actively involved in the *labor market*, where they hire and fire skilled and unskilled laborers, managers, and other professionals, and in the various *markets for raw materials and other inputs* required for the business. Thus, Dell Computer Corporation, for instance, has many purchasing managers who actively seek out new and varied sources for inputs to their production, including semiconductor chips, disk drives, monitors, modems, etc. Firms also trade in the *capital goods market*. When ExxonMobil buys a new offshore oil rig or American Airlines buys new jetliners or disposes of old ones, they are engaging in transactions in the capital goods markets. Finally, firms are ac-

Figure 2.1
The Business Environment of the Firm

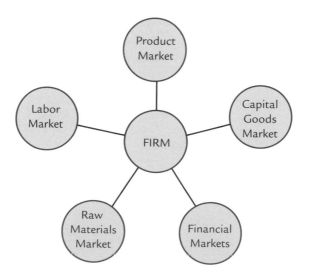

tive participants in the *financial markets.* The financial markets are where firms raise additional funds and invest their excess funds. We need a thorough understanding of the role, scope, and functioning of the financial markets since a number of the financial manager's responsibilities require interaction with them.

FINANCIAL MARKETS

The Financial System

Trading in financial assets takes place in financial markets. Although money is the most obvious financial asset, there are other financial assets that represent *claims* against assets and future earnings of firms, government entities, or even individuals. The credit card balances and mortgage loans of individuals, Treasury security obligations of the U.S. government, debt and equity securities of corporations all are examples of financial assets that are generated and traded in the financial markets. Financial markets are generally classified into primary and secondary markets. ***Primary markets*** are where *new* securities or primary claims are issued, resulting in cash inflow to the issuer. ***Secondary markets*** are markets where *already existing* financial claims such as stocks and bonds are bought and sold, with no resulting cash inflow to the issuer of the claim. Figure 2.2 graphically depicts the major elements of financial markets.

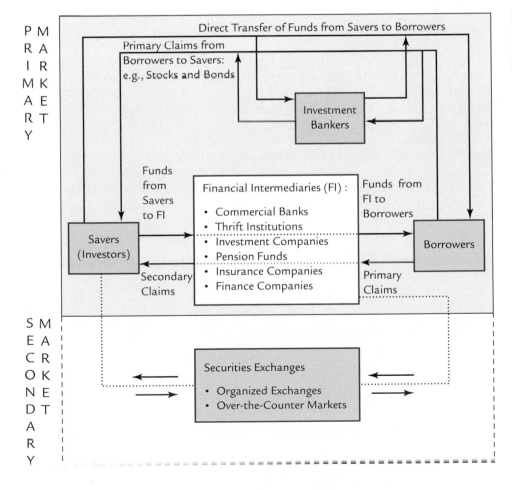

Figure 2.2
Diagram of the Financial Market System

Primary Markets

The basic purpose of the primary markets is to channel funds from *saving units* to *borrowing units.* These units could be households, businesses, or government entities. Generally, households as a group are net savers, while businesses and government entities, as a group, tend to be net borrowers. However, the terms *net saver* or *net borrower* do not necessarily connote anything about a particular entity's financial health. Businesses as a group are generally net borrowers because they often invest in growth opportunities that cannot be financed by internally generated funds alone. They have to obtain funds through the sale of stock or debt issues to finance new projects. The federal government, more often than not, is a net borrower because the tax revenues it generates are less than its spending, resulting in a net deficit. Households generally are net savers since as a group they earn more than they spend on current consumption.

We have been talking in terms of groups, but it should be noted that on an individual basis, some units might include both net savers and net borrowers. So, not all households are net savers; a young family may be a net borrower while an older, retired couple may be classified as a net saver. Likewise, a start-up company in a growth industry, such as biotechnology, may be a net borrower; but a large firm in a mature industry, such as oil exploration and refining, is likely to be a net saver. Furthermore, a firm or an entity that is a net saver (borrower) doesn't necessarily mean it does not borrow (invest) funds. A firm that has an excess of cash flow over its spending may still borrow over the course of a year to finance seasonal needs such as the buildup in inventory in anticipation of the year-end holiday selling season.

Our focus in this chapter is on *primary claims* issued by the corporation rather than by governments and individuals. Primary claims of corporations include various debt securities, such as mortgage and debenture bonds, commercial paper, and lines of credit and equity offerings, including common stock and preferred stock.

Direct and Indirect Flow of Funds from Savers to Borrowers

As shown in Figure 2.2, firms may issue primary claims *directly* to investors (savers), often with the help of *investment bankers.* The role of the investment banker is to assist firms with the issuance process. Funds may also be transferred directly from savers to borrowers *without* the intervention of an investment banker—as when a current shareholder of Intel Corporation buys additional shares in the company through its dividend reinvestment plan. Another example might involve a family-owned corporation borrowing funds from family members or friends for business purposes. However, for most publicly held corporations, direct transfers involve the help of investment bankers. Their basic function is to find buyers for the primary claim issue. The issue could be a type of corporate bond, preferred stock, common stock, or some other type of security. The investment banker helps the firm in deciding such things as the size of the issue, timing of the issue, and what features the issue should have. Investment bankers also may *underwrite* the issue, in which case they buy the entire issue and resell it to the public at a slightly higher price—thereby taking over the risk of selling the issue. Primary claims can be sold either as a *public offering* or as a *private placement.* In a public offering, as the term implies, the securities are sold to individual investors or institutional investors in general. In a private placement, the entire issue is placed with a single investor or a small group of investors.

Investment bankers usually form a *syndicate* when deciding to underwrite an issue. A group of investment bankers (the syndicate) get together to engage in a particular transaction to reduce the risk exposure for individual members and also to get a broad marketing exposure. Firms issuing common shares to the public for the first time—also known as ***initial public offerings (IPOs)***, or subsequently, as ***seasoned equity offerings***, usually do so on an underwritten basis with an investment banking syndicate. For example, the advertisement in Figure 2.3 shows that on July 19, 2000, StorageNetworks, Inc. sold 10.35 million shares of common stock in an initial public offering (IPO) underwritten by an investment banking syndicate led by Goldman, Sachs & Co. Investment bankers also help firms sell debt securities.

Figure 2.2 shows that funds also may flow from savers to borrowers (firms) *indirectly* through ***financial intermediaries***. Financial intermediaries include commercial banks, thrift institutions, investment companies, pensions funds, insurance companies, and finance companies. In this instance, savers invest in the ***secondary claims*** of financial intermediaries, which in turn invest in primary claims of the borrowers.

**Figure 2.3
Sample of Initial
Public Offering**

Secondary claims are the claims issued by the financial intermediary. The deposit an investor makes into a savings account in a bank is an example of a secondary claim. Other examples of secondary claims are certificates of deposit issued by a bank, life insurance policies, investments in a mutual fund, and contributions to a pension fund. Financial intermediaries take the proceeds of these secondary claims and in turn invest the funds in primary claims of the ultimate borrowers. For example, banks take the funds pooled from many depositors and invest them in primary claims, such as loans to companies. Investment bankers may be involved in this indirect channel by helping firms sell their primary claims to the financial intermediaries. Table 2.1 provides a brief description of the various financial intermediaries.

Financial intermediaries facilitate the transfer of funds from savers to borrowers by offering potential benefits to investors:

1. Diversification. For many investors with limited funds it would be difficult to diversify by directly purchasing the primary claims of firms. For instance, an individual with only $1,000 savings would be hard-pressed to purchase shares in more than one firm. IBM shares, for example, were trading for approximately $80 per share at the beginning of 2003; at that price, you would not be able to afford more than 12 shares, let alone invest in other companies. On the other hand, if you invest the $1,000 through a mutual fund, such as the Fidelity Magellan stock fund, your money is pooled with that of many other investors, enabling the portfolio manager of the fund to invest in a well-diversified combination of securities—thereby reducing the risk to you.

2. Expertise. Since most financial intermediaries are experts in their lines of business, your funds generally are managed by individuals who can make choices informed by their skills and the resources at their disposal.

Table 2.1 Description of Different Financial Intermediaries

Commercial Banks:	Savings institutions that take deposits in the form of checking accounts, savings accounts, certificates of deposit, etc., and invest in primary claims such as mortgage loans, consumer loans, commercial loans, or government debt securities.
Thrift Institutions:	Savings institutions that take deposits and invest mainly in consumer loans and mortgage loans.
Investment Companies:	Mutual funds that pool savings of many individuals and invest in portfolios of securities. They invest in a wide variety of primary claims including bonds and stocks. Mutual funds are set up to meet different objectives, such as income, growth, tax-free, international diversification, etc.
Pension Funds:	Organizations that take pension contributions while a person is gainfully employed and provide benefits upon retirement. The pension contributions are invested in primary claims usually of a long-term nature, such as long-term bonds, stocks, and real estate.
Insurance Companies:	A wide variety of companies that provide insurance coverage for life, casualty, theft, and medical losses. The insurance companies charge premiums that are invested in both real and financial assets. The returns from the investments are used to pay any future claims made by policyholders.
Finance Companies:	Non-deposit-taking institutions that specialize in consumer loans, commercial loans, and equipment leasing. Finance companies obtain funds by issuing their own debt claims and stocks.

3. Liquidity. Generally, secondary claims of financial intermediaries are more liquid than primary claims of firms. Banks stand ready to redeem your account at a moment's notice, but the same cannot be said of an investment in the common stock of smaller firms. Further, you do not incur any transactions costs (commissions) in closing an account, whereas you pay commissions in selling shares in a company.

4. Convenience. Financial intermediaries such as banks, thrifts, and even mutual funds provide the added convenience of check-writing privileges, record-keeping services, and the convenience of "one-stop" shopping service for other personal financial services. Banks, for example, in addition to providing traditional checking services may offer you credit cards, mortgage lending, trust management, and other services.

5. Risk management. Financial intermediaries also provide an important risk management function. For example, a life insurance policy on the breadwinner of the family can eliminate some of the extreme consequences associated with loss of life on household income. Likewise by investing in an FDIC-insured bank deposit an investor can virtually eliminate any default risk that he or she would otherwise experience if the money were invested directly in a corporation.

The distinction between different types of financial intermediaries is slowly disappearing. In the aftermath of the great 1929 stock market crash the U.S. government enacted legislation that severely restricted the activities of various types of financial intermediaries. For example, banks were not allowed to engage in investment banking activities or to sell insurance policies. This was done to ensure that financial institutions did not misuse the funds entrusted to them—a major contributing factor to the 1929 crash. However, in the last two decades there has been a steady liberalization of the regulatory environment, especially in broadening the activities that the different types of financial intermediaries may engage in. As a result, the different types of financial intermediaries are increasingly encroaching onto each other's turfs. For example, Citicorp merged with Travelers Insurance and Salomon Smith Barney to form Citigroup—combining one of the largest commercial banks with one of the largest insurance companies and one of the largest investment banking firms. This trend toward breaking down the distinction between different types of financial intermediaries is expected to continue and even accelerate in the future.

Money and Capital Markets The market for primary claims consists of money markets and capital markets. *Money markets* deal in short-term securities, which are customarily defined as securities having maturities of one year or less *when first issued*. Firms enter the money market to borrow funds for the short term and also to invest funds in the short term. Short-term borrowing needs arise for a variety of reasons including seasonal increases in inventory to meet, say, the demand during the peak year-end holiday season. Firms also invest their excess cash in the money markets until they have a need for the funds. *Capital markets* deal in long-term securities having maturities greater than 1 year *when first issued*. The capital markets are used to obtain long-term funds through the issuance of various debt and equity instruments. Table 2.2 shows examples of money and capital market instruments. The distinction between money market and capital market instruments is based on the original maturity of the instrument. Thus, a corporate bond issued with an original maturity of 15 years, with 6 months remaining to maturity, is still considered a capital market instrument and not a money market instrument.

Table 2.2 Examples of Money and Capital Market Instruments

Money Market Instruments

Treasury Bills:	Short-term obligations of the U.S. government. They are issued with initial maturities of 13, 26, and 52 weeks.
Commercial Paper:	Short-term, unsecured promissory notes issued by large well-known corporations and finance companies. Maturities range up to 270 days.
Checking Account:	Deposits maintained by individuals and businesses with commercial banks against which checks are written.
Certificates of Deposit (CDs):	Issued by commercial banks and entitling the holder to receive the amount deposited plus accrued interest.

Capital Market Instruments

Corporate Bonds:	Long-term debt obligations of corporations with maturities extending usually from 10 to 30 years. Interest is usually paid semiannually.
Treasury Bonds:	Debt obligations of the U.S. government with maturities extending from 10 to 30 years. Interest is paid semiannually.
Common Stock:	A financial asset that provides an equity ownership stake in a business. Returns are in the form of dividends declared by the firm and capital gains (or losses) on the sale of the common stock.
Mortgage Loans:	Loans taken by an individual or firm to finance the purchase of real property using the property as security or collateral.
Municipal Bonds:	Long-term bonds issued by state and local governments to finance various projects, such as a new school.

Secondary Markets

We said earlier that financial markets are comprised of primary and secondary markets. Our discussion up to this point has focused on primary markets used by companies and other borrowers to raise new funds. Thus, when a company transacts in the primary market it results in a net cash inflow to the firm. We now turn to a discussion of the secondary markets. Figure 2.2 shows that secondary markets are where the savers (investors) and intermediaries trade in *previously* issued securities: organized exchanges and over-the-counter markets. Familiar examples of a secondary market is the New York Stock Exchange (NYSE) or the ***over-the-counter market (OTC)***. The OTC market consists of numerous *security dealers* linked together by an electronic network of computer terminals and telephones through which they make offers to buy and sell securities for their clients and for their own accounts as well.

In secondary markets trading takes place in already issued corporate stocks and bonds. For example, if you had been lucky enough to purchase some shares of the initial public offering of eBay Inc. at $18.00/share on September 24, 1998, when the issue was first sold to the public, you would have been transacting in the primary market. Suppose you decided to sell it the same day in the OTC market where the stock was listed at the opening market price of $53.50. You would have entered into a transaction in the secondary market. Note that when you sell the shares in the OTC market to another investor the firm receives no money since the transaction is entirely between the two investors.

In addition to secondary markets for stocks and bonds, there is also a secondary market for virtually every type of primary claim including commercial paper, home mortgage loans, credit card balances, bankers acceptances, municipal bonds, and U.S. Treasury bonds. These other secondary markets are generally not as well known because trading in them is confined to big institutional players rather than individual investors. These markets are, however, extremely important to the economy.

Benefits of Secondary Markets Although secondary markets do not result in any direct cash inflow into a firm, their existence and effectiveness is crucial to the efficient functioning of the primary claims market and the economy as a whole. They provide a number of benefits:

1. Liquidity. One of the most important benefits of a secondary market is the liquidity that it provides to potential investors. Can you imagine investing in shares of Wal-Mart if you knew that there was no organized secondary market where you could easily sell the security? Or buying a bond issued by General Electric Corporation if you knew that when the time came to sell the security you would have to search for a buyer yourself? An organized secondary market brings together all the buyers and sellers interested in transacting in particular types of securities, thus increasing the chances that an interested buyer (seller) will meet an interested seller (buyer).

2. Efficient pricing and information disclosure. With a concentration of buyers and sellers in one "location" there is greater likelihood for more information generation and dissemination, with the consequent result that security prices will reflect their true intrinsic worth. For example, in the U.S. stock markets you will find that there is no dearth of information about companies. Numerous businesses have been formed with the sole purpose of providing analysis of companies. These businesses find that investors (markets) are willing to pay for such valuable information. Firms such as Value Line, Standard & Poor's, and Moody's have high-quality research staffs who put out information and analyze various securities and firms on a timely basis. This is in addition to the information and analyses conducted by professional money management firms and brokerage houses. In fact, companies have a vested interest in ensuring that pertinent information about them is made available to the market in a timely manner. Companies like Motorola, Intel, and Merck continually report the latest developments through the news wires, press bulletins, regular meetings with financial analysts, and other means. By doing so, these companies help ensure that their stocks are trading at a price that reflects the future prospects of the firm.

3. Efficient allocation of capital. From a macroeconomic perspective, secondary markets enable the proper allocation of capital by facilitating an efficient primary market. An effective secondary market ensures that funds will go to those businesses and industries that have bright prospects, while firms with ineffective management or those in declining industries will be choked out of existence unless significant remedies are instituted. By doing so, overall social welfare is increased and the economy as a whole is better off.

Security Exchanges We next discuss briefly the secondary markets for corporate stocks and bonds. As noted before, there exists a secondary market for virtually every type of primary claim. Our focus here is on corporate equities and bonds, as these tend to be the most important sources of long-term capital for firms. The secondary markets may be classified into organized securities exchanges, over-the-counter markets, and electronic communications networks.

Organized Securities Exchanges Organized securities exchanges operate from a centralized location. A prime example of an organized exchange is the New York

Click on this button at **http://finance. swlearning.com** *for links to exchanges and indexes.*

Security and OTC exchanges support Web sites describing themselves, the stocks they trade, how to be listed on their exchanges, and more. **http://www.nyse.com http://www.nasdaq.com http://www.amex.com**

Stock Exchange (NYSE), which operates from its landmark location at 11 Wall Street, New York. The NYSE along with the American Stock Exchange (AMEX), also located in New York, make up the two national securities exchanges in the United States. They are referred to as national exchanges because of the scope of the firms listed on them and because they attract buyers and sellers from throughout the country and internationally. There are also *regional* exchanges located around the country. The largest are the Chicago Stock Exchange, the Pacific Stock Exchange, the Boston Stock Exchange, the Cincinnati Stock Exchange, and the Philadelphia Stock Exchange. Most of the trading in the regional exchanges is confined to firms that have a regional presence and a limited number of shareholders.

The organized stock exchanges are like private clubs where memberships are restrictive. Only listed securities can be traded on these exchanges, and listing requirements vary. The NYSE has stringent requirements to be listed, while the NASDAQ, AMEX and the regional stock exchanges have less restrictive conditions. The NYSE, sometimes referred to as the Big Board, had ***preferred*** and ***common stocks*** from 2,862 companies listed on the exchange (as of the end of year 2000). In addition, corporate bonds issued by 375 companies are traded on the NYSE. In general, the larger, more prestigious companies and firms with a longer operating history seek to be listed on the NYSE. Table 2.3 presents some of the listing requirements for the NYSE. The smaller, newer, and more regional companies usually obtain a listing on one of the other exchanges; as they grow bigger and more profitable they often graduate to the more prestigious exchanges. For example, Outback Steakhouse, Inc. was listed on the NASDAQ but in year 2000 decided to move to the NYSE.

Trading on the organized exchanges takes place among members of the stock exchanges who own "seats" in the exchange. There are 1,366 seats on the NYSE, a number that has remained constant since 1953. The members who own these seats have the right to buy and sell the listed securities in the exchange. Thus, if you were interested in selling your shares in The Walt Disney Company, which is listed on the NYSE, you would contact your broker, such as Charles Schwab, which is a member of the exchange, and give instructions to sell your shares. Charles Schwab in turn transmits your sell order to its representative on the stock exchange floor, who attempts to sell your shares to other members in the exchange who are ready to buy Disney shares. Obviously, your representative will sell your Disney shares to the highest bidder. Thus, the transaction involves an auction process where buyers seek out the seller with the lowest price and sellers seek out the highest bidder. Consequently, organized exchanges also are sometimes referred to as ***auction markets***.

A discussion of organized exchanges would not be complete without mentioning the role of specialists. **Specialists** are members of the exchange who play an im-

Table 2.3 Listing Requirements for NYSE

Earnings:	Earnings before tax of at least $2.5 million for the most recent year and $2 million for the preceding 2 years.
Assets:	Net tangible assets of at least $18 million.
Market Capitalization:	Market value for publicly held shares must equal at least $100 million.
Shares Outstanding:	Total shares outstanding of at least 1.1 million.
Shareholders:	At least 2,000 shareholders, each owning at least 100 shares.

Source: 2000 NYSE Fact Book.

portant role in maintaining a fair and orderly market in the stocks assigned to them. Among other things specialists ensure sufficient liquidity and minimal volatility in their specialty stocks. For example, if there is an order imbalance in the Disney stock with a large number of sell orders but few buy orders, the specialist for Disney would step in and buy the stock for his own account. On the other hand, if the Disney stock was subject to a buying pressure, the specialist would sell some of the stock from his inventory to meet the excess demand.

Over-the-Counter Market. Stocks and other securities that are not listed on the organized exchanges are said to trade in the OTC market. Generally speaking, the stocks trading in the OTC market are smaller, less widely followed, and have shorter trading histories than their counterparts in the national listed exchanges. But this is by no means the rule. Although their stock could trade on the NYSE, Microsoft, Intel, and Apple Computer prefer to trade in the OTC markets. In addition, most corporate bonds, preferred stocks, U.S. Treasuries, and municipal bonds are traded in the OTC markets. (Remember, the OTC market, unlike the organized exchanges, is not characterized by a physical location where all the trading is concentrated.) The OTC dealers who are willing to buy and sell a security for their own account are said to ***make a market*** in that security. These dealers maintain an inventory of particular securities from which they sell to interested buyers and to which they add by buying from interested sellers. The dealers post *bid* and *ask* prices on the securities in which they make a market. The bid price is the price at which the dealer is willing to buy a given security and the ask price is the price the dealer is willing to sell a given security. For any given dealer the ask price is going to be greater than the bid price. This difference is known as the ***spread,*** which is how the dealer makes a profit.

As an investor if you are interested in buying a security that trades in the OTC market, your broker will find out which dealers are making a market in that particular security and attempt to buy the security from the dealer posting the lowest ask price. On the other hand, if you are in the market to sell a security, your broker will seek to transact with the dealer posting the highest bid price.

A specific example of an OTC market is the NASDAQ stock market, or simply NASDAQ. ***NASDAQ*** is an acronym for National Association of Securities Dealers Automated Quotation. It is a wholly owned subsidiary of the National Association of Security Dealers (NASD), a self-regulated body of brokers and dealers that licenses its members and regulates how trading is to be conducted. Recently NASDAQ was reorganized to become a for-profit organization just like any publicly held corporation. NASDAQ is a network of dealers and brokers scattered all over the country that conduct business through a system of electronic terminals. The terminals display, among other things, dealers' bid and ask prices for various stocks and allow participants to transact their trades electronically rather than in a particular physical location (as in the case of organized stock exchanges). As in the case of organized stock exchanges, only securities meeting certain requirements are eligible to be listed in the NASDAQ. Further, a subsection of these stocks may be considered for inclusion as a ***National Market Security (NMS)*** issue if more stringent qualifications are met. The NMS stocks basically are stocks that are national in scope, have a wide following, and are the most liquid. There are currently over 6,000 actively traded issues in the NASDAQ.

http://www.nasdaq.com

Electronic Communications Networks. Electronic communications networks or ECNs represent the latest development in how stocks are traded. The growth of this alternate stock market is directly attributable to the rise of the Internet. The first ECNs appeared in 1997. Unlike the auction-based organized stock exchanges or the OTC dealer markets, ECNs are designed to bring buyers and sellers together directly. Buyers and sellers enter the amount and the prices at which they are willing to trade and the ECN automatically matches the buyers and sellers. Participants are levied a charge of 0.25 cents to 1.5 cents per share by the ECN for this service. However, the potential savings for investors can be very significant because there are no dealer spreads and no broker commissions to be incurred. The ECN also provides complete anonymity to the participants. In the event the ECN is unable to find a match internally, it has the capability to link to the NASDAQ and execute the trade there.

There are currently 14 ECNs that trade mostly in the more liquid NASDAQ stocks. Some of the better known ECNs are Archipelago, Island, INSTINET, Tradebook, BRUT, and REDIBook. They have become such a major force that estimates indicate that ECNs now account for approximately 30 to 40 percent of NASDAQ volume. A limited number of NYSE stocks are also traded on the ECNs. Many consider INSTINET (Institutional Networks Corporation), formed in 1969, to be the original electronic trading network; it was created to link large institutional buyers and sellers, such as mutual funds and insurance companies, thereby saving them significant amounts in commissions. This system of direct trading is sometimes known as *the fourth market.*

Decimalization Stocks had been quoted in minimum increments of one eighth of a dollar, meaning that the minimum price change was 12.5 cents. However, as a result of a U.S. congressional mandate, all exchanges were required to implement decimal pricing by August 2, 2001, which meant that that all securities must trade in minimum increments of a penny. The motivation for the legislation is research that indicated that the minimum increment of one eighth resulted in unnecessarily high spreads and therefore high transactions costs to investors. Preliminary evidence indicates that since the decimalization program was implemented, spreads and consequently transactions costs have declined, benefiting investors.

After-Hours Trading Currently, trading in the NYSE and NASDAQ is generally restricted to weekdays between 9:30 A.M. and 4:00 P.M. Eastern Standard Time. One of the problems with such restrictive trading times is that investors are unable to trade based on news that may be released after trading hours. For example, companies often release earnings announcements after the exchanges have closed. An investor who wants to transact based on that news has to wait until the following morning, by which time the stock price may be impacted by other news released overnight. However, investors now have the ability to trade after hours on certain stocks listed in the NYSE and the NASDAQ. Some of the ECNs permit trading in certain stocks before the market opens from 8:00 A.M. to 9:30 A.M. and after hours from 4:30 P.M. to as late as 8:00 P.M. The handwriting is on the wall. It is only a matter of time before all trading can be done round-the-clock including on weekends.

REGULATION OF FINANCIAL MARKETS

A number of state and federal agencies are involved in regulating various aspects of financial markets. However, the most dominant role from a corporation's perspective is that of the *Securities and Exchange Commission (SEC).* Created in the aftermath of the 1929 stock market crash, the SEC was entrusted with the enforcement

FINANCE &The Real World

Congress Cracks Down on Corporate Swindlers

The century started out with a rash of corporate scandals, from Enron to WorldCom to Tyco International, and many others. While their so-called independent auditors looked the other way, these companies and their top managers cooked the books, causing investors to lose millions of dollars when the deceptions were finally uncovered. This type of management fraud is seen as a major threat to the integrity of the U.S. stock market.

As a result of these scandals, Congress passed and President Bush signed the Sarbanes–Oxley Act into law in mid-2002, which affects the more than 12,000 publicly traded companies in the United States. Its aim is to raise the standards of corporate accountability by, among other things, requiring chief executives and chief financial officers to accept criminal liability for the accuracy of their companies' financial statements. The new law also improves disclosure of financial performance, requiring companies to use strict accounting standards, not jazzy methods cooked up during the late 1990s that put a positive spin on results.

The provisions also establish tough new rules for CPA firms who audit their books—such as severe limitations on the amount of consulting they can perform. Congress established the Public Company Accounting Oversight Board, which has the job of conducting regular inspections of accounting firms, and the power to revoke an individual's or firm's license to practice accounting. In addition, public companies are required to elect a professionally competent board of directors that is truly independent, including a separate audit committee that will review the work of the independent auditors.

Not to be outdone, the Securities & Exchange Commission, a government agency that oversees public companies, added even more regulations to the integrity of the stock market. It ordered companies to report what they pay their accountants for auditing and consulting services, to let investors know when auditors might be tempted to give in to management to protect their consulting fees. The SEC is also imposing tough new restrictions on tax services that auditors can provide—such as the sale of tax shelters—although CPA firms can still prepare a client's tax returns and audit the company in the same year.

Between Congress and the SEC, there are many new laws and regulations designed to prevent corporate fraud along the lines of Enron. To be sure, the amount of chicanery should decline. But human nature being what it is, there will always be swindlers in our midst—they'll just have to work harder to pull it off.

Sources: The Wall Street Journal, February 24, 2003, "Corporate Governance, A Special Report"; The Business Forum Online, "The Significance of the Sarbanes-Oxley Act"; *Business Week,* January 30, 2003, "A Fact Sheet on the SEC's New Rules."

---

of the Securities Act of 1933. The primary purpose of the existence of SEC is to ensure full disclosure of security information so that investors, individuals, and institutions alike have credible and timely information on which to base their investment decisions. This is accomplished by requiring firms to file comprehensive reports (called *Forms*) periodically or as needed. For example, firms with publicly held securities are required to file annual reports (known as the *10-K Form*) and quarterly reports (known as the *10-Q Form*) with the SEC within a specified time after the end of the fiscal period. Firms are also required to file **proxy statements** prior to annual shareholder meetings detailing, among other things, matters to be discussed and voted upon. Firms also have to file special forms prior to the issuance of new securities (e.g., new stock or bond issues) to the public and report other unusual events of material importance (e.g., potential merger or divestiture) in a timely manner. The SEC is also responsible for enforcing insider trading laws which

Visit the SEC Web site for regulations, filings, forms, and other information.
http://www.sec.gov

are designed to prevent insiders from taking advantage of their "inside" knowledge at the expense of all other outside shareholders. For example, under insider trading laws the chief executive officer (CEO) of a firm is barred from trading on the firm's stock in anticipation of news that the CEO is aware of but has not been released to the public. Finally, the SEC is involved in governing the activities of investment bankers and certain other financial intermediaries including mutual funds, investment management companies, and purveyors of financial advice and research.

Comprehension Check Questions

1. What is the purpose of financial markets?
2. What is the difference between primary markets and secondary markets?
3. What useful role do secondary markets perform?
4. What is the SEC?

MARKET EFFICIENCY

A central theme of much of academic finance and financial economics research since the 1960s has been the efficiency of the capital markets. Capital market efficiency is an implicit assumption in many decision models widely used in finance. Consequently, this concept is important to a full understanding of these decision models.

Security markets are considered to be ***efficient capital markets*** if *prices instantaneously reflect in an unbiased manner all relevant information about that security*. In understanding the concept of market efficiency we first need to recognize that security prices change only when there is new information, or information that is *different from what was anticipated*. For example, on November 15, 2001, Microsoft's much-anticipated game machine, X-Box, was finally made available for sale through various retail outlets. Microsoft's stock price closed the day before at $65.95, and on the day the new product was released the stock closed at $66.12. There was hardly any change in the stock price despite the significance of the event—because it had been widely anticipated. The market had already reflected the benefits of the revenue stream from X-Box in Microsoft's stock price before the actual release of the new product. Participants in the market were well aware of the development of the product through previous press releases from Microsoft and other industry and media sources. Thus, in an efficient market security prices adjust to information when it *first* becomes available.

Another example of market efficiency is the reaction to earnings releases. Firms periodically release information on their actual earnings or forecasted earnings. If the earnings information released is different from what the market expected, then there is likely to be a significant stock price reaction. If the market is efficient, the stock price should react to this announcement within a few moments of its release. If it takes several days or even a few hours to fully absorb this information, then the market may be considered to be *inefficient*. Inefficiency implies that one can easily buy shares of this stock upon announcement and sell it a few hours or few days later and earn an abnormally high return.

To illustrate the market efficiency phenomenon consider the example of Merck & Co., which announced on December 11, 2001 that their earnings per share for 2002 would be less than anticipated. Specifically, management revised their earnings per share projections downward to $3.02—considerably lower than the $3.40 earnings per share analysts had projected. As a result, analysts and other investors assigned Merck stock a lower valuation. This decrease in stock value was reflected

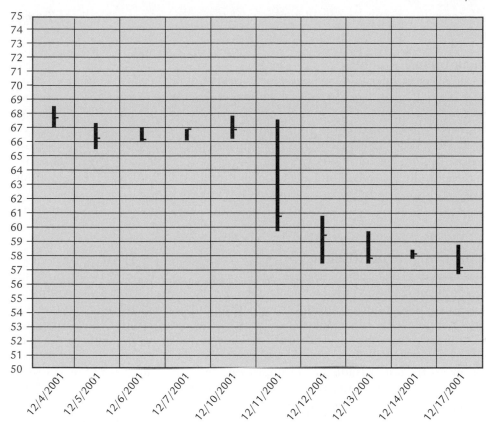

Source: MSN Money

**Figure 2.4
Daily Stock Prices
for Merck & Co.
around Forecasted
Earnings
Announcement**

very quickly in the stock price. Figure 2.4 shows a chart of the daily price (high–low range and closing prices) of the stock for several days on either side of December 11, 2001 when Merck announced its revised projections. Note that in the days prior to the announcement date the stock prices hovered in the $66–$68 range. On the day of the announcement, there was a downward spike with the stock price closing at $60.70, which is 9.4 percent lower than the previous day's closing price of $66.99. Thereafter, Merck's stock price appears to move randomly about a new equilibrium price level in the range of $58–$59. Note that the stock price did not take several days to completely react to the negative news release on December 11; rather the stock price seems to have reacted swiftly on the day of the news release.

If markets are inefficient, or slow to react to new information, a person could easily attain abnormal profits by trading on the stock after the release of information. Specifically, if the information is positive you would buy the stock when the information is released and then sell it a few days later after the stock has risen to its new equilibrium level. You can also profit from negative news releases by selling the stock first and then buying it back a few days later when the stock has settled to a new lower level. The latter type of transaction is called ***short-selling***. In a short sale you essentially sell a stock that you do not own by "borrowing" it from another investor (this is done by the stockbroker on your behalf) and then replacing it later by purchasing it, presumably, at a lower price.

The above example of Merck illustrates the concept of market efficiency with respect to publicly available information such as company news releases. The finance discipline recognizes several degrees of market efficiency based on the type of information set under consideration: *weak-form efficiency, semistrong-form efficiency,* and *strong-form efficiency.*

Weak-form Efficiency

Markets are considered to be **weak-form efficient** if no investor can consistently earn **excess (or abnormal) returns** based on an investment strategy using historical stock market information such as past prices, returns, or volume of trading. Excess or abnormal returns are defined as returns over and above those expected based on the risk of the stock. Basically, this means that one cannot look at historical trends in prices and other stock market data and forecast what will happen next. Thus mechanical trading rules are unlikely to generate abnormal returns. For example, an investor cannot assume that a stock that has gone up in price 3 days in a row is likely to go up in price on the following day. A trading strategy based on this rule is not likely to generate excess returns.

Semistrong-form Efficiency

Markets are considered to be **semistrong efficient** if no investor can consistently earn *excess* returns based on an investment strategy using any publicly available information (such as announcements of earnings, dividends, sales, annual report releases, mergers, etc.). This means that once information is made public, security prices very quickly reflect this new information. Thus, it would be too late for an individual to buy or sell stock based on some announcement and hope to make an abnormal profit from that trade. For example, one trading strategy is to buy stocks in firms that announce better-than-expected profits. If markets are semistrong-form efficient, such a strategy of buying stocks right after a firm announces unexpectedly positive earnings is unlikely to yield excess returns because by the time you buy the stock it would have already reflected the new information.

Strong-form Efficiency

Strong-form efficiency reflects a theory that security prices reflect *all* information, both public and private. Thus, in a strong-form efficient capital market, no individual or group should be able to consistently earn abnormal profits, including insiders possessing private information about the economic profits of the firm.

Overall, evidence suggests that security markets are weak-form and semistrong-form efficient. However, it is questionable that the markets are strong-form efficient. Several individuals gained notoriety in the 1980s for their illegal insider trading including Ivan Boesky, Dennis Levine, and Michael Milken. More recently Martha Stewart has come under scrutiny for her alleged insider trading of ImClone stock. The abnormal profits these individuals made from becoming privy to (illegally obtained) insider information is evidence that strong-form efficiency probably does not hold.

Comprehension Check Questions

1. What is meant by market efficiency?

2. Differentiate between, weak-, semistrong-, and strong-forms of market efficiency.

READING *THE WALL STREET JOURNAL*

As a student of corporate finance, you should be able to read and understand financial information regularly reported in the financial section of newspapers, business magazines, the television media, and increasingly on Internet sites (e.g., http://www.msn.com and http://www.yahoo.com). We use *The Wall Street Journal (WSJ)* as a reference since it is the most widely circulated business newspaper and because most other sources quote information using a similar format. While there is considerable information in the *WSJ*, we focus here on common stock and corporate bond quotes. In addition, we will get acquainted with some of the common stock and bond indexes and interest rates.

Understanding Corporate Stock Quotations

Figure 2.5 shows a portion of the stock price quotations as they appear in the Wednesday, January 8, 2003 issue of the *WSJ*. The data pertains to trading information as of the day before (in this case, Tuesday, January 7, 2003). If the *WSJ* was published on Monday, the information would refer to the previous Friday's trading data. We will focus on the stock quote for Wal-Mart Corporation, one of the largest discount department store chains in the world. Going from left to right, the first column shows the percentage change in the stock price from the beginning of the year. Wal-Mart stock decreased in price 0.1 percent between the beginning of the year and January 7. Given that only a few days have elapsed since the beginning of the year, the

YTD % CHG	52-WEEK HI	LO	STOCK (SYM)	DIV	YLD %	PE	VOL 100s	CLOSE	NET CHG
5.3	39.88	28.57	Wachovia WB	1.04	2.7	15	29332	38.36	-0.33
-4.1	17.50	10.27	WacknhutCorr WHC		...	11	138	10.65	-0.44
6.1	33.10	15.30	WadlRed A WDR	.53	2.5	19	3045	20.87	-0.24
9.4	40.70	27.70	Walgreen WAG	.15	.5	31	58392	31.94	0.49
1.1	22.62	15.80	WallaceCS WCS	.66	3.0	31	1986	21.74	-0.03
-0.1	63.94	43.72	WalMart WMT	.30	.6	29	65117	50.46	0.27
-5.4	15.15	8.51	WalterInd WLT	.12	1.2	6	746	10.25	-0.03
5.1	39.98	27.80	WashMut WM	1.08f	3.0	10	32315	36.30	-0.30
2.2	764	516	WashPost B WPO	5.60	.7	53	117	754.50	-4.50
0.4	30.15	20.42	♣WashREIT WRE	1.41	5.5	19	794	25.60	-0.35
-3.6	39.98	23.49	WsteConn WCN		...	21	3809	37.22	-0.78
2.9	31.10	20.20	WasteMgt WMI	.01	...	20	17740	23.59	-0.17
8.8	12.59	7	WtrPikTch PIK		...	9	201	8	-0.02
-2.2	39.25	17.86	WatersCp WAT		...	26	12079	21.29	-0.63
1.5	19.48	12.65	Watsco WSO	.12	.7	16	935	16.62	0.09
4.4	33.25	17.95	WatsnPharm WPI		...	18	8355	29.50	-0.10
0.6	27.50	17.31	WatsonWyatt A WW		...	16	1582	21.88	-0.08
1.3	20.45	13.70	WattsInd A WTS	.24	1.5	14	358	15.95	-0.57
2.1	14	8.14	WausaMosin WMO	.34	3.0	27	810	11.46	-0.25
4.4	33.60	7.50	WCI Commun WCI n		...	...	288	10.65	0.12
-7.6	54.25	32.55	♣Weatherford WFT		...	cc	23713	36.88	-2.74
4.1	40.10	30.28	WebstrFnl WBS	.76	2.1	11	2135	36.23	-0.20
13.8	2.25	1.31	WderNutrtn A WNI		...	12	90	1.65	...
-8.6	50.39	31.35	WgtWtchrs WTW		...	23	16732	42.03	-2.75
0.0	39.20	29.29	WngtnRlty WRI s	2.22	6.0	17	1255	36.85	-1.00
0.9	39.50	26.90	WeisMkts WMK	1.08	3.4	15	115	31.33	-0.65
-9.2	28.50	19.40	WellChoice WC n		...	...	6776	21.75	0.25
1.9	18.22	9.20	Wellman WLM	.36	2.6	dd	600	13.74	-0.26
-1.0	89.20	57.58	♣WelptHlth WLP s		...	17	17088	70.46	-2.07
3.6	54.84	38.10	WellsFargo WFC	1.12	2.3	15	32211	48.54	-0.30
0.8	26.61	24.60	WlsFargoCap WPD n	1.74	6.6	...	360	26.44	0.14
2.2	41.60	26.15	Wendys WEN	.24	.9	15	11087	27.67	0.20
-2.4	7.58	2.85	Wescolnt WCC		...	11	203	5.36	-0.17
0.0	32.50	16.25	WstPharmSvc WST	.80	3.3	dd	139	24.39	0.45
0.5	18	8.50	♣WestarEngy WR	1.20	12.1	...	5799	9.95	-0.31
0.9	8.08	4.90	WstCstHspty WEH		...	11	220	5.75	0.05
6.0	32	15.74	Westcorp WES	.48	2.2	12	190	22.26	-0.16
27.5	8.96	2.98	WstnDgtl WDC		...	23	38663	8.15	0.38
-4.0	40.12	25	♣WestGasRes WGR	.20	.6	33	4537	35.38	-1.22
4.7	48	35.60	WpacBk ADS WBK	1.89e	4.7	...	58	40.41	-0.22
-1.7	6.05	0.39	WstptStvn WXS		...	dd	1435	0.58	-0.04
-3.5	21.40	13.20	WestportRes WRC		...	dd	4351	20.08	-0.83
2.9	17.27	11.40	Westwood wi n	.04e	.3	...	31	13.80	0.08
4.5	40.50	24.41	WestwdOne WON		...	46	3742	39.04	0.03
5.6	68.09	37.35	Weyerhsr WY	1.60	3.1	cc	9514	51.99	-0.11
3.4	79.80	29.32	Whirlpool WHR	1.36	2.5	14	3308	54.02	-0.90

Figure 2.5
Common Stock Quotations from the New York Stock Exchange

Source: The Wall Street Journal, *January 8, 2003. Reprinted with permission.*

small change in price is not very meaningful. However, note that some stocks experienced significant gains and losses during this period, such as Walgreen (a nationwide drug store chain), which experienced a 9.4 percent increase. Other stocks such as Walter Industries (WalterInd) declined in price during this time. The next two columns show the stock's price range for the previous 52 weeks. Wal-Mart's common stock price ranged from a low (*Lo*) of 43.72 to a high (*Hi*) of 63.94 in the preceding 52 weeks. Immediately to the right of the name is the **ticker** symbol used to identify the stock. The ticker symbol is a 1–4 letter symbol assigned by an exchange to identify a particular stock. Wal-Mart's ticker symbol is WMT. The next column shows the stock's annual dividend (cash) rate. Normally, cash dividends are paid every quarter. In reporting the annual dividend rate, *WSJ* takes the most recent quarterly dividend paid and multiplies it by 4 to obtain the annualized rate. Wal-Mart shareholders can expect an annual cash dividend of $0.30 per share. To the right of the dividend is the **current dividend yield** in percent, defined as the annual dividend divided by the closing price of the stock times one hundred: $0.30/$50.46 × 100 = 0.6%.

The **price-earnings** or **P/E** ratio is shown next. This is simply the closing market price divided by the sum of the latest four quarters of earnings per share. Wal-Mart's P/E ratio of 29 indicates that investors are willing to pay $29 for every dollar of earnings per share. The P/E ratio is a relative valuation measure that is very widely used by investors. P/E ratios depend on many factors including growth prospects, size of the firm, and risk inherent in the firm. Higher P/E ratios are associated with larger firms, firms with lower risk, and firms with greater growth prospects, holding everything else constant. The next figure is the *trading volume* in the stock in hundreds of shares. In the case of Wal-Mart, 6,511,700 shares traded hands on January 7, 2003. This is followed by the closing price, which is the last price at which trade was executed for that day. On January 7, 2003, Wal-Mart's closing price was $50.46. The final column shows the *net change* in the day's closing price compared to the previous day's closing price. Wal-Mart's common stock closed $0.27 higher than on January 6, 2003.

Understanding Corporate Bond Quotations

For information on bonds, visit e-Trade and click on Plan & Advice, then the Knowledge Center.
http://www.etrade.com

Corporate bonds are debt obligations of firms. While most corporate bonds are not listed on an exchange, there is still an active secondary market for many corporate bonds. The WSJ gives trading information on the 40 most actively traded bonds. An excerpt of the corporate bond quotes taken from the WSJ for Friday, September 5, 2003 is shown in Figure 2.6. As in the case of stocks the information pertains to the previous trading day, i.e., Thursday, September 4, 2003.

Let us take a close look at the first bond listed in Figure 2.6—a bond issued by General Motors (GM). Note that unlike common stocks, a firm may have several bonds outstanding, each with different characteristics. Figure 2.6 shows two other bonds belonging to General Motors—the third (issued by General Motors Acceptance Corporation, the financing subsidiary of GM) and seventh bonds listed in the figure. In addition to these bonds, GM has many other bonds that may not be as actively traded (therefore, not reported by WSJ) or may be privately held and not listed on an exchange. The GM bond in question has a **coupon rate** of 8.375 percent and *matures* on July 15, 2033. The coupon rate is the interest rate paid on the bond. The interest is typically paid semi-annually, but the rate is quoted as an annual rate. The dollar amount of interest to be received is equal to the coupon rate times the **face** (or **principal**) amount of the bond. Unless otherwise stated, the face amount of corporate bonds is $1,000. The 8.375 percent coupon rate on the GM bond means that an investor will receive $83.75 in interest every year (0.08375 x $1,000). The **maturity** date shows the length of the debt obligation. In this case the bond matures

Thursday, September 4, 2003

Forty most active fixed-coupon corporate bonds

COMPANY (TICKER)	COUPON	MATURITY	LAST PRICE	YIELD	*EST SPREAD	UST†	EST $ VOL (000's)
General Motors (GM)	8.375	Jul 15, 2033	100.614	8.317	301	30	203,944
Ford Motor Credit (F)	6.700	Jul 16, 2004	103.633	2.367	47	2	121,099
General Motors Acceptance (GMAC)	6.875	Aug 28, 2012	99.799	6.905	240	10	117,747
AT&T Wireless Services (AWE)	8.125	May 01, 2012	114.646	5.933	142	10	97,537
Ford Motor Credit (F)	7.250	Oct 25, 2011	101.517	7.000	249	10	88,689
ConocoPhillips (COP)	5.900	Oct 15, 2032	95.972	6.200	90	30	88,510
General Motors (GM)	7.125	Jul 15, 2013	101.201	6.952	245	10	83,122
FirstEnergy (FE)	6.450	Nov 15, 2011	98.610	6.671	217	10	81,484
AOL Time Warner (AOL)	6.875	May 01, 2012	107.853	5.710	120	10	76,480
Conoco Global Funding (COP)	6.350	Oct 15, 2011	108.667	5.033	53	10	76,464
Ford Motor (F)	7.450	Jul 16, 2031	89.340	8.449	314	30	70,123
Sprint Capital (FON)	8.375	Mar 15, 2012	113.982	6.234	173	10	68,280
Wells Fargo & (WFC)	7.250	Aug 24, 2005	109.645	2.191	30	2	66,050
AOL Time Warner (AOL)	7.700	May 01, 2032	108.213	7.029	172	30	57,265
Travelers Property Casualty (TAP)	5.000	Mar 15, 2013	97.408	5.351	84	10	57,002
Conoco (COP)	6.950	Apr 15, 2029	108.852	6.252	94	30	56,687
Albertson's (ABS)	7.500	Feb 15, 2011	111.489	5.589	109	10	56,100
Amerada Hess (AHC)	7.125	Mar 15, 2033	100.145	7.113	179	30	55,000

Source: The Wall Street Journal, *January 8, 2003. Reprinted with permission.*

**Figure 2.6
Corporate Bond
Quotations from
the New York
Stock Exchange**

on July 15, 2033, which results in a time remaining to maturity of slightly under 30 years relative to the trading date of September 4, 2003. On the maturity date the firm will have to pay back the principal or face amount in addition to the final interest payment due. Following the maturity date is the **last price** at which the bond traded on the trading date in question. The last price is reported as a percent of face value following the convention used by brokers to quote bond prices. The closing price on the GM bond is 100.614. If you had actually bought a bond at this price you would have paid $1,006.14 (100.614 x 10). The next column shows the **yield-to-maturity** (**YTM**) of the bond. The YTM tells an investor what rate of return (annual) he or she can expect to receive if the bond is purchased at the last price indicated and is held to maturity. Details of how YTM is calculated will be discussed in Chapter 7. In this instance an investor buying the GM bond at the quoted last price of $100.614 can expect to earn a rate of return of 8.317 percent if the bond is held to maturity. The next column shows the *estimated spread* between the YTM of the bond in question and a Treasury bond with similar time remaining to maturity. In other words, the spread is calculated as the YTM of the corporate bond minus the YTM of the Treasury bond. This difference or spread is also known as the **default risk spread**. The default risk spread tells the investor how much additional yield can be expected because of the assumption of default risk. Default risk is the risk that the issuer will be unable to pay its debt obligation including interest and principal payments. All corporate bonds are subject to some default risk while Treasury bonds, because they are issued by the U.S. government, are assumed to have no risk of default. Thus, default risk spreads increase as the risk of default of an issue increases. Default risk spreads may change over time with spreads increasing when the economy is more uncertain. Default risk is discussed in more detail in Chapter 7. For the GM bond we are examining, the spread is 301 basis points or 3.01 percent. It is the convention to quote spreads in terms of basis points where 100 basis points is equal to 1 percent. Thus, the GM bond has a yield that is 301 basis points greater than a U.S. Treasury bond of similar maturity. Following the column on estimated spread is length of maturity of the U.S. Treasury bond used to compute the default risk spread. In this case the U.S. Treasury bond has 30 years remaining to maturity, which is equivalent to the time remaining to maturity on the GM bond. The final column shows the *estimated volume of trading* (in thousands of dollars of face amount of debt). A total of $203,944,000 face amount of GM bonds were traded on September 4, 2003. You will note that, in general, the volume of trading in bonds is considerably less than the volume of trading in the common shares of the same company.

Understanding Stock and Bond Market Averages

We have discussed how to interpret prices of individual stocks and bonds. It is also important to know how the overall market for stocks and bonds are doing because, as we shall find out in Chapter 6, stocks and bonds generally move up and down together. Thus, you will find that even though IBM did not announce or release any material news on a given day, their stock price may have gone up or down because the "market" went up or down. The same is true for IBM bonds.

Stock Market Averages To find out how the entire market is performing, investors and analysts need an indicator that captures how stocks from different *sectors* of the economy are performing. Figure 2.7 shows several stock market indicators that appear in the *WSJ*. We will discuss a few of the more commonly used indicators. Probably the most popular indicator of the stock market is the ***Dow Jones Industrial Average (DJIA)***. The DJIA, as other market indicators, is an index that attempts to measure the movement across a class of securities. The DJIA is a *price-weighted* index consisting of 30 large, well-known (blue-chip) stocks from different sectors of the economy. Table 2.4 presents the composition of the DJIA 30 index. The index is basically calculated as the sum of the prices on the 30 stocks divided by the number of stocks. The divisor, however, has changed over time due to stock splits and changes in the composition of the index.

While the DJIA is a very popular index and gets much attention in the press and television news, it has certain limitations, especially for the serious investor. First, because the DJIA is price-weighted index, a 10 percent change in price of a $100 stock would have a much bigger impact on the index than a similar 10 percent change in the price of a $20 stock. Second, the DJIA is composed of only 30 very large companies. Thus, it may not reflect the broad movement across various size firms. From Figure 2.7 we observe that the DJIA 30 Index closed at a level of 8,740.59 on January 7, 2003 and that the index level dropped 13.89 percent in the previous 52 weeks. In addition to the industrial average, the Dow Jones series also includes averages for the transportation, utilities, and a composite of the three indexes. These are shown in Figure 2.7. The numbers preceding each of the indexes is the number of stocks used in the average.

Table 2.4 Stocks Included in the Dow Jones Industrial Average

3M Co.	Honeywell International Inc.
Alcoa Inc.	Intel Corp.
American Express Co.	International Business Machines Corp.
AT&T Corp.	International Paper Co.
Boeing Co.	J.P. Morgan Chase & Co.
Caterpillar Inc.	Johnson & Johnson
Citigroup Inc.	McDonald's Corp.
Coca-Cola Co.	Merck & Co. Inc.
E.I. DuPont de Nemours & Co.	Microsoft Corp.
Eastman Kodak Co.	Philip Morris Cos. Inc.
ExxonMobil Corp.	Procter & Gamble Co.
General Electric Co.	SBC Communications Inc.
General Motors Corp.	United Technologies Corp.
Hewlett-Packard Co.	Wal-Mart Stores Inc.
Home Depot Inc.	Walt Disney Co.

Source: Dow Jones, January 8, 2003

(http://www.djindexes.com/jsp/industrialAverages.jsp?sideMenu=true.html)

Major Stock Indexes

Figure 2.7
Stock Market
Indicators

Dow Jones Averages	DAILY HIGH	LOW	CLOSE	NET CHG	% CHG	52-WEEK HIGH	LOW	% CHG	YTD % CHG
30 Industrials	8802.64	8713.03	8740.59	−32.98	−0.38	10635.25	7286.27	−13.89	+ 4.78
20 Transportations	2421.58	2382.11	2396.89	−24.82	−1.02	3049.96	2013.02	−15.10	+ 3.76
15 Utilities	230.95	223.18	225.78	− 5.49	−2.37	310.75	167.57	−22.74	+ 4.93
65 Composite	2505.87	2471.73	2483.02	−22.38	−0.89	3093.84	2033.44	−15.95	+ 4.55
Dow Jones Indexes									
US Total Market	215.96	213.46	214.16	− 1.48	−0.69	271.69	179.60	−20.59	+ 4.72
US Large-Cap	205.40	202.97	203.62	− 1.33	−0.65	261.42	172.31	−22.11	+ 5.04
US Mid-Cap	237.96	235.18	235.97	− 1.92	−0.81	291.12	192.15	−16.47	+ 4.16
US Small-Cap	256.49	253.23	254.40	− 1.94	−0.76	320.03	209.81	−17.12	+ 3.00
US Growth	826.11	814.09	818.46	− 0.55	−0.07	1181.77	687.99	−30.74	+ 5.55
US Value	1142.36	1127.82	1130.23	−12.06	−1.06	1352.27	938.11	−13.03	+ 4.60
Global Titans 50	159.04	156.66	157.61	− 1.39	−0.87	200.55	134.76	−21.41	+ 4.25
Asian Titans 50	85.72	83.43	83.48	− 1.21	−1.43	107.20	78.96	−14.47	+ 1.18
DJ STOXX 50	2544.79	2479.06	2504.27	−22.46	−0.89	3707.12	2274.60	−30.84	+ 4.02
Nasdaq Stock Market									
Composite	1442.26	1416.23	1431.57	+10.25	+0.72	2055.74	1114.11	−30.36	+ 7.19
Nasdaq 100	1082.52	1057.16	1071.85	+10.37	+0.98	1666.58	804.64	−35.69	+ 8.89
Biotech	515.60	508.30	509.89	− 4.72	−0.92	874.93	403.98	−41.72	+ 2.62
Computer	691.53	674.32	686.47	+14.45	+2.15	1070.28	503.26	−35.86	+10.26
Telecommunications	119.65	116.83	118.55	+ 0.35	+0.30	242.89	81.43	−51.19	+ 8.97
Standard & Poor's Indexes									
500 Index	930.65	919.98	922.93	− 6.08	−0.65	1170.29	776.76	−20.49	+ 4.90
MidCap 400	446.64	440.63	442.08	− 4.55	−1.02	550.38	372.88	−13.80	+ 2.86
SmallCap 600	203.22	200.08	201.02	− 2.15	−1.06	257.81	170.73	−15.04	+ 2.24
SuperComp 1500	204.90	202.53	203.20	− 1.42	−0.69	256.74	171.10	−19.82	+ 4.65
New York Stock Exchange									
Composite	495.71	490.11	490.89	− 4.82	−0.97	609.53	421.09	−16.76	+ 3.81
Industrials	607.25	600.74	601.65	− 5.60	−0.92	763.43	532.91	−18.14	+ 3.03
Finance	539.40	532.89	534.51	− 4.67	−0.87	622.09	437.72	− 9.71	+ 4.71
Others									
Russell 2000	397.36	391.19	393.95	− 3.04	−0.77	522.95	327.04	−20.87	+ 2.83
Wilshire 5000	8782.37	8684.78	8713.70	−58.52	−0.67	10953.64	7342.84	−19.55	+ 4.44
Value Line	275.98	272.63	274.06	− 1.79	−0.65	382.26	219.50	−27.04	+ 3.82
Amex Composite	839.08	828.42	828.73	−10.88	−1.30	962.69	771.87	− 0.89	+ 0.53

Source: The Wall Street Journal, *January 8, 2003. Reprinted with permission.*

A broader index than the DJIA is the *S&P 500*, provided by the Standard & Poor's Corporation. As the name implies it consists of 500 stocks from various sectors of the economy. It is a *market value-weighted* index. Thus, if the market value of all the 500 companies is $100 billion and IBM has a total market value of its common stock of $2.5 billion, then IBM's weight in the index is 2.5 percent. The S&P 500 index is a composite of four other indexes (not shown in Figure 2.7) provided by S&P:

1. S&P Industrial (400 stocks)
2. S&P Transportation (20 stocks)
3. S&P Utilities (40 stocks)
4. S&P Financials (40 stocks).

The sample of 500 stocks is taken largely from the NYSE, but includes some stocks from the AMEX and the NASDAQ. The aggregate market value of all the

S&P 500 stocks represents approximately 80 percent of the market value of all stocks listed in the NYSE. Because of its broader representation, many professionals use the S&P 500 as a proxy for the entire "market."

Other popular, but less well known, indexes include the *NYSE Composite*, the *AMEX Composite* and *NASDAQ Composite* indexes based on all stocks trading in their respective exchanges. Similar to the S&P 500, these indexes are market value-weighted indexes. One of the broadest stock market indexes is the **Wilshire 5000,** which is also a market value-weighted index consisting of all NYSE, AMEX, and the larger more active OTC stocks; in all over 6,500 stocks are included.

Bond Market Averages   The *WSJ* is also a valuable source of information for average yields on various short- and long-term debt instruments. Information on short-term debt instruments is provided in the Money Rates section of the newspaper; an

**Figure 2.8
Short-term
Interest Rates**

Money Rates

Thursday, February 13, 2003

The key U. S. and foreign annual interest rates below are a guide to general levels but don't always represent actual transactions.

Commercial Paper

Yields paid by corporations for short-term financing, typically for daily operation

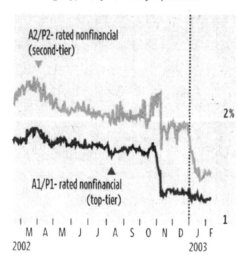

A2/P2- rated nonfinancial (second-tier)

2%

A1/P1- rated nonfinancial (top-tier)

1

M A M J J A S O N D J F
2002   2003

Source: Federal Reserve

Prime Rate: 4.25% (effective 11/07/02).
Discount Rate: 2.25% (effective 01/09/03).
Federal Funds: 1.750% high, 1.250% low, 1.438% near closing bid, 1.750% offered. Effective rate: 1.28%. Source: Prebon Yamane (USA) Inc. Federal-funds target rate: 1.250% (effective 11/06/02).
Call Money: 3.00% (effective 11/07/02).
Commercial Paper: Placed directly by General Electric Capital Corp.: 1.26% 30 to 41 days; 1.20% 42 to 49 days; 1.26% 50 to 132 days; 1.20% 133 to 144 days; 1.26% 145 to 223 days; 1.20% 224 to 231 days; 1.26% 232 to 270 days.
Euro Commercial Paper: Placed directly by General Electric Capital Corp.: 2.75% 30 days; 2.71% two months; 2.66%

three months; 2.62% four months; 2.57% five months; 2.53% six months.
Dealer Commercial Paper: High-grade unsecured notes sold through dealers by major corporations: 1.22% 30 days; 1.22% 60 days; 1.22% 90 days.
Certificates of Deposit: 1.26% one month; 1.26% three months; 1.26% six months.
Bankers Acceptances: 1.26% 30 days; 1.26% 60 days; 1.26% 90 days; 1.26% 120 days; 1.26% 150 days; 1.26% 180 days. Source: Prebon Yamane (USA) Inc.
Eurodollars: 1.25% - 1.27% one month; 1.25% - 1.27% two months; 1.26% - 1.28% three months; 1.26% - 1.29% four months; 1.26% - 1.29% five months; 1.26% - 1.29% six months. Source: Prebon Yamane (USA) Inc.
London Interbank Offered Rates (Libor): 1.3400% one month; 1.3400% three months; 1.3400% six months; 1.3900% one year. Effective rate for contracts entered into two days from date appearing at top of this column.
Euro Libor: 2.79763% one month; 2.70463% three months; 2.56613% six months; 2.48500% one year. Effective rate for contracts entered into two days from date appearing at top of this column.
Euro Interbank Offered Rates (Euribor): 2.796% one month; 2.707% three months; 2.569% six months; 2.485% one year. Source: Reuters.
Foreign Prime Rates: Canada 4.50%; European Central Bank 2.75%; Japan 1.375%; Switzerland 2.63%; Britain 3.75%.
Treasury Bills: Results of the Monday, February 10, 2003, auction of short-term U.S. government bills, sold at a discount from face value in units of $1,000 to $1 million: 1.150% 13 weeks; 1.165% 26 weeks. Tuesday, February 11, 2003 auction: 1.155% 4 weeks.
Overnight Repurchase Rate: 1.27%. Source: Garban Intercapital.
Freddie Mac: Posted yields on 30-year mortgage commitments. Delivery within 30 days 5.39%, 60 days 5.46%, standard conventional fixed-rate mortgages: 3.625%, 2% rate capped one-year adjustable rate mortgages.
Fannie Mae: Posted yields on 30 year mortgage commitments (priced at par) for delivery within 30 days 5.50%, 60 days 5.58%, standard conventional fixed-rate mortgages: 3.25%, 6/2 rate capped one-year adjustable rate mortgages. Constant Maturity Debt Index: 1.251% three months; 1.255% six months; 1.288% one year.
Merrill Lynch Ready Assets Trust: 0.89%.
Consumer Price Index: December, 180.9, up 2.4% from a year ago. Bureau of Labor Statistics.

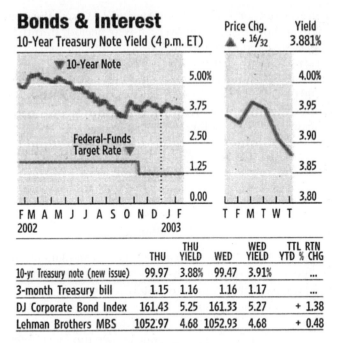

Figure 2.9
Long-term Bond
Rates

Bonds & Interest
10-Year Treasury Note Yield (4 p.m. ET)

	THU	THU YIELD	WED	WED YIELD	TTL RTN YTD % CHG
10-yr Treasury note (new issue)	99.97	3.88%	99.47	3.91%	...
3-month Treasury bill	1.15	1.16	1.16	1.17	...
DJ Corporate Bond Index	161.43	5.25	161.33	5.27	+ 1.38
Lehman Brothers MBS	1052.97	4.68	1052.93	4.68	+ 0.48

Source: The Wall Street Journal, *February 14, 2003. Reprinted with permission.*

example of which is shown in Figure 2.8. Take particular note of the ***prime rate,*** the rate at which banks lend to their best or "prime" customers on a short-term basis, and the T-bill rate. The T-bill refers to short-term debt obligations of the U.S. Treasury with maturities less than 1 year. The *WSJ* also presents information on yields in the long-term bond market. An excerpt is shown in Figure 2.9. The average price and yield on the 10-year Treasury note is shown. Also of interest is the Dow Jones Corporate Bond Index (DJ Corporate Bond Index). The DJ Corporate Bond Index is an average of a sample of corporate bonds with 2, 5, 10, and 30 years to maturity.

Comprehension Check Questions

1. What does the P/E ratio measure?
2. How is current dividend yield defined?
3. *The Wall Street Journal* lists the price of a corporate bond at 99.38. If you purchased a bond at this price, what actual amount would you have paid for the bond?

CALCULATING HOLDING PERIOD RETURNS

Knowing how to calculate **the rate of returns** on various investments is important in order to make proper investment decisions. Returns may be calculated for any given holding period such as 1 day, 5 days, 1 week, 6 weeks, 1 month, 3 months, 1 year, 2 years, etc. The general formula for the ***holding period return*** is:

$$K_t = \frac{P_t - P_{t-1} + C_t}{P_{t-1}}$$

where K_t is the holding period return for period t, P_t is the price of the asset at the end of period t, P_{t-1} is the price at the end of the previous period, and C_t is any cash distribution received from the investment in period t. We will illustrate how to calculate the return from holding an asset over a 1-year period, thus the subscript t in the above formula is assumed to represent 1 year. As an example let us evaluate the returns on Procter & Gamble stock for 2002. The stock closed at a price of $85.94 on the last day of trading in 2002 (December 31) and at $79.13 on the last trading day in 2001 (December 31). During the course of the year, Procter & Gamble paid out four quarterly dividends, which totaled $1.64. Plugging in these values into the formula yields a holding period return of 10.68 percent:

$$K_t = \frac{P_t - P_{t-1} + C_t}{P_{t-1}}$$

$$K_t = \frac{85.94 - 79.13 + 1.64}{79.13}$$

$$K_t = 0.1068 \text{ or } 10.68\%$$

In addition to stocks, the above formula can be used to calculate the returns on any other security or asset. For instance, in the case of a bond investment, the calculation would be similar except that coupon or interest payments would be substituted for the cash distribution in the formula.

The return just calculated is also called a *realized* (or *ex-post* after the fact) *return.* Realized returns differ from *expected* (or *ex-ante,* before the fact), *returns.* Although ex-ante returns are calculated in the same manner as ex-post returns, ending prices (P_t) and cash distributions (C_t) for expected returns are estimated values, whereas ending prices and cash distributions for realized returns are actual values.

Comprehension Check Questions

1. How are holding period returns calculated?
2. In the formula for calculating holding period returns what do cash distributions refer to?

HISTORICAL RECORD OF CAPITAL MARKET RETURNS

We close this chapter by presenting a historical record of how various capital market returns have fared. Figure 2.10 shows the average market returns for several asset classes including Treasury securities, corporate bonds, and stocks for the period 1926–2002. Also shown is the average inflation rate per year. The right side of the figure contains a frequency distribution chart for each asset group. The chart is a summary of the annual returns for each asset class and the corresponding frequency of occurrence. The frequency distribution gives an indication of how risky the returns are. The concept of risk will be covered in more detail in Chapter 6. From the table you will note that T-bills on average yielded a market return of 3.8 percent, which is slightly more than the average rate of inflation. Long-term government bonds and corporate bonds yielded an average return of 5.8 and 6.2 percent, respectively. The average market return on large-company stocks was 12.2 percent, while the average return on small-company stocks was even greater at 16.9 percent. However, you will note that investments with higher returns are also associated with higher risk. For instance, the dispersion of returns for small- and large-company stocks are much wider than for the various classes of bonds. The risk–return trade-off is a basic principle of finance that investors require and are rewarded, on average, with higher returns for assuming greater levels of risk.

Figure 2.10
Annual Historical
Rates of Return:
1926–2002

Series	Arithmetic Mean	Standard Deviation	Distribution
Large-Company Stocks	12.2%	20.5%	
Small-Company Stocks*	16.9	33.2	
Long-Term Corporate Bonds	6.2	8.7	
Long-Term Government	5.8	9.4	
Intermediate-Term Government	5.6	5.8	
U.S. Treasury Bills	3.8	3.2	
Inflation	3.1	4.4	

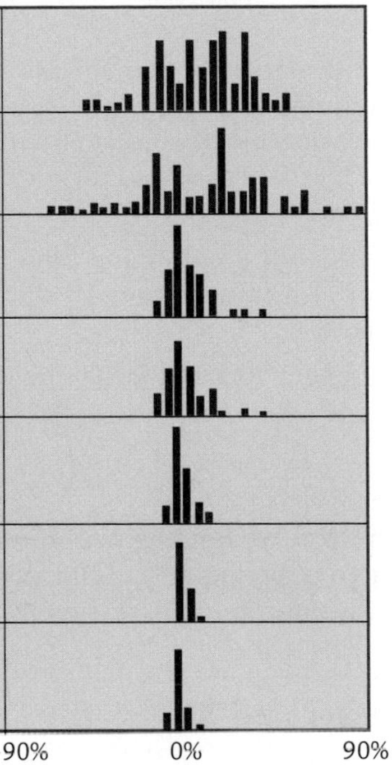

-90%   0%   90%

Source: Stocks, Bonds, Bills, and Inflation, 2003 Yearbook *(Chicago, Ill.: R.G. Ibbotson Associates)*

Summary

> A firm's business environment consists of the different markets it interacts with, including the labor market, product market, raw materials market, capital goods market, and the financial market.

> Financial markets are where trading in financial assets takes place. Financial assets represent claims against assets and future earnings of firms, government entities, and individuals. Financial assets include money, debt obligations, and stocks.

> Financial markets can be classified into money and capital markets and into primary and secondary markets. Money markets deal in securities with maturities of approximately 1 year or less, while capital markets deal in securities with maturities greater than 1 year. Primary markets are those in which new securities are issued; secondary markets are those in which existing securities are traded.

> An important function of the primary market is to transfer funds from savers (such as individuals) to borrowers (such as corporations). The transfer of funds may occur directly, usually with the help of investment bankers, or indirectly, through financial intermediaries. Investment bankers help corporations and other entities in selling their primary claims (e.g., stocks and bonds) to savers. Financial intermediaries, such as commercial banks, issue secondary claims (e.g., savings deposits) and invest in primary claims of borrowers.

> Secondary markets for stocks and bonds consist of organized exchanges, such as the New York and American Stock Exchanges, and the over-the-counter market, which is a network of securities dealers linked together electronically and by telephone.

➤ The existence of secondary markets provides several benefits including liquidity, efficient pricing, information disclosure, and efficient allocation of capital.

➤ Security markets are considered to be efficient if prices instantaneously reflect in an unbiased manner all relevant information about that security. There are several degrees of market efficiency depending on the information set being considered: weak-form efficiency, semistrong-form efficiency, and strong-form efficiency.

➤ *The Wall Street Journal* provides useful information on corporate stocks and bonds and information on the overall performance of the stock and debt markets.

➤ The general formula for the holding period return is:

$$K_t = \frac{P_t - P_{t-1} + C_t}{P_{t-1}}$$

where K_t is the holding period return for period t, P_t is the price of the asset at the end of period t, P_{t-1} is the price at the end of the previous period, and C_t is any cash distribution received from the investment in period t.

Questions and Topics for Discussion

1. What is the basic purpose of a financial market?
2. How is a direct transfer of funds from savers to borrowers accomplished?
3. How do money and capital markets differ?
4. Describe the various types of financial intermediaries, including the sources of their funds and the types of investments they make.
5. How do primary and secondary financial markets differ?
6. What is the primary distinction between the trading process on the New York Stock Exchange and the over-the-counter markets?
7. Describe the concept of market efficiency. What are the three different levels of market efficiency?
8. What are electronic communications networks?
9. What is a stock market index?
10. What are some benefits of financial intermediaries?

Self-Test Problems

ST1. Three months ago, you purchased 100 shares of TCBY Enterprises for $11 per share. The stock has just paid a 10-cent-per-share dividend, and the current price per share is $8.75. What has been your holding period return on this stock?

ST2. Using the information in Figure 2.5, calculate your expected holding period return over the next 12 months if you purchased a share of Wal-Mart stock at the closing price shown, received the indicated dividend over the next year, and the stock doubled in value at the end of the 12-month period.

ST3. What rate of return would you have made on the AT&T Wireless Services (AWE) bond with a coupon rate of 8.125 percent and maturing on May 01, 2012 shown in Figure 2.6 if you sold it at the last price shown and had bought the bond 12 months ago for $102.50?

Problems

1. Using the data contained in Figure 2.7, what 12-month rate of return, excluding dividend yields, would an investor have received by purchasing the following group of stocks?

   a. The stocks in the Dow Jones 30 Industrial average?

   b. The stocks in the New York Stock Exchange Industrial average?

   c. The stocks in the NASDAQ Computer Industry average?

   d. The stocks in the Wilshire 5000 index?

   Assume you purchased the stocks in the various averages in the same proportions that they are in the averages.

   BASIC

2. An investor bought 100 shares of Venus Corporation common stock 1 year ago for $40 per share. She just sold the shares for $44 each, and during the year, she received four quarterly dividend checks for $40 each. She expects the price of the Venus shares to fall to about $38 over the next year. Calculate the investor's realized percentage holding period return.

   BASIC

3. An investor bought 10 Ellis Industries, Inc. long-term bonds 1 year ago, when the company first issued them. In addition, he bought 200 shares of the company's common stock at the same time for $30 per share. He paid $1,000 each for the bonds, and today the bonds are selling at $950 each (long-term interest rates have increased slightly over the past year). The bonds have a stated interest rate of 12 percent per year. The investor received an interest payment equaling $60 per bond 6 months ago and has just received another $60 interest payment per bond. Calculate the investor's percentage holding period return for the 1 year he has held the bonds.

   BASIC

4. Suppose a Midwest Telephone and Telegraph (MTT) Company bond, maturing in 1 year, can be purchased today for $975. Assuming that the bond is held until maturity, the investor will receive $1,000 (principal) plus 6 percent interest (that is, $0.06 \times \$1,000 = \$60$). Determine the percentage holding period return on this investment.

   BASIC

5. **a.** National Telephone and Telegraph (NTT) Company common stock currently sells for $60 per share. NTT is expected to pay a $4 dividend during the coming year, and the price of the stock is expected to increase to $65 a year from now. Determine the *expected* (ex-ante) percentage holding period return on NTT common stock.

   INTERMEDIATE

   b. Suppose that 1 year later, NTT's common stock is selling for $75 per share. During the 1-year period, NTT paid a $4 common stock dividend. Determine the *realized* (ex-post) percentage holding period return on NTT common stock.

   c. Repeat (b) given that NTT's common stock is selling for $58 1 year later.

   d. Repeat (b) given that NTT's common stock is selling for $50 1 year later.

INTERMEDIATE **6.** Six months ago, you purchased a tract of land in an area where a new industrial park was rumored to be planned. This land cost you $110,000, and the seller offered you an interest-free loan for 70 percent of the land cost. Today, the industrial park project was formally announced, and an attorney for the developer has just offered you $190,000 for your land. If you accept this offer, what will be your holding period return on this investment?

CHALLENGE **7.** The stock of Tips, Inc., a new firm operating a chain of sports betting parlors, has just been sold in an initial public offering at a price of $25 per share. One week after this offering, the stock has risen in value to $35. You believe the stock will rise to $45 over the coming year. You do not expect Tips to pay any dividends over the year. If you require a rate of return on this stock of 18 percent, do you believe this is a good investment at the current price of $35?

CHALLENGE **8.** Over the past 10 years, your $15,000 in gold coins has increased in value by 200 percent. You plan to sell these coins today. You have paid annual storage and insurance costs of $500 per year. Assay expenses at the time of sale are expected to total $400. What is your 10-year (not annualized) holding period return on this investment?

BASIC **9.** Assume the following stock quotations were recently reported in *The Wall Street Journal*:

33.9	52.60	16.99	BestBuy BBY		...	18	42792	32.34	1.55
−4.2	48.30	34.71	DuPont DD	1.40	3.4	22	25898	40.63	0.38
17.0	34.15	21.30	GenElec GE	.76	2.7	19	160221	28.49	0.66

   a. What are the dividend yields on the common stock of Best Buy, DuPont, and General Electric?

   b. By what percentage did the stock of Best Buy appreciate from the beginning of the year?

   c. What is the current price-earnings ratio for General Electric and DuPont?

   d. What was the closing price of Best Buy stock on the previous trading day?

   e. If you had purchased a share of General Electric at the closing price, what would you have paid for it?

   f. What was the difference between the lowest and the highest price at which General Electric stock traded in the preceding 52 weeks?

BASIC **10.** The following bond quotations recently appeared in *The Wall Street Journal*:

Lucent 6½ 28	12.6	229	51.50	+5.50
IBM 6½ 28	6.1	25	105.75	−0.50

   a. What is the coupon rate and year of maturity for each bond?

   b. How much would you have had to pay to buy one IBM bond at the closing trade?

   c. Why do you think the yield on the Lucent bond is higher than the yield on the IBM bond?

   d. How much did the price of one IBM bond change from the prior day's closing price?

11. The following bond quotations recently appeared in *The Wall Street Journal*:

ConocoPhillips (COP)	5.900	Oct 15, 2032	95.972	6.200	90	30	88,510
Amerada Hess (AHC)	7.125	Mar 15, 2033	100.145	7.113	179	30	55,000

a. How much in annual interest payment would an investor in each of these bonds receive?

b. How much would you have to pay to buy one COP bond at the last price shown?

c. Why do you think the yield-to-maturity on the AHC bond is higher than the yield to maturity on the COP bond?

THOMSON ONE—Business School Edition

Go to the text Web site at http://moyer.swlearning.com, select your book, and click on the Thomson ONE button. Enter Thomson ONE—Business School Edition by using the username and password you created when you registered the serial number on your access card. Use the "Prices" tab, "Overviews" option, and "Detailed Quote Report" sub-option in the Thomson ONE—BSE database to compare the performance of Boeing (BA) to the performance of the broader market as measured by the S&P 500 stock average. What factors can you cite that may help to explain this relative performance? What returns did an investor in Boeing stock receive over the past 6 months, past one year, and past 3 years?

CHAPTER

3 Review of Financial Statements

This chapter provides a brief review of financial statements that are covered in more depth in accounting courses. An understanding of the financial statements is critical because of their role in effective financial decision making. Financial statements are one key source of information that management, investors, creditors, analysts, employees, and other interested parties rely on to make decisions. A sampling of some decisions that require the use of financial statements are:

- ➤ Analysts use financial statements to assess the value of a firm and make recommendations on whether to buy, hold, or sell a stock.
- ➤ Financial statements are useful for long-term planning purposes. For example, financial statements may be used to see whether enough internally generated funds will be available to meet future growth targets.
- ➤ Financial statements are used by labor unions to assess a firm's financial condition while negotiating for better pay/benefit packages for their members.
- ➤ Bond investors use financial statements to assess the long-term safety of the firm.
- ➤ Managers may use financial statements to identify problem areas in the firm (for example, a slowdown in collections).
- ➤ Investment bankers use financial statements to help determine an appropriate offering price for a security.
- ➤ Rating agencies rely on financial statements to assess business risk of the firm.

In addition to financial statements, this chapter also provides a brief exposition of the federal income tax structure as it applies to corporations.

Chapter Objectives

After reading this chapter, students should have an understanding of the following:

1. The major financial statements

2. The information contained in the financial statements

3. The limitations of financial statements

4. The federal income tax structure as it applies to corporations

THE ACCOUNTING FUNCTION

The *accounting function* is concerned with the gathering, processing, and reporting of data on business transactions of the firm. The end result of the accounting function is a set of *financial statements*. While financial statements are varied and generated at different levels of the organization, our focus is on financial statements at the firm level. Specifically, we focus on four financial statements that appear in the company's *annual report.*

The annual report is a document that corporations provide to their shareholders summarizing the operations of the firm over the preceding year. The four major statements typically included in the annual report are: the *balance sheet,* the *income statement,* the *statement of retained earnings,* and the *statement of cash flows.* These same statements also are provided to the Securities and Exchange Commission in annual Form *10-K* reports required by the agency of all large publicly traded firms. The Form 10-K reports filed with the SEC, however, contain more details and additional schedules and information not found in the annual reports. The annual reports may be thought of as the summary version of the report filed with the SEC.

We use the annual report as the basis of discussion since it is the most widely disseminated document, and discuss each of the above-mentioned main components in detail. We use the 2000 annual report of Furniture Brands International, Inc. for illustrative purposes (the complete annual report may be downloaded from the company's Web site: http://www.furniturebrands.com/pdfs/2000annual.pdf). Furniture Brands is the largest manufacturer of residential furniture in the United States. The firm sells furniture under several well-known brand names including Broyhill, Lane, and Thomasville. Major competitors of Furniture Brands include Ethan Allen Interiors, Inc., La-Z-Boy Inc., and LifeStyles Furnishings International, Inc. Furniture Brands stock is listed on the NYSE under the ticker symbol FBN.

http://www.
furniturebrands.com/
pdfs/2000annual.pdf

THE ANNUAL REPORT

Table 3.1 provides an outline of the typical annual report. The annual report generally begins with a page containing the *financial highlights* of the firm's performance. The report may highlight a few key financial figures such as sales, net income, and earnings per share. Usually these are presented in a tabular as well as a graphical format.

This is followed by the *letter to the stockholders from the chief executive officer* (CEO). The letter to shareholders is an important part of the annual report. In the letter, the CEO communicates with the shareholders, providing his assessment of the firm's performance in the year past. A well-written letter would address both positive and negative developments in the firm. In this section, the CEO also

Table 3.1 Outline of the Annual Report

I. Financial Highlights
II. Letter to Stockholders from the CEO
III. Operations Review
IV. Financial Performance
  Summary of Financial Ratios
  Balance Sheet
  Income Statement
  Statement of Retained Earnings
  Statement of Cash Flows
  Report from the Independent Auditor
V. Members of the Management Team and Board of Directors

communicates information about strategic plans for the future. Investors can glean important information about various aspects of the company's management from the letter, including such things as the quality of the top management, leadership, vision, and planning for the future.

The letter from the CEO is sometimes followed by a section on *operations review.* Basically, this section contains a description of the various business/product lines of the firm and their competitive position in the industry—discussed primarily from marketing and production standpoints. Growth in sales of various products, market shares, and new product developments are among the topics included here.

Next in the annual report is the all-important section on *financial performance.* The financial performance section usually begins with a table containing common financial ratios (discussed in Chapter 4) and key figures from the different financial statements over a 5- to 10-year period. This is followed by the balance sheet, income statement, statement of retained earnings, and the statement of cash flows. The statements are followed by a section of notes that include details not covered by the financial numbers in the various statements and explanations of various items in the financial statements. An important part of the financial performance section of the annual report is a letter from an independent auditor. This letter certifies that the firm has used *Generally Accepted Accounting Principles* in developing the financial statements. It basically serves to inform the public that the auditors have not uncovered any obvious misrepresentations in the statements.

The final section of the report contains information about the individuals on the board of directors and the top management team of the firm.

Comprehension Check Questions

1. What are the typical parts of an annual report?
2. What are the four financial statements included in the annual report?

THE BALANCE SHEET

e-Lecture

Overview of Finance and Raising Money

The **balance sheet** provides a "snapshot" of a firm's financial condition as of a particular date. As can be seen from the model provided as Table 3.2, the balance sheet shows what the firm owns (*assets*) and how they were financed between *liabilities* and **stockholders' equity.** The assets may be classified as current and fixed assets. The liabilities consist of current and long-term liabilities. Liabilities refer to claims owed

Table 3.2 Major Components of the Balance Sheet

Assets		Liabilities and Stockholders' Equity	
Current assets	$	Current liabilities	$
		Long-term liabilities	$
Fixed assets	$	Stockholders' equity	$
Total Assets	$	**Total Liabilities, Stockholders' Equity**	$

to outsiders such as the trade suppliers, the Internal Revenue Service, bondholders, banks, employees, etc. The stockholders' equity refers to funds provided by or that belong to the stockholders of the company. *A basic principle in the construction of the balance sheet is that the assets must equal the liabilities and stockholders' equity.*

Table 3.3 presents the consolidated balance sheet for Furniture Brands for the year 2000 along with the comparative statement for 1999. Our discussion focuses on the 2000 information. Note that the balance sheet reflects information as of December 31, since Furniture Brands' fiscal year ends on that date.

Assets

Assets are usually divided into *current assets* (cash and other assets that are likely to be converted to cash in the near term, typically defined as less than 1 year) and *fixed assets* (property, plant, and equipment). The major components of current assets are *cash and cash equivalents*, *accounts receivable*, and *inventories*.

Cash and Cash Equivalents *Cash*, of course, refers to exactly that—cash in the possession of the firm, including balances deposited at a bank. Cash balances do not earn any interest. *Cash equivalents*, also known as *marketable securities*, refers to funds invested in short-term securities such as T-bills, commercial paper, and the like. These are funds the firm does not need immediately and therefore have been "parked" in a marketable securities account, earning interest. However, because marketable securities are short-term accounts, the firm has quick access to these funds whenever it requires them. In some instances the balances for cash and cash equivalents are shown separately. Furniture Brands has chosen to present the combined balance for cash and cash equivalents. At the end of 2000, Furniture Brands had $14.6 million in cash and cash equivalents, which is approximately 1 percent of the firm's total assets.

Accounts Receivable The *accounts receivable* balance for Furniture Brands is $351.8 million or nearly 51 percent of its current assets and 27 percent of its total assets. This represents the single largest category of assets for the firm. The accounts receivable captures the funds owed to the company by its customers. Furniture Brands sells its products through furniture centers, independent dealers, national and local chains, and department stores. As with most manufacturing businesses, customers buy on credit. Depending upon industry practice, customers typically have 30 to 45 days to pay for the merchandise. In terms of the accounting treatment, when the merchandise is shipped it is recognized as a sale and *the amount invoiced becomes an accounts receivable that is owed to the firm by the customer.*

Inventory Another major current asset category is the *inventory*. This is especially true for manufacturing firms. Service-oriented firms require very little inventory balances as part of their business operations. In the case of manufacturing firms, the inventory consists of three types: raw materials, work in process, and finished

Table 3.3 Furniture Brands' Balance Sheet

(Dollars in thousands)	December 31, 2000	December 31, 1999
Assets		
Current assets:		
Cash and cash equivalents	$ 14,606	$ 7,409
Receivables, less allowances of $23,075 ($19,057 at December 31, 1999)	351,804	345,385
Inventories	294,454	285,395
Prepaid expenses and other current assets	30,717	33,711
Total current assets	691,581	671,900
Property, plant and equipment:		
Land	19,206	18,930
Buildings and improvements	226,096	204,177
Machinery and equipment	345,040	322,527
	590,342	545,634
Less accumulated depreciation	287,107	247,888
Net property, plant and equipment	303,235	297,746
Intangible assets	289,895	303,446
Other assets	20,127	15,742
	$1,304,838	$1,288,834
Liabilities and Shareholders' Equity		
Current liabilities:		
Accounts payable	$ 65,483	$ 73,617
Accrued employee compensation	24,822	28,450
Accrued interest expense	7,646	1,762
Other accrued expenses	45,167	50,035
Total current liabilities	143,118	153,864
Long-term debt	462,000	535,100
Other long-term liabilities	115,815	125,673
Shareholders' equity:		
Preferred stock, authorized 10,000,000 shares, no par value – issued, none	—	—
Common stock, authorized 100,000,000 shares, $1.00 stated value – issued 52,277,066 shares at December 31, 2000 and 1999	52,277	52,277
Paid-in capital	118,360	120,326
Retained earnings	462,473	356,572
Treasury stock at cost (2,601,759 shares at December 31, 2000 and 2,907,059 shares at December 31, 1999)	(49,205)	(54,978)
Total shareholders' equity	583,905	474,197
	$1,304,838	$1,288,834

goods, depending on the stage of the production process. Furniture Brands has a total inventory balance of $294.5 million; accounting for approximately 43 percent of the current asset account and 23 percent of total assets. Inventory is usually valued either on a **FIFO** (first-in, first-out) or **LIFO** (last-in, first-out) basis. In the FIFO method, it is assumed that the first units produced are those that are sold first, while in LIFO the last units produced are the ones that are sold first. In an inflationary setting, the LIFO method yields the higher cost of goods sold and therefore a lower tax liability. However, the balance sheet values for inventory in this case (LIFO) appear undervalued. It is therefore a more conservative accounting practice. The use of FIFO in an inflationary setting yields exactly the opposite results. The particular method a firm uses to value its inventory is disclosed in the footnotes to the financial statements. (Footnotes to the financial statement under discussion show that Furniture Brands employs the LIFO method.)

Prepaid Expenses and Other Current Assets In addition to the above current asset accounts, Furniture Brands also has a relatively small amount of current assets categorized as *prepaid expenses and other current assets*. Prepaid expenses refer to expenses, such as insurance and rent, which may be paid in advance. Prepaid expenses are considered an asset as they have not been "consumed" yet. *Other current assets* refers to those that do not neatly fit into one of the major categories discussed previously. One such other current asset account many firms have is *deferred income taxes*. Deferred income taxes can be both an asset and a liability. We will discuss deferred taxes when we cover the liabilities section of the balance sheet.

Fixed Assets Besides current assets, the other major category of assets is *fixed assets* or property, plant, and equipment. Furniture Brands reports land, buildings and improvements, and machinery and equipment under this category. Fixed assets are usually carried at cost (what the firm paid for it) less accumulated **depreciation.** The accumulated depreciation is subtracted from the original cost of the asset to reflect the fact that assets, such as equipment, lose their value or *depreciate* over time. The depreciation amounts are based on a predetermined schedule. For financial reporting purposes, most firms use the *straight-line method* of depreciation. The formula for calculating the annual depreciation using the straight-line method is:

$$Depreciation = \frac{(\textit{cost of the asset} - \textit{expected salvage value})}{\textit{economic life of asset}} \qquad \textbf{(3.1)}$$

where the cost of the asset is installed cost of the asset (including any shipping and installation charges), expected salvage value is the amount that can be recovered from the sale of the asset at the end of its economic life, and the economic life is the length of time the asset is expected to be in use. For an asset that originally cost $100,000, with an expected salvage value of $10,000 and useful life of 5 years, the annual straight-line depreciation would equal:

$$= \frac{(\$100,000 - \$10,000)}{5} = \$18,000$$

For tax purposes, firms often use an *accelerated depreciation* schedule permissible under the tax laws. The main feature of the accelerated depreciation method is that a heavier depreciation rate is incurred in the beginning years of the asset's use and less in the later years. The net result is reduced tax liabilities in the early years of the asset usage, but higher taxes in the later years. The total tax payments over the life of the asset are unaffected. However, from a time value of money standpoint, you would prefer to delay the payment of taxes rather than accelerate it.

Furniture Brands reported net property, plant, and equipment of $303.2 million—or about 23 percent of total assets. Note that the original cost of property, plant, and equipment totaled $590.3 million and that accumulated depreciation was $287.1 million. The difference yields the reported net property, plant, and equipment. Thus, a significant portion of the firm's assets has already been depreciated—from an accounting perspective. The size of the accumulated depreciation relative to the original cost provides a clue as to how long the firm has been in business and to the age of the fixed assets. Furniture Brands apparently has been in business for a while.

The next asset category reported by Furniture Brands is *intangible assets.* Intangible assets consist of the value of trademarks and patents acquired by the firm. It can also include goodwill arising from the acquisition of firms for more than their book values. Furniture Brands reports intangible assets of $289.9 million. As a proportion of total assets it is equal to approximately 22 percent. Most firms do not report such sizable amounts for intangible assets.

The final item under assets is *other assets.* Furniture Brands reports $20.1 million in other assets, consisting of miscellaneous long-term assets that do not fit into any of the other categories reported.

Summing up all the different assets, Furniture Brands has total assets of $1,304.8 million. Next, we examine the "right-hand side" of the balance sheet, which shows how Furniture Brands *financed* its total assets (the "left-hand side" of the balance sheet). The right-hand side or the financing side of the balance sheet consists of liabilities and shareholders' equity.

Liabilities

The liabilities side of the balance sheet, similar to assets, may be broken down into current and long-term portions. *Current liabilities* are obligations of the firm that have to be settled in the short term, typically within 1 year. Current liabilities usually consist of *accounts payable, notes payable,* and *accrued liabilities.*

Accounts Payable   *Accounts payable* refers to obligations of the firm incurred as a result of purchasing goods and services from suppliers. For instance, Furniture Brands may purchase upholstery fabric from a supplier on credit terms that require payment within 45 days. This purchase would result in an increase in accounts payable for Furniture Brands. (Note: The transaction would result in an increase in accounts receivable for the supplier.) When the account is paid, the accounts payable account is reduced by that amount and the cash account is also decreased, thereby keeping the balance sheet "balanced." Furniture Brands has $65.5 million in accounts payable, making up almost 46 percent of all current liabilities.

Notes Payable   *Notes payable* refers to short-term loan obligations of the firm that are typically used by the firm to meet seasonal requirements. From the balance sheet it does not appear that Furniture Brands has any notes payable.

Accrued Liabilities   Another type of current liabilities is *accrued liabilities.* Accrued liabilities arise because the accounting profession follows what is generally referred to as the *accrual basis of accounting.* This means that revenues and expenses are recognized when they are incurred rather than when the cash is received or paid. In the case of accrued liabilities, expenses are recognized prior to the actual payment of cash.

Accrued employee compensation is one example of an accrued liability. Because employees are not paid on a daily but rather on a monthly, or some other periodic, basis, the firm accrues a liability until the obligation is paid off. For example, let us assume that a firm pays its employees monthly and the monthly payroll is $30,000. In other words, the daily payroll obligation the firm incurs is $1,000 (for simplicity let's assume that there are 30 working days in a month). If we were to construct a balance sheet at the end of the tenth day of the month, our accrued employee compensation will equal $10,000 ($1,000 per day × 10 days). From the current liabilities section of Furniture Brands' balance sheet, we note the firm has $24.8 million in accrued employee wages.

Furniture Brands also has accrued interest expense in the amount of $7.6 million. Just like accrued employee compensation, accrued interest expenses arise because interest on debt obligations are paid on a periodic basis rather than on a daily basis. For example, consider a firm that has $10 million in debt outstanding on which it incurs $100,000 in interest every month. If interest is paid quarterly, the accrued interest expense 2 months into the quarter is $200,000 ($100,000 interest per month × 2 months). Thus, a balance sheet constructed at the end of the second month of the quarter would show an accrued interest expense of $200,000.

Another type of accrued liability firms report is accrued taxes. One example of accrued tax is that associated with corporate income tax. Firms estimate and pay corporate income taxes every quarter. However, they accrue taxes leading up to the end of the quarter. In addition to income taxes, corporations are obligated to pay other taxes including property, excise, or sales taxes, which are remitted at different frequencies: Some are paid annually while others are remitted quarterly or monthly. Furniture Brands does not report a separate accrued tax expense but it is probably included in the *other accrued expenses* category.

Summing up all the current liabilities, Furniture Brands has $143.1 million in current liabilities, or nearly 11 percent of total liabilities and shareholders' equity (or total assets). In other words, Furniture Brands financed 11 percent of its total assets through current liability sources.

Long-term Liabilities Following the current liabilities are *long-term liabilities*, which are obligations that extend beyond 1 year. These generally consist of *long-term debt* (also known as *funded debt*), such as mortgage bonds and debentures. Furniture Brands has $462 million in long-term debt, accounting for approximately 35 percent of total liabilities and shareholders' equity. For most companies this would be considered high. For example, Ethan Allen Inc., a major competitor of Furniture Brands, had long-term debt of only $9.487 million in its 2000 fiscal year balance sheet, which amounted to just 1.7 percent of the firm's total liabilities and shareholders' equity. If a firm has too much debt, it runs the risk of being unable to pay its debt obligation (interest and/or principal payment) on time and being forced into bankruptcy. On the other hand, firms may want to have a moderate amount of debt in order to take advantage of the tax deductibility of interest expense. The tax deductibility of interest expense makes the effective cost of debt even lower. In Chapters 12 and 13 we explore more fully the issues surrounding choice of appropriate debt policy.

Furniture Brands also reports *other long-term liabilities* of $115.8 million. Footnotes to the financial statements reveal that much of this consists of *deferred income tax liability*. Deferred income taxes arise because of what are referred to as "temporary" differences in the income reported to shareholders and income reported for tax purposes. These differences occur for many reasons, but one major source is the use of accelerated depreciation methods for tax purposes and straight-line depreciation methods for reporting purposes. The result is a lower tax liability for tax purposes and a higher tax amount in statements reported to stockholders.

Table 3.4 provides an example. Shown are the taxes for reporting purposes based on straight-line depreciation and the actual taxes paid based on an accelerated depreciation method. The actual taxes amount to $6.12 million, but the taxes reported to shareholders is $6.80 million. The difference of $0.68 million is a deferred tax liability. Note that this difference is only temporary. The actual taxes ultimately paid will be no different from those assumed to be paid using straight-line depreciation. Consequently, the financial income reported is higher than the taxable income. In order to reconcile the difference between the reported tax liability of $6.80 million and the actual tax cash outflow of $6.12 million, the difference of $0.68 million ($6.80 million − $6.12 million) is placed into a deferred tax liability account. Sometimes a *deferred tax asset* rather than, or in addition to, deferred tax liability is reported. A deferred tax asset occurs when reported financial income is less than the taxable income. This might occur, for example, if a firm is expecting a liability judgment in a current litigation for which it has taken a charge in its reported income. However, for tax purposes the liability is not deductible until it is paid. The footnotes to the Furniture Brands statement reveal that the firm has a deferred tax asset, but it is reported under other current assets.

The total long-term liabilities for Furniture Brands are $577.8 million (long-term debt + other long-term liabilities). The total long-term liabilities account for approximately 44 percent of total liabilities and shareholders' equity. The total of *all* liabilities is $720.9 million or about 55 percent of total liabilities and sharehold-

---

Table 3.4 Illustration of Deferred Federal Income Taxes

(A) Calculation of Taxes for Financial Reporting and Tax Purposes (in Millions of Dollars)

	Financial Reporting Purposes	Tax Purposes
Sales	$100.00	$100.00
Expenses, Excluding Depreciation	70.00	70.00
Depreciation:		
Straight-line	10.00	
MACRS*		12.00
Earnings Before Taxes	$ 20.00	$ 18.00
Taxes (34%)	6.80	6.12
Earnings After Taxes	$ 13.20	$ 11.88

(B) Partial Income Statement Reported to Stockholders (in Millions of Dollars)

Earnings Before Taxes	$ 20.00
Federal Income Taxes @ 34%:	
Current	$ 6.12
Deferred	0.68
Total Federal Income Tax	$ 6.80
Earnings After Taxes	$ 13.20

*MACRS stands for Modified Accelerated Cost Recovery System, a form of accelerated depreciation used for tax purposes.

ers' equity. That is, Furniture Brands has financed 55 percent of its total assets with some form of liability—current and long-term liabilities.

Stockholders' Equity

The final account in the balance sheet we will examine is the *stockholders' equity* account, which follows the liabilities section of the balance sheet. The stockholders' equity account represents the ownership interest in the firm and consists of preferred stock and common stock ownership interests. Both preferred stockholders and common stockholders are considered as having an ownership stake in the firm, although effectively it is the latter that assume that role.

Preferred Stock The *preferred stock account* reflects the proceeds from the sale of preferred stock at the time it was issued. Evidently, Furniture Brands has no preferred stock outstanding.

Common Stock at Par or Stated Value and Paid-in Capital The next two accounts, *common stock at par value* or *stated value* and the *paid-in capital* in excess of par value—together capture the proceeds from the sale of common stock. Firms usually assume an arbitrary par value per share, which has little to do with the actual price the stock sold for. To show how these two accounts work, assume a company sold 200,000 shares of common stock at $3.50 per share with a par value per share of $2.00. The entries then would be $400,000 in the common stock at par value account (200,000 shares × $2.00 par value per share) and $300,000 in the paid-in capital in excess of par value account: ($3.50 selling price − $2.00 par value) × 200,000 shares. The paid-in capital account captures the difference between the actual selling price and the par value.

Furniture Brands has approximately 52.3 million common shares outstanding, each with a par or stated value per share of $1.00, yielding a total of $52.3 million in common stock at stated value. The paid-in capital is $118.4 million.

Note that the values in the preferred stock and common stock accounts are based on the price at which these securities were *issued*. These prices may have little resemblance to the current trading price of the stock. The current trading price of the stock may be less than, equal to, or greater than the original selling price of these securities.

Retained Earnings The next item under the stockholders' equity category is *retained earnings*. Retained earnings refer to net income that was retained in the firm and is net of all dividends paid. The retained earnings figure is the cumulative amount from the inception of the firm. The increase in retained earnings in the balance sheet from one year to the next is equal to the net income generated in the year less all dividends paid out to preferred and common stockholders in the year. Retained earnings for Furniture Brands is $462.5 million, which is the amount of net income plowed back into the firm since inception.

Treasury Stock at Cost The final item under stockholders' equity is *treasury stock at cost*. **Treasury stock** is stock that the firm bought back. Firms frequently buy back shares that were previously issued. Shares are bought back for a variety of reasons (this topic is covered more fully in Chapter 14). Firms engage in buyback programs in order to give the shares to employees as part of an employee stock option plan. Firms also buy back stock because they want to "send a signal" to the marketplace. By buying back shares, the firm is sending a message that they are so confident in the firm's future prospects that they are investing in it themselves. Furniture Brands has a total of $49.2 million in treasury stock. Note that treasury stock has the effect of reducing the stockholders' equity since it effectively reduces outstanding shares.

1. What are assets and liabilities?
2. What is meant by deferred tax liability?
3. What are accruals?

THE INCOME STATEMENT

Finance in the News

Click on this button at **http://finance. swlearning.com** *for synopses of recent articles on Financial Statements and Analysis.*

Unlike the balance sheet, which is a snapshot of the firm at a given point in time, the *income statement* captures the operating results of the firm *over a period of time.* The income statement details the *earnings generated by the firm after all expenses have been subtracted from the revenues.* Income statements can be generated for any period of time. The annual reports, of course, present annual income statements. In addition, firms also provide quarterly income statements to their shareholders. Internally, firms may also generate monthly or even weekly income statements.

Furniture Brands' income statement (also known as the *statement of operations*) for fiscal year 2000 with comparative data for years 1999 and 1998 is shown in Table 3.5.

Sales

The income statement begins with the *sales* or *revenues*, net of returns and allowances. In the 2000 fiscal year Furniture Brands had sales of $2,116.2 million.

Cost of Operations

The next item is the *cost of operations* (also referred to as *cost of sales* or *cost of goods sold*). The cost of sales reflects the direct cost of producing the merchandise and includes such things as the cost of raw materials and labor that goes into the manufacturing process. The cost of goods sold is affected by the inventory valuation used by the firm. In an inflationary setting the use of the LIFO method results in a higher cost of goods sold, while a FIFO method will yield a lower cost of goods sold.

For Furniture Brands, the cost of operations was $1,529.9 million. The difference between sales and cost of sales is the *gross margin* or *gross profit margin*. This is the amount that is available to meet all the other expenses of the firm. The gross margin for Furniture Brands in year 2000 was $586.4 million.

Operating Expenses

The next group of expenses is operating expenses. These include: *selling, general, and administrative expenses, depreciation*, and *research and development costs.* However, not all firms report every item separately, especially research and development costs.

Selling, General, and Administrative Expenses *Selling, general, and administrative expenses* refer to overhead costs of doing business and include marketing expenses, advertising costs, salaries to management, general utilities, etc. Sometimes depreciation, instead of being shown separately, is reflected in the selling, general, and administrative expenses. Furniture Brands' income statement shows selling, general, and administrative expenses of $335.6 million in 2000.

Depreciation *Depreciation* expense, as we have seen earlier in this chapter, is a way to allocate the cost of fixed assets, such as buildings and equipment, over time. Since fixed assets are expected to have a useful life of more than 1 year, they are

Table 3.5 Furniture Brands' Income Statement

(Dollars in thousands except per share data)	2000	1999	1998
	Year Ended December 31,		
Net sales	$2,116,239	$2,088,112	$1,960,250
Costs and expenses:			
Cost of operations	1,529,874	1,498,622	1,406,434
Selling, general, and administrative expenses	335,596	321,205	314,837
Depreciation and amortization (includes $13,546, $13,155 and $13,670 related to fair value adjustments)	58,155	56,528	55,469
Earnings from operations	192,614	211,757	183,510
Interest expense	36,389	37,577	43,455
Other income, net	9,772	2,584	12,088
Earnings before income tax expense and extraordinary item	165,997	176,764	152,143
Income tax expense	57,574	64,854	54,205
Earnings before extraordinary item	108,423	111,910	97,938
Extraordinary item – early extinguishment of debt, net of income tax benefit	(2,522)	—	—
Net earnings	$ 105,901	$ 111,910	$ 97,938
Net earnings per common share – basic			
Earnings before extraordinary item	$ 2.19	$ 2.20	$ 1.88
Extraordinary item – early extinguishment of debt	(0.05)	—	—
Net earnings per common share – basic	$ 2.14	$ 2.20	$ 1.88
Net earnings per common share – diluted			
Earnings before extraordinary item	$ 2.15	$ 2.14	$ 1.82
Extraordinary item – early extinguishment of debt	(0.05)	—	—
Net earnings per common share – diluted	$ 2.10	$ 2.14	$ 1.82

not expensed in the year they are purchased; rather their expense is spread over more than 1 year. Consequently, depreciation expense is not a cash expense but an accounting treatment to allocate the cost of fixed assets over their estimated life. For reporting purposes most firms use the straight-line depreciation method (see page 61). However, for tax purposes firms use an accelerated depreciation method. As noted in our previous discussion, the accelerated depreciation method allows the firm to use higher depreciation rates in the early years of the asset's life, decreasing sharply in the later years.

Another noncash expense that firms may report in their income statement along with depreciation—or separately—is *amortization expense*. Amortization usually arises in connection with the purchase of intangible assets such as the value of patents, trademarks, copyrights, and goodwill. For accounting purposes such expenses are amortized or allocated over their useful lives. Goodwill refers to the accumulated value paid for acquisitions in excess of the recorded book value of acquired assets, and can be a significant amortization expense for firms making major acquisitions. However, it is important to note that recent accounting rule changes in the United States have eliminated the amortization requirement for intangible assets with indefinite lives (See FASB Statement 142, http://www.fasb.org). The rule applies to firms with fiscal years after December 15, 2001. Instead of amortizing intangible assets, firms now have to report an impairment loss if a loss in value of the intangible asset is experienced. The above ruling only applies to intangible assets with indefinite lives like goodwill associated with acquisitions. In the case of intangible assets with finite lives (e.g., a patent on a drug) firms continue to amortize an asset over its useful life.

Furniture Brands reported a combined depreciation and amortization expense of $58.2 million in 2000.

Research and Development Costs Another operating expense firms report is *research and development (R&D) costs*. As the term implies, R&D costs refer to expenses incurred in developing new products. R&D expense is not always shown as a separate amount. Indeed Furniture Brands does not have a separate line item for R&D expense. However, in some industries R&D costs account for a significant portion of the expenses and are highlighted as a separate expense item in the income statement. For example, Adaptec Inc., which manufactures specialized computer hardware, reported research and development expense of 19 percent of sales in its 2001 fiscal year income statement.

After subtracting the operating expenses, the resulting figure is *operating profit* or *earnings from operations*. In 2000 Furniture Brands generated earnings from operations of $192.6 million.

Nonoperating Expenses

Following the operating profit, firms typically disclose *interest expenses* and *other expenses*. Sometimes firms also report interest income and other income, such as interest earned on marketable securities or income from rental property the firm may own. Furniture Brands incurred an interest expense of $36.4 million and generated other income of $9.8 million. The resulting *earnings before income tax and extraordinary item* for Furniture Brands is $166 million.

Income Tax

The next item is the *income tax expense*. For Furniture Brands income tax (federal, state, etc.) amounted to $57.6 million. The federal income tax structure for corporations is discussed more fully in a separate section at the end of this chapter (page 78). After subtracting the income tax expense, Furniture Brands reported earnings before extraordinary item of $108.4 million.

Extraordinary Items

Before presenting the net income, firms subtract any *extraordinary expense items*. Extraordinary items, as the phrase implies, refer to significant nonrecurring, one-time expenses a firm may incur. Examples include costs associated with plant closings, fire, or corporate restructuring charges. These are reported separately, rather than as part of operating expenses, so that investors treat them as one-time charges that are unlikely to recur in the future. Furniture Brands' income statement includes an extraordinary expense of $2.5 million related to the early extinguishment (elimination) of debt.

Net Earnings

The *net earnings* (also sometimes referred to as *net income* or *earnings after taxes*) are the earnings remaining after all expenses have been charged. In street terminology net income is sometimes referred to as the "bottom line." The net income figure is very important to common stock investors in gauging the performance of the firm. As residual owners of the firm, the net earnings are what accrue to the shareholders. In the event a firm has preferred stock, the relevant net earnings figure is the net earnings after subtracting preferred stock dividends, also known as *earnings available to common shareholders*. Furniture Brands' net earnings equaled $105.9 million in 2000. Since the firm has no preferred stock outstanding, the net earnings shown is what is available to the common stockholders.

The income statement also shows earnings or net income on a per common share basis. Firms are required to report both *basic* and *diluted earnings per common share*. The basic earnings per share is calculated as net income after payment of preferred dividends divided by the average number of common shares outstanding. For Furniture Brands the basic earnings per share equaled $2.14. If we eliminated the effect of the extraordinary item, the equivalent basic earnings per share is $2.19.

The diluted earnings per share calculation takes into account the potential dilutive effect of convertible securities and/or stock options outstanding. Firms sometimes issue **convertible securities,** such as convertible bonds or convertible preferred stock, which are likely to be converted into the underlying common shares sometime in the future. When the conversion takes place the outstanding share balance increases. Consequently, conversion results in net earnings being spread over a larger share balance and decreases the proportional claim of existing shareholders on the future income stream.

Firms also issue stock options as part of employee stock option plans. As mentioned in Chapter 1, stock options are securities that entitle the holder to purchase the underlying shares at a particular price (known as the exercise price) within some stated time period. As part of the compensation package, top management and others often receive options to buy shares of the firm at attractive exercise prices if certain conditions and performance targets are met. When employees exercise their stock options, the outstanding share balances will increase resulting in *dilution*. To reflect this future potential conversion, firms are required to calculate a diluted earnings per share figure, which assumes that the convertible securities and stock options will result in additional shares outstanding. It should be noted that the diluted earnings per share that firms are required to provide is a "worst case" scenario, since not all convertible securities get converted and not all stock options get exercised. Furthermore, some firms satisfy the conversion and stock option exercise requirements by purchasing shares in the open market, thereby leaving the outstanding share balance unaffected.

The diluted earnings per share for Furniture Brands is $2.10 after the extraordinary item and $2.15 if the extraordinary item is not taken into account. Evidently, the dilutive impact is minimal for Furniture Brands. However, for some firms, especially in high-tech industries, where employee stock options are a significant component of compensation, the dilutive impact of stock options can be significant. For example, Apple Computer during its 2000 fiscal year reported basic earnings per share of $2.42 but diluted earnings per share of $2.18—a difference of approximately 10 percent.

STATEMENT OF RETAINED EARNINGS AND STATEMENT OF SHAREHOLDERS' EQUITY

Following the income statement, annual reports usually include a *statement of retained earnings* or statement of shareholders' equity. The purpose of the statement of retained earnings is to reconcile the retained earnings number in the balance sheet with the net income figure from the income statement. The statement of shareholders' equity has a similar purpose but, in addition, also shows changes in the various shareholders' equity accounts over the year.

A typical format for the statement of retained earnings is shown in Table 3.6. The statement begins with the retained earnings from the previous year's balance sheet. To this is added the net income from the current income statement. Cash dividends are then subtracted, yielding retained earnings at the end of the current year. In the example in Table 3.6, the previous year's retained earnings is $1,000,000. To this we add the current year's net income and then subtract all cash dividends that were paid. In the example, the firm paid out $25,000 in preferred dividends and $75,000 in common stock dividends. The resulting retained earnings at the end of the current year is $1,200,000. Thus, the firm added $200,000 to its retained earnings account this year.

Furniture Brands' annual report includes a statement of shareholders' equity (which reflects changes in each of the stockholders' equity accounts—not just changes in retained earnings) as shown in Table 3.7. The statement shows that Furniture Brands' retained earnings increased from $356.6 million at the end of 1999 to $462.5 million at the end of 2000. Note that the increase ($105.9 million) in retained earnings is equal to the net earnings in 2000. The statement also shows that the treasury stock account decreased by $5.8 million. (Recall that the treasury stock accounts for shares bought back by the firm from the market.) The notes to the financial statements reveal the firm used some of its treasury stock to meet stock option plan requirements. This transaction also impacted the paid-in capital account resulting in a decrease of $2 million. There was no change in the common stock account (stated value or par value account).

Comprehension Check Questions

1. What is the purpose of the statement of retained earnings?
2. How are the statements of shareholders' equity and retained earnings different?
3. What is the difference between basic and diluted earnings per share?

Table 3.6 Illustrative Example of Statement of Retained Earnings

Retained earnings at beginning of year (same as retained earnings from prior year's balance sheet)	$1,000,000
Net income	$ 300,000
Cash dividends paid to preferred stockholders	($25,000)
Cash dividends paid to common stockholders	($75,000)
Retained earnings at end of year (figure that is shown in the current year's balance sheet)	**$1,200,000**

Table 3.7 Furniture Brands' Statement of Shareholders' Equity

(Dollars in thousands)	Common Stock	Paid-In Capital	Retained Earnings	Treasury Stock	Total
Balance December 31, 1997	$52,003	$124,595	$146,724	$ —	$323,322
Net earnings			97,938		97,938
Common stock activity:					
Stock plans activity	274	2,918			3,192
Purchase of treasury stock – 525,000 shares				(10,943)	(10,943)
Balance December 31, 1998	52,277	127,513	244,662	(10,943)	413,509
Net earnings			111,910		111,910
Common stock activity:					
Stock plans activity		(7,187)		15,685	8,498
Purchase of treasury stock – 3,123,200 shares				(59,720)	(59,720)
Balance December 31, 1999	52,277	120,326	356,572	(54,978)	474,197
Net earnings			105,901		105,901
Common stock activity:					
Stock plans activity		(1,966)		5,773	3,807
Balance December 31, 2000	$52,277	$118,360	$462,473	$(49,205)	$583,905

THE STATEMENT OF CASH FLOWS

The *statement of cash flows* shows the effects of a *company's operating, investing, and financing activities on its cash balance.* The principal purpose of the statement of cash flows is to provide relevant information about a company's cash receipts and cash payments during a particular accounting period. It is useful in answering such questions as:

➤ How much cash did the firm generate from operations?
➤ How did the firm finance fixed capital expenditures?
➤ How much new debt did the firm add?
➤ Was the cash from operations sufficient to finance fixed asset purchases?

The statement of cash flows is a supplement to the balance sheet and income statements. One of the limitations of the income and balance sheet statements is that they are based on accrual accounting. Recall that in accrual accounting, revenues and expenses are recorded when incurred—not when cash changes hands. For example, if a sale is made for credit, under accrual accounting the sale is recognized but cash has not been received. Similarly a tax expense may be shown in the income statement but it may not be paid until later. The statement of cash flows permits the

For a brief refresher on accounting, visit **http://warren. swlearning.com**, *select the Corporate and Financial Accounting text, and take the quiz for the chapter of your choice at the Interactive Study Center.*

analyst to reconcile the accrual-based figures in the income and balance sheet statements to the actual cash balance reported in the balance sheet.

The statement of cash flows is broken down into *operating, investing,* and *financing* activities. Table 3.8 provides an outline of a statement of cash flows. *Operating cash flows* refer to cash generated from or used in the course of business operations of the firm. For most firms the net operating cash flows will be positive as their operating inflows (primarily from revenue collections) will exceed operating cash outflows (for example, payment for raw materials and wages). As we will see, there are two ways to determine operating cash flows: the *direct* method and the *indirect* method.

Investing activities refer to cash flow effects from long-term investing activities, such as purchase or sale of plant and equipment. The net cash flow from investing activities can be either positive or negative. A firm that is still in the growth phase would be building up fixed assets (installing new equipment or building new plants) and therefore show negative cash flows from investing activities. On the other hand, a firm that is divesting unprofitable divisions may realize cash inflows from the sale of assets and therefore show a positive cash flow from investing activities.

Financing activities refer to cash flow effects of financing decisions of the firm, including sale of new securities, such as stocks and bonds, repurchase of securities, and payment of dividends. Note that payment of interest to lenders is *not* included under financing activities. Accounting convention in determining the statement of cash flows assumes that interest payments are part of operating cash flows. Once the cash flows from the three different sources—operating, investing, and financing—are identified, the beginning and ending cash balances are reconciled.

In the *direct method* of generating operating cash flows, the firm reports cash inflows and cash outflows from operating activities. Table 3.9 illustrates the format for

Table 3.8   Format of Statement of Cash Flows

Cash flows from operating activities	$
Cash flows from investing activities	$
Cash flows from financing activities	$
Net increase (decrease) in cash	$
Cash at beginning of period	$
Cash at end of period	$

Table 3.9   Illustrative Format for Direct Method of Determining Cash Flow from Operations

Cash flows from operating activities:	
Cash received from customers	$10,000
Cash paid to suppliers and employees	(8,400)
Interest received on marketable securities account	450
Interest paid on loans	(215)
Income taxes paid	(1,250)
Net cash provided by (used in) operating activities	**$585**

doing this. Cash inflows include collections from customers and interest received on security investments. Cash outflows include payments to suppliers and employees, interest payments, and tax payments. The net cash flow from operating activities is the resulting amount after summing the various cash inflows and outflows.

In the *indirect method*, you begin with the net income and *convert* it to cash flow from operating activities by adjusting for transactions that affect the reported income but that did not affect the cash balance of the firm. A typical format for the indirect method is shown in Table 3.10. The net income shown of $800 is adjusted for noncash expenses including depreciation and amortization. In Table 3.10 the depreciation expense of $1,200 is added back to the net income. Next we adjust for changes in noncash and non-interest-earning current assets and non-interest-charging liabilities. The adjustments are made to undo the accrual-based nature of these accounts. For example, under accrual-based accounting, an increase in accounts receivable results in higher income than on a cash basis; the sale is recognized even though it is not collected. Consequently increases in accounts receivable are deducted from net income to arrive at the cash flow from the operations figure.

A similar rationale applies for increases in inventories. If you add to inventory beyond what is sold, then the cost of goods sold reported is less than what you paid for inventory on a cash basis. Alternatively, you can think of increases in accounts receivable and inventory as "using up" cash, and they have to be deducted from net income to arrive at the *cash balance.* Increases in prepaid expenses are deducted from net income as these have been paid for but not recognized in the income statement. So essentially what is done is to *deduct* from net income any increases in noncash and non-interest-earning current asset accounts. If there were a decrease in the noncash and non-interest-earning current assets, then the appropriate adjustment would be to *add* them to net income. In the example shown in Table 3.10, the adjustment consists of adding the decrease in accounts receivable of $200, subtracting the increase in inventory of $250, and adding the decrease in prepaid expenses of $200.

On the liabilities side, any increases in non-interest-charging liabilities are *added* to net income to arrive at cash flow from operations. Under accrual-based accounting the expense associated with an increase in accounts payable has already been included in the reported net income, but from a cash standpoint it has not been paid; therefore increases in accounts payable are added to the net income to

Table 3.10 Illustrative Format for Indirect Method of Determining Cash Flow from Operations

Cash flows from operating activities:		
Net income		$800
Adjustments to reconcile net income to net cash		
provided by operating activities:		
Depreciation expense	$1,200	
(Increase) decrease in accounts receivable	$ 200	
(Increase) decrease in inventory	(250)	
(Increase) decrease in prepaid expenses	$ 200	
Increase (decrease) in accounts payable	$ 200	
Increase (decrease) in taxes payable	($ 100)	$1,450
Net cash provided by (used in) operating activities		$2,250

FINANCE &The Real World

How to Distort the Books Enron Style

You may have heard the phrase "cooking the books." It refers to the efforts of a company, despite the presence of outside auditors, to distort its financial statements to make investors think things are better than they really are. It's nothing new—only the recipe has changed. More attention has been paid to this problem in recent years because of a roller-coaster stock market and news of accounting fraud at such companies as Enron and WorldCom. In the vast majority of cases, the companies aren't guilty of law violations—but rather, just enough distortion to throw off investors.

For example, according to a study of the largest 1,000 U.S. companies by REL Consultancy Group, a London-based management consulting firm, some companies manipulate balance sheets by artificially reducing inventory levels and accounts receivable at year end. The study found that the companies under study were able to cut their inventories by a total of $70 billion on December 31, 2001, or 12% from the prior quarter, by shipping out more of their products at year end. But there is evidence that the customers didn't really want the inventory. Three months later, the inventories rose by $70 billion, suggesting that either customers returned inventory or they cut back on their purchases in the new year because they had too much sitting in warehouses.

The study also showed that companies pushed to get their customers to pay their bills by the end of the year. Accounts receivable fell $20 billion, or 2%, in the fourth quarter, only to jump $60 billion, or 5%, in the first quarter of 2002. At the same time, accounts payable fell $45 billion, or 7%, in the fourth quarter, only to rise $75 billion, or 12%, by the end of the first quarter.

The net result is that working capital fell $45 billion, or 4% in the fourth quarter, making the companies look more efficient because they had less money tied up in these accounts. The trend reversed itself in the first quarter when net working capital rose $55 billion, or 5%.

True, retailers typically make much of their sales during Christmas and would be expected to have lower inventory at the end of the year. But in other cases, it could mean that the company is trying to make itself look good for the annual report. If inventories are really rising, then it could be a sign of trouble—a sign that the company is having trouble selling its product.

Another example of a distortion was the increased use of something called "EBITDA," or earnings before interest expense, taxes, depreciation and amortization. Proponents argued that EBITDA, which became fashionable in the mid-1990s, was supposed to be a more appropriate measure of earnings than net income. Instead, it became a vehicle for shifting the attention of investors away from a company's burdensome debt. A case in point: AOL Time Warner, which reported fourth quarter 2002 EBITDA of $8.8 billion, but a net loss of $53 billion.

As you read through this chapter, keep in mind that virtually every item on the financial statements is subject to some reasonable interpretation or "wiggle room." But it's up to top management and the outside auditors to make sure that the numbers fairly represent the true health of the company. In the cases of Enron and WorldCom, management and their auditors obviously fell down on the job.

Sources: The Wall Street Journal, February 14, 2003, "How to Spot Some Dirt in Rosy Annual Reports"; *Business Week,* January 14, 2003, "EBITDA's Foggy Bottom Line."

	4th quarter 2001		1st quarter 2002	
	$ in billions	%	$ in billions	%
Accounts Receivable	−$20	2%	+$60	5%
Accounts Payable	−$45	7%	+$75	12%
Working Capital	−$45	4%	+$55	5%

arrive at the cash balance. A similar logic applies to various accruals and deferred tax liabilities. If there is a decrease in the non-interest-charging liability accounts, then the adjustment would entail a *deduction* from the net income figure. In Table 3.10 the increase in accounts payable of $200 increases cash flow, so it is added back to net income; the decrease in taxes payable of $100 results in a reduction of cash flow, so it is subtracted from net income.

Let us now examine Furniture Brands' statement of cash flows shown in Table 3.11. The first thing we notice is that Furniture Brands uses the indirect method in determining the cash flows from operating activities. The Financial Accounting Standards Board (the governing body of the accounting profession that sets accounting standards) recommends that firms use the direct method for determining cash flows from operations yet most firms prefer the indirect method. The reason for this is that most accounting systems in place are not equipped to gather the information needed to calculate cash flows using the direct method.

We begin with Furniture Brands' net income of $105.9 million. After adjusting for noncash expenses and various accruals and deferrals, Furniture Brands reports net cash from operating activities of $132.1 million. Under investing activities, the firm realized negligible cash inflows from the disposal of assets, while it had cash outflows of $53.3 million due to additions to property, plant and equipment. The net cash outflow from investing activities was $53 million. The major cash flows under financing activities include a payment of $559.6 million in long-term debt and an increase of $486.5 million in long-term debt. Evidently, the firm used the entire proceeds from the new debt to pay off existing long-term debt. The firm also incurred $2.1 million in issuance costs associated with the new long-term debt and raised some funds through issuance of some of the stock from the firm's treasury stock account. The net cash outflow from financing activities was $72 million, most of it going towards a loan payment. Summarizing, the firm raised $132.1 million from operating activities and incurred cash outflows of $53 million in investing activities and cash outflows of $72 million in financing activities. The resulting net change in cash and cash equivalents is $7.2 million. When added to the beginning cash and cash equivalent balance, this results in an ending cash and cash equivalents balance of $14.6 million.

The statement of cash flows for Furniture Brands is notable in that the firm had significant net cash inflows from operating activities that it used to pay off some long-term debt and to make additions to property, plant and equipment. It is evident that the firm is not experiencing any serious financial problems and is generating ample cash flows from its operations. Furniture Brands' statement of cash flows is typical of large profitable firms in a mature industry.

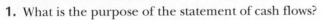

Comprehension Check Questions

1. What is the purpose of the statement of cash flows?
2. What are operating, financing, and investing activities?

LIMITATIONS OF FINANCIAL STATEMENTS

In producing the financial statements contained in the annual report, firms adhere to accounting standards collectively referred to as ***Generally Accepted Accounting Principles (GAAP)***. The GAAP are set by the Financial Accounting Standards Board (FASB) which is a private body entrusted with setting standards for the practice of

Table 3.11 Furniture Brands' Statement of Cash Flows

(Dollars in thousands)	Year Ended December 31, 2000	1999	1998
Cash flows from operating activities:			
Net earnings	$ 105,901	$ 111,910	$ 97,938
Adjustments to reconcile net earnings to net cash provided by operating activities:			
Net loss on early extinguishment of debt	2,522	—	—
Depreciation of property, plant and equipment	46,095	44,468	43,409
Amortization of intangible and other assets	12,060	12,060	12,060
Noncash interest and other expense	1,602	2,172	2,107
Increase in receivables	(6,419)	(21,221)	(30,189)
(Increase) decrease in inventories	(9,059)	21,987	(20,336)
Increase in prepaid expenses and intangible and other assets	(7,737)	(2,872)	(3,055)
Increase (decrease) in accounts payable, accrued interest expense and other accrued expenses	(9,226)	(12,861)	29,704
Increase (decrease) in net deferred tax liabilities	(2,788)	(5,390)	2,624
Decrease in other long-term liabilities	(807)	(1,687)	(2,956)
Net cash provided by operating activities	132,144	148,566	131,306
Cash flows from investing activities:			
Proceeds from the disposal of assets	316	451	1,233
Additions to property, plant and equipment	(53,310)	(48,951)	(44,358)
Net cash used by investing activities	(52,994)	(48,500)	(43,125)
Cash flows from financing activities:			
Payments for debt issuance costs	(2,090)	—	(1,684)
Additions to long-term debt	486,500	—	218,000
Payments of long-term debt	(559,600)	(54,100)	(295,800)
Proceeds from the issuance of common stock	—	—	3,192
Proceeds from the issuance of treasury stock	3,237	7,943	—
Purchase of treasury stock	—	(59,720)	(10,943)
Net cash used by financing activities	(71,953)	(105,877)	(87,235)
Net increase (decrease) in cash and cash equivalents	7,197	(5,811)	946
Cash and cash equivalents at beginning of period	7,409	13,220	12,274
Cash and cash equivalents at end of period	$ 14,606	$ 7,409	$ 13,220
Supplemental Disclosure:			
Cash payments for income taxes, net	$ 63,120	$ 68,100	$ 49,889
Cash payments for interest	$ 30,873	$ 40,070	$ 42,974

accounting in the United States. In addition to FASB, the Securities and Exchange Commission (SEC) has the authority to establish accounting policies. However, although on occasion it has imposed its own views on some issues, the SEC prefers to defer such decisions to FASB.

To ensure that GAAP has been followed, firms are required to have their annual financial statements audited by an external auditor—that is, a public accounting firm. Such a firm conducts an audit to verify that the statements are in conformity with GAAP and that on the basis of their tests the data and information presented in the financial statements are not misrepresented. The external auditor's judgment is reflected in their "opinion," which becomes a part of the annual report. Furniture Brands' annual report was audited by KPMG, one of the "Big 4" accounting firms. The auditor's opinion for Furniture Brands is reproduced in Figure 3.1. As can be seen, Furniture Brands has a "clean" opinion. In contrast some firms may have a "qualified" opinion indicating that the external auditor finds or has raised significant questions regarding information contained in the financial statements.

**Figure 3.1
Report from
Independent
Auditor**

INDEPENDENT AUDITORS' REPORT

The Board of Directors and Shareholders
Furniture Brands International, Inc.:

We have audited the accompanying consolidated balance sheets of Furniture Brands International, Inc. and subsidiaries as of December 31, 2000 and 1999, and the related consolidated statements of operations, shareholders' equity, and cash flows for each of the years in the three-year period ended December 31, 2000. These consolidated financial statements are the responsibility of the Company's management. Our responsibility is to express an opinion on these consolidated financial statements based on our audits.

We conducted our audits in accordance with auditing standards generally accepted in the United States of America. Those standards require that we plan and perform the audit to obtain reasonable assurance about whether the financial statements are free of material misstatement. An audit includes examining, on a test basis, evidence supporting the amounts and disclosure in the financial statements. An audit also includes assessing the accounting principles used and significant estimates made by management, as well as evaluating the overall financial statement presentation. We believe that our audits provide a reasonable basis for our opinion.

In our opinion, the consolidated financial statements referred to above present fairly, in all material respects, the financial position of Furniture Brands International, Inc. and subsidiaries as of December 31, 2000 and 1999, and the results of their operations and their cash flows for each of the years in the three-year period ended December 31, 2000, in conformity with accounting principles generally accepted in the United States of America.

KPMG LLP

St. Louis, Missouri
January 25, 2001

Although adherence to GAAP standards provides some assurance as to the accounting standards being followed, it still leaves a considerable amount of latitude to the firm in developing the financial statements. Thus, some firms may follow relatively conservative policies, while other firms may apply fairly aggressive polices in developing the financial statements. This, in turn, leads to the question of *balance sheet quality* and *earnings quality*. For example, there may be a question of whether inventory or accounts receivable have been written down to reflect a lower realizable value. In the case of banks there is the issue of whether adequate loan loss reserves have been taken.

Similar questions may be raised about earnings quality. For example, sales may be booked even when there is a question of whether they may be realized. In 1994, Bausch and Lomb, a large manufacturer of contact lenses, found that many of their managers were shipping merchandise to their customers at the end of the year with the understanding that they may return the merchandise for credit. This practice allowed the managers, and the firm, to show improved sales for the year. This revelation ultimately caused the firm to steeply revise downward the earnings for the year. Other examples may be more subtle. Some firms expense their research and development costs yearly, while others spread them over several years. The former practice is considered more conservative, thus exhibiting a "better" quality of earnings.

The wide latitude that firms have in following GAAP makes financial statement comparison both across firms and for the same firm over time difficult. Firms may change their policies over time and different firms may adhere to different policies within the same industry.

Another limitation of financial statements concerns the existence of *hidden liabilities and assets*. Examples of hidden liabilities may include potential costs of litigation, certain lease and debt obligations, and inadequate reserves for future obligations. Enron Corporation, the high-flying energy-producing and -trading concern that failed in 2001, was supposed to have hidden more than a billion dollars in liabilities in a web of partnerships and subsidiaries that were not reflected in the consolidated balance sheet of the parent corporation.

On the other hand, there may also be hidden assets. Firms may have real estate property that is recorded on a historical costs basis but may have experienced considerable appreciation in market value. Similarly, a firm may have intangible assets, such as brand value, that are not captured in the balance sheet. For example, Philip Morris was willing to pay over 10 times the fair value of Kraft's physical assets in order to obtain the brands (e.g., Velveeta cheese and Miracle Whip salad dressing) and consumer loyalty that Kraft had spent decades building up.

The limitations of financial statements we discussed have important implications for finance, because finance deals with the notion of market value and expected cash flows, rather than the notion of historical cost and expected net income.

Comprehension Check Questions

1. What does the acronym GAAP refer to and who determines GAAP?
2. What are some limitations of using financial statements?

FEDERAL INCOME TAXES FOR CORPORATIONS

Both individuals and businesses must pay taxes on their taxable income. The type and rates of taxation that businesses must pay depend on the form of business organization. Generally, when organized as a corporation, business income is taxed at corporate rates, whereas business income of sole proprietorships and partnerships is taxed at the rates of the individual owners or partners. Since corporations are the dominant form of business organization (in terms of sales), this section focuses on corporate income taxes.

Federal income tax laws were first enacted by the government in 1913 and have been changed numerous times since then. This section contains a brief introduction to some tax law concepts and provides the background needed for understanding tax issues discussed later in the book.

Corporate Income Taxes

In general, the taxable income of a corporation is calculated by subtracting business expenses from revenues. Tax-deductible business expenses normally include the cost of goods sold, selling and administrative expenses, depreciation allowances, and interest expenses. Federal income taxes are computed on the resulting taxable income. For tax years beginning on or after December 31, 2002, the tax rates imposed on corporations are shown in Table 3.12. Generally, the corporate tax code follows a *progressive tax* structure just like the tax schedule for individuals. In other words, tax rates increase as taxable income increases. For example, the tax rate is only 15 percent for taxable incomes up to $50,000, but it is 25 percent for taxable incomes over $50,000 and up to $75,000, and it is 34 percent for taxable incomes over $75,000 and up to $100,000. However, the benefits of the 15 percent and 25 percent rates are phased out (or "recaptured") by imposing an additional 5 percent tax (i.e., 39% instead of 34%) on taxable income between $100,001 and $335,000. The benefit of the 34 percent rate on taxable income between $335,000 and $10,000,000 is phased out by imposing an additional 3 percent tax (i.e., 38% instead of 35%) on taxable income between $15,000,001 and $18,333,333. The effect of these provisions is that corporations with taxable incomes in excess of $18,333,333 pay a flat rate of 35 percent on all taxable income.

The calculation of the total tax for various levels of taxable income is shown in Table 3.13. The *average tax rate* of a corporation is calculated by dividing the total tax by taxable income. The **marginal tax rate** of a corporation is defined as the tax

Table 3.12 2002 Corporate Tax Rates

Taxable Income	Marginal Tax Rate	Tax Calculation Base Tax + (Marginal Tax Rate × Amount Over Base Income)
Up to $50,000	15%	$ 0 + (15% × Amount over $0)
$50,001–$75,000	25%	$ 7,500 + (25% × Amount over $50,000)
$75,001–$100,000	34%	$ 13,750 + (34% × Amount over $75,000)
$100,001–$335,000	39%*	$ 22,250 + (39% × Amount over $100,000)
$335,001–$10,000,000	34%	$ 113,900 + (34% × Amount over $335,000)
$10,000,001–$15,000,000	35%	$3,400,000 + (35% × Amount over $10,000,000)
$15,000,001–$18,333,333	38%**	$5,150,000 + (38% × Amount over $15,000,000)
Over $18,333,333	35%	35% × Taxable Income

*Includes additional 5% "recapture" tax under the Tax Reform Act of 1986.

**Includes additional 3% "recapture" tax under the Revenue Reconciliation Act of 1993.

Source: Taxable income and marginal tax rates are taken from Internal Revenue Service Publication 542.

Table 3.13 Computation of Corporate Income Taxes

Taxable Income	Marginal Tax Rate	Tax Calculation	Average Tax Rate
$ 25,000	15%	$0 + (.15 × $25,000) = $3,750	15%
75,000	25	$7,500 + (.25 × $25,000) = $13,750	18.33
100,000	34	$13,750 + (.34 × $25,000) = $22,250	22.25
250,000	39	$22,250 + (.39 × $150,000) = $80,750	32.3
1,250,000	34	$113,900 + (.34 × $915,000) = $425,000	34.0
2,500,000	34	$113,900 + (.34 × $2,165,000) = $850,000	34.0
12,500,000	35	$3,400,000 + (.35 × $2,500,000) = $4,275,000	34.2
17,500,000	38	$5,150,000 + (.38 × $2,500,000) = $6,100,000	34.86
25,000,000	35	.35 × $25,000,000 = $8,750,000	35.0
$125,000,000	35	.35 × $125,000,000 = $43,750,000	35.0

rate on the next dollar of taxable income. For large corporations with taxable incomes exceeding $18,333,333, the effective marginal and average tax rates are equal to 35 percent.

In addition to paying taxes on *operating* or *ordinary income*, corporations must also pay taxes on *capital gains income* and *dividend income.*

Capital Gains Income Corporate *capital gains* income currently (2003) is taxed at the same marginal tax rate as ordinary income. Corporate *capital losses* are deductible only against capital gains. Net capital losses may be carried back and applied against net gains in the prior 3 years. Any remaining net capital loss may be carried forward for 5 years and applied against capital gains in those years.

Dividend Income Dividends received by a corporation are normally entitled to a 70 percent exclusion from federal income taxes. (The actual dividend exclusion depends on the extent of stock ownership. Corporations that own less than 20 percent of a dividend-paying corporation can exclude 70 percent of the dividends received from taxes. The dividend exclusion is 80 percent if the corporation owns 20 to 80 percent of the dividend-paying corporation. The dividend exclusion is 100 percent if the corporation owns more than 80 percent of the dividend-paying corporation.) To illustrate, suppose that the Hastings Corporation owns less than 20 percent of the stock in the Fremont Corporation and that Fremont pays $100,000 in dividends to Hastings during 2003. Hastings has to pay taxes on only 30 percent of the $100,000, or $30,000. (The other 70 percent, or $70,000, is excluded—that is, received tax-free. However, Fremont has to pay taxes on its income before paying the $100,000 to Hastings, because *dividends paid by a firm are not considered tax-deductible expenses.*) The $30,000 of taxable dividend income is taxed at ordinary income tax rates. Assuming that Hastings is large enough to have a marginal tax rate of 35 percent, the tax on the dividends is $30,000 × 0.35 = $10,500. For corporations having a marginal tax rate of 35 percent, intercompany dividends are taxed at an effective rate of 10.5 percent—that is, $(1 - 0.7) \times 35\%$.

Loss Carrybacks and Carryforwards

Corporations that sustain net operating losses during a particular year are permitted by tax laws to apply the losses against any taxable income in other years, thereby lowering the taxes owed in those years. If such a loss is applied against a previous year, it is called a *loss carryback*; if it is applied against a succeeding year, it is called a *loss carryforward*.

The tax laws specify that a corporation's net operating loss may be carried back 2 years and forward 20 years to offset taxable income in those years. For example, suppose the NOL Corporation incurs a net operating loss totaling $200,000 in 20X6. This loss may be carried back 2 years to 20X4. If the NOL Corporation had 20X4 taxable income of $125,000, for example, it could receive a tax refund equal to the taxes it paid for that year. The remaining $75,000 portion of the 20X6 net operating loss next could be carried back to 20X5.

Comprehension Check Questions

1. What is the difference between marginal and average tax rates?
2. How is taxable income determined?
3. How are loss carryback and carryforward used?

Summary

> The annual report typically consists of five parts. These are: (1) Financial highlights, (2) Letter to the stockholders from the CEO, (3) Operations review, (4) Financial performance, and (5) Members of the management team.

> The financial performance section of the annual report includes four financial statements: the balance sheet, the income statement, the statement of retained earnings or statement of shareholders' equity, and the statement of cash flows.

> The balance sheet summarizes the firm's assets, liabilities, and stockholders' equity as of a given point in time. Total assets must equal the sum of the liabilities and the stockholders' equity. The major categories of assets are current assets and fixed assets. Current assets typically include cash, marketable securities, accounts receivable, and inventory. Liabilities consist of current liabilities and long-term liabilities. Current liabilities include accounts payable, notes payable, current portion of long-term debt, and accruals such as wages and taxes payable. Long-term liabilities include long-term debt obligations, lease obligations, convertible debt, and deferred tax liabilities. Stockholders' equity includes preferred stock, common stock at par value, paid-in capital in excess of par, and retained earnings.

> The income statement summarizes the sales, expenses, and profit generated by a firm over a period of time. Expenses include the following: (1) cost of goods sold, (2) selling, general, and administrative expenses, (3) depreciation, (4) interest expense, and (5) taxes.

> The statement of retained earnings reconciles the beginning and ending retained earnings with the net income. The statement of shareholders' equity shows the changes in the various accounts under shareholders' equity during the course of the year.

> The statement of cash flows summarizes the cash flows from operating, investing, and financing activities of the firm.

> Firms may maintain several different financial statements. Most firms have one set of statements for tax purposes and another for reporting purposes.

➤ Annual financial statements of publicly held firms have to be audited by an external auditor. The auditor ensures that the statements are based on Generally Accepted Accounting Principles. The GAAP standards are set by the accounting profession's standards-setting body, the Financial Accounting Standard Board. In addition to FASB, the SEC can also mandate that firms use certain accounting conventions.

➤ Investors need to be careful in interpreting financial statements. Although GAAP ensures that firms follow certain rules, firms still have considerable latitude in developing the various financial statements. Within the GAAP guidelines, firms can follow conservative or aggressive policies in developing the balance sheet and income statements. This makes for difficult comparisons of financial statements across firms, even those in the same industry. Firms also may change their accounting policies, which makes it difficult to interpret financial statements of the same firm over time. Financial statements are beset by other problems such as hidden assets and liabilities. Hidden assets may include the value of certain patents or the value of real estate property. An example of a hidden liability is the potential cost of litigation from a class action product liability lawsuit.

➤ The marginal federal tax rate for corporations varies from 15 percent to 39 percent. The marginal tax rate is defined as the tax on the next dollar of taxable income. The average tax rate is calculated by dividing the total tax by the taxable income.

Questions and Topics for Discussion

1. What are the four types of financial statements found in most annual reports and what information does each provide?

2. Why is the net income not the same as the amount of cash generated by the firm?

3. Define each of the following terms:
   a. total assets
   b. current assets
   c. fixed assets
   d. current liabilities
   e. accounts payable
   f. accrued expenses
   g. accounts receivable
   h. inventory
   i. deferred income taxes
   j. shareholders' equity
   k. gross margin
   l. operating earnings
   m. cost of sales
   n. earnings per share—basic
   o. earnings per share—diluted

p. cash flow from operating activities

q. cash flow from investing activities

r. cash flow from financing activities

4. Why is the balance sheet referred to as a "snapshot" of the firm at a point in time?

5. Contrast the income statement with the balance sheet.

6. What is meant by "aggressive" and "conservative" accounting practice?

7. Why do companies maintain two sets of financial statements?

8. How are total assets financed?

9. Define common stock par or stated value, paid-in capital, retained earnings, and treasury stock.

10. What is an extraordinary item and why is it shown separately on the income statement?

11. What effect does the LIFO vs. the FIFO method of inventory valuation have on the firm's gross profits?

12. What is the difference between operating income, capital gains income, and dividend income? At approximately what rates are these different types of income taxed?

13. What are deferred taxes, and how do they come into being?

14. What purpose does the letter from the auditor serve in the annual report?

Self-Test Problems

ST1. Prepare a balance sheet for Trident Corporation using the following data:

	(in thousands of dollars)
Cash	$ 1,500
Accounts payable	?
Marketable securities	$ 2,500
Accrued salaries and wages	$12,500
Accounts receivable	$15,000
Total current liabilities	$25,000
Accounts receivable	$15,000
Inventory	?
Current liabilities	$25,000
Long-term debt	$22,000
Total liabilities	$47,000
Fixed assets (net)	$35,000
Common stock (par value)	$ 5,000
Total assets	$87,000
Paid-in capital	$18,000
Retained earnings	?
Total stockholders' equity	$40,000
Total liabilities and stockholders' equity	?

ST2. Based on the following information prepare an income statement for Skymobile Corporation:

	(in thousands of dollars)
Sales	$130,000
Cost of sales	?
Gross margin	$ 27,000
Selling, general, and administrative expenses	$ 14,000
Research & development costs	$ 2,000
Operating profit	?
Interest expense	?
Earnings before tax	$ 8,000
Income tax average rate is 37.5%	

ST3. DF Bicycles Company expects sales next year of $5,000. The projected cost of sales is $2,800, while selling, general, and administrative expenses and depreciation expense are expected to be $900 and $400, respectively. What is the maximum in interest expense the firm can incur if it wants to target a net income of $300? Assume a corporate tax rate of 40 percent.

ST4. Complete the following statement of cash flows for OnLine Trading Corporation and then answer the questions that follow:

		(in thousands of dollars)
Cash flows from operating activities		
Net income		$(4,500)
Adjustments to reconcile net income to net		
cash provided by operating activities		
Depreciation	$3,500	
Increase in receivables	(1,400)	
Increase in accounts payable	1,000	
Increase in deferred income tax liability	500	3,600
Net cash provided by operating activities		?
Cash flows from investing activities		
Increase in fixed assets	(3,000)	
Net cash provided by investing activities		?
Cash flows from financing activities		
Issuance of common stock	3,000	
Issuance of long-term debt	1,200	
Net cash provided by financing activities		$4,200
Net increase in cash		300
Cash, January 1, 2001		250
Cash, December 31, 2001		$550

a. Were the net cash flows from operating activities positive or negative? Explain.

b. How was the increase in fixed assets financed?

c. If you were a loan officer, would you have extended the loan of $1,200?

ST5. During the past year, Alcore Enterprises, Inc. had sales of $3 million, cost of goods sold of $1.8 million, operating expenses of $800,000, and interest expenses of $200,000. Alcore paid preferred stock dividends of $100,000 and common stock dividends of $200,000 during the year. Alcore also retired maturing debt totaling $1.5 million during the year. Using the U.S. federal corporate tax rates shown in Table 3.12, what was Alcore's taxable income and its total tax liability for the year? What are Alcore's average and marginal tax rates?

Problems

1. Prepare a balance sheet for Ventures Incorporated using the following data: **BASIC**

Cash	$ 3,000
Accounts payable	$ 25,000
Marketable securities	$ 5,000
Accrued salaries and wages	?
Accounts receivable	?
Total current liabilities	$ 50,000
Inventory	$ 66,000
Current assets	$104,000
Long-term debt	?
Total liabilities	$ 94,000
Fixed assets (net)	?
Common stock (par value)	$ 10,000
Total assets	$174,000
Paid-in capital	$ 36,000
Retained earnings	?
Total stockholders' equity	$ 80,000
Total liabilities and stockholders' equity	$174,000

2. Based on the following information prepare an income statement for Ductron **BASIC**
Castings Corporation:

Sales	$260,000
Cost of sales	?
Gross margin	$ 54,000
Selling, general, and administrative expenses	$ 28,000
Research & development costs	$ 4,000
Operating profit	?
Interest expense	?
Earnings before tax	$ 16,000
Income tax average rate is 37.5%	

3. SKF Bearings Company expects sales next year of $10,000. The projected cost **INTERMEDIATE**
of sales is $5,600 while selling, general, and administrative expenses and depreciation expense are expected to be $1,800 and $800, respectively. What is the maximum in interest expense the firm can incur if it wants to target a net income of $400. Assume a corporate tax rate of 40 percent.

4. Banner Corporation is a new manufacturing firm that will start operations in **BASIC**
3 months producing flags for the domestic and international market. The owners project the following figures for the various balance sheet accounts:

Current assets = $275,000
Fixed assets = $175,000
Current liabilities = $150,000
Shareholders' equity = $225,000

For the balance sheet to "balance," what is the amount of long-term debt that is needed?

BASIC   **5.** Krispy Doughnuts Inc. had the following shareholders' equity balances on December 31, 2000:

Shareholders' equity	
Preferred stock, par value $50.00 per share, 10,000 shares outstanding	$ 500,000
Common stock, par value $1.00 share, 2,000,000 shares outstanding	2,000,000
Paid-in capital	1,750,000
Retained earnings	800,000
Total shareholders' equity	**$3,550,000**

During 2001, Krispy Doughnuts generated net income of $500,000. Management paid out $3.00 per share in preferred stock dividends. In addition, common shareholders received $0.25 in cash dividends per share. Show Krispy Doughnuts' new balances under stockholders' equity for the fiscal year ending December 31, 2001.

INTERMEDIATE   **6.** Complete the following statement of cash flows for Skycomm Corporation and then answer the questions that follow:

Cash flows from operating activities		
Net income		$(9,000)
Adjustments to reconcile net income to net cash		
provided by operating activities		
Depreciation	$7,000	
Increase in receivables	(2,800)	
Increase in accounts payable	2,000	
Increase in deferred income tax liability	1,000	7,200
Net cash provided by operating activities		?
Cash flows from investing activities		
Increase in fixed assets	(6,000)	
Net cash provided by investing activities		?
Cash flows from financing activities		
Issuance of common stock	6,000	
Issuance of long-term debt	2,400	
Net cash provided by financing activities		8,400
Net increase in cash		600
Cash, January 1, 2001		500
Cash, December 31, 2001		$1,100

a. Was the net cash flows from operating activities positive or negative? Explain.

b. How was the increase in fixed assets financed?

c. If you were a loan officer, would you have extended the loan of $2,400?

INTERMEDIATE   **7.** Following are Coloma Beverages' balance sheet for the prior year, 2002, and the statement of cash flows for the current year, 2003. Based on this information re-create Coloma Beverages' balance sheet for the current year, 2003.

Balance Sheet
December 31, 2002

Assets

Cash and cash equivalents	$ 50,000
Accounts receivable	100,000
Inventory	150,000
Total current assets	300,000
Property, plant, and equipment	
Less accumulated depreciation	400,000
Total assets	$700,000

Liabilities and shareholder's equity

Accounts payable	$ 60,000
Notes payable	50,000
Accrued expenses	40,000
Total current liabilities	150,000
Long-term debt	180,000
Deferred income taxes	20,000
Shareholders' equity	
Common stock at par	50,000
Paid-in capital	125,000
Retained earnings	175,000
Total shareholders' equity	$350,000
Total liabilities and shareholders' equity	**$700,000**

Statement of Cash Flows
Year 2003

Cash flows from operating activities		
Net income		$80,000
Adjustments to reconcile net income to		
net cash provided by operating activities		
Depreciation	$25,000	
Increase in receivables	(12,000)	
Increase in accounts payable	14,000	
Increase in deferred income tax liability	5,000	32,000
Net cash provided by operating activities		112,000
Cash flows from investing activities		
Increase in fixed assets	(40,000)	
Net cash provided by investing activities		(40,000)
Cash flows from financing activities		
Cash dividends paid on common stock	(12,000)	
Payment of principal on notes payable	(50,000)	
Issuance of long-term debt	35,000	
Net cash provided by financing activities		(27,000)
Net increase in cash		45,000
Cash, January 1, 2002		50,000
Cash, December 31, 2003		**$95,000**

INTERMEDIATE   **8.** Reproduced below is Drugstore.com's statement of cash flows.

DRUGSTORE.COM, INC.

CONSOLIDATED STATEMENTS OF CASH FLOWS

(in thousands)

Year Ended
December 31, 2000

Operating Activities:	
Net loss	$(193,015)
Adjustments to reconcile net loss to net cash used in operating activities:	
Noncash expenses:	
Depreciation	11,715
Marketing and sales	18,191
Charitable contributions	—
Amortization of intangible assets	34,774
Amortization of stock-based compensation	15,115
Changes in:	
Accounts receivable	(1,683)
Inventories	(4,799)
Prepaid marketing expenses	(649)
Other current assets	(300)
Deposits and other assets	(5,812)
Accounts payable and accrued expenses	(16,117)
Other	269
Net cash used in operating activities	(142,311)
Investing Activities:	
Purchases of marketable securities	(39,119)
Sales of marketable securities	123,491
Purchases of fixed assets	(22,972)
Purchases of intangible assets	(32)
Business acquisition, net of cash received	(335)
Issuance of note receivable to officer	—
Net cash provided by (used in) investing activities	61,033
Financing Activities:	
Net proceeds from sales of common stock	141,180
Net proceeds from exercise of stock options, warrants, and employee stock purchase plan	2,106
Net proceeds from sales of preferred stock	22,683
Proceeds from capital lease obligations	127
Principal payments on capital lease obligations	(3,312)
Net cash provided by financing activities	162,784
Net increase in cash and cash equivalents	81,506
Cash and cash equivalents at beginning of period	26,526
Cash and cash equivalents at end of period	$ 108,032
Supplemental Cash Flow Information:	
Cash paid for interest	$ 395
Equipment acquired through capital lease agreements	$ 3,254
Issuance of equity and debt instruments in exchange for prepaid marketing, intangible assets, software, and a vendor agreement	$ 49,498
Issuance of common stock in connection with business acquisition	$ 37,619

a. What was Drustore.com's net income in 2000?

b. What was the company's cash flows from operating activities?

c. What were the major sources of cash used to fund the deficit in cash flows from operating activities?

d. What was Drugstore.com's year-end cash balance for 2000?

9. Reproduced on page 90 is the balance sheet for Krispy Kreme Doughnuts for fiscal year 2000 and 2001.   INTERMEDIATE

a. What are the total assets of the firm and how were they financed between liabilties and shareholders' equity in each of the two years.

b. How much of the net income generated in fiscal year 2001 did Krispy Kreme retain?

c. What was the increase in total assets from fiscal year 2000 to 2001? Just from looking at the balance sheet (i.e., you do not have the benefit of the statement of cash flows), where do you think Krispy Kreme got the funds from to support the increase in total assests?

10. Last year, Idaho Steel Corporation had taxable ordinary income of $2 million   **BASIC**
and capital gains income of $500,000. The company also had $50,000 in dividend income and paid its stockholders $150,000 in dividends. Calculate the Idaho Steel Corporation's tax bill.

11. Last year the Selling Corporation had earnings before interest and taxes (op-   **INTERMEDIATE**
erating income) equal to $1 million. It paid $200,000 in dividends to its stockholders and $100,000 in interest to its creditors. During the year the company also repaid a bank loan of $150,000. Assuming a corporate income tax rate of 40 percent on all taxable income, calculate the Selling Corporation's tax bill.

12. Clapper Industries reported taxable income of $290,000.   **INTERMEDIATE**

a. What is Clapper's marginal tax rate?

b. What is Clapper's average tax rate?

c. If Clapper's taxable income increases to $410,000, what will be the company's marginal and average tax rates?

THOMSON ONE—Business School Edition

Go to the text Web site at http://moyer.swlearning.com, select your book, and click on the Thomson ONE button. Enter Thomson ONE—Business School Edition by using the username and password you created when you registered the serial number on your access card. Use the "Financials" tab in the Thomson ONE—BSE database to determine the following information for Xerox Corporation (XRX):

a. Operating income for the past 4 years.

b. Net income available to common for the past 4 years.

c. The major sources of cash used to fund the deficit in "net cash flow from operating activities in the year 2000.

d. The trend in "Cash & Equivalents" over the past 5 years. Compare this trend with the trend in "Accounts Receivable" over the same period.

e. The trend in "Capital Expenditures" over the past 5 years. What factors do you think might have impacted this trend?

KRISPY KREME DOUGHNUTS, INC.
CONSOLIDATED BALANCE SHEETS

IN THOUSANDS, EXCEPT PAR VALUE AMOUNTS

YEAR ENDED	Jan. 30, 2000	Jan. 28, 2001
ASSETS		
Current Assets:		
Cash and cash equivalents	$ 3,183	$ 7,026
Short-term investments	—	18,103
Accounts receivable, less allowance for doubtful accounts of $1,324 (2000) and $1,302 (2001)	17,965	19,855
Accounts receivable, affiliates	1,608	2,599
Other receivables	794	2,279
Inventories	9,979	12,031
Prepaid expenses	3,148	1,909
Income taxes refundable	861	—
Deferred income taxes	3,500	3,809
Total current assets	41,038	67,611
Property and equipment, net	60,584	78,340
Deferred income taxes	1,398	—
Long-term investments	—	17,877
Investment in unconsolidated joint ventures	—	4,695
Other assets	1,938	2,970
Total assets	$104,958	$171,493
LIABILITIES AND SHAREHOLDERS' EQUITY		
Current Liabilities:		
Accounts payable	$ 13,106	$ 14,697
Accrued expenses	14,080	19,904
Revolving line of credit	—	3,526
Current maturities of long-term debt	2,400	—
Income taxes payable	—	41
Total current liabilities	29,586	38,168
Deferred income taxes	—	579
Compensation deferred (unpaid)	990	1,106
Long-term debt, net of current portion	20,502	—
Accrued restructuring expenses	4,259	3,109
Other long-term obligations	1,866	1,735
Total long-term liabilities	27,617	6,529
Minority interest	—	1,117
Shareholders' Equity:		
Preferred stock, no par value, 10 million shares authorized; none issued and outstanding	—	—
Common stock, no par value, 100,000 shares authorized; issued and outstanding — 0 (2000) and 25,916 (2001)	—	85,060
Common stock, $10 par value, 1,000 shares authorized; issued and outstanding — 467 (2000) and 0 (2001)	4,670	—
Paid-in capital	10,805	—
Unearned compensation	—	(188)
Notes receivable, employees	(2,547)	(2,349)
Nonqualified employee benefit plan asset	—	(126)
Nonqualified employee benefit plan liability	—	126
Accumulated other comprehensive income	—	609
Retained earnings	34,827	42,547
Total shareholders' equity	47,755	125,679
Total liabilities and shareholders' equity	$104,958	$171,493

CHAPTER

4 Evaluation of Firm Performance

I n the previous chapter, we reviewed the four basic financial statements that are contained in the annual report. This chapter deals with financial ratio analysis, which uses information contained in financial statements. *Financial ratios* are statistical yardsticks that relate two numbers generally taken from a firm's income statement, balance sheet, or both. They enable interested parties to make relative comparisons of firm performance over time as well as compare performance across different firms.

PURPOSE OF FINANCIAL RATIOS

Financial ratios are used by management for analysis, monitoring, and planning purposes.

> ➤ As an *analytical* tool, financial ratios can assist management in identifying strengths and weaknesses in a firm. They can indicate whether a firm has enough cash to meet obligations; a reasonable accounts receivable collection period; an efficient inventory management policy; sufficient property, plant, and equipment; and an adequate capital structure—all of which are necessary if a firm is to achieve the goal of maximizing shareholder wealth. Financial analysis also can be used to assess a firm's viability as an ongoing enterprise and to determine whether a satisfactory return is being earned for the risks taken.

> ➤ Financial ratios are also a useful *monitoring* device. On the basis of financial ratio analysis, management may uncover a problem in a certain area of the firm's operations and institute remedial action. Through a regular review of relevant financial ratios, management can monitor whether or not the remedial actions are working.

> ➤ Financial ratios provide a very effective role in *planning*. In Chapter 1 we said that the objective of every firm's managers should be to maximize shareholder wealth. For this appropriate objective to be successful, it needs to be *operationalized*. Financial ratios allow management to translate goals into operational objectives. In other words, simply urging all employees to maximize shareholder wealth will probably not be very effective. On the other hand, setting targets in terms of specific ratios, such as the average collection period or inventory turnover, will likely yield better results, because financial ratios are specific, measurable, and easy to relate to.

An excellent source for financial ratio analysis assistance, including a free ratio analysis spreadsheet, is provided by the Small Business Administration at **http://www.onlinewbc. gov/docs/finance/index. html**

Financial ratio analyses are used also by persons other than financial managers. For example, credit managers may examine some basic financial ratios concerning a prospective customer when deciding whether to extend credit. Security analysts and investors use financial analysis to help assess the investment worth of different securities. Bankers use the tools of financial analysis when deciding whether to grant loans. Financial ratios have been used successfully to forecast such financial events as impending bankruptcy. Unions, such as the United Auto Workers (UAW), refer to financial ratios when negotiating collective bargaining agreements with employers. Finally, students and other job hunters may perform financial analyses of potential employers to determine career opportunities.

INTERPRETING FINANCIAL RATIOS

A *financial ratio* is a relationship that indicates something about a firm's activities, such as the ratio between the firm's current assets and current liabilities or between its accounts receivable and its annual sales. Financial ratios enable an analyst to make a comparison of a firm's financial condition over time or in relation to other firms. Ratios essentially standardize various elements of financial data for differences in the size of a series of financial data when making comparisons over time or between firms. For example, the total profits of IBM normally are many times those of Apple Computer, because IBM is much larger than Apple. By computing ratios, such as net profits divided by total assets, the relative performance of the two companies can be assessed more accurately.

Successful financial ratio analysis requires that an analyst keep in mind the following points:

➤ Any discussion of financial ratios is likely to include only a representative sample of possible ratios. Many other ratios can be developed to provide additional insights. In some industries (such as banking), an analyst will use special ratios unique to the activities of firms in those industries.

➤ Financial ratios serve only as "*flags*" indicating potential areas of strength or weakness. A thorough analysis requires the examination of other data as well.

➤ Frequently a financial ratio must be dissected to discover its true meaning. For example, a low ratio may be caused by either a low numerator or a high denominator. A good financial analyst will examine both the numerator and the denominator before drawing any conclusions.

➤ A financial ratio is meaningful only when it is compared with some standard, such as an industry ratio trend, a ratio trend for the specific firm being analyzed, or a stated management objective.

➤ When financial ratios are used to compare one firm with another, it is important to remember that differences in accounting techniques may result in substantial differences in financial ratios. Failure to keep this in mind can lead to incorrect conclusions.

Comprehension Check Questions

1. What are financial ratios?
2. How does management use financial ratios for analysis, planning, and monitoring?
3. Why is it important to compare ratios to industry standards or over time?

BASIC CATEGORIES OF FINANCIAL RATIOS

Much as the human body is made up of different systems that are interconnected, such as the circulatory system, the nervous system, the immune system, and so on, a firm also is made up of different systems. To evaluate the efficient functioning of different systems within the body, a physician may order specific tests. For example, your doctor may order a stress test to see how well your heart is functioning, or she may ask for a blood test to check your immune system. Similarly, there are different groups of ratios to evaluate different aspects of a firm's operations. These ratio groupings include:

1. *Liquidity ratios:* indicate a firm's ability to meet short-term financial obligations
2. *Asset management ratios:* indicate how efficiently a firm is using its assets to generate sales
3. *Financial leverage management ratios:* indicate a firm's capacity to meet short- and long-term debt obligations, and how risky is the firm's financial structure

4. *Profitability ratios:* measure how effectively a firm's management generates profits on sales, assets, and stockholders' investments

5. *Market-based ratios:* measure the financial market's evaluation of a company's performance

It is important to keep in mind that it is not necessary to use all of these ratios in performing a ratio analysis. Selection of the ratios to be examined will depend on the particular individual's perspective and objectives. For example, suppliers and short-term creditors are likely to be most concerned with a firm's current liquidity and near-term cash-generating capacity. Bondholders and holders of preferred stock, who have long-term claims on a firm's earnings and assets, focus on the firm's cash-generating ability over the long run and on the claims other investors have on the firm's cash flows. Common stockholders and potential investors are especially interested in measures of profitability and risk, because common stock prices are dependent on the amount and stability of a firm's future earnings, possible appreciation in value, and dividends. Management is concerned with all aspects of financial analysis, both short term and long term, because it is responsible for conducting the firm's day-to-day operations and earning a competitive rate of return for risks taken.

The calculation and interpretation of financial ratios is illustrated in this chapter by using the financial statements for Furniture Brands International Corporation covered in Chapter 3. In interpreting the ratios for Furniture Brands we compare the ratios to an industry average. This is known as **comparative analysis.** We will also conduct a **trend analysis,** where ratio trends over time are analyzed.

There are two ways to obtain an industry average. The first, and easier approach, is to use an industry average calculated by a third-party source such as Standard and Poor's, Value Line, or Moody's. The second is to construct your own industry average. While useful, third-party sources of industry averages have certain limitations associated with them:

1. How the industry is defined may be different from what is preferred by the analyst. For example, Value Line defines the furniture industry to include manufacturers of residential and commercial furniture and also includes certain suppliers (e.g., producers of upholstery fabric, coils and springs, etc.). As an analyst you may want to compare Furniture Brands to companies that are engaged primarily in the manufacture of residential furniture rather than commercial furniture as the two markets are characterized by fundamental differences. Producing and marketing chairs and desks for commercial offices is very different from producing and marketing sofas and dining sets for the residential market. The profit margins, production methods, marketing plans, and distribution mechanisms differ considerably between the two markets. Consequently the financial ratios may be different for firms engaged in these two segments of the furniture industry.

2. In the use of externally generated industry average ratios, the definition and calculation of ratios may vary. While the variations for the most part are slight, in some cases they could be significant. For example, some sources define debt ratio as including current liabilities and long-term liabilities; other sources define debt ratio as including only long-term debt. The analyst must make sure that the definition he or she is employing for the firm being evaluated matches that used in the computation of the industry average. For example, if the analyst calculates the debt ratio to include current liabilities and long-term debt, then the resulting debt ratio may appear to be significantly higher than the industry average if the latter was based on long-term debt alone.

In view of the above limitations, we chose to construct our own furniture industry average ratios to serve as a benchmark for comparing Furniture Brands' financial ratios. The industry financial ratios are calculated by averaging the ratios for Ethan Allen Interiors, La-Z-Boy, Bassett, Chromcraft, and Flexsteel—all firms that primarily manufacture residential furniture.

Comprehension Check Questions

1. Are all ratios important for all users of ratios?
2. What are the limitations of third-party industry average ratios?
3. What is the difference between comparative and trend ratio analysis?

Liquidity Ratios

A firm that intends to remain a viable business entity must have enough cash on hand to pay its bills as they come due. In other words, the firm must remain *liquid*. One way to determine whether this is the case is to examine the relationship between a firm's current assets and near-term obligations (or current liabilities). It is important to keep in mind that while current liabilities are ultimately discharged with cash, the firm need not have the entire amount of cash today. From a liquidity perspective, the firm needs to ensure that it has *sufficient cash to meet current payments and that it has sufficient near-term liquid assets (e.g., accounts receivable and inventory) to meet payments for other maturing obligations as they come due in the near term.* As inventory gets converted to accounts receivable and accounts receivable into cash in the normal course of business, the firm will generate enough cash to pay off current liabilities as they come due. We consider two liquidity ratios: the *current ratio* and the *quick ratio*.

Current Ratio *Current ratio* is defined as:

$$\text{Current ratio} = \frac{\text{Current assets}}{\text{Current liabilities}} \qquad (4.1)$$

Current assets include the cash a firm already has on hand and in the bank, plus any assets that can be converted into cash within a "normal" operating period of 12 months, such as marketable securities held as short-term investments, accounts receivable, and inventories. Current liabilities include any financial obligations expected to fall due within the next year, such as accounts payable, notes payable, the current portion of long-term debt due, other payables, and various accruals such as taxes and wages due.

Using data from Furniture Brands' balance sheet statement shown in Chapter 3 (page 60), the current ratio is determined as:

$$\frac{\$691.581}{\$143.118} = 4.83 \text{ times}$$

Furniture Brands therefore has $4.83 in current assets for every $1 of current liabilities.

The ratio is interpreted to mean that to satisfy the claims of short-term creditors exclusively from existing current assets, Furniture Brands must be able to convert each dollar of current assets into at least $0.21 of cash ($1.00/$4.83 = $0.21). The industry average for the current ratio is 3.12 times, meaning that the average firm in the industry must convert $0.32 ($1.00/$3.12 = $0.32) of each dollar of current assets into cash to meet short-term obligations. Thus, Furniture Brands' current ratio appears to be well above the industry average and hence less risky.

However, one must be careful in making any strong judgments without undertaking a more thorough analysis. A higher current ratio is not necessarily indicative of better liquidity. For example, a higher current ratio may be due to greater inventory levels compared to the industry, which, in turn, could be indicative of the firm having trouble moving things "off the shelf." The financial analyst must dissect, or "go behind," the ratio to discover why it differs from the industry average and determine whether a serious problem exists.

Quick Ratio   The *quick ratio* is defined as follows:

$$(4.2) \qquad \text{Quick ratio} = \frac{\text{Cash} + \text{Marketable securities} + \text{Accounts receivable}}{\text{Current liabilities}}$$

This ratio, sometimes called the "acid test," is a more stringent measure of liquidity than the current ratio. Sometimes the numerator of the quick ratio is defined simply as the current ratio minus inventory. The quick ratio takes into account only the most liquid of current assets (defined as cash, marketable securities, and accounts receivable) and eliminates all others (including inventory and prepaid expenses) from consideration. By subtracting inventories from current assets, this ratio recognizes that a firm's inventories are often one of its least liquid current assets. This is, of course, more applicable to some industries than to others. For example, if you are an apparel manufacturer, the ability to liquidate your inventory at fair value is highly doubtful. On the other hand, if you manufacture a commodity product such as newsprint, you may have greater confidence in the value of the inventory, especially if the prices are stable. Referring to the figures on Furniture Brands' balance sheet, the firm's quick ratio at year-end 2000 is calculated as:

$$\frac{\$14.606 + \$351.804}{\$143.118} = \frac{\$366.41}{\$143.118} = 2.56 \text{ times}$$

The industry average is 1.75 times. Consistent with the current ratio, Furniture Brands' quick ratio is above the industry average and appears to be less risky.

Asset Management Ratios

One objective of financial management is to determine how a firm's resources can be best distributed among the various asset accounts. If a proper mix of cash, receivables, inventories, property, plant, and equipment can be achieved, the firm's asset structure will be more effective in generating sales revenue.

Asset management ratios indicate how much a firm has invested in a particular type of asset (or group of assets) relative to the revenue the asset is producing. *By comparing asset management ratios for the various asset accounts of a firm with established industry norms, an analyst can determine how efficiently a firm is allocating its resources.*

This section discusses several types of asset management ratios, including the *average collection period*, the *inventory turnover ratio*, the *fixed-asset turnover ratio*, and the *total asset turnover ratio*.

Average Collection Period   The *average collection period* is the average number of days an account receivable remains outstanding. It usually is determined by dividing a firm's year-end receivables balance by the average daily credit sales (based on a 365-day year):

$$\text{Average collection period} = \frac{\text{Accounts receivable}}{\text{Annual credit sales}/365} \qquad \textbf{(4.3)}$$

Assuming all sales for Furniture Brands are for credit, the average collection period ratio at year-end 2000 can be calculated as $\$351.804/(\$2,116.239/365 \text{ days}) = \$351.804/\$5.798$ per day $= 60.7$ days. The industry average for this ratio is 49.4 days. Furniture Brands' ratio is well above the industry average. This may not necessarily be alarming. There may be legitimate reasons why the average collection period for Furniture Brands is higher than the industry average. Some reasons would be:

➢ The difference in ratios between Furniture Brands and the industry average could be due to differences in the credit terms offered by Furniture Brands and the industry in general. Furniture Brands, for instance, may give their customers a longer time period—say, 60 days—to pay for the merchandise purchased, while the industry norm may call for a shorter credit term—say, 45 days. We don't know this for sure, since this information is not always available from the annual reports, but it is a possible explanation.

➢ The difference may be due to differences in the customer composition. Firms in a given industry may operate in several different segments, each with their own collection policies. For example, Ethan Allen, one of the larger competitors of Furniture Brands, sells a significant portion of its output through company-owned outlets. Thus, Ethan Allen is both a manufacturer and a retailer, unlike Furniture Brands, which has no retail presence. Indeed, Ethan Allen's average collection period is only 14.6 days, which may explain why the industry average we calculated is comparatively lower. Flexsteel, another firm in the industry, manufactures residential furniture but is also a major supplier of upholstered sofas and other furniture to the recreational vehicle market. The collection terms in that industry may be shorter than in the residential furniture market, again yielding a lower industry average.

Consequently, there are may be perfectly valid reasons why a firm may have a higher-than-average collection period. This is where additional investigation is needed. If Furniture Brands' higher collection period does not have a sound basis, this could indicate problems with the firm's credit terms and their collection effort. Assuming that there is a problem with the collections effort, an analyst could conclude that by bringing the average collection period for Furniture Brands down to the industry average of 49.4 days, the firm can release funds that are tied up in accounts receivable. The released funds would amount to $(60.7 \text{ days} - 49.4 \text{ days}) \times \$5.798$ million average credit sales per day $= \$65.52$ million. The firm can more profitably employ these funds elsewhere, for example, retiring long-term debt and/or adding to plant and equipment.

Inventory Turnover Ratio The *inventory turnover ratio* is defined as follows:

$$\text{Inventory turnover} = \frac{\text{Cost of sales}}{\text{Average inventory}} \qquad \textbf{(4.4)}$$

Whereas the cost of sales is usually listed on a firm's income statement, the average inventory has to be calculated. This can be done in a number of ways. For example, if a firm has been experiencing a significant and continuing rate of growth in sales, the average inventory may be computed by adding the figures for the beginning and ending inventories for the year and dividing by 2. If sales are seasonal or otherwise subject to wide fluctuations, however, it would be better to add the month-end inventory balances for the entire year and divide by 12. However, obtaining month-end inventory balances is a problem, as firms do not report these in the annual reports. An alternative is to use quarterly balances from the quarterly financial statements, which most firms do provide.

Some analysts calculate inventory turnover as simply the ratio of annual sales to ending inventory. Although the *sales-to-inventory ratio* is technically inferior and gives results different from those of more commonly used ratios, it may be satisfactory if used consistently when making comparisons between one firm and the industry as a whole. However, the problem with this ratio is that it tends to differ from one firm to another, depending on policies regarding markups on the cost of sales.

Since the furniture industry is not highly seasonal, we will use the beginning and end-of-the-year inventory balances to calculate average inventory. Note that the beginning inventory value is the same as the ending inventory balance for the preceding year. For Furniture Brands, the average inventory balance is: ($294.454 + $285.395)/2 = $289.925. Dividing the cost of sales by this figure, $1,529.874/$289.925, gives an inventory turnover ratio of 5.28 times. This compares with an average of 5.49 for the industry. The difference is probably not significant.

A very high or a very low inventory turnover ratio relative to the industry average may have negative implications. A low inventory turnover ratio could be indicative of excessive inventory balances, or that some of the inventory is slow moving or even obsolete.

If a firm's inventory turnover ratio is too high, it may mean the firm is frequently running out of certain items in stock and may be losing sales to competitors. In the 1980s Pratt and Whitney, a well-known manufacturer of jet engines, decided to cut down on inventory of finished engines, resulting in disastrous market share consequences and profitability. Because downtime is costly for airline operators, they require ready availability of engines, if one has to be replaced. Airlines using Pratt and Whitney engines started experiencing longer downtimes because of a shortage of inventory with the jet engine maker. Consequently many of these airlines took their business to other manufacturers, notably General Electric, who gained market share at the expense of Pratt and Whitney.

Fixed Asset Turnover Ratio   The *fixed asset turnover ratio* is defined as follows:

(4.5)
$$\text{Fixed asset turnover} = \frac{\text{Sales}}{\text{Net fixed assets}}$$

It indicates the extent to which a firm is utilizing existing property, plant, and equipment to generate sales. It is important to note that this ratio is especially vulnerable to a number of factors that may influence the value of net fixed assets in the denominator. The balance sheet figures that indicate how much a firm has invested in property, plant, and equipment are affected by the following:

- ➤ The cost of the assets when acquired. If the firm came into existence many years ago, its cost basis would be lower than that of another firm that started operations more recently.
- ➤ The depreciation policies adopted by the firm. An accelerated depreciation policy compared to a straight-line depreciation policy will cause net fixed assets to decrease more rapidly with time.
- ➤ The extent to which fixed assets are leased rather than owned.

➢ The choice of technology. Two firms in the same industry, producing similar products, may adopt different technologies; one firm may rely on a considerable level of automation, while another firm may adopt a more labor-intensive manufacturing process. Also some firms may rely more heavily on subcontractors to do part of the manufacturing, consequently reducing the amount of investment needed in property, plant, and equipment.

Because of these factors, it is possible for firms manufacturing virtually identical products to have significantly different fixed asset turnover ratios. Thus, the ratio should be used primarily for year-to-year comparisons within the same company, rather than for intercompany comparisons.

Furniture Brands fixed asset turnover ratio is $2,116.239/$303.235 = 6.98 times, slightly above the industry average of 6.3 times.

Total Asset Turnover Ratio The *total asset turnover ratio* is defined as follows:

$$\text{Total asset turnover} = \frac{\text{Sales}}{\text{Total assets}} \qquad (4.6)$$

It indicates how effectively a firm uses its total resources to generate sales and is a summary measure influenced by each of the asset management ratios previously discussed.

Furniture Brands' total asset turnover ratio is $2,116.239/$1,304.838 = 1.62 times, almost identical to the industry average of 1.63.

Comprehension Check Questions

1. What is the rationale for computing the quick ratio?
2. Is a lower average collection period more desirable than a higher one? Explain.
3. What are some problems with the fixed asset turnover ratio?

Financial Leverage Management Ratios

Whenever a firm finances a portion of its assets with any type of fixed-charge financing—such as debt, preferred stock, or leases—the firm is said to be using financial leverage. *Financial leverage management ratios measure the degree to which a firm is employing financial leverage* and, as such, are of interest to creditors and owners alike.

Both long- and short-term creditors are concerned with the amount of leverage a firm employs, because it indicates the firm's risk exposure in meeting debt service charges (that is, interest and principal repayment). A firm that is heavily financed by debt offers creditors less protection in the event of bankruptcy. For example, if a firm's assets are financed with 85 percent debt, the value of the assets can decline by only 15 percent before creditors' funds are endangered. In contrast, if only 15 percent of a firm's assets are debt-financed, asset values can drop by 85 percent before jeopardizing the creditors.

Owners are interested in financial leverage because it influences the rate of return they can expect to realize on their investment and the degree of risk involved. For example, if a firm is able to borrow funds at 9 percent and employ them at 12 percent, the owners earn the 3 percent difference and may view financial leverage favorably. On the other hand, if the firm can earn only 3 percent on the borrowed funds, the -6 percent difference ($3\% - 9\%$) will result in a lower rate of return to the owners.

Either balance sheet or income statement data can be used to measure a firm's use of financial leverage. The balance sheet approach gives a *static* measure of financial leverage at a specific point in time and emphasizes *total* amounts of debt, whereas the income statement approach provides a more *dynamic* measure and relates required interest payments on debt to the firm's ability to pay. Both approaches are employed widely in practice.

There are several types of financial leverage management ratios, including the debt ratio, the debt-to-equity ratio, the times interest earned ratio, and the fixed-charge coverage ratio.

Debt Ratio The *debt ratio* is defined as follows:

$$(4.7) \qquad \text{Debt ratio} = \frac{\text{Total debt}}{\text{Total assets}}$$

It measures the proportion of a firm's total assets that is financed with creditors' funds. As used here, the term *debt* encompasses all short-term liabilities and long-term liabilities. Some individuals prefer to use a narrower definition of debt and consider only interest-charging liabilities such as long-term debt or bonds, notes payable, and lines of credit.

Bondholders and other long-term creditors are among those likely to be interested in a firm's debt ratio. They tend to prefer a low debt ratio, because it provides more protection in the event of liquidation or some other major financial problem. As the debt ratio increases, so do a firm's fixed-interest charges. If the debt ratio becomes too high, the cash flows a firm generates during economic recessions may not be sufficient to meet interest payments. Thus, a firm's ability to market new debt obligations when it needs to raise new funds is crucially affected by the size of the debt ratio and by investors' perceptions about the risk implied by the level of the ratio.

Debt ratios are stated in terms of percentages. Furniture Brands' debt ratio as of year-end 2000 is ($143.118 + $462.000 + $115.815)/$1,304.838 = $720.933/ $1,304.838 = 0.55251, or about 55 percent. The numerator is the sum of all current liabilities, long-term debt, and other long-term liabilities. The ratio is interpreted to mean that Furniture Brands' creditors are financing 55 percent of the firm's total assets. Furniture Brands' debt ratio is considerably greater than the 32 percent industry average. Evidently Furniture Brands' management has relied on debt to a much greater extent than does the industry on average in financing assets. The high leverage ratio also means that shareholders of Furniture Brands may be subject to significantly greater bankruptcy risk than other firms in the industry.

Debt-to-Equity Ratio The *debt-to-equity ratio* is defined as follows:

$$(4.8) \qquad \text{Debt-to-equity} = \frac{\text{Total debt}}{\text{Total equity}}$$

It is similar to the debt ratio and relates the amount of a firm's debt financing to the amount of equity financing. Actually, the debt-to-equity ratio is not really a new ratio; it is simply the debt ratio in a different format. The debt-to-equity ratio also is stated as a percentage. Furniture Brands' debt-to-equity ratio at year-end 2000 is $720.933/$583.905 = 1.235, or 123.5 percent. The industry average is 48 percent. In other words, the average firm in the industry raised approximately $0.48 in liabilities for each dollar of equity in the firm. In contrast, Furniture Brands uses $1.24 of liabilities for every dollar of equity financing. This shows that Furniture Brands has been following a very aggressive financing policy and probably has little flexibility in terms of future borrowing capacity. From the perspective of creditors, it means that Furniture Brands is probably not a good credit risk relative to the average firm in the industry, and creditors either would not be eager to lend to Furniture Brands or would do so only by charging higher interest rates than for the average firm in the industry.

Because most interest costs are incurred on long-term borrowed funds (greater than 1 year to maturity) and because long-term borrowing places multiyear, fixed financial obligations on a firm, some analysts also consider the ratio of *long-term debt-to-total assets*, or *long-term-debt-to-equity*. For Furniture Brands the long-term-debt-to-total-assets ratio is 35.4 percent. The comparable industry average is 9.2 percent. The long-term-debt-to-equity ratio for Furniture Brands is 79.1 percent. The corresponding industry average is 14.6 percent. These figures once again confirm the aggressive financing policy of Furniture Brands. Some analysts consider all noncurrent liabilities as long-term debt, in our calculations we only consider liabilities identified as long-term debt.

Times Interest Earned Ratio The *times interest earned (TIE) ratio* is defined as follows:

$$\text{Times interest earned} = \frac{\text{Earnings before interest and taxes (EBIT)}}{\text{Interest charges}} \qquad \textbf{(4.9)}$$

Often referred to as simply *interest coverage*, this ratio employs income statement data to measure a firm's use of financial leverage. It tells the analyst the extent to which the firm's current earnings are able to meet current interest payments. The **EBIT** figures are used because the firm makes interest payments out of operating income, or EBIT. When the times interest earned ratio falls below 1.0, the continued viability of the enterprise is threatened because the failure to make interest payments when due can lead to bankruptcy.

From Furniture Brands' income statement we note that the company incurred interest expense of $36.389 million in 2000. The firm's operating earning or EBIT was $192.614 million. In other words, Furniture Brands covers annual interest payments 5.29 times; this figure is significantly below the industry average of 31.8 times. It is clear from the debt, debt-to-equity, and times interest earned ratios that Furniture Brands has followed an aggressive financing policy.

Fixed-Charge Coverage Ratio The *fixed-charge coverage ratio* is defined as follows:

$$\text{Fixed-charge coverage} = \frac{(\text{EBIT}) + \text{lease payments}}{\text{Interest} + \text{lease payments} + \text{preferred dividends before tax} + \text{before tax sinking fund}} \qquad \textbf{(4.10)}$$

It measures the number of times a firm is able to cover total **fixed charges,** which include (in addition to interest payments) preferred dividends and payments required under long-term lease contracts. Many corporations also are required to make **sinking fund** payments on bond issues; these are annual payments aimed at either retiring a portion of the bond obligation each year or providing for the ultimate redemption of bonds at maturity. Under most sinking fund provisions, the firm either may make these payments to the bondholders' representative (the **trustee**), who determines through a lottery process which of the outstanding bonds will be retired, or deliver to the trustee the required number of bonds purchased by the firm in the open market. Either way, the firm's outstanding indebtedness is reduced.

In calculating the fixed-charge coverage ratio, an analyst must consider each of the firm's obligations on a *before-tax* basis. However, because sinking fund payments and preferred stock dividends are not tax deductible and therefore must be paid out of after-tax earnings, a mathematical adjustment has to be made. After-tax payments must be divided by $(1 - T)$, where T is the marginal tax rate. This effectively converts such payments to a before-tax basis, or one that is comparable to the EBIT. And, since lease payments are deducted in arriving at the EBIT, they must be added back into the numerator of the ratio, because the fixed charges (in the denominator) also include lease payments.

The fixed-charge coverage ratio is a more severe measure of a firm's ability to meet fixed financial obligations. It is not always easy to calculate the fixed-charge coverage ratio because information, especially on lease payments and sinking fund payments, is not always readily available from the financial statements. For Furniture Brands, the notes to the financial statements reveal that the firm incurred lease payments of $18.514 million in 2000 and that there were no sinking fund payments. From the balance sheet we know that the firm did not have any preferred shares outstanding, therefore no preferred dividends were paid out. Using these numbers, Furniture Brands' fixed-charge coverage ratio is: ($192.614 + $18.514)/ ($36.389 + $18.514) = $211.128/$54.903 = 3.8 times. We do not have a comparable industry average, as the necessary information was not available in the financial statements for all five firms used in constructing the industry average.

Profitability Ratios

More than any other accounting measure, a firm's profits demonstrate how well the firm is making investment and financing decisions. If a firm is unable to provide adequate returns in the form of dividends and share price appreciation to investors, it may be unable to maintain, let alone increase, its asset base. *Profitability ratios measure how effectively a firm's management is generating profits on sales, total assets, and, most importantly, stockholders' investment.* Therefore, anyone whose economic interests are tied to the long-run survival of a firm will be interested in profitability ratios.

There are several types of profitability ratios, including the *gross profit margin ratio*, the *net profit margin ratio*, the *return on investment ratio*, and the *return on stockholders' equity ratio*.

Gross Profit Margin Ratio The *gross profit margin ratio* is defined as follows:

$$(4.11) \qquad \text{Gross profit margin} = \frac{\text{Sales} - \text{Cost of sales}}{\text{Sales}}$$

It measures the relative profitability of a firm's sales after the cost of sales has been deducted, thus revealing how effectively the firm's management is making decisions regarding pricing and the control of production costs. Furniture Brands' gross profit margin ratio is ($2,116.239 − $1,529.874)/$2,116.239 = 27.7%, which is in line with the industry average of 27.2 percent. This percentage indicates that Furniture Brands' cost of production is consistent with the industry's experience.

Net Profit Margin Ratio The *net profit margin ratio* is defined as follows:

$$(4.12) \qquad \text{Net profit margin} = \frac{\text{Earnings after tax (EAT)}}{\text{Sales}}$$

It measures how profitable a firm's sales are after all expenses, including taxes and interest, have been deducted. Furniture Brands' net profit margin ratio is $105.901/$2,116.239 = 5.0%, which is below the industry average of 5.70 percent. Since the gross profit margin was nearly identical to the industry, the below-average net profit margin is indicative of above-average operating expenses and/or interest expenses. We noted previously that Furniture Brands relies heavily on debt financing, which entails significant interest expense. The significant interest expense associated with the high debt ratio appears to have depressed Furniture Brands' net profit margin relative to the industry average.

Some analysts also compute an *operating profit margin ratio*, defined as earnings before interest and taxes (EBIT) or operating earnings/sales. It measures the profitability of a firm's operations before considering the effects of financing decisions. Because the operating profit margin is computed before considering interest charges, this ratio often is more suitable for comparing the profit performance of different firms that may utilize varying amounts of debt financing.

Return on Investment (Total Assets) Ratio The *return on investment ratio (ROI)* is defined as follows:

$$\text{Return on investment} = \frac{\text{Earnings after tax (EAT)}}{\text{Total assets}} \qquad (4.13)$$

It measures a firm's net income in relation to the total asset investment. Furniture Brands' return on investment ratio, $105.901/$1,304.838, is 8.1 percent, which is somewhat below the industry average of 9.4 percent and consistent with the below-average net profit margin for the firm.

Some analysts also like to compute the ratio of EBIT to total assets (EBIT/Total Assets). This measures the operating profit rate of return for a firm. An after-tax version of this ratio is earnings before interest and after tax (EBIAT) divided by total assets. These ratios are computed before interest charges and may be more suitable when comparing the operating performance of two or more firms that are financed differently. Another variant of the operating performance ratio is the ratio of earnings before interest, depreciation, and amortization (EBITDA)/total assets. Many analysts prefer the EBITDA/total assets, since noncash expenses (depreciation and amortization expense) are ignored, giving a measure of operating profits that is based more on cash flows.

Return on Stockholders' Equity Ratio The *return on stockholders' equity ratio (ROE)* is defined as follows:

$$\text{Return on stockholders' equity} = \frac{\text{Earnings after tax (EAT)}}{\text{Stockholders' equity}} \qquad (4.14)$$

It measures the rate of return that the firm earns on stockholders' equity. Because only the stockholders' equity appears in the denominator, the ratio is influenced directly by the amount of debt a firm is using to finance assets. Furniture Brands' return on stockholders' equity ratio is $105.901/$583.905 = 18.1%. The comparable industry average is 13.7 percent. Furniture Brands' above-average performance on return on stockholders' equity but not on return on investments is attributable to the heavy debt load taken on by the firm. With relatively higher debt financing, the firm is able to spread its net income over a smaller base of stockholders' equity, thereby increasing the return on stockholders' equity. (In a later section we will explain the relation between return on investment and return on stockholder's equity more completely.)

Market-based Ratios

The financial ratios discussed in the previous four groups all are derived from accounting income statement and balance sheet information provided by the firm. *Market-based ratios provide an assessment of performance as perceived by the financial market.* The market-based ratios for a firm should parallel the accounting ratios of that firm. For example, if the accounting ratios suggest that the firm has more risk than the average firm in the industry and has lower profit prospects, this information should be reflected in a lower market price of that firm's stock.

Price-to-Earnings (P/E) Ratio The *price-to-earnings ratio* (**P/E**) is defined as follows:

$$(4.15) \qquad P/E = \frac{\text{Market price per share}}{\text{Current earnings per share}}$$

(Some security analysts use next year's projected earnings per share in the denominator; this is called a forward P/E. There is nothing wrong with this alternative definition as long as comparisons between firms are done on the same basis.)

In general, *the lower a firm's risk, the higher its P/E ratio should be.* In addition, *the better the growth prospects of its earnings, the greater is the P/E multiple.* For example, Merck & Co., a major drug company facing a number of patent expirations and, therefore, questionable growth prospects, had a P/E multiple of approximately 18 in mid-2003. In contrast, Abbott Laboratories, another major player in the drug industry that did not face the same risk of lower growth prospects as Merck, enjoyed a P/E multiple of approximately 27 in mid-2003.

Furniture Brands' current (2000) earnings per share is $2.03 (net earnings of $105.901 million divided by the 52.277 million shares outstanding reported in the stockholders' equity portion of the balance sheet). Note that this is different from the basic earnings per share of $2.10 and diluted earnings per share of $2.14 reported at the bottom of Furniture Brands' income statement. Both the basic and diluted earnings per share measures are based on accounting conventions that take into account shares outstanding over the course of the year, adjustments for stock repurchases, and adjustments for the dilutive effects of convertible securities and stock options (Furniture Brands does not have any convertible securities but does have stock options outstanding). The measure of earnings per share we calculate simply divides the net income to common shareholders by the actual number of shares issued as reported in the balance sheet; this is common practice among financial analysts. Furniture Brands' year-end closing price was $21.0625 per share. The price is for December 29, 2000, the last day of trading in the year 2000. Dividing the market price per share by the earnings per share yields Furniture Brands' P/E ratio of 10.4 times ($21.06/$2.03). Furniture Brands' P/E ratio is about the same as the industry average of 10.0 times. This suggests that the market's assessment of Furniture Brands' stock is about the same as the industry average.

As a supplement to the price-to-earnings ratio, financial analysts sometimes also examine a firm's *stock-price-to-free-cash-flow ratio*. Free cash flow represents the portion of a firm's total cash flow available to pay common stock dividends, to invest in other projects (e.g., capital expenditures and/or acquisition of other companies), and to service additional debt. Free cash flow often is viewed as a better measure than earnings of the financial soundness of a firm. Earnings data sometimes can be misleading because accounting rules give companies discretion in such areas as the recognition of revenues that have not been received and the allocation of costs over different time periods. For example, Integrated Resources and Todd Shipyards had good earnings, but had negative cash flow and were forced to file for bankruptcy.

Market-to-Book Value or Price-to-Book Value (P/BV) Ratio The *market-to-book* or *price-to-book ratio* is defined as follows:

$$P/BV = \frac{\text{Market price per share}}{\text{Book value per share}} \qquad (4.16)$$

Generally, the higher the rate of return a firm is earning on its common equity relative to the return required by investors (the cost of common equity), the higher will be the *P/BV* ratio.

The book value per share of common stock is determined by dividing the total common stockholders' equity for a firm by the number of shares outstanding. In the case of Furniture Brands at year-end 2000, the book value per share is equal to $11.17 (common stockholders' equity of $583.905 million divided by 52.277 million shares outstanding). With a market price per share of $21.0625, the market-to-book ratio for Furniture Brands is 1.89 ($21.06/$11.17). Furniture Brands' P/BV ratio is considerably better than the industry average of 1.33. It should be noted that, because the market-to-book ratio contains the book value of the common stockholders' equity in the denominator (remember that, for firms with no preferred stock, common stockholders' equity is equal to total assets minus total liabilities), it is affected by the accounting treatments used by a firm in such crucial areas as inventory valuation and depreciation. For this reason, comparisons between firms often can be misleading.

In general the P/E and P/BV ratios for Furniture Brands compare favorably to the industry average. The better-than-average market-based ratios may be surprising in view of the higher-than-average debt ratios. Evidently the market thinks that the risk associated with the higher-than-average debt ratios may be offset by other positive factors. For example, growth prospects for Furniture Brands may be better than for other competitors.

Comprehension Check Questions

1. How are the debt and debt-to-equity ratios different from times interest earned and fixed-charge coverage ratios?

2. Can the net profit margin of a firm decline over time, while the gross margin increases or stays the same? Explain.

3. What do the market-based ratios measure that is not captured in the other four categories of ratios?

Summary of Financial Ratio Analysis

Table 4.1 lists all the financial ratios calculated for Furniture Brands along with the corresponding industry average (see the assessment column on the right of the table). For example, the firm's liquidity ratios are ranked above average relative to industry measures. With respect to asset management ratios, the average collection period appears to be significantly worse than the industry average and the inventory turnover ratio is also below average. However, the fixed asset turnover ratio is better than the industry average, while the total asset turnover ratio is about the same as the industry average.

The financial leverage position of the firm is of concern, given that they appear to be significantly greater than the industry average. This is apparent from the much higher than average debt and debt-to-equity ratios and the much-lower-than-average times interest earned ratio. The firm has been following a rather aggressive

Table 4.1 Summary of Ratios for Furniture Brands

Ratio	Definition	Calculation	Industry Average	Assessment
LIQUIDITY				
1. Current ratio	$\dfrac{\text{Current assets}}{\text{Current liabilities}}$	$= \dfrac{691.581}{143.118} = 4.83$	3.12	Better than industry average
2. Quick ratio (acid test)	$\dfrac{\text{Cash + Marketable securities + Accounts receivable}}{\text{Current liabilities}}$	$= \dfrac{14.606 + 351.804}{143.118} = 2.56$	1.75	Better than industry average
ASSET MANAGEMENT				
3. Average collection period	$\dfrac{\text{Accounts receivable}}{\text{Credit sales/365}} <$	$= \dfrac{351.804}{2,116.239/365} = \dfrac{351.804}{5.798}$ $= 60.7$ days	49.4 days	Worse than industry average
4. Inventory turnover	$\dfrac{\text{Cost of sales}}{\text{Average inventory}}$	$= \dfrac{1,529.874}{289.925} = 5.28$ times	5.49	Worse than industry average
5. Fixed asset turnover	$\dfrac{\text{Sales}}{\text{Fixed assets}}$	$= \dfrac{2,116.239}{303.235} = 6.98$ times	6.3	Better than industry average
6. Total asset turnover	$\dfrac{\text{Sales}}{\text{Total assets}}$	$= \dfrac{2,116.239}{1,304.838} = 1.62$ times	1.63	Average
FINANCIAL LEVERAGE MANAGEMENT				
7. Debt ratio	$\dfrac{\text{Total debt}}{\text{Total assets}}$	$= \dfrac{720.933}{1,304.838} = .5525$ or 55.25%	32%	Worse than industry average
8. Debt-to-equity	$\dfrac{\text{Total debt}}{\text{Total equity}}$	$= \dfrac{720.933}{583.905} = 1.235$ or 123.5%	48%	Worse than industry average
9. Times interest earned	$\dfrac{\text{Earnings before interest and taxes (EBIT)}}{\text{Interest charges}}$	$= \dfrac{192.614}{36.389} = 5.29$ times	31.8 times	Worse than industry average
10. Times fixed charges earned	$\dfrac{\text{EBIT + Lease payments}}{\text{Interest + Lease payments + Before-tax sinking fund + Preferred stock dividends before tax}}$	$= \dfrac{211.128}{54.903} = 3.8$ times	—	—
PROFITABILITY				
11. Gross profit margin	$\dfrac{\text{Sales − Cost of sales}}{\text{Sales}}$	$= \dfrac{2,116.239 - 1,529.874}{2,116.239} = 27.7\%$	27.2%	Better than industry average
12. Net profit margin	$\dfrac{\text{Earnings after taxes (EAT)}}{\text{Sales}}$	$= \dfrac{105.901}{2,116.239} = 5.0\%$	5.7%	Worse than industry average
13. Return on investment	$\dfrac{\text{Earnings after taxes (EAT)}}{\text{Total asset}}$	$= \dfrac{105.901}{1,304.838} = 8.1\%$	9.4%	Worse than industry average
14. Return on stockholders' equity	$\dfrac{\text{Earnings after taxes (EAT)}}{\text{Stockholders' equity}}$	$= \dfrac{105.901}{583.905} = 18.1\%$	13.7%	Better than industry average
MARKET-BASED				
15. Price-to-earnings ratio	$\dfrac{\text{Market price per share}}{\text{Current earnings per share}}$	$= \dfrac{21.0625}{2.03} = 10.4$ times	10.0 times	Better than industry average
16. Market-to-book ratio	$\dfrac{\text{Market price per share}}{\text{Book value per share}}$	$= \dfrac{21.0625}{11.17} = 1.89$	1.33	Better than industry average

FINANCE & The Real World

Assessment of Financial Performance

Ultimately, the results of operating decisions appear in a firm's financial statements. The methods used to interpret financial statements can vary, with the perspective of the interpreter determining what areas are emphasized. For example, if a banker and an entrepreneur were analyzing the same financial statements, they might focus on different data. But whatever perspective is taken, the issues are fundamentally the same and are captured in the following four questions:

- *Does the firm have the capacity to meet its short-term (one-year or less) financial commitments?*
- *Is the firm producing adequate operating profits on its assets?*
- *How is the firm financing its assets?*
- *Are the stockholders receiving an acceptable return on their equity investment?*

Source: Adapted from Small Business Management: An Entrepreneurial Emphasis, 12th Edition, Longenecker, Moore, and Petty. © 2003 South-Western, p. 522. Reprinted by permission.

---

financing policy, which could limit the firm's future financing flexibility, making it more difficult to obtain additional debt and reasonable rates. Additionally, the higher bankruptcy risk associated with high leverage ratios would be of concern to creditors and shareholders alike.

The profitability measures are mixed, with a slightly above-average gross profit margin, a below-average net profit margin and return on investment, and an above-average return on stockholders' equity. The worse-than-average net profit margin and return on investment are likely due to the excessive financial leverage assumed by the firm. The higher-than-average return on stockholders' equity is also attributable to the high debt ratio, which permits the firm to spread the net income over a smaller shareholder equity base.

The market-based ratios on balance are in line with the industry ratios. It is slightly above average for the P/E ratio and about average for the market-to-book ratio. The P/E and P/BV ratios suggest that the market is not overly concerned about Furniture Brands' high debt ratio—possibly because the market sees offsetting positive factors such as better liquidity and perhaps better future prospects. Although future prospects are difficult to measure and assess, it is an important element of market-based ratios. Both the P/E and P/BV ratios have the market price in the numerator, which should reflect future prospects for the firm. Therefore, even though certain fundamentals may not look favorable for Furniture Brands relative to industry norms, the stock price is a forward-looking measure that reflects the firm's condition in the future.

TREND ANALYSIS

Thus far, the analysis of Furniture Brands has focused solely on the year 2000. This has provided a fairly complete, if rather static, picture of the company's situation at that particular point in time in comparison with industry standards. To gain insight into the direction the company is moving, however, a trend analysis should be performed. A trend analysis indicates a firm's performance over time and reveals whether its position is improving or deteriorating relative to other companies in the industry.

A trend analysis requires that a number of different ratios be calculated over several years and plotted to yield a graphic representation of the company's performance. Figure 4.1 depicts a trend analysis for Furniture Brands for the years 1996 to 2000. Selected ratios from four different categories of ratios are plotted for the firm and the industry. Specifically, a *measure of liquidity* (current ratio), *asset structure* (total asset turnover), *financial leverage* (debt ratio), and three measures of *profitability* (net profit margin, ROI, ROE) are shown. Furniture Brands' current ratio has exceeded four times in each of the years and has been consistently greater than the industry average. The total asset turnover ratio tells an interesting story. Furniture Brands has consistently improved its total asset turnover ratio from 1996 to 2000 to the point where it is now equal to the industry. It is evident that the firm was well below industry average in 1996 but has steadily narrowed the gap over time. The steady improvement over time shows that management has paid conscious attention to improve the total asset ratio over time.

In the cross-sectional analysis we noted that the debt ratio for Furniture Brands was of some concern (see page 105). Figure 4.1 reveals that the excessive

**Figure 4.1
Trend Analysis of
Financial Ratios for
Furniture Brands
1996–2000**

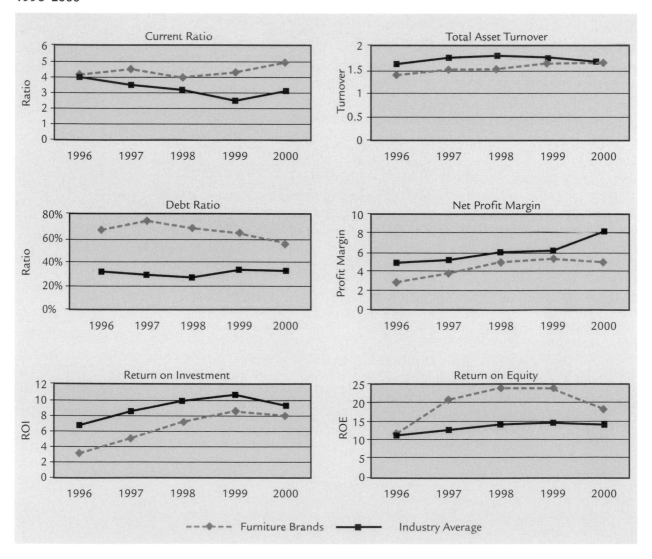

debt ratio appears to have been a problem for some time. While the industry average debt ratio appears to be stable around 30 percent, Furniture Brands' ratio was as high as about 75 percent in 1997. However, management has been aware of the high debt ratio as revealed by the firm's attempt to steadily pare down the debt ratio from the high of 75 percent to approximately 55 percent in 2000. The net profit margin for the firm has improved steadily over time but is still below the industry average, which also has improved steadily over time (with the slight exception of the last year). The below-average net profit margin performance of Furniture Brands is likely due to the higher interest costs experienced by the firm as a result of the high debt ratios. Note that the improvement in net profit margin over time is associated with the decrease in the debt ratio over time. Consistent with the trend analysis of the net profit margin ratio, Furniture Brands' return on investment has been below the industry average but is significantly improved over time.

The final ratio we examine is the return on stockholders' equity. Unlike the other two profitability measures examined, net profit margin and return on investments, Furniture Brands compares very favorably with the industry over time with respect to return on stockholders' equity. The firm has consistently exceeded the industry average in each of the five years although the gap has narrowed in the last year.

In summary, the comparative financial ratio analysis *combined with* the trend analysis provide the financial analyst with a fairly clear picture of Furniture Brands' performance. The firm's liquidity is above average as revealed by the current and quick ratios. The asset management ratios are on par with the industry although the average collection period was of some concern. The financial leverage ratios suggest that the firm has an excessively high debt ratio and low interest coverage ratio. However, the trend analysis reveals that the firm has been steadily paring down the debt ratio and in time may reach the industry average. The profitability measures are mixed. The gross profit margin is just above the industry average, implying that the cost of production for Furniture Brands is competitive with the industry. The net profit margin and return on investment are below the industry averages—probably a result of the high debt ratio assumed by the firm. The trend analysis reveals that both the net profit margin and the return on investments have improved over time coinciding with the steady decline in the debt ratios and corresponding decrease in interest costs over time. The return on stockholders' equity has consistently beaten industry averages. Finally, the market-based ratios reveal that the firm's stock is viewed favorably relative to the industry average as revealed in the P/E and P/BV ratios.

ANALYSIS OF PROFITABILITY: A COMPREHENSIVE FRAMEWORK

The ROI and ROE profitability ratios discussed above can be broken down into their constituent elements. Doing so gives us a better understanding of how different factors combine to determine the overall profitability of the firm.

Return on Investment

We had previously defined the *return on investment (ROI)* as the ratio of earnings after taxes (EAT) to total assets. The ROI ratio can be examined more closely to provide additional insights into its significance. The ROI also can be viewed as a function of the net profit margin times the total asset turnover, because the net profit margin ratio = EAT/sales and the total asset turnover ratio = sales/total assets:

(4.17)
$$\text{ROI} = \frac{\text{Earnings after tax (EAT)}}{\text{Total assets}} = \frac{\text{EAT}}{\text{Sales}} \times \frac{\text{Sales}}{\text{Total assets}}$$

It is important to examine a firm's ROI in terms of "margin" and "turnover," because each plays a major role in contributing to profitability. *Margin* measures the profit earned per dollar of sales but ignores the amount of assets used to generate sales. The ROI relationship brings these two components together and shows that a deficiency in either one will lower a firm's return on investment.

Using the figures from the net profit margin ratio and total asset turnover ratio calculated previously for Furniture Brands, the firm's ROI for 2000 can be computed as 5.0% × 1.62 = 8.1%. Figure 4.2, called a modified ***DuPont chart*** or ***analysis*** because it was developed and is used by the DuPont Corporation, illustrates this relationship. For purposes of comparison, the industry average ROI = 5.70% × 1.63 = 9.3%. The ROI relationship shows that the lower ROI for Furniture Brands relative to the industry is due to the lower net profit margin relative to the industry. The DuPont chart illustrates the relationship between a firm's ROI and the factors that determine it. By working back through the DuPont chart, an analyst can begin to pinpoint potential areas for improvement that will enhance the firm's ROI.

The relative contributions of the net profit margin and the asset turnover ratio in the ROI relationship differ from industry to industry. Specifically, the turnover ratio is dependent largely on a firm's investment in property, plant, and equipment. Firms with large investments in fixed assets tend to have low turnover ratios; public utilities, railroads, and large industrial firms fall into this category. If these companies are to succeed, their relatively low turnover ratios must be offset by correspondingly high margins to produce competitive ROIs. For example, electric and gas utilities typically have net profit margins of 10 to 15 percent. In contrast, other industries require much lower investments in fixed assets, resulting in higher turnover ratios. A typical example is the retail grocery chain industry, which has margins of only 1 or 2 percent. Firms in this industry often achieve turnovers of 10 times or more. If a grocery chain had a lower turnover, its ROI probably would not be sufficient to attract investors.

Return on Stockholders' Equity

Figure 4.2 also shows Furniture Brands' return on stockholders' equity, which is computed as 18.1 percent. If the firm were financed solely with common equity (stock), the return on stockholders' equity would equal the return on investment. Furniture Brands' stockholders have supplied about 55 percent of the firm's total capital, whereas creditors have supplied the remaining 45 percent. Because the entire 8.1 percent return on investment belongs to the stockholders (even though they only supplied 55 percent of the total capital), Furniture Brands' return on common equity is higher than its return on investment.

To clarify how the return on stockholders' equity is determined, a new ratio, the *equity multiplier ratio*, is defined as follows:

(4.18)
$$\text{Equity multiplier} = \frac{\text{Total assets}}{\text{Stockholders' equity}}$$

Furniture Brands' equity multiplier ratio is computed from figures found in the balance sheet as \$1,304.838/\$583.905 = 2.24 times. The industry average for the ratio is 1.47 times. Once again, it can be seen that Furniture Brands has financed a significantly greater proportion of assets with debt than the average firm in the industry.

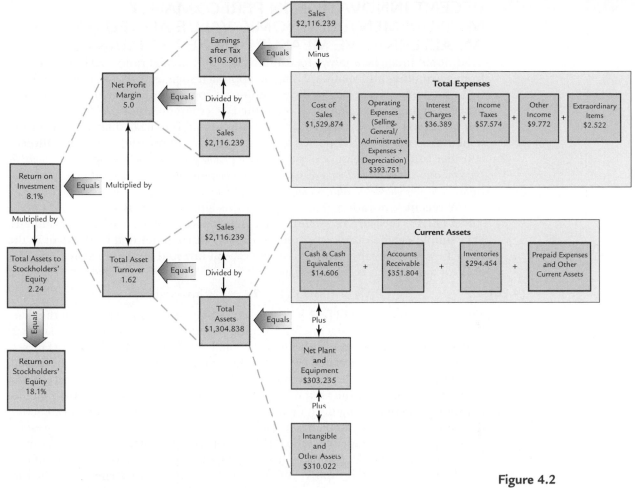

Figure 4.2
DuPont Chart Analysis of Furniture Brands' ROE and ROI

The equity multiplier ratio may be used to show how a firm's use of debt to finance assets affects the return on equity, as follows:

$$\text{Return on stockholders' equity} = (\text{Net profit margin}) \times (\text{Total asset turnover}) \times (\text{Equity multiplier}) \qquad (4.16)$$

$$= \frac{\text{Earnings after tax}}{\text{Sales}} \times \frac{\text{Sales}}{\text{Total assets}} \times \frac{\text{Total assets}}{\text{Stockholder's equity}}$$

In Furniture Brands' case, the return on stockholders' equity is 5.00% × 1.62 × 2.24 = 18.1%. For the industry, the corresponding calculation is 5.70% × 1.63 × 1.47 = 13.7%. Although these figures are the same as the return on equity computed directly by dividing earnings after tax by stockholders' equity, the calculations shown illustrate more clearly how the return on investment is magnified into a larger return on stockholders' equity through the use of financial leverage. The more debt a firm uses, the greater the equity multiplier effect. We can clearly see here that Furniture Brands' below-average ROI has been offset by the use of greater financial leverage to yield an above-average return on stockholders' equity. Although increased use of debt can increase the return on equity, it comes at the expense of greater risk.

RECENT INNOVATION IN PERFORMANCE MEASUREMENT: ECONOMIC VALUE ADDED (EVA®)— AN ALTERNATIVE MEASURE OF PERFORMANCE

Traditional financial analysis focuses on a set of financial ratios derived primarily from accounting information. Using an approach such as DuPont analysis, a firm's financial performance can be dissected into its component elements. The ultimate measure of firm performance is the return on common equity. Although insights can be gained from this type of analysis, traditional financial analysis suffers from weaknesses inherent in reported accounting information, and it does not directly consider risk in the measure of performance. *The greatest shortcoming of traditional financial analysis is the lack of a direct tie between performances, as measured using financial ratios, and shareholder wealth, as measured by the market price of a firm's stock.*

A recent innovation that addresses this shortcoming is the *Economic Value Added (**EVA®**)* measure of performance developed by Stern Stewart & Company. Very simply the measure compares the dollar return generated by the firm to the return expected by the investors on the capital invested by them in the firm. The EVA for a given year is calculated as:

(4.20)
$$EVA = (EBIT)\ (1 - T) - k \times \text{invested capital}$$

The first component $(EBIT)(1 - T)$ is the after-tax operating earnings of the firm. Note that this is before any interest expense because we are interested in earnings that will be distributed to *all* providers of capital—debt and equity holders. The second component $(k \times \text{invested capital})$ is the product of the average cost of capital, k, and the amount of invested capital at the beginning of the year. The average cost of capital depends on the various sources of capital employed by the firm including short-term debt, long-term debt, preferred stock, and common equity. Each of the various sources of capital has its own associated cost of capital, and k represents the composite or average of all the different sources of capital. The invested capital refers to sum total of all capital contributed by each of the different sources of capital. Thus, $(k \times \text{invested capital})$ refers to the dollar return expected by all the capital holders taken together. Based on this formula, EVA is positive if the return generated exceeds the return expected by the capital holders.

EVA is a very comprehensive measure of performance. What EVA says is that a firm's earnings must exceed what it costs to raise the capital employed in the firm. In other words, good management not only generates sufficient earnings to meet the business expenses of firm (cost of production, operating expenses) but also provides for compensation to the various capital holders. A positive EVA therefore signifies that management has generated earnings over and above what the capital holders require. When that happens, share prices will increase.

Calculating the EVA is somewhat involved as we need to know cost of capital, k. (The cost of capital will be discussed in Chapter 11.) In addition to k, we need to measure operating earnings and invested capital. Stern Stewart points out that the measure of operating earnings, or EBIT, is an adjusted measure of the operating earnings seen in the accounting statements. Stern Stewart adjusts for a number of accounting treatments before coming up with the proper measure of operating earnings. Conceptually though, as can be seen from the formula, it is very straightforward. For example, let us assume we want to calculate EVA for Music Box Corporation for 2001. Let's assume that Music Box employed several sources of capital, including debt and common equity, and that we are provided with the following information:

Invested capital at the beginning of year 2001: $2.5 billion

Average cost of capital: 8.5%

Corporate tax rate: 40%

EBIT generated in 2001: $450 million

Plugging in the corresponding values into the EVA formula:

$$EVA = EBIT\ (1 - T) - k \times \text{invested capital}$$
$$= \$450 \text{ million} (1 - .4) - .085 \times \$2,500 \text{ million}$$
$$= \$270 \text{ million} - 212.5 \text{ million}$$
$$= \$57.5 \text{ million}$$

Thus, Music Box's management generated additional wealth in 2001 of $57.5 million over and above what the various sources of capital cost the firm.

It is important to note that management should not be penalized if the EVA is negative in a given year because it may be due to circumstances beyond their control. For example, airlines do poorly when the economy is in a recession regardless of the efforts of management to increase traffic. Consequently, despite all efforts, the after-tax EBIT for airlines may not exceed their cost of capital, yielding negative EVAs. However, if an airline is yielding consistently negative EVAs year after year, then serious questions may be raised regarding the management's competence. In addition to EVA, Stern Stewart also calculates what it refers to as the *market value added* (MVA), which is a cumulative measure of EVA since the inception of the firm. Stern Stewart's Web site (http://www.sternstewart.com) provides a ranking of the MVAs of 1,000 firms. A selection of firms with the best and worst MVAs along with their EVAs for the year 1999 is provided in Table 4.2.

COMMON-SIZE FINANCIAL STATEMENTS

In addition to financial ratios, it is also useful to examine common-size financial statements. A *common-size balance sheet* shows the firm's assets and liabilities as a percentage of total assets, rather than in dollar amounts. Table 4.3 shows Furniture Brands' common-size balance sheet at year-end 2000 and 1999. A *common-size income statement* lists the firm's income and expense items as a percentage of net sales, rather than in dollar amounts. Table 4.4 contains Furniture Brands' common-size income statement for the year 2000 and 1999. Common-size financial statements allow trends in financial performance to be detected and monitored more easily than do financial statements showing only dollar amounts. These can also be compared to common size statements for the industry as a whole.

A comparison of Furniture Brands' common-size balance sheets for 2000 and 1999 reveals that all of the asset accounts maintained fairly stable proportions to total assets during the 2 years. Accounts receivable, as a percent of total assets was stable at around 27 percent while inventories as a percent of total assets was approximately 22 percent. Property, plant, and equipment remained stable at about 23 percent. On the liabilities we note a drop in the proportion of total liabilities to total assets from approximately 63 percent in 1999 to about 55 percent in 2000. This decrease is almost entirely attributable to the decrease in the proportion of long-term debt to total assets, which dropped from approximately 42 percent to approximately 35 percent of total assets. The decrease in the proportion of total liabilities to total assets is consistent with the trend analysis showing that management has been working hard to steadily pare down Furniture Brands' reliance on debt financing over the past several years.

Table 4.2 Best and Worst 1999 MVA rankings from Stern Stewart & Co.

MVA Rank 1999	MVA Rank 1998	MVA Rank 1994	TIC	Company Name	MVA 1999	EVA (Average) Capital) 1999	Capital (Year-End Operating Capital) 1999	Return on Capital[R] 1999	Cost of Capital (WACC) 1999
1	1	10	MSFT	Microsoft	629,407	5,796	20,034	51.78	12.62
2	2	2	GE	General Electric	467,510	3,499	75,830	17.20	12.47
3	8	50	CSCO	Cisco Systems	348,442	182	23,653	13.72	12.78
4	5	3	WMT	Wal-Mart Stores	282,655	1,528	54,013	14.31	10.99
5	3	26	INTC	Intel	253,907	4,695	29,825	30.55	12.19
6	9		LU	Lucent Technologies	200,540	−1,828	65,594	9.81	13.69
7	23	425	AOL	America Online	187,558	−156	4,482	11.10	15.53
8	41	38	ORCL	Oracle	154,263	605	5,413	24.59	12.42
9	11	78	IBM	IBM	154,219	1,349	66,827	13.33	11.40
10	19	25	HD	Home Depot	148,358	884	16,145	16.60	10.49
11	10	6	XOM	ExxonMobil	144,687	4,440	180,040	11.67	8.16
12	4	5	MRK	Merck	143,001	3,449	29,553	23.09	10.72
13	6	1	KO	Coca-Cola	134,149	1,562	18,120	21.80	12.31
14	47	307	SUNW	Sun Microsystems	133,953	595	5,954	23.85	13.03
15	14	430	DELL	Dell Computer	132,609	1,330	7,302	46.33	14.79
16	43		YHOO	Yahoo!	128,748	−862	8,847	−2.66	15.99
17	15	11	PG	Procter & Gamble	127,222	1,782	31,587	15.52	9.72
18	362	393	QCOM	QUALCOMM	126,323	78	3,521	15.80	13.05
19	30	133	AIG	American International Group	118,726	−119	48,774	10.44	10.70
20	12	18	BMY	Bristol-Myers Squibb	115,411	2,589	17,811	24.90	10.08
980	983	986	ORI	Old Republic International Corporation	−2,186	−195	3,851	4.87	9.93
981	528	474	GT	Goodyear Tire & Rubber	−2,321	−407	13,453	4.65	8.02
982	998	999	NGH	Nabisco	−2,329	−869	11,207	1.98	6.22
983	967	993	CB	Chubb Corporation	−2,602	−677	12,484	4.38	10.14
984	338	449	S	Sears Roebuck	−3,019	−82	34,269	6.70	6.94
985	309	152	MAT	Mattel	−3,277	−4	10,652	7.81	7.87
986	479	496	CNC	Conseco	−3,298	5	9,135	12.89	12.82
987	302	96	JCP	JCPenney	−3,830	−278	21,746	5.45	6.68
988	850	984	AET	Aetna	−3,958	−646	11,922	6.18	11.86
989	996	174	GLK	Great Lakes Chemical	−3,981	242	6,967	11.82	8.07
990	994	994	KM	Kmart	−4,721	−560	19,727	4.82	7.70
991	212	130	RTN.B	Raytheon	−4,803	−689	26,628	5.26	7.91
992	535	990	UNM	UNUM Corporation	−5,782	−2	13,487	11.71	11.73
993	991	857	HRC	HEALTHSOUTH	−6,102	−487	12,147	6.02	10.12
994	923	979	ACL	ACE Limited	−6,233	−1,297	9,862	−5.08	11.40
995	365	961	WM	Washington Mutual	−6,591	−730	21,381	9.37	12.87
996	997	996	SPS	St. Paul Companies	−6,703	−1,266	14,277	1.81	10.58
997	86	281	ONE	BankOne Corporation	−8,857	−1,577	45,561	8.47	11.98
998	75	501	FTU	First Union Corporation	−10,412	−1,425	42,965	8.20	11.61
999	1000	527	3VCRIQ	Vencor	−11,877	−1,090	14,896	−1.08	6.22
1000	999	1000	LTR	Loews Corporation	−13,607	−2,546	19,948	−2.42	9.50

Table 4.3 Common-size Balance Sheets for Furniture Brands

	2000	1999
ASSETS		
Current assets		
Cash and cash equivalents	1.2%	0.6%
Accounts receivable	27.0	26.8
Inventories	22.6	22.1
Prepaid expenses and other current assets	2.4	2.6
Total current assets	53.2	52.1
Net Property, plant, and equipment, less accumulated depreciation	23.2	23.1
Intangible assets	22.2	23.5
Other assets	1.5	1.2
Total assets	100.0	100.0
LIABILITIES AND STOCKHOLDERS' EQUITY		
Current liabilities		
Accounts payable	5.0%	5.7%
Accrued expenses	6.0	6.2
Total current liabilities	11.0	11.9
Long-term debt	35.4	41.5
Other long-term liabilities	8.9	9.8
Total liabilities	55.3	63.2
Stockholders' equity (total)	44.7	36.8
Total liabilities and stockholders' equity	100.0	100.0

Table 4.4 Common-size Income Statements for Furniture Brands

	2000	1999
Sales	100.0%	100.0%
Cost of operations	72.3	71.8
Selling, general, and administrative expenses	15.9	15.1
Depreciation and amortization	2.7	2.7
Earnings from operations	7.8	10.1
Interest expense	1.7	1.8
Other income, net	0.5	0.1
Earnings before income tax expense and extraordinary item	7.8	8.5
Income tax expense	2.7	3.1
Earnings before extraordinary item	5.1	5.4
Extraordinary item	.1	-
Net earnings	5.0	5.4

A comparative analysis of the common-size income statements of Furniture Brands for 2000 and 1999 shows a slight increase in the cost of production (cost of operations) and selling, general, and administrative expenses as a percent of sales. The increase in production costs and selling, general, and administrative expenses resulted in the operating profit declining from 10.1 percent of sales in 1999 to 7.8 percent of sales in 2000. Interest expense as a percent of sales declined slightly as a result of the decline in the debt ratio. Net profit declined from 5.4 percent to 5.0 percent of sales, which is consistent with the decline in the operating profit margin.

Comprehension Check Questions

1. How is the DuPont framework useful?
2. What are common-size statements?
3. What is EVA and how is it different from accounting measures of profitability?

SOURCES OF COMPARATIVE FINANCIAL DATA

An analyst may refer to a number of sources of financial data when preparing a comparative financial analysis, including the following:

Dun and Bradstreet. Dun and Bradstreet (D&B) prepares a series of 14 key business ratios for 800 different lines of business based on the SIC codes (a numeric industry classification system). The ratios are based on the financial statements of some 400,000 companies. D&B reports three values for each ratio—the *median*, the *upper quartile*, and the *lower quartile*. The median is the figure that falls in the middle when individual ratios of sampled firms are arranged by size. The figure halfway between the median and the ratio with the highest value is the upper quartile, and the figure halfway between the median and the ratio with the lowest value is the lower quartile. By reporting three values for each ratio, D&B enables the analyst to compare a particular firm with the "average" (median) firm, as well as with the "typical" firms in the top and bottom halves of the sample. The D&B publication containing the data is titled *Industry Norms and Key Business Ratios.*

Risk Management Association (RMA). This national association of bank loan and credit officers uses information provided from loan applications to compile 16 ratios for over 250 lines of business based on the SIC codes. Like D&B, RMA reports the median, upper quartile, and lower quartile for each ratio. Data are presented for four categories of firm size. This source is especially useful to the analyst gathering information about smaller firms. The RMA publication containing the data is titled *Statement Studies.*

Quarterly Financial Report for Manufacturing Companies. The Federal Trade Commission (FTC) and the Securities and Exchange Commission (SEC) cooperate in publishing quarterly reports on balance sheet and income statement data of various manufacturing companies. These include analyses of the firms by industry and asset size, along with presentations of financial statements in ratio form.

Almanac of Business and Industrial Financial Ratios. This annual almanac of business and industrial financial ratios, based on Internal Revenue Service data, reports 22 ratios for many industries. It also includes the number of establishments in the sampled industry, the number without net income, and the total dollar receipts for each of the 13 size groups into which firms in each industry are classified.

Financial Studies of Small Business. This annual publication of Financial Research Associates is particularly valuable for the evaluation of small firms.

Moody's or Standard and Poor's Industrial, Financial, Transportation, and Over-the-Counter Manuals. These contain a large amount of balance sheet and income statement data, as well as other relevant background information about a firm.

Dun and Bradstreet
http://www.dnb.com
Risk Management Association
http://www.rmahq.org

The Federal Trade Commission
http://www.ftc.gov
The Securities and Exchange Commission
http://www.sec.gov

Moody's
http://www.moodys.com
Standard and Poor's
http://www.standardandpoors.com

Table 4.5 Sample Industry Data from Thomson ONE—Business School Edition

Company Ticker	Furniture Brands International Inc U:FBN	Peer Weight	Peer Aggregate	Peer Mean	Peer Median	Peer Std Dev
Last Fiscal Yr End Date	12/31/2002					
Profitability Ratios						
Return on Per Share	14.47	42.73 %	33.86	5.64	14.50	20.22
Return on Assets	8.86	28.55 %	31.03	5.17	7.16	6.71
Cash Flow to Sales	7.62	17.79 %	42.86	7.14	8.49	2.92
Gross Profit Margin	26.14	22.27 %	117.35	19.56	24.50	11.89
Operating Profit Margin	8.44	27.22 %	31.01	5.17	8.58	7.30
Pretax Margin	7.69					
Net Margin	4.96					
Sales per Employee	101,597.84					
Net Income per Employee	0.01					
Asset Utilization Ratios						
Asset Turnover	1.53	18.95 %	8.07	1.35	1.33	0.21
Inventory Turnover	4.29	16.60 %	25.86	4.31	4.08	1.41
Leverage Ratios						
Total Debt to Common Equity	43.10	13.16 %	327.52	54.59	27.08	71.52
LT Debt to Common Equity	43.10	18.51 %	232.86	38.81	22.17	44.72
LT Debt to Total Capital	30.12	22.54 %	133.63	22.27	18.15	17.99
Dividend Payout	0.00	0.00 %	12.12	2.42	0.00	4.85
Cash Dividend Coverage Ratio	n/a	NaN	14.66	7.33	7.33	5.88
Liquidity Ratios						
Quick Ratio	1.98	24.11 %	8.20	1.37	1.40	0.42
Current Ratio	4.30	22.71 %	18.95	3.16	3.20	1.09
Cash and Equivalent to Current Assets	1.77	8.40 %	21.14	3.52	2.37	2.84
Accounts Receivable Days	55.14	15.77 %	349.64	58.27	56.24	13.81
Inventories Days Held	83.83	14.80 %	566.43	94.41	88.36	35.39
Market Value Ratios						
Current P/E Ratio	11.64					
Price/Book Ratio	1.48	16.20 %	9.12	1.52	1.67	0.68
Price/Cash Flow Ratio	8.22	16.26 %	50.57	8.43	8.47	2.48

Annual Reports. Most corporations publish an annual report containing income statement and balance sheet data, along with other information of interest.

10K Reports. Every widely held firm is required annually to file a 10K report with the SEC. These reports contain income statement and balance sheet data, plus a wide range of other relevant information dealing with the firm's past and current performance and expected future prospects.

Trade Journals. These are published by trade associations and contain a great deal of financial and other types of information on member firms.

Commercial Banks. Banks frequently compile financial reports on selected industries.

Computerized Data Sources. A number of computerized databases are also available to assist in financial analysis. The *Research Insight* database is available from Standard and Poor's and widely used in academic institutions and the professional investing community. It contains complete balance sheet, income statement, stock price, and dividend information for several thousand companies, covering a period of up to 20 years. Value Line provides summary financial data and forecasts of future performance for over 1,700 firms. The Value Line database is available in both hard copy and for personal computers. In addition to these Internet sources, students with access to Thomson ONE–Business School Edition can find information on financial ratios for individual firms, as well as for industry groups and other user customized peer groups. Table 4.5, for example, shows key industry financial ratios based on Furniture Brands' SIC industry code (2511) for 2002.

Most of the above data sources can be accessed via the Internet but some may require subscription. There are far too many Internet sources of corporate financial data to enumerate here. The interested student could use any of several popular Internet search engines to locate useful data. For example, by entering the search for financial ratios, most search engines would list from several dozen to hundreds of possible sites. Some of the more popular search engines are: http://www.yahoo.com, http://www.altavista.com, http://www.google.com, and http://www.lycos.com. A few specific sites students may find useful are:

http://www.sec.gov: This is the site of SEC's EDGAR database, which provides access to many of the filings required by the SEC of most publicly held corporations. The forms include the 10K annual and 10Q quarterly filings. Most corporations file these statements electronically; they are available to the public within minutes of filing.

http://www.yahoo.com: The finance section of this Internet portal has many resources to search for a wide variety of financial information including financial statement data, ratios, current and historical prices, corporate news, and much more.

http://www.hoovers.com: Provides corporate history and financial and business information for many corporations. Also provides industry information such as major competitors.

http://www.reportgallery.com: Popular Internet site to search for annual reports that are available online. The site also has links to other popular financial Web sites.

A WORD OF CAUTION ABOUT RATIO ANALYSIS

Throughout the analysis of Furniture Brands International Corporation, we emphasized that an analyst must exercise caution when evaluating a firm's financial ratios. Although ratios can provide valuable information, they also can be misleading for a number of reasons.

First, ratios are only as reliable as the accounting data on which they are based. As noted in the previous chapter, the financial statements of most U.S. companies are prepared in accordance with *generally accepted accounting principles (GAAP)* laid out by the Financial Accounting Standards Board. Even though careful financial analysis can provide excellent insights into the direction and relative strength of the firm, the financial analyst must keep in mind that GAAP gives firms considerable latitude in reporting their financial positions. Different firms follow different accounting procedures for inventory valuation, depreciation, reporting long-term leases, pension fund contributions, and mergers and acquisitions, to name just a few. These, in turn, affect reported earnings, assets, liabilities, and stockholders' equity. Unless the analyst makes adjustments for accounting reporting differences, ratio comparisons between individual companies and with various industry norms cannot be viewed as definitive.

Second, with the exception of disclosing upper and lower quartile values, firms that compile industry norms often do not report information about the *dispersion*, or distribution, of the individual values around the mean ratio. If the reported ratios are dispersed widely, the industry average will be of questionable value, because it may not reflect the "typical" firm in the industry. Furthermore, the standard of comparison probably should not be the "typical" firm but rather the better-performing firms in the industry. Without some measure of dispersion, however, ratios for these better-performing firms cannot be determined.

Third, valid comparative analysis depends on the availability of data for appropriately defined industries. Some industry classifications are either too broad or too narrow to be reliable sources of comparative data when an analyst is evaluating a particular firm. Most firms operate in more than one industry, which makes analysis more difficult. To some extent forming a peer group, as we did for Furniture Brands, may alleviate industry classification problems.

Fourth, it is important to remember that financial ratios provide a *historic* record of the performance and financial condition of a firm. Further analysis is required before this historic record can be used as a basis for *future* projections.

Finally, comparisons of a firm's ratios with industry norms may not always be what they seem. Ratios comparing unfavorably with industry norms should be construed as "red flags" indicating the need for further investigation—not signals of impending doom. On the other hand, even if a firm's ratios compare favorably with those of the better-performing firms in the industry, it does not necessarily mean the firm is performing adequately. If, for example, the industry itself is experiencing a declining demand for its goods and services, favorable ratio comparisons simply may indicate that a firm is not decaying as rapidly as the typical firm in the industry. Thus, comparisons of selected ratios—particularly those relating to profitability—must be made with *national* industry averages in order to determine whether a particular firm in a particular industry is justified in making further investments.

In summary, ratios should not be viewed as substitutes for sound business judgment. Instead, they are simply tools that can help management make better decisions.

1. How can industry classification pose a problem for ratio analysis?
2. Why should we question ratios based on financial statements that use GAAP standards?
3. How does the fact that financial statements are based on historical data pose a limitation on financial ratio analysis?

Summary

➤ Financial ratios are statistical yardsticks that relate two numbers generally taken from a firm's income statements and balance sheets.

➤ Financial ratios fall into five categories:

- Liquidity ratios, which measure a firm's ability to meet its maturing obligations

- Asset management ratios, which measure how efficiently a firm is using resources to generate sales

- Financial leverage management ratios, which indicate a firm's capacity to meet short- and long-term debt obligations

- Profitability ratios, which measure the firm's ability to generate profits on sales, assets, and stockholders' investment

- Market-based ratios, which measure the market's (investors') perceptions of a firm's performance and risk

➤ Trend analysis introduces the element of time into financial ratio analysis. It gives the analyst a more dynamic view of a company's situation than does a pure comparative financial ratio analysis alone.

➤ The relationship of the return on investment (ROI) to "margin" and "turnover" can be used to determine if one or both of the two is deficient in contributing to the profitability of a firm.

➤ Common-size financial statements, which express financial items in percentages, are helpful in detecting and monitoring financial trends.

➤ To gain further insight into the relative financial position of a firm, the analyst must compare the financial ratios with industry averages. The more diversified the firm, the more difficult it will be to make such a comparison. Two major sources of industry ratios are Dun and Bradstreet and Risk Management Association.

➤ Financial ratio analysis is only as good as the quality of the financial statements on which it is based.

➤ The Economic Value Added (EVA®) is a measure of performance developed by Stern Stewart & Company. It compares the dollar return generated by the firm to the return expected by the investors in the various sources of capital utilized by the firm.

Questions and Topics for Discussion

1. What are the primary limitations of ratio analysis as a technique of financial statement analysis?

2. What is the major limitation of the current ratio as a measure of a firm's liquidity? How may this limitation be overcome?

3. What problems may be indicated by an average collection period that is substantially above or below the industry average?

4. What problems may be indicated by an inventory turnover ratio that is substantially above or below the industry average?

5. What factors limit the use of the fixed asset turnover ratio in comparative analyses?

6. Why are there separate asset structure ratios for inventory, fixed assets, and accounts receivable?

7. Are higher current, quick, inventory turnover, fixed asset turnover, and total asset turnover ratios better than lower ones?

8. What are the three most important determinants of a firm's return on stockholders' equity?

9. What specific effects can the use of alternative accounting procedures have on the validity of comparative financial analyses?

10. What is the relationship between a firm's P/E multiple and that firm's risk and growth potential?

11. Discuss the general factors that influence the quality of a company's reported earnings and its balance sheet.

12. Why would you anticipate a lower P/E ratio for a typical natural gas utility than for a computer technology firm, such as Dell Computer?

13. According to the DuPont framework, can a firm show a stable ROE pattern despite declining net profit margins and total asset turnovers? Explain.

14. How is Economic Value Added (EVA) different from accounting measures of profitability?

Self-Test Problems

The following financial data for the Freemont Corporation are to be used in answering the first six self-test problems.

Balance Sheet ($000)

Assets		Liabilities & Stockholders' Equity	
Cash	$ 1,500	Accounts payable	$12,500
Marketable securities	2,500	Notes payable	12,500
Accounts receivable	15,000	Total current liabilities	$25,000
Inventory	33,000	Long-term debt	22,000
Total current assets	$52,000	Total liabilities	$47,000
Fixed assets (net)	35,000	Common stock (par value)	5,000
Total assets	$87,000	Contributed capital in excess of par	18,000
		Retained earnings	17,000
		Total stockholders' equity	$40,000
		Total liabilities and stockholders' equity	$87,000

Income Statement ($000)

Sales (all on credit)	$130,000
Cost of sales	103,000
Gross margin	27,000
Operating expenses*	16,000
Earnings before interest and taxes	$ 11,000
Interest expense	3,000
Earnings before taxes	$ 8,000
Income tax	3,000
Earnings after taxes	$ 5,000

*includes $200 (000) in lease payments.

Other Information

Stock price	$ 9.50
Book value per share	$ 8.00
Number of shares	5,000(000)

ST1. Calculate the following liquidity ratios:

   a. Current ratio

   b. Quick ratio

ST2. Calculate the following asset management ratios:

   a. Average collection period

   b. Inventory turnover

   c. Fixed asset turnover

   d. Total asset turnover

ST3. Calculate the following financial leverage management ratios:

   a. Debt ratio

   b. Debt-to-equity ratio

   c. Times interest earned ratio

   d. Fixed-charge coverage ratio

ST4. Calculate the following profitability ratios:

   a. Gross profit margin

   b. Net profit margin

   c. Return on investment

   d. Return on stockholders' equity

ST5. Calculate the following market-based ratios:

   a. Price-to-earnings ratio

   b. Market price-to-book value ratio

ST6. Express the return on investments as a function of the net profit margin and the total asset turnover ratio. Next, calculate the return on stockholders' equity ratio as a function of the net profit margin, total asset turnover, and equity multiplier ratios.

Problems

1. Vanity Press, Inc. has annual sales of $1,600,000 (assume all sales are on credit) and a gross profit margin of 35 percent.

   BASIC

   a. If the firm wishes to maintain an average collection period of 50 days, what level of accounts receivable should it carry? (Assume a 365-day year.)

   b. The inventory turnover for this industry averages six times. What average level of inventory should the firm maintain to achieve the same inventory turnover figure as the industry?

2. Pacific Fixtures lists the following accounts as part of its balance sheet.

   BASIC

Total assets	$10,000,000
Accounts payable	$ 2,000,000
Notes payable (8%)	1,000,000
Long-term debt (10%)	3,000,000
Common stock at par	1,000,000
Contributed capital in excess of par	500,000
Retained earnings	2,500,000
Total liabilities and stockholders' equity	$10,000,000

   Compute the return on stockholders' equity if the company has sales of $20 million and the following net profit margin:

   a. 3 percent

   b. 5 percent

3. Clovis Industries had sales in 20X1 of $40 million, 20 percent of which were cash. If Clovis normally carries 45 days of credit sales in accounts receivable, what are its average accounts receivable balances? (Assume a 365-day year.)

   BASIC

4. Williams Oil Company had a return on stockholders' equity of 18 percent during 20X1. Its total asset turnover was 1.0 times, and its equity multiplier was 2.0 times. Calculate the company's net profit margin.

   BASIC

5. Using the data in the following table for a number of firms in the same industry, do the following:

   CHALLENGE

   a. Compute the total asset turnover, the net profit margin, the equity multiplier, and the return on equity for each firm.

   b. Evaluate each firm's performance by comparing the firms with one another. Which firm or firms appear to be having problems? What corrective action would you suggest the poorer performing firms take? Finally, what additional data would you want to have on hand when conducting your analyses?

	Firms			
(millions of dollars)	A	B	C	D
Sales	$20	$10	$15	$25
Net income after tax	3	0.5	2.25	3
Total assets	15	7.5	15	24
Stockholders' equity	10	5.0	14	10

6. Tarheel Furniture Company is planning to establish a wholly owned subsidiary to manufacture upholstery fabrics. Tarheel expects to earn $1 million after taxes on the venture during the first year. The president of Tarheel wants to know what the subsidiary's balance sheet would look like. The president believes that it would be advisable to begin the new venture with ratios that are similar to the industry average.

Tarheel plans to make all sales on credit. All calculations assume a 365-day year. In your computations, you should round all numbers to the nearest $1,000. Based upon the industry average financial ratios presented here, complete the projected balance sheet for Tarheel's upholstery subsidiary.

Industry Averages

Current ratio	2:1
Quick ratio	1:1
Net profit margin ratio	5 percent
Average collection period	20 days
Debt ratio	40 percent
Total asset ratio	2 times

Forecasted Upholstery Subsidiary Balance Sheet

Cash	_____	Total current liabilities	_____
Accounts receivable	_____	Long-term debt	_____
Inventory	_____	Total debt	_____
Total current assets	_____	Stockholders' equity	_____
Net fixed assets	_____	Total liabilities and	
Total assets	_____	stockholders' equity	_____

7. The Jamesway Printing Corporation has current assets of $3.0 million. Of this total, $1.0 million is inventory, $0.5 million is cash, $1.0 million is accounts receivable, and the balance is marketable securities. Jamesway has $1.5 million in current liabilities.

a. What are the current and the quick ratios for Jamesway?

b. If Jamesway takes $0.25 million in cash and pays off $0.25 million of current liabilities, what happens to its current and quick ratios? What happens to its real liquidity?

c. If Jamesway sells $0.5 million of its accounts receivable to a factor (a type of specialized financial institution that buys accounts receivable; for details see Chapter 17) and uses the proceeds to pay off short-term debt obligations, what happens to its current and quick ratios?

d. If Jamesway sells $1.0 million in new stock and places the proceeds in marketable securities, what happens to its current and quick ratios?

e. What do these examples illustrate about the current and quick ratios?

8. Gulf Controls, Inc., has a net profit margin of 10 percent and earnings after taxes of $600,000. Its current balance sheet follows:

Current assets	$1,800,000	Current liabilities	$ 600,000
Fixed assets	2,200,000	Long-term debt	1,000,000
Total assets	$4,000,000	Common stock	500,000
		Retained earnings	1,900,000
		Total liabilities and stockholders' equity	$4,000,000

a. Calculate Gulf's return on stockholders' equity.

b. The industry average ratios are as follows:

Net profit margin	6 percent
Total asset turnover	2.5 times
Equity multiplier	1.4 times

Compare Gulf Controls with the average firm in the industry. What is the source of the major differences between the Gulf and the industry average ratios?

9. Using the following data for Jackson Products Company, answer Parts a through g:

CHALLENGE

Jackson Products Company's Balance Sheet
December 31, 20X1

Cash	$ 240,000	Accounts payable	$ 380,000
Accounts receivable	320,000	Notes payable (9%)	420,000
Inventory	1,040,000	Other current liabilities	50,000
Total current assets	$1,600,000	Total current liabilities	$ 850,000
Net plant and equipment	800,000	Long-term debt (10%)	800,000
Total assets	$2,400,000	Stockholders' equity	750,000
		Total liabilities and stockholders' equity	$ 2,400,000

Income Statement for the Year Ended
December 31, 20X1

Net sales (all on credit)	$3,000,000
Cost of sales	1,800,000
Gross profit	$1,200,000
Selling, general, and administrative expenses	860,000
Earnings before interest and taxes	$ 340,000
Interest:	
Notes	$37,800
Long-term debt	80,000
Total interest charges	117,800
Earnings before taxes	$ 222,200
Federal income tax (40%)	88,880
Earnings after taxes	$ 133,320

Industry Averages

Current ratio	2.5 times
Quick ratio	1.1 times
Average collection period (365-day year)	35 days
Inventory turnover ratio	2.4 times
Total asset turnover ratio	1.4 times
Times interest earned ratio	3.5 times
Net profit margin ratio	4.0 percent
Return on investment ratio	5.6 percent
Total assets/stockholders' equity (equity multiplier) ratio	3.0 times
Return on stockholders' equity ratio	16.8 percent
P/E ratio	9.0 times

a. Evaluate the liquidity position of Jackson relative to that of the average firm in the industry. Consider the current ratio, the quick ratio, and the net working capital (current assets minus current liabilities) for Jackson. What problems, if any, are suggested by this analysis?

b. Evaluate Jackson's performance by looking at key asset management ratios. Are any problems apparent from this analysis?

c. Evaluate the financial risk of Jackson by examining its times interest earned ratio and its equity multiplier ratio relative to the same industry average ratios.

d. Evaluate the profitability of Jackson relative to that of the average firm in its industry.

e. Give an overall evaluation of the performance of Jackson relative to other firms in its industry.

f. Perform a DuPont analysis on ROI and ROE for Jackson. What areas appear to have the greatest need for improvement?

g. Jackson's current P/E ratio is 7 times. What factor(s) are most likely to account for this ratio relative to the higher industry average ratio?

INTERMEDIATE　**10.** Given the following data for Profiteers, Inc., and the corresponding industry averages, perform a trend analysis of the return on investment and the return on stockholders' equity. Plot the data and discuss any trends that are apparent. Also, discuss the underlying causes of these trends.

Years	20X1	20X2	20X3	20X4	20X5
Profiteers, Inc.					
Net profit margin	14%	12%	11%	9%	10%
Asset turnover	1.26x	1.22x	1.20x	1.19x	1.21x
Equity multiplier	1.34x	1.40x	1.61x	1.65x	1.63x

Years	20X1	20X2	20X3	20X4	20X5
Industry Averages					
Net profit margin	12%	11%	11%	10%	10%
Asset turnover	1.25x	1.27x	1.30x	1.31x	1.34x
Equity multiplier	1.42x	1.45x	1.47x	1.51x	1.53x

CHALLENGE　**11.** If a company sells additional common stock and uses the proceeds to increase its inventory level and to increase its cash balances, what is the near-term (immediate) impact (increase, decrease, no change) of this transaction on the following ratios?

a. Current ratio

b. Return on stockholders' equity

c. Quick ratio

d. Debt to total assets

e. Total asset turnover

12. Keystone Resources has a net profit margin of 8 percent and earnings after taxes of $2 million. Its current balance sheet is as follows: **INTERMEDIATE**

Current assets	$ 6,000,000	Current liabilities	$ 3,500,000
Fixed assets	10,000,000	Long-term debt	5,500,000
Total assets	$16,000,000	Common stock	2,000,000
		Retained earnings	5,000,000
		Total liabilities and stockholders' equity	$16,000,000

   a. Calculate Keystone's return on stockholders' equity.

   b. Industry average ratios are

Net profit margin	10%
Total asset turnover	2.0 times
Equity multiplier	1.5 times

   What does a comparison of Keystone to these averages indicate about the firm's strengths and weaknesses?

   c. Keystone has inventories of $3.2 million. Compute the firm's quick ratio.

13. The stock of Jenkins Corporation, a major steel producer, currently is selling for $50 per share. The book value per share is $125. In contrast, the price per share of Dataquest's stock is $40, compared to a book value per share of $10. Dataquest, a leading software developer, has a copyright on the best-selling database management program. Why do these two firms have such dramatically different market-to-book ratios? **BASIC**

14. Fill in the balance sheet for the Jamestown Company presented below based on the following data (assume a 365-day year): **INTERMEDIATE**

Sales	$3,650,000
Total asset turnover	4x
Current ratio	3.1
Quick ratio	2:1
Current liabilities to stockholders' equity	30%
Average collection period	20 days
Total debt to total assets	0.4

Balance Sheet

Cash	_____	Accounts payable	_____
Accounts receivable	_____	Total current liabilities	_____
Inventory	_____	Long-term debt	_____
Total current assets	_____	Stockholders' equity	_____
Fixed assets	_____		
Total assets	_____	Total liabilities and equity	_____

CHALLENGE **15.** The Southwick Company has the following balance sheet ($000):

Assets		Liabilities & Stockholders' Equity	
Cash	$ 500	Accounts payable	$ 1,750
Marketable securities	750	Notes payable	1,250
Accounts receivable	2,000	Total current liabilities	$ 3,000
Inventory	2,500	Long-term debt	1,750
Total current assets	$ 5,750	Total liabilities	$ 4,750
Plant and equipment (net)	5,000	Common stock ($1 par)	1,000
Total assets	$10,750	Contributed capital in excess of par	2,000
		Retained earnings	3,000
		Total stockholders' equity	$ 6,000
		Total liabilities and stockholders' equity	$10,750

Financial Ratios

Current ratio	1.92
Quick ratio	1.08
Debt-to-equity ratio	0.79

Evaluate the impact of each of the following (independent) financial decisions on Southwick's current, quick, and debt-to-equity ratios:

a. The firm reduces its inventories by $500,000 through more efficient inventory management procedures and invests the proceeds in marketable securities.

b. The firm decides to purchase 20 new delivery trucks for a total of $500,000 and pays for them by selling marketable securities.

c. The firm borrows $500,000 from its bank through a short-term loan (seasonal financing) and invests the proceeds in inventory.

d. Southwick borrows $2,000,000 from its bank through a 5-year loan (interest due annually, principal due at maturity) and uses the proceeds to expand its plant.

e. The firm sells $2,000,000 (net) in common stock and uses the proceeds to expand its plant.

INTERMEDIATE **16.** Armbrust Corporation is the maker of fine fitness equipment. Armbrust's bank has been pressuring the firm to improve its liquidity. Which of the following actions proposed by the CFO do you believe will actually achieve this objective? Why or why not?

a. Sell new equity and use the proceeds to purchase a new plant site.

b. Use cash and marketable securities to pay off short-term bank borrowings and accounts payable.

c. Borrow long-term and use the proceeds to pay off short-term debt.

d. Sell surplus fixed assets and invest the proceeds in marketable securities.

BASIC **17.** From Stern Stewart's Web site (http://www.sternstewart.com) identify the five best performing firms in terms of EVAs and the five worst performing firms. Do the same with MVAs.

18. Go to finance page of Yahoo!'s Web site (http://www.yahoo.com) and update the ratio analysis for Furniture Brands using data for the latest year available. The data to calculate the ratios can be found in the financials section. Make sure you request the annual data (not quarterly). Specifically calculate the following ratios for Furniture Brands and compare them to those presented in the chapter for year 2000:

Current ratio

Total asset turnover

Average collection period

Debt ratio

Gross profit margin

Net profit margin

Return on investment

Return on stockholders' equity

THOMSON ONE—Business School Edition

Go to the text Web site at http://moyer.swlearning.com, select your book, and click on the Thomson ONE button. Enter Thomson ONE—Business School Edition by using the username and password you created when you registered the serial number on your access card. Use the "Financials" tab and the "Growth Ratios" menu item (Worldscope Annual Growth Ratios) from the Thomson ONE database to determine the following information for Adolph Coors, Inc (RKY):

a. What has been the trend in debt usage by the company over the past 5 years?

b. What has been the trend in "asset turnover" over the past 5 years?

c. What has been the trend in "accounts receivable days" over the past 5 years?

d. What has been the trend in "return on total equity" over the past 5 years?

e. How would you characterize the performance of Adolph Coors over the past 5 years?

DETERMINANTS OF VALUATION

PART TWO

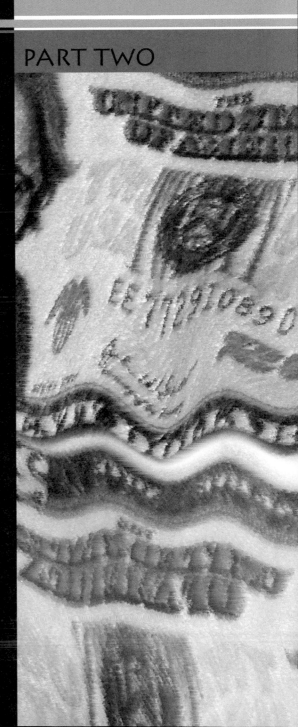

Valuation is the central theme of financial management and finance in general. Chapter 5 develops the concept of the time value of money. This concept is used in the valuation of securities and the evaluation of investment projects expected to provide benefits over a number of years. Chapter 6 provides a comprehensive introduction to the concept of risk in finance and the relationship between risk amd required return. Chapter 7 discusses long term debt including the characteristics of long term debt and the valuation of bonds. Chapter 8 deals with the valuation of common stocks and preferred stocks.

CHAPTER
5 The Time Value of Money

An understanding of the time value of money is important for businesses as well as individuals: Both must make investment decisions and choose among alternatives that have varying cash flow patterns over time.

To illustrate the importance of time value of money, let us assume that you are confronted with the choice of investing in three alternatives with the following cash flow benefits over a 3-year period:

Year	A	B	C
1	$20	$0	$0
2	20	0	0
3	20	60	70

Let us also assume that the risk associated with these alternatives is identical. Alternative A is expected to generate cash flows of $20 each year for 3 years, alternative B has no payoffs in the first 2 years but is expected to generate $60 in year 3, while alternative C is similar to B except that the payoff in year 3 is $70. By comparing A and B it is evident that a rational individual would choose A over B. Although the total cash flow benefit is the same for A and B, alternative A generates the cash flows earlier relative to B.

Choosing between A and B was fairly easy; now let us compare A and C. It is apparent that the choice between A and C is not all that clear. Although A has cash flows each year that sum to $60, C has a single cash flow of $70 in year 3. Your preference for A or C would depend upon whether or not A's cash flows in year 1 and 2 can be invested to yield a total cash flow at the end of year 3 that exceeds the cash flow from alternative C in year 3. Whether this is possible would depend on the interest rate at which you can invest the funds.

The above example is typical of the decisions firms and individuals have to make. Businesses have to make investment decisions that require huge outlays today in exchange for future benefits. For example, DaimlerChrysler may decide to refurbish its plant in Toledo, Ohio that manufactures Jeep Grand Cherokees. This would entail a major commitment *now* for savings in the *future*. In making this decision management would have to figure what these *future savings are worth in terms of today's dollars* and compare it to the *outlay required today for the renovation*. Alternatively, the firm can calculate the returns implied in the savings given the investment required, and compare that to returns the company can generate if the money were put to use elsewhere.

Individuals are confronted with similar decisions. For example, in purchasing an automobile you may have several options for financing. A dealer may give you the choice of a loan or a lease option with different cash flow patterns. Another example is an investment decision that requires choosing between a ***zero coupon bond*** and a bond with annual coupon payments—again with different cash flow patterns over time. The concepts in this chapter are applied by businesses and individuals to make meaningful comparisons among alternatives with varying cash flow patterns over time.

Although an understanding of the time value of money is useful in and of itself, it also is a necessary prelude to the following topics:

➢ Valuation of securities and other assets
➢ Capital budgeting (the analysis of long term corporate investments)
➢ Cost of capital
➢ Working capital (short-term asset and liability) management

By putting effort into a careful reading and a mastery of concepts in this chapter, you will find that tackling the topics listed above and discussed throughout this book will be that much easier.

Chapter Objectives

After reading this chapter, you should have an understanding of the following:

1. The meaning of interest and discount rates

2. The concept of future and present values and how to calculate these values

3. The meaning and implication of compounding and compounding frequency

4. How to calculate the future and present values of an annuity and the present value of a perpetuity

5. The meaning and calculation of effective interest rates

6. The application of present and future value concepts to special situations such as growth rates and loan amortization

THE USE OF FINANCIAL CALCULATORS AND SPREADSHEETS

The concepts in this chapter are illustrated using four methods: Time value of money problems may be solved using *mathematical formulas, special interest factor tables* provided at the end of the textbook, *financial calculators,* and *spreadsheet software.* The serious business student should plan on becoming adept at the use of financial calculators and spreadsheet software, such as Microsoft Excel, to solve time value of money problems efficiently. Spreadsheet software also has many applications across all business disciplines. In addition to applications in this chapter, spreadsheets are useful in solving *security valuation, capital budgeting,* and *financial forecasting problems.* Most employers consider it an asset if a potential employee is already familiar with the use of spreadsheets.

While the use of financial calculators and spreadsheets are encouraged, we urge students to familiarize themselves as well with the formulas and the use of the tables in solving the basic time value of money problems. Solving problems initially by using formulas and the tables provides a better appreciation of what is happening on a conceptual level. We have found that going straight to the calculators or to spreadsheets often results in students thinking in mechanical terms—inputting numbers into a calculator or a spreadsheet with little appreciation for what it is you are really trying to do in the problem.

If you need to calculate present value and future value but don't have access to a handheld calculator or a spreadsheet, try one of many Web sites that have built-in time-value calculators, such as the one at Salem Five.
http://www.salemfive.com

Calculator Solution

The calculator solutions are illustrated in special boxes throughout the chapter. The same basic steps are involved regardless of which financial calculator you use. There are five basic keys that are utilized for solving time value of money problems. You can think of each key as a specific variable. While the location and specific notation may vary between calculators, usually the five keys are grouped together.

The five basic keys are:

N	I/Y	PV	PMT	FV

N	= Number of periods
I/Y	= Interest rate per period
PV	= Present value amount
PMT	= Payment
FV	= Future value amount

Calculator Solution

As a general guideline, you should do the following before using a financial calculator to solve a time value of money problem:

1. Set number of payments per year to 1.
2. Clear the time value of money registers so that values held over from a previous problem do not affect your current calculations.
3. Set payments to end-of-period mode.
4. Some calculators are preset to display only two decimal places; while this may be sufficient in most instances, we suggest removing this feature, to use floating-decimal.

Spreadsheet Solution

Spreadsheet solutions are presented for selected problems in special boxes throughout the chapter. Although a variety of spreadsheets exist, we will be illustrating problems in this chapter using Microsoft Excel. Spreadsheets are simply a series of the rows and columns making up a matrix of cells. The rows are identified by numbers while the columns are referenced by alphabetical characters. A sample spreadsheet is shown here:

	A	B	C	D	E	F	G	H
2								
3								
4								
5								
6								
7								
8								
9								
10								
11								
12								
13								
14								
15								
16								
17								
18								
19								

Spreadsheet strategies

Individual cells are identified by the row and column in which they are located, for example, the highlighted cell in the sample spreadsheet above is B4—column B, row 4. The cells may contain text material, numbers, or formulas. In solving time value of money problems we will be using several time value of money *functions* built into the spreadsheet software. Functions are formulas built into the spreadsheet, sparing us the need to actually enter the formulas. The functions we will be using are:

PV—to calculate present value

FV—to calculate future value

PMT—to calculate payments

NPER—to calculate the number of periods

RATE—to calculate the interest rate or discount rate

These functions are used to calculate the corresponding variable given other known values for the problem.

THE CONCEPTS OF INTEREST, FUTURE VALUE, AND PRESENT VALUE

This chapter is titled "Time Value of Money" for a good reason. Money can be thought of as having a **time value.** In other words, *an amount of money received today is worth more than the same dollar amount if it were received a year from now.* The primary reason for this is that the current dollar can be invested to earn a rate of return. (This holds true even if risk and inflation are not considerations.) Suppose, for example, that you had $100 and decided to put it into a savings account for a year. By doing this, you temporarily give up, or forgo, spending the $100 however you wished, or you might forgo the return that the $100 might earn from some alternative investment, such as U.S. Treasury bonds. Similarly, a bank that loans money to a firm forgoes the opportunity to earn a return on some alternative investment.

Interest is the return earned by or the amount paid to someone who has forgone current consumption or alternative investment opportunities and "rented" money in a creditor relationship. *Interest rate* refers to interest stated on a percentage basis and is usually stated on a per annum (year) basis. Sometimes the interest rate is referred to by other names including **opportunity rate, discount rate,** and **required rate of return.**

This chapter is basically concerned with two concepts—*future value* and **present value.** In *future value* you are interested in finding out the value at some point in the future of a deposit made today or of a series of deposits to be made in the future. Since these deposits are assumed to earn a rate of interest, we know that the future value of a deposit or a series of deposits to be made will equal more than the simple sum of all the deposits. The *present value* concept is the mirror image of the future value concept. In a present value you are interested in finding out the value today of a cash flow or a series of cash flows to be received in the future. Given the concept of interest, we know that a dollar to be received in the future is worth less than a dollar today, therefore, the present value of a cash flow or a series of cash flows in the future will be less than the simple sum of these cash flows.

Comprehension Check Questions

1. Why is it said that money has "time value"?

2. How are the terms interest and interest rate different?

3. What is the basic difference between future value and present value?

FUTURE VALUE OF A SINGLE CASH FLOW

e-Lecture

The future value of a single cash flow answers the question: *How much will money deposited today be worth at some specified time in the future at a given interest rate?* For example, assume that Jerry Jones deposits $1,000 in a savings account paying 6 percent interest compounded annually and that you wish to find out the value of his deposit at the end of 1 year. Before we can tackle this problem we need to understand the notion of *compounding.* **Compound interest** is interest earned not only on the initial deposit (or the **principal,** in this case the $1,000) *but also on interest.* Therefore, when making a deposit that earns a given interest rate per year, the future value consists of three components: (1) the *principal value* (or initial deposit), (2) the *interest on the original principal* (this is also known as **simple interest**), and (3) *interest on interest.* For now, in our Jerry Jones example, we will assume that interest is compounded *annually,* paid once at the end of each year. Later, we will consider situations where interest is compounded more frequently—say, every 6 months or every month.

Going back to our example, if Jerry leaves the $1,000 deposit for 1 year, at the end of the year he will get back the principal and the interest on the principal. There will be no interest on interest component since the deposit is kept for only

1 year and we are assuming annual compounding (interest is paid only once a year). Specifically, the future value at the end of 1 year will equal:

$$FV_1 = PV_0(1 + i) \qquad (5.1)$$
$$= \$1,000(1 + 0.06)$$
$$= \$1,000 + \$60$$
$$= \$1,060$$

where FV_1 stands for the future value at the end of first period (year 1), PV_0 is the present value at time 0 (or principal amount), and i is the interest rate per year. Note that the future value at the end of year 1 is composed of the principal or initial deposit ($1,000) and the simple interest on the principal ($60).

Let's now illustrate the above example using a *time line,* a very useful device for illustrating and solving time value of money problems. You will find that the time line helps to eliminate much confusion and makes solving problems much easier. For the above example, the time line is drawn as follows:

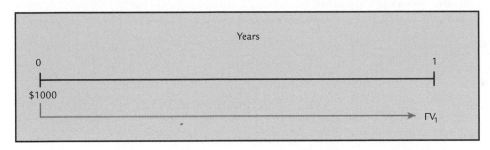

A time line, as the phrase denotes, is a line drawn in time space with tick marks denoting the time periods. The tick marks denote the end of each time period, which may be yearly, as in this case, or it may represent some other interval, such as quarterly or semiannual periods. Also shown on the time line are the relevant cash flows. At time 0 (now) a deposit of $1,000 ($PV_0$) is shown. At the end of time period 1 the future value of the deposit (FV_1) is shown as an unknown. Notice that we have an arrow going to the right from the time 0 deposit ($1,000) to the unknown future value in time period 1 (FV_1), indicating that we wish to find the future value of the deposit.

Now, let us consider what happens if Jerry leaves the principal plus the accumulated interest in the account an additional year. The future value at the end of second year is calculated as follows:

$$FV_2 = FV_1(1 + i) \qquad (5.2)$$
$$= \$1,060(1 + 0.06)$$
$$= \$1,060 + \$63.60$$
$$= \$1,123.60$$

Note that the interest earned in year 2, $63.60, consists of simple interest (interest on original principal) of $60 ($1,000 × .06) and interest on first year's interest of $3.60 ($60 × .06). Thus, FV_2 can be broken down into the following three components:

1. Principal $\qquad\qquad\qquad\qquad\qquad\qquad = \$\quad 1,000$
2. Simple interest for 2 years = $1,000 × .06 × 2 $\quad = \$\quad\quad 120$
3. Interest on interest earned in year 1 = $60 × .06 = $\underline{\$\quad\quad 3.60}$
$$FV_2 = \$1,123.60$$

Let's extend the above example to year 3. If Jerry makes no withdrawals from the account for another year, it will total the following at the end of the third year:

(5.3)
$$FV_3 = FV_2(1 + i)$$
$$= \$1,123.60(1 + 0.06)$$
$$= \$1,191.02$$

The future value at the end of year 3, $1,191.02, consists of $1,000.00 in original principal, $180.00 in simple interest, and $11.02 in interest on interest. The simple interest consists of the interest on the original principal earned in each of the 3 years: $60 × .06 × 3 = $180.00. The interest on interest consists of the interest earned on interest in year 3: $123.60 × .06 = $7.42, plus the interest earned on interest in year 2: $60 × 0.06 = $3.60, or a total of $11.02.

From the preceding example, we can now develop a general formula for computing the future value of any given present value amount compounded at a given interest rate for a given length of time. Substituting Equation 5.2 into Equation 5.3 yields the following equation:

$$FV_3 = FV_1(1 + i)\,(1 + i)$$

(5.4) or

$$FV_3 = FV_1(1 + i)^2$$

Substituting Equation 5.1 into Equation 5.4 yields the following:

$$FV_3 = PV_0(1 + i)\,(1 + i)^2$$

(5.5) or

$$FV_3 = PV_0(1 + i)^3$$

It is apparent that the above equation can be further generalized to calculate the future value at the end of period n for any payment compounded at interest rate i:

$$FV_n = PV_0(1 + i)^n$$

To gain familiarity with the Equation 5.6, let us solve the following example: What is the future value at the end of year 20 of a savings deposit of $1,000 made today if interest is compounded annually at 6 percent? Plugging in the known values into Equation 5.6, we have:

$$FV_{20} = \$1,000(1 + .06)^{20}$$
$$= \$1,000(3.207)$$
$$= \$3,207$$

Thus, at the end of 20 years, your original deposit of $1,000 has accumulated to $3,207. Note from the above steps that the figure 3.207 is the result of raising 1.06 to the power of 20. On a calculator it is obtained by raising 1.06 to the power of 20. Most calculators have a power key usually labeled y^x. You would enter 1.06, then press the y^x key and then enter 20. Upon pressing the = key you should get the resulting answer. The 3.207 figure has a special significance; it is the *future value interest factor* for 6 percent and 20 periods (years). The future value interest factor is a number that tells you how much $1 would be worth at some point in the future, if it were compounded at some given rate of interest. Thus, $1 today compounded at 6 percent would be worth $3.207 at the end of 20 years. Therefore, if we deposit $1,000 today, it would be worth $1,000 × 3.207 or $3,207 in 20 years.

As an alternative to the mathematical formula for calculating the future value of a single cash flow presented in Equation 5.6, we can use a formula employing specially constructed tables containing future value interest factors. From our discussion above, we noted that $(1 + i)^n$ is the future value interest factor at a rate i for n periods. Consequently, Equation 5.6 may be rewritten as follows:

$$FV_n = PV_0(FVIF_{i, n}) \qquad \text{(5.7)}$$

where FVIF is the future value interest factor, $i =$ the interest rate per period, and $n =$ the number of periods.

Table I at the end of the book provides a listing of future value interest factors for various interest rates covering up to 60 periods (for now we will assume that each period pertains to a year). A portion of Table I is reproduced as Table 5.1. Table 5.1 can be used to determine the value of $1,000 compounded at 6 percent for 20 years:

$$FV_{20} = PV_0(FVIF_{6, 20})$$
$$= \$1,000 \ (3.207)$$
$$= \$3,207$$

The 3.207 figure is arrived at by reading down the 6 percent column and across the 20 row under the "End of Period(n)" heading to where they meet.

We can also solve the future value of a single sum using the financial calculator. Recall that the five basic time value of money keys on the calculator are:

N	I/Y	PV	PMT	FV

Solving future value of a single sum requires that we use all of the above keys except PMT. Continuing with the same example, we *enter the known values* for number of periods (N), interest rate per period (I/Y) and the present value (PV). We then *compute for the unknown future value.*

Enter:	20	6	−1,000
	N	I/Y	PV

Compute: FV = 3,207.14

Calculator

Solution

Note that the answer using the calculator, $3,207.14, is slightly different from the $3,207 obtained using the interest factor tables. The difference is attributable to the rounding error in the interest factor tables, which are rounded to three decimal places. Also note that in solving the problem on a financial calculator the pres-ent value or principal amount is entered as a negative value. In using a financial calculator it is important to keep in mind that cash flows should be entered with the "correct" sign. *Cash outflows are considered to be negative while cash inflows are considered to be positive.* Thus, any outflows are reflected in the calculator as negative values. In our example the savings deposit in year 0 is considered a cash outflow from the individual hence PV is −1,000. The computed future value, $3,207.14, on the other hand is returned as a positive sum denoting that it is a cash inflow to the individual. If we were to enter the present value amount as a positive figure (1,000), then the

Table 5.1 Future Value Interest Factors (FVIFs) for $1 at Interest Rate *i* for *n* Periods*

End of Period (*n*)	Interest Rate (*i*)				
	1%	**5%**	**6%**	**8%**	**10%**
1	1.010	1.050	1.060	1.080	1.100
2	1.020	1.102	1.124	1.166	1.210
3	1.030	1.158	1.191	1.260	1.331
4	1.041	1.216	1.262	1.360	1.464
5	1.051	1.276	1.338	1.469	1.611
8	1.083	1.477	1.594	1.851	2.144
9	1.094	1.551	1.689	**1.999**	2.358
10	1.105	**1.629**	1.791	2.159	2.594
20	1.220	2.653	**3.207**	4.661	6.728
25	1.282	3.386	4.292	6.848	10.835

*The values in this and similar tables in this text have been rounded off to three places. When large sums of money are involved, more accurate tables or financial calculators should be used.

calculator would return the future value as a negative sum (−3,207.14). So using the "wrong" sign for present value does not do any serious harm as long we realize that the resulting future value would have the "incorrect" sign.

The solution itself is unaffected as long as we remember to interpret the final answer using the correct sign. However, entering cash flows with the correct signing convention becomes critical later on when we deal with problems involving multiple cash flows with different signs. Using incorrect signs when dealing with complex cash flows will result in answers that are numerically wrong. *It is therefore worthwhile to make it a habit to enter values into the calculator with the appropriate sign: + for inflows and − for outflows.* Note that by default all values entered are assumed to be positive, so only the negative values need to be preceded by the minus sign.

Compound Interest and Future Value

From our preceding examples you may have noticed that the interest-on-interest component of the future value becomes larger as we leave the deposit in the account for a longer period of time. To further illustrate the impact of compounding, in Figure 5.1 we decompose the future value into its constituent elements—principal, simple interest, and interest on interest—for an initial deposit of $1,000 left in an account earning 6 percent per year for various lengths of time.

From Figure 5.1 it is apparent that the *longer you leave the deposit in the interest bearing account, the bigger is the proportion of the interest on interest on the future value.* At the end of 5 years, the interest on interest component accounts for only 3 percent of the future value of $1,338—($38/$1,338) × 100%—but at the end of 25 years the interest on interest portion has become the dominant component accounting for 42 percent of the total ending value of $4,292—($1,792/$4,292) × 100%. This illustrates why personal financial planners urge individuals to make regular, even if small, contributions toward their retirement because the power of compounding can translate even modest savings into a fairly substantial amount in the future.

The compounding effect will be bigger for higher interest rates and, conversely, smaller for lower interest rates. This is illustrated in Figure 5.2.

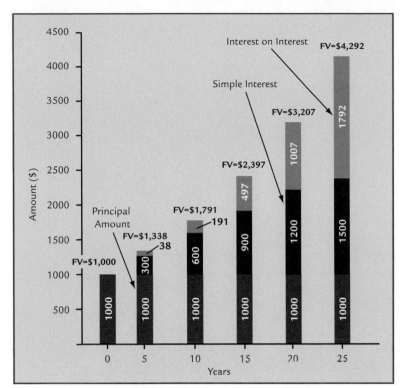

Figure 5.1
Effect of Compounding Over Time of a $1,000 Initial Deposit at 6 Percent Interest per Year (Figures rounded to nearest dollar)

Solving for the Interest Rate

In some problems, the present value (PV_0) and future value (FV_n) are given and the object is to determine the interest rate (i). For example, you are presented with the opportunity to invest $1,000 today in exchange for receiving $1,629 at the end of 10 years. Before you decide to part with the $1,000 you would like to know what rate or return you are expected to make. To solve this problem you can enter the known values for PV, FV_n, and n in Equation 5.6 and solve for i mathematically. However, it would be much easier to solve for i using Equation 5.7 and the tables, or using the calculator. Substituting the known values into Equation 5.7, we have:

$$\$1,629 = \$1,000 \ (FVIF_{i,\,10})$$

$$FVIF_{i,\,10} = \frac{\$1,629}{\$1,000}$$

$$FVIF_{i,\,10} = 1.629$$

Next, we look up 1.629 in the future value interest factor tables (Table 5.1 or Table I on the insert to this book) across the row labeled 10 (for 10 years) and read off the corresponding interest rate from the column label. In this case, the interest rate is 5 percent. Thus, the investment yields a 5 percent rate of return—that is, by paying $1,000 for this investment today and receiving $1,629 in 10 years, you will be earning a 5 percent rate of return per annum (year) on your investment.

Besides being slow, the use of tables to solve interest rate problems is of limited use since we cannot identify interest rates that are not whole percentages. If the interest rate is a fractional number, the best we can do with tables is to identify the closest whole percent number (however, table values may be interpolated to arrive at a more precise but still approximate answer).

**Figure 5.2
Future Value of a
$100 Investment at
Various Compound
Interest Rates**

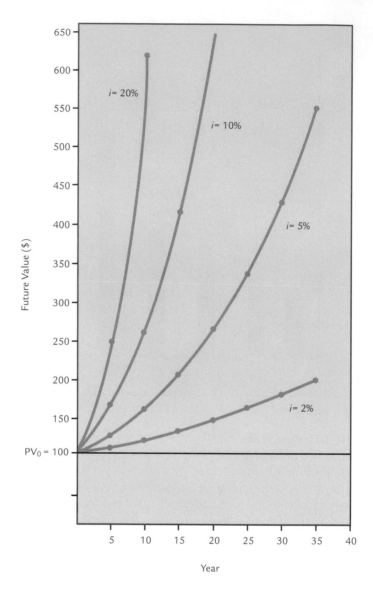

Solving the above problem using a calculator is much faster and yields a precise answer. We enter the known values and compute for interest rate:

Calculator

Solution

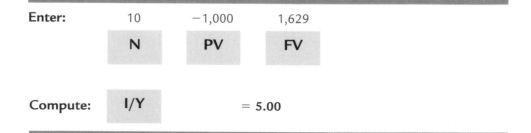

Enter:	10	−1,000	1,629
	N	PV	FV
Compute:	I/Y		= 5.00

Note that the present value amount is entered as a negative (cash outflow), while the future value is entered as positive amount (cash inflow).

Solving for the Number of Periods

Just as we solved for the interest rate given all other known values, we can solve for the number of periods, given all other known values. Specifically, if we know the interest rate per period, the present value, and the future value, we can solve for the length of time or number of periods. For example, Terry Jalbert has $5,000 that he would like to deposit in a savings account. How long would it take Terry to double his money if the savings account pays 8 percent interest per annum? As in the case of solving for the interest rate, we can use Equation 5.6 and solve for n mathematically, but it would be easier to solve the problem using Equation 5.7 and the tables or using the calculator. Plugging in the known values into Equation 5.7, we have the following:

$$\$10,000 = \$5,000(\text{FVIF}_{8,\,n})$$

$$\text{FVIF}_{8,\,n} = \frac{\$10,000}{\$5,000}$$

$$\text{FVIF}_{8,\,n} = 2.000$$

Next, we look up 2.000 in the future value interest factor tables (Table 5.1 or Table I) down the column labeled 8 percent and read off the corresponding length of time (years) across the row. The closest value we observe under the column labeled 8 is 1.999, which corresponds to 9 years. Thus, at an 8 percent rate of interest, it will take Terry 9 years to double his savings.

An easier, but approximate, way to calculate how long it takes to double a sum is given by the **Rule of 72**. Practitioners use this rule of thumb to figure out quickly how long it takes to double any sum at a given interest rate. The Rule of 72 says to find out how long it takes to double a given sum, simply divide 72 by the interest rate. Let's apply the rule to Terry's question:

$$\text{Number of years to double money} = \frac{72}{i}$$

$$= \frac{72}{8}$$

$$= 9 \text{ years}$$

As in the case of other time value of money problems, using a calculator is much faster and yields a precise answer. We enter the known values and compute for n:

Enter:	8	−5,000	10,000
	I/Y	PV	FV

Compute:	N	= 9.01

Calculator
Solution

Comprehension Check Questions

1. How is the future value of a single cash flow calculated?
2. What is a time line?

3. What does the Future Value Interest Factor (FVIF) represent?

4. What is the *Rule of 72?*

PRESENT VALUE OF A SINGLE CASH FLOW

Click on the Investment Analysis Calculator button at **http://finance. swlearning.com** *for an interactive financial calculator for future and present value calculations.*

The future value calculations answer the question: What will be the future value of X dollars invested today, compounded at some rate of interest, i? The financial decision maker, however, often is faced with another type of problem: Given some future value, FV_n, what is its equivalent value today? That is, what is its *present value,* PV_0? The solution requires present value calculations, which are used to determine the dollar amount today, PV_0, that is equivalent to some promised future dollar amount, FV_n. The equivalence depends upon the rate of interest (return) that can be earned on investments during the time period under consideration.

The future value of a sum invested today (FV_n) and the present value today (PV_0) of a sum to be received at some point in the future are mirror images of each other. The present value of a future sum can be calculated from the equation used to determine the future value of a sum invested today. Recall Equation 5.6:

(5.6)
$$FV_n = PV_0(1 + i)^n$$

or, expressing it in terms of PV_0

(5.8)
$$PV_0 = FV_n\left[\frac{1}{(1 + i)^n}\right]$$

where $1/(1 + i)^n$ is known as the *present value interest factor.* Note that the present value interest factor is the reciprocal of the future interest factor for any given interest rate i and length of time n. The process of finding present values frequently is called *discounting.* Equation 5.8 is the basic discounting formula.

To illustrate the use of Equation 5.8, suppose you are presented with an investment opportunity that pays $255.20 in 5 years. To decide how much this investment is worth to you in today's dollars will depend on what rate of return or interest rate you expect. The interest rate used in the discounting process is known as the *discount rate.* Let's assume that your discount rate is 5 percent. We can solve this problem using Equation 5.8, but before we do, let's first draw the time line for the problem:

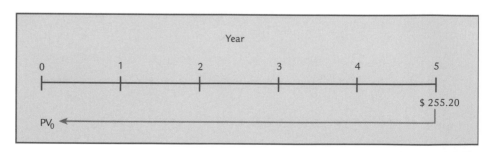

The time line shows that we have an investment that promises to pay $255.20 at the end of 5 years. The problem is to solve the present value at time 0. Note that the arrow is pointing to the left, indicating that we are discounting. Recall that in determining the future value of a sum to be deposited today, the arrow was pointing to the right: We were compounding to the future.

To solve the problem using Equation 5.8, we have

$$PV_0 = \$255.20 \left[\frac{1}{(1 + .05)^5} \right]$$

$$= \$255.20(0.784)$$

$$= \$200.08$$

Thus, an investment that pays $255.20 at the end of 5 years is worth $200.08 today if the discount rate is 5 percent. In other words, an investor who pays $200.08 for this investment today and receives $255.20 in 5 years would be earning a rate of return of 5 percent per year.

In the above problem note that the present value interest factor is 0.784, which tells us that $1 to be received 5 years from now is worth $0.784 today, given an interest rate or discount rate of 5 percent. If we use a higher discount rate, the present value interest factor, and present value PV_0, would be lower. If we hold the discount rate constant but move the future value amount further into the future, the present value would be lower. Figure 5.3 shows the effect of time, n, and interest rate, i, on the present value of $100 to be received in the future.

As an alternative to solving the present value problem mathematically using Equation 5.8, we can rewrite the equation in terms of the present value interest factor:

$$PV_0 = FV_n(PVIF_{i,\,n}) \tag{5.9}$$

where $PVIF_{i,\,n}$ is the *present value interest factor* for a given interest i and number of periods n. The present value interest factor tells you how much a dollar to be received n periods in the future is worth today at a given interest or discount rate i. The present value interest factors are provided in Table II on the insert. A portion of the present value interest factor tables is reproduced here as Table 5.2.

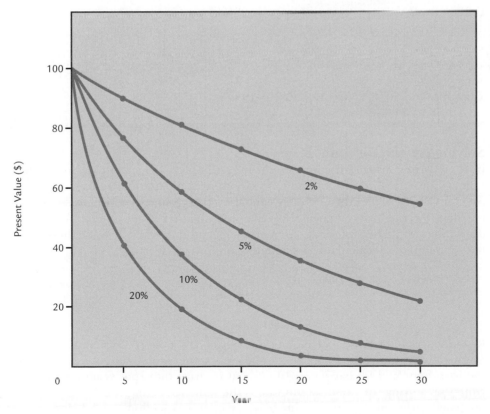

Figure 5.3
Present Value of a $100 Investment at Various Discount Rates

Table 5.2 Present Value Interest Factors (PVIFs) for $1 at Interest Rate *i* for *n* Periods

End of Period (*n*)	Interest Rate (*i*)					
	1%	5%	6%	8%	10%	13%
1	0.990	0.952	0.943	0.926	0.909	0.885
2	0.980	0.907	0.890	0.857	0.826	0.783
3	0.971	0.864	0.840	0.794	0.751	0.693
4	0.961	0.823	0.792	0.735	0.683	0.613
5	0.951	**0.784**	0.747	0.681	0.621	**0.543**
8	0.923	0.677	0.627	0.540	0.467	0.376
10	0.905	0.614	0.558	0.463	0.386	0.295
20	0.820	0.377	0.312	0.215	0.149	0.087
25	0.780	0.295	0.233	0.146	0.092	0.047

Applying Equation 5.9 to the problem described in the time line, we have

$$PV_0 = \$255.20(PVIF_{5,5})$$
$$= \$255.20(0.784)$$
$$= \$200.08$$

We can also solve present value of single cash flow problems using the financial calculator. The steps are exactly the same as solving the future value of a single cash flow except we now compute for the present value (PV) rather than the future value (FV).

Calculator

Solution

Enter:	5	5	255.20
	N	I/Y	FV

Compute:	PV	= −199.96

Solving for the Discount Rate

In some problems the discount rate is the unknown. For example, the Friendly Loan Company is willing to lend Fred Goodtime $5,000 today in exchange for a payment of $11,439 at the end of 5 years. If Fred takes the loan, what rate of interest (discount rate) is Fred paying? We can use Equation 5.8 to solve for *i* mathematically but it would be easier to use Equation 5.9 and the PVIF tables, or alternatively to use the financial calculator. Using Equation 5.9 we have:

$$\$5,000 = \$11,439(PVIF_{i,5})$$
$$PVIF_{i,5} = \frac{\$5,000}{\$11,439}$$
$$PVIF_{i,5} = 0.4371$$

Reading across the row labeled 5 periods (years) in Table II, we find the PVIF factor equal to 0.4371 under the column labeled 18 percent. Thus, if Fred takes out the loan he would be paying an 18 percent interest rate (per year) on the loan. Note that solving for the discount rate is the same as solving for the interest rate discussed earlier in the future value of single cash flow section (page 141).

The above problem can be solved much more easily with the financial calculator. The steps are similar to the ones shown for determining the interest rate in the future value of single cash flow section (see page 142). The steps using the calculator are shown below.

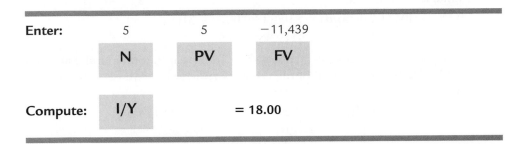

Enter:	5	5	−11,439
	N	PV	FV

| Compute: | I/Y | | = 18.00 |

Calculator

Solution

Comprehension Check Questions

1. How is present value different from future value of a single sum?
2. What does the Present Value Interest Factor (PVIF) represent?
3. What is a discount rate?

FUTURE VALUE OF A STREAM OF CASH FLOWS

By now you know how to determine the future value of a single cash flow or deposit. However, many problems in real life involve a series or *stream of cash flows over time*. For example, you may be planning for retirement in 30 years and expect to set aside $5,000 in a savings account every year; you would like to know how much your savings program would amount to at the end of 30 years at a given interest rate. Alternatively, a company may wish to retire $10,000,000 in debt at the end of 15 years and would like to know how much they must set aside each year to attain that goal assuming the deposits earn a given rate of interest per year.

For convenience we will divide our discussion of the future value of a stream of cash flows into cash flows that are *uneven* and cash flows that are *even* (**annuities**).

Future Value of Uneven Cash Flows

Uneven cash flows refer to deposits that are not uniform over time. For example consider the following deposits made at the end of each of the next 3 years:

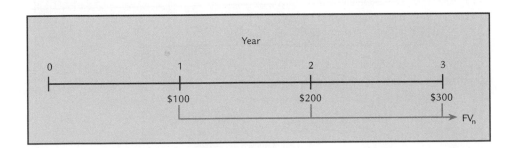

What is the future value of these deposits at the end of year 3, if they are deposited into an account earning 6 percent per year compounded annually? The best way to answer this problem is to think of the three deposits as three single cash flow deposits.

The first deposit of $100, made at the end of year 1, will be in the account earning interest for 2 full years before the end of the 3-year period. Therefore its future value is the following:

$$FV_3(\text{1st deposit}) = \$100(1+0.06)^2 \text{ or } \$100(FVIF_{6,\,2})$$
$$= \$112.36$$

The second deposit of $200, made at the end of year 2, will be in the account for one full year before the end of the 3-year period, and it will earn interest for 1 year. Thus, its future value is as follows:

$$FV_3(\text{2nd deposit}) = \$200(1+0.06)^1 \text{ or } \$200(FVIF_{6,\,1})$$
$$= \$212.00$$

The final deposit of $300, made at the end of year 3, will earn no interest since the deposit coincides with the time when we want to measure the future value. In other words, the final deposit has no time to earn interest consequently its future value at the end of year 3 is the same as the amount of deposit:

$$FV_3(\text{3rd deposit}) = \$300(1 + 0.06)^0 \text{ or } \$300(FVIF_{6,\,0})$$
$$= \$300(1)$$
$$= \$300.00$$

The future value at the end of year 3 of all three deposits combined is:

$$FV_3 = FV_3(\text{1st deposit}) + FV_3(\text{2nd deposit}) + FV_3(\text{3rd deposit})$$
$$FV_3 = \$112.36 + \$212 + \$300$$
$$FV_3 = \$624.36$$

This solution is summarized in Figure 5.4.

The problem may also be solved using the financial calculator. The procedure involves calculating the future value at the end of year 3 of each of the deposits and then summing the resulting values. To save time and reduce the potential for making mistakes, it is advisable that instead of writing down the future value of each deposit and then summing them, the future value of each deposit should be stored in the calculator's memory and cumulated. The solution below outlines the steps involved.

Figure 5.4
Illustration of Future Value of Uneven Cash Flows

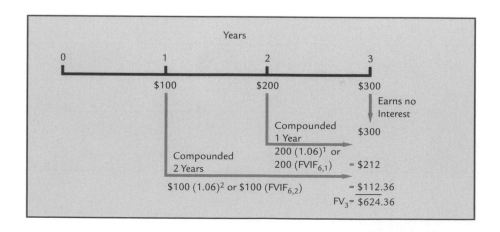

Calculate future value of year 1 deposit:

Enter: 2   −100   6

N	PV	I/Y

Compute: | FV | = 112.36

Store value in memory.

Calculate future value of year 2 deposit:

Enter: 1   −200   6

N	PV	I/Y

Calculator

Solution

Compute: | FV | = 212

Add to previous value in memory.

Calculate future value of year 3 deposit:

Enter: 0   −300   6

N	PV	I/Y

Compute: | FV | = 300

Add to previous value in memory.

Recall memory   = 624.36

Because the year 3 deposit of $300 does not earn any interest, we can forgo the calculation of the future value of the third deposit (shown above) and simply add $300 to the recalled value from the memory.

The solution for the future value of an uneven stream of cash flows using the spreadsheet is illustrated on the next page.

Future Value of an Annuity

We now discuss how to find the future value of a stream of cash flows that are uniform. Such cash flows are referred to as an *annuity*. An annuity is the payment or receipt of equal cash flows per period for a specified amount of time. There are two types of annuities. An *ordinary annuity* is one in which the payments or receipts occur at the *end* of each period. An *annuity due* is one in which payments or receipts occur at the *beginning* of each period. Most lease payments, such as apartment rentals, as well as life insurance premiums, are annuities due.

The following time lines illustrate the difference between an ordinary annuity and an annuity due.

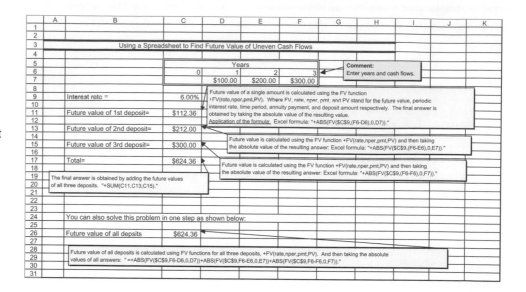

Spreadsheet strategies

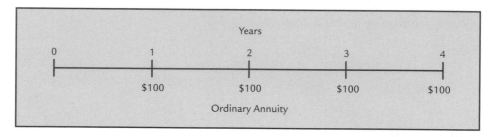

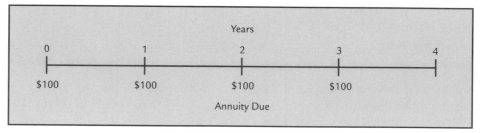

Both time lines describe a $100 annuity for 4 years. In the ordinary annuity the deposits or cash flows occur at the end of each year—the first cash flow or deposit occurs at the end of year 1 (or 1 year from today), while the fourth deposit or cash flow occurs at the end of year 4 (or 4 years from today). In the annuity due illustration, the cash flows occur at the beginning of each year—the first cash flow or deposit occurs at the beginning of year 1 (or at time 0, today) and the fourth deposit occurs at the beginning of year 4 (or at the end of year 3).

Future Value of an Ordinary Annuity A future value of an ordinary annuity ($FVAN_n$) problem asks the question: If *PMT* dollars are deposited in an account at the end of each year for *n* years and if the deposits earn interest rate *i* compounded annually, what will be the value of the account at the end of *n* years? To illustrate, suppose Nadya receives a 3-year ordinary annuity of $1,000 per year and deposits the money in a savings account at the end of each year. The account earns interest at a rate of 6 percent compounded annually. How much will her account be worth at the end of the 3-year period? The following time line illustrates the problem:

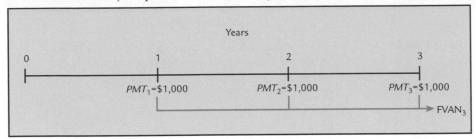

As in the case of calculating the future value of a stream of uneven cash flows, we can calculate the future value of the ordinary annuity as the sum of the future values of each of the cash flows in the annuity stream. We can use the mathematical formula (Equation 5.6) or the formula using the future value interest factor tables (Equation 5.7) to calculate the future value of each of the deposits. This is illustrated in Figure 5.5. As can be seen, the future value of the 3-year $1,000 ordinary annuity compounded at 6 percent is $3,184.

The approach illustrated in Figure 5.5 can become cumbersome, especially if we are dealing with rather long annuities—say, for example, a 20-year annuity. An easier way to calculate the future value of an ordinary annuity is to use the specially constructed future value interest factor of annuity tables. The future value interest factor of annuity tells you what a $1 annuity is worth at the end of the annuity period given an interest rate.

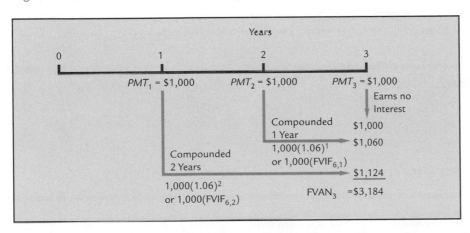

**Figure 5.5
Illustration of Future Value of Ordinary Annuity**

Table III on the insert provides the future value interest factor of an annuity for various combinations of the interest rates and time periods. A portion of Table III is reproduced here as Table 5.3. Note that the future value of annuity interest factor (FVIFA) is the sum of the future value interest factors presented in Table I. For example, the future value of an annuity interest factor for a 3-year ordinary annuity at 6 percent is:

$$FVIFA_{6,3} = FVIF_{6,2} + FVIF_{6,1} + FVIF_{6,0}$$
$$= 1.124 + 1.060 + 1.000$$
$$= 3.184$$

Using the annuity factors, the future value of an ordinary annuity ($FVAN_n$) may be calculated by multiplying the annuity payment, *PMT*, by the appropriate interest factor,

End of Period (n)	Interest Rate (i)			
	1%	**5%**	**6%**	**10%**
1	1.000	1.000	1.000	1.000
2	2.010	2.050	2.060	2.100
3	3.030	3.152	**3.184**	3.310
4	4.060	4.310	4.375	4.641
5	5.101	5.526	5.637	6.105
10	10.462	12.578	13.181	15.937
20	22.019	33.066	36.786	57.275
25	28.243	47.727	54.865	98.347

Table 5.3 Future Value of an Ordinary Annuity Interest Factors (FVIFA) for $1 per Period at Interest Rate *i* for *n* Periods

(5.10)
$$FVAN_n = PMT(FVIFA_{i, n})$$

Let's use the above formula to figure the future value of Nadya's annuity:

$$FVAN_3 = PMT(FVIFA_{6, 3})$$
$$= \$1,000(3.184)$$
$$= \$3,184$$

We can also solve future value of ordinary annuity problems using the financial calculator. The steps are similar to those used for solving the future value of a single sum problem except that instead of a present value or principal amount we have an ordinary annuity which is entered using the PMT (or payment) key. The calculator steps to solve Nadya's problem are as follows:

Calculator Solution

Enter:

3	6	−1,000
N	I/Y	PMT

Compute: FV = 3,183.60

The spreadsheet solution is shown below.

Spreadsheet strategies

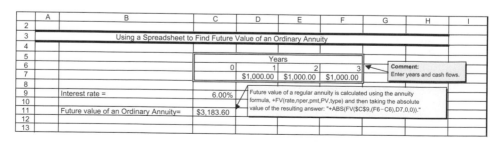

	A	B	C	D	E	F	G	H	I
2									
3		Using a Spreadsheet to Find Future Value of an Ordinary Annuity							
4									
5				Years					
6			0	1	2	3		Comment:	
7				$1,000.00	$1,000.00	$1,000.00		Enter years and cash flows.	
8									
9		Interest rate =	6.00%	Future value of a regular annuity is calculated using the annuity					
10				formula, +FV(rate,nper,pmt,PV,type) and then taking the absolute					
11		Future value of an Ordinary Annuity=	$3,183.60	value of the resulting answer: "+ABS(FV($C$9,(F6−C6),D7,0,0))."					
12									
13									

Future Value of an Annuity Due Consider the case of Nadya's problem cited earlier. If she deposits $1,000 in a savings account at the *beginning* of each year for the next 3 years and the account earns 6 percent interest, compounded annually, how much will be in the account at the end of 3 years? (Recall that when the deposits were made at the *end* of each year, the account totaled $3,184 at the end of 3 years.)

Figure 5.6 illustrates this problem as an *annuity due*. Note that with an annuity due, PMT_1 is compounded for 3 years, PMT_2 for 2 years, and PMT_3 for 1 year. *Thus, each deposit now is compounded for one additional year at 6 percent.* Note that the answer we get (see below) for an annuity due ($3,375) is also equal to the future value of an ordinary annuity compounded for 1 additional year at 6 percent: $3,184 $(1.06)^1$. Thus, a simple way to figure the future value of annuity due is to first calculate the future value of an ordinary annuity due and multiply the resulting answer by $(1+ i)$:

$$FVAND_n = FVAN_n(1 + i) \qquad\qquad (5.11)$$

If you are using the tables, the future value of an annuity due may be stated as follows:

$$FVAND_n = PMT[FVIFA_{i, n}(1 + i)] \qquad\qquad (5.12)$$

Applying this to the illustration in Figure 5.6, we have:

$$FVAND_3 = \$1,000[(3.184)(1.06)]$$
$$= \$1,000(3.375)$$
$$= \$3,375$$

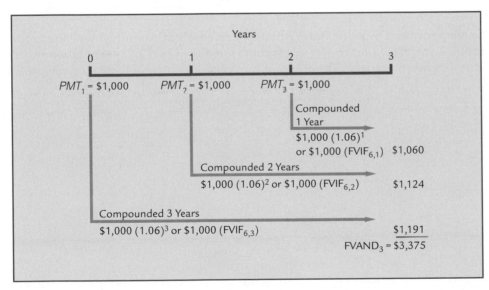

Figure 5.6
Illustration of Future Value of an Annuity Due

If one is using a calculator, there are two options. The first option is to solve the problem assuming an ordinary annuity and then using Equation 5.11 to adjust the resulting answer to an annuity due. The second option is to change the default setting of the calculator to an annuity due mode. By default the calculator assumes that the cash flows (annuity payments) entered occur at the *end of the period*. The default setting can be changed to *beginning of the period* mode. Once the default setting is changed the problem can be solved just as an ordinary annuity problem. The following steps illustrate the second option.

Step 1:

Change default setting to beginning of period cash flows.

Step 2:

Solve the problem.

Calculator

Solution

Enter: 3   6   −1,000

| N | I/Y | PMT |

Compute: FV   = 3,374.62

The spreadsheet solution is shown below.

Spreadsheet strategies

	A	B	C	D	E	F	G	H	I
2									
3		Using a Spreadsheet to Find Future Value of an Annuity Due							
4									
5				Years					
6			0	1	2	3	Comment:		
7				$1,000.00	$1,000.00	$1,000.00	Enter years and cash flows.		
8									
9		Interest rate =	6.00%	Note:					
10				Future value of an annuity due is calculated using the annuity					
11		Future value of an Annuity Due=	$3,374.62	formula, +FV(rate,nper,pmt,PV,type) and then taking the absolute					
12				value of the resulting answer: "+ABS(FV($C$9,(F6−C6),D7,0,1))."					
13									

Solving for the Discount Rate, Annuity, or Length of Annuity In solving for the future value of an annuity we were given the annuity (PMT), length of annuity (n), and the interest rate (i). However, we can just as easily solve for PMT, or i, or n, if we have information on the other three variables. For example, Robert Ho would like to save enough money to buy his dream car, a Porsche Carrera, in 8 years. The car is expected to cost $125,000 at that time. How much must Robert save at the end of each of the next 8 years if the savings earn 8 percent per year?

Using Equation 5.10 we have

$$\$125,000 = PMT(FVIFA_{8,8})$$

$$PMT = \frac{\$125,000}{10.637}$$

$$= \$11,751.43$$

Therefore, Robert Ho needs to set aside $11,751.43 every year so that he will have $125,000 at the end of 8 years to buy his dream car.

We can solve Robert's problem using the financial calculator by entering all the known values and then computing for the annuity (PMT).

Calculator

Solution

Enter: 8   8   125,000

| N | I/Y | FV |

Compute: PMT   = −11,751.85

The spreadsheet solution (not shown) is determined in similar fashion using the PMT function and supplying the known values for number of periods, interest rate, and the future value.

Now, let's try a problem where the length of time, n, is the unknown. Assume that Robert Ho feels he can manage to set aside $8,500 every year but not the $11,751.43 (answer based on future value interest factor of annuity formula) determined earlier. How long would it take Robert to achieve the target savings amount of $125,000? Assume that the savings earn an 8 percent rate of return per year.

Using Equation 5.10 we have

$$\$125,000 = \$8,500 \ (\text{FVIFA}_{8, \, n})$$

$$\text{FVIFA}_{8, \, n} = \frac{\$125,000}{\$8,500}$$

$$\text{FVIFA}_{8, \, n} = 14.706$$

From Table III on the insert, if we look down the column labeled 8 percent, the FVIFA equal to 14.706 occurs somewhere between the interest factors for 10 (14.487) and 11 years (16.645). Thus, it will take Robert somewhere between 10 and 11 years (closer to 10 years since 14.706 is closer to 14.487 than to 16.645) to save the needed amount.

Using the calculator we obtain a more precise answer of 10.11 years.

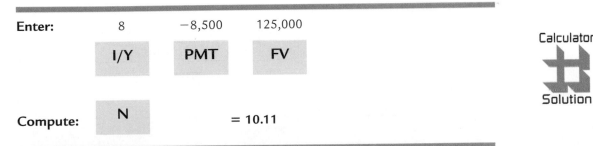

The spreadsheet solution (not shown) is solved using the NPER function and supplying the known values for interest rate, payment or annuity, and the future value.

Comprehension Check Questions

1. What is meant by the future value of a stream of cash flows?
2. How is an ordinary annuity different than an annuity due?
3. What does the Future Value Interest Factor of an Annuity (FVIFA) represent?

PRESENT VALUE OF A STREAM OF CASH FLOWS

As in the case of future value, we also can determine the present value of a stream of cash flows that is received in the future. From a financial management perspective these situations are more prevalent than situations requiring the calculation of a future value of stream of cash flows. For example, business investments, such as expansion of plant capacity, involve cash flow benefits over the life of the project lasting several years. An evaluation of the project would require calculating the present value of the stream of future benefits. Alternatively, if you are an investor contemplating the value of a corporate bond, you will want to calculate the present value of the cash flow stream expected from the bond investment. We will illustrate how to determine the present value of uneven streams and annuities.

Present Value of an Uneven Stream

Consider an investment that yields the following unequal cash flows over time:

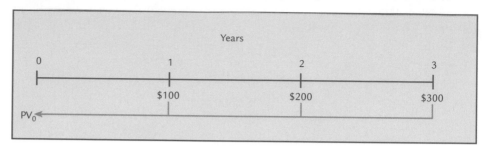

Assuming the discount rate is 10 percent, the present value of this stream of unequal cash flows is simply the sum of the present values of the individual cash flows in each of the years discounted at the 10 percent rate:

$$PV_0 = \frac{\$100}{(1 + .10)^1} + \frac{\$200}{(1 + .10)^2} + \frac{\$300}{(1 + .10)^3}$$

Or, using the tables this is equal to:

$$PV_0 = \$100(PVIF_{10,1}) + \$200(PVIF_{10,\,2}) + \$300(PVIF_{10,\,3})$$
$$= \$100(0.909) + \$200(0.826) + \$300(0.751)$$
$$= \$481.40$$

This solution also is illustrated in Figure 5.7.

**Figure 5.7
Illustration of
Present Value of
Uneven Cash Flows**

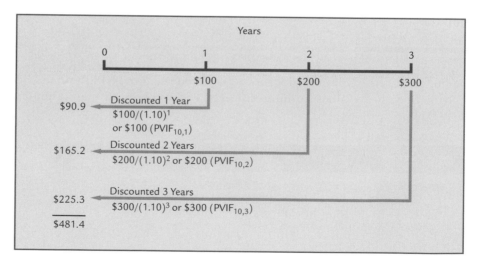

The significance of the $481.40 present value is that if you were to pay this amount for the investment, the future cash flows from the investment represent a 10 percent rate of return (annualized) on your investment.

Solving for the present value of a stream of uneven cash flows using a calculator is similar to that of solving for the present value of an uneven stream of cash flows. Simply calculate the present value of each cash flow and sum the resulting values. Spreadsheets are very useful in calculating the present value of uneven cash flow streams as illustrated on the following page.

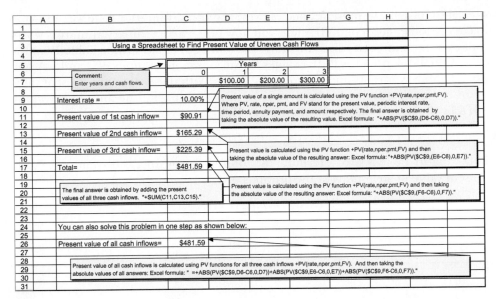

Present Value of an Annuity

In this section we will discuss how to determine the present value of an ordinary annuity and the present value of an annuity due. In addition, we also will show how to calculate the present value of *deferred annuities* and the present value of a *perpetuity.*

Present Value of an Ordinary Annuity The present value of an ordinary annuity $(PVAN_0)$ is the sum of the present value of a series of uniform cash flows that occur at the end of each period for a certain number of periods. For example, Andy Prevost is presented with an opportunity to invest in a business that will generate cash flows of $1,000 at the end of each year for the next 5 years. What is the value of this business opportunity to Andy if his discount rate is 6 percent? The value of the business would be equal to the sum of the present values of each of the $1,000 cash flows to be received over the next 5 years. Mathematically, this could be solved as follows:

$$PVAN_0 = \frac{\$1000}{(1+.06)^1} + \frac{\$1000}{(1+.06)^2}$$
$$+ \frac{\$1000}{(1+.06)^3} + \frac{\$1000}{(1+.06)^4} + \frac{\$1000}{(1+.06)^5}$$

Alternatively, we can use the present value interest factor tables:

$$PVAN_0 = \$1,000(PVIF_{6,1}) + \$1,000(PVIF_{6,2})$$
$$+ \$1,000(PVIF_{6,3}) + \$1,000(PVIF_{6,4}) + \$1,000(PVIF_{6,5})$$
$$= \$1,000(0.943) + \$1,000(0.890) + \$1,000(0.840)$$
$$+ \$1,000(0.792) + \$1,000(0.747)$$
$$= \$943 + \$890 + \$840 + \$792 + \$747$$
$$= \$4,212$$

Figure 5.8 illustrates this concept. This approach becomes tedious especially with a long annuity. As in the case of future value of ordinary annuity, we can make use of specially constructed present value of ordinary annuity interest factors (PVIFA) to make the job easier. The PVIFA tells you how much a $1 ordinary annuity is worth today given an interest (discount) rate, i, and length of annuity, n. Table IV at the end of the book presents PVIFA values for various combinations of n and i. A portion of Table IV is reproduced here as Table 5.4. With these tables the present value of an ordinary annuity can be determined by multiplying the annuity payment, *PMT*, by the appropriate interest factor, $\text{PVIFA}_{i,\,n}$:

(5.13)
$$\text{PVAN}_0 = PMT(\text{PVIFA}_{i,\,n})$$

Referring to Table 5.4 to determine the interest factor for $i = 6\%$ and $n = 5$, the present value of an annuity in the previous problem can be calculated as follows:

$$\text{PVAN}_0 = PMT(\text{PVIFA}_{6,\,5})$$
$$= \$1{,}000(4.212)$$
$$= \$4{,}212$$

**Figure 5.8
Illustration of
Present Value of
an Ordinary Annuity**

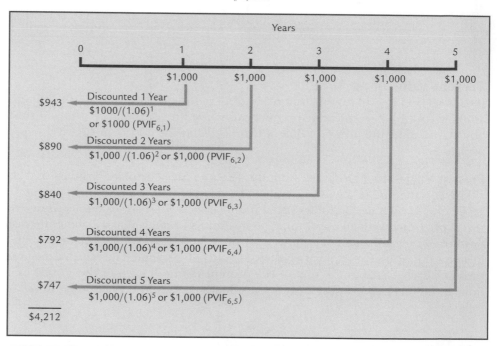

Table 5.4	Present Value of an Ordinary Annuity Interest Factors (PVIFA) for $1 per Period at Interest Rate i for n Periods			
	Interest Rate (i)			
End of Period (n)	**1%**	**5%**	**6%**	**10%**
1	0.990	0.952	0.943	0.909
2	1.970	1.859	1.833	1.736
3	2.941	2.723	2.673	2.487
4	3.902	3.546	3.465	3.170
5	4.853	4.329	**4.212**	3.791
10	9.471	7.722	7.360	6.145
20	18.046	12.462	11.470	8.514
25	22.023	14.094	12.783	9.077

We can also solve present value of ordinary annuity problems using the financial calculator. The steps are similar to those used for solving the future value of an ordinary annuity problem. The calculator steps to solve Andy's problem are as follows:

Enter:	5	6	1,000
	N	I/Y	PMT

Compute:	PV	= −4,212.36

Calculator Solution

The present value of an ordinary annuity using a spreadsheet is shown next.

	A	B	C	D	E	F	G	H	I
2									
3		Using a Spreadsheet to Find Present Value of an Ordinary Annuity							
4									
5		Comment:			Years				
6		Enter years and cash flows.	0	1	2	3	4	5	
7				$1,000.00	$1,000.00	$1,000.00	$1,000.00	$1,000.00	
8									
9		Interest rate =	6.00%		Present value of a regular annuity is calculated using the PV function				
10					+PV(rate,nper,pmt,FV,type). Where PV, rate, nper, pmt, and FV stand				
11		Present Value of an Ordinary Annuity=	$4,212.36		for the present value, periodic interest rate, number of periods in an				
12					an annuity, annuity value, and future value, respectively. And, type is				
13					zero for regular annuity and one for annuity due. The final answer is				
14					obtained by taking the absolute value of the resulting answer:				
15					Excel formula. "+ABS(PV($C$9,(H6−C6),D7,0,0))"				
16									

Spreadsheet strategies

Present Value of an Annuity Due

Consider the case of the 5-year annuity of $1,000 each year, discounted at 6 percent, that we used earlier to illustrate the calculation of present value of an ordinary annuity. What is the present value of this stream if it is assumed to be an annuity due rather than an ordinary annuity—that is, the annuity cash flows occur at the beginning of the year rather than at the end of each year? Figure 5.9 illustrates the time line and solution to this problem by discounting the yearly cash flows individually.

The first payment received at the beginning of year 1 (end of year 0) is already in its present value form and therefore requires no discounting. PMT_2 is discounted for 1 period, PMT_3 is discounted for 2 periods, PMT_4 is discounted for 3 periods, and PMT_5 is discounted for 4 periods. The discounted sum of the individual year cash flows is $4,465. Note that each of the payments was discounted *1 year less* compared to the equivalent ordinary annuity problem in Figure 5.8. Note, consequently, that the present value of the annuity due ($4,465) is greater than the present value of the ordinary annuity ($4,212) by a factor of (1+0.06) or the compounded value for 1 year. So, an easier way to calculate the present value of an annuity due is to take the present value of an ordinary annuity and multiply it by (1+*i*):

$$PVAND_0 = PVAN_0(1 + i) \tag{5.14}$$

Using the present value interest factor of an annuity we can restate the above equation as:

$$PVAND_0 = [PMT(PVIFA_{i, n})](1 + i) \tag{5.15}$$

or

$$PVAND_0 = PMT [PVIFA_{i, n}(1 + i)]$$

Buying a home, leasing a car, borrowing money, and many other transactions are based on the time value of money. For handy worksheets on mortgages, loans, etc., in English and Spanish, visit FinanCenter at **http://www.financenter. com**

Figure 5.9
Illustration of
Present Value of
an Annuity Due

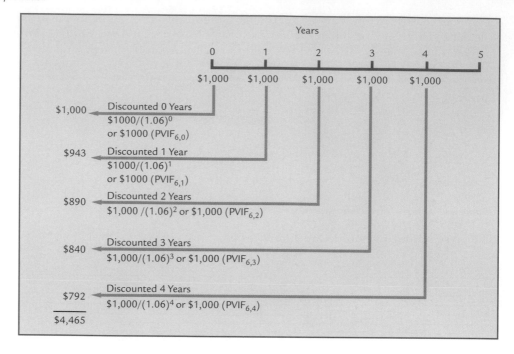

Applying the formula to the problem illustrated in Figure 5.9, we have:

$$PVAND_0 = \$1,000[PVIFA_{6,5}(1 + .06)]$$
$$= \$1,000[4.212(1.06)]$$
$$= \$4,465$$

If using a calculator, there are two options similar to calculating the future value of an annuity due. The first option is to solve the problem assuming an ordinary annuity and then using Equation 5.15 to adjust the resulting answer to an annuity due. The second option is to change the default setting of the calculator to an annuity due mode. The following steps illustrate the second option.

Step 1:
Change default setting to beginning of period cash flows.

Step 2:
Solve the problem.

Calculator
Solution

Enter:	5	6	1,000
	N	I/Y	PMT

Compute:	PV		= −4,465.11

Solving for present value of an annuity due using a spreadsheet is illustrated on the next page.

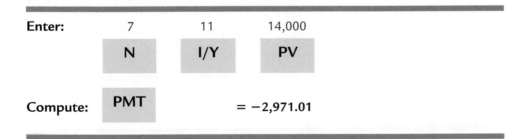

	A	B	C	D	E	F	G	H	I
2									
3		Using a Spreadsheet to Find Present Value of an Annuity Due							
4									
5					Years				
6		Comment:	0	1	2	3	4	5	
7		Enter years and cash flows.		$1,000.00	$1,000.00	$1,000.00	$1,000.00	$1,000.00	
8									
9		Interest rate =	6.00%						
10									
11		Present Value of an Annuity Due	$4,465.11						
12									
13									
14									
15									
16									

Present value of an annuity due is calculated using the PV function +PV(rate,nper,pmt,FV,type). Where PV, rate, nper, pmt, and FV stand for the present value, periodic interest rate, number of periods in an annuity, annuity value, and future value, respectively. And type is zero for regular annuity and one for annuity due. The final answer is obtained by taking the absolute value of the resulting value. Excel formula: "+ABS(PV($C$9,(H6−C6),D7,0,1))"

Spreadsheet strategies

Solving for the Discount Rate, Annuity, or Length of Annuity

In solving for the present value of an annuity we were given the annuity, *PMT*, length of annuity, *n*, and the interest rate, *i*. However, we can just as easily solve for *PMT*, or *i*, or *n*, if we have information on the other three variables. For example, the EasyLoan Company has offered to extend a loan to Ray Romano at an interest rate of 11 percent per annum over a 7-year period. The loan would require that Ray make equal annual payments at the end of each of the next 7 years. If Ray wants to borrow $14,000 from EasyLoan, what will his annual payments be over the next 7 years?

Using Equation 5.13 we have

$$\$14,000 = PMT(\text{PVIFA}_{11,7})$$

$$PMT = \frac{\$14,000}{4.712}$$

$$PMT = \$2,971.14$$

Therefore, Ray would have to make annual payments of $2,971.14 at the end of each of the next 7 years.

The loan problem can be solved using the financial calculator by entering all the known values and then computing for the annuity (*PMT*).

Enter: 7 → **N**   11 → **I/Y**   14,000 → **PV**

Compute: **PMT** = −2,971.01

Calculator Solution

Now, let's try a problem where the interest rate, *i*, is the unknown. Assume that Bill Sharpe was presented with an investment opportunity from All Star Investment Corporation that will generate $800 every year for the next 15 years. Bill would receive these cash flows at the end of each year. The cost of this investment is $5,500. If Bill decides to invest in this opportunity, what rate of return would he be earning?

Using Equation 5.13 we have

$$\$5,500 = \$800(\text{PVIFA}_{i,15})$$

$$\text{PVIFA}_{i,15} = \frac{\$5,500}{\$800}$$

$$\text{PVIFA}_{i,15} = 6.875$$

From Table IV at the end of the book, if we look across the row labeled 15 periods, the PVIFA equal to 6.875 occurs somewhere between the interest factors for 11 (7.191) and 12 percent (6.811). Thus, Bill would be earning somewhere between 11 and 12 percent (closer to 12 percent since 6.875 is closer to 6.811 than to 7.191) if he were to accept the investment offer from All Star Investment Corporation.

Using the calculator we obtain a more precise answer of 11.82 percent.

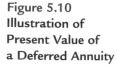

Calculator

Solution

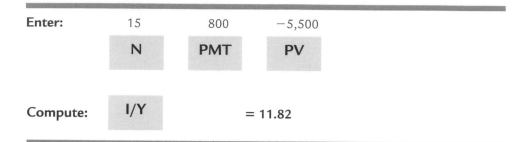

Present Value of a Deferred Annuity

In finance, one frequently encounters problems where an annuity begins more than 1 year in the future—in other words a *deferred annuity*. For example, suppose that David Carter wishes to provide for the college education of his daughter. She will begin college 6 years from now, and Carter wishes to have $15,000 available for his daughter at the beginning of each year in college. How much must be invested today at an 8 percent annual rate of return in order to provide the 4-year, $15,000 annuity for David's daughter?

The time line and the solution using the present value interest factors are illustrated in Figure 5.10. Note that the first payment or cash flow occurs at the end of year 6, which is the beginning of the first year of college, and the last payment occurs at the end of year 9, which is the beginning of the senior year of college. As you can see from the figure, the solution involves breaking the problem into two steps. In the first step we determine the present value of the 4-year $15,000 annuity as of the end of year 5. We do this by multiplying the annuity by the present value interest factor of annuity at 8 percent for 4 years. The resulting present value of annuity, $49,680, gives you the single cash flow equivalent of the $15,000 annuity as of

**Figure 5.10
Illustration of
Present Value of
a Deferred Annuity**

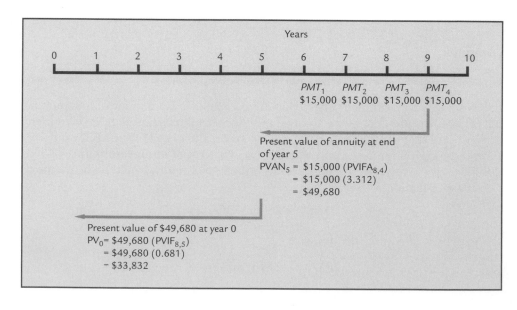

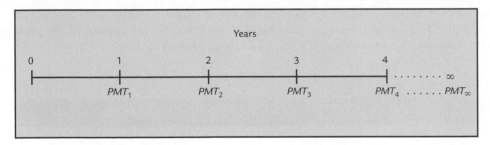

the end of year 5 assuming a discount rate of 8 percent. This is only an intermediate step. Remember, our goal is to find the equivalent of the $15,000 annuity in terms of today's (year 0) dollars.

In the second step we take the year 5 single cash flow equivalent of the annuity and discount it back to year 0. This is done by multiplying $49,680 by the present value interest factor at 8 percent for 5 years. This results in a present value of $33,832. If David has $33,832 today and invests it in an account earning 8 percent per year, there will be exactly enough money in the account to withdraw $15,000 at the beginning of each of the 4 years of his daughter's college education. After the last withdrawal, the account balance will be zero.

Present Value of a Perpetuity

A *perpetuity* is an annuity that goes on forever; that is, a perpetuity is an infinite annuity. The following time line describes a perpetuity. The symbol ∞ indicates that the series goes to infinity.

Determining the present value of a perpetuity (PVPER_0) is very simple. It is equal to the perpetuity divided by the discount rate:

$$\text{PVPER}_0 = \frac{PMT}{i}$$

(5.16)

Perpetuities are useful in valuing certain types of bonds and preferred stock that pay a fixed cash flow forever. Perpetuities are also useful in setting up endowments for scholarships and other purposes. For example, let's assume Pete Sampras wants to set up a tennis scholarship for a deserving student at Becker State University. The scholarship endowment should be of sufficient size to provide an annual scholarship of $6,000 forever. If the scholarship fund can earn 7 percent compounded annually, what size gift should Pete give to Becker State University? Substituting $6,000 for *PMT* and 0.07 for *i* into Equation 5.16, we have

$$\text{PVPER}_0 = \frac{\$6,000}{.07}$$

$$\text{PVPER}_0 = \$85,714$$

With the $85,714, Becker State University can set up a scholarship fund that would generate $6,000 annually to perpetuity. You may wonder: How can the fund exist in perpetuity? The reason is the perpetuity is exactly equal to the amount of interest generated every year: $85,714 × .07 = $6,000. Consequently, the principal amount remains untouched.

The present value of perpetuity formula is useful in valuing certain types of financial instruments. Some preferred stocks take the form of a perpetuity because these special securities never mature; that is, there is no obligation on the part of the issuer to redeem these securities at their face value at any time in the future. A financial instrument such as this provides the holder with a series of equal, periodic payments into the indefinite future. The application of the present value of perpetuity formula to the case of preferred stock is examined in Chapter 8.

Comprehension Check Questions

1. What is meant by the present value of a stream of cash flows?

2. If you have the same number of cash flows, which will have a greater present value—ordinary annuity or an annuity due?

3. What does the Present Value Interest Factor of an Annuity (PVIFA) represent?

4. What is the formula for the present value of a perpetuity?

EFFECT OF COMPOUNDING PERIODS ON PRESENT AND FUTURE VALUES

Thus far, it has been assumed that compounding (and discounting) occur annually. Recall the general compound interest equation

(5.6)
$$FV_n = PV_0(1 + i)^n$$

where PV_0 is the initial deposit, i is the annual interest rate, n is the number of years, and FV_n is the future value that will accumulate from the annual compounding of PV_0. An interest rate of i percent per year for n years is assumed. The rate i is the annual rate assuming the interest is paid, or compounded, annually. This rate is also known as the **nominal rate.**

In some circumstances, interest on an account may be paid or compounded more frequently than annually. The effect of increasing the frequency of compounding is that it increases the interest-on-interest component and thus the future value of the cash flow. For example, you may have a savings account where the interest is compounded semiannually instead of annually. Let's say that the nominal annual interest rate is 10 percent and that you deposit $1,000 into this savings account for 1 year. Since the savings account pays and compounds interest semiannually, your future value at the end of the first 6 months ($\frac{1}{2}$ year) is equal to:

$$FV_{\frac{1}{2}} = \$1,000(1 + \tfrac{.10}{2})$$
$$= \$1,000 + \$50$$
$$= \$1,050$$

Note that at the end of the first 6 months you receive half of the nominal annual interest or 5 percent ($\frac{i}{2} = \frac{.10}{2}$). At the end of the year, the future value is equal to:

$$FV_1 = \$1,050(1 + \tfrac{.10}{2})$$
$$= \$1,050 + \$52.5$$
$$= \$1,102.50$$

Alternatively, FV_1 can be determined as:

$$FV_1 = \$1,000(1 + \tfrac{.10}{2})^2$$
$$= \$1,102.50$$

Note that at the end of the year, you have earned an extra $2.50 from interest on the interest paid in the first 6 months. Recall that if the interest were compounded annually the future value at the end of the year would amount to just $1,100. Thus, compounding frequency has the effect of increasing the future value by enhancing the interest-on-interest component of future value. What would happen if the interest on the savings account were compounded quarterly? Using the same logic shown above when interest is paid semiannually, the future value at the end of the 1-year deposit period if interest is paid quarterly is equal to:

$$FV_1 = \$1,000(1 + \tfrac{.10}{4})^4$$
$$= \$1,103.81$$

In general, the future value of a single sum can be calculated for any compounding frequency and length of time using the following formula:

$$FV_n = PV_0\left(1 + \frac{i}{m}\right)^{mn} \tag{5.17}$$

where m is the number of times during the year the interest is compounded and n is the number of years.

Table 5.5 contains the future value, FV_1, of $1,000 earning a nominal interest of 10 percent for several different compounding frequencies. For example, the future value (FV_1) of $1,000 compounded monthly ($m = 12$) at a nominal interest rate (i) of 10 percent per year by Equation 5.17 is

$$FV_1 = \$1,000(1 + \tfrac{.10}{12})^{12 \times 1}$$

$$= \$1,104.71$$

As Table 5.5 shows, the more frequent the compounding, the greater the future value of the deposit. You can see that there appears to be a limit to the future value as compounding frequency increases. As the table shows, at the maximum if we assume continuous compounding the future value is $1,105.17. The formula for future value with continuous compounding is given by:

$$FV_n = PV_0(e)^{in} \tag{5.18}$$

where e is a constant equal to 2.71828. (On your calculator use the e^x key.)

It is fairly simple to solve future values with nonannual compounding frequency on the financial calculator or Excel spreadsheet. We can use the same steps as those for computing the future value of a single sum with annual compounding except that the interest rate and number of periods are expressed in terms of the *compounding frequency*. That is, for the number of periods we enter the value of mn and for the interest rate we enter the value $\frac{i}{m}$. Let's solve the following problem using the calculator:

Table 5.5 Effects of Different Compounding Frequencies on Future Values of $1,000 at a 10 Percent Interest Rate

Initial Amount	Compounding Frequency	Future Value, FV_1 (End of Year 1)
$1,000	Yearly	$1,100.00
1,000	Semiannually	1,102.50
1,000	Quarterly	1,103.81
1,000	Monthly	1,104.71
1,000	Daily	1,105.16
1,000	Continuously*	1,105.17

*The future value of a cash flow when interest is continuously compounded is given by: $FV_n = PV_0(e)^{in}$ where e is the exponential number having the approximate value 2.71828.

What is the future value at the end of 8 years of a deposit today of $5,000, if the annual (nominal) interest rate is 8 percent and the account compounds quarterly? Note that the value entered for N is 32 ($mn = 4 \times 8$) and for I/Y it is 2 ($\frac{i}{m} = \frac{8}{4}$).

Calculator Solution

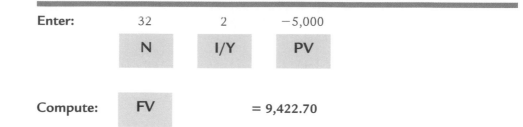

Enter: 32   2   −5,000

| N | I/Y | PV |

Compute: FV   = 9,422.70

The relationship between present values and compound values suggests that present values will also be affected by the frequency of compounding. In general, the present value of a sum to be received at the end of year n, discounted at the rate of i percent and compounded m times per year, is as follows:

(5.19)
$$PV_0 = \frac{FV_n}{\left(1 + \dfrac{i}{m}\right)^{mn}}$$

Table 5.6 contains a number of present values, PV_0, for $1,000 received 1 year in the future discounted at a nominal interest rate of 10 percent with several different compounding frequencies. For example, the present value (PV_0) of $1,000 compounded quarterly ($m = 4$) at a nominal interest rate (i) of 10 percent per year by Equation 5.19 is

$$PV_0 = \frac{\$1,000}{(1 + \frac{.10}{4})^{4 \times 1}}$$

$$= \$905.95$$

As shown in Table 5.6, the more frequent the compounding, the smaller the present value of a future amount. The steps for using the calculator for solving present value of a single sum with nonannual compounding frequency are similar to those for calculating the future value except that now you are computing for the present value.

Table 5.6 Effects of Different Compounding Frequencies on Present Values of $1,000 at a 10 Percent Interest Rate

Amount	Compounding Frequency	Present Value, PV_0
$1,000	Yearly	$909.09
1,000	Semiannually	907.03
1,000	Quarterly	905.95
1,000	Monthly	905.21
1,000	Daily	904.85
1,000	Continuously	904.84

*The present value of a single cash flow when interest is continuously compounded is given by: $PV_0 = FV_n / e^{in}$ where e is the exponential number having the approximate value 2.71828.

EFFECT OF COMPOUNDING PERIODS ON FUTURE AND PRESENT VALUES OF ANNUITIES

In calculating the future and present values of annuities we have assumed that the annuities occur on an annual basis. However, many annuities involve periodic cash flows on a nonannual basis. For example, many bonds pay fixed interest that are stated on an annual basis but are paid semiannually. Another example involves mortgage payments on home loans, which are paid on a monthly frequency. In this section we show you how to calculate future and present values of annuities involving cash flows that are paid in nonannual intervals. We will first discuss future value of an annuity and then the present value of an annuity.

Let's assume that Cindy Capriati wants to set aside $500 every 6 months into a savings account. The account pays 10 percent interest per year but is compounded semiannually. How much will Cindy have in her savings account at the end of 10 years? Recall that the future value of an ordinary annuity with annual payments and compounding is given by Equation 5.10:

$$FVAN_n = PMT(FVIFA_{i, n})$$

To change the above formula to accommodate nonannual payment and compounding, all we need to do is express i and n in terms of the compounding frequency:

$$FVAN_n = PMT(FVIFA_{\frac{i}{m}, mn}) \tag{5.19}$$

Applying this to Cindy's problem we have:

$$
\begin{aligned}
FVAN_{10} &= \$500(FVIFA_{\frac{10}{2}, 2\times10}) \\
&= \$500(FVIFA_{5, 20}) \\
&= \$500(33.066) \\
&= \$16,533
\end{aligned}
$$

So Cindy would have $16,533 at the end of 10 years. This can also be solved using the calculator or the spreadsheet just as we would solve any future value of an ordinary annuity problem except that the number of periods and the interest rate are expressed in terms of the compounding frequency. For number of periods we enter $20(2 \times 10)$ and for interest rate we enter $5(\frac{10}{2})$.

Now let us examine present value of an annuity where the discount rate and payments occur at nonannual frequencies. Let's assume that Moe Sann has an investment opportunity that will pay him $50 every quarter for the next 15 years. How much are these cash flows worth to Moe if he requires an annual rate of 12 percent compounded quarterly? Recall the present value of an ordinary annuity assuming annual compounding is given by Equation 5.13:

$$PVAN_0 = PMT(PVIFA_{i, n})$$

To reflect the frequency of compounding we make the following adjustment similar to what we did in Equation 5.19 in the case of future values:

$$PVAN_0 = PMT(PVIFA_{\frac{i}{m}, mn}) \tag{5.20}$$

Applying the above formula to Moe's problem we have

$$
\begin{aligned}
PVAN_0 &= \$50(PVIFA_{\frac{12}{4}, 4\times15}) \\
&= \$50(PVIFA_{3, 60}) \\
&= \$50(27.676) \\
&= \$1,383.80
\end{aligned}
$$

So, the maximum Moe should pay for this investment is $1,383.80. To solve this using the calculator you would follow the same steps as in solving the present value of an ordinary annuity except that the values for the number of periods and the interest rate are expressed in terms of the frequency interval. That is, with respect to the above problem, you would enter 60 for the number of periods and 3 for interest rate.

EFFECTIVE RATE OF RETURN

Suppose you come across the following two investment opportunities. First Investment Corporation advertises a 10 percent annually compounded rate of return on their savings certificate program. True Investment Corporation offers a similar investment program with a stated annual rate of interest of 10 percent but the compounding is quarterly. Who is offering you the better deal? From the previous section we know that the more frequently an annual *nominal* rate of interest is compounded, the greater is the actual or **effective interest rate** being earned or charged. Thus, investing with True Investment Corporation where your interest is compounded quarterly at a 2.5 percent rate every 3 months is a better deal than investing with First Investment Corporation where the interest is compounded annually at a 10 percent rate.

In this section we show how to compare interest rates with various compounding frequencies. We do this by calculating the *effective annual rate of interest*. The effective annual rate of interest (i_{eff}) can be calculated as follows:

(5.21)
$$i_{eff} = \left(1 + \frac{i}{m}\right)^m - 1$$

where m is the number of compounding intervals per year. Using Equation 5.21, what is the effective annual interest rate for True Investment Corporation? Substituting .10 for i and 4 for m into the right-hand side of Equation 5.21, we have

$$i_{eff} = \left(1 + \frac{.10}{4}\right)^4 - 1$$

$$= .1038 \text{ or } 10.38 \text{ percent}$$

Thus investing with True Investment Corporation yields an effective annual interest rate of 10.38 percent, which exceeds the 10 percent effective annual interest rate of First Investment Corporation. By law firms have to report the **annual percentage rate** or **APR.** APR is simply the stated rate per period annualized by multiplying the rate by the compounding frequency. Thus, if a credit card company charges 1.5 percent interest per month and interest is charged on the monthly balance, the APR is simply 1.5×12, or 18 percent. The APR is a standardized way to calculate the annual interest rate. However, many consumers are led astray because of the mistaken notion that comparing the APRs is sufficient to identify the best deal. That is not so. It is the *effective annual interest rate* that *tells you whether you are getting the best deal or not.*

Using the example of the credit card company, what is the effective rate of interest given that the rate per month is 1.5 percent or that the APR is 18 percent? Using the effective interest rate formula we have:

$$i_{eff} = \left(1 + \frac{.18}{12}\right)^{12} - 1$$

or

$$i_{eff} = (1 + .015)^{12} - 1$$
$$= .1956 \text{ or } 19.56 \text{ percent}$$

Thus, the effective or true interest rate you are being charged is 19.56 percent—*not* the 18 percent APR that is advertised and disclosed in the monthly credit card statement.

Comprehension Check Questions

1. What effect does compounding frequency have on future and present values?
2. What is the relation between effective rate of interest and compounding frequency?
3. What is the difference between effective rate and the nominal rate?

APPLICATION OF PRESENT VALUES AND FUTURE VALUES TO SPECIAL SITUATIONS

In this section we discuss two special applications of the compounding and discounting concepts.

Loan Amortization Problem

One useful application of the present value of an annuity formula is in determining the payments necessary to pay off a loan. ***Loan amortization*** refers to the schedule of payments that are to be made over the life of the loan. While loans can be structured in many ways, most consumer loans (auto, appliances, and home mortgages) are structured so that the borrower pays an equal amount periodically over the term of the loan. In this section we will show you how to determine the loan amortization on a typical consumer loan. For simplicity we will assume that the payments are annual although most consumer loans require monthly payments.

Finance in the News

Click on this button at **http://finance. swlearning.com** *for synopses of recent articles on Time Value of Money.*

For example, suppose you borrowed $10,000 from Lexington State Bank. The loan is for a period of 4 years at an interest rate of 9 percent. It requires that you make four equal, annual, end-of-year payments that include both principal and interest on the outstanding balance. The first step to doing the loan amortization table is to determine the four equal, annual, end-of-year payments. Since this is an ordinary annuity we can use Equation 5.13 to calculate the amount of the payment:

$$\$10,000 = PMT(\text{PVIFA}_{9,\,4})$$

$$PMT = \frac{\$10,000}{3.240}$$

$$= \$3,086$$

Alternatively, we can use the calculator to solve the problem:

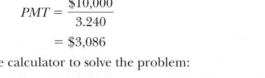

Enter:	4	9	10,000
	N	**I/Y**	**PV**

Compute:	**PMT**	= −3,086.69

Calculator

Solution

FINANCE &The Real World

Bankers use time value of money concepts for loans of all types including home mortgages. When you buy a house, the bank sets up a monthly payment schedule that takes into account interest rates as well as the life of the loan. To calculate the payment, the banker plugs in the interest rate and the number of payment periods into a calculator or computer. As the years go by, your monthly mortgage payment pays interest on the loan and reduces the loan balance, thus boosting your home equity.

In recent years, a new type of mortgage has emerged to help people who own their homes but need cash for living expenses. It's called a "reverse" mortgage. Reverse mortgages have become extremely popular as people approach retirement without the nest egg that they thought they would have from the poorly-performing stock market. It is a way to generate cash without having to pay the money back.

Here's how it works: A person approaching retirement whose home is largely paid off receives payments from the bank, thus relinquishing equity in the home. In one scenario, the person can receive income for life. In another, the income can be taken over a fixed period of time, as a line of credit or as a lump sum. The money is tax-free because it is a loan that is essentially paid off at death when the bank reclaims the house. At the homeowner's death, the bank owns the house.

The amount of the loan depends on the value of the house and the person's age. For example, a 77-year old couple with a home worth $250,000 would qualify for a reverse mortgage of $175,600. It could be paid out in a lump sum or a monthly payout that would add up to that amount by the time both died, less loan costs. In this case, the couple would net $1,069 per month. Again, the banker uses a calculator or computer to come up with the payment, plugging in such variables as interest rates as well as the person's life expectancy.

One catch is that the person must continue to live in the house. Once that no longer is the case, the loan comes due. So it wouldn't be a good idea if, say, your parents want to sell you their house at some time in the future, or if they want to sell it to retire to Arizona. Another catch is that the person must be at least 62 years of age when signing up.

Because the homeowner makes no monthly payments, the loan isn't amortized in the traditional way. Instead, the amount owed grows larger over time—and the equity in the home shrinks. In the meantime, the homeowner is still responsible for property taxes, insurance, and repairs. The bank will make sure that the home is kept in good shape so that it can be sold at a later date.

Sources: Business Week Online, April 5, 2001, "Forward Thinking About Reverse Mortgages"; *Time* magazine, February 17, 2003, p. 99, "The Backwards Loan"; http://www.aarp.org/revmort

The slight difference between the interest factor and calculator solutions is due to the rounding error induced by the tables. By making four annual, end-of-year payments to the bank of $3,086 each, you will completely pay off your loan, plus provide the bank with its 9 percent interest return. The loan amortization schedule is developed in Table 5.7. Note that the table shows, for each year, the beginning balance, annual payment, annual interest, payment towards principal, and the ending balance. At the beginning of year 1, your loan balance is $10,000. At the end of year 1 you make a payment of $3,087 (value from calculator rounded to the nearest dollar). Of this annual payment, the interest portion is $900 determined as the beginning balance times the annual interest rate ($10,000 × .09). The portion going toward principal reduction, $2,187, is the difference between the annual payment and the interest amount ($3,087 − $900). Similar calculations are done for years 2, 3, and 4. Note that although the payments are fixed, *the amount going towards interest and principal varies over time.* Specifically, the interest component diminishes with time while the

Table 5.7 Loan Amortization Table

Year	Beginning Balance	Annual Payment	Interest Amount	Principal Reduction	Ending Balance
1	$10,000	$3,087	$900	$2,187	$7,813
2	7,813	3,087	703	2,384	5,429
3	5,429	3,087	489	2,598	2,831
4	2,831	3,087	255	2,832	0

amount applied towards principal reduction increases with time. This problem illustrates why homeowners find that in the early years of their mortgage loan very little equity is built up—most of the payment goes toward interest and relatively little toward principal reduction.

The spreadsheet is very handy in solving loan amortization problems. The loan amortization shown in Table 5.7 can be solved using the spreadsheet below.

Calculating Growth Rates

A common application of the compounding formula is the calculation of growth rates. In the context of the present and future values, the notion of interest rates and growth rates are similar.

Some stock valuation models require estimates of the growth rates in dividends or earnings per share. One way to estimate growth rates is by examining historical data. For example, assume Sara Lee Corporation had earnings per share of $0.96 in fiscal year ending June 30, 1997 and $1.62 in fiscal year ending June 30, 2002. We can calculate Sara Lee's compound annual growth rate in earnings per share over this 5-year period by applying the future value of a single cash flow

	A	B	C	D	E	F	G	H
3								
4			Using a Spreadsheet to Amortize an Annual Loan					
5								
6		Loan amount=		$10,000				
7		Interest rate=		9%	Comment:			
8		Loan term=		4	Payment is calculated using the PMT function (PMT(rate,nper,PV)) and			
9		Loan payment=		$3,086.69	then taking the absolute value of the resulting answer:			
10					"+ABS(PMT(D7,D8,D6))."			
11								
12								
13				Amortization Table				
14		Year	Beginning		Interest	Principal	Ending	
15			Balance	Payment	Paid	Paid	Balance	
16		1	$10,000.00	$3,086.69	$900.00	$2,186.69	$7,813.31	
17		2	7,813.31	$3,086.69	$703.20	$2,383.49	$5,429.82	
18		3	5,429.82	$3,086.69	$488.68	$2,598.00	$2,831.82	
19		4	2,831.82	$3,086.69	$254.86	$2,831.82	$0.00	
20		Totals		$12,346.75	$2,346.75	$10,000.00		
21								
22				Formulas Used in the Amortization Table:				
23		Year	Beginning		Interest	Principal	Ending	
24			Balance	Payment	Paid	Paid	Balance	
25		1	=+D6	=+$D$9	=+C16*$D$7	=+D16-E16	=+C16-F16	
26		2	=+G16	=+$D$9	=+C17*$D$7	=+D17-E17	=+C17-F17	
27		3	=+G17	=+$D$9	=+C18*$D$7	=+D18-E18	=+C18-F18	
28		4	=+G18	=+$D$9	=+C19*$D$7	=+D19-E19	=+C19-F19	
29		Totals		=+SUM(D16:D19)	=+SUM(E16:E19)	=+SUM(F16:F19)		
30								
31		Comment:						
32		Ending balance must be zero. Addition of interest paid and principal paid must be equal to total of payments.						
33								
34								

Spreadsheet strategies

formula. We can think of the earnings per share in fiscal year 1997 as the present value and the earnings per share in fiscal year 2002 as the future value 5 years later. Using the mathematical formula for the future value of a single cash flow, we have:

$$\$1.62 = \$0.96 \, (1 + i)^5$$
$$(1+i)^5 = \frac{\$1.62}{\$0.96}$$
$$i = (1.6875)^{\frac{1}{5}} - 1$$
$$i = 0.11 \text{ or } 11\%$$

Or, using the tables:

$$\$1.62 = \$0.96(\text{FVIF}_{i, 5})$$
$$\text{FVIF}_{i, 5} = 1.6875$$

From Table I, we find this future value interest factor in the 5-year (period) row under the 11 percent interest (or growth rate) column. Hence, Sara Lee's earnings per share have grown at an annual compound rate of growth of 11 percent over the past 5 years.

We could also have solved this using the present value of a single sum formulation. Mathematically, this would be equal to:

$$\$0.96 = \$1.62/(1 + i)^5$$
$$(1 + i)^5 = \frac{\$1.62}{\$0.96}$$
$$i = (1.6875)^{\frac{1}{5}} - 1$$
$$i = 0.11 \text{ or } 11\%$$

Using the present value tables:

$$\$0.96 = \$1.62(\text{PVIF}_{i, 5})$$
$$\text{PVIF}_{i, 5} = 0.5926$$

From Table II, we find this present value interest factor in the 5-year (period) row under 11 percent interest, or growth rate, column.

Alternatively, the problem may be solved using the calculator:

Calculator Solution

Enter:	5	−0.96	1.62
	N	PV	FV

Compute:	I/Y	= 11.03

Comprehension Check Questions

1. What is a loan amortization schedule?
2. How can you use present and future value formulas to calculate the growth rate in a variable?

Summary

➤ The time value of money plays an important role in many areas of financial decision making. The time value of money refers to the fact that a dollar to be received or paid in the future is worth less than that today.

➤ Interest is the return earned by or the amount paid to someone who has forgone current consumption. Sometimes the interest rate is referred to by other names including opportunity rate, discount rate, required rate of return, and compound rate of return.

➤ Simple interest is interest earned or paid on the principal only. Compound interest is interest paid not only on the principal but also on any interest earned but not withdrawn during earlier periods.

➤ An annuity is the payment or receipt of a series of equal cash flows per period for a specified number of periods. In an ordinary annuity, the cash flows occur at the *end* of each period. In an annuity due, the cash flows occur at the *beginning* of each period.

➤ Table 5.8 summarizes the equations used to compute the future and present values of the various cash flow streams.

Table 5.8 Summary of Future Value and Present Value Formulas

Type of Problem	Equation	Interest Factor Table	Equation Number in Text
Future value of a single cash flow	$FV_n = PV_0(1 + i)^n$ or $FV_n = PV_0(FVIF_{i,n})$	I	5.6, 5.7
Present value of a single cash flow	$PV_0 = FV_n\left[\dfrac{1}{(1 + i)^n}\right]$ or $PV_0 = FV_n(PVIF_{i,n})$	II	5.8, 5.9
Future value of an ordinary annuity	$FVAN_n = PMT(FVIFA_{i,n})$	III	5.10
Future value of an annuity due	$FVAND_n = FVAN_n(1 + i)$ or $FVAND_n = PMT[FVIFA_{i,n}(1 + i)]$	III	5.11, 5.12
Present value of an ordinary annuity	$PVAN_0 = PMT(PVIFA_{i,n})$	IV	5.13
Present value of an annuity due	$PVAND_0 = PVAN_0(1 + i)$ or $PVAND_0 = [PMT(PVIFA_{i,n})](1 + i)$	IV	5.14, 5.15
Present value of a perpetuity	$PVPER_0 = \dfrac{PMT}{i}$	—	5.16

Definitions:
n = *number of time periods of discounting or compounding (usually years).*
i = *annual rate of interest (i.e., annual nominal interest rate).*
PMT = *annuity cash flow (i.e., amount of cash flow paid or received for a specified number of years or forever in the case of a perpetuity). In an ordinary annuity, the cash flows are received at the end of each year. In an annuity due, the cash flows are received at the beginning of each year.*

➤ The future value interest factor tells you how much $1 today is worth at some point in the future given a length of time and interest rate. The future value interest factor of annuity tells you how much a $1 annuity is worth at a particular interest rate at the end of a given length of time.

➤ The present value interest factor tells you how much $1 to be received at some point in the future is worth today at a given interest (discount) rate. The present value interest factor of annuity tells you how much a $1 annuity over a given length of time is worth today at a given interest rate.

➤ The more frequently compounding occurs during a given period, the higher is the effective interest rate on an investment. More frequent compounding results in higher future values and lower present values than less frequent compounding at the same interest rate.

➤ A loan amortization schedule shows the dollar amount and total number of periodic payments owed on a debt obligation. It also shows the loan balance after each payment and gives the breakdown of interest and principal of each payment.

Questions and Topics for Discussion

1. Which would you rather receive: the proceeds from a 2-year investment paying 5 percent simple interest per year or from one paying 5 percent compound interest? Why?

2. Which is greater: the future value interest factor (FVIF) for 10 percent and 2 years or the present value interest factor (PVIF) for 10 percent and 2 years?

3. What happens to the present value of an annuity as the interest rate increases? What happens to the future value of an annuity as the interest rate increases?

4. Which would you prefer to invest in: a savings account paying 6 percent compounded annually or a savings account paying 6 percent compounded daily? Why?

5. What type of contract might require the use of annuity due computations?

6. What effect does more frequent compounding have on present values?

7. Explain what is meant by the *Rule of 72*?

8. What is the relationship between present value and future value?

9. What is the difference between an ordinary annuity and an annuity due? Give examples of each.

10. If you have the same number of cash flows, which will have a greater future value—ordinary annuity or an annuity due?

11. If the required rate of return increases, what is the impact on the following?
    a. A present value of an annuity
    b. A future value of an annuity

12. Describe how to set up a loan amortization schedule.

13. Give an example of a perpetuity. How does a perpetuity differ from an annuity?

14. Explain how to determine the present value of an uneven cash flow stream.

Self-Test Problems

ST1. Calculate the value in 5 years of $1,000 deposited in a savings account today if the account pays interest at a rate of:

a. 8 percent per year, compounded annually

b. 8 percent per year, compounded quarterly

ST2. A business is considering purchasing a machine that is projected to yield cash savings of $1,000 per year over a 10-year period. Using a 12 percent discount rate, calculate the present value of the savings. (Assume that the cash savings occur at the end of each year.)

ST3. You own a small business and have put it up for sale. You have been offered $2,000 per year for 5 years, with the first receipt at the end of 4 years. Calculate the present value of this offer, using a 14 percent discount rate.

ST4. Simpson Peripherals earned $0.90 per share in 1998 and $1.52 in 2003. Calculate the annual growth rate in earnings per share over this period.

ST5. Yolanda Williams is 35 years old today and is beginning to plan for her retirement. She wants to set aside an equal amount at the *end* of each of the next 25 years so that she can retire at age 60. She expects to live to an age of 80 and wants to be able to withdraw $50,000 per year from the account on her 61st through 80th birthdays. The account is expected to earn 10 percent per year for the entire period of time. Determine the size of the annual deposits that she must make.

Problems

1. How much will $1,000 deposited in a savings account earning a compound annual interest rate of 6 percent be worth at the end of the following number of years? **BASIC**

a. 3 years

b. 5 years

c. 10 years

2. If you require a 9 percent return on your investments, which would you prefer? **BASIC**

a. $5,000 today

b. $15,000 five years from today

c. $1,000 per year for 15 years

3. The Lancer Leasing Company has agreed to lease a hydraulic trencher to the Chavez Excavation Company for $20,000 a year over the next 8 years. Lease payments are to be made at the beginning of each year. Assuming that Lancer invests these payments at an annual rate of 9 percent, how much will it have accumulated by the end of the 8th year? **INTERMEDIATE**

4. The Mutual Assurance and Life Company is offering an insurance policy under either of the following two terms: **INTERMEDIATE**

a. Make a series of 12 payments of $1,200 at the beginning of each of the next 12 years (the first payment being made today)

b. Make a single lump-sum payment today of $10,000 and receive coverage for the next 12 years

If you had investment opportunities offering an 8 percent annual return, which alternative would you prefer?

BASIC **5.** How much must you deposit at the end of each year in an account that pays a nominal annual rate of 20 percent, if at the end of 5 years you want $10,000 in the account?

BASIC **6.** A leading broker has advertised money multiplier certificates that will triple your money in 9 years; that is, if you buy one for $333.33 today, it will pay you $1,000 at the end of 9 years. What rate of return will you earn on these money multiplier certificates?

BASIC **7.** What is the present value of $800 to be received at the end of 8 years, assuming the following annual interest rate?

   a. 4 percent, discounted annually

   b. 8 percent, discounted annually

   c. 20 percent, discounted quarterly

   d. 0 percent

BASIC **8.** Mr. Jones bought a building for $60,000, payable on the following terms: a $10,000 down payment and 25 equal annual installment payments to include principal and interest of 10 percent per annum. Calculate the amount of the installment payments. How much of the first year's payment goes toward reducing the principal amount?

BASIC **9.** A firm purchases 100 acres of land for $200,000 and agrees to remit 20 equal annual end-of-year installments of $41,067 each. What is the effective annual interest rate on this loan?

BASIC **10.** Susan Robinson is planning for her retirement. She is 30 years old today and would like to have $600,000 when she turns 55. She estimates that she will be able to earn a 9 percent rate of return on her retirement investments over time; she wants to set aside a constant amount of money every year (at the end of the year) to help achieve her objective. How much money must Robinson invest at the end of each of the next 25 years to realize her goal of $600,000 at the end of that time?

BASIC **11.** A life insurance company offers loans to its policyholders against the cash value of their policies at a (nominal) annual interest rate of 8 percent, compounded quarterly. Determine the effective annual percentage interest rate on these loans.

BASIC **12.** Your great-uncle Claude is 82 years old. Over the years, he has accumulated savings of $80,000. He estimates that he will live another 10 years at the most and wants to spend his savings by then. (If he lives longer than that, he figures you will be happy to take care of him.) Uncle Claude places his $80,000 into an account earning 10 percent annually and sets it up in such a way that he will be making 10 equal annual withdrawals—the first one occurring 1 year from now—such that his account balance will be zero at the end of 10 years. How much will he be able to withdraw each year?

INTERMEDIATE **13.** You decide to purchase a building for $30,000 by paying $5,000 down and assuming a mortgage of $25,000. The bank offers you a 15-year mortgage requiring annual end-of-year payments of $3,188 each. The bank also requires you to pay a 3 percent loan origination fee, which will reduce the effective amount the bank lends to you. Compute the annual percentage rate of interest on this loan.

14. An investment promises to pay $6,000 at the end of each year for the next
5 years and $4,000 at the end of each year for years 6 through 10.

    a. If you require a 12 percent rate of return on an investment of this sort, what is the maximum amount you would pay for this investment?

    b. Assuming that the payments are received at the *beginning* of each year, what is the maximum amount you would pay for this investment, given a 12 percent required rate of return?

15. Your parents have discovered a $1,000 bond at the bottom of their safe deposit
box. The bond was given to you by your late great-aunt Hilda on your second birthday. The bond pays interest at a rate of 5 percent per annum, compounded annually. Interest accumulates and is paid at the time the bond is redeemed. You are now 27 years old. What is the current worth of the bond (principal plus interest)?

16. Your mother is planning to retire this year. Her firm has offered her a lump-
sum retirement payment of $50,000 or a $6,000 lifetime annuity—whichever she chooses. Your mother is in reasonably good health and expects to live for at least 15 more years. Which option should she choose, assuming that an 8 percent interest rate is appropriate to evaluate the annuity?

17. Construct a loan amortization schedule for a 3-year, 11 percent loan of
$30,000. The loan requires three equal, end-of-year payments.

18. Mitchell Investments has offered you the following investment opportunity:

- $6,000 at the end of each year for the first 5 years, plus
- $3,000 at the end of each year from years 6 through 10, plus
- $2,000 at the end of each year from years 11 through 20.

    a. How much would you be willing to pay for this investment if you required a 12 percent rate of return?

    b. If the payments were received at the beginning of each year, what would you be willing to pay for this investment?

19. Upon retirement, your goal is to spend 5 years traveling around the world. To
travel in the style to which you are accustomed will require $250,000 per year at the beginning of each year. If you plan to retire in 30 years, what are the equal, annual, end-of-year payments necessary to achieve this goal? The funds in the retirement account will compound at 10 percent annually.

20. You deposit $4,500 per year at the end of each of the next 25 years into an ac-
count that pays 10 percent compounded annually. How much could you withdraw at the end of each of the 20 years following your last deposit? (The 25th and last deposit is made at the beginning of the 20-year period. The first withdrawal is made at the end of the first year in the 20-year period.)

21. You deposit $10,000 at the end of each of the next 4 years into an account that
pays 12 percent annually. What is the account balance at the end of 10 years?

22. Determine the value at the end of 3 years of a $10,000 investment (today) in a
bank certificate of deposit (CD) that pays a nominal annual interest rate of 8 percent, compounded

    a. Semiannually

    b. Quarterly

    c. Monthly

CHALLENGE **23.** An investment offers the following year-end cash flows:

End of Year	Cash Flow
1	$20,000
2	$30,000
3	$40,000

Using a 15 percent interest rate, convert this series of irregular cash flows to an equivalent (in present value terms) 3-year annuity.

CHALLENGE **24.** James Street's son, Harold, is 10 years old today. Harold, a studious young fellow, already is making plans to go to college on his 18th birthday, and his father wants to start putting money away now for that purpose. Street estimates that Harold will need $18,000, $19,000, $20,000, and $21,000 for his freshman, sophomore, junior, and senior years, respectively. He plans on making these amounts available to Harold at the beginning of each of these years.

Street would like to make eight annual deposits (the first of which would be made on Harold's 11th birthday, 1 year from now, and the last on his 18th birthday, the day he leaves for college) in an account earning 10 percent annually. He wants the account to eventually be worth enough to *just* pay for Harold's college expenses. Any balances remaining in the account will continue to earn the 10 percent.

How much will Street have to deposit in this "planning" account each year to provide for Harold's education?

INTERMEDIATE **25.** How much must you deposit at the end of each quarter in an account that pays a nominal interest rate of 20 percent, compounded quarterly, if at the end of 5 years you want $10,000 in the account? (Hint: You may need to adjust the interest rate and the number of compounding periods to reflect quarterly, rather than annual, compounding.)

INTERMEDIATE **26.** IRA Investments develops retirement programs for individuals. You are 30 years old and plan to retire on your 60th birthday. You want to establish a plan with IRA that will require a series of equal, annual, end-of-year deposits into the retirement account. The first deposit will be made 1 year from today on your 31st birthday. The final payment on the account will be made on your 60th birthday. The retirement plan will allow you to withdraw $120,000 per year for 15 years, with the first withdrawal on your 61st birthday. Also at the end of the 15th year, you wish to withdraw an additional $250,000. The retirement account promises to earn 12 percent annually.

What periodic payment must be made into the account to achieve your retirement objective?

CHALLENGE **27.** You have just had your 30th birthday. You have two children. One will go to college 10 years from now and require four beginning-of-year payments for college expenses of $10,000, $11,000, $12,000, and $13,000. The second child will go to college 15 years from now and require four beginning-of-year payments for college expenses of $15,000, $16,000, $17,000, and $18,000. In addition, you plan to retire in 30 years. You want to be able to withdraw $50,000 per year (at the end of each year) from an account throughout your retirement. You expect to live 20 years beyond retirement. The first withdrawal will occur on your 61st birthday.

What equal, annual, end-of-year amount must you save for each of the next 30 years to meet these goals, if all savings earn a 13 percent annual rate of return?

28. Steven White is considering taking early retirement, having saved $400,000. **INTERMEDIATE** White desires to determine how many years the savings will last if $40,000 per year is withdrawn at the end of each year. White feels the savings can earn 10 percent per year.

29. Your son, Charlie, has just turned 15. Charlie plans to go to college to study **CHALLENGE** electronics on his 18th birthday. College is expected to cost Charlie $15,000, $16,000, $17,000, and $18,000 for each of his 4 years in school. You want these funds to be available to him at the beginning of each year in college. In addition, you want to give Charlie a $25,000 graduation gift on his 22nd birthday so that he can get a start on his career or on graduate school.

    You currently have $8,000 to meet these obligations. You want to save an equal amount at the end of each of the next 6 years to meet the remaining obligations. If your investments earn 7 percent per annum, how much must you save at the end of each of the next 6 years?

30. Crab State Bank has offered you a $1,000,000 5-year loan at an interest rate of **INTERMEDIATE** 11.25 percent, requiring equal annual end-of-year payments that include both principal and interest on the unpaid balance. Develop an amortization schedule for this loan.

31. Try using one of the many Internet savings calculators (such as the one on **INTERMEDIATE** msn.com: http://moneycentral.msn.com/investor/calcs/n_savapp/main.asp) to solve the following savings problems:

    a. How much will you have at the end of 25 years if you save $300 each month for the next 25 years and the savings earn 7 percent per year?

    b. How long would it take to attain $30,000 if you set aside $200 per month in an account earning 8 percent per year?

32. Using one of the mortgage loan calculators available on the Internet (e.g., **INTERMEDIATE** http://www.bankrate.com), do a loan amortization for a $150,000, 30-year mortgage loan at a rate of 5 percent and answer the following questions:

    a. How much is the monthly payment?

    b. How much of the first payment (i.e., year 1, month 1) goes towards interest? towards principal reduction?

    c. How much of the 180th payment (i.e., year 15, month 12) goes towards interest? towards principal reduction?

    d. What is the remaining balance on the loan at the end of the fifth year?

CHAPTER
6 Analysis of Risk and Return

In this chapter we discuss the concepts of risk and the relationship between risk and return. The last section of Chapter 2 provides an excellent starting point for a discussion of these concepts. In Chapter 2 we noted that U.S. Treasury bills and government bonds historically had the lowest volatility in returns but also had the lowest returns. Corporate bonds had a comparatively greater dispersion of returns and higher returns than government bonds. And, common stocks exhibited the highest returns, but these were associated with the highest risk. Thus, it appears that investors require, and are rewarded with, higher rates of return for assuming greater risk.

In this chapter we further expand upon the notion of risk and how to measure it. We look at risk from the perspective of an individual asset held in isolation as well as when it is part of a large portfolio of assets. We also discuss a model *(Capital Asset Pricing Model)* that relates risk to required rate of return. This model is important because, as we shall learn in later chapters, the value of any asset is a function of the future cash flows from the asset and the rate of return required on the investment. Thus, the required rate of return plays an important part in determining the value of an asset. Specifically, we will show that the required rate of return depends on the riskiness of the returns from the asset.

FINANCIAL MARKET HISTORICAL RETURNS

As an introduction to the concepts in this chapter it would serve us well to briefly review the historical record of returns for various classes of securities. We will examine the historical returns to large-company stocks, small-company stocks, Treasury bills, and long-term government bonds. These returns were tabulated by Ibbotson and Associates and are widely used by finance professionals. Large-company stocks consist of firms in the S&P 500 Composite Index. Recall from Chapter 2 that this index is constructed of 500 very large companies. Small-company stocks are defined as companies with a market capitalization of $604 million or less and included in the DFA Micro Cap Fund. Treasury bill returns are based on U.S. Treasury securities with a maturity of 30 days. Long-term government bonds refer to obligations of the U.S. government that have a maturity of approximately 20 years.

Figure 6.1 shows how much $1 invested in each of these classes of securities in 1925 (year-end) would have grown to by 2002 (year-end). A dollar invested in T-bills in 1925 would amount to $17.48 by the end of 2002. The same dollar invested in long-term government bonds would be worth $59.70 by the end of 2002. On the other hand a dollar invested in large-company stocks in 1925 would have an ending value of $1,775.34 by the end of 2002 while the same dollar invested in small-company stocks would have translated to a whopping $6,816.41 by the end of 2002. Why are the ending values so dramatically different for government bonds versus common stocks? Also, why do they differ between small-company and large-company stocks? The answer may be found partially in Figure 6.2. The figure shows the average annual returns for the four classes of securities and their standard deviations and frequency distributions over the period 1926–2002. Let's focus on the average annual returns and the frequency distributions. The average annual return on T-bills is 3.8 percent while on long-term government securities it is 5.8 percent. Large-company stocks yielded an average annual return of 12.2 percent and small-company stocks had an average annual return of 16.9 percent. These returns mirror the findings observed in Figure 6.1. Now let's examine the frequency distributions. The frequency distribution diagram is a histogram of the probability or frequency of occurrence of the return outcome. Note that in the case of T-bills the frequency distribution is relatively "tight"—there is not much dispersion. Further, note that there are only few instances where the return is negative. The long-term government bonds have a somewhat wider distribution. However, compared to the two government securities distributions (i.e., T-bills and long-term government bonds) the large- and small-company stocks exhibit a much wider distribution. The small-company stocks evidence the widest swings in annual returns. Also, note that

Figure 6.1
Value at the End of 2002 of $1 Invested at the End of 1925 in Various Classes of Securities

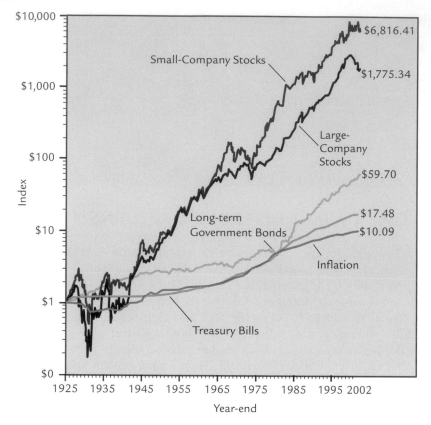

Source: Stocks, bonds, bills, and inflation, 2003 yearbook *(Chicago, Ill.: R.G. Ibbotson Associates)*

there are comparatively more instances where the large- and small-company stocks exhibit negative returns. It appears that while small-company stocks yield the highest average returns, they are accompanied by the most dispersion. In fact comparing the average returns, to the frequency distribution we see a pattern of increased returns being associated with the increased dispersion of returns. This is one of the basic principles of finance: *Higher returns are associated with higher risk.* The rest of this chapter is devoted to developing the notion of risk and the relationship between risk and return.

THE MEANING OF RISK

Most people probably have some idea of risk. Although our focus is from a financial perspective, we also experience risk in our personal lives. In common parlance, risk may be viewed as a chance that some unfavorable event will occur. It could be, for example, the chance that you will be involved in an auto accident on your way to work, or the chance that a hurricane will hit the city where you live. From the perspective of finance, **risk** is defined as *the possibility that actual future returns will deviate from expected returns.* In other words, it represents the *variability* of returns. The returns may be measured in different ways: net income, cash flows, earnings per share, return on investment, holding period returns, etc. Regardless of how you define returns, most financial assets will exhibit risk in their returns.

Table 6.1 shows the annual earnings per share that were forecast for Delta Air Lines common stock for the period 1993–2002. These forecasts were made just before the start of the year by financial analysts at Value Line. Value Line is one of

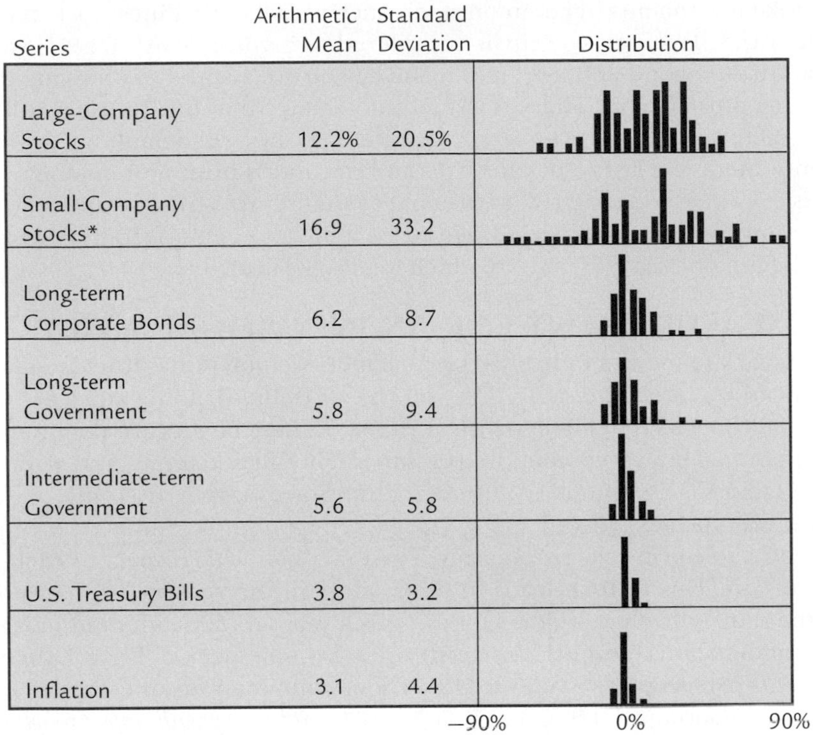

Series	Arithmetic Mean	Standard Deviation	Distribution
Large-Company Stocks	12.2%	20.5%	
Small-Company Stocks*	16.9	33.2	
Long-term Corporate Bonds	6.2	8.7	
Long-term Government	5.8	9.4	
Intermediate-term Government	5.6	5.8	
U.S. Treasury Bills	3.8	3.2	
Inflation	3.1	4.4	

−90%   0%   90%

Figure 6.2
Average Annual Returns and Standard Deviation of Returns of Various Classes of Securities 1926–2002

*The 1933 Small Company Stocks Total Return was 142.9 percent.

Source: Stocks, bonds, bills, and inflation, 2003 yearbook *(Chicago, Ill.: R.G. Ibbotson Associates)*

many firms that provide research services, which include earnings projections, to investors. Table 6.1 also shows the actual earnings per share for each year. Note that the actual values never match the forecasted values. In some years the actual earnings per share were better than the forecasted values and in other years, worse. Thus, it is evident that common stockholders of Delta Air Lines are subject to risk.

Table 6.1 Forecasted and Actual Earnings per Share for Delta Air Lines Common Stock

Year	Forecasted Earnings per Share	Actual Earnings per Share
2002	$ −8.95	$ −7.89
2001	$ 7.80	$ −8.46
2000	$ 7.31	$ 6.87
1999	$ 6.60	$ 7.20
1998	$ 6.00	$ 6.34
1997	$ 9.25	$ 5.51
1996	$ 8.00	$ 0.71
1995	$ 2.60	$ 2.01
1994	$ 1.20	$ −1.87
1993	$ −5.45	$ −5.27

Source: Various issues of Value Line Investment Survey

Unlike investments in common stock, such as Delta Air Lines stock, an investment in a U.S. Treasury security is considered to be **default risk**–free. If you purchase a Treasury bond and hold it to maturity, you are assured of receiving the maturity value plus interest. There is virtually no chance that the Treasury will fail to redeem these securities at maturity or that the Treasury will default on any interest payments owed. As a last resort, the Treasury can always print more money.

Basically we can define risk as the chance that returns from an investment will be different from those expected. However, a more precise definition of risk requires the use of *probability concepts,* which we discuss next.

RISK MEASUREMENT FOR AN INDIVIDUAL ASSET

Let us go back to the example of Delta Air Lines. We noted that forecasted and actual returns are rarely the same. The returns on Delta Air Lines stock are a function of many factors that affect the firm. Some of these factors are the outlook for the economy, oil prices, competitive pressures, labor negotiations, and so on. Each of these factors is associated with uncertainty. For example, the outlook for the economy over the next year may be good, moderate, or poor. Similarly, the price of oil may be stable or it may rise sharply. The outcomes with respect to each factor are uncertain. This in turn leads to uncertainty in the returns to shareholders. Thus, the returns to shareholders for any given year are dependent upon the particular combination of events that occur over that time period. From a finance or investments perspective we refer to the various combinations of events as **states of nature.** It is important to recognize that it is the *uncertainty with respect to which state of nature will occur that causes the riskiness in the returns.* Thus, if we could know for sure that the economy will be moderate, oil prices will be low, and labor cost will be stable, then there is no risk because we know what the returns are going to be given these outcomes. However, given that we do *not* know with certainty which states of nature will occur, the returns are going to be uncertain.

Probability Distribution

We now develop a measure of risk based on the concept of probability distributions. A **probability distribution** shows the possible unique outcomes and their associated probabilities. Let us assume that returns to Delta Air Lines stockholders are a function of the *state of the economy* and the *state of oil prices.* Also, let us assume that the state of the economy is either going to be good or bad and that the oil prices will be stable or increase. (This is an oversimplification of what occurs in reality, but it helps to illustrate the concept of risk.) In the real world there are, of course, many more factors than just the two considered here. Furthermore, these factors may have many outcomes, rather than a few discrete values as we have assumed; for example, the state of the economy as measured by the rate of growth of GDP assumes values over a continuum rather than just two possibilities—good or bad. Next, let us assign probabilities to these different events. The probability that a particular outcome or event will occur is defined as the percentage chance (or likelihood) of its occurrence. The sum of all the outcomes should equal 100 percent. Let us assume that the probability of a good economy is .6 (60%) and the probability of a poor economy is .4 (40%). In other words, we are saying that the odds are 6 out of 10 that the economy over the next year will be good. Conversely, there is 4 in 10 chance of a poor economy during this time. Similarly, let us assume that the probability that oil prices will remain stable or increase is .4 and .6, respectively. This gives us a total of four possible combinations of outcomes with corresponding returns and associated probabilities. These four distinct combinations are summarized in Table 6.2. The table shows a two-by-two matrix that reflects the four possible combinations: (1) good economy and stable

Table 6.2 Forecasted Returns for Delta Air Lines Stock		
	State of Oil Prices	
State of the Economy	Stable (0.4)	High (0.6)
Good (0.6)	20% (0.24)	10% (0.36)
Poor (0.4)	5% (0.16)	−5% (0.24)

oil price, (2) good economy and higher oil price, (3) poor economy and stable oil price, and (4) poor economy and higher oil price.

From the table we observe that the projected return is 20 percent if the economy is good and oil price is stable, 10 percent if the economy is good but oil price increases, 5 percent if the economy is poor but oil price is stable, and −5 percent if the economy is poor and oil price increases. The variation in returns from −5 percent to 20 percent—depending on which combination of outcomes will occur—is indicative of the risk inherent in this stock. Another stock may be characterized by less (or more) dispersion if its returns were less (or more) sensitive to the two risk factors: economy and oil price.

While a visual inspection of the range of returns provides a useful indication of the risk, comparing risk across a large number of stocks would be much easier if risk could be captured in a single number. To do this we first need to calculate the probability of each of the four outcomes. The probability of each of the four outcomes, shown in parenthesis next to each of the return outcomes in Table 6.2, is the *joint probability* that the particular state of the economy and the state of oil prices will occur. If we assume that the state of the economy and the state of oil prices are *independent* factors, then their joint probability is simply the product of their respective probabilities. Recall from your knowledge of statistics that two factors or variables are considered independent if the value of one does not systematically depend on the value for the other. The assumption that oil prices and the economy are independent may not be a reasonable one. However, for the purposes of this discussion we will assume the two are independent. Thus, the probability of a good economy and stable oil price is calculated as the product of the probability of a good economy and the probability of stable oil price ($0.60 \times 0.40 = 0.24$). In similar manner, the joint probabilities of the other three combinations may be calculated.

The returns in Table 6.2 may be viewed as outcomes arising from a **subjective distribution.** It is a subjective distribution because the return estimates are based on (subjective) opinions of an individual, for example, a financial analyst following Delta Air Lines stock. Using the possible return outcomes and their associated probabilities, we can draw the *discrete probability distribution* as shown in Figure 6.3. We refer to this as a **discrete distribution** because the returns take on only certain specific values and are not continuous. The distribution shows the possible unique outcomes of returns and their associated probabilities. There are two statistics that are commonly used to describe a distribution: the expected value and the standard deviation.

Expected Value The *expected value* is a *statistical measure of the mean or average value of possible outcomes.* Operationally, it is defined as the weighted average of possible outcomes, with the weights being the probabilities of occurrence.

Figure 6.3
Discrete Probability
Distribution for Delta
Air Lines Stock Using
Forecasted Returns

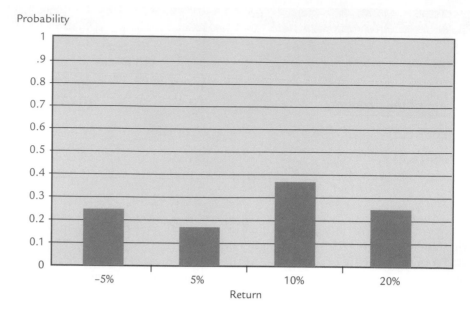

Algebraically, the expected returns from an asset or security may be defined as follows:

$$\hat{r} = \sum_{j=1}^{n} r_j p_j$$

(6.1)

where $\hat{r}$ is the expected return; r_j is the jth possible outcome out of n total outcomes; and p_j is the probability that the jth outcome will occur. The Σ symbol indexed over j going from 1 to n is a short-form notation, which means that the operation following this notation ($r_j \times p_j$) should be summed over the n possible outcomes. Table 6.3 shows the calculation of expected return for Delta Air Lines. The expected return based on the subjective distribution is 8.0 percent.

Standard Deviation The second statistic we wish to calculate is the **standard deviation**. *It is a statistic that captures the degree of dispersion around the mean or the expected value.* It is defined as the square root of the sum of the squared differences of the individual outcomes around the expected value weighted by their corresponding probabilities. It is computed as follows:

$$\sigma = \sqrt{\sum_{j=1}^{n} (r_j - \hat{r})^2 p_j}$$

(6.2)

where σ is the standard deviation.

Table 6.3 Expected Return Calculation Using Forecasted Returns for Delta Air Lines Stock

r_j	p_j	$r_j \times p_j$
20%	0.24	4.8%
10%	0.36	3.6%
5%	0.16	0.8%
−5%	0.24	−1.2%

$$\text{Expected Return} = \hat{r} = \sum_{j=1}^{n} r_j p_j = 8.0\%$$

Table 6.4 Standard Deviation Calculation Using Forecasted Returns for Delta Air Lines Stock

r_j	$\hat{r}$	$r_j - \hat{r}$	$(r_j - \hat{r})^2$	p_j	$(r_j - \hat{r})^2 \times p_j$
20%	8%	12%	144	0.24	34.56
10%	8%	2%	4	0.36	1.44
5%	8%	3%	9	0.16	1.44
−5%	8%	−13%	169	0.24	40.56

$$\sum_{j=1}^{n} (r_j - \hat{r})^2 p_j = 78.0$$

$$\sigma = \sqrt{\sum_{j=1}^{n} (r_j - \hat{r})^2 p_j}$$

$$= \sqrt{78}$$

$$= 8.8\%$$

The standard deviation can be used to measure the variability of returns from an investment. As such, it gives an indication of the risk involved in the asset or security. *The larger the standard deviation, the more variable is an investment's returns and the riskier is the investment.* A standard deviation of zero indicates no variability and thus no risk. Table 6.4 shows the calculation of the standard deviation for Delta Air Lines stock. The standard deviation is 8.8 percent. Standard deviations may be calculated for any probability distribution, but they are particularly useful when dealing with a *normal probability distribution.* A normal probability distribution is best described as a continuous distribution that is symmetric and bell shaped. A *continuous distribution* is a distribution that describes probabilities for outcomes over a continuum rather than a few discrete outcomes. A continuous normal probability distribution representation for Delta Air Lines is shown in Figure 6.4.

The standard deviation has special significance in statistics. One standard deviation unit on either side of the expected value of a normal probability distribution covers 68.26 percent of the area under the curve. Two standard deviations on either side of the expected value covers 95.44 percent of the area under the curve, while three standard deviations on either side of the expected value accounts for 99.74 percent of the area under the curve. This provides useful information on the

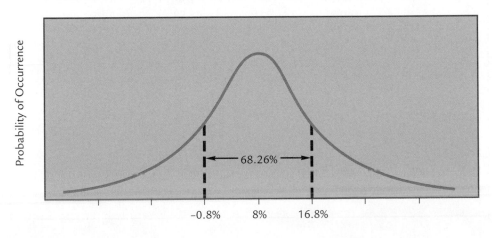

**Figure 6.4
Continuous Probability
Distribution for Delta
Air Lines Stock**

risk of an asset. For Delta Air Lines, one standard deviation unit on either side of the expected value covers the range −0.8 percent to 16.8 percent (8.0% ± 8.8%). Thus, there is an approximately 68 percent probability that Delta's stock returns will range between −0.8 percent and 16.8 percent.

Objective Distributions We have illustrated the concepts of expected value and standard deviation using a subjective distribution. We can also apply these concepts to *objective distributions*. Objective distributions are based on objective data, an example of which is historical data. In the case of stock returns, we can take the historical returns on Delta Air Lines stock. In Table 6.5 we show annual holding period returns on Delta Air Lines stock for 1993–2002. Using objective or historical data, the *mean or average* return is estimated using the following formula:

$$(6.3) \qquad \hat{r}(\text{historical}) = \frac{\sum_{t=1}^{n} r_t}{n}$$

where t is an index for the year and n is the number of years of data. Note that all we do is add up the returns over the different years and divide by the number of years. The formula is similar to the mean return of a subjective distribution, except here we implicitly assume that the weight of each of the outcomes is exactly equal: $1/n$. Table 6.5 shows the calculation for the mean return.

The mean return over the 10-year period 1993–2002 for Delta Air Lines stock is −0.50 percent. We can consider this to be the *expected* return as well, if we assume that the future distribution for Delta Air Lines will mirror the past distribution. This may or may not be a reasonable assumption. If it is safe to assume that there have been no fundamental changes in the firm or its environment, it may be reasonable to use the historical mean return as indicative of the firm's future expected return. On the other hand, if there have been dramatic changes within the company or its environment, this may not be a valid assumption. In the case of Delta Air Lines, given the dramatic events of 2001 and 2002 (World Trade Center attacks and the Iraq War) and their impact on Delta's and other airline stocks, the histori-

Table 6.5 Mean Return Calculation Using Historical Returns for Delta Air Lines Stock

t	r_t
1993	7.57
1994	−7.37
1995	45.99
1996	−3.60
1997	68.04
1998	−12.56
1999	−4.16
2000	0.80
2001	−41.46
2002	−58.24

$$\sum_{t=1}^{n} r_t = -4.99$$

Mean of Average Return $= \hat{r}(\text{historical}) = \sum_{t=1}^{n} r_t/n = -4.99/10 = -0.50\%$

cal average return may not be a good forecast of the future expected return. In addition to the mean, the standard deviation of returns using historical data may also be calculated. This is computed as follows:

$$\sigma(\text{historical}) = \sqrt{\frac{\sum_{t=1}^{n} (r_t - \hat{r})^2}{n - 1}} \tag{6.4}$$

where σ is the standard deviation based on historical returns. Note that, similar to the case of subjective distributions, we use the squared deviations of the outcomes from the mean, except that in the case of historical data we weight each of the outcomes by the number of observations minus 1. The divisor is 1 less than n in order to correct for a bias arising from the use of a sample of observations to estimate the true population mean (see any introductory statistics textbook for a more detailed explanation). The calculation of standard deviation from objective historical returns for Delta Air Lines is illustrated in Table 6.6. The standard deviation of returns for Delta is found to be 36.75 percent.

In Table 6.7 we present the standard deviations of historical returns using data for the period 1993–2002 for a sample of firms. Notice that standard deviations tend to be lower for large firms in mature industries such as Consolidated Edison (utilities), General Mills (food products), Dow Chemical (chemicals), and International Paper (paper products). On the other hand firms in high-tech areas, such as Intel (semiconductor manufacturing), Dell Computer (computer hardware), and JDS Uniphase (telecommunications equipment), tend to have considerably higher standard deviations. The standard deviation of returns calculated using historical data are useful measures of risk but one has to be careful in using them to assess riskiness in the future. The historical data give us an indication of how risky a stock was in the past, but this may not necessarily indicate its riskiness in the future. The stock may be less or more risky in the future depending on changes in the firm and its environment. To the extent that no fundamental changes are expected in the future, standard deviations based on past data may be reasonable approximations

Table 6.6 Standard Deviation Calculation Using Historical Returns for Delta Air Lines Stock

t	r_t	$\hat{r}$	$r_t - \hat{r}$	$(r_j - \hat{r})^2$
1993	7.57	−0.50	8.07	65.12
1994	−7.37	−0.50	−6.87	47.20
1995	45.99	−0.50	46.49	2161.32
1996	−3.60	−0.50	−3.10	9.61
1997	68.04	−0.50	68.54	4697.73
1998	−12.56	−0.50	−12.06	145.44
1999	−4.16	−0.50	−3.66	13.40
2000	0.80	−0.50	1.30	1.69
2001	−41.46	−0.50	−40.96	1677.72
2002	−58.24	−0.50	−57.74	3333.91

$$\sum_{t=1}^{n} (r_t - \hat{r})^2 = 12153.14$$

$$\text{Standard deviation} = \sigma(\text{historical}) = \sqrt{\frac{\sum_{t=1}^{n} (r_t - \hat{r})^2}{n - 1}} = \sqrt{\frac{12153.14}{(10 - 1)}} = 36.75\%$$

Table 6.7 Standard Deviation of Historical Returns for a Sample of Firms (1993–2002)

Company	Industry	Standard Deviation
Albertson's Inc.	Retail—Grocery	26.98%
Alcoa Inc.	Metal and Mining—Aluminum	42.40%
Amazon.com Inc.	Specialty—Retail	435.62%
American Airlines Inc.	Transportation—Airlines	37.62%
Anheuser-Busch Inc.	Beverages	18.76%
AOL-Time Warner Inc.	Media	188.04%
BankOne Corp.	Banking	26.52%
Barnes & Noble Inc.	Specialty—Retail	54.21%
Best Buy Co.	Retail—Consumer Electronics	110.04%
Boeing Co.	Aerospace—Defense	36.81%
Caterpillar Inc.	Manufacturing—Machinery	22.33%
Cisco Systems Inc.	Computer—Hardware	71.21%
Consolidated Edison	Utilities	23.36%
Dell Computer Corp.	Computer—Hardware	111.04%
Disney (Walt) Co.	Media	21.55%
Dow Chemical	Chemicals	20.90%
ExxonMobil Corp.	Energy	15.78%
FedEx Corp.	Transportation—Delivery	20.58%
Furniture Brands Intl, Inc.	Consumer Products—Durables	37.27%
Gap Inc.	Retail—Clothing	55.98%
General Mills Inc.	Food products	12.62%
General Motors	Automotive—Manufacturers	29.39%
Heinz Co.	Food	24.42%
Intel Corp.	Electronics—Semiconductor mfg.	53.55%
Intl Business Machines	Computer—Hardware	34.92%
Intl Paper Co.	Manufacturing—Paper Products	14.39%
JDS Uniphase Corp.	Telecom equipment	266.53%
McDonald's Corp.	Leisure—Restaurants	31.32%
McGraw-Hill Co. Inc.	Media—Publishing	21.26%
Merck & Co.	Pharmaceutical	33.21%
Microsoft Corp.	Computer—Software	53.50%
Nokia Corp.	Telecom equipment	112.70%
PepsiCo. Inc.	Food, Beverages	23.65%
Pfizer Inc.	Pharmaceutical	39.10%
Procter & Gamble Co.	Consumer Products—Nondurables	21.03%
Wal-Mart Stores	Retail—Discount	46.50%

Source: Compiled from data taken from http://www.yahoo.com.

of the riskiness of assets in the future. In fact many investment professionals use such measures as screening devices to identify potentially desirable stocks to own or recommend.

Comprehension Check Questions

1. What is the definition of risk from a financial perspective?
2. What are some factors that account for riskiness in investments?
3. Why are Treasury securities considered to be default risk–free?

RISK OF AN ASSET IN A PORTFOLIO CONTEXT

e-Lecture

While the standard deviation is a very useful measure of risk, it may not be an appropriate measure of risk when an asset or security is held as part of a ***portfolio***. A portfolio is a collection of two or more assets or securities. In this section we develop a more relevant way to measure risk when an asset is only one of many assets held by an individual or entity.

Most individuals and institutions invest in a portfolio of assets. Commercial banks invest in many different types of financial assets when they make loans to consumers and businesses; individuals invest in many different types of financial assets when they buy securities, such as bank certificates of deposit, corporate bonds, and stocks; and corporations invest in many different kinds of physical assets when they acquire production and distribution facilities (i.e., plant and equipment). Consequently, it is important to know how the returns from *portfolios* of investments behave over time and how to measure risk when an asset is held as part of a portfolio of investments. However, before we can discuss risk in a portfolio context, we first need to get acquainted with the calculation of portfolio returns.

Calculating Portfolio Returns

Since a portfolio is a combination of several securities, the return on a portfolio is simply the weighted average of the returns on the individual securities that make up the portfolio. The weights of the individual securities will equal the proportion of each security in the portfolio. The formula for the return on the portfolio is as follows:

$$r_p = \sum_{j=1}^{n} w_j r_j \qquad (6.5)$$

where r_p is the return on the portfolio, w_j is the proportion of security j in the portfolio consisting of n different securities, and r_j is the return on security j.

As an example, let's calculate the return for year 2000 for a portfolio consisting of equal investments in Delta Air Lines, American Airlines, and United Airlines stock. The year 2000 stock returns for Delta, American, and United were 0.80, 29.02, and −49.40 percent, respectively. Since the portfolio consists of equal investments in the three airline stocks, the proportion (weight) of each stock in the portfolio is 1/3. Plugging in the weights and returns for the individual securities into Equation 6.5 we have:

$$r_p = \left(\frac{1}{3}\right)(0.80\%) + \left(\frac{1}{3}\right)(29.02\%) + \left(\frac{1}{3}\right)(-49.40\%)$$

$$r_p = -6.53\%$$

Thus, the return on an equally weighted portfolio of Delta, American, and United Airlines' stock was −6.53 percent in year 2000.

Total Risk, Systematic Risk, and Unsystematic Risk

In developing the appropriate measure of risk in a portfolio context, let us begin by recalling the concept of standard deviation of an individual asset or security. The standard deviation of returns for an individual security captures the dispersion around the mean or expected return. We had said earlier that security returns deviate around their expected value because of uncertainty in the states of nature or the inability to forecast exactly which set of events will occur. We can think of standard deviation of individual stock returns as capturing the *total risk* of individual stocks. Let's examine some of the specific factors that contribute to total risk. In

Table 6.8 Examples of Events That Contribute to Total Risk

Federal Reserve announces easing of monetary policy
CEO resignation
University of Michigan Consumer Confidence Index shows an increase
Announcement of class-action product liability lawsuit against a manufacturer
Factory shutdown due to labor strike
Discovery of new drug with significant potential
Increase in unemployment rates
Congress passes legislation decreasing marginal tax rates for all businesses
Hurricane destroys businesses and homes in South Florida
Firm declares bankruptcy
Federal deficit increases significantly
Increase in productivity due to greater use of computers in the workplace
Increase in energy prices
Global recession
Competitor slashes prices
U.S. Treasury rates decline
Firm receives offer to be acquired at a significant premium
Firm announces omission of dividends

other words, what are some specific events that cause the returns on individual stocks (such as those in Table 6.7) to deviate about their expected values? Table 6.8 provides a listing of some of the unexpected events that contribute to total risk of a security. The list is by no means exhaustive. A close look at the list reveals that the risky events could be dichotomized into two categories. One category consists of risk factors having a broad impact on virtually *all* firms in the economy (these are *italicized* in Table 6.8); the other includes risky events having a narrower impact on just a firm or a group of firms (firms in a specific industry).

Events such as unexpected Federal Reserve policy announcements, unemployment figure releases, or tax law changes are likely to have an impact that will be felt by virtually all economic sectors. For instance, if the Federal Reserve were to announce a significant rate cut that was unanticipated by the market, it would cause interest rates in general to decline, with implications to a wide variety of industries. The cost of borrowing would decline for all businesses and individuals. This could spur new capital spending by many businesses and consumer spending as well. Thus, virtually every sector may feel the impact. *Events that impact the entire market are known as* **systematic risk** *events.*

On the other hand, some of the risk factors listed have a very localized effect. Take, for example, the declaration of bankruptcy by a firm. Consider the filing for bankruptcy by Kmart Corporation, a large discount department store chain, in early 2002. The bankruptcy decision was accompanied by a decline in Kmart's stock price. However, the decision to declare bankruptcy by Kmart had no impact on other stocks such as IBM, General Motors, AOL-TimeWarner, etc. *Events with a localized impact on a firm or a group of firms are known as* **unsystematic risk** *events.* Note that Kmart's bankruptcy was an "unsystematic" risk factor with negative consequences for Kmart investors but not for all firms in general. The purchase of Lotus by IBM in June 1995 is another example of an unsystematic risk factor—in this case with a positive impact. Lotus shares closed at $32.50 the day before the announcement and rose on the next day to over $61.00 when IBM announced its intention to acquire Lotus at

$60.00 per share. This transaction had no effect on other firms such as General Motors, Coca-Cola Enterprises, etc. Unsystematic risk factors may also include events that may affect a particular industry, but not the entire economy. An example might be new wage contracts in the auto industry that will affect most of the automobile manufacturing firms, but will have no measurable effect in unrelated industries such as pharmaceutical or restaurant industries.

Unsystematic risk is sometimes referred to as ***diversifiable risk*** because diversifying one's investments can easily eliminate its effects. On the other hand, systematic risk is referred to as *nondiversifiable risk* or ***market risk*** because systematic risk affects stocks throughout the economy. In conclusion we can say that

$$\text{Total risk} = \text{Unsystematic risk} + \text{Systematic risk}$$

Diversification and Portfolio Risk

Let us expand upon the concept of unsystematic (diversifiable) risk and systematic (nondiversifiable) risk. Figure 6.5 shows a plot of Delta Air Lines stock holding period returns for the 10 years 1993–2002. The figure also shows stock returns for two of its rival firms, AMR (holding corporation for American Airlines) and United Airlines. The dispersion of the returns over time gives you an indication of the total risk involved in each of these stocks. Notice that all three airline stocks tend to move together, more or less. This is not surprising since they are all in the business of transporting passengers by air and are affected by similar risk factors. Therefore, it is likely that you will derive little benefit from diversifying your holdings across the three airline stocks. For example, all three airlines will experience increased traffic and profits due to economic expansion. By the same token all three airlines will experience declines in profitability because of shocks to oil prices.

The bold or heavier line in Figure 6.5 traces the returns from a portfolio consisting of equal dollar amounts of the three airline stocks. Note what happens to the dispersion of the returns. The portfolio returns are not as volatile as the three individual stocks' returns. This indicates that there is some reduction in risk when you diversify across the three airline stocks, but evidently not very much. The reduction

An excellent source of economic and financial data is the Federal Reserve Bank of St. Louis Web site. **http://www.stls.frb.org**

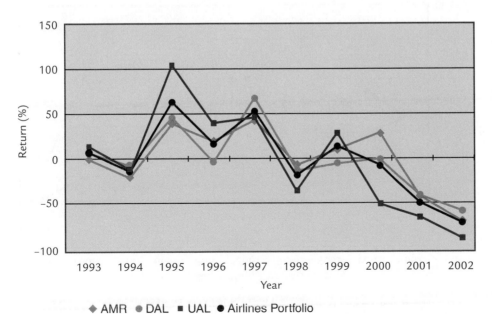

**Figure 6.5
Annual Returns of
Delta Air Lines
(DAL), American
Airlines (AMR),
United Airlines
(UAL), and Airline
Portfolio**

in risk occurs because negative unsystematic risk effects in a stock are offset, to some degree, by positive unsystematic gains in another stock(s). For example, losses in American Airlines due to a strike by the flight attendants may be offset by increased traffic in the other two airlines in the portfolio. However, since all three stocks are in the same industry, their fortunes overall are tied together by common factors in the industry. In other words, these stocks are highly correlated with each other.

In Figure 6.6 we show annual returns from 1993 to 2002 for Delta Air Lines and several other stocks from different industries. Stock returns for Bristol-Myers Squibb (pharmaceutical drugs), McDonald's Corporation (fast food restaurant), International Business Machines (computers), Procter & Gamble Company (consumer products) are shown. Note that the pattern of returns for the five stocks are much less correlated compared to the pattern of returns for the three airline stocks. This is because the firms operate in different industries and respond to different risk factors. However, there are some common elements that all stocks respond to regardless of the industry they are in (such as the overall economic cycle, interest rates, etc.). The portfolio line in Figure 6.6 shows the return to a portfolio with equal dollar investments in these five stocks. Note that the volatility of returns for the portfolio appears to be less than for the individual stocks. This clearly illustrates the benefit of **diversification.** *By holding securities in industries that are not highly positively correlated we can reduce the effects of unsystematic risk.* The more we diversify across different industries, the more we are able to eliminate unsystematic risk.

Figure 6.7 illustrates what happens to portfolio risk as we increase portfolio size. Portfolio risk is measured as the standard deviation of returns of the portfolio. Note that portfolio risk declines very rapidly at first and then tapers off. This reduction in risk occurs because as we add stocks, randomly chosen from the different industries, we are able to eliminate the unsystematic risk effects. Thus, unsystematic losses in some stocks are offset by unsystematic gains elsewhere in the portfolio. The shaded area is the risk reduction through elimination of unsystematic risk. The risk level tapers off but cannot be completely eliminated because the portfolio will always be

**Figure 6.6
Annual Returns of
Delta Air Lines
(DAL), Bristol-Myers
Squibb (BMY), Procter & Gamble (PG),
International Business
Machines (IBM),
McDonald's (MCD),
and Portfolio**

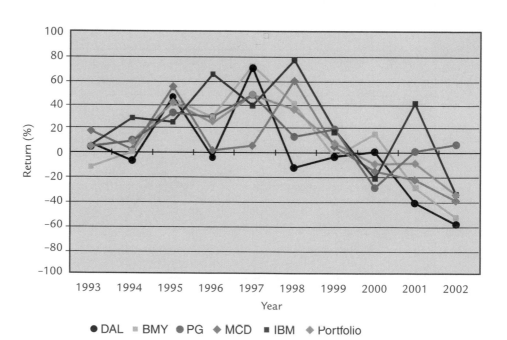

● DAL   ▪ BMY   ● PG   ◆ MCD   ▪ IBM   ◆ Portfolio

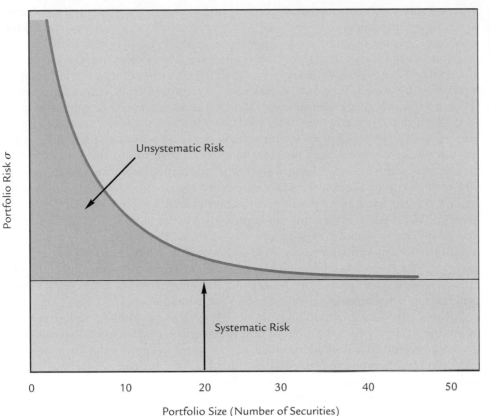

Figure 6.7
**Effect of Portfolio
Size on Portfolio Risk**

subject to the effects of systematic risk factors. The area that is not shaded represents the systematic risk of the portfolio. Studies have shown that it takes as few as 40 randomly chosen stocks to virtually eliminate unsystematic risk.

The Relevant Risk

The above discussion suggests that the relevant risk is the systematic risk because unsystematic risk can be easily diversified away by holding a collection of stocks from across different sectors of the economy. If we accept the notion that most investors are well diversified, then in considering individual assets or stocks, the focus should be on the systematic component of the risk rather than the total risk. The question we now have to tackle is: How do we measure the systematic risk of a stock?

Measuring Systematic Risk As we add more stocks to a portfolio, the unsystematic risk is reduced, and if we carry this diversification far enough we can eliminate *all* unsystematic risk. For this to happen, however, we must invest in all assets that exist in the economy. In finance we refer to this as the ***market portfolio***. *The market portfolio in theory consists of all assets that exist in the universe.* Thus, it would not only include stocks, bonds, and other financial instruments but also real estate, art, and precious metals. Theoretical work reveals that each asset in the market portfolio must be held in the same proportion as its market capitalization weight to total market capitalization of all assets. In other words, if IBM has a market capitalization of $4.5 billion and the market value of all assets in the universe is $300 billion, then IBM should have a weight of 1.5 percent in the market portfolio. However, constructing an all-encompassing market portfolio would be difficult if not impossible. As you can imagine it would be an impossible task to identify every possible asset and its market value. Consequently, in practice we *approximate* the market portfolio with a *proxy* whose value and returns are easy to calculate. One such popular proxy is the S&P 500 stock index. Recall from Chapter 2 that the S&P 500 is a market value–weighted index of 500 very large stocks from various industries. Thus, the finance profession views the S&P 500 as *a market value-weighted portfolio.*

Given that the market portfolio (S&P 500) is subject *only* to systematic risk, we can use it as a reference point for measuring the systematic risk of any given stock. In other words, by comparing an individual stock's pattern of behavior vis-à-vis the market, one can obtain a relative measure of systematic risk for any given stock. To illustrate, we plot the annual holding period returns of Delta Air Lines stock against the annual holding period returns on the S&P 500 portfolio for the 10-year period, 1993–2002. This is shown in Figure 6.8. We use annual returns for illustrative purposes. In actual practice monthly—or even weekly and daily—returns are used rather than annual returns, so as to have enough observations to capture a meaningful relationship between the two series. The scattergram in Figure 6.8 shows an approximately positive relationship between Delta Air Lines stock returns and the market returns proxied by the S&P 500 index.

Using regression methodology we can obtain a more precise relationship. The solid line in Figure 6.8 is the line of best fit using the *Ordinary Least Squares (OLS)* procedure. The OLS is simply a statistical procedure to capture the linear relationship between a dependent variable (in this case the returns on Delta Air Lines stock) and an independent variable (in this case the returns on the market portfolio proxied by the S&P 500 Index). In finance we refer to this regression line as

**Figure 6.8
Determining the Beta
(characteristic line)
for Delta Air Lines
Stock**

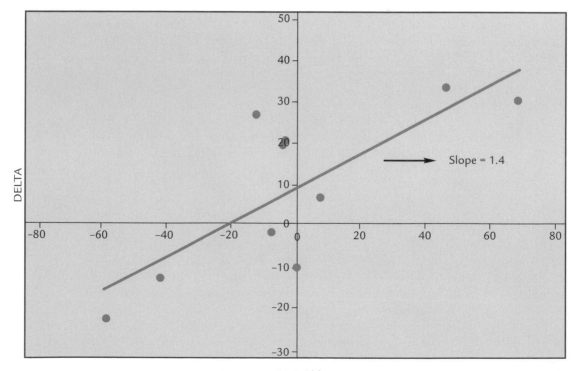

S & P 500

Table 6.9 Interpretation of Selected Beta Values

Beta Value	Direction of Movement in Returns	Interpretation
2.0	Same as market	Twice as risky (responsive) as market
1.0	Same as market	Risk equal to that of market
0.5	Same as market	Half as risky as market
0	Uncorrelated with market	No market-related risk
−0.5	Opposite of market	Half as responsive as the market but in opposite direction

the *characteristic line*. The slope of the characteristic line, commonly referred to as *beta* (or β), is 1.4 for Delta Air Lines stock. The beta value for Delta Air Lines tells us that the stock is 1.4 times as risky as the market. Since the market itself is subject only to systematic risk, this implies that Delta Air Lines stock has systematic risk that is 1.4 times that of the market. *The beta is, therefore, an index of the systematic risk.* The market, by definition, has a beta equal to 1. A beta of less than 1 indicates that the firm has less systematic risk than does the market. Typically firms that are very large and that operate in very stable and mature industries may have betas less than the market. Table 6.9 summarizes the interpretation of selected betas. Betas for a number of firms, taken from Value Line Investment Survey, are shown in Table 6.10. Value Line uses a similar regression procedure to the one outlined for Delta Air Lines in calculating the betas.

We now know how to determine the beta of a single asset or stock. This is, of course, useful information so that we can appropriately value individual stocks. However, most individuals and institutions own many stocks or assets so it would be of interest to determine the beta of a *portfolio*. Calculating the beta of a portfolio is fairly easy; it is simply the weighted average of the betas of the individual stocks or assets that make up the portfolio. The weights are based on the market value proportion of each asset or stock to the total value of the portfolio. Thus,

$$\beta_p = \sum_{j=1}^{n} w_j\beta_j \tag{6.6}$$

where β_p is the beta of the portfolio, w_j is the weight of the jth asset or stock in the portfolio, and β_j is the beta of the jth stock or asset in the portfolio. To illustrate the use of Equation 6.6, let's assume that you have a portfolio with equal investments in Best Buy Corporation, General Motors, Intel, and PepsiCo. Using data contained in Table 6.10, the beta of this portfolio is calculated as follows:

$$\beta_p = (0.25)\,(1.35) + (0.25)\,(1.20) + (0.25)\,(1.30) + (0.25)\,(.60)$$
$$\beta_p = 1.1125$$

Comprehension Check Questions

1. What is systematic risk?
2. What is unsystematic risk?
3. What is the market portfolio and what type of risk does it contain?
4. What is beta?

Table 6.10 Beta Values for Selected Firms

Company	Industry	Beta
Albertson's Inc.	Retail—Grocery	0.65
Alcoa Inc.	Metal and Mining—Aluminum	1.15
Amazon.com Inc.	Specialty—Retail	1.80
American Airlines Inc.	Transportation—Airlines	—
Anheuser-Busch Inc.	Beverages	0.60
AOL-Time Warner Inc.	Media	1.70
BankOne Corp.	Banking	1.25
Barnes & Noble Inc.	Specialty—Retail	1.20
Best Buy Co.	Retail—Consumer Electronics	1.35
Boeing Co.	Aerospace—Defense	1.00
Caterpillar Inc.	Manufacturing—Machinery	1.10
Cisco Systems Inc.	Computer—Hardware	1.45
Consolidated Edison	Utilities	0.55
Dell Computer Corp.	Computer—Hardware	1.25
Disney (Walt) Co.	Media	1.20
Dow Chemical	Chemicals	1.00
ExxonMobil Corp.	Energy	0.80
FedEx Corp.	Transportation—Delivery	1.10
Furniture Brands Intl, Inc.	Consumer Products—Durables	1.40
Gap Inc.	Retail—Clothing	1.45
General Mills Inc.	Food	0.50
General Motors	Automotive—Manufacturers	1.20
Heinz Co.	Food	0.55
Intel Corp.	Electronics—Semiconductor	1.30
Intl Business Machines	Computer—Hardware	1.05
Intl Paper Co.	Manufacturing—Paper Products	1.00
JDS Uniphase Corp.	Telecommunications	1.65
Lockheed Martin Corp.	Aerospace—Defense	0.55
McDonald's Corp.	Leisure—Restaurants	0.95
McGraw-Hill Co. Inc.	Media—Publishing	0.80
Merck & Co.	Pharmaceutical	0.95
Microsoft Corp.	Computer—Software	1.15
Nokia Corp.	Telecommunications	1.40
PepsiCo. Inc.	Food, Beverages	0.60
Pfizer Inc.	Pharmaceutical	0.95
Procter & Gamble Co.	Consumer Products—Nondurables	0.60
Wal-Mart Stores	Retail—Discount	1.05

Source: Value Line Investment Survey, March 28, 2003

RELATIONSHIP BETWEEN REQUIRED RATE OF RETURN AND RISK

Our final objective for this chapter is to develop a relationship between the required rate of return and risk. Intuitively we know that investors need to be compensated for risk; otherwise, no one would invest in risky assets. Historical data also confirms this relationship. At the beginning of this chapter we observed that the average historical returns for various classes of securities increased as risk increased. Specifically, we noted that U.S. Treasury and government securities had the lowest dispersion (risk) but also the lowest average returns. Corporate bonds were riskier than government securities but also had higher average returns. Finally, common stocks, which are characterized by relatively higher risk, were associated with the highest average returns. This pattern is consistent with the view that, on average, higher-risk assets are associated with higher required rates of return. That is, investors are rewarded with higher returns for assuming greater risk.

The question now is what kind of risk should investors be compensated for? In other words, while we know that required returns increase as risk increases, we need a precise definition of risk. The discussion in the previous section suggests that the relevant measure of risk is systematic risk. This is the risk investors cannot diversify away. Given that beta is a relative measure of systematic risk, it is reasonable to assume that there exists a relationship between required rate of return and beta. The nature of this relationship is captured in the equation of the *Security Market Line (SML)*. The SML is a part of the body of theory known in finance as the *Capital Asset Pricing Model (CAPM)*. The CAPM provides a strong analytical basis for evaluating risk–return relationships in a portfolio context.

The Security Market Line

The SML is a functional model that relates the required rate of return to systematic risk as captured by beta. The SML equation is given as follows:

$$k_j = \underbrace{\hat{r}_f}_{\substack{\text{risk-free} \\ \text{rate of} \\ \text{return}}} + \underbrace{\beta_j \, (\hat{r}_m - \hat{r}_f)}_{\text{risk premium}} \qquad (6.7)$$

where k is the required rate of return on a given asset j, $\hat{r}_f$ is the risk-free rate of return, β is the beta of asset j, and $\hat{r}_m$ is the required return on the market portfolio. Note that the formula has two components: a *risk-free rate of return* and a *risk premium*. The SML equation tells us that for any given asset or security, investors should be compensated with a risk-free rate of return plus a premium for risk.

The risk-free rate of return may be thought of as the compensation for postponing consumption. In other words, when an individual invests in, say, a corporate bond, he or she forgoes the opportunity to spend that money now and thus should be compensated for postponing spending to a later time. The risk-free rate is proxied by the yield on a Treasury security such as a T-bill or a T-bond. The second part of the formula, risk premium, refers to additional compensation for assuming risk. The risk premium is made of two components:

$$\beta_j \, (\hat{r}_m - \hat{r}_f)$$

The first component is the beta of the security, β_j, which measures systematic risk of the security relative to the market portfolio. The second component is the term inside the parenthesis, $\hat{r}_m - \hat{r}_f$, which is defined as the *market risk premium*. It is the premium required for holding the market portfolio, which is *subject only to systematic risk and has a beta equal to 1*. Therefore the risk premium for any given asset is going to be some multiple of the market risk premium, depending on the beta. Take the example of Delta Air Lines stock. Recall that Delta's common stock has a beta of 1.4 calculated by regressing annual returns of Delta's common stock against those of the S&P 500 Index over the period 1993–2002. The beta of 1.4 means the Delta stock has systematic risk that is 1.4 times that of the market portfolio. Consequently an investor in Delta stock would require a risk premium that is 1.4 times that of the market portfolio. Based on historical stock market data over the time period 1926–2002, the average market risk premium (average return on stocks minus the return on long-term government bonds) has been 6.4 percent. The risk premium for Delta stock is then equal to:

$$\underbrace{1.4}_{\text{beta}} \times \underbrace{(6.4)}_{\text{market risk premium}} = \underbrace{8.96\%}_{\text{risk premium for Delta stock}}$$

Note that the risk premium is a function only of the systematic risk of the asset and not the total risk. Thus, according to the CAPM, investors should not be rewarded—that is, expect compensation—for unsystematic risk.

To figure the required rate of return on Delta's common stock, we also need data on the risk-free rate of return. If the current risk-free rate is 5 percent, using the Security Market Line equation, the required rate of return for Delta's common stock would equal:

$$= 5 + 1.4 \ (6.4)$$
$$= 13.96\%$$

Figure 6.9 graphically depicts the SML equation assuming a risk-free rate of 5 percent and a market risk premium of 6.4 percent:

$$k_j = 5 + \beta_j \ (6.4)$$

The vertical axis is the required rate of return on an asset and the horizontal axis is the beta of the asset. The intercept is the risk-free rate while the slope is the market risk premium. The SML line shows, at a glance, what the required rate of return should be for any given beta. The required rate of return on a stock with a beta of 0.5, which is half as risky as the market portfolio, is 8.2 percent. A stock which has the same risk as the market portfolio (i.e., beta = 1) will have a required rate of return of 11.4 percent. A stock with systematic risk that is twice that of the market portfolio will have a required rate of return of 17.8 percent.

Although we have assumed the values that go into the SML equation as given, the required rate of return may change over time as the inputs to the SML equation change. First, the required rate of return may change because the risk-free rate of return changes. $\hat{r}_f$ may change because of Federal Reserve policy action, federal deficits, and the inflation outlook, among other things. Second, the required rate of return may change because the market risk premium changes. Changes in the market risk premium occur because of the investors' outlook for the future. If investor confidence is fairly low and the outlook for the economy is gloomy, investors may require a higher compensation for assuming systematic risk and, therefore, a higher market risk

Figure 6.9
Security Market Line with Risk-Free Rate of 5 Percent and Market Risk Premium of 6.4 Percent

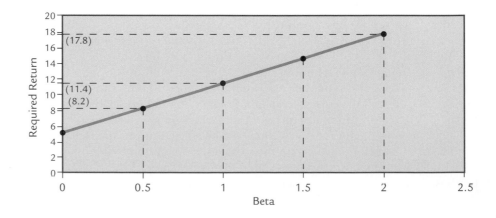

premium. On the other hand, if the outlook for the economy is good and the market in general is confident about the future, then investors may be satisfied with a lower market risk premium for systematic risk. Finally, the required rate of return may change because of changes in the beta of the stock. The beta, which captures the relative sensitivity of the stock to the market portfolio, may change due to fundamental changes in the firm because of management actions, or it may change because of factors outside the control of management. For example, if the firm diversifies into businesses that have less systematic risk than its current business, then the beta of the firm will go down. On the other hand, beta of the firm may go up because the firm takes on a lot of debt. Beta may also change due to industry factors. For instance, when the airline industry was deregulated in the 1980s, the betas for airline stocks generally went up because the deregulation resulted in unfettered competition between the airlines.

Criticisms of the CAPM and a Discussion of Some New Models

There have been many empirical tests of the CAPM and its implications but one of the most basic tests involves the relationship between systematic risk (beta) and return. If the CAPM is a valid representation of how investors view risk, then on average one should observe a positive relationship between stock returns and their beta. Some researchers have found positive relationships between systematic (beta) risk and return. However, the explanatory power has been very low. It appears that the market factor (systematic risk) on average explains less than 5 percent of the observed returns for individual stocks.

Criticisms of the CAPM have lead researchers to develop other models of asset pricing. One such model is the *Arbitrage Pricing Theory*.[1] The APT model is a multifactor model which explains asset returns as a function of the risk-free rate of return and several systematic risk factors:

$$k_j = \hat{r}_f + \beta_{j1}(rp_1) + \beta_{j2}(rp_2) + \ldots + \beta_{jn}(rp_n) \qquad (6.8)$$

Where k_j is the required return for security j, $\beta_{j1} \ldots \beta_{jn}$ denote the sensitivity of security j to each of the n systematic risk factors and $rp_1 \ldots rp_n$ denote the risk premiums associated with each of the n systematic risk factors. Note the similarity between this model and the security market line equation of the CAPM (Equation 6.7). In the CAPM there is only one risk factor—the market systematic risk factor—and asset return is a function of the risk-free rate of return and the risk premium associated with the market risk factor. In the case of APT there are multiple systematic risk factors (n risk factors) and the asset returns are a function of the risk-free rate of return and the risk premiums associated with each of the n systematic risk factors. The problem with the APT is that the theory is too general; it does not specify the number of factors nor what they are specifically. There have been several empirical investigations of the APT to determine the number of systematic risk factors and what they are. One study finds the empirical APT consists of four risk factors that include industrial production, default risk premium (risk of bankruptcy), inflation, and changes in the yield curve.[2]

One model that has gained prominence in the literature of late is the *Fama-French Three Factor Model,* based on the works of Eugene Fama and Kenneth French.[3]

[1]Ross, S.A., 1976, "The Arbitrage Theory of Capital Asset Pricing," *Journal of Economic Theory* 13 [December], pp. 341–360.

[2]Chen, N.F., R. Roll, and S. Ross, 1986, "Economic Forces and the Stock Market: Testing the APT and Alternative Asset Pricing Theories," *Journal of Business* 59 [July], pp. 383–403.

[3]Fama, E.F., and K.R. French, 1993, "Common Risk Factors in the Returns on Stocks and Bonds," *Journal of Financial Economics* 33 [February], pp. 3–56.

Fama and French found in their empirical investigations that stock returns are closely related to the size of the firm and the book-to-market ratio of the stock. These two variables were more significant than market risk in explaining the cross-section of stock returns. The Fama-French model assumes that the required rate of return on a security is a function of a market risk factor, a firm-size risk factor, and a book-to-market ratio risk factor. According to the model, firm size and growth (proxied by the book-to-market ratio) are important determinants of a security's risk in addition to, or perhaps even more significant than, the market systematic risk factor.

Despite the controversy concerning the validity of the CAPM, it is still used extensively. For example, most corporations, in estimating their weighted average cost of capital, use the CAPM to estimate their cost of equity.

Comprehension Check Questions

1. What is the Security Market Line?
2. What is the measure of risk used in the Security Market Line?
3. What is the Arbitrage Pricing Theory model?

Summary

➢ From the perspective of finance, risk refers to the possibility that outcomes can be different from what is expected. Most financial assets are characterized by risk to some degree. However, Treasury securities are default risk-free. They are risk-free because the interest payments and the principal are guaranteed by the U.S. government.

➢ The probability distribution refers to the possible outcomes for an asset with the corresponding probabilities of occurrence. Probability distributions may be either subjective or objective. Subjective distributions refer to outcomes and probabilities based on subjective estimates of an individual, such as a financial analyst. Objective distributions are based on historical data, such as historical stock returns.

➢ The standard deviation of returns is a useful measure of total risk for assets viewed in isolation (i.e., when the asset is not part of a portfolio). The standard deviation is a statistical concept that is defined as the square root of the weighted average of squared deviations about the expected value. Standard deviations may be calculated using subjective or objective distributions.

➢ Total risk may be broken down into systematic and unsystematic risk. Unsystematic risk refers to risk factors that affect only a given firm or group of firms (examples include factory shutdown due to strike, discovery of a new block-buster drug, a class-action product liability lawsuit against a manufacturer). Systematic risk refers to risk factors that are broad-ranging in their impact, affecting all firms to some degree or another (examples include the tightening of monetary policy by the Federal Reserve, legislation that would change the marginal tax rate for all businesses, an increase in consumer confidence).

➢ Unsystematic risk is also referred to as diversifiable risk because diversifying one's holdings can eliminate it. Systematic risk or market risk, on the other hand, is nondiversifiable risk because all firms are subject to it to some degree.

Thus, systematic risk or market risk is the relevant risk since unsystematic risk can be eliminated by diversifying.

➣ The market portfolio is a portfolio that consists of all assets that have value. It is all-encompassing; it includes stocks, bonds, real estate, collectibles, and other assets of value. The assets are contained in the market portfolio in proportions equal to their market capitalization value relative to the value of all assets. The market portfolio is perfectly diversified—that is, it contains no unsystematic risk. Unsystematic risk in the market portfolio is completely eliminated because unsystematic losses in the portfolio (e.g., loss due to litigation) are offset by unsystematic gains in the portfolio (e.g., discovery of a significant new drug). The market portfolio is subject only to systematic risk. In practice, the S&P 500 Index is a popular proxy for the market portfolio.

➣ The Capital Asset Pricing Model is a theory that provides a model to relate the required rate of return to risk. The equation that embodies this relationship is referred to as the Security Market Line. According to the SML, the required rate of return on any asset is equal to the risk-free rate of return plus a risk premium that depends on the systematic risk of the asset.

➣ In the SML equation, systematic risk is captured by beta. The beta is a measure of the volatility of an asset's returns relative to the volatility of the returns on the market portfolio. The market, by definition, has a beta of 1.

➣ The Arbitrage Price Theory and the Fama-French Three Factor models are examples of multifactor models of stock returns. These models assume that the required rate of return on an asset is a function of more than one risk factor.

Questions and Topics for Discussion

1. Define the following terms:
   a. Probability distribution
   b. Standard deviation
   c. Required rate of return
   d. Systematic risk
   e. Unsystematic risk
   f. Portfolio
   g. Security Market Line
   h. Characteristic line
   i. State of nature
2. Compare objective and subjective probability distributions.
3. Explain why U.S. government bonds are considered risk-free.
4. Distinguish between unsystematic and systematic risk. Under what circumstances are investors likely to ignore the unsystematic risk characteristics of a security?
5. The stock of Amrep Corporation has a beta value estimated to be 1.4. How would you interpret this beta value? How would you evaluate the firm's systematic risk?
6. How is a security's beta value computed?
7. What are the two components of the required rate of return according to the Capital Asset Pricing Model?
8. According to the Capital Asset Pricing Model why is unsystematic risk irrelevant to diversified investors?

9. What type of risk does diversification eliminate?

10. What is the market risk premium?

11. What impact does a change in a security's beta have on its required rate of return?

12. How is risk defined in a financial sense?

13. Discuss the general relationship between risk and return (required rate of return).

14. What are some of the alternative models to the Capital Asset Pricing Model?

Self-Test Problems

ST1. Given are the following possible dollar returns (dividends plus capital gains) over the coming year from a $10,000 investment in General Motors common stock:

State of Economy	Probability	Return
Recession	0.20	$-1,000
Normal year	0.60	1,500
Boom	0.20	2,500

Convert the dollar returns to percentage returns and then determine the

a. Expected return

b. Standard deviation of returns

ST2. Determine the expected return on the portfolio and the beta of a portfolio consisting of equal investments in the following common stocks:

Security	Expected Return	Beta
Boeing	10.7%	.95
DaimlerChrysler	12.5%	1.25
Intel	11.9%	1.15
Wal-Mart Stores	11.3%	1.05

ST3. Assume that the risk-free rate of return is 4 percent and the market risk premium is 7 percent.

a. Determine the required rate of return on Wisconsin Public Service (WPS) common stock whose beta is 0.60.

b. Assume that the market risk premium remains constant but that the risk-free rate of return increases from 4 percent to 6 percent. Determine the required rate of return on WPS common stock.

c. Assume that the risk-free rate of return remains the same at 4 percent but that the market risk premium increases to 9 percent. Determine the required rate of return on WPS common stock.

d. Assume that the beta of WPS stock rises from 0.60 to 0.85 but that the risk-free rate is 4 percent and the market risk premium is 9 percent. Determine the required rate of return on WPS common stock.

Problems

BASIC   **1.** You have estimated the following probability distributions of expected future returns for Stocks X and Y:

Stock X Probability	Return	Stock Y Probability	Return
0.1	−10%	0.2	9%
0.2	10%	0.2	12%
0.4	15%	0.3	15%
0.2	20%	0.2	19%
0.1	40%	0.1	22%

a. What is the expected rate of return for Stock X? Stock Y?

b. What is the standard deviation of expected returns for Stock X? for Stock Y?

c. Which stock would you consider to be riskier? Why?

2. The expected rate of return for the stock of Concrete Enterprises is 20 percent, **BASIC** with a standard deviation of 15 percent. The expected rate of return for the stock of Brick Corporation is 20 percent, with a standard deviation of 11 percent.

a. Which stock would you consider to be riskier? Why?

b. If you knew that the beta coefficient of Concrete Enterprises stock is 1.4 and the beta of Brick Corporation is 1.6, how would your answer to Part a change?

3. You have the following information on two securities in which you have invested: **INTERMEDIATE**

	Expected Return	Standard Deviation	Security Beta	% Invested (w)
Xerox	15%	4.5%	1.20	35%
Kodak	12%	3.8%	0.98	65%

a. Which stock is riskier in a portfolio context? Which stock is riskier if you are considering them as individual assets (not part of a portfolio)?

b. Compute the expected return on the portfolio.

c. Compute the beta of the portfolio.

4. Given a risk-free rate ($\hat{r}_f$) of 6 percent and a market risk premium ($\hat{r}_m - \hat{r}_f$) of **BASIC** 7.5 percent, calculate the required rate of return on each of the following stocks, based on the betas given in Table 6.10:

a. Caterpillar

b. Microsoft

c. General Motors

d. ExxonMobil

5. The stock of Pizza Hot, Inc., a Mexican pizza chain, has an estimated beta of **INTERMEDIATE** 1.5. The current risk-free rate is 6 percent and the market risk premium is 6.4 percent.

a. Calculate the required rate of return for Pizza Hot stock.

b. What is the risk premium for Pizza Hot stock.

6. Using Equation 6.7, suppose you have computed the required rate of return **INTERMEDIATE** for the stock of Bulldog Trucking to be 16.6 percent. Given the current stock price, the current dividend rate, and analysts' projections for future dividend growth, you expect to earn a rate of return of 18 percent.

a. Would you recommend buying or selling this stock? Why?

b. If your expected rate of return from the stock of Bulldog is 15 percent, what would you expect to happen to Bulldog's stock price?

CHALLENGE   **7.** The stock of Jones Trucking is expected to return 13 percent annually with a standard deviation of 8 percent. The stock of Bush Steel Mills is expected to return 17 percent annually with a standard deviation of 14 percent. The beta of the Jones' stock is 0.9, and the beta of the Bush stock is 1.2. The risk-free rate of return is expected to be 8 percent, and the expected return on the market portfolio is 15 percent. The current dividend for Jones is $4. The current dividend for Bush is $6.

a. What is the expected return from a portfolio containing the two securities if 40 percent of your wealth is invested in Jones and 60 percent is invested in Bush?

b. Which stock is the better buy in the current market? Why?

BASIC   **8.** The annual historical returns for American Airlines stock for 1996 to 2000 are shown below. Calculate the standard deviation and mean returns for American Airlines stock.

Year	Return
1996	18.7
1997	45.8
1998	−7.6
1999	12.8
2000	29.0

CHALLENGE   **9.** Three Rivers Investment Company desires to construct a portfolio with a 20 percent expected return. The portfolio is to consist of some combination of Security X and Security Y, which have the following expected returns and betas:

	Security X	Security Y
Expected return	15%	26%
Beta	0.94	1.33

a. Determine the proportion of X and Y to achieve an expected portfolio return of 20 percent.

b. What is the beta of the portfolio determined in (a)?

INTERMEDIATE   **10.** The required rate of return on a stock is 14.5 percent. If the risk-free rate is 5.5 percent and the beta of the stock is 1.15, what is the market risk premium?

INTERMEDIATE   **11.** Suppose that a portfolio consists of the following stocks:

Stock	Amount	Beta
Pepsi Co	$20,000	.70
Intel	$40,000	1.30
General Motors	$40,000	1.10

The risk-free rate $(\hat{r}_f)$ is 5 percent and the market risk premium $(\hat{r}_m - \hat{r}_f)$ is 8.8 percent.

a. Determine the beta for the portfolio.

b. Determine the expected return on the portfolio in part (a).

THOMSON ONE—Business School Edition

Go to the text Web site at http://moyer.swlearning.com, select your book, and click on the Thomson ONE button. Enter Thomson ONE—Business School Edition by using the username and password you created when you registered the serial number on your access card. Use the "Prices" tab, "Overviews" option and the "Detailed Quote Report" sub-option from the Thomson ONE database to determine the beta for Starwood Hotels (HOT), Dell Computer (@Dell), Freddie MAC (FRE), Abbott Laboratories (ABT), and Lockheed Martin (LMT). Discuss possible reasons for the differences you observe among these companies.

CHAPTER
7 Characteristics and Valuation of Bonds

At the end of 2002 U.S. corporate business assets (nonfarm and nonfinancial corporations) were financed by nearly $4.9 trillion in credit market debt (mostly long-term debt) and nearly $6.5 trillion in equities. These two sources provided the bulk of financing for U.S. corporate businesses. Examples of long-term debt include bonds and loans from financial institutions. Generally speaking, debt financing entails a relatively constant distribution of interest and has a prior claim on the assets of the firm in the event of bankruptcy.

Equity instruments include *preferred stock* and *common stock*. Preferred stock is sometimes referred to as a **hybrid security** because it shares features of debt as well as common stock. Common stock, however, is the primary source of equity capital. It confers an ownership stake in the firm. Unlike the situation with debt, there is no contractual obligation to pay a fixed dividend. Common stocks are characterized by a residual claim on earnings.

In this chapter and the next we discuss the characteristics of various types of long-term capital instruments and we develop valuation models for these securities. An understanding of the sources of long-term capital and their characteristics is critically important for the financial manager. The finance manager is responsible for evaluating them and raising funds in a manner consistent with the firm's objectives. In addition, the valuation of long-term securities is important to a firm's top management, as well as to current owners, prospective investors, and security analysts. In Chapter 1 we concluded that shareholder wealth maximization is the appropriate goal for firms. Without an understanding of the factors that affect share prices it would be difficult for management to undertake policies consistent with maximizing share price. Current owners and prospective investors should be able to compare their own valuations of the firm's securities with actual market prices to make rational security purchase and sale decisions. Likewise, security analysts use valuation techniques in evaluating long-term corporate securities when making investment recommendations.

This chapter focuses on the characteristics and valuation of long-term debt. The next chapter contains a discussion of the characteristics and valuation of common and preferred stocks.

Chapter Objectives

After reading this chapter, you should have an understanding of the following:

1. Types, features, and characteristics of long-term debt instruments

2. Valuation of bonds

3. Determining the yield to maturity of bonds

4. Determinants of the required rate of return on bonds

DEFINITION OF LONG-TERM DEBT AND BONDS

Long-term debt refers to any promissory note that a borrower executes with a lender wherein he or she agrees to repay the borrowed funds and to compensate the lender for the borrowed funds over a period of time greater than 1 year. Promissory notes with a duration of less than 1 year are classified as short-term debt. Companies generally obtain long-term debt either by seeking a loan from a financial institution or by issuing **bonds**. Bonds are simply long-term debt instruments sold by issuing corporations in the capital markets. Although this chapter focuses on bonds, it should be noted that, in principle, the characteristics and valuation of bonds and other types of long-term debt are similar.

The basic elements of a bond include the *face amount* or **par value**, *maturity date*, and the *coupon* or *coupon rate*. We will illustrate these elements using the sample *bond certificate* in Figure 7.1. A bond certificate is a document that serves as proof of ownership of the bond and provides details of the obligations of the bond issuer. The bond in Figure 7.1 was issued by The Sparta Supply Company on September 14, 1978. In addition to the maturity date, coupon, and face amount of the bond, the bond certificate also shows the name of the investment banker who underwrote the issue, the name of the trustee, and the obligations of the issuer.

The *face amount, par value,* or *maturity value* of a bond is the amount that the issuer promises to pay back to the bondholder on the maturity date. For corporate bonds the par value is typically $1,000. Note that the Sparta Supply Co. bond has a face amount of $1,000.

The *maturity date* is when the issuer promises to pay back the face amount. In the case of the Sparta Supply bond, the bond matured on December 15, 1982.

The *coupon rate* refers to the interest rate *as a percentage of the face amount* that the issuer promises to pay at fixed intervals until the maturity of the bond. For corporate bonds the coupon amount or interest amount is paid on a semiannual basis. The coupon rate on the Sparta Supply bond is $9\frac{3}{4}$ percent or $97.50 per year. The Sparta Supply bond pays interest semiannually on June 15 and December 15. Thus the Sparta Supply bond pays $48.75 every 6 months ($1,000 $\times$ .0975/2).

There are many different types of long-term debt. The type or types a company chooses to use will depend on its own particular financial situation, prevailing market demands, and the characteristics of the industry as a whole.

TYPES OF LONG-TERM BONDS

Long-term bonds generally are classified according to whether or not they are secured by specific physical assets of the issuing company. Secured debt issues usually are called **mortgage bonds,** while issues not secured by specific assets are called **debentures** or, occasionally, *debenture bonds.*

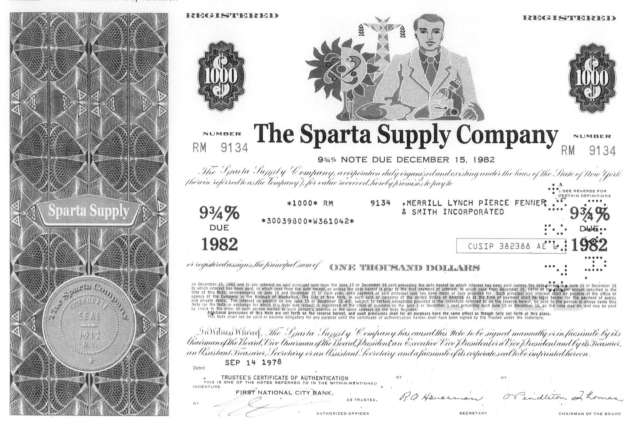

Figure 7.1
Sample Bond
Certificate

At the present time, utility companies are the largest issuers of mortgage bonds. In recent years, the use of mortgage bonds relative to other forms of long-term debt has declined, whereas the use of debentures has increased. Because debentures are unsecured, their quality depends on the general creditworthiness of the issuing company. As a result, they are usually issued by large, financially strong firms.

The interest rate differential between the mortgage bond and debenture alternatives is another example of the risk–return trade-off that occurs throughout finance. For example, suppose Midstates Oil Company could issue either mortgage bonds or debentures. If the mortgage bonds could be sold with a 6 percent interest rate, the debentures would have to be sold at a higher rate—for example, $6\frac{1}{4}$ percent—to attract investors. This is due to the fact that investors require a higher return on debentures, which are backed only by the unmortgaged assets of the company and the company's earning power, than they do on mortgage bonds, which are secured by specific physical assets as well as the company's earning power.

Debt issues also are classified according to whether they are *senior* or *junior*. *Senior debt* has a higher priority claim to a firm's earnings and/or assets than junior debt. Occasionally, the actual name of the debt issue will contain a "junior" or "senior" qualifier. In most instances, however, identification of how a particular company's debt issues are ranked requires an analysis of the restrictions placed on the company by the purchasers of the issue.

Unsecured debt also may be classified according to whether it is *subordinated* to other types of debt. In the event of a liquidation or reorganization, the claims of *subordinated debenture* holders are considered only *after* the claims of unsubordinated debenture holders. In general, subordinated debentures are junior to other types of debt, including bank loans, and may even be junior to *all* of a firm's other debt.

Banks and finance companies often issue bonds backed by a stream of payments from consumer and commercial obligations, known as *receivables*. These securities are known as *asset-backed securities*. Credit card and automobile loan payments are the two primary types of receivables used in the market for asset-backed securities.

FEATURES OF LONG-TERM BONDS

Long-term bonds have a number of unique features:

- ➢ Coupon rates
- ➢ Maturity
- ➢ Calls
- ➢ Puts
- ➢ Sinking fund
- ➢ Links to equity

Many of their features are common to other types of debt as well, such as loans from banks and other financial institutions.

Coupon Rates

The coupon rates on new bonds normally are fixed and set equal to market interest rates on bonds of comparable quality and maturity so that the bonds sell at or near par value. However, some bonds have *floating* coupon rates. These became especially popular during the inflationary period of the early 1980s when a number of highly rated financial institutions as well as other corporations used them to raise substantial sums of money. In a floating rate bond, the coupon is reset periodically (usually, twice a year) depending upon prevailing interest rates.

At the other extreme are the bonds that do not pay any coupon; these are called *zero coupon bonds*. At the end of the maturity the buyer of the bond receives the face value. Since no coupon is paid, these bonds sell at a deep *discount* from face value. Coca-Cola Enterprises, Inc. for example, in 1995 issued over $1.9 billion face amount in zero coupon bonds that mature in 2020. One of the advantages of these types of bonds to the issuing firm is the reduction in (or elimination of) interest payments (a cash outflow) during the life of the bonds. Another advantage is the slightly lower cost (yield to maturity) of these issues compared with bonds that are issued at or near par value. The primary disadvantage of these types of bonds is the large cash outflow required by the firm at maturity. A variant of the zero coupon bond is a bond that has low coupon rates compared to prevailing interest rates and therefore sells at a significant discount from face value. These bonds and zero coupon bonds are also known as *original-issue deep discount* (OID) bonds.

Maturity

The typical maturity on long-term debt is about 20 to 30 years. Occasionally, companies borrow money for as long as 40 years or, in rare cases, even longer. In 1997, Bristol-Myers Squibb and Motorola issued 100-year bonds maturing in 2097. Evidently these companies were attempting to take advantage of what was then considered to be very low interest rates. On the other end of the scale, companies in need of financing often are willing to borrow for as few as 10 years, especially if they feel that interest rates are temporarily high, as was true in the environment of the early 1980s—an environment characterized by high rates of inflation and historically high interest rates. But in the past decade or so, when generally low inflation and moderate interest rates prevailed, many large companies were issuing fixed-rate debt securities with 25- and 30-year maturities.

Call Feature and Bond Refunding

A *call feature* is an optional retirement provision that permits the issuing company to redeem, or *call*, a debt issue prior to its maturity date at a specified price termed the *redemption*, or *call price*. Many firms use the call feature because it provides them with the potential flexibility to retire debt prior to maturity if, for example, interest rates decline and the issuer wants to refinance at the lower rates.

When a bond is called, the issuer pays the bondholder the call price rather than the face amount. The call price is greater than the par value of the debt, and the difference between the two is the *call premium*. Most bonds are not immediately callable after issuance, that is, they have a *deferred call feature*. With a deferred call feature, the bond issuer must wait several years after issuing the bonds, typically 3 to 5 years, before being entitled to call the bonds before maturity. The call premium usually is equal to about 1 year's interest but declines the closer it gets to the maturity date. For example, in November 1995 McDonald's Corporation issued $150 million of 7.05 percent, 30-year debentures with a deferred call feature. McDonald's Corporation could call the bonds starting in 2006 at a call price of 103.26 percent of par value (or $1,032.60). The call price declines each year to 100 percent of par if the bonds are called in 2016 or later.

Because a call feature gives the company significant flexibility in its financing plans, while at the same time potentially depriving the lenders of the advantages they would gain from holding the debt until maturity, the issuing company has to offer the investors compensation in the form of the *call premium* in exchange for the call privilege. In addition, the interest rate on a callable debt issue usually is slightly higher than the interest rate on a similar noncallable issue.

Because of the interest savings that can be achieved, a firm is most likely to call a debt issue when prevailing interest rates are appreciably lower than those that existed at the time of the original issue. When a company calls a relatively high interest rate issue and replaces it with a lower interest rate issue, the procedure is called *bond refunding*. For example, in 1996 Chevron Corp. called its 9.38 percent debentures due 2016. The firm hoped to replace these bonds with new debt at a lower interest rate. The prevailing interest rate in 1996 for bonds of similar risk was approximately 7.5 percent. Thus, by issuing new bonds, Chevron could reduce interest costs by nearly 2 percent.

Put Feature

Some bonds have a *put* feature or *option* that entitles the bondholder to sell the bond back ("put" back) to the issuer before maturity at a predetermined price. In an inflationary setting where interest rates have risen, the put feature enables investors to put the lower coupon bond back to the issuer and reinvest the proceeds in new bonds with higher coupon rates. More recently bonds have been issued with put features that are triggered by specific events. One common trigger is a change of control provision: if a firm is taken over, then the target firm bondholder has the option of putting the bond back to the issuer. Because the bondholder has the put flexibility, the yield is lower than on similar bonds without the put feature.

Sinking Fund

Often lenders require that a borrowing company gradually reduce the outstanding balance of a debt issue over its life instead of having the entire principal amount come due on a particular date 20 or 30 years into the future. The usual method of providing for a gradual retirement is a *sinking fund*, so called because a certain amount of money is put aside annually, or "sunk," into a sinking fund account. For example, in 1991 McDonald's Corporation issued $100 million face amount of 7.3 percent bonds with a sinking fund provision that mature in 2006. The sinking fund required that the firm redeem a certain percentage of the bonds each year beginning in 1991 and through 2005. The percentage to be redeemed each year varied, starting at 2.5 percent of outstanding bonds in 1991 and gradually increasing to 8.4 percent in 2005. By the time of the maturity date, 97.7 percent of the bonds would have been redeemed.

In practice, sinking fund requirements are satisfied either by purchasing a portion of the debt each year in the open market or, if the debt is callable, by using a lottery technique to determine which actual numbered certificates will be called and retired within a given year. The alternative chosen depends on the current market price of the debt issue. In general, if current interest rates are above the issue's coupon rate, the current market price of the debt will be less than $1,000, and the company should meet its sinking fund obligation by purchasing the debt in the open market. If, on the other hand, market interest rates are lower than the issue's coupon rate, and if the market price of the debt is above the call price, the company should use the call procedure.

Equity-Linked Debt

Some debt issues (and some preferred stock issues) are linked to the equity (common stock) of the firm through a *conversion feature* that allows the holder at his or her option to exchange the security for the company's common stock at a predetermined price known as the **conversion price.** In some instances, a **conversion ratio** rather than a conversion price is specified. The conversion ratio is the number of shares into which a convertible bond can be converted. The conversion price may be derived from the convertible ratio by dividing the par value of the bond (typically $1,000) by the conversion ratio. The interest cost (coupon rate) of a **convertible bond (debt)** issue is usually less than an otherwise similar **straight bond (debt)** issue without the conversion option because investors are willing to accept the value of the conversion privilege as part of their overall return. For example, in 2000, Kerr-McGee Corporation issued $550 million face amount of convertible bonds with a coupon rate of 5.25 percent and a conversion price of $61.07. If Kerr-McGee were to have issued a straight bond instead, the coupon rate probably would have been around 8.5 percent. At the time the convertible bond was issued in 2000, Kerr-McGee's common stock was trading for approximately $35.00; thus the conversion option did not have any immediate value. However, the *prospect* that the stock price would exceed the conversion price of $61.07 at some point in the future (before the maturity date of the bond) makes the convertibility feature a valuable option for the bondholder. Another form of equity-linked debt is the issuance of **warrants** along with straight debt; this combination is called a **unit.** A warrant is an option to purchase shares of a company's common stock at a specified price during a given time period.

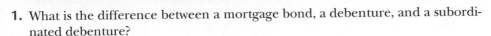

Comprehension Check Questions

1. What is the difference between a mortgage bond, a debenture, and a subordinated debenture?
2. What is an original-issue deep discount (OID) bond?
3. What is the call feature and how do firms benefit from it?

BOND RATINGS

The most significant aspect of the risk of any debt is the *risk of default.* Default risk refers to the likelihood that the issuer will be unable to make the interest and principal

For more detail on bond rating methodologies see
http://www.moodys.com
http://www.standardandpoors.com

payments on time. Fortunately for most bond investors, they do not have to carry out an independent assessment of default risk for every bond they are interested in. There are special financial organizations, known as **bond rating** *agencies,* that provide an independent assessment of default risk for many of the outstanding bonds. Two of the more widely known bond rating agencies that deal with corporate debt are Moody's Investor Services and Standard and Poor's (S&P) Corporation.

These agencies consider a variety of factors when rating a firm's securities, including earnings stability, coverage ratios, the relative amount of debt in the firm's capital structure, the degree of subordination, and management quality as well as past experience. According to Moody's rating scale, the highest-quality, lowest-risk issues are rated Aaa, and the scale continues down through Aa, A, Baa, Ba, B, Caa, Ca, and C. On the Standard and Poor's ratings scale, AAA denotes the highest-quality issues, and this rating is followed by AA, A, BBB, BB, B, and so on. S&P also has various C and D classifications for high-risk issues; the majority of debt issues, however, fall into one of the A or B categories. Within each letter rating class, the agencies also use qualifiers to make finer distinctions in default quality. For instance, Standard and Poor's uses + and − qualifiers; thus, a AA+ has lower default risk than an AA or AA− bond. Moody's uses 1, 2, 3 as the qualifiers; thus a Baa1 has lower default risk than a Baa2 or Baa3 rated bond. Figure 7.2 shows the Moody's and S&P's bond-rating definitions.

In general, firms with the most favorable profitability and leverage ratios tend to have the highest credit ratings. Let's compare the bond ratings for two department store chains—Wal-Mart and JCPenney. Wal-Mart bonds were rated AA while JCPenney bonds were rated BBB− by Standard and Poor's in early 2003. Table 7.1 gives selected leverage and profitability ratios for the two companies. Note the poorer profitability, debt, and interest coverage ratios for JCPenney compared to Wal-Mart.

Bonds rated in the top four categories (Aaa, Aa, A, and Baa in the case of Moody's ratings and AAA, AA, A, and BBB in the case of Standard and Poor's ratings) are considered to be **investment grade**. Bonds that fall into the lower rating categories (Ba and below in the case of Moody's and BB and below in the case of Standard and Poor's) are known as *noninvestment grade, speculative grade, high-yield,* or **junk bonds.** The top four categories are known as investment grade because many financial institutions are not permitted to invest in the lower-rated bonds or face severe restrictions if they do.

Table 7.1 Selected Leverage and Profitability Ratios for Wal-Mart and JCPenney for Year 2002

	Wal-Mart	JCPenney
Standard and Poor's bond rating	AA	BBB−
Sales	$217,800 million	$32,004 million
Total assets	$83,451 million	$18,048 million
Net profit margin	3.2%	0.9%
ROA	8.0%	1.7%
Long-term debt to total assets ratio	22.4%	28.7%
Total debt to total assets ratio	26.2%	33.9%
Interest coverage ratio	11.9x	2.0x

Source: Ratings are from Standard and Poor's Web site (http://www.standardandpoors.com), Feb. 14, 2003. Financial variables and ratios are obtained from or calculated from information contained in the 2002 annual reports of the respective companies.

Figure 7.2
Moody's and Standard and Poor's Bond Ratings Definitions

Moody's Bond Ratings

Moody's long-term obligation ratings are opinions of the relative credit risk of fixed-income obligations with an original maturity of one year or more. They address the possibility that a financial obligation will not be honored as promised. Such ratings reflect both the likelihood of default and any financial loss suffered in the event of default.

Moody's Long-Term Rating Definitions:

Aaa
Obligations rated Aaa are judged to be of the highest quality, with minimal credit risk.

Aa
Obligations rated Aa are judged to be of high quality and are subject to very low credit risk.

A
Obligations rated A are considered upper-medium grade and are subject to low credit risk.

Baa
Obligations rated Baa are subject to moderate credit risk. They are considered medium-grade and as such may possess certain speculative characteristics.

Ba
Obligations rated Ba are judged to have speculative elements and are subject to substantial credit risk.

B
Obligations rated B are considered speculative and are subject to high credit risk.

Caa
Obligations rated Caa are judged to be of poor standing and are subject to very high credit risk.

Ca
Obligations rated Ca are highly speculative and are likely in, or very near, default, with some prospect of recovery of principal and interest.

C
Obligations rated C are the lowest rated class of bonds and are typically in default, with little prospect for recovery of principal or interest.

Note: Moody's appends numerical modifiers 1, 2, and 3 to each generic rating classification from Aa through Caa. The modifier 1 indicates that the obligation ranks in the higher end of its generic rating category; the modifier 2 indicates a mid-range ranking; and the modifier 3 indicates a ranking in the lower end of that generic rating category.

(Continued)

**Figure 7.2
(Continued)**

Standard and Poor's Ratings

Issue credit ratings are based, in varying degrees, on the following considerations:

> Likelihood of payment-capacity and willingness of the obligor to meet its financial commitment on an obligation in accordance with the terms of the obligation
>
> Nature of and provisions of the obligation
>
> Protection afforded by, and relative position of, the obligation in the event of bankruptcy, reorganization, or other arrangement under the laws of bankruptcy and other laws affecting creditors' rights

The issue-rating definitions are expressed in terms of default risk. As such, they pertain to senior obligations of an entity. Junior obligations are typically rated lower than senior obligations, to reflect the lower priority in bankruptcy, as noted above. (Such differentiation applies when an entity has both senior and subordinated obligations, secured and unsecured obligations, or operating company and holding company obligations.) Accordingly, in the case of junior debt, the rating may not conform exactly with the category definition.

AAA

An obligation rated AAA has the highest rating assigned by Standard & Poor's. The obligor's capacity to meet its financial commitment on the obligation is extremely strong.

AA

An obligation rated AA differs from the highest rated obligations only to a small degree. The obligor's capacity to meet its financial commitment on the obligation is very strong.

A

An obligation rated A is somewhat more susceptible to the adverse effects of changes in circumstances and economic conditions than are obligations in higher-rated categories. However, the obligor's capacity to meet its financial commitment on the obligation is still strong.

BBB

An obligation rated BBB exhibits adequate protection parameters. However, adverse economic conditions or changing circumstances are more likely to lead to a weakened capacity of the obligor to meet its financial commitment on the obligation.

Note: Obligations rated BB, B, CCC, CC, and C are regarded as having significant speculative characteristics. BB indicates the least degree of speculation and C the highest. While such obligations will likely have some quality and protective characteristics, these may be outweighed by large uncertainties or major exposures to adverse conditions.

BB

An obligation rated BB is less vulnerable to nonpayment than other speculative issues. However, it faces major ongoing uncertainties or exposure to adverse business, financial, or economic conditions which could lead to the obligor's inadequate capacity to meet its financial commitment on the obligation.

B

An obligation rated B is more vulnerable to nonpayment than obligations rated BB, but the obligor currently has the capacity to meet its financial commitment on the obligation. Adverse business, financial, or economic conditions will likely impair the obligor's capacity or willingness to meet its financial commitment on the obligation.

CCC

An obligation rated CCC is currently vulnerable to nonpayment and is dependent upon favorable business, financial, and economic conditions for the obligor to meet its financial commitment on the obligation. In the event of adverse business, financial, or economic conditions, the obligor is not likely to have the capacity to meet its financial commitment on the obligation.

CC

An obligation rated CC is currently highly vulnerable to nonpayment.

(Continued)

Figure 7.2
(Continued)

C

A subordinated debt or preferred stock obligation rated C is *currently highly vulnerable* to nonpayment. The C rating may be used to cover a situation where a bankruptcy petition has been filed or similar action taken, but payments on this obligation are being continued. A C also will be assigned to a preferred stock issue in arrears on dividends or sinking fund payments, but that is currently paying.

D

An obligation rated D is in payment default. The D rating category is used when payments on an obligation are not made on the date due even if the applicable grace period has not expired, unless Standard & Poor's believes that such payments will be made during such grace period. The D rating also will be used upon the filing of a bankruptcy petition or the taking of a similar action if payments on an obligation are jeopardized.

Plus (+) or minus (−)

The ratings from AA to CCC may be modified by the addition of a plus or minus sign to show relative standing within the major rating categories.

Source: http://www.moodys.com *and* http://www.standardandpoors.com

Companies with weak financial positions (e.g., highly leveraged balance sheets or low earnings) often issue high-yield or junk bonds to obtain capital needed for internal expansion or for corporate acquisitions and buyouts. Junk bonds typically yield 3 percent or more than the highest-quality corporate debt. For example, Campeau Corporation had to pay over 17 percent in November 1988 to obtain some of the funds it needed to pay for the acquisition of Federated Department Stores. These bonds were rated CCC+ by Standard and Poor's. Junk bonds came to prominence in the 1980s when Michael Milken and the investment banking firm he worked for, Drexel Burnham Lambert, Inc., marketed them as a significant source of funds for corporations looking to restructure or acquire other firms. Although not nearly as popular today, junk bonds are still an important source of funds for some firms.

INDENTURE

An *indenture* is a contract between a firm that issues long-term debt securities and the lenders. In general, an indenture does the following:

> ➢ Thoroughly details the nature of the debt issue
> ➢ Carefully specifies the manner in which the principal must be repaid
> ➢ Lists any restrictions placed on the firm by the lenders

Covenants

The restrictions cited above are called *covenants*, and the firm must satisfy them to keep from defaulting on its obligations. Typical restrictive covenants include the following:

1. Maintain a minimum coverage, or times interest earned, ratio
2. Maintain a minimum level of working capital
3. Restriction on the maximum amount of dividends the firm can pay on its preferred and common stock
4. Restrictions on the firm's ability to sell or dispose off existing assets
5. Restrictions on the firm's ability to acquire or merge with another company
6. Other restrictions that effectively limit how much additional debt the firm may incur

Restrictive covenants can be used to safeguard the position of debt holders by prohibiting certain actions by shareholders or managers that might be detrimental to the market value of the debt securities and the ability of the firm to repay the debt at maturity. Strong debt covenants can reduce managerial flexibility and thus impose opportunity costs on the firm. For example, by requiring prior approval from bondholders for an acquisition or merger, the firm may miss a significant opportunity to increase shareholder wealth. At the same time, strong covenants can result in higher credit ratings and lower borrowing costs to the firm by limiting transfers of wealth from bondholders to stockholders and placing limits on the bargaining power of management in any future debt renegotiations. The optimal package of covenants minimizes the sum of these costs.

Trustees

Because the holders of a large firm's long-term debt issue are likely to be scattered widely geographically, the Trust Indenture Act of 1939 requires that a trustee represent the debt holders in dealings with the issuing company. A trustee usually is a commercial bank or trust company that is responsible for ensuring that all the terms and covenants set forth in the indenture agreement are adhered to by the issuing company. The issuing company must pay the trustee's expenses.

Comprehension Check Questions

1. What are bond ratings?
2. What are junk bonds?
3. What is an indenture?
4. What are covenants and what purpose do they serve?

BOND VALUATION

e-Lecture

The value of any asset is based on the expected future benefits, or cash flows, the owner will receive over the life of the asset. For example, assume that you are trying to value a business that is for sale. The value of that business would depend on the future cash flows— cash generated from sales less the expenses of running the business—that it is expected to generate. Conceptually, the cash flow time line may be depicted as follows:

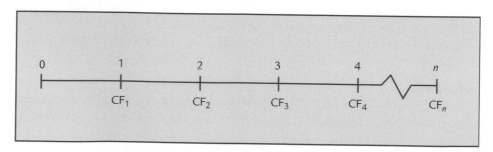

where CF_1, CF_2, . . . , CF_n are the annual cash flows up to year n when the business is assumed to be terminated or sold. Valuing this business boils down to the following question: How much are you willing to pay *today* for the *future stream of cash flow benefits* CF_1, CF_2, . . . , CF_n? Having successfully mastered the concepts in the discussion of the time value of money (Chapter 5), the answer is fairly simple: The value of the business or asset is equal to the discounted value (present value) of the future stream of cash flows. Algebraically, the value of the asset is equal to:

(7.1)
$$V_0 = \frac{CF_1}{(1+i)^1} + \frac{CF_2}{(1+i)^2} + \frac{CF_3}{(1+i)^3} + \ldots + \frac{CF_n}{(1+i)^n}$$

Alternatively, using the summation notation, as follows:

$$V_0 = \sum_{t=1}^{n} \frac{CF_t}{(1+i)^t} \qquad (7.2)$$

where V_0 is the value of the asset at time zero, CF_t the expected cash flow in period t, i the required rate of return or discount rate, and n the length of the holding period. The required rate of return, i, depends on the *risk* of the cash flows. From Chapter 6 we know that investors require higher rates of return for investments with riskier cash flows. The approach to valuation illustrated in Equation 7.2 is referred to as the **capitalization of cash flow** or the *discounted cash flow* method.

Using the Capitalization of Cash Flow Method

Applying this conceptual model to the valuation of bonds is relatively straightforward. In the case of bonds, the future cash flows are contractually specified. These include the interest (coupon) payment each period, $I_1, I_2, \ldots , I_n$, until it matures n periods from now and the principal payment, M, received at the time of maturity in period n. The cash flows are illustrated in the following time line:

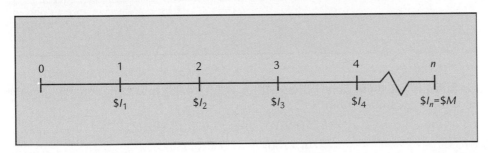

These cash flows are then discounted at an appropriate required rate of return. This would depend, among other things, upon the general level of interest rates prevailing in the economy and the riskiness of the bonds. For example, bonds with higher default risk (e.g., bonds issued by JCPenney in Table 6.1) will require a higher discount rate than otherwise similar bonds issued by firms with lower risk of default (e.g., bonds issued by Wal-Mart in Table 6.1). The determinants of the required rate of return are discussed more fully in the "Key Determinants of Bond Yields" section later in this chapter.

Click on the Investment Analysis Calculator button at **http://finance. swlearning.com** *for an interactive financial calculator for bond valuation.*

Using the capitalization of cash flow method, the value of a bond is equal to:

$$P_0 = \frac{I_1}{(1+k_d)^1} + \frac{I_2}{(1+k_d)^2} + \frac{I_3}{(1+k_d)^3} + \ldots + \frac{I_n + M}{(1+k_d)^n} \qquad (7.3)$$

where P_0 is the present value of the bond at time zero, or its purchase date, and k_d is the investor's required rate of return on this particular bond issue.

Because all of the interest payments on a bond normally are equal (that is $I_1 = I_2 = \ldots = I_{n-1} = I_n = I$), Equation 7.3 can be simplified as follows:

$$P_0 = \sum_{t=1}^{n} \frac{I}{(1+k_d)^t} + \frac{M}{(1+k_d)^n} \qquad (7.4)$$

The first term in Equation 7.4 represents the present value of an annuity of I (interest or coupon payment) per period for n periods; the second term represents the present value of a *single payment* of M (face or maturity amount) in period n. Using the interest factor tables, Equation 7.4 can be restated as:

$$P_0 = I(\text{PVIFA}_{k_d,n}) + M(\text{PVIF}_{k_d,n}) \qquad (7.5)$$

To illustrate the use of Equation 7.5, consider the following example. Tasty Food Company issued $300 million of 7 percent bonds maturing on May 15, 2011. The bonds were issued in $1,000 denominations (par value) and pay interest on May 15 each year.

An investor who wishes to purchase one of these Tasty bonds on May 15, 2004 and requires an 8 percent rate of return on this particular bond issue would compute the value of the bond as follows. These calculations assume that the investor will hold the bond until maturity and receive seven annual ($n = 7$) interest payments of $70 each ($I = \$1,000 \times 0.07$) plus a principal payment, M, of $1,000 at the end of the seventh year, May 15, 2011. The expected cash flows from this bond are shown on the time line below:

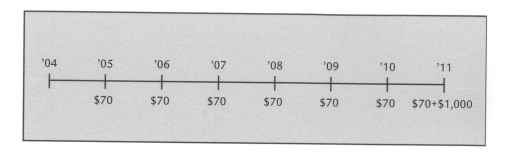

Substituting these values along with $k_d = 8\%$ (0.08) into Equation 7.5 gives the following value for the bond:

$$P_0 = \$70(\text{PVIFA}_{8,\,7}) + \$1,000(\text{PVIF}_{8,\,7})$$
$$= \$70(5.206) + \$1,000(0.583)$$
$$= \$947.42 \text{ (or } \$947)$$

In other words, an investor requiring an 8 percent return on this Tasty Food Company bond would be willing to pay approximately $947 for it on May 15, 2004.

The calculator solution to the above problem is as follows:

Calculator
Solution

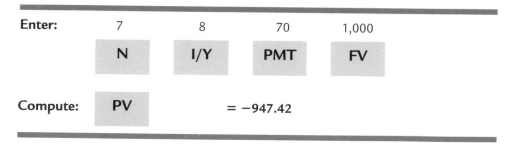

Bond valuation problems may also be solved using Excel spreadsheet software as illustrated on the next page.

In the problem shown, you may wonder why investors would require an 8 percent rate of return on bonds that pay only 7 percent interest. The answer is that the required rate of return has increased since the bonds originally were issued. At the time of issue, the prevailing rate of interest (that is, the required rate of return) on bonds of this maturity and quality was approximately 7 percent. Hence, the coupon rate was set at 7 percent. Because of such factors as tight credit market conditions, higher inflation, increased firm risk, and so on, investors now require a higher rate of return to induce them to purchase these bonds.

	A	B	C	D	E	F	G	H	I	J
1										
2										
3		Using a Spreadsheet to Find the Price of a Bond with Annual Interest Payments								
4										
5		Years								
6			2004	2005	2006	2007	2008	2009	2010	2011
7				$70.00	$70.00	$70.00	$70.00	$70.00	$70.00	$70.00
8										$1,000.00
9										
10		Required rate of return =	8.00%		Present value of the coupon payments is calculated using the PV function PV(rate,nper,PMT,FV) and then take the absolute value of the resulting answer: "+ABS(PV($C$10,(I6-B6),C7,0))."					
11										
12		Present value of coupon payments=	$364.45							
13					Present value of the maturity amount is calculated using the PV function PV(rate,nper,PMT,FV) and then take the absolute value of the resulting answer: "+ABS(PV($C$10,(I6-B6),0,I8))."					
14		Present value of maturity amount=	$583.49							
15										
16		Price of bond =	$947.94							
17										
18		Price of a bond is the sum of the present values of the coupon payments and maturity amount. "+SUM(C12,C14)."								
19										
20										
21										
22		You can also solve this problem in one step as shown below:								
23										
24		Price of bond =	$947.94							
25										
26		Calculate the present value of the coupon payments and maturity amount in one step, and then take the absolute value of the resulting answer: "=+ABS(PV($C$10,I6-B6,C7,I8))."								
27										
28										
29										

Spreadsheet strategies

Semiannual Interest Payments

Most corporate bonds pay interest semiannually. Modifying Equations 7.4 and 7.5 to accommodate the semiannual nature of interest is quite straightforward. Instead of receiving I of interest every year, you now receive $I/2$ of interest semiannually. Similarly, the discount rate and the number of periods need to be expressed in semiannual terms rather than as annual figures. Thus, the discount rate is $k_d/2$ and the number of periods to maturity is $2n$. Equation 7.4 and 7.5 can be expressed in the semiannual form as:

$$P_0 = \sum_{t=1}^{2n} \frac{I/2}{(1 + k_d/2)^t} + \frac{M}{(1 + k_d/2)^{2n}} \qquad (7.6)$$

$$P_0 = I/2(\text{PVIFA}_{k_d/2n}) + M(\text{PVIF}_{k_d/2,2n}) \qquad (7.7)$$

With semiannual interest and compounding, the value for the Tasty Food Company bond is calculated as follows (using Equation 7.7):

$$P_0 = \$35(\text{PVIFA}_{4, 14}) + \$1,000(\text{PVIF}_{4, 14})$$
$$= \$35(10.563) + \$1,000(0.577)$$
$$= \$946.71 \text{ (or } \$947)$$

In this problem, the annual required rate of return is divided by 2 ($k_d/2 = 8/2 = 4$) and the number of periods is multiplied by 2 ($n \times 2 = 7 \times 2 = 14$). The calculated bond value differs only slightly from the solution obtained previously assuming annual interest payments and compounding.

BOND PRICING PRINCIPLES

Now that we know how to value a bond, we should become familiar with some of the basic *principles of bond pricing*. There are four in particular that we will consider:

First Principle: *Bond values are inversely related to the required rate of return.* Figure 7.3 and the accompanying table shows the value of the Tasty bond for various required rates of return. Note that as the required rate of return increases, the value of the bond drops. The value has to drop because the coupon rate is fixed; thus the only way the investor will earn the required rate of return is to offer less for the bond.

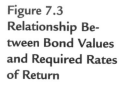

Required Rate of Return %	Bond Value ($)
3	1249
5	1116
6	1056
7	1000
8	948
9	899
11	812

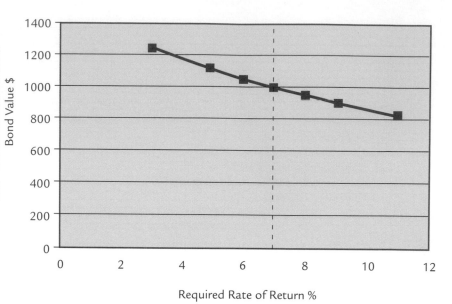

Figure 7.3
Relationship Between Bond Values and Required Rates of Return

Second Principle: *If the required rate of return is greater than the coupon rate then the bond value is less than the par value. If the required rate of return is less than the coupon rate then the bond value is greater than the par value.* From the table in Figure 7.3, note that the value of the Tasty bond is exactly equal to the par value ($1,000) when the required rate of return is equal to the coupon rate (7%). When the required rate of return is greater than 7 percent, the value of the bond drops below the par value. When this happens the bond is known to *trade at a discount.* Conversely, when the required rate of return is less than the coupon rate, bond values are greater than the par value. Bonds trading above the par value are said to be trading at a premium.

Third Principle: *The sensitivity of bond prices to a given change in the required rate of return increases with the maturity of the bond.* This principle states that, holding all other things constant, the value of a longer-term bond is affected more by changes in required rates of return than the value of a shorter-term bond is. We refer to the relative change in bond price to a given change in the required rate of return as ***interest rate risk.*** Thus, according to the third bond pricing principle, interest rate risk for longer maturity bonds is greater than for shorter maturity bonds. Figure 7.4 illustrates this principle using a 15-year and a 3-year maturity bond, each with a 7 percent coupon rate. If we assume that the initial required rate of return is 7 percent, both bonds would be priced at $1,000.

The accompanying table in Figure 7.4 shows what happens to values of the two bonds as interest rate (required return) changes. The table also shows the percentage change in price relative to the beginning value ($1,000). As is evident from the figure and the table, the variation in the value of the 15-year bond is considerably greater than the variation of the 3-year bond. For example, if the interest rate (required rate of return) increases from 7 percent to 9 percent, the value of the 15-year bond drops from $1,000 to $839 or a 16 percent drop: (($1,000 − $839)/ $1,000) × 100. On the other hand, the value of the 3-year bond drops from $1,000 to $949 or just a drop of 5 percent: (($1,000 − 949)/$1,000) × 100. The larger drop for the 15-year bond, in contrast to the 3-year bond, occurs because the in-

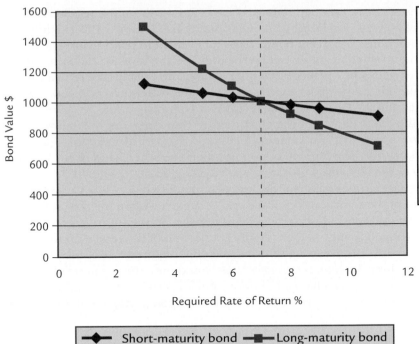

Required Rate of Return %	Short-maturity bond (3 years) price ($)	Long-maturity bond (15 years) price ($)
3	1113	1478
5	1054	1208
6	1027	1097
7	1000	1000
8	974	914
9	949	839
11	902	712

**Figure 7.4
Sensitivity of Bond Prices to Maturity for a Given Change in Interest Rates**

vestor is locked into a lower coupon rate (7 percent) compared to the required rate of return (9 percent) for a longer period of time. Conversely, when the required rate of return drops from 7 percent to, say, 6 percent, the longer-maturity bond increases in price more than the shorter-maturity bond because you are receiving a higher coupon rate than the required rate of return for a longer period of time.

Fourth Principle: *The sensitivity of bond prices to a given change in the required rate of return decreases the higher the coupon rate.* This principle states that a bond with a higher-coupon rate exhibits a smaller change in price than an otherwise identical lower-coupon rate bond for a given change in the required rate of return. Table 7.2 illustrates this principle using two bonds with identical maturities of 15 years but one with a coupon of 2 percent and the other with a coupon of 7 percent. Let's assume

Table 7.2 Sensitivity of Bond Prices to Coupon for a Given Change in Interest Rates

Required rate of Return %	Low-Coupon Bond (2%) Price $	Percent Change %	High-Coupon Bond (7%) Price $	Percent Change
3	881	61.7	1478	47.8
5	689	26.4	1208	20.8
6	612	12.3	1097	9.7
7	545	0	1000	0
8	486	−10.8	914	−8.6
9	436	−20	839	−16.1
11	353	−35.2	712	−28.8

Note: Percent change is change in bond price relative to the initial price based on a 7 percent required rate of return

that the interest rate or required return is 7 percent initially. At this required rate of return, the lower-coupon bond (2 percent bond) has a value of $545 while the higher-coupon bond (7 percent bond) has a value equal to par, $1,000. The lower-coupon bond is valued at a discount, as the only way the investor can earn the required rate of return of 7 percent is to offer a lower price. Thus, the return for the lower-coupon bond consists of the coupon and the difference between the discounted price and the face value to be received at maturity.

When the required rate of return increases from 7 percent to 9 percent, the lower-coupon bond drops in value to $436 or a drop of 20 percent: (($436 − $545)/$545) × 100. The higher-coupon bond on the other hand drops in value from $1,000 to $839 or a drop of 16 percent: (($839 − $1,000)/$1,000) × 100. The larger percentage drop in value for the lower-coupon bond occurs because a significant portion of the return occurs at the end of maturity when the face amount is received. Given that cash flows to be received farther in the future are worth less today, lower-coupon bonds, where a significant portion of the return occurs at maturity, will be more sensitive to a given change in the required rate of return.

Based on this principle, *zero coupon bonds* would have the greatest volatility in prices. That is, for a given change in interest rates a zero coupon bond would exhibit the greatest change in price compared to a coupon paying bond, holding all else constant.

YIELD TO MATURITY

As a bond investor, you are often presented with alternative bonds that are trading at different prices. To decide whether to invest in a bond you would like to know what rate of return you are likely to earn if you were to purchase the bond at a particular price. In other words you would like to know the **yield to maturity (YTM)** of the bond. The yield to maturity of a bond is the *discount rate that equates the present value of all expected interest payments (until maturity) and the repayment of principal (at maturity) from a bond to the present bond price.* In other words, the YTM *tells a bond investor what he or she is likely to earn if a bond is purchased for a given price and held to maturity.* If the current price of a bond, P_0, the uniform annual interest payments, I, the maturity value, or principal, M, and length of maturity, n, are known, the yield to maturity of a bond can be calculated by solving for k_d in Equation 7.4 or 7.5. These equations are reproduced below:

$$(7.4) \qquad P_0 = \sum_{t=1}^{n} \frac{I}{(1 + k_d)^t} + \frac{M}{(1 + k_d)^n}$$

$$(7.5) \qquad P_0 = I(\text{PVIFA}_{k_d,n}) + M(\text{PVIF}_{k_d,n})$$

Given values for any four of the five variables in this equation (P_0, I, M, k_d, n) one can solve for the value of the fifth variable. Recall that the above equations were used to determine the value of a bond (P_0) when the value of k_d is known (along with the values of I, M, and n). In the yield to maturity calculation, which follows, the above equations are used to determine k_d when the value of P_0 is known (along with the values of I, M and n).

We will illustrate the calculation of YTM using the AT&T Wireless Services bond that appeared in the *WSJ* quotes discussed in Chapter 2 (Figure 2.7). The relevant section of *The Wall Street Journal* quote as it appeared on Friday, September 5, 2003 (recall that the information is for Thursday, September 4, 2003 trading date) is reproduced in Figure 7.5. Note that the AT&T Wireless bond has a coupon rate of 8.125 percent and matures on May 1, 2012. Let's assume that you purchased one

Thursday, September 4, 2003

Forty most active fixed-coupon corporate bonds

COMPANY (TICKER)	COUPON	MATURITY	LAST PRICE	YIELD	*EST SPREAD	UST†	EST $ VOL (000's)
General Motors (GM)	8.375	Jul 15, 2033	100.614	8.317	301	30	203,944
Ford Motor Credit (F)	6.700	Jul 16, 2004	103.633	2.367	47	2	121,099
General Motors Acceptance (GMAC)	6.875	Aug 28, 2012	99.799	6.905	240	10	117,747
AT&T Wireless Services (AWE)	8.125	May 01, 2012	114.646	5.933	142	10	97,537

**Figure 7.5
Bond Quote from *The Wall Street Journal***

Source: The Wall Street Journal, January 7, 2003.

of these bonds on September 4, 2003 at the last price indicated—$1,146.46. To keep things simple we will assume that the bond matures on September 4, 2012 (rather than the May 1, 2012 shown in the figure) and that interest is paid every year on September 4. The calculation of YTM will be illustrated using (1) present value tables (Equation 7.5), (2) the financial calculator, and (3) Excel Spreadsheet.

Using the present value tables is essentially a trial-and-error process. The method requires that we identify the discount rate that equates the present value of future cash flows of a bond (the right-hand side of Equation 7.5) to the bond price (left-hand side of Equation 7.5). The steps in the trial-and-error procedure are as follows:

Step 1. Make an approximate estimate of the yield to maturity. Note that if the current price of the bond is above (or below) the maturity value—i.e., if the bond is selling at a premium (discount)—then the trial rate should be less than (greater than) the coupon rate.

Step 2. Use this rate to compute the present value of the bond's cash flows (that is, interest payments and principal payment).

Step 3. Try a higher (lower) rate if the present value of the bond's cash flows is greater (less) than the current bond price.

Step 4. Repeat the process (attempting to "bracket" the yield to maturity) until a rate is found at which the present value of the bond's cash flows is equal to the current bond price.

Let's apply the trial-and-error method to the AT&T Wireless Services (AWE) bond. The bond's price is at a premium, so we know that the YTM must be less than the coupon rate of 8.125 percent. As a starting point, let's calculate the value of the bond using a discount rate of 5 percent:

$$P_0 = \$81.25 \ (\text{PVIFA}_{5,9}) + \$1,000 \ (\text{PVIF}_{5,9})$$
$$= \$81.25 \ (7.108) + \$1,000 \ (0.645)$$
$$= \$1,222.53$$

Since this is greater than the quoted price of $1,146.46 we know the YTM must be higher than 5 percent. Substituting 6 percent for the discount rate, we get a bond value of

$$P_0 = \$81.25 \ (\text{PVIFA}_{6,9}) + \$1,000 \ (\text{PVIF}_{6,9})$$
$$= \$81.25 \ (6.802) + \$1,000 \ (0.592)$$
$$= \$1,144.66$$

Obviously the value just obtained is less than the closing price of the bond. Thus, we have "bracketed" the YTM between 5 and 6 percent. It is evident from the values obtained that the actual bond price of $1,146.46 is closer to the bond value at 6 percent than it is to the bond value at 5 percent, so the YTM is just below 6 percent.

Using a financial calculator we can obtain the more precise answer of YTM = 5.97 percent:

Calculator Solution

Enter:	9	−1,146.46	81.25	1,000
	N	PV	PMT	FV

Compute:	I/Y	= 5.97

The spreadsheet solution for calculating YTM is as follows:

Spreadsheet strategies

	A	B	C	D	E	F	G	H	I	J
1										
2										
3		Using a Spreadsheet to Find the Yield to Maturity of a Bond with Annual Interest Payments								
4										
5		Years								
6			2003	2004	2005	2006	....	.....	....	2012
7				$81.25	$81.25	$81.25	$81.25	$81.25	$81.25	$81.25
8										$1,000.00
9										
10		Price of bond =		$1,146.46						
11										
12		Yield to maturity =		5.97%		Note: Yield to maturity is calculated using the RATE function (RATE(nper,PMT,-PV,FV)).				
13						Excel formula: "=RATE((I6-B6),C7,-C10,I8)"				
14										
15										

Thus, if you purchased the AT&T Wireless Services bond for $1,146.46 and held it to maturity you would have *realized a rate of return of 5.97 percent.* An implicit assumption of the YTM calculation is that the coupon payments received every year are reinvested at the rate equal to the YTM. This may or may not be true. If the coupon payments are reinvested at a rate less than the YTM, then your realized yield will be *less* than the original YTM; on the other hand, if you reinvest the coupon payments at rates in excess of the YTM, then your realized yield will be *greater* than the original YTM.

The yield to maturity can be used to compare the risk of two or more bonds that are similar *in all other respects* including time to maturity. The bond with the higher yield to maturity is the one perceived to be the riskier by investors. Also, the yield to maturity on existing bonds can be used as an estimate of the required returns of investors on any new (and similar) bonds the firm may issue.

Comprehension Check Questions

1. Describe the capitalization of cash flow or discounted cash flow method approach to valuing bonds.
2. What are the four principles of bond pricing?
3. What information does the yield to maturity of a bond provide?

KEY DETERMINANTS OF BOND YIELDS

A key element of the bond valuation equation (Equation 7.3 or 7.4) is the discount rate or the yield to maturity. In general, the yields on bonds move up and down together as they are impacted by a number of common factors. However, yields also vary depending upon the particulars of the issue and the firm. In this section we explore some of the determinants of the required rate of return on debt.

From Chapter 6 we know that the required rate of return for any asset depends on the risk-free rate of return and a risk premium:

(7.8)
$$k = r_f + \text{risk premium}$$

where k is the required rate of return and r_f is the risk-free rate of return. Recall that the risk-free rate of return compensates the investor for postponing consumption. The risk premium is the additional compensation expected by the investor for assuming risk in the asset's cash flows. In Chapter 6 the risk premium was defined as the systematic risk of the asset relative to the market portfolio. While this definition of risk premium can be used for any asset, in the case of bonds the risk premium is commonly broken down into *maturity risk premium, default risk premium,* and *marketability risk premium.* Thus, the conceptual framework for determining the required rate of return on debt, k_d, is given by:

$$k_d = r_f + \text{risk premium} \begin{cases} \text{maturity risk premium} \\ \text{default risk premium} \\ \text{marketability risk premium} \end{cases} \tag{7.9}$$

We now discuss each of the components of the required rate of return.

Risk-Free Rate of Return

As we said earlier, the risk-free rate of return is the compensation to the investor for postponing consumption. For example, assume that you decide to invest $1,000 in a particular bond *today.* By doing so you are forgoing the opportunity to consume that $1,000 *today.* You could have used the $1,000 to buy clothes, pay for college tuition, buy new furniture, etc. By choosing to invest that money you are postponing consumption for which you should be compensated. *The risk-free rate of return compensates you for postponing current consumption.* In practice we use the return available on a security with no risk of default to substitute for the risk-free rate of return. Short-term U.S. government securities, such as Treasury bills, generally are considered to be risk-free investments and are used as a proxy for the risk-free rate.

The risk-free rate of return, r_f, that we observe is the *nominal* risk-free rate. The nominal risk-free rate depends on the *real risk-free rate* and the *expected inflation premium.* The **Fisher effect** captures the relation between the nominal risk-free rate and the real risk-free rate and inflation premium:

$$(1 + r_f) = (1 + r'_f)(1 + i_n) \tag{7.10}$$

$$r_f = r'_f + i_n + r'_f i_n \tag{7.11}$$

where r'_f is the real risk-free rate and i_n is the expected inflation premium. The last term on the right-hand side is very small, so the nominal risk-free rate is usually depicted as simply the sum of the real risk-free rate and the expected inflation premium:

$$r_f = r'_f + i_n \tag{7.12}$$

The *real risk-free rate of return* is the return that investors would require from a security having no risk of default in a period of *no expected inflation.* It is the return necessary to convince investors to postpone current, real consumption opportunities. The real rate of return is determined by the interaction of the supply of funds made available by savers and the demand for funds for investment. Historically, the real rate of return has been estimated to average in the range of 2 to 4 percent.

The second component of the risk-free rate of return is an *inflation premium* or *purchasing power loss premium.* Investors require compensation for expected losses in purchasing power when they postpone current consumption and lend funds. For example, let's assume you have $100 with which you can buy 100 cans of Coke. Instead of purchasing the Coke and consuming it, you choose instead to loan the money in exchange for $103 a year from now. If there is no inflation, then at the end of the year you have enough money to buy 103 cans of Coke. So you have made a real rate of return of 3 percent. Now assume that during the course of the year Coke prices increased to $1.04 per can. How many cans of Coke can you buy at the end of the year? The answer is 99 cans ($103/$1.04). At the end of the year the $103 dollars that the borrower gives is not sufficient to even buy the 100 cans of Coke you could have purchased and consumed a year ago. In other words not only did you not gain anything for sacrificing current consumption but also you did not even retain the same purchasing power you had a year ago. Consequently, the nominal risk-free return must include a premium for expected inflation.

Using Equation 7.12, if the real rate of return is 3 percent and the expected inflation rate is 4 percent, the nominal risk-free rate should equal 7 percent:

$$r_f = 3 + 4$$
$$= 7 \text{ percent}$$

At any point in time, the required risk-free rate of return on any security can be estimated from the yields on short-term U.S. government securities, such as 90-day Treasury bills. When considering return requirements on all types of securities, it is important to remember that *increases in expected inflation rates normally lead to increases in the required rates of return on all securities.*

Risk Premium

The risk premium implicitly assigned by an investor to a given security in determining the required rate of return (Equation 7.9) is a function of several different risk elements. These risk elements (and premiums) include:

➢ Maturity risk premium
➢ Default risk premium
➢ Marketability risk premium

Each of these risk elements is examined below.

Maturity Risk Premium The return required on a security is influenced by the maturity of that security or the ***term structure of interest rates***. The term structure of interest rates is the pattern of interest rate yields (required returns) for securities that differ only in the length of time to maturity. Plotting interest rate yields (percent) on the vertical axis and the length of time to maturity (years) on the horizontal axis results in a *yield curve*. Yield curves can assume different shapes. Usually they are *upward sloping,* that is, the longer the maturity the higher the yield—although it is not uncommon to observe *downward sloping, flat,* or even *hump-shaped* yield curves. Figure 7.6 shows the yield curve on Friday, January 24, 2003 to be upward sloping. The yield on 3-month U.S. government Treasury bills was 1.14 percent. In contrast, the yield on 10-year U.S. government bonds was 3.92 percent, and the yield on 30-year U.S. government bonds was 4.86 percent. Occasionally, as in August 1981 the yield may slope downward as shown in Figure 7.7, indicating that the longer the time to maturity, the lower is the required return on the security. At that time, the Federal Reserve had drastically "tightened" the money supply and a deep recession followed.

A number of theories have been advanced to explain the shape of the yield curve, including the *expectations theory,* the *maturity premium theory,* and *market segmentation theory.*

According to the expectations theory, *long-term interest rates are a function of expected future (that is, forward) short-term interest rates.* In other words, you can think of long-term rates as being the average of a series of short-term rates. For example, the yield on a 10-year bond can be thought of as the average of the yield on the cur-

Figure 7.6
Upward-Sloping Yield Curve

Source: Bloomberg.com

U.S. Treasuries Sat., 25 Jan 2003, 12:26am EST

Bills		Mat Date	Previous Price/Yield	Current Price/Yield	Yld Chg	Prc Chg
3month		4/24/03	1.12 (1.14)	1.12 (1.14)	0.00	+0
6month		7/24/03	1.15 (1.17)	1.15 (1.18)	0.00	+0

Notes/ Bonds	Coupon	Mat Date	Previous Price/Yield	Current Price/Yield	Yld Chg	Prc Chg
2year	1.750	12/31/04	100-06+ (1.64)	100-07+ (1.63)	-0.02	+0-01
5year	3.000	11/15/07	100-18 (2.87)	100-21 (2.85)	-0.02	+0-03
10year	4.000	11/15/12	100-18+ (3.93)	100-21+ (3.92)	-0.01	+0-03
30year	5.375	2/15/31	107-26 (4.86)	107-27 (4.86)	0.00	+0-01

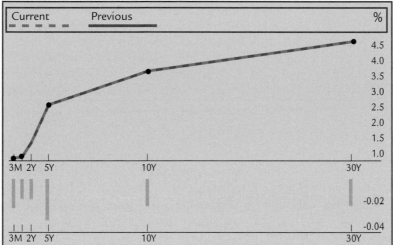

rent 1-year bond plus the expected yield on a 1-year bond issued 1 year from now, plus the expected yield on a 1-year bond issued 2 years from today, and so on, until we have factored in the expected yield on a 1-year bond 9 years from today. If future short-term interest rates are expected to rise, the yield curve will tend to be upward sloping. In contrast, a downward-sloping yield curve reflects an expectation of declining future short-term interest rates. According to the expectations theory, current and expected future interest rates are dependent on expectations about future rates of inflation. Many economic and political conditions can cause expected future inflation and interest rates to rise or fall. These conditions include expected future government deficits (or surpluses), changes in Federal Reserve monetary policy (that is, the rate of growth of the money supply), and cyclical business conditions.

The liquidity (or maturity) premium theory of the yield curve holds that *required returns on long-term securities tend to be greater the longer the time to maturity*. The maturity premium derives from the higher interest rate risk associated with longer-term securities. From the bond pricing principles, we know that the value of a bond tends to vary more as interest rates change, the longer the term to maturity. Thus, if interest rates rise, the holder of a long-term bond will find that the value of the investment has declined substantially more than that of the holder of a short-term bond. In addition, the short-term bond holder has the option of holding the bond for the short time remaining to maturity and then reinvesting the proceeds from that bond at the new higher interest rate. The long-term bondholder must wait much longer before this opportunity is available. Accordingly, it is argued that whatever the shape of the yield curve, a maturity premium is reflected in it.

**Figure 7.7
Downward-Sloping
Yield Curve**

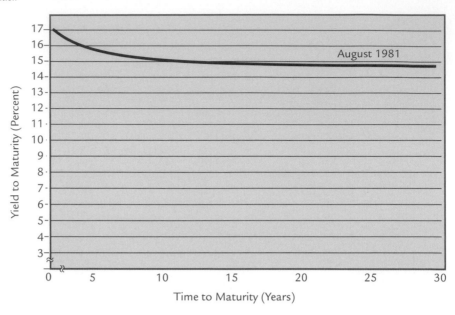

Finance in the News

Click on this button at
http://finance.
swlearning.com *for*
synopses of recent articles
on Bonds.

Finally, according to the market segmentation theory, *the securities markets are segmented by maturity.* That is, interest rates within each maturity segment are determined to a certain extent by *the supply and demand interactions of the segment's borrowers and lenders.* If strong borrower demand exists for long-term funds and these funds are in short supply, the yield curve will be upward sloping. Conversely, if strong borrower demand exists for short-term funds and these funds are in short supply, the yield curve will be downward sloping. The segmentation theory assumes that borrowers and lenders are not free to substitute between various maturity instruments. Thus a lender wanting to provide long-term funds would not be willing to lend in the short-term market. Similarly a borrower wanting to borrow long-term funds would not consider borrowing in the short-term market.

Several factors limit the choice of maturities by lenders. One such restriction is the legal regulations that limit the types of investments commercial banks, savings and loan associations, insurance companies, and other financial institutions are permitted to make. Another limitation faced by lenders and borrowers is the desire (or need) to match the maturity structure of their liabilities with assets of equivalent maturity. For example, life insurance companies and pension funds, because of the long-term nature of their contractual obligations to clients, are interested primarily in making long-term investments. Commercial banks and money market funds, in contrast, are primarily short-term lenders because a large proportion of their liabilities are in the form of deposits that can be withdrawn on demand.

At any point in time, the term structure of interest rates is the result of the interaction of the factors just described. All three theories are useful in explaining the shape of the yield curve.

Default Risk Premium U.S. government securities generally are considered to be free of default risk—that is, the risk that interest and principal will not be paid as promised in the bond indenture. In contrast, corporate bonds are subject to varying degrees of default risk. Investors require higher rates of return on securities subject to default risk. Earlier in the chapter we noted that bond ratings provide a summary measure of the default risk of bonds. Figure 7.8 shows the monthly aver-

FINANCE & The Real World

When Stocks Went South, Bonds Boomed

During the early part of this decade, when stocks were in the midst of the worst bear market in 30 years, an investor in bonds could have posted double-digit returns. But many investors ignored a basic principle of investing: never put all your eggs in one basket.

True, most young people are turned off by bonds because they don't offer growth in capital like stocks. And it's a lot more interesting to invest in the stocks of dynamic companies and follow their ups and downs. With bonds, all you get is an interest payment every six months. And you hope the company stays in business so that it can pay off its bondholders. Still, if the company gets in trouble, bond investors are paid first, whereas the stock may become worthless.

In many ways, bonds are a very different investment than stocks, and for that reason alone, they make good sense. If you invest some of your money in stocks and some in bonds, then you're investing in at least two baskets, not one.

Typically, a young investor would have more of his or her money in the stock market and less in bonds because stocks tend to do better over a long time horizon such as 30 years. But as people start nearing retirement, bonds begin to look more attractive because they pay a steady income—and the closer to retirement we are, the less time we have to wait for the stock market to rebound. People in high tax brackets like municipal bonds, which offer tax-free income. Regard-less of investor age, though, bonds offer stability to a portfolio, and that can be attractive at any age. When bonds mature, they pay back the whole investment. With stocks, one never knows how much money will come back. It could be double, or it could be zero.

Of course, no one can predict whether stocks are going up or bonds are going down. But one thing is fairly consistent: bonds often perform well when stocks do poorly. One reason is that bond prices rise when interest rates fall, which in turn is typical during periods of economic sluggishness. That's what happened during 2001–2002—bonds posted excellent results because interest rates fell sharply. On the other hand, stocks typically need economic growth to do well, since they are driven by corporate profits. Therefore, a prudent "asset allocation" decision is to put some of your money in stocks and some in bonds, on the theory that no one can predict the future. If nothing else, bonds offer diversification to your portfolio.

If you're worried about a company's ability to pay its debts, then you might want to avoid corporate bonds and buy government bonds such as U.S. Treasury securities, which are considered risk free from a credit standpoint. If you're worried about rising interest rates, and falling bond prices, then hold the bond until maturity when you'll get all your money back. Or, own bonds with short maturities. They're less price sensitive to rising interest rates than bonds with long maturities.

Source: Newsweek, December 10, 2001, "Bonding with Your Money . . ."

age yields for 2002 on corporate bonds in various rating classes and also average yield for long-term U.S. Treasury bonds. It is clear that the yields on bonds increase as the risk of default increases, reflecting the positive relationship between risk and required return. For example, in December 2002 the average yield on long-term Treasury bonds was 4.28 percent, while the yield on AAA corporate industrial bonds was 5.29 percent and on BBB bonds was 7.3 percent. Note that over time, the spread between the required returns on bonds having various levels of default risk varies, reflecting the economic prospects and the resulting probability of default. The variations over time are especially noticeable when we examine data at various points of the economic cycle. For example, during the relative prosperity the country was

Figure 7.8
Average Monthly Bond Yields for Various Default Rating Classes and Treasury Bonds, 2002

Source: Based on data taken from Standard & Poor's Bond Guide, January 2003 issue.

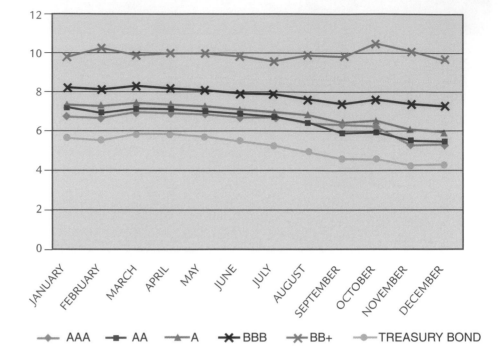

enjoying at the end of 1997, the average yield on BBB-rated corporate bonds was approximately 7.19 percent while the average yield on AAA-rated bonds was 6.61 percent—a premium of .58 percentage points or 58 basis points (standard industry practice is to refer to fractional percentage points in terms of basis points; one percent is equal to 100 basis points). However, at the end of 2002 with an uncertain economy, the average yield on BBB-rated bonds was 7.3 percent while the average yield on AAA-rated bonds was 5.29 percent or a premium of 2.01 percentage points.

Marketability Risk Premium Marketability risk refers to the ability of an investor to buy and sell a company's securities quickly, without a significant loss of value. For example, there is very little marketability risk for the bonds of ExxonMobil, which are very widely held. On the other hand, bonds of a relatively small oil refining company, such as Holly Corporation, may be more difficult to unload as the firm is not well known and may not be owned widely. For firms whose securities have an active secondary market, trades can be executed almost instantaneously with low transaction costs at the current market price. In contrast, if you own bonds of a relatively unknown firm, you might find it difficult to locate a buyer for those bonds. When a buyer is found, that buyer may not be willing to pay the price that you could get for similar bond of a larger well-known company. The marketability risk premium can be significant for securities that are not regularly traded.

Comprehension Check Questions

1. What is the Fisher effect?
2. What are the components of a bond's risk premium?
3. What are some of the theories used to explain the shape of the yield curve?

Summary

➤ Bonds are a type of long-term debt, usually sold in denominations of $1,000, and they constitute a promise by the issuing company to repay a certain amount of money (the $1,000 principal) on a particular date (the maturity date) and to pay a specified amount of interest at fixed intervals (usually twice a year). Bonds are sometimes referred to as fixed income securities because the interest (coupon) paid on the bond remains constant over the life of the bond. This is unlike common stock, which is known as a variable income security, because common stock dividends can change over time.

➤ Long-term debt and bonds generally are classified according to whether or not they are secured by specific physical assets of the issuing company. Secured debt issues are known as mortgage bonds, whereas debt issues backed only by un-mortgaged assets and the company's earning power are known as debentures.

➤ The indenture is the contract between the issuing company and the debt holders. It spells out the details and nature of the debt issue and lists restrictions or covenants placed on the firm by the lenders.

➤ The trustee is usually a commercial bank that represents the debt holders in dealings with the company.

➤ Most bonds have a call feature, which gives the issuing company the option to retire the debt prior to maturity.

➤ Bonds commonly have a sinking fund requirement, which, in practice, means the company must gradually reduce the outstanding balance of the debt issue over its life.

➤ Bond ratings provide a summary measure of the risk of default of a bond issue. The top four rating categories are referred to as investment grade bonds. Bonds below the top four rating classes are known as noninvestment grade, speculative grade, high-yield, or junk bonds.

➤ Using the capitalization of cash flow method, the value of a bond is equal to the present value of the stream of interest and principal payments discounted at the investor's required rate of return.

➤ The yield to maturity on a bond is the rate of return the investor expects to earn if the bond is purchased at a given price and held until maturity.

➤ The four bond pricing principles are:

  Bond prices are inversely related to the required rate of return.

  If the required rate of return is greater than the coupon rate, then the bond value is less than the face value. If the reported rate of return is less than the coupon rate, then the bond value is greater than the face value.

  The sensitivity of bond prices to a given change in the required rate of return increases with the maturity of the bond.

  The sensitivity of bond prices to a given change in the required rate of return decreases the higher the coupon rate.

➤ The required rate of return on debt is equal to the risk-free rate of return plus a risk premium. The risk premium consists of the maturity risk premium, default risk premium, and marketability risk premium.

➤ The Fisher effect captures the relation between the nominal risk-free rate and the real risk-free rate and inflation premium.

➢ The *term structure of interest rates* or *the shape of the yield curve* may be explained by the expectations theory, liquidity premium theory, and/or the market segmentation theory.

Questions and Topics for Discussion

1. Define the following terms associated with long-term debt:
   a. Indenture
   b. Trustee
   c. Call feature
   d. Sinking fund
   e. Put feature
   f. Conversion feature
   g. Coupon rate

2. Describe the basic features of each of the following types of bonds:
   a. Mortgage bonds
   b. Debentures
   c. Subordinated debentures

3. Suppose a company simultaneously sold two long-term debt issues at par value: $6\frac{1}{8}$ percent senior debentures and $6\frac{3}{8}$ percent subordinated debentures. What risk–return trade-off would an investor face who was considering one of these issues?

4. What variables must be known (or estimated) in applying the capitalization of cash flow/discounted cash flow method of valuation to a physical or financial asset?

5. Describe the relationship between the coupon rate and the required rate of return that will result in a bond selling at
   a. A discount
   b. Face value
   c. A premium

6. What is yield to maturity?

7. Explain why bondholders often prefer a sinking fund provision in a bond issue.

8. Explain what is meant by interest rate risk.

9. Describe the basic features of each of the following types of bonds:
   a. Floating-rate bonds
   b. Original issue deep discount bonds
   c. Zero coupon bonds

10. Explain the term structure of interest rates using the expectations theory.

11. What is the Fisher effect?

12. Compare the bond ratings for Continental Airlines and Southwest Airlines. Use the *Standard & Poor's Bond Guide* or the *Moody's Bond Record* from your library to get information on the bond ratings. What reasons can you cite for the differences in bond ratings between the firms?

Self-Test Problems

ST1. What is the yield to maturity of a $1,000 par value bond that is selling for $884, matures in 12 years, and has a coupon rate of $7\frac{3}{8}$ percent?

ST2. AlliedSignal Corporation has a series of zero coupon bonds outstanding that mature on August 1, 2015. Calculate the yield to maturity if an investor purchases one of these bonds on August 1, 2004 at a price of $2,250. The bond is expected to pay $5,000 at maturity.

ST3. Bankers Trust has bonds outstanding ($1,000 par value) that mature 10 years from today and have a coupon interest rate of 9 percent. Calculate the maximum price an investor should be willing to pay if the investor desires a 10 percent yield to maturity.

ST4. What is the real risk-free rate if the nominal risk-free rate is 6 percent and the inflation premium is 3.4 percent?

Problems

1. Determine the value of a $1,000 denomination Bell South bond with a 7 percent coupon rate maturing in 20 years for an investor whose required rate of return is: **BASIC**

    a. 8 percent

    b. 7 percent

    c. 5 percent

2. Consider Allied Signal Corporation's $9\frac{7}{8}$ percent bonds that mature on June 1, 2010. Assume that the interest on these bonds is paid and compounded annually. Determine the value of a $1,000 denomination Allied Signal Corporation bond as of June 1, 2004, to an investor who holds the bond until maturity and whose required rate of return is **INTERMEDIATE**

    a. 7 percent

    b. 9 percent

    c. 11 percent

    d. What would be the value of the Allied Signal Corporation bonds at an 8 percent required rate of return if the interest were paid and compounded *semiannually*?

3. Southern Bell has issued $4\frac{3}{8}$ percent bonds that mature on August 1, 2011. Assume that interest is paid and compounded annually. Determine the yield to maturity if an investor purchases a $1,000 denomination bond for $853.75 on August 1, 2004. **BASIC**

4. American Telephone & Telegraph has issued $8\frac{1}{8}$ percent debentures that will mature on July 15, 2032. Assume that interest is paid and compounded annually. If an investor purchases a $1,000 denomination bond for $1,025 on July 15, 2004, determine the bond's yield to maturity. Explain why an investor would be willing to pay $1,025 for a bond that is going to be worth only $1,000 at maturity. **BASIC**

5. Consider the Allied Signal Corporation zero coupon money multiplier notes of 2008. The bonds were issued on July 1, 1990 for $100. Interest is paid every **INTERMEDIATE**

July 1 and the bond matures on July 1, 2008. Determine the yield to maturity if the bonds are purchased at the

a. Issue price in 1990

b. Market price as of July 1, 2004, of $750

c. Explain why the returns calculated in (a) and (b) are different.

BASIC **6.** If you purchase a zero coupon bond today for $225 and it matures at $1,000 in 11 years, what rate of return will you earn on that bond (to the nearest 10th of 1 percent)?

INTERMEDIATE **7.** In 1990, Packard Motors issued 10.95 percent debentures that will mature on August 1, 2025. If an investor purchased one of these bonds ($1,000 denomination) on August 1, 2004, for $1,086.25, determine the yield to maturity. Explain why an investor would be willing to pay $1,086.25 in 2004 for one of these bonds when he or she is going to receive only $1,000 when the bond matures in 2025.

INTERMEDIATE **8.** AT&T Corporation has several issues of bonds outstanding. One of the outstanding bonds has a $5\frac{1}{8}$ percent coupon and matures in 2004. The bonds mature on April 1 in the maturity year. Suppose an investor buys this bond on April 1, 1999, and assume interest is paid annually on April 1. Calculate the yield to maturity assuming the investor buys the bond at the following price, as quoted in the financial press:

a. 100

b. 90

c. 105

BASIC **9.** If the nominal interest rate is 5.75 percent and the real risk-free rate is 3.25 percent, what is the inflation premium according to the Fisher effect (use Equation 7.12)?

INTERMEDIATE **10.** Dooley, Inc., has outstanding $100 million (par value) bonds that pay an annual coupon rate of interest of 10.5 percent. Par value of each bond is $1,000. The bonds are scheduled to mature in 20 years. Because of Dooley's increased risk, investors now require a 14 percent rate of return on bonds of similar quality with 20 years remaining until maturity. What price would the bonds sell for now?

INTERMEDIATE **11.** The following bond quotations are taken from *The Wall Street Journal* dated Friday, September 5, 2003:

Company	Coupon	Maturity	Last Price	Yield
International Paper (IP)	6.750	Sep 01, 2011	108.198	5.468
Sara Lee (SLE)	3.875	Jun 15, 2013	89.700	5.235
Wells Fargo (WFC)	7.250	Aug 24, 2005	109.645	2.191
General Motors (GM)	7.125	Jul 15, 2013	101.201	6.952
Lincoln National (LNC)	6.200	Dec 15, 2011	105.903	5.307

a. Explain why the International Paper bond is selling at a premium but the Sara Lee is selling at a discount.

b. Why is the yield (yield to maturity) on the General Motors bond so much higher than the yield on the Sara Lee bond?

c. Why is the yield (yield to maturity) on the Wells Fargo Bank bond so much less than the yield on the Lincoln National Corp. bond?

12. Calculate the yield to maturity on the Lincoln National Bank bond shown in Problem 11 assuming you paid the last price indicated and the bond matures on September 4, 2011 (rather than the actual maturity date of December 15, 2011, so as to avoid complications with fractional years).

BASIC

13. Go to http://www.bondsonline.com and from the bond quote page search for Wal-Mart bond (type "Wal Mart" for the issue name). From the list of Wal-Mart bonds provided pick one bond—preferably one with more than 10 years remaining to maturity—and copy down the current price, annual coupon rate, and maturity year. Using the current price, annual coupon amount, and maturity year, compute the yield to maturity for the bond.

INTERMEDIATE

CHAPTER

8 Characteristics and Valuation of Common Stocks and Preferred Stocks

As mentioned in the introduction to the previous chapter, common stock and preferred stock issues are sources of equity for a firm. Common stocks confer an ownership stake in the firm. Unlike debt, there is no contractual obligation upon the company to pay a fixed dividend. Common stocks are characterized by a residual claim on earnings and assets; all earnings, net of all expenses, accrue to common shareholders. Thus, common shareholders do well if the firm has good earnings but they also bear most of the losses if earnings are poor. The residual claim on assets means that in the event of a bankruptcy all other claim holders have to be satisfied first before consideration can be given to owners of common stock.

Although preferred stocks are classified as an equity instrument, they have many attributes similar to debt instruments. Like debt, preferred stocks promise to pay the holder a prespecified income (called the *preferred dividend*) on a periodic basis. Most preferred stocks today have many other features similar to debt, such as a call feature, floating dividend rate, and convertibility feature. For most firms preferred stock issues are not a significant source of financing. Public utilities and financial institutions occasionally raise funds in the preferred stock market, but it is uncommon for industrial firms to rely on this source of financing.

In this chapter we discuss the characteristics of common and preferred stocks and develop valuation models for these securities. For reasons mentioned in the previous chapter, an understanding of long-term sources of capital including common and preferred stocks is critically important for the financial manager, who is responsible for raising the funds to enable the firm to pursue its objectives. The finance manager also needs to have a good understanding of the valuation of securities so that the firm may follow policies consistent with the objective of maximizing shareholder wealth.

Chapter Objectives

After reading this chapter, you should have an understanding of the following:

1. Features and characteristics of common stocks

2. The valuation of common stocks

3. Features and characteristics of preferred stocks

4. The valuation of preferred stocks

COMMON STOCK

A firm's common stockholders are its true owners. Common stock is a *residual form of ownership* because the claims of common stockholders on the firm's earnings and assets are considered only after all other claims have been paid. For example, earnings that accrue to shareholders are the residual or net earnings after paying out all operating expenses (including salaries to employees and purchases of raw materials), interest expenses to debt holders and other creditors, taxes to the government, and dividends to preferred stockholders. In similar fashion, if a firm declares bankruptcy and decides to liquidate its assets, the claim of common stockholders against the assets of the firm comes last after claims of employees, governments (e.g., taxes owed to federal and state government agencies), debt holders, other general creditors (e.g., suppliers of raw materials), and preferred stockholders have been satisfied. Because of the residual nature of their claims, common stockholders bear most of the risk of the firm. However, *in exchange for bearing the residual risk of the firm, common stockholders have the potential to earn very high returns*. Unlike debt holders, who are limited to the interest rate that a firm is contractually obligated to pay, there is no limit to the earnings that accrue to shareholders. In addition to potentially high returns, common stockholders are entitled to certain rights not available to other security holders.

Figure 8.1 shows a copy of the stock certificate for Sara Lee. Stock certificates are issued to common stock investors as evidence of ownership in the firm. The stock certificate shows the name and address of the owner and the number of shares owned. The reverse side of the certificate usually spells out the rights of the stockholder. Most shareholders do not take physical possession of stock certificates but rather leave it in *street name,* which is essentially a book entry maintained by the firm showing the holders of the firm's shares at any given time. Leaving the shares in street name allows for quicker sale of the stock; otherwise the stockowner must first deliver the stock certificate to his or her broker before selling the shares.

The New York Stock Exchange has an excellent tutorial on stocks covering the history of stocks; how stocks are bought and sold; how a stock exchange works; why stock prices "go up and down"; regulation; strategies; lots of pictures; and much more. It also has a comprehensive glossary of financial terms.
http://www.nyse.com/about/about.html

Stockholders' Rights

Common stockholders have a number of general rights, including the following:

1. Dividend Rights. Stockholders have the right to share equally on a per-share basis in any distribution of corporate earnings in the form of dividends.

2. Asset Rights. In the event of liquidation, stockholders have the right to assets that remain after the obligations to the government (taxes), employees, debt holders, and other creditors have been satisfied.

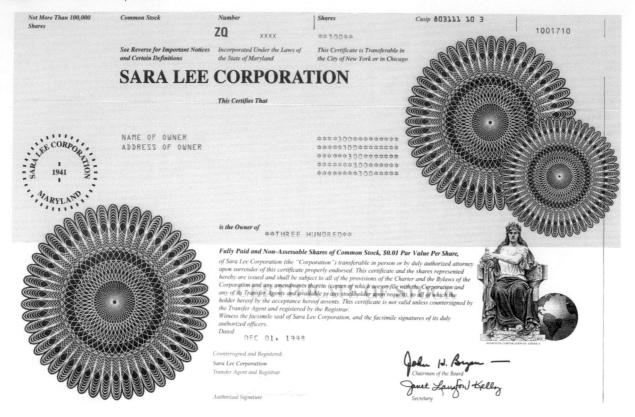

**Figure 8.1
Sample Stock
Certificate**

3. Preemptive Rights. Stockholders may have the right to share proportionately in any new stock sold. For example, a stockholder who owns 20 percent of a corporation's stock may be entitled to purchase 20 percent of any new issue. Preemptive rights exist in a relatively small minority of firms in the United States at the present time.

4. Voting Rights. Stockholders have the right to vote on matters such as the selection of the board of directors, whether to retain a particular auditing firm, whether to increase the number of shares authorized, and whether to merge with another firm. Probably the most significant voting right is the right to vote for the board of directors. Because the board has the ultimate authority to hire and fire top management, the right to elect its members confers ultimate control of the firm to the common shareholders.

The election of directors and other voting normally occurs at the annual stockholders' meeting. Prior to the meeting firms are required to mail a *proxy statement* to its shareholders, which contains material information regarding matters to be voted on. Shareholders need not be physically present to vote; ballots attached to the proxy statement may be mailed. Shareholders may also authorize the management—or anyone else—to vote on their behalf, in other words, they can vote by *proxy*. It is not uncommon for management or another stockholder or group of stockholders to actively solicit proxies from shareholders. This is especially true when there is a contentious issue up for a vote. In the rather unlikely event that another stockholder or group of stockholders sends out their own proxy statement, a

proxy fight is said to occur. Proxy fights are most common when a company is performing poorly or in the midst of a hostile takeover attempt. For example, in early 2002 the management of Hewlett-Packard recommended to its shareholders that they vote in favor of the merger with Compaq Corporation. However, a dissident group lead by Mr. William Hewlett, grandson of the cofounder of Hewlett-Packard, recommended that shareholders vote against the merger proposal. A proxy fight ensued with management winning the vote narrowly.

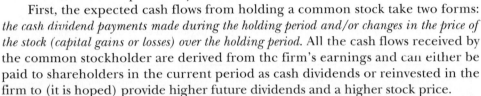

Comprehension Check Questions

1. What are some of the rights that accompany common stock ownership?
2. Why is common stock known as a residual form of ownership?
3. What is a proxy?

Valuation of Common Stock

In principle, the valuation of common stock is no different from the valuation of other types of securities, such as bonds, that we discussed in the preceding chapter. The basic procedure involves *capitalizing* (that is, discounting) the expected stream of cash flows to be received from holding the common stock. In the case of common stock, this is complicated by several factors.

e-Lecture

First, the expected cash flows from holding a common stock take two forms: *the cash dividend payments made during the holding period and/or changes in the price of the stock (capital gains or losses) over the holding period.* All the cash flows received by the common stockholder are derived from the firm's earnings and can either be paid to shareholders in the current period as cash dividends or reinvested in the firm to (it is hoped) provide higher future dividends and a higher stock price.

Second, because common stock dividends normally are expected to grow rather than remain constant, the relatively simple annuity formulas used in the valuation of bonds generally are not applicable, and more complicated models must be used.

Finally, the expected cash flows from common stock are more uncertain than are the cash flows from bonds. Common stock dividend payments are related to the firm's earnings in some manner, and it can be difficult to forecast long-term earnings and dividend payments with a high degree of accuracy.

To better understand the application of the capitalization of cash flow valuation method to common stock, let us begin with a simple example where an investor is considering the purchase of a stock and hopes to hold it for exactly one period. At the end of that one period the investor expects to receive a cash dividend, D_1, and sell the stock for a price, P_1. These cash flows may be shown on a time line as follows:

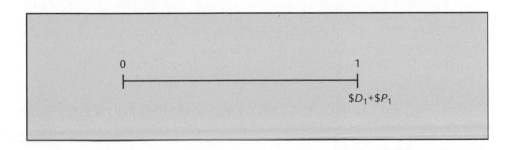

The problem is to determine the value of this stock to the investor today (that is, time 0), given a required rate of return on the investment, k_e. The required rate of return, of course, depends upon the risk of the stock. It may be estimated by utilizing the **Capital Asset Pricing Model (CAPM)** formula in Chapter 6 (Equation 6.7).

Applying the capitalization of cash flow method (discounted cash flow), the value of this stock is determined as the present value of the cash flows to be received during the holding period:

(8.1)
$$P_0 = \frac{D_1}{(1 + k_e)^1} + \frac{P_1}{(1 + k_e)^1}$$

For example, if Diversified Corporation common stock is expected to pay a $1 dividend and sell for $27.50 at the end of one period, what is the value of this stock to an investor who requires a 14 percent rate of return? The answer is calculated as follows:

$$P_0 = \frac{\$1.00}{(1 + 0.14)^1} + \frac{\$27.50}{(1 + 0.14)^1}$$

$$= \$0.88 + \$24.12$$

$$= \$25.00$$

Thus, the investor who purchases the stock for $25 today, collects the $1 dividend and sells the stock for $27.50 at the end of one period will earn the 14 percent required rate of return.

The one-period model shown above may be generalized to holding periods longer than one period. For an investor who is expected to hold on to the stock for n periods, the time line of cash flows is given by:

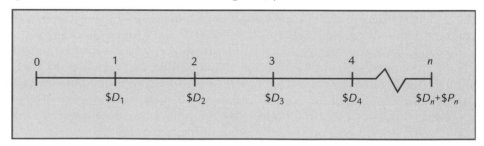

The value of the stock, using the capitalization of cash flow method, is then given by

(8.2)
$$P_0 = \frac{D_1}{(1 + k_e)^1} + \frac{D_2}{(1 + k_e)^2} + \frac{D_3}{(1 + k_e)^3} + \ldots + \frac{D_n}{(1 + k_e)^n} + \frac{P_n}{(1 + k_e)^n}$$

where $D_1, D_2, \ldots, D_n$ are the dividends expected to be received in each of the next n periods, P_n is the expected amount from the sale of the stock at the end of the nth period, and k_e is the investor's required rate of return for this investment.

Continuing with our previous example, suppose that the Diversified Corporation stock expects to pay dividends of $1.00, $1.00, and $1.50 in years 1, 2, and 3 respectively. Also, assume that the stock can be sold for $33.10 at the end of year 3. The value of this stock today, for an investor whose required rate of return on this investment is 14 percent would equal:

$$P_0 = \frac{\$1.00}{(1 + 0.14)^1} + \frac{\$1.00}{(1 + 0.14)^2} + \frac{\$1.50}{(1 + 0.14)^3} + \frac{\$33.10}{(1 + 0.14)^3}$$

$$= \$0.88 + \$0.77 + \$1.01 + \$22.34$$

$$= \$25.00$$

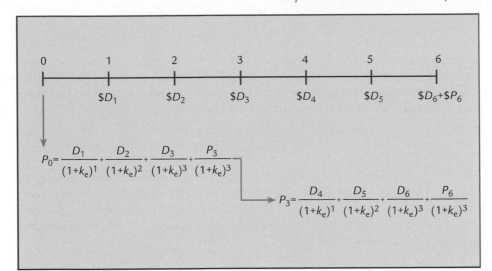

Figure 8.2
Illustration of Dividend Capitalization Model

In both of the previous examples we were silent on how the selling price at the end of the holding period is determined. Upon reflection it should be evident that the selling price would depend upon the dividends and the ending price over the subsequent holding period. Thus, if we have two successive holding periods of, say, 3 years, the price at the end of the first holding period, P_3, is equal to the present value of cash flows in the subsequent holding period: D_4, D_5, D_6, and P_6. This is illustrated in Figure 8.2. If we extend this chain it is evident that the price at the end of each holding period should equal the present value of cash flows from the subsequent holding period, *ad infinitum*. Therefore, *the value today of a firm's common stock to an investor is equal to the present value of the expected future dividend stream to infinity*. The generalized formula for the current value of a stock is:

$$P_0 = \frac{D_1}{(1+k_e)^1} + \frac{D_2}{(1+k_e)^2} + \frac{D_3}{(1+k_e)^3} + \frac{D_4}{(1+k_e)^4} + \ldots \infty, \tag{8.3}$$

or alternatively, using the summation notation,

$$P_0 = \sum_{t=1}^{\infty} \frac{D_t}{(1+k_e)^t} \tag{8.4}$$

As a practical model, Equation 8.4 is of little use since it requires the investor to forecast dividends into the infinite future. This is obviously impossible to do. However, we can make the model practical by assuming that the dividend payments over time are expected to grow at a constant rate. This model is generally referred to as the *constant growth dividend model*, which is described below.

Constant Growth Dividend Valuation Model

If a firm's future dividend payments (per share) are expected to grow at a *constant rate, g,* per period forever, then the dividend at any future time period t can be forecasted as follows:

$$D_t = D_0(1+g)^t \tag{8.5}$$

where D_0 is the dividend in the current period ($t = 0$). The expected dividend in period 1 is $D_1 = D_0(1+g)^1$, the expected dividend in period 2 is $D_2 = D_0(1+g)^2$, and so on. Substituting Equation 8.5 for D_t in the general dividend valuation model (Equation 8.4) yields the following:

(8.6)
$$P_0 = \sum_{t=1}^{\infty} \frac{D_0(1 + g)^t}{(1 + k_e)^t}$$

Assuming that the required rate of return, k_e, is greater than the dividend growth rate, g, Equation 8.6 can be transformed algebraically to obtain the following simplified common stock valuation model (The interested reader can find the derivation of Equation 8.7 in most intermediate corporate finance texts):

(8.7)
$$P_0 = \frac{D_0(1 + g)}{k_e - g}$$

Note that in the above constant growth valuation model the dividend value in the numerator is D_1 (or $D_0 (1+g)^1$)—that is, the dividend expected to be received 1 year from now. The model assumes that D_0, the current dividend, has just been paid and does not enter the (forward-looking) valuation process. Consequently, Equation 8.7 is also expressed as:

(8.8)
$$P_0 = \frac{D_1}{k_e - g}$$

The constant growth valuation model (Equation 8.7 or 8.8) assumes that a firm's *earnings, dividends, and stock price are all expected to grow at a constant rate, g, into the future.* Hence to apply this model to a specific common stock, it is necessary to estimate the expected future growth rate, g.

To illustrate the application of the constant growth valuation model, consider the common stock of Lilly and Co., a well-known pharmaceutical company. Assume that you are trying to value Lilly common stock at the beginning of 2003. Dividends for Lilly arc expected to be $1.34 per share in the coming year, D_1 (2003). You are also informed that the dividends are expected to grow at 8.5 percent annually. To determine the value of a share of this stock to an investor who requires an 11 percent rate of return, substitute $1.34 for D_1, 8.5 percent (0.085) for g, and 11 percent (0.11) for k_e in Equation 8.8. This yields a value for a share of Lilly's common stock of

$$P_0 = \frac{\$1.34}{0.11 - 0.085}$$

$$P_0 = \$53.60$$

Estimating the Inputs to the Constant Growth Model As we have seen, using the constant growth model (Equation 8.7 or 8.8) is fairly easy. The model requires that we estimate three variables: D_1, g, and k_e. D_1 can be expressed in terms of D_0, a value that is known, and the growth rate, g:

$$D_1 = D_0 (1+g)$$

Thus, the only two variables that we need to spend some effort in estimating are g and k_e. We first discuss the estimation of the growth rate, g, and then the estimation of the required rate of return, k_e. The growth rate in dividends can be estimated using two general approaches:

1. Historical Growth Rate. A historical growth rate can be easily calculated from past dividend data. Table 8.1 shows past dividend per share data for Lilly and Co. from 1992 to 2002. While there are several approaches to calculating growth rates from historical data, a common approach that is advocated is to calculate the growth rate over a 5- or 10-year period. Using the compounding formula from

Table 8.1	Historical Dividend per Share Data for Lilly and Co.
2002	$1.24
2001	$1.12
2000	1.04
1999	0.92
1998	0.80
1997	0.74
1996	0.69
1995	0.66
1994	0.63
1993	0.61
1992	0.55

Source: Value Line Investment Survey, April 25, 2003

Chapter 5 (Equation 5.6) and applying it to Lilly's dividend per share data over the 10-year period, 1992–2002, we have:

$$\$1.24 = \$0.55 \ (1+i)^{10}$$

$$i = g = 0.085$$

Thus, based on historical data, an investor in Lilly's common stock can expect an 8.5 percent growth rate in dividends per share. Note that this is the growth rate we used in evaluating Lilly's stock earlier.

2. *Projected Growth Rate.* The problem with growth rates estimated from historical data is precisely that: They are *historical* in nature and may not reflect what will happen in the *future*. Recall that the discounted cash flow model discounts future expected dividends. That is why it is preferable to use forecasted or projected dividend growth rates rather than historical growth rates. There are several sources of projected growth rates. The widely available *Value Line Investment Survey* provides short-run (next year) and long-run (typically, 5 years) dividend growth projections for over 1,800 stocks followed by Value Line analysts as part of the firm's standard service (excludes expanded coverage stocks). In addition there are a number of sources of consensus analysts, forecasts defined as the average forecasts of reporting analysts following a stock. Unlike the Value Line forecasts that rely upon a single analyst following a given stock, consensus forecasts represent an average of several analysts following a given stock. Consensus forecasts are provided by several sources including Zacks and Thomson Financial/First Call. These are now widely available through a number of Internet sources (e.g., http://www.yahoo.com; clicking on Research from the individual stock quote page will provide detailed consensus earnings forecast information).

In the case of Lilly stock, the Value Line analyst assigned to the stock forecasted that dividends would increase from $1.24 actually paid in 2002 to a projected amount of $1.74 in 2007 (the projection is for the 2006–2008 time period, but for convenience we will assume that the projection is for the midpoint of the range, 2007). Applying the compound growth rate formula, we have:

$$\$1.74 = \$1.24 \ (1+i)^{5}$$

$$i = g = 0.070 \text{ or } 7.0\%$$

So, rather than the historical growth rate we could have substituted the estimated projected growth rate of 7 percent into the constant growth model in determining the value of Lilly stock. It is evident that the resulting stock value will be different. Which growth rate to use depends on the investor's subjective preference and experience.

The required rate of return, k_e, can be estimated using the **Security Market Line equation (SML)** (Equation 6.7) discussed in Chapter 6:

$$k_e = \hat{r}_f + \beta \, (\hat{r}_m - \hat{r}_f)$$

where k_e is the required rate of return for the stock, $\hat{r}_f$ is the risk-free rate of return, β is the beta of the stock, and $\hat{r}_m$ is the required return on the market portfolio. In Chapter 11 we discuss in greater detail how these variables are estimated. For now, let's assume that the risk-free rate at the beginning of 2003 was 5 percent, the beta of Lilly stock was 0.85, and the market risk premium $(\hat{r}_m - \hat{r}_f)$ was 7 percent. Using these values in the SML equation, we have:

$$k_e = 5 + 0.85 \, (7)$$
$$k_e = 11\%$$

Recall that this is the value we used for k_e to determine the constant dividend growth rate value for Lilly stock.

Comprehension Check Questions

1. Why are common stocks more difficult to value than bonds?
2. Conceptually, describe the capitalization of cash flow (discounted cash flow) approach to valuing common stock.
3. What are the basic assumptions of the constant growth model?

Insights from the Constant Growth Dividend Valuation Model

The constant growth model is useful in deriving important insights on the determinants of stock value and stock returns.

What Factors Influence Stock Prices? From Chapter 1 we know that the goal of management is to maximize shareholder wealth. The constant growth model (Equation 8.7 or 8.8) is a very simple yet intuitive model that holds some important lessons for the finance manager who wants to maximize shareholder wealth. The model tells us that stock prices are influenced by:

1. Dividend Next Period, D_1. Holding everything else constant, the higher the next period dividend, the higher the current stock price will be. Thus an expectation of an increase in the next period dividend will result in an increased share price. Assuming dividends are a fixed proportion of earnings, higher next period earnings will have a positive influence on share prices.

2. The Required Rate of Return, k_e. Holding everything else constant, the higher the rate of return required by investors, the lower the current stock price is. Recall from Chapter 6 that the required return, k_e, to investors may be determined by the Security Market Line equation (Equation 6.7). From this equation we know that k_e is affected by the risk-free rate of return, market risk premium, and beta of the security. An increase in the risk-free rate, holding everything else constant, will increase k_e, and in turn result in a drop in the stock price. Similarly an increase in the market risk premium, holding all else constant, will result in an increase in k_e and a drop in the value of the stock. Finally, an increase in the beta of the stock, holding everything else constant, will cause k_e to increase with a consequent drop in the stock price.

3. Growth Rate in Dividends. An increase in the growth rate of dividends, g, will result in an increase in the stock price, holding everything else constant. Since dividends are paid out of earnings, an increase in the growth rate of earnings should result in an increase in share price as well.

What Are the Components of Stock Returns? The constant growth dividend valuation model can be used to illustrate the two forms of returns that an investor can expect to receive from holding a common stock. Solving Equation 8.8 for k_e yields the following:

$$k_e = \frac{D_1}{P_0} + g \qquad\qquad (8.9)$$

The investor's expected rate of return, k_e, is equal to the expected dividend yield, D_1/P_0, plus the expected growth rate of dividends, g. The growth rate is also equal to the expected return from price appreciation. *Thus, expected returns to shareholders consist of a dividend income portion and a capital gain portion.* To illustrate, let's take the case of Lilly stock. Applying Equation 8.9, the required rate of return of 11 percent can be broken down into the following dividend yield and price appreciation components:

$$0.11 - \frac{\$1.34}{\$53.60} + .085$$

$$0.11 = 0.025 + 0.085$$

It is evident that most of the returns on Lilly stock are expected to come from price appreciation (8.5 percent) and only a moderate amount from dividends (2.5 percent). In the chapter on dividend policy (Chapter 14) you will learn that there is usually a trade-off between these two forms of returns. Stocks that have a higher dividend yield are also the ones that tend to have a smaller capital gain. Conversely, stocks that exhibit significant capital gains on average are also the ones that have a small dividend or no dividend yield.

Limitations of the Constant Growth Dividend Valuation Model

The constant dividend growth rate model is very useful for valuing common stock, but applying it successfully requires that we understand the limitations of the model. The model requires that the stock *pay dividends* and that *dividends grow at a constant rate.* Numerous stocks pay dividends but finding one whose dividends (expected) grow at a constant rate every year could be very difficult. However, there are many stocks that exhibit *stable growth* in dividends over time—that is, follow a policy of regular increases in their dividends. These stocks most likely belong to large firms operating in mature industries. As a practical matter, it has been shown that the constant growth model can work well for such stocks. For example, constant growth dividend models traditionally have been used successfully in valuing public utility stocks (e.g., electric utility and natural gas utility stocks) that typically are very large and operate in a mature industry with stable growth.

The only other limitation of the model is that the *required rate of return must exceed the expected growth rate in dividends*; otherwise the resulting stock price is infinite. The intuitive explanation is that if a stock's dividends grow forever at a rate faster than the required rate of return the present value of the stream keeps increasing the further we extend the stream into the future.

The first limitation—constant dividend growth rate—could be easily overcome. A variant of the constant growth model—known commonly as the non–constant dividend growth model—can be used to value stocks that are expected to have different dividend growth rates over time. For example, dividends initially may grow at an above average rate and then follow a more stable constant growth rate. Under this model the value of the stock is simply the sum of the present value of the dividends during the initial above normal growth phase and the present value of dividends during the subsequent constant growth phase. A detailed illustration of the non–constant growth model is beyond the scope of this book but may be found in any intermediate corporate finance textbook.

Other Models of Valuation

Click on the Investment Analysis Calculator button at **http://finance. swlearning.com** *for an interactive financial calculator for common stock valuation.*

How do we value a stock that does not pay dividends? The dividend valuation models discussed above require that the stock pay dividends. In the case of non-dividend-paying stocks there are several alternative models that may be used. These models may also be used to value dividend-paying stocks.

The first model is the *price-earnings (PE) multiple model*. The model is very simple to apply and is intuitively appealing. The model is very widely used in practice, even among sophisticated professional investors. The PE model relies on the notion that common stock investors *buy the earnings stream* of the stock. As such, the value of the stock depends on how much the investor is willing to pay per dollar of earnings per share. According to the PE model the value of a stock is equal to:

(8.10)
$$P_0 = \text{(appropriate PE multiple)} \times \text{(earnings per share)}$$

As can be seen, there are two components to the formula: earnings per share and the appropriate price-earnings multiple. The earnings per share can be the current earnings per share (annual) or it can be the expected earnings per share for the coming year. Most professional investors prefer to use the latter inasmuch as the investor is really buying the future stream and not the past earnings. The more difficult element of the formula is *determining the appropriate PE multiple ratio*. Unfortunately there is no rigorous theory that we can rely on to determine the appropriate PE multiple. It is generally acknowledged that the appropriate PE multiple decreases with the riskiness of the stock and increases with higher growth in earnings. One approach to determining the appropriate PE ratio is to start with the average PE multiple for a given industry and adjust it upward or downward, depending on the relative standing of the particular firm being evaluated within the industry in terms of its risk and growth prospects.

For example, let's assume you want to value Lilly Corporation's common stock using the PE model. Your research reveals that financial analysts expect Lilly's earnings per share to equal $2.55 in the coming year. You also determine that the average PE ratio based on forward earnings (next year earnings) in the pharmaceutical industry is 22 and that Lilly's riskiness and growth in earnings are similar to the average firm in the industry. Given that Lilly is similar to the average firm in the industry we can assume that an appropriate PE multiple for the stock is the industry average. Applying Equation 8.10 we have

$$= 22 \times \$2.55$$
$$= \$56.10$$

Thus, an appropriate value for Lilly stock is $56.10.

Another model to value common stock is the *enterprise valuation model*. Warren Buffet and Peter Lynch, two legendary investors, have been known to use this model in their investment decisions. Many firms use this approach in determining an offer price in a potential acquisition or merger.

The first step is to forecast cash flows for the entire business and then discount them back at the firm's average cost of capital to arrive at a present value of the entire business. From the enterprise value, the value of all debt and preferred stock is subtracted, yielding the value of common equity. Dividing the value of common equity by the number of shares outstanding gives the appropriate value per share of common stock. Implementing the enterprise valuation model is beyond the scope of this textbook, but it is usually covered in most intermediate textbooks in the chapter on mergers and acquisitions.

Common Stock Valuation and Accounting

In this section we discuss stock value from an accounting perspective. Bear in mind that, from our perspective, *market value* is what is relevant. However, because financial statements serve such an important role in finance, it is useful to discuss stock value from an accounting perspective and contrast it with valuation from a finance perspective. Common stock appears on the right-hand side of a firm's balance sheet as part of the stockholders' equity. This is shown for the Lawrence Company in Table 8.2. ***Stockholders' equity*** includes both preferred stock (if any exists) and common equity. The total equity attributable to the common stockholders of the Lawrence Company is equal to the total stockholders' equity less the preferred stock:

$$\$117,820,000 - \$37,500,000 = \$80,320,000$$

In other words, the sum of the common stock, contributed capital in excess of par value, and retained earnings equals the total common stockholders' equity.

The amount shown in the common stock par value account is calculated by multiplying the number of shares actually outstanding by the ***par value***, an arbitrary value assigned to shares of common stock. The Lawrence Company has 6.675 million shares outstanding and a $2 par value, resulting in a balance of $13.35 million.

The contributed capital in excess of par value account is the amount of capital raised by selling the common shares for more than the stated par value. In the case of Lawrence Company, the firm sold the 6.675 million shares at a price that yielded $28.713 million in addition to the par value. Assuming all 6.675 million shares were sold at one time, the firm must have sold the shares at a price of $6.23 per share—($13,350,000 common stock par value + $28,713,000 capital in excess of par value)/6,750,000 shares. Thus, out of the $6.23 initial selling price per share, $2 is the par value per share, and the remaining $4.23 is the contributed capital in excess of par value on a per share basis.

Additions to the retained earnings account occur as a result of earnings retained in the business, as opposed to earnings paid out to the stockholders as dividends. Retained earnings, which are internally generated funds, are one of the

Table 8.2 Lawrence Company Stockholders' Equity, December 31, 2002 (in thousands of dollars)

Preferred stock; $25 par value; authorized, 2,000,000 shares; issued and outstanding, 1,500,000 shares	$37,500
Common stock; $2 par value; authorized, 10,000,000 shares; issued and outstanding, 6,675,000 shares	13,350
Contributed capital in excess of par value	28,713
Retained earnings	38,257
Total stockholders' equity	**$117,820**

most important sources of capital for business. In the case of Lawrence Company, retained earnings as of December 31, 2002 amounted to $38.257 million. It is important to remember that the retained earnings shown in the balance sheet does not represent cash available to the firm. As we said earlier, it is simply earnings that have been reinvested in the firm; the retained earnings, for example, may have been used to add to plant capacity, inventory, or accounts receivable.

The **book value** *per share* of common stock is calculated as follows:

(8.11)
$$\text{Book value per share} = \text{Total common stockholders' equity}/\text{Number of shares outstanding}$$

In the case of the Lawrence Company,

$$\text{Book value per share} = \$80,320,000/6,675,000$$
$$= \$12.03$$

Note that a common stock's book value is simply the result of a calculation based on certain balance sheet figures, which are primarily the result of historical transactions and accounting conventions used to report retained earnings. *The book value per share does not necessarily have any relationship to the common stock's market price or value derived from one of the financial models.* The latter are based on expectations of future earnings. However, for most well-managed companies the market price of the stock tends to be greater than its book value.

Comprehension Check Questions

1. What are the two sources of returns to common stock investors?

2. What is the impact of each of the following on the value of a common stock: growth rate in dividends, the size of the dividend per share, and the required rate of return?

3. How is the PE model used to value common stocks?

4. What is the relation between book value per share and market price per share or the value determined using a financial model?

PREFERRED STOCK

For more on preferred stock, visit a company that deals in preferred stock funds at **http://www.preferredincome.com/pfd.htm**

Preferred stock bears its name because it usually has preference, or priority, over common stock with regard to the company's dividends and assets. For example, if a company's earnings in a given year are insufficient to pay dividends on preferred stock, the company is not permitted to pay dividends on its common stock. In the event of a liquidation following bankruptcy, the claims on the firm's assets by preferred stockholders are subordinate to those of creditors but have priority over those of common stockholders.

Preferred stock is considered a **hybrid security** because it shares certain characteristics of debt as well as those of common stock. Like common stock, preferred stock is part of the stockholders' equity. However, preferred stockholders do not have the voting rights of common shareholders. Like long-term debt, preferred stock is considered a fixed-income security, although preferred stockholders receive dividends instead of interest payments. Because the issuing firm often does not promise repayment at a specific date, preferred stock tends to be a more permanent form of financing than long-term debt. However, unlike with debt, the nonpayment of dividends will not normally result in forced bankrutpcy.

Unlike interest payments on debt that are tax deductible, preferred dividends cannot be deducted from income for corporate income tax purposes. This means

FINANCE & The Real World

Preferring Dividends

In the exploding stock market of the 1990s, investors in stocks didn't care about dividends. They just wanted shares of fast-growing companies that would reinvest profits rather than pay out dividends to shareholders. But once the stock market bubble burst in 2000, investors rekindled their interest in dividend-paying stocks. That way, they would at least get paid some income for their investment.

Then, the government made dividends even more popular. It changed the way dividends are taxed, reducing the tax rate from a maximum of nearly 40 percent to just 15 percent. That really made dividends attractive. In contrast, bonds paid interest, but those investors received no such tax break.

Still, investors were shaken by the turmoil in the stock market, and even though dividends received a tax break, bonds seemed safer. If the company got into trouble, bondholders were paid off first, whereas the stockholders could get nothing.

Was there a way to receive the tax benefits of dividends and some of the security of bonds? Yes. Preferred stock fit the bill. Preferred shares have some of the characteristics of stocks and some of bonds. They usually pay a dividend that gets the favorable tax treatment. But as a "preferred" security, investors receive more guarantees in terms of payments than do regular "common" shareholders.

Preferred shares are available, but they can be hard to find. For many years, corporations shied away from issuing them because dividend payments aren't tax deductible like bond interest payments.

Sources: Forbes, March 3, 2003, "How to Buy a Preferred"; The Wall Street Journal, May 2, 2003, "Mutual-Fund Investors Find Preferred Play."

---

that the after-tax cost of preferred stock is greater than that of long-term debt, assuming that the pretax preferred stock and long-term debt rates are about the same.

Features of Preferred Stock

Like debt, preferred stock has its own unique distinguishing characteristics. A number are discussed here.

1. Preferred Dividend. The dividend on a preferred stock issue is usually stated as dollar amount, but it is sometimes stated as a percentage of the par value. The par value for preferred stocks is usually $25, $50, or $100. For example, Alcoa Inc. $3.75 preferred stock has a par value of $100 per share while the Duke Energy 6.375% 'A' preferred stock has a par value of $25 per share. The Alcoa preferred stock pays a dividend of $3.75 per year while the Duke preferred stock pays a dividend of $1.59 per year (0.06375 dividend rate × $25 par value).

2. Adjustable Rate Preferred Stock. Many preferred stocks today have an adjustable rate provision. This type of preferred stock became popular in the early 1980s. With these issues, dividends are reset periodically and offer returns that vary with interest rates. For example, Citicorp (now "Citigroup") issued 4 million shares of adjustable rate preferred stock on February 18, 1983, with an initial dividend rate of 9.75 percent per annum until August 31, 1983. The annual dividend rate thereafter was to be set quarterly depending on an index based on various Treasury securities.

3. Cumulative Feature. Most preferred stock is cumulative. This means that if, for some reason, a firm fails to pay its preferred dividend, it cannot pay dividends on its common stock until it has satisfied all or a prespecified amount of preferred dividends in arrears. The principal reason for this feature is that investors are generally unwilling to purchase preferred stock that is not cumulative.

4. Participation. Preferred stock is said to be participating if the holders share in any increased earnings the company might experience. Virtually all preferred stock, however, is nonparticipating; that is, the preferred dividend remains constant, even if the company's earnings increase. Any dividend increases resulting from higher earnings accrue directly to the common stockholders.

5. Maturity. Preferred stock technically is part of a firm's equity capital. As such, some firms issue preferred stock that is intended to be perpetual—that is, a permanent portion of the stockholders' equity having no specific maturity date. Many preferred stock investors, however, desire sinking fund provisions, which guarantee that the issue will be retired over a specified time period.

6. Call Feature. Like long-term debt, preferred stock can sometimes be redeemed, or called, at the issuing firm's option at some specified price. For example, the Citicorp adjustable rate preferred stock discussed above was callable (deferred call) from February 28, 1988 to February 28, 1993 at $103 per share and thereafter at $100 per share. As in the case of debt the call feature allows the issuing company a measure of flexibility in its financing plans. With a call provision, the firm can replace a higher rate preferred stock with a lower-cost issue when rates fall.

7. Voting Rights. As a general rule, preferred stockholders are not entitled to vote for the company's board of directors. However, special voting procedures frequently take effect if the company omits its preferred dividends or incurs losses for a period of time. In such a case, the preferred stockholders often vote as a separate group to elect one or more members of the company's board of directors. This ensures that the preferred holders will have direct representation on the board.

Valuation of Preferred Stock

Let's consider the case of preferred stock that pays regular, fixed dividends and has no maturity date (i.e., fixed dividends are paid to infinity). Recall the constant growth dividend valuation model for common stock (Equation 8.8):

$$P_0 = \frac{D_1}{k_e - g}$$

This equation may be easily adapted to calculate the value of preferred stock that pays fixed dividends indefinitely. In the case of preferred stock, g will equal zero since dividends are assumed to be fixed; instead of D_1 we now have a fixed dividend, D_p; and the discount rate will equal the rate suitable for the particular preferred stock, k_p. Making these substituions into the above equation we have

(8.12)
$$P_0 = \frac{D_p}{k_p}$$

where D_p is the dividend per period, and k_p is the investor's required rate of return. Note that this formula is simply the present value of a perpetuity that we studied in Chapter 5 (Equation 5.16).

To illustrate the use of Equation 8.12, take the case of Great Plains Energy 3.8 percent preferred stock with a $100 par value per share. What is the value of this stock to an investor who requires a 7 percent annual rate of return on the investment? Substituting $3.80 ($0.038 \times 100) for D_p and 0.07 for k_p yields the following:

$$P_0 = \frac{\$3.80}{0.07}$$
$$= \$54.29$$

Comprehension Check Questions

1. How is preferred stock distinct from common stock and long-term debt?
2. How do you value preferred stock that pays a fixed dividend and has no maturity?

Summary

- The common stockholders are the true owners of the firm; and, as such, common stock is a permanent form of financing.

- Common stocks are considered to be a residual form of ownership in that the claims of common stockholders on the firm's earnings and assets are considered only after all other claims have been paid. Because of the residual nature of ownership, common stockholders bear most of the risk of the firm but they also have the potential to make very high returns.

- Because of their ownership position, common stockholders have certain rights. Common stockholder rights include the following:

   The right to dividends, if one is paid.

   The right to any assets remaining after senior claims are satisfied in a liquidation.

   The right to vote on important corporate matters including the right to vote for board members.

   The preemptive right, or the right to share proportionately in any new stock sold. Common stocks of very few firms in the United States have this right.

- The valuation of common stock is considerably more complicated than the valuation of bonds for the following reasons:

   The cash flows can take two forms: cash dividend payments and price appreciation.

   Common stock dividends normally are expected to grow and not remain constant.

   The cash flows from common stocks generally are more uncertain than the cash flows from other types of securities.

- In the general dividend valuation model, the value of a common stock is equal to the present value of all the expected future dividends discounted at the investor's required rate of return.

- If we assume that dividends continue to grow indefinitely at a constant rate, g, then the value of a common stock is equal to the next year's dividend, D_1, divided by the difference between the investor's required rate of return, k_e, and the growth rate in dividends, g.

- A simple stock valuation model that is often used in practice is the PE model. To apply the PE model, we multiply the stock's earnings per share (either the current earnings per share or next year's expected earnings per share) by the appropriate PE ratio.

➤ The book value per share is the value per share reflected in the financial statements of the firm. It is determined as the stockholders' equity (less preferred stock) divided by common shares outstanding. The book value per share is not necessarily related to the market price of the stock or to the value of the stock as determined by financial models.

➤ Preferred stock occupies an intermediate position between long-term debt and common stock as a source of capital. Like common stock, preferred stock is part of the stockholders' equity, and preferred stockholders receive returns in the form of dividends. Preferred stock is similar to long-term debt in that preferred dividends, like the interest on long-term debt, usually remain constant over time.

➤ Preferred stock usually has the following features:

Preferred stocks pay a dividend that is usually fixed. It may be stated as a fixed dollar amount per share or as a percentage of the par value. Most preferred stocks have a par value of $25, $50, or $100.

Most preferred stock is cumulative; that is, dividends on common stock cannot be paid as long as any past or present preferred dividends remain unpaid.

Virtually all preferred stock is nonparticipating; that is, preferred stock does not share in any increased earnings of the firm.

Some preferred stock is perpetual, whereas other preferred stock is gradually retired by the firm.

Preferred stock often is callable.

➤ The principal disadvantage of preferred stock financing is that dividends are not tax deductible, which, all other things being equal, causes the after-tax cost of preferred stock to the firm to be higher than the cost of long-term debt.

➤ The value of a preferred stock with fixed dividend and infinite maturity is given by the present value of a perpetuity. That is, the value of a preferred stock is equal to the annual preferred dividend divided by the investor's required rate of return.

Questions and Topics for Discussion

1. Why is common stock referred to as a residual form of ownership?

2. Explain the differences between par value, book value, and market value per share of common stock.

3. Discuss the various stockholder rights.

4. What factor or factors make the valuation of common stocks more complicated than the valuation of bonds?

5. Explain the relationship between financial decisions and shareholders' wealth or stock price.

6. Explain how *each* of the following factors would affect the valuation of a firm's common stock, assuming that all other factors remain constant:

   a. The general level of interest rates shifts upward, causing investors to require a higher rate of return on securities in general.

   b. Increased foreign competition reduces the future growth potential of the firm's earnings and dividends.

   c. Investors reevaluate upward their assessment of the risk of the firm's common stock as the result of increased South American investments by the firm.

7. In the context of the constant growth dividend valuation model, explain what is meant by

   a. Dividend yield

   b. Capital gain or price appreciation yield

8. Explain how the book value per share of common stock can change over time.

9. Define the following terms associated with preferred stock:

   a. Par value

   b. Call feature

   c. Cumulative dividends

   d. Participation

   e. Adjustable rate preferred

10. Why is preferred stock known as a hybrid security?

Self-Test Problems

ST1. What is the current value of a share of Commonwealth Edison common stock to an investor who requires a 12 percent annual rate of return, if next year's dividend, D_1, is expected to be $3 per share and dividends are expected to grow at an annual rate of 4 percent for the foreseeable future?

ST2. The Edgar Corporation expects to pay a $2 per share dividend next year (D_1). The required rate of return on the stock is 12 percent and the stock is currently selling for $24.00. Assuming the constant growth valuation model is appropriate, what is the implied growth rate of dividends for Edgar stock?

ST3. Atlas Energy Corporation preferred stock has a par value of $25 and carries a preferred dividend rate of 4.5 percent. If an investor requires a rate of return of 8 percent on this stock, what would be an appropriate value for this Atlas Energy preferred stock?

Problems

1. General Cereal common stock dividends have been growing at an annual rate **BASIC** of 7 percent per year over the past 10 years. Current dividend (D_0) is $1.70 per share. What is the current value of a share of this stock to an investor who requires a 12 percent rate of return if the following conditions exist?

   a. Dividends are expected to continue growing at the historic rate for the foreseeable future.

   b. The dividend growth rate is expected to *increase* to 9 percent per year.

   c. The dividend growth rate is expected to *decrease* to 6.5 percent per year.

2. The Foreman Company's earnings and common stock dividends have been **BASIC** growing at an annual rate of 6 percent over the past 10 years and are expected to continue growing at this rate for the foreseeable future. The firm currently (D_0) pays an annual dividend of $5 per share. Determine the current value of a share of Foreman common stock to investors with each of the following required rates of return:

a. 12 percent

b. 14 percent

c. 16 percent

d. 6 percent

e. 4 percent

BASIC 3. The common stock of General Land Development Company (GLDC) is expected to pay a dividend of $1.25 next year and currently sells for $25. Assume that the firm's future dividend payments are expected to grow at a constant rate for the foreseeable future. Determine the implied growth rate of GLDC's dividends (and earnings), assuming that the required rate of return of investors is 12 percent.

INTERMEDIATE 4. Over the past 5 years, the dividends of the Gamma Corporation have grown from $0.70 per share to the current level of $1.30 per share ($D_0$). This growth rate is expected to continue for the foreseeable future. What is the value of a share of Gamma Corporation common stock to an investor who requires a 20 percent return on an investment?

BASIC 5. What is the current per-share value of JRM Corporation to an investor who requires a 16 percent annual rate of return, if JRM's current per-share dividend is $2 and is expected to remain at $2 for the foreseeable future?

INTERMEDIATE 6. The chairman of Heller Industries told a meeting of financial analysts that he expects the firm's earnings and dividends to double over the next 6 years. The firm's current (that is, as of year 0) earnings and dividends per share are $4 and $2, respectively.

a. Estimate the compound annual dividend growth rate over the 6-year period.

b. Assuming the forecasted growth rate in (a) will go on forever, how much is this stock worth today if investors require an 18 percent rate of return?

c. Why might the stock price calculated in (b) not represent an accurate valuation to an investor with an 18 percent required rate of return?

INTERMEDIATE 7. Takeshi's Takeout Inc. stock is currently trading at $32 per share. An analyst following this stock projects next year's dividends to equal $1.25 per share. The analyst thinks that at the current price the stock will yield a return of 14 percent. If the constant growth model is appropriate for this stock, what is the rate of growth implied in the current stock price?

INTERMEDIATE 8. Lavonne has been watching the share price of Piedmont Enterprises with an eye to investing in it at the right price. The stock experienced a dip in price recently to where Lavonne thinks it might make a good investment. The stock was quoted on the over-the-counter market at an ask price of $28. The analysts' consensus earnings forecast for this stock for next year is $2.25 per share. The industry average PE ratio is 12x using next year's forecasted earnings. If Piedmont is comparable to the average firm in the industry, would you advise Lavonne to buy Piedmont shares at the quoted ask price?

INTERMEDIATE 9. Calculate the book value per share based on the reported stockholders' equity account for Bridgford Foods in fiscal year ending November 2, 2001 shown on the following page:

('000)

Shareholders' equity:

Preferred stock, without par value	
Authorized—1,000 shares	
Issued and outstanding—none	
Common stock, $1.00 par value	$10,505
Capital in excess of par value	17,475
Retained earnings	29,355
Total shareholders' equity	$57,335

10. Saturated Meat Corporation preferred stock is currently selling for $32 per share. The preferred dividend, which is fixed, amounts to $2.50 per share. If Jennifer requires a return of 9 percent on this stock, should she invest in this stock? **BASIC**

11. The Kummins Engine Company common stock has a beta of 0.9. The current risk-free rate of return is 5 percent and the market risk premium is 8 percent. The CEO of the company is quoted in a press release as saying that the firm will pay a dividend of $0.80/share in the coming year and expects the dividends to grow at a constant rate of 7 percent for the foreseeable future. Using the constant growth model, what value would you assign to this stock? **INTERMEDIATE**

12. In the problem above, assume that, along with the forecast of dividends, the CEO announced that the firm would increase its debt ratio to 45 percent from 35 percent. As a trained financial analyst, you think the resulting increase in debt ratio will raise Kummins' beta to 1.15 and also increase the growth rate of dividends to 9.5 percent. If all other information is the same as in the above problem, what impact would this have on the stock price? If you were the CEO what would you do? **CHALLENGE**

13. Bragg's Fort Corporation has experienced rapidly growing earnings per share at a rate of 20 percent per annum over the past 15 years. The price of the stock of Bragg's is $50 per share. Earnings per share is $3. The current dividend rate is $2 per share. Bragg's has a beta of 1.3. The long-term risk-free rate is 6.9 percent and the expected return on the overall market is 14 percent. The company's bonds are rated Aa by Moody's and currently sell to yield 9 percent. The average tax rate of Bragg's is 30 percent, but its marginal rate is 40 percent. A new financial analyst has suggested that Bragg's can be valued using a constant growth dividend valuation model. What constant growth rate would that analyst recommend using if she believes in capital market efficiency and the capital asset pricing model? Do you agree with her valuation recommendation? Why or why not? **CHALLENGE**

14. The following stock quotations were reported in *The Wall Street Journal* (interpretation of stock market quotes was covered in Chapter 2): **INTERMEDIATE**

8.1	21.96	8.70	Office Depot **ODP**	...		30	47221	20.05	−1.69
8.5	51.55	38.70	PubSvcEnt **PEG**	2.16	4.7	14	7844	45.77	0.85
−1.2	23.35	18.26	SaraLee **SLE**	0.60	2.7	11	13575	21.97	−0.14
15.7	54.48	43	PhlpMor **MO**	2.32	4.4	14	44305	53.07	−0.29

  a. What are the dividend yields on the common stock of Office Depot, Public Service Enterprises, and Sara Lee?

  b. What possible explanation can you give for the differences in the common stock dividend yields observed in (a)?

  c. What is the current price-earnings ratio for Philip Morris and for Office Depot?

  d. What possible explanation can you give for the differences in the price-earnings ratios observed in (c)?

INTERMEDIATE **15.** The current dividend, D_0, of the stock of Sun Devil Corporation is $3 per share. Under present conditions, this dividend is expected to grow at a rate of 6 percent annually for the foreseeable future. The beta of Sun Devil's stock is 1.5. The risk-free rate of return is 7 percent, and the expected market rate of return is 14 percent.

  a. At what price would you expect Sun Devil's common stock to sell?

  b. If the risk-free rate of return declines to 6 percent, what will happen to Sun Devil's stock price? (Assume the expected market rate of return remains at 14 percent.)

  c. Sun Devil's management is considering acquisitions in the machine tool industry. Management expects the firm's beta to increase to 1.6 as a result of these acquisitions. The dividend growth rate is expected to increase to 7 percent annually. Would you recommend this acquisition program to management? (Assume the same initial conditions that existed in (a)).

CHALLENGE **16.** Caledonia Minerals has an estimated beta of 1.6. The company is considering the acquisition of another firm that has a beta of 1.2. Both companies are exactly the same size.

  a. What is the expected new beta value for the combined firm?

  b. The risk-free rate of return is estimated at 7 percent, and the market return is estimated as 12 percent. What is your estimate of the required return of investors in Caledonia before and after the merger?

  Caledonia Minerals is expected to pay a $1 dividend next year ($D_1 = \$1$). This dividend is expected to grow at a rate of 6 percent per year for the foreseeable future if the merger is not completed. The merger is not expected to change the dividend for next year, that is, D_1 is expected to be $1.00, but future dividends are expected to grow at a 7 percent rate as a result of the merger.

  c. What is the value of a share of stock in Caledonia Minerals prior to the merger?

  d. What is the new value of a share of stock, assuming that the merger is completed?

  e. Would you recommend that Caledonia go ahead with the merger?

CHALLENGE **17.** Tucker Manufacturing Company has a beta estimated at 1.0. The risk-free rate is 6 percent, and the expected market return is 12 percent. Tucker expects to pay a $4 dividend next year ($D_1 = \$4$). This dividend is expected to grow at 3 percent per year for the foreseeable future. The current market price for Tucker is $40.

  a. Is the current stock price an equilibrium price, based upon the SML calculation of k_e for Tucker?

  b. What do you think the appropriate equilibrium price is? How will that price be achieved?

INTERMEDIATE **18.** Find the current stock price for Lilly Corporation (Ticker symbol: LLY) from the finance page of http://www.yahoo.com. Also get the current earnings per share for Lilly Corp. and the industry PE ratio. The earnings per share can be obtained by requesting the *detailed* quote for the stock. The industry PE ratio may be obtained by clicking on the Research key once you get the detailed quote. Assuming Lilly Corp. is similar to the industry average firm, what is the appropriate value for a share of Lilly Corp? Using the PE model is Lilly Corp. stock undervalued or overvalued?

THOMSON ONE—Business School Edition

Go to the text Web site at http://moyer.swlearning.com, select your book, and click on the Thomson ONE button. Enter Thomson ONE—Business School Edition by using the username and password you created when you registered the serial number on your access card. Use the "Prices" tab, "Overviews" option, "Worldscope Market Data" sub-option, to look at a valuation analysis for AT&T Corporation(I). What reasons can you give for the volatility in the PE ratio over the past 10 years? Compare your results from AT&T with those for Bellsouth (BLS).

THE CAPITAL
INVESTMENT DECISION

PART THREE

This portion of the text focuses on capital expenditures—that is, investments in long-term assets. Chapter 9 deals with the measurement of the cash flows (benefits and costs) associated with long-term investment projects. Chapter 10 considers various decision-making criteria that can be used when choosing projects that will maximize the value of the firm.

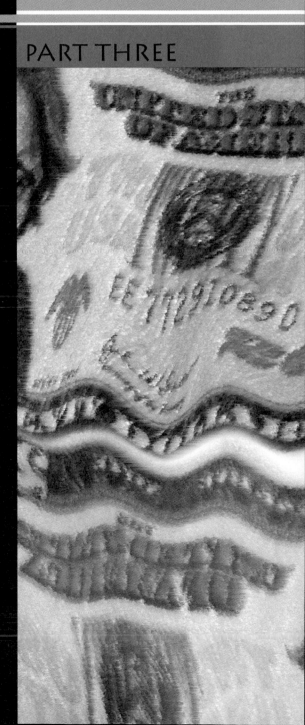

CHAPTER

9 Capital Budgeting and Cash Flow Analysis

I n this and the following chapter we discuss the capital budgeting decision-making aspect of financial management. *Capital budgeting is the process of planning for capital expenditures. A capital expenditure is a cash outlay that is expected to generate a flow of future benefits lasting longer than 1 year.* It is distinguished from a normal operating expenditure, which is expected to result in benefits during the coming 1-year period. (The choice of a 1-year period is arbitrary, but it does serve as a useful guideline.) Table 9.1 shows the annual capital expenditures for year 2002 for companies that comprise the Dow Jones 30 Index. The table also shows the annual sales and the proportion of capital expenditures to sales. Intel Corporation, for example, spent $4.7 billion on its capital expenditure program in 2002, amounting to over 17 percent of sales for the year.

The capital budgeting decision, perhaps more than any other decision, has the greatest long-term significance to the firm and its shareholders. For new firms, it is what determines the product or service they are going to provide—that is, the industry in which it operates. For new and existing firms alike, capital expenditures determine the future direction and relative prosperity of the firm. For example, Wal-Mart's decision in the early 1990s to expand the discount retail operation to include groceries led to a major capital expenditure program that ushered in a period of increased prosperity to the firm. On the other hand, Webvan invested over $100 million to develop the on-line grocery delivery market, but it failed miserably in developing the concept to profitability, ultimately ending in bankruptcy. Thus, the stakes in capital budgeting can be very high. An incorrect decision may lead to significant losses and, in extreme cases, even financial distress and bankruptcy.

Table 9.1 Capital Expenditures by Firms Listed on the Dow Jones 30 Index for Year 2002 (in millions of dollars)

	Company	Capital Expenditures ($ millions)	Sales ($ millions)	Capital Expenditures as Percent of Sales
1	3M Co.	763	16,332	4.7
2	Alcoa Inc.	1,270	20,263	6.3
3	Altria Group Inc.	2,009	80,408	2.5
4	American Express Co.	670	23,807	2.8
5	AT&T Corp.	3,878	37,827	10.3
6	Boeing Co.	1,001	54,069	1.9
7	Caterpillar Inc.	1,773	20,152	8.8
8	Citigroup Inc.	1,377	93,041	1.5
9	Coca-Cola Co.	851	19,564	4.4
10	E.I. DuPont de Nemours & Co.	1,280	24,522	5.2
11	Eastman Kodak Co.	577	12,835	4.5
12	ExxonMobil Corp.	11,437	204,506	5.6
13	General Electric Co.	13,351	131,698	10.1
14	General Motors Corp.	7,443	186,763	4.0
15	Hewlett-Packard Co.	1,710	56,588	3.0
16	Home Depot Inc.	2,749	58,247	4.7
17	Honeywell International Inc	671	22,274	3.0
18	Intel Corp.	4,703	26,764	17.6
19	International Business Machines Corp.	4,753	81,186	5.9
20	International Paper Co.	1,009	24,976	4.0
21	J.P. Morgan Chase & Co.	NA	44,118	NA
22	Johnson & Johnson	2,577	36,298	7.1
23	McDonald's Corp.	2,004	15,406	13.0
24	Merck & Co. Inc.	2,370	51,790	4.6
25	Microsoft Corp.	770	28,365	2.7
26	Procter & Gamble Co.	1,679	40,238	4.2
27	SBC Communications Inc.	6,808	43,138	15.8
28	United Technologies Corp.	586	28,212	2.1
29	Wal-Mart Stores Inc.	9,355	246,525	3.8
30	Walt Disney Co.	1,086	25,329	4.3

Source: Calculated from data taken from Yahoo Finance (http://www.yahoo.com)

Several different types of outlays may be classified as capital expenditures and evaluated using the framework of capital budgeting models, including the following:

➢ The purchase of a new piece of equipment, real estate, or a building in order to expand an existing product or service line or enter a new line of business
➢ The replacement of an existing capital asset, such as a drill press
➢ Investments in permanent increases of target inventory levels or levels of accounts receivable
➢ The refunding of an old bond issue with a new lower-interest issue
➢ Lease-versus-buy analysis

➤ Expenditures for an advertising campaign designed to generate overall corporate awareness (as opposed to short-term promotional campaigns)
➤ Investments in employee education and training
➤ Expenditures for a research and development program
➤ Merger and acquisition evaluation

In view of the risks associated with these projects, management should exercise great care in generating and analyzing capital budgeting proposals. Capital budgeting analysis is essentially a two-step procedure:

1. In the first step, cash flows associated with the capital budgeting project must be estimated. In a typical project, there is an initial investment, followed by a series of net cash flows over the life of the project.
2. The second step is to assess the feasibility of the project. Basically, this requires the determination of whether the future cash flows generated from the project (net cash flows) justify the required investment.

In this chapter we discuss the cash flow aspects of capital budgeting analysis. In the following chapter we discuss several evaluation criteria to assess the feasibility of a given capital budgeting project.

Chapter Objectives

After reading this chapter, you should be able to do the following:

1. Understand and apply the principles of estimating cash flows.
2. Identify and estimate the initial and net cash flows.

PRINCIPLES OF ESTIMATING CASH FLOWS

The typical capital expenditure requires an initial cash outflow, termed the **net investment.** The initial investment is followed by a series of **net cash flows,** which are essentially cash inflows minus cash outflows generated as a result of engaging in the project. In the *conventional* case the net cash flows are all positive (i.e., inflows exceed outflows). In the *nonconventional* case the net cash flows may change signs, sometimes more than once. The net cash flows are estimated for the duration of the project. Conceptually, the cash flow diagram may be illustrated as follows:

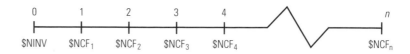

where NINV is the net investment, NCF is net cash flow, and n is the duration of the project.

In determining the cash flows associated with a capital budgeting project, certain basic principles should be adhered to. These principles should be applied to the determination of net investment as well as of net cash flows. They include:

1. Cash Flows Should Be Measured on an Incremental Basis. In other words, the cash flow stream for a particular project should be estimated from the perspective of how the entire cash flow stream of the firm will be affected if the project is adopted—as compared with the stream if the project is not adopted. Therefore, *all* changes in the firm's revenue stream, cost stream, and tax stream that would result from the acceptance of the project should be included in the analysis. In contrast, cash flows that would not be changed by the investment should be disregarded.

For example, assume that Singapore Airlines wants to replace its fleet of 747 Boeing jets that service its Pacific routes with a new generation of 747s that have identical capacity but significant gains in fuel economy. Since the passenger capacities are identical, it is unlikely that the replacement will have any meaningful impact on the revenues. Therefore, the project is not likely to result in any cash flow increases from revenue changes. However, because of the fuel savings there will be a positive cash flow impact from reduced operating costs, and this should be recognized.

The incremental cash flow perspective should be applied to the determination of the net investment as well. Continuing with the Singapore Airlines replacement example, let us assume that the existing fleet will be sold if the decision to replace the fleet is accepted. Consequently, the net investment associated with the replacement decision is not the cost of the new aircraft; rather, it is the cost of the new aircraft reduced by the amount of the proceeds (after tax) from the sale of the old aircraft.

2. Cash Flows Should Be Measured on an After-Tax Basis. Because the initial investment made on a project requires the outlay of after-tax cash dollars, the returns from the project should be measured in the same units—namely, after-tax cash flows.

3. Changes in Net Working Capital Should Be Included in the Determination of Cash Flows. It is easy to forget to include the working capital investments that are needed to start or expand a business. As we shall find out in Chapter 16, most businesses require substantial investments in current asset accounts in addition to investments in fixed assets. It would be difficult for manufacturing or even service businesses to operate without cash, marketable securities, accounts receivable, or inventories. However, businesses need not raise capital to fund the *entire* investment in current assets: Some of the investment in current assets is automatically financed by spontaneous increases in current liabilities such as accounts payable, accrued wages, and taxes. Thus, the additional investment we are concerned with is the portion of current assets *not* financed by spontaneous increases in current liabilities— that is, net working capital.

It is important to keep in mind that changes in net working capital affect not only the net investment (NINV) calculation but also the net cash flows (NCF). In addition to an initial investment in net working capital, a firm would have to provide for further increases in the future as sales increase. These additional working capital requirements should be included in the net cash flow calculations as outflows. However, as the project winds down, net working capital balances decline; these should be included as inflows when determining the net cash flows.

4. All the Indirect Effects of a Project Should Be Included in the Cash Flow Calculations. An example of an indirect effect is what the marketing profession sometimes refers to as the "cannibalization" effect. A good illustration of the cannibalization effect is the Saturn car project of General Motors (GM). Let us assume that GM projected annual revenues of $2.5 billion for the new Saturn cars. Not all of this may represent net additional revenue to GM: Some of the sales may come from customers who otherwise would have purchased another GM model, such as Chevrolet Cavalier or Pontiac Sunbird. If we assume that the Saturn car is expected to take away (cannibalize) $400 million in sales from these other models, the incremental sales from Saturn cars is only $2.1 billion and not the full $2.5 billion. Cannibalization effects are common in firms with multiple brand names (e.g., Procter & Gamble, Kellogg's, RJR Nabisco) or locations (McDonald's, Wal-Mart).

5. Sunk Costs Should Not Be Considered When Evaluating a Project. A *sunk cost* is an outlay that already has been made (or committed to be made). Because sunk costs cannot be recovered, they should not be considered in the decision to accept or reject a project. For example, let us assume that Metalcraft, Inc., a manufacturer of steel furniture, is contemplating the manufacture and sale of steel doors for commercial and residential applications. The existing manufacturing facility was built a year ago at a cost of $800,000. The current operations occupy only half of the space; the remaining space is left vacant with no foreseeable alternative use. Management feels that the steel door venture can be housed in the currently unoccupied factory space. From a capital budgeting analysis perspective, should the firm take 50 percent of the cost of the facility (.5 × $800,000 = $400,000) and assign it to the net investment in the new project? The answer is no, since the factory building is a *sunk cost*. Another example of a sunk cost is if Metalcraft commissioned an outside consultant to study the feasibility of manufacturing steel doors for which it had paid $25,000 a year ago. The $25,000 payment for the feasibility study is a sunk cost and should not be included in the evaluation of the project today.

The notion of sunk cost also can be applied to net cash flows over the life of the project. Continuing with the Metalcraft example, assume that the firm's production manager is paid $60,000 per year. He will be given the additional task of overseeing the production of the new steel door product line with no increase in compensation. However, it is expected that the production manager will spend one-third of his time on the new venture. A similar question to the one posed earlier arises here: Do we take one-third of the production manager's salary (1/3 × $60,000 = $20,000) as an operating cash outflow of the new project? Again, the answer is no, because the salary is a sunk cost—it has to be paid regardless of whether or not the new venture is undertaken.

6. The Value of Resources Used in a Project Should Be Measured in Terms of Their Opportunity Costs. *Opportunity costs* of resources (assets) are the cash flows those resources could generate if they are not used in the project under consideration. To illustrate this concept, let's return to the example of Metalcraft. Suppose that the currently unoccupied portion of the factory can be partitioned and sold to another interested user for $600,000. By utilizing this space for the steel door venture, Metalcraft is forgoing the *opportunity* to realize $600,000 from the sale of the factory space. Thus, the opportunity cost of $600,000 (after adjustment for tax effects) should be included as part of the net investment.

Comprehension Check Questions

1. In the context of capital budgeting analysis, what is meant by incremental cash flows?
2. Why should changes in net working capital be considered in capital budgeting analysis?

3. Why are sunk costs considered irrelevant in calculating project cash flows?

4. What are opportunity costs?

ESTIMATING PROJECT CASH FLOWS

In this section we discuss details of how to calculate the net investment and net cash flows for capital budgeting projects. We will consider two examples. The first is a *new business project* and the second is a *replacement project*. In the new business project all of the cash flows are *new* or *incremental*, since there are no existing cash flows to consider. The replacement type project, on the other hand, involves replacing a piece of equipment with a newer, more efficient one. Consequently, in analyzing a replacement project, the cash flow analysis must take into account a comparison of the replacement cash flows with the existing cash flows (cash flows assuming no replacement is undertaken) so that *only the incremental* cash flows are considered.

The new business project could be thought of as a special case of the replacement project—with the existing cash flows assuming a value of zero. However, for our purposes it is easier to illustrate the cash flow concepts by first applying it to a new business project, and then to a replacement project.

Estimating Cash Flows for a New Business

Assume that after intensive research, you have developed a new golf ball that is very forgiving of golfers' mistakes. It has some very desirable aerodynamic properties compared to the competition, and you expect it to command a significant share of the market. You want to capitalize on your invention by manufacturing and marketing this new golf ball under the brand name Hole-in-One.

Engineering studies indicate that the equipment needed for the business will cost $275,000. In addition, there will be a $15,000 charge for shipping and installation. Finally, the firm will have to provide for initial net working capital in the amount of $50,000—consisting of $10,000 cash balance, $20,000 accounts receivable from dealers (golf pro-shops), $20,000 in raw material inventory, $5,000 in work-in-progress inventory, and $10,000 in finished goods inventory less $10,000 accounts payable and $5,000 in accrued wages and other accrued expenses.

This venture is expected to last 5 years, after which time the business will terminate and the equipment will be sold. The equipment will be depreciated to zero using the straight-line method over the 5-year life of the project. It is estimated that the equipment can be sold for $10,000 when the business is terminated in 5 years.

Marketing analysis indicates the following revenue stream can be generated over the next 5 years:

Year 1	Year 2	Year 3	Year 4	Year 5
$250,000	$300,000	$325,000	$300,000	$225,000

Sales are expected to increase at first, and then to decline as competitors introduce similar improvements to their products.

Cash operating costs are estimated to equal 45 percent of the revenues. The operating costs include cost of manufacturing and overhead expenses such as salaries, utilities, advertising, and rent. In addition, it is estimated that beginning in year 1, the firm's net working capital every year is going to equal 20 percent of the following year's revenues.

Calculating the Net Investment (NINV) For a new business, the net investment is calculated as follows:

New project cost plus installation and shipping costs
PLUS
Investment in net working capital initially required
EQUALS
Net investment (NINV)

For Hole-In-One, Inc. the net investment calculation is shown in Table 9.2.

Calculating the Net Cash Flows (NCF) The annual net cash flows (NCF) are simply cash inflows minus cash outflows associated with the project. The cash flows consist primarily of *operating cash flows* (OCF)—that is, cash flows associated with the operating aspects of the project such as revenues and expenses. The operating cash flows are then adjusted to take into account changes in net working capital requirements, yielding the net cash flow. In addition, in the terminal year of the project, cash flows associated with the end of the project must be considered. These cash flows are sometimes referred to as *terminal cash flows*. An example of a terminal cash flow is the proceeds realized (after-tax) from the sale of equipment.

Operating cash flows for any given period are determined as follows:

> **Cash inflows from revenues**
> **2 Cash operating expenses**
> **2 Depreciation**
> _____
>
> **Operating earnings before taxes**
> **2 Taxes**
> _____
>
> **Operating earnings after taxes**
> **1 Depreciation**
> _____
>
> **Operating cash flows**

Table 9.3 shows the operating cash flows for the Hole-in-One project. In Year 1, cash inflows from revenues arc $250,000. Cash outflows for operating expenses are $112,500, equal to 45 percent of the revenues.

Depreciation expense is $58,000 per year. The depreciation amount was determined using the straight-line method. Under the straight-line depreciation method, the annual amount of an asset's depreciation (*Dep*) is calculated as follows:

(9.1)
$$\text{Annual depreciation expense } (Dep) = \frac{\text{Installed cost}}{\text{Number of years over which asset is depreciated}}$$

Table 9.2 Net Investment Calculation for Hole-in-One New Business Project	
Cost of equipment	$275,000
Installation and shipping charges	$ 15,000
Increase in initial net working capital	$ 50,000
NINV	**$340,000**

Table 9.3 Cash Flow from Operations for Hole-in-One New Business Project

	Year 1	Year 2	Year 3	Year 4	Year 5
Revenues (R)	$250,000	$300,000	$325,000	$300,000	$225,000
− Operating costs (O)	$112,500	$135,000	$146,250	$135,000	$101,250
− Depreciation expense (Dep)	$ 58,000	$ 58,000	$ 58,000	$ 58,000	$ 58,000
Operating earnings before taxes	$ 79,500	$107,000	$120,750	$107,000	$ 65,750
− Taxes (T)	$ 31,800	$ 42,800	$ 48,300	$ 42,800	$ 26,300
Operating earnings after taxes	$ 47,700	$ 64,200	$ 72,450	$ 64,200	$ 39,450
+ Depreciation expense (Dep)	$ 58,000	$ 58,000	$ 58,000	$ 58,000	$ 58,000
Cash flow from operations (OCF)	**$105,700**	**$122,200**	**$130,450**	**$122,200**	**$ 97,450**

The depreciable basis of the equipment is $290,000 (cost of equipment plus installation and shipping charges). Since we are depreciating the equipment to a zero salvage value over 5 years using the straight-line method, the annual depreciation expense is $58,000 ($290,000/5 years). Although depreciation is a noncash expense item, we should include it in order to calculate the tax expense correctly: Depreciation is a deductible expense for tax purposes. Note, however, from Table 9.3, that the depreciation expense is subsequently added back to obtain the operating cash flow. For Hole-in-One, after subtracting depreciation expense, the operating earnings before taxes for year 1 equal $79,500. Subtracting taxes at an assumed rate of 40 percent gives us operating earnings after taxes of $47,700. We then add back the noncash depreciation expense of $58,000 to yield operating cash flows of $105,700 in year 1. The same sequence of steps is repeated to determine the operating cash flows for the remaining years of the project life, also shown in Table 9.3.

The next step is to calculate the cash flow effects from changes in the net working capital. We previously included an initial net working capital investment of $50,000 in the net investment calculation. However, most firms have to add to their net working capital investments as the business grows over time. For example, with expanding sales and increased production, firms will be required to commit additional funds to support higher accounts receivable and inventory balances. Table 9.4 shows a worksheet to calculate the additional net working capital investment in each year. We start by projecting the *level* of the net working capital in each year. The year 0 amount of $50,000 is the initial net working capital requirement. Starting in year 1 net working capital is assumed to equal 20 percent of the revenues in the following year. Thus, year 1 net working capital level is $60,000 (.2 × $300,000),

Table 9.4 Working Capital Investment Worksheet for Hole-in-One New Business Project

	Year 0	Year 1	Year 2	Year 3	Year 4	Year 5
Revenues		$250,000	$300,000	$325,000	$ 300,000	$ 225,000
Net working capital (20% of next year's revenues)	$50,000	$ 60,000	$ 65,000	$ 60,000	$ 45,000	$ 0
Increase in net working capital (Net working capital in a given year *minus* net working capital the year before)	$50,000	$ 10,000	$ 5,000	$−5,000	$−15,000	$−45,000

year 2 net working capital level is $65,000 (.2 × $325,000), etc. Note that the total investment in net working capital begins to decline in year 3 as future sales decrease. The decline occurs because lower sales for the firm translate into smaller accounts receivable balances and also because the firm need not maintain as high a finished and raw material inventory balance as before.

Once the net working capital balances are projected, the incremental investment in net working capital can be easily determined. In year 1 the *additional* increase in net working capital is $10,000, which is simply the net working capital level in the year minus the net working capital level in the preceding year ($60,000 − $50,000). Similarly, in year 2 the additional investment in net working capital is $5,000 ($65,000 − $60,000). In year 3, note that the incremental investment in net working capital is a negative number: −$5,000 ($60,000 − $65,000 = $−5,000). The negative number indicates that the firm is actually divesting, or recovering prior investments in net working capital as accounts receivable and other current assets are reduced due to lower sales. Thus, a decrease in net working capital has the effect of increasing the net cash flow. In year 4 there is a further decrease in net working capital of $15,000 ($45,000 − $60,000 = −$15,000). Finally, at the end of year 5, all remaining net working capital balance is assumed to be recovered ($0 − $45,000 = −$45,000). As a check, note that the sum of all the net working changes from year 0 through the terminal year must equal zero: + $50,000 + $10,000 + $5,000 − $5,000 − $15,000 − $45,000 = $0.

In the final year of the project there is an additional consideration in determining the net cash flow. Specifically, we should add the after-tax salvage value on the sale of the fixed assets. The after-tax salvage value is calculated as follows:

Salvage value from sale of asset

PLUS or MINUS

Tax effects on sale of asset

EQUALS

After-tax salvage value

Note from the above that the cash flow effects on the sale of the asset at the end of the project life must take into account the tax consequences of the sale. The tax effects may be positive or negative depending upon the sale price relative to the book value. There are four possibilities we need to consider.

Case 1: Sale of an Asset for Its Book Value. If a company disposes off an asset for an amount exactly equal to the asset's tax book value, there is neither a gain nor a loss on the sale and thus there are no tax consequences. For example, if Hole-in-One sells the equipment for $50,000 and it has a book value for tax purposes of $50,000, no taxes are associated with this disposal. (In general, the tax book value of an asset equals the installed cost of the asset less accumulated tax depreciation.)

Case 2: Sale of an Asset for Less than Its Book Value. If Hole-in-One sells the equipment for $20,000 and it has a tax book value of $50,000, the firm incurs a $30,000 pretax loss. This operating loss may be offset against prior year earnings, or if a firm has multiple businesses the loss may be offset against taxable income elsewhere, effectively reducing the company's taxes by an amount equal to the loss times the company's marginal tax rate.

Assume that the company's earnings before taxes is $100,000 (before consideration of the operating loss from the disposal of the asset). Taxes on these earnings are $100,000 times the company's marginal (40%) tax rate, or $40,000. Because of the operating loss of $30,000 incurred by selling the asset for $20,000, the company's taxable income is reduced to $70,000, and the taxes decline to $28,000 (40% of $70,000). The $12,000 difference in taxes is equal to the tax loss on the sale of the old asset times the company's marginal tax rate ($30,000 × 40%).

Case 3: Sale of an Asset for More than Its Book Value but Less than Its Original Cost. If Hole-in-One sells the asset for $60,000—$10,000 more than the current tax book value—$50,000 of this amount constitutes a tax-free cash inflow and the remaining $10,000 is taxed as operating income. As a result, the firm's taxes increase by $4,000, or the amount of the gain times the firm's marginal tax rate ($10,000 × 40%). The $4,000 in taxes represents the *recapture of depreciation* by the IRS—that is, it is the amount by which the firm benefited in tax savings previously as a result of depreciating the asset *more* than it should have.

Case 4: Sale of an Asset for More than Its Original Cost. If Hole-in-One sells the asset for $300,000 (assuming an original asset cost of $290,000), part of the gain from the sale is treated as ordinary income (recapture of depreciation) and part is treated as a long-term capital gain. The gain receiving ordinary income treatment is equal to the difference between the original asset cost and the current tax book value, or $240,000 ($290,000 − $50,000). The capital gain portion is the amount in excess of the original asset cost, or $10,000. Under current U.S. tax law (early 2003), both ordinary income and capital gains are taxed at the same corporate rate. In this case then, the total tax consists of the tax on the capital gain ($10,000 × 40%), $4,000, and the tax on the ordinary income gain ($240,000 × 40%), $96,000 or a total of $100,000.

In the case of our Hole-in-One example, the equipment is assumed to have a salvage value of $10,000. Table 9.5 illustrates the calculation of the after-tax cash flows from the salvage value. Since the book value at the end of year 5 is $0, the $10,000 salvage value is a *gain* (recapture of depreciation) on which taxes at the marginal rate for the firm must be paid. At 40 percent, the tax amounts to $4,000 (.4 × $10,000). The resulting after-tax cash flow from salvage value is $6,000.

Table 9.6 pulls together all the elements of the net cash flows. Specifically, the table details the operating cash flow, the cash flow effects from changes in the net working capital investment, the cash flow from salvage value, and the resulting net cash flow. In year 1 the net cash flow is $95,700, which is equal to the operating cash flow of $105,700 less the increase in net working capital of $10,000. For the terminal year, the cash flow effects from salvage value are included in determining the net cash flow.

Table 9.5 Cash Flow from Salvage Value for Hole-in-One New Business Project

Salvage value from sale of asset	$10,000
Tax on sale of asset (40%)	−$ 4,000
After-tax salvage value (ATSV)	$ 6,000

Calculation of tax on sale of asset:	
Book value of asset:	$ 0
Gain on sale of asset:	$10,000
(selling price − book value)	
Tax liability (gain × tax rate: $10,000 × .4)	$ 4,000

Table 9.6 Net Cash Flow Calculation for Hole-in-One New Business Project

	Year 1	Year 2	Year 3	Year 4	Year 5
Revenues (R)	$250,000	$300,000	$325,000	$300,000	$225,000
− Operating costs (O)	$112,500	$135,000	$146,250	$135,000	$101,250
− Depreciation expense (Dep)	$58,000	$58,000	$58,000	$58,000	$58,000
Operating earnings before taxes	$79,500	$107,000	$120,750	$107,000	$65,750
− Taxes	$31,800	$42,800	$48,300	$42,800	$26,300
Operating earnings after taxes	$47,700	$64,200	$72,450	$64,200	$39,450
+ Depreciation expense (Dep)	$58,000	$58,000	$58,000	$58,000	$58,000
Cash flow from operations (OCF)	$105,700	$122,200	$130,450	$122,200	$97,450
− Increase in net working capital (NWC)	$10,000	$5,000	$−5,000	$−15,000	$−45,000
+ Salvage value					$10,000
− Tax on salvage value					$4,000
Net cash flow (NCF)	**$95,700**	**$117,200**	**$135,450**	**$137,200**	**$148,450**

The net cash flows could also have been computed using an equation. In equation form, the operating cash flow is determined as follows:

(9.2)
$$OCF = (R - O - Dep)(1 - T) + Dep$$

where:

OCF = operating cash flow
R = cash inflow from revenue
O = cash outflow due to cash operating expense
Dep = depreciation expense
T = marginal tax rate of the firm

To obtain the net cash flow, NCF, the operating cash flow is adjusted for changes in net working capital investment. Thus, NCF or net cash flow is equal to:

(9.3)
$$NCF = (R - O - Dep)(1 - T) + Dep - \Delta NWC$$

where ΔNWC ("delta NWC") is the increase in net working capital.

Equation 9.3 can be used to estimate the annual net cash flow for any given year of the project life. However, in the terminal year of the project life, the after-tax salvage value also must be included (ATSV):

(9.4)
$$NCF \text{ (terminal year)} = (R - O - Dep)(1 - T) + Dep - \Delta NWC + ATSV$$

Applying the equation format to the Hole-in-One golf project, the yearly net cash flows are calculated as follows:

$NCF_1 = (\$250,000 - \$112,500 - \$58,000)(1 - .40) + \$58,000 - \$10,000$
$\quad = \$95,700$
$NCF_2 = (\$300,000 - \$135,000 - \$58,000)(1 - .40) + \$58,000 - \$5,000$
$\quad = \$117,200$
$NCF_3 = (\$325,000 - \$146,250 - \$58,000)(1 - .40) + \$58,000 - (\$-5,000)$
$\quad = \$125,450$
$NCF_4 = (\$300,000 - \$135,000 - \$58,000)(1 - .40) + \$58,000 - (\$-15,000)$
$\quad = \$137,200$
$NCF_5 \text{ (terminal year)} = (\$225,000 - \$101,250 - \$58,000)(1 - .40) + \$58,000 -$
$(\$-45,000) + \$10,000 \text{ (salvage value)} - \$4,000 \text{ (tax on salvage value)} = \$148,450$

Note in year 3 and subsequent years the increase in net working capital is a negative number, implying that net working capital is being liquidated—consequently, *adding* to the net cash flow.

Spreadsheets can be very handy in estimating project cash flows. There is less potential for making arithmetic errors and also it is more efficient as formulas can be used to project the variable. For example, if operating expenses are growing at 5 percent per year, one need only specify the operating expense for the first year; the values for the remaining years can be expressed in terms of the variable's value for the preceding year and the growth rate for the variable. Cash flows for the Hole-in-One project using the Excel spreadsheet are shown here.

Spreadsheet strategies

	A	B	C	D	E	F	G	H
1	Using the Spreadsheet to Estimate Net Investment for Hole-in-One New Business Project							
3			Year 0					
4	New Machine		$275,000		Excel formula: +SUM(C4:C6)			
5	Installation		15000					
6	Increase in NWC		50000					
7	Net Investment (Year 0)		$340,000					
10	Using the Spreadsheet to Estimate Net Cash Flows for Hole-in-One New Business Project							
11	(Excel Formulas are shown for column H only. But similar formulas are used in columns D to G)							
13						Years		
14				1	2	3	4	5
19	Revenue			$250,000	$300,000	$325,000	$300,000	$225,000
20	-Operating Cost	45%		112,500	135,000	146,250	135,000	101,250
21	-Depreciation			58,000	58,000	58,000	58,000	58,000
22	Earnings before taxes			79,500	107,000	120,750	107,000	65,750
23	-Taxes	40%		31,800	42,800	48,300	42,800	26,300
24	Earnings after taxes			47,700	64,200	72,450	64,200	39,450
25	+Depreciation			58,000	58,000	58,000	58,000	50,000
26	Cash Flow from operations			105,700	122,200	130,450	122,200	97,450
27	-Increase in NWC			10,000	5,000	-5,000	-15,000	-45,000
28	+Salvage value							10,000
29	-Tax on salvage value							4,000
31	Net Cash Flow			$95,700	$117,200	$135,450	$137,200	$148,450

Annotations:
- 45 percent of revenues. Excel formula: "+$B$20*H19"
- Straight line depreciation for 5 years. Excel formula: = "+SUM($C$4:$C$5)/5"
- Excel formula: "+H19-H20-H21"
- Tax rate=40%. Excel formula: "+$B$23*H22"
- Excel formula: "+H22-H23"
- Add back depreciation.
- Excel formula: "+H24+H25"
- 20 percent of the next year's sales minus accumulated NWC of the last year. Excel formula: "=0.2*I19-SUM(C6,D27:G27)". Note I19 has no value so the first term of the formula is = 0.
- Tax rate times salvage value (since book value=0). Excel Formula: "+$B$23*H28"
- Note: Cash flow from Operations minus increase in NWC plus after tax salvage value. Excel Fromula: "+SUM(H26-H27+H28-H29)"

Comprehension Check Questions

1. How is the net investment for a new business project calculated?
2. How are operating cash flows different from net cash flows?
3. Why is depreciation, a noncash item, considered in the calculation of net cash flows?
4. Why must net working capital investments be considered in the determining project cash flows?

Calculating Cash Flows for an Asset Replacement Project

The previous example of a *new business project* illustrated the key elements for the calculation of a project's net investment and its annual net cash flows. In this section, we consider an *asset replacement project*. Asset replacements involve retiring one asset and replacing it with another, more efficient asset.

Estimating cash flows for asset replacement projects is somewhat different from estimating cash flows for a new business. In the case of a replacement decision we have to compare *projected cash flows with the project in place against cash flows that would continue to be generated had the replacement project not been undertaken.* The reason we do this is because the only cash flows that are relevant are the *incremental differences between the two.*

To illustrate, let us take the example of Briggs & Stratton. Suppose Briggs & Stratton purchased an automatic drill press 6 years ago. The drill press originally cost $160,000 and was being depreciated to a zero salvage value over a 10-year period using the straight-line method. The existing machine, though 6 years old, can last another 6 years. The firm is considering replacing the existing machine with a newer one costing $200,000 plus shipping and installation cost of $10,000. The new machine will be depreciated to a zero value over a 6-year period using the straight-line method. If the replacement is undertaken, the existing machine can fetch a price of $40,000.

Briggs & Stratton expects annual revenues during the project's first year to rise to $85,000 from $75,000 if the new drill press is purchased. The increased revenue is the result of higher output from the new press, and management is confident there is sufficient demand to sell the additional output. After the first year, revenues from the new project are expected to increase at a rate of $2,000 a year for the remainder of the project life compared to revenues without the replacement.

We will further assume that while the old drill press required two operators, the new drill press is more automated and needs only one, thereby reducing annual operating costs from $40,000 to $20,000 during the project's first year. After the first year, annual operating costs of the new drill press are expected to increase by $1,000 a year for the remaining life of the project (operating costs for the old drill press, if kept, are assumed to remain constant over the next 6 years). The firm's marginal tax rate is 40 percent. It is anticipated that initially (year 0) an additional investment in net working capital of $5,000 is required with a further increase of $3,000 in year 1. Thereafter, no additional investment in net working capital is required. At the end of year 6, it is expected that the drill press can be sold for $25,000 salvage value.

Calculating the Net Investment (NINV) The calculation of net investment is similar to that of the new business project with the exception that the cost of the new project is *reduced* by any proceeds from the sale of the old asset net of any tax effects associated with that sale. The tax effects may be positive or negative. If the asset is sold for more than book value the transaction will result in a tax liability (cash outflow). On the other hand a sale price that is less than the book value will result in a tax credit (cash inflow) to the firm. The general format for calculating the net investment for a replacement project is:

New project cost plus installation and shipping costs

PLUS

Investment in net working capital initially required

MINUS

Proceeds from the sale of old asset

PLUS or MINUS

Tax effects on sale of old asset

EQUALS

Net Investment (NINV)

Table 9.7 illustrates the calculation of net investment for the Briggs & Stratton replacement project. The cost of the new drill press including shipping and installation is $210,000. Net working capital initially required is $5,000. Proceeds from the sale of the existing drill press are $40,000. The tax consequences of the sale are shown in the lower half of Table 9.7. The book value of the existing drill press is

Table 9.7 Net Investment Calculation for Briggs & Stratton Replacement Project

Cost of new drill press	$ 200,000
+ Shipping and installation charges	$ 10,000
− Proceeds from sale of old drill press	$ 40,000
− Tax credit from loss on sale of old drill press	$ 9,600
+ Investment in initial net working capital	$ 5,000
NINV	**$165,400**

Calculation of tax credit from loss on sale of old machine:

Book value of existing asset: (Original cost minus accumulated depreciation: $160,000 − $16,000 annual depreciation × 6 years)	$64,000
Loss on sale of old asset: (selling price − book value: $40,000 − $64,000)	$24,000
Tax credit (loss × tax rate: $24,000 × .4)	$9,600

$64,000 computed as the cost of the equipment ($160,000) less accumulated depreciation ($16,000 depreciation per year × 6 years). The sale price of the drill press ($40,000) represents a loss relative to book value resulting in a tax credit to the firm (amount of loss × tax rate: $24,000 × .4). The NINV is equal to $165,400.

Calculating the Net Cash Flows (NCF) The relevant measure of net cash flows for a replacement project is the incremental difference in the cash flows with and without the project. Table 9.8 illustrates the operating cash flows with and without the project for year 1 of the project life. The format is identical to the one utilized for the new business project (Table 9.3). If the replacement decision is undertaken, next year's revenues will equal $85,000 while operating expenses will be $20,000. The depreciation expense for the new drill press will equal $35,000 per year. The depreciation expense is determined as the depreciable basis of the new asset (cost of equipment plus installation and shipping) divided by the number of years over which the asset is being depreciated: ($200,000 + $10,000)/ 6 years = $35,000. The resulting after-tax operating cash flow is equal to $53,000.

On the other hand, if the firm were to continue operating with the existing drill press, next year's revenues will equal $75,000, while operating costs will be $40,000. Depreciation expense on the existing asset is $16,000 ($160,000/10 years) per year. Note that if the old drill press were kept it would be on its *seventh year* of depreciation in year 1—a fact that will become relevant when we determine cash flows for subsequent years. The resulting after-tax operating cash flow is equal to $27,400. This compares to the after-tax operating cash flow of $53,000 if the replacement project is undertaken.

The *relevant* cash flow is the *difference* between these two cash flows—that is, the after-tax operating cash flow with the project minus the after-tax operating cash flow without the project. From Table 9.8 this difference is equal to $25,600 ($53,000 − $27,400). Thus, if a new drill press is purchased to replace the old one, Briggs & Stratton's after-tax operating cash flow will improve by $25,600 in year 1. The $25,600 represents the incremental cash flow for year 1 from taking on the replacement project.

Table 9.8 Cash Flow Projection for Briggs & Stratton with and without Replacement Project for Year 1

	Cash Flow with Replacement	Cash Flow without Replacement
Revenues (R)	$ 85,000	$ 75,000
− Operating costs (O)	20,000	40,000
− Depreciation (Dep)	35,000	16,000
Operating earnings before taxes	30,000	19,000
− Taxes (40%)	12,000	7,600
Operating earnings after taxes	18,000	11,400
+ Depreciation (Dep)	35,000	16,000
Cash flow from operations (OCF)	$53,000	$27,400

Instead of developing two statements of cash flows—one with the new project and the other without the new project—we could have simply developed one cash flow statement expressed in a *change* format. Such a statement is shown in Table 9.9 for year 1. Note that all the changes are expressed as the *variable with the project (w) minus the variable without the project (wo)*. For example, change in revenues is equal to the revenue with the replacement project minus the revenue without the replacement project. The table begins with the change in revenue, and then subtracts the change in cash operating expense and the change in depreciation expense. The resulting figure is the change in operating cash flow before tax. Subtracting taxes and adding back the change in the depreciation expense yields the change in after-tax operating cash flow. In the final step we subtract the increase in net working capital to obtain the net cash flow. The incremental cash flow from operations in year 1 of $25,600 is identical to the value obtained when cash flows were determined separately with and without the replacement project. After subtracting the increase in net working capital of $3,000, the net cash flow in year 1 is determined to be $22,600.

Table 9.10 shows the net cash flow calculations for all 6 years. In year 5 note that the change in depreciation expense has increased from $19,000 to $35,000. The difference is due to the fact that the existing asset, if kept, would have been fully depreciated by year 4. Thus, in year 5 you only have the depreciation for the new asset but not the existing asset ($35,000 − $0 = $35,000). Also in year 5, note

Table 9.9 Incremental Operating Cash Flows for Briggs & Stratton Replacement Project for Year 1

Change in revenues ($R_w - R_{wo}$)	$10,000
− Change in operating costs ($O_w - O_{wo}$)	−20,000
− Change in depreciation ($Dep_w - Dep_{wo}$)	19,000
Change in operating earnings before taxes	11,000
− Change in taxes (40%)	4,400
Change in Operating earnings after taxes	6,600
+ Change in depreciation ($Dep_w - Dep_{wo}$)	19,000
Change in cash flow from operations	25,600
− Increase in net working capital (ΔNWC)	3,000
Net cash flow	**$22,600**

Table 9.10 Net Cash Flow Calculation for Briggs & Stratton Replacement Project

	Year 1	Year 2	Year 3	Year 4	Year 5	Year 6
Change in revenues ($R_w - R_{wo}$)	$10,000	$12,000	$14,000	$16,000	$18,000	$20,000
− Change in operating costs ($O_w - O_{wo}$)	$−20,000	$−19,000	$−18,000	$−17,000	$−16,000	$−15,000
− Change in depreciation expense ($Dep_w - Dep_{wo}$)	$19,000	$19,000	$19,000	$19,000	$35,000	$35,000
Change in operating earnings before taxes	$11,000	$12,000	$13,000	$14,000	$−1,000	$0
− Change in Taxes (40%)	$4,400	$4,800	$5,200	$5,600	$−400	$0
Change in operating earnings after taxes	$6,600	$7,200	$7,800	$8,400	$−600	$0
+ Change in depreciation expense ($Dep_w - Dep_{wo}$)	$19,000	$19,000	$19,000	$19,000	$35,000	$35,000
Change in cash flow from operations	$25,600	$26,200	$26,800	$27,400	$34,400	$35,000
− Increase in net working capital (ΔNWC)	$3,000					$−8,000
+ Salvage value						$25,000
− Tax on salvage value						$10,000
Net cash flow (NCF)	**$22,600**	**$26,200**	**$26,800**	**$27,400**	**$34,400**	**$58,000**

that the operating earnings before tax is $−1,000. The negative value is assumed to result in a tax credit of $400; the firm can use the loss to offset gains elsewhere in the firm to yield a tax saving.

In the terminal year of the project we need to factor in the after-tax effects of the salvage value and recovery of the net working capital. The recovery of net working capital in year 6 amounts to $8,000 ($5,000 initial net working capital investment and $3,000 in additional net working capital investment in year 1). The salvage value from sale of the drill press is $25,000. Since the drill press is fully depreciated by the end of year 6, the sale price represents a gain that is taxed at the firm's marginal tax rate ($25,000 × .4 = $10,000).

In equation form, the net cash flows for a replacement project may be determined as:

$$NCF = [(R_w - R_{wo}) - (O_w - O_{wo}) - (Dep_w - Dep_{wo})] (1 - T) \quad \text{(9.5)}$$
$$+ (Dep_w - Dep_{wo}) - \Delta NWC.$$

where

R_w = Revenues of the firm *with* the project
R_{wo} = Revenues of the firm *without* the project
O_w = Operating costs exclusive of depreciation for the firm *with* the project
O_{wo} = Operating costs exclusive of depreciation for the firm *without* the project
Dep_w = Depreciation charges for the firm *with* the project
Dep_{wo} = Depreciation charges for the firm *without* the project
ΔNWC = increase in net working capital

The terminal year net cash flow has to be adjusted to reflect the after-tax salvage value. Also the recovery in net working capital would manifest itself as a negative value for the change in net working capital. Thus, in the terminal year the net cash flow is equal to:

$$NCF \text{ (terminal year)} = [(R_w - R_{wo}) - (O_w - O_{wo}) - (Dep_w - Dep_{wo})] (1 - T)$$
$$+ (Dep_w - Dep_{wo}) - \Delta NWC + ATSV$$

where

ATSV is the after-tax salvage value.

Applying the equation format to the determination of NCFs for Briggs & Stratton, we get:

$$NCF_1 = [(\$85,000 - \$75,000) - (\$20,000 - \$40,000) - (\$35,000 - \$16,000)]$$
$$(1 - .4) + (\$35,000 - \$16,000) - \$3,000 = \$22,600$$

$$NCF_2 = [(\$87,000 - \$75,000) - (\$21,000 - \$40,000) - (\$35,000 - \$16,000)]$$
$$(1 - .4) + (\$35,000 - \$16,000) - \$0 = \$26,200$$

$$NCF_3 = [(\$89,000 - \$75,000) - (\$22,000 - \$40,000) - (\$35,000 - \$16,000)]$$
$$(1 - .4) + (\$35,000 - \$16,000) - \$0 = \$26,800$$

$$NCF_4 = [(\$91,000 - \$75,000) - (\$23,000 - \$40,000) - (\$35,000 - \$16,000)]$$
$$(1 - .4) + (\$35,000 - \$16,000) - \$0 = \$27,400$$

$$NCF_5 = [(\$93,000 - \$75,000) - (\$24,000 - \$40,000) - (\$35,000 - \$0)]$$
$$(1 - .4) + (\$35,000 - \$0) - \$0 = \$34,400$$

$$NCF_6 \text{ (terminal year)} = [(\$95,000 - \$75,000) - (\$25,000 - \$40,000) -$$
$$(\$35,000 - \$0)] (1 - .4) + (\$35,000 - \$0) - (\$-8,000)$$
$$+ \$25,000 \text{ (salvage value)} - \$10,000$$
$$\text{(tax on salvage value)} = \$58,000$$

The net cash flows obtained above are identical to those shown in Table 9.10.

Note that the equation for determining net cash flows for asset replacement projects (Equation 9.5) may also be used to determine net cash flows for new business projects. In the latter case, values for variables subscripted with a *wo* are set equal to zero since there are no existing cash flows to which the new business project is being compared to.

As in the case of the new business project example, calculating the cash flows for a replacement project may be more easily accomplished using a spreadsheet software. Cash flow estimates for the Briggs & Stratton replacement project using the Excel spreadsheet are shown here.

Spreadsheet strategies

	A	B	C	D	E	F	G	H
2	Using the Spreadsheet to Estimate Net Investment for Briggs and Stratton Replacement Project							
4			Year 0					
5	Cost of new drill press		$200,000					
6	Shipping and installation		10,000					
7	Sale of old drill press		-40,000					
8	Tax credit on sale of old press		-9,600					
9	Increase in NWC		5,000					
10	Net Investment		$165,400					
12	Additional data:							
13	Book value of old drill press		$64,000					
14	Sale price of old press		$40,000					
15	Tax rate		40%					
16	Cost of old press		$160,000					
18	Using the Spreadsheet to Estimate Net Cash Flows for Briggs and Stratton Replacement Project							
19	(Excel formulas are shown for column H only. But similar formulas are used in columns C to G)							
28						Years		
29			1	2	3	4	5	6
31	Increase in Revenue		$10,000	$12,000	$14,000	$16,000	$18,000	$20,000
32	- Change in operating costs		-20,000	-19,000	-18,000	-17,000	-16,000	-15,000
33	- Change in depreciation		19,000	19,000	19,000	19,000	35,000	35,000
34	Earnings before taxes		11,000	12,000	13,000	14,000	-1,000	0
35	-Taxes	40%	4,400	4,800	5,200	5,600	-400	0
36	Earnings after taxes		6,600	7,200	7,800	8,400	-600	0
37	+Depreciation		19,000	19,000	19,000	19,000	35,000	35,000
38	Cash flow from operations		25,600	26,200	26,800	27,400	34,400	35,000
39	-Increase in NWC		3,000	0	0	0	0	-8,000
40	+Salvage value							25,000
41	-Tax on salvage value							10,000
43	Net Cash Flow		$22,600	$26,200	$26,800	$27,400	$34,400	$58,000

Annotations (callouts in spreadsheet):
- (Row 8) Tax rate x Loss relative to book value. Excel formula: C15*(C14-C13)
- (Row 19) Last year's figure plus $2,000. Excel formula: "G31+2000"
- Note: Operating savings decrease by $1,000 each year. Excel formula: "G32+1000"
- Note: Old machine has 4 years of Dep remaining. Excel formula: "=+IF(H29>4,SUM($C$5:$C$6)/6,SUM($C$5:$C$6)/6-$C$16/10)"
- Excel formula: "+H31+H32-H33"
- Tax rate times earnings before taxes. Excel formula: "+$B$35*H34"
- Excel formula: "+H34-H35"
- Add back depreciation.
- Excel formula: "+H36+H37"
- Recovery of NWC invested in year 0 and year 1. Excel formula: "=-SUM(C39:C9)"
- Note: Book value = 0 therefore tax is equal to tax rate times salvage value. Excel formula: "+$B$35*H40"
- Excel formula: "+SUM(H38-H39+H40-H41)"

Comprehension Check Questions

1. How is the calculation of net investment for replacement projects different from that for new business projects?
2. How is the calculation of net cash flows for replacement projects different from that for new business projects?

INTEREST CHARGES AND NET CASH FLOWS

In the two sample projects used to illustrate the estimation of cash flows, you may have noticed that no interest or other financing costs were deducted in determining the net cash flows. Often the purchase of a particular asset is tied closely to the creation of some debt obligation, such as the sale of mortgage bonds or a bank loan. Nevertheless, it is generally considered *incorrect* to deduct the interest charges associated with a particular project from the estimated cash flows. This is true for two reasons.

First, the decision about how a firm should be financed can—and should—be made independently of the decision to accept or reject one or more projects. Instead, the firm should seek some combination of debt, equity (common stock), and preferred stock capital that it considers optimal. In many cases, this will result in a capital structure with the cost of capital (discussed in Chapter 11) at or near its minimum. Because investment and financing decisions normally should be made independently of one another, each new project can be viewed as being financed with the same proportions of the various sources of capital funds used to finance the firm as a whole.

Second, when a discounting framework is used for project evaluation, the discount rate, or cost of capital, already incorporates the cost of funds used to finance a project. Thus, deducting interest charges in the net cash flow calculations essentially would result in a double counting of costs.

PROBLEMS IN CASH FLOW ESTIMATION

Because project cash flows occur in the future, there are varying degrees of *uncertainty* about the value of these flows. Therefore, it is difficult to predict the actual cash flows of a project. The capital budgeting process assumes the decision maker is able to estimate cash flows accurately enough that these estimates can be used in project evaluation and selection. For this assumption to be realistic, project proposals should be based on inputs from appropriate personnel who have the expertise to accurately estimate the various elements of project cash flows. It is important to note that the accuracy of forecasts may also be dependent on the nature of the capital budgeting project. For example, the cash flows for asset replacement projects generally are easier to forecast than the cash flows for projects dealing with new product introductions.

Another problem often encountered in practice is *biased forecasts*. An individual or a division in a firm that has a vested interest in a project may bias the net cash flow forecasts upward (and/or the net investment downward) to improve the acceptability of the project. To prevent or reduce such biased forecasts, it is important that forecasts be verified and that firms have an incentive structure that rewards unbiased forecasts and penalizes biased forecasts.

Comprehension Check Questions

1. Why is interest expense not included in the calculation of cash flows for capital budgeting projects?
2. What are some problems of cash flow estimation?

Summary

➤ Capital budgeting is the process of planning for purchases of assets whose returns are expected to continue beyond 1 year.

➤ Capital budgeting analysis involves two basic steps: (1) to estimate cash flows, comprised of net investment and net cash flows; and (2) to evaluate the feasibility of the project on the basis of the net cash flows and the net investment required to generate the cash flows.

➤ Project cash flows should be measured on an incremental after-tax basis.

➤ Net working capital requirements and indirect cash flow effects associated with a project should be included in the calculation of net investment and net cash flows.

➤ Resources of a firm used in an investment project should be valued at their opportunity cost based on the cash flows these resources could generate in their next best alternative use.

➤ Sunk costs represent outlays that already have been made or committed and that cannot be recovered. Sunk costs should not be considered when evaluating an investment project.

➤ The net investment (NINV) in a project is the net cash outlay required to place the project in service. It includes the project cost *plus* any necessary increases in initial net working capital *minus* proceeds from the sale of the old asset (in the case of replacement decisions) *plus* or *minus* the taxes associated with the sale of the old asset (in the case of replacement decisions).

➤ The net cash flows (NCF) from a project are the incremental changes in a firm's operating cash flows that result from investing in the project. These flows include the changes in the firm's revenues, operating costs, depreciation, taxes, and net working capital with and without the project. In the terminal year of the project life, the after-tax salvage value also needs to be considered.

Questions and Topics for Discussion

1. Define capital expeditures and provide examples of capital expenditures.

2. Cash flows for a particular project should be measured on an incremental basis. What does that mean?

3. How does the opportunity cost concept affect capital budgeting cash flow determination?

4. What factors should be considered when estimating a new business's NINV? Is it any different for an asset replacement project?

5. Why is depreciation, a noncash expense, considered when estimating a project's net cash flows?

6. What are the potential tax consequences of selling an old asset in an asset replacement investment decision?

7. How is the determination of net cash flows different for an asset replacement project compared to a new business project?

8. Why should changes in net working capital be considered in capital budgeting cash flows? How do net working capital changes impact net investment? Net cash flows?

9. Why is it generally incorrect to consider interest charges when computing a project's net cash flows?

Self-Test Problems

ST1. The Fleming Company, a food distributor, is considering replacing a filling line at its Oklahoma City warehouse. The existing line was purchased several years ago for $600,000. The line's book value is $200,000, and Fleming management feels it could be sold at this time for $150,000. A new, increased capacity line can be purchased for $1,200,000. Delivery and installation of the new line are expected to cost an additional $100,000. Assuming Fleming's marginal tax rate is 40 percent, calculate the net investment for the new line.

ST2. Ocean Foods Corporation (OFC) currently processes seafood with a unit it purchased several years ago. The unit, which originally cost $500,000, currently has a book value of $250,000. OFC is considering replacing the existing unit with a newer, more efficient one. The new unit will cost $700,000 and will require an additional $50,000 for delivery and installation. The new unit also will require OFC to increase its investment in initial net working capital by $40,000 followed by an increase of $10,000 in net working capital in year 1; no further increases in net working capital are anticipated. The new unit will be depreciated on a straight-line basis over 5 years to a zero balance. OFC expects to sell the existing unit for $275,000. OFC's marginal tax rate is 40 percent.

If OFC purchases the new unit, annual revenues are expected to increase by $100,000 in the first year and by $150,000 in the second year relative to the old unit. The increases are attributable to greater processing capacity. Sales in year 3 and beyond are anticipated to remain at the same level as year 2's projections. The annual operating costs (exclusive of depreciation) for the new unit are expected to be $20,000 less than if the old unit were kept. After 5 years, the new unit will be completely depreciated and is expected to be sold for $70,000. (Assume that the existing unit is being depreciated at a rate of $50,000 per year.)

a. Calculate the project's net investment.

b. Calculate the annual net cash flows for the project.

Problems

1. Johnson Products is considering purchasing a new milling machine that costs $100,000. The machine's installation and shipping costs will total $2,500. If accepted, the milling machine project will require an initial net working capital investment of $20,000. Johnson plans to depreciate the machine on a straight-line basis over a period of 8 years. About a year ago, Johnson paid $10,000 to a consulting firm to conduct a feasibility study of the new milling machine. Johnson's marginal tax rate is 40 percent.

BASIC

a. Calculate the project's net investment (NINV).

b. Calculate the annual straight-line depreciation for the project.

BASIC

2. A new machine costing $100,000 is expected to save the McKaig Brick Company $15,000 per year for 12 years before depreciation and taxes. The machine will be depreciated on a straight-line basis for a 12-year period to an estimated salvage value of $0. The firm's marginal tax rate is 40 percent. What are the annual net cash flows associated with the purchase of this machine? Also compute the net investment (NINV) for this project.

BASIC

3. The Taylor Mountain Uranium Company currently has annual cash revenues of $1.2 million and annual cash expenses of $700,000. Depreciation amounts to $200,000 per year. These figures are expected to remain constant for the foreseeable future (at least 15 years). The firm's marginal tax rate is 40 percent.

A new high-speed processing unit costing $1.2 million is being considered as a potential investment designed to increase the firm's output capacity. This new piece of equipment will have an estimated usable life of 10 years and a $0 estimated salvage value. If the processing unit is bought, Taylor's annual revenues are expected to increase to $1.6 million and annual expenses (exclusive of depreciation) will increase to $900,000. Annual depreciation will increase to $320,000. Assume that no increase in net working capital will be required as a result of this project. Compute the project's annual net cash flows for the next 10 years, assuming that the new processing unit is purchased. Also compute the net investment (NINV) for this project.

INTERMEDIATE

4. A firm has an opportunity to invest in a new device that will replace two of the firm's older machines. The new device costs $570,000 and requires an additional outlay of $30,000 to cover installation and shipping. The new device will require the firm to increase its net working capital by $20,000. Both the old machines can be sold—the first for $100,000 (book value equals $95,000) and the second for $150,000 (book value equals $75,000). The original cost of the first machine was $200,000, and the original cost of the second machine was $140,000. The firm's marginal tax bracket is 40 percent. Compute the net investment for this project.

INTERMEDIATE

5. Five years ago, the Mori Foods Company acquired a bean-processing machine. The machine cost $30,000 and is being depreciated using the straight-line method over a 10-year period to an estimated salvage value of $0. A new, improved processor is now available, and the firm is considering making a switch. The firm's marginal tax rate is 40 percent. What are the after-tax cash flow effects of selling the old processing unit if it can be sold for the following prices?

a. $15,000

b. $5,000

c. $26,000

d. $32,000

INTERMEDIATE

6. Nguyen, Inc. is considering the purchase of a new computer system (ICX) for $130,000. The system will require an additional $30,000 for installation. If the new computer is purchased it will replace an old system that has been fully depreciated. The new system will be depreciated over a period of 10 years using straight-line depreciation. If the ICX is purchased, the old system will be sold for $20,000. The ICX system, which has a useful life of 10 years, is expected to increase revenues by $32,000 *per year* over its useful life. Operating costs are expected to decrease by $2,000 *per year* over the life of the system. The firm is taxed at a 40 percent marginal rate.

a. What net investment is required to acquire the ICX system and replace the old system?

b. Compute the annual net cash flows associated with the purchase of the ICX system.

7. Two years ago, Agro, Inc. purchased an ACE generator that cost $250,000. Agro had to pay an additional $50,000 for delivery and installation, and the investment in the generator required the firm to increase its net working capital position by $25,000. The generator, which is being depreciated over a period of 5 years using straight-line depreciation, has a current market value of $79,550. The firm's marginal tax rate is 40 percent. If the firm liquidates the asset for its current market value, compute the after-tax proceeds from the sale of the asset.

8. Benford, Inc. is planning to open a new sporting goods store in a suburban mall. Benford will lease the needed space in the mall. Equipment and fixtures for the store will cost $200,000 and be depreciated over a 5-year period on a straight-line basis to $0. The new store will require Benford to increase its net working capital by $200,000 at time 0, thereafter, net working capital balances are expected to equal 20 percent of the following year's sales. First-year sales are expected to be $1 million and to increase at an annual rate of 8 percent over the expected 10-year life of the store. Operating expenses (including lease payments and excluding depreciation) are projected to equal 70 percent of sales. The salvage value of the store's equipment and fixtures is anticipated to be $10,000 at the end of 10 years. Benford's marginal tax rate is 40 percent.

a. Compute the net investment required for Benford.

b. Compute the annual net cash flows for the 10-year projected life of the store.

9. Argyl Manufacturing is evaluating the possibility of expanding its operations. This expansion will require the purchase of land at a cost of $100,000. A new building will cost $100,000 and be depreciated on a straight-line basis over 20 years to a salvage value of $0. Actual land salvage at the end of 20 years is expected to be $200,000. Actual building salvage at the end of 20 years is expected to be $150,000. Equipment for the facility is expected to cost $250,000. Installation costs will be an additional $40,000 and shipping costs will be $10,000. This equipment will be depreciated using the straight-line method over a 10-year period. Actual estimated salvage at the end of 20 years is $0. The project will require net working capital of $70,000 initially (year 0), an additional $40,000 at the end of year 1, and an additional $40,000 at the end of year 2. The project is expected to generate increased EBIT (operating income) for the firm of $100,000 during year 1. Annual EBIT is expected to grow at a rate of 4 percent per year until the project terminates at the end of year 20. The marginal tax rate is 40 percent. Compute the initial net investment and the annual net cash flow from the project in year 20.

10. Homecraft Stores (HSI), which operates a chain of retail warehouse-type stores, is considering opening a new store in the Tampa area. The store itself will cost $7,000,000 to build. In addition, fixtures for the store are expected to cost $700,000 and installation of the fixtures is estimated to cost another $50,000. Initial net working capital (primarily due to inventory) is expected to be $600,000. HSI plans to build the Tampa store on land it purchased 5 years

ago for $200,000. The land currently is worth $500,000 and it is assumed that if the store were not built the land would be sold. Calculate the net investment for the proposed Tampa store.

CHALLENGE **11.** Ralph's Bow Works (RBW) is planning to add a new line of bow ties that will require the acquisition of a new knitting and tying machine. The machine will cost $1,000,000. It will be depreciated over 10 years to a zero salvage value using the straight-line method. Interest costs associated with financing the equipment purchase are estimated to be $50,000 per year. The expected salvage value of the machine at the end of 10 years is $50,000. The decision to add the new line of bow ties will require additional net working capital of $50,000 immediately, $25,000 at the end of year 1, and $10,000 at the end of year 2. RBW expects to sell $300,000 worth of the bow ties during each of the 10 years of product life. RBW expects the sales of its other ties to decline by $25,000 (in year 1) as a result of adding this new line of ties. The lost sales level will remain constant at $25,000 over the 10-year life of the proposed project. The cost of producing and selling the ties is estimated to be $50,000 per year. RBW will realize savings of $5,000 each year because of lost sales on its other tie lines. The marginal tax rate is 40 percent. Compute the net investment (year 0) and the net cash flows for years 1 and 10 for this project.

INTERMEDIATE **12.** Bratton Stone Works is considering an expansion proposal that will require an outlay of $1 million for land and $5 million for equipment. The equipment will be depreciated over 8 years to a zero salvage value using the straight-line method. The life of the project is expected to be 10 years. The actual salvage value of the equipment at the end of 10 years is expected to be $1 million. At the end of 10 years, Bratton hopes to sell the land for $1,800,000. Revenues from the project are expected to be $700,000 per year. Operating costs are expected to be $200,000 per year. The ordinary and capital gains tax rate for Bratton is 40 percent. The project will require an additional investment in working capital of $250,000 in year 0 and $150,000 at the end of year 1. What net cash flow will this project produce in year 10?

CHALLENGE **13.** Clyne Industries wants to market its new Slammin Jammin Basketball Goal Set. To bring this product to the market will require the purchase of equipment costing $650,000. Shipping and installation expenses associated with the equipment are estimated to be $50,000. Additional net working capital investments of $50,000 will be required at time 0, $25,000 in year 1, and $10,000 in year 2. Revenues are expected to be $250,000 in year 1 and grow at a rate of $25,000 per year through year 5, and then decline by $25,000 per year until the project is terminated at the end of year 10. Annual operating expenses are expected to be $80,000 in year 1 and to grow at a rate of $10,000 per year until the end of the project life. Depreciation will be determined using the straight-line method over 10 years with an assumed zero salvage value. The actual salvage value of the equipment at the end of 10 years is expected to be $50,000. The marginal, ordinary tax rate is 40 percent and the capital gains tax rate is 30 percent. Compute the expected net cash flow for year 10, the last year in the life of the project.

CHALLENGE **14.** Hurley's Winery is planning to acquire a new grape masher. The masher will cost $100,000 including shipping and installation and will be depreciated over 8 years using the straight-line method. At the time the masher is purchased, Hurley will have to invest $5,000 in net working capital. Additional investments in net working capital are required at the end of year 1 of $3,000 and year 2 of $2,000. Net revenues attributable to the masher are expected to total $25,000 during year 1 and to grow by 5 percent per annum through the end of year 6. After that time, revenues are expected to decline by 10 percent per annum. Annual year 1 cash operating expenses are expected to total $10,000 and grow at an annual rate of 10 percent per annum. Hurley expects to sell the masher at the end of year 7 for $10,000. The marginal tax rate for Hurley is 40 percent for ordinary income and 28 percent for capital gains. Compute the expected net cash flows for year 7. Include in your year 7 calculations the proceeds from the salvage value of the masher and recovery of net working capital at the end of year 7.

CHAPTER

10 Capital Budgeting Decision Criteria and Risk Analysis

This chapter looks at some widely used capital budgeting decision models, discussing and illustrating their relative strengths and weaknesses. In addition, we explore some of the available methods for evaluating the risk of capital budgeting projects. When combined with the cash flow procedures developed in Chapter 9 and the time value of money procedures developed in Chapter 5, the models we cover in this chapter provide the basis for making capital expenditure decisions. As mentioned in the previous chapter, there are two steps in capital budgeting analysis. The first step, covered in the last chapter, is the estimation of the cash flows. The second step, the focus of this chapter, is the evaluation of the feasibility of the project on the basis of the cash flows estimated.

Chapter Objectives

Upon completion of this chapter, you should have mastered the following:

1. Know and be able to apply several widely used capital budgeting evaluation methods.

2. Be aware of the relative merits and limitations of the different capital budgeting evaluation methods.

3. Have an understanding of how to account for and evaluate differences in riskiness of projects.

4. Understand the effects of inflation in capital budgeting analysis.

SOME TERMS AND CONCEPTS IN CAPITAL BUDGETING

Before proceeding with the discussion of the capital budgeting evaluation methods, it is necessary to introduce a number of terms and concepts encountered in this chapter.

Cost of Capital

A firm's cost of capital (or weighted average cost of capital) *is defined as the cost of the funds supplied to it.* It also is termed the *required rate of return* or *hurdle rate,* because it specifies the minimum necessary rate of return required by the firm's investors. In this context, the firm's cost of capital serves as a hurdle rate in deciding which capital investment projects are acceptable. However, this assumes that the projects being evaluated are of average risk relative to the projects the firm is currently engaged in. In this chapter, it is assumed that the cost of capital is a known value. Chapter 11 explores the methods used to determine the cost of capital.

How Projects Are Classified

A firm usually encounters several different types of projects when making capital expenditure decisions, including *independent projects* and *mutually exclusive projects.*

An *independent project is one whose acceptance or rejection does not directly eliminate other projects from consideration.* For example, a firm may be considering the installation of a new telephone communications system in its headquarters and replacing a drill press at a factory location around the same time. In the absence of a constraint on the availability of funds, both projects could be adopted if they meet minimum investment criteria.

A *mutually exclusive project is one whose acceptance precludes the acceptance of one or more alternative proposals.* Because two or more mutually exclusive projects have the capacity to perform the same function for a firm, only one should be chosen. For example, in 2002 the Dutch airline, KLM, was considering replacing its fleet of long-haul planes with Boeing 767s, Airbus A320s, or a combination of both. The three alternatives are mutually exclusive.

Availability of Funds

When a firm has adequate funds to invest in all projects that meet some capital budgeting selection criterion, such as has been true for Philip Morris (now Altria) in recent years, the firm is said to be operating without a *funds constraint*. Frequently, however, firms have acceptable projects whose total initial cost is greater than the total funds the firm has available to invest in capital projects. This necessitates *capital rationing,* or setting limits on capital expenditures, and results in some special capital budgeting problems.

DECISION MODELS FOR EVALUATING CAPITAL EXPENDITURES

Four criteria are commonly used for evaluating and selecting investment projects. These are:

➤ Net Present Value (NPV)
➤ Internal Rate of Return (IRR)
➤ Profitability Index (PI)
➤ Payback Period (PB)

The first three approaches are all based on the capitalization of cash flow/ discounted cash flow technique. The last approach is a much simpler view of project feasibility that does not rely upon the discounted cash flow technique. In the remainder of the chapter we will cover the mechanics of how to apply these techniques to project evaluation and their relative merits and problems.

Net Present Value

The *net present value (NPV)* of a capital expenditure project is defined as the *present value of the stream of net cash flows from the project minus the project's net investment*. The cash flows are discounted at the firm's required rate of return—at its cost of capital. As we said earlier, a firm's cost of capital is defined as its minimum acceptable rate of return for projects of average risk.

The net present value of a project may be expressed as

(10.1)
$$\text{NPV} = \sum_{t=1}^{n} \frac{\text{NCF}_t}{(1 + k)^t} - \text{NINV}$$

or, using the present value interest factor tables, as

(10.2)
$$\text{NPV} = \sum_{t=1}^{n} \text{NCF}_t \times \text{PVIF}_{k,t} - \text{NINV}$$

where NCF_t is the net cash flow for year t of the project's life which extends over n years, k is the cost of capital, and NINV is the net investment that occurs in year 0.

e-Lecture

To illustrate net present value calculations, suppose a firm is considering two projects, A and B, having net investments and net cash flows as shown in Table 10.1. The net present value computations for the two projects are presented in Table 10.2. These calculations assume a 14 percent cost of capital. The calculations in these tables also assume that cash flows are received at the end of each year, rather than as a flow during the year. This assumption, although a normal one, tends to slightly understate a project's net present value (and its internal rate of return and profitability index). Project A is shown in Table 10.2 to have a negative net present value ($-1,387$), and Project B has a positive net present value ($7,735$). The NPV also may be calculated using a financial calculator as shown below, yielding $-1,391.66$ and $7,738.23$ for Projects A and B, respectively. (Note that these values differ from those calculated in Table 10.2 because of round off errors in the present value tables.)

Table 10.1 Sample Project Cash Flows

Year	Project A Net Cash Flows (NCF)	Project B Net Cash Flows (NCF)
1	$12,500	$ 5,000
2	12,500	10,000
3	12,500	15,000
4	12,500	15,000
5	12,500	25,000
6	12,500	30,000
Net investment (NINV)	$50,000	$50,000

Table 10.2 Sample Net Present Value Calculations

Project A

Present value (PV) of an annuity of
$12,500 for 6 years at 14 percent:

$$\text{PV of NCF} = \$12,500 \,(\text{PVIFA}_{14,6})$$
$$= \$12,500 \,(3.889)^{\dagger}$$
$$- \$48,613$$

Project B

Year	NCF	$PVIF_{14,t}$*	PV of NCF
1	$5,000	0.877	$ 4,385
2	10,000	0.769	7,690
3	15,000	0.675	10,125
4	15,000	0.592	8,880
5	25,000	0.519	12,975
6	30,000	0.456	13,680
			57,735

Project A:
Less Net investment (NINV) 50,000
Net Present Value (NPV) $−1,387

Project B:
Less Net investment (NINV)   50,000
Net Present Value (NPV) $ 7,735

*From the PVIF table (Table II).
†From the PVIFA table (Table IV).

To calculate the NPV of a project using the calculator, you will need to use the cash flow (CF) keys or the cash flow worksheet.

Project A:

Enter: −50,000   12,500   14

| CF_0 | CF_{1-6} | I/Y |

Calculator

Solution

Compute: NPV   = − 1,391.66

Project B:

Enter: −50,000   5,000   10,000

| CF_0 | CF_1 | CF_2 |

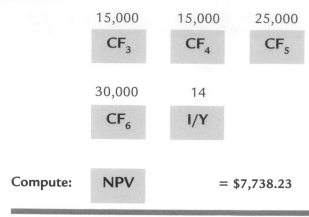

15,000		15,000		25,000	
CF₃		**CF₄**		**CF₅**	

$$CF_3 \quad CF_4 \quad CF_5$$

30,000　　　14

$$CF_6 \qquad I/Y$$

Compute:　**NPV**　　　= **$7,738.23**

Spreadsheet software may also be used to solve for NPV as illustrated.

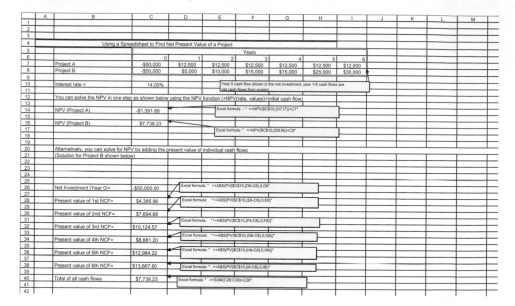

	A	B	C	D	E	F	G	H	I	J	K	L	M
4		Using a Spreadsheet to Find Net Present Value of a Project											
5						Years							
6			0	1	2	3	4	5	6				
7		Project A	-$50,000	$12,500	$12,500	$12,500	$12,500	$12,500	$12,500				
8		Project B	-$50,000	$5,000	$10,000	$15,000	$15,000	$25,000	$30,000				
10		Interest rate =	14.00%		Year 0 cash flow shown is the net investment, year 1-6 cash flows are								
11					net cash flows from project.								
12		You can solve the NPV in one step as shown below using the NPV function (+NPV(rate, values)+initial cash flow)											
14		NPV (Project A)	-$1,391.66		Excel formula : " =+NPV($C$10,(D7:I7))+C7"								
16		NPV (Project B)	$7,738.23										
17					Excel formula: " =+NPV($C$10,(D8:I8))+C8"								
20		Alternatively, you can solve for NPV by adding the present value of individual cash flows											
21		(Solution for Project B shown below)											
26		Net Investment (Year 0)=	-$50,000.00	Excel formula: " =+ABS(PV($C$10,(D6-C6),0,D8"									
28		Present value of 1st NCF=	$4,385.96	Excel formula: " =+ABS(PV($C$10,(E6-C6),0,E8)"									
30		Present value of 2nd NCF=	$7,694.68										
32		Present value of 3rd NCF=	$10,124.57	Excel formula: " =+ABS(PV($C$10,(F6-C6),0,F8))"									
34		Present value of 4th NCF=	$8,881.20	Excel formula: " =+ABS(PV($C$10,(G6-C6),0,G8))"									
36		Present value of 5th NCF=	$12,984.22	Excel formula: " =+ABS(PV($C$10,(H6-C6),0,H8))"									
38		Present value of 6th NCF=	$13,667.60	Excel formula: " =+ABS(PV($C$10,(I6-C6),0,I8))"									
40		Total of all cash flows	$7,738.23	Excel formula: " =+SUM(C28:C38)+C26"									

Decision Rule In general, a project should be accepted *if its net present value is greater than or equal to zero and rejected if its net present value is less than zero.* This is so because a positive net present value in principle translates directly into increases in stock prices and increases in shareholders' wealth. In the previous example, Project A would be rejected because it has a negative net present value, and Project B would be accepted because it has a positive net present value. The adoption of Project B would increase the firm's shareholder wealth by $7,735, while the adoption of Project A would result in decreasing shareholder wealth by $1,387.

To illustrate the impact on a per-share basis, assume that the firm adopting the project has 1,000 shares outstanding and that each share was trading for $50 prior to the announcement of the project adoption. The announcement of the adoption of Project B theoretically should result in an increase in stock price of $7.74 (net present value of project/number of shares outstanding or $7,735/1,000) to $57.74. This is the theoretical impact; the actual impact will depend on whether the announcement was previously anticipated by the market and by the market's assessment of the profitability of the project, which may differ from the firm's. If the adoption of the project was anticipated by the market (e.g., due to news leakage), then the actual announcement may be associated with only a slight or even no impact on share price. Also, if the market does not have the same information as the firm in assessing the profitability of Project B or if the market is more or less optimistic in its assessment of the information, then the actual share price reaction may differ from the theoretical impact. In the case of Project A, a similar announcement should result in a decline in share price of $1.39 ($1,387/1,000) to $48.61.

If two or more mutually exclusive investments have positive net present values, the project having the largest net present value is the one selected. Assume, for example, that a firm has three mutually exclusive investment opportunities (G, H, and I), each requiring a net investment of $10,000 and each having a 5-year expected economic life. Project G has a net present value of $2,000; H has a net present value of $4,000; and I has a net present value of $3,500. Of the three, H would be preferred over the other two because it has the highest net present value and therefore is expected to make the largest contribution to the objective of shareholder wealth maximization.

Advantages and Disadvantages of the Net Present Value Method The net present value of a project, as illustrated above, is the expected number of dollars by which the present value of the firm is increased as a result of adopting the project. Consequently, the net present value method is consistent with the goal of shareholder wealth maximization. The net present value approach considers both the magnitude and the timing of cash flows over a project's entire expected life.

The net present value approach also indicates whether a proposed project will yield the rate of return required by the firm's investors. The cost of capital represents this rate of return; when a project's net present value is greater than or equal to zero, the firm's investors can expect to earn at least their required rate of return.

The net present value criterion has a weakness: Many people find it difficult to work with a present value dollar return rather than with a percentage return. As a result, many firms use another present value–based method that is interpreted more easily; namely, the internal rate of return method.

Internal Rate of Return

The ***internal rate of return (IRR)*** is defined as the *discount rate that equates the present value of the net cash flows from a project with the present value of the net investment.* In other words, IRR is the discount rate that causes a project's net present value to equal zero. The internal rate of return for a capital expenditure project is conceptually similar to the yield to maturity for a bond investment that we covered in Chapter 7. Like the yield to maturity, the IRR tells you the yield you are receiving on an investment.

A project's internal rate of return can be determined by solving for r in the following equation:

$$0 = \sum_{t=1}^{n} \frac{\text{NCF}_t}{(1 + r)^t} - \text{NINV} \tag{10.3}$$

or, using the present value interest factor tables,

$$0 = \sum_{t=1}^{n} \text{NCF}_t \times \text{PVIF}_{r,t} - \text{NINV} \tag{10.4}$$

Note that this equation is identical to the equation for solving for NPV except that we are solving for the discount rate, r (the internal rate of return), that yields an NPV equal to zero. Equation 10.3 may be restated as

$$\text{NINV} = \sum_{t=1}^{n} \frac{\text{NCF}_t}{(1 + r)^t} \tag{10.5}$$

Figure 10.1
NPV Profiles: Relationship between the Net Present Value and the Internal Rate of Return for Projects A and B

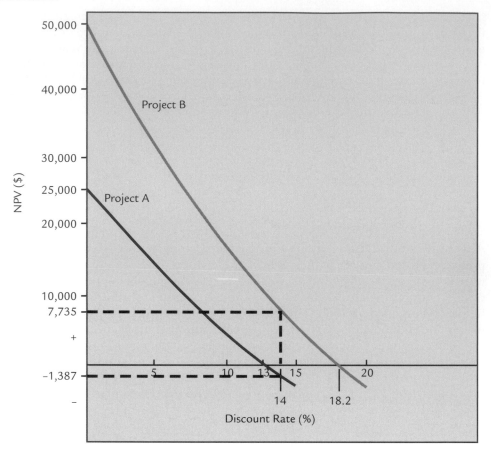

In this form, the internal rate of return is the discount rate that yields a present value of net cash flows *equal* to the net investment. The internal rate of return tells you the average annual rate of return the company would be earning over the life of the project if it were to invest an amount equal to the net investment on the project (this is true subject to the reinvestment rate assumption of the IRR, which is discussed later in the chapter).

Figure 10.1 illustrates the relationship between net present value and internal rate of return. The figure plots the net present values of Project B and Project A (from Table 10.2) at various discount rates. This type of graph is known as an *NPV profile*. Note that at a 14 percent cost of capital, the net present value of B is $7,735—the same figure that resulted from the computations performed in Table 10.2. The internal rate of return for Project B is approximately equal to 18.2 percent, which is the discount rate at which the NPV is equal to zero. Thus, the internal rate of return is a special case of the net present value computation. In the case of Project A note that the discount rate at which the NPV is equal to zero, or the IRR, is approximately 13 percent.

We will now demonstrate the calculation of the internal rate of return for Projects A and B. Because Project A is an annuity of $12,500 for 6 years requiring a net investment of $50,000, its internal rate of return may be computed directly with the aid of a PVIFA table, such as Table IV on the insert to this book. In this case, the present value of the annuity, $PVAN_0$, is $50,000; the annuity payment, PMT, is $12,500; and $n = 6$ years. The following equation,

$$PVAN_0 = PMT(PVIFA_{r,n}) \qquad\qquad (10.6)$$

can be rewritten to solve for the PVIFA:

$$PVIFA_{r,n} = \frac{PVAN_0}{PMT} \qquad\qquad (10.7)$$

In this case, PVIFA = \$50,000/\$12,500 = 4.000. Referring to Table IV and reading across the table for $n = 6$, it can be seen that the interest factor of 4.000 occurs near 13 percent, where the value is 3.998. Thus, the internal rate of return for Project A is about 13 percent.

The internal rate of return for Project B is more difficult to calculate because the project is expected to yield uneven cash flows. In this case calculating the internal rate of return is a trial-and-error procedure. The steps to this algorithm are as follows:

1. Select a starting value for the discount rate; 10 percent is as a good a starting point as any.
2. Next, calculate the NPV using Equation 10.1 or 10.2.
3. If the NPV is positive, you know that the discount rate should be adjusted higher in order to obtain an NPV of zero. On the other hand, if the resulting NPV is negative, you should use a lower discount rate to get the NPV to equal zero. Accordingly, increment the discount rate up or down until you have identified the discount rate that yields an NPV equal to zero.

Let's apply this algorithm to Project B. The NPV for Project B at a discount rate of 10 percent is given by:

$$= \$5,000\ (PVIF_{10,1}) + \$10,000\ (PVIF_{10,2}) + \$15,000\ (PVIF_{10,3}) + \$15,000$$
$$(PVIF_{10,4}) + \$25,000\ (PVIF_{10,5}) + \$30,000\ (PVIF_{10,6}) - \$50,000$$
$$= \$66,760 - \$50,000$$
$$= \$16,760$$

Since this is positive let's try a higher discount rate, say 14 percent:

$$= \$5,000\ (PVIF_{14,1}) + \$10,000\ (PVIF_{14,2}) + \$15,000\ (PVIF_{14,3}) + \$15,000$$
$$(PVIF_{14,4}) + \$25,000\ (PVIF_{14,5}) + \$30,000\ (PVIF_{14,6}) - \$50,000$$
$$= \$57,735 - \$50,000$$
$$= \$7,735$$

The NPV is still positive, therefore let's try an even higher discount rate of 19 percent:

$$= \$5,000\ (PVIF_{19,1}) + \$10,000\ (PVIF_{19,2}) + \$15,000\ (PVIF_{19,3}) + \$15,000$$
$$(PVIF_{19,4}) + \$25,000\ (PVIF_{19,5}) + \$30,000\ (PVIF_{19,6}) - \$50,000$$
$$= \$48,675 - \$50,000$$
$$= -\$1,325$$

The NPV is now negative, so try a lower discount rate of 18 percent:

$$= \$5,000\ (PVIF_{18,1}) + \$10,000\ (PVIF_{18,2}) + \$15,000\ (PVIF_{18,3}) + \$15,000$$
$$(PVIF_{18,4}) + \$25,000\ (PVIF_{18,5}) + \$30,000\ (PVIF_{18,6}) - \$50,000$$
$$= \$50,315 - \$50,000$$
$$= \$315$$

The NPV now is positive. Because the present value factors are provided only for whole percentages, the best we can do using the tables is to show that the IRR for project B is between 18 and 19 percent.

Using a financial calculator yields the precise answers of 12.98 percent and 18.19 percent for the IRR of Projects A and B as shown below, not to mention that it is also quicker to calculate.

To calculate the IRR of a project using the calculator enter the cash flows as you would for NPV and then compute the IRR.

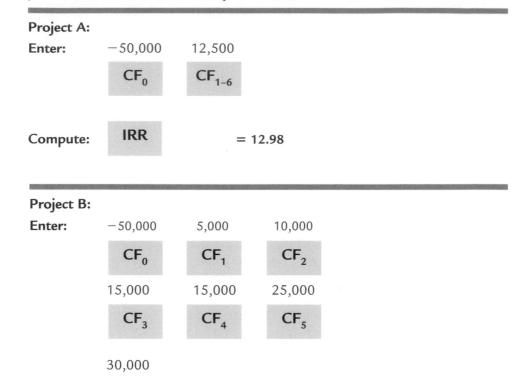

Calculator

Solution

Project A:

Enter: −50,000   12,500

                CF$_0$ CF$_{1-6}$

Compute: IRR   = 12.98

Project B:

Enter: −50,000   5,000   10,000

                CF$_0$ CF$_1$ CF$_2$

           15,000   15,000   25,000

                CF$_3$ CF$_4$ CF$_5$

           30,000

                CF$_6$

Compute: IRR   = 18.19

The IRR may also be solved using spreadsheet software as shown on next page.

Decision Rule Generally, when considering independent projects, the internal rate of return method indicates that a *project whose internal rate of return is greater than or equal to the firm's cost of capital should be accepted, whereas a project whose internal rate of return is less than the firm's cost of capital should be rejected.* In the case of Projects A and B, using a cost of capital of 14 percent, B would be acceptable and A would be unacceptable.

When two or more *mutually exclusive projects* are being considered, it is *generally* preferable to accept the project having the highest internal rate of return as long as it is greater than or equal to the cost of capital. Assuming Projects A and B were mutually exclusive and the *cost of capital were 12 percent*, B would be chosen over A as it has the higher IRR even though both projects meet the minimum required rate of return standard.

Advantages and Disadvantages of the Internal Rate of Return Method The internal rate of return and net present value methods are the two most widely used capital budgeting techniques used in industry. In a 1999 survey of 392 Chief Financial

	A	B	C	D	E	F	G	H	I
1									
2									
3		Using a Spreadsheet to Find Internal Rate of Return of a Project							
4					Years				
5			0	1	2	3	4	5	6
6		Project A	-$50,000	$12,500	$12,500	$12,500	$12,500	$12,500	$12,500
7		Project B	-$50,000	$5,000	$10,000	$15,000	$15,000	$25,000	$30,000
8									
9		Interest rate =	14.00%						
10					Excel formula used (+IRR (Values, Guess)):				
11					"=+IRR(C6:I6,10)"				
12		IRR (Project A)	12.98%						
13									
14		IRR (Project B)	18.19%						
15									
16					Excel formula used (+IRR (Values, Guess)):				
17					"=+IRR(C7:I7,10)"				
18									

Officers (CFOs) from a broad cross section of firms in the United States, two researchers, Graham and Harvey, document that 74.9 percent of the respondents always or almost always use the NPV and 75.7 percent always or almost always use the IRR to evaluate capital budgeting proposals.[1] Although the NPV is theoretically superior, the popularity of the internal rate of return method may be due to the fact that some people feel more comfortable dealing with the concept of a project's percentage rate of return than with its dollar amount of net present value. Like the net present value approach, the internal rate of return technique takes into account both the magnitude and the timing of cash flows over the entire life of a project in measuring the project's economic desirability.

However, some potential problems are involved in using the internal rate of return technique. The possible existence of *multiple internal rates of return* is one such problem. Whereas equating the net present value of a project to zero will yield only one internal rate of return, *r*, for projects with *conventional cash flows*, there are times when two or more rates may be obtained. Recall that conventional cash flows occur when an initial cash outlay (net investment) is followed by a stream of positive net cash flows. If for some reason—such as large abandonment costs at the end of a project's life or a major shutdown and rebuilding of a facility sometime during its life—the initial net investment is followed by one or more positive net cash flows (inflows) that then are followed by a negative cash flow, it is possible to obtain more than one internal rate of return.

Consider the following investment, which has three internal rates of return— 0, 100, and 200 percent:

Year	Net Cash Flows
0	$-1,000
1	+6,000
2	-11,000
3	+6,000

Using a calculator to solve the IRR for the above cash flow yields 0 percent; however, 100 and 200 percent are also valid. To convince yourself, enter 100 and 200 as

Spreadsheet strategies

[1]Graham, John R., and Campbell R. Harvey, 2001, "The Theory and Practice of Corporate Finance: Evidence from the Field," *Journal of Financial Economics*, 60 (May/June), pp. 187–243.

the discount rates and solve for the NPVs, they should both yield an NPV of $0. In some instances where cash flows have multiple IRRs, the calculator may return an error message.

Unfortunately, none of these rates can be compared to the firm's cost of capital to determine the project's acceptability. Although several techniques have been proposed for dealing with the multiple internal rate of return problem, none provide a simple, complete, and generally satisfactory solution. The best approach in this case is to use the net present value criterion. If a project's net present value is positive, it is acceptable; if it is negative, it is not acceptable. Many financial calculators and software packages are available that compute internal rates of return, and they will usually warn the user when a potential multiple internal rate of return problem exists. Whenever this is a possibility, the use of the net present value method is preferred.

Net Present Value versus Internal Rate of Return: The Reinvestment Rate Assumption

Both the net present value and the internal rate of return methods result in identical decisions to either accept or reject an independent project with conventional cash flows. This is true because the net present value is greater than (less than) zero if—and only if—the internal rate of return is greater than (less than) the required rate of return, k. In the case of mutually exclusive projects with conventional cash flows, however, the two methods may yield contradictory results; one project may have a *higher* internal rate of return than another and, at the same time, a *lower* net present value.

Consider, for example, mutually exclusive Projects L and M, described in the following table. Both require a net investment, NINV, of $1,000. Using the internal rate of return approach, Project L, with an IRR of 21.6 percent, is preferred compared with Project M with an IRR of 18.3 percent. Using the net present value approach with a discount rate of 5 percent, Project M is preferred to Project L. Hence, it is necessary to determine which technique is the correct one to use in this situation.

	Project L	Project M
NINV	$1,000	$1,000
NCF:		
Year 1	$667	$0
Year 2	$667	$1,400
NPV at 5%	$240	$270
IRR	21.6%	18.3%

The outcome depends on what *assumptions* the decision maker chooses to make about the *implied reinvestment rate* for the net cash flows generated from each project. Both the NPV and the IRR methods assume that the net cash flows generated by the projects are reinvested at an assumed rate of return. The net present value assumes that the *cash flows are reinvested at the cost of capital, k*, whereas the internal rate of return assumes that the *cash flows are reinvested at the computed internal rate of return, r*. The difference in the reinvestment rate assumptions between the net present value and the internal rate of return can lead to conflicts in the rankings between the two methods. This can be seen in Figure 10.2, which shows the NPV profiles for Project M and Project L. Note that the NPV profiles for the two projects *cross over* (at a discount rate of 10 percent), suggesting a potential conflict in the rankings between the NPV and IRR methods. For discount (reinvestment) rates below 10 percent, Pro-

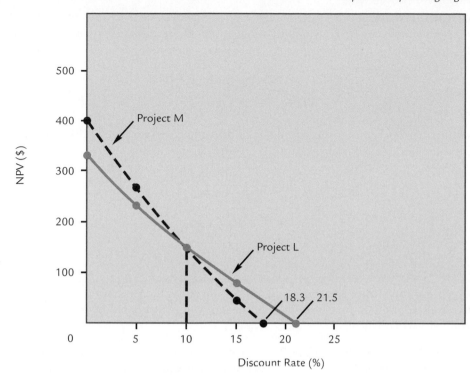

Figure 10.2
NPV Profiles: Net Present Value versus Internal Rate of Return for Mutually Exclusive Alternatives

ject M has a higher net present value than Project L and therefore is the preferred project. For discount rates greater than 10 percent, Project L is preferred using both the net present value and internal rate of return approaches. Hence, a conflict only occurs in this case for discount (cost-of-capital) rates below 10 percent. Generally, the cost of capital is considered to be a more *realistic* reinvestment rate than the computed internal rate of return because the cost of capital is the ***opportunity cost*** of capital for the firm. This is the rate the market expects the firm to earn based on its risk. Alternatively, if we think of a particular project as being a one-shot project— that there is no scope for further expansion or reinvestment at the same rate of return as the original investment—then it does not make sense to assume that the cash flows from the project can be reinvested to yield the internal rate of return. It would be more reasonable to assume that the cash flows can be reinvested elsewhere in the firm or in some other project at the firm's cost of capital.

In view of these problems, *the net present value approach is normally superior to the internal rate of return when choosing among mutually exclusive investments.*

Comprehension Check Questions

1. Distinguish between independent and mutually exclusive projects.
2. What is capital rationing?
3. How do you interpret a positive (negative) NPV?
4. What is the decision rule when using the IRR to assess a project?
5. What is the reinvestment rate assumption for IRR and NPV? How does the difference in reinvestment rate assumption between NPV and IRR affect their relative merits?

Profitability Index

The *profitability index (PI),* or benefit–cost ratio, is the *ratio of the present value of expected net cash flows over the life of a project to the net investment.* It is expressed as follows:

(10.8)
$$PI = \frac{\sum_{t=1}^{n} NCF_t / (1 + k)^t}{NINV}$$

Assuming a 14 percent cost of capital, *k,* and using the data from Table 10.2, the profitability index for Projects A and B can be calculated as follows:

$$PI_A = \frac{\$48,613}{\$50,000}$$
$$= 0.97$$

$$PI_B = \frac{\$57,735}{\$50,000}$$
$$= 1.15$$

The profitability index is interpreted as the present value return *for each dollar of initial investment.* In comparison, the net present value approach measures *the total present value dollar return.*

Decision Rule According to the PI criterion, a project whose *profitability index is greater than or equal to 1 is considered acceptable, whereas a project having a profitability index less than 1 is considered unacceptable.* In the case of the illustrative problem above, Project B is acceptable; Project A is not. When two or more independent projects with conventional cash flows are considered, the profitability index, net present value, and internal rate of return approaches all will yield identical accept–reject signals; this is true, for example, with Projects A and B.

When dealing with mutually exclusive investments, conflicts may arise between the net present value and the profitability index criteria. This is most likely to occur if the alternative projects require significantly different net investments. Consider, for example, the following information on Projects J and K. According to the net present value criterion, Project J would be preferred because of its larger net present value. According to the profitability index criterion, Project K would be preferred.

	Project J	**Project K**
Present value of Net cash flows	$25,000	$14,000
Less Net investment	20,000	10,000
NPV	$5,000	$4,000
PI	1.25	1.40

When a conflict arises, the final decision must be made on the basis of other factors. For example, if a firm has no constraint on the funds available to it for capital investment—that is, no capital rationing—the net present value approach is preferred because it will select the projects that are expected to generate the largest *total dollar* increase in the firm's wealth and, by extension, maximize shareholder wealth. If, however, the firm is in a capital rationing situation and capital budgeting is being done for only one period, the profitability index approach may be preferred because it will indicate which projects will maximize the returns *per dollar of investment*—an appropriate objective when a funds constraint exists.

Payback Period

The *payback period (PB)* of an investment is the *period of time required for the cumulative net cash flows from a project to equal the net investment.* In other words the PB tells you how many years it would take to recover the initial investment. If the expected net cash flows are *equal* each year, then the payback period is equal to the ratio of the net investment to the annual net cash flows of the project:

$$PB = \frac{NINV}{NCF} \qquad (10.9)$$

When the annual net cash flows are not equal each year, slightly more complex calculations are required to compute the payback period. In this case, the analyst must add up the yearly net cash flows until the cumulative total equals the net investment. The number of years it takes for this to occur is the project's payback period.

Table 10.3 illustrates the calculation of payback periods for projects A and B, which were presented earlier in this section. The computed PB period is 4 years for Project A and 4.20 years for Project B.

Decision Rule The PB decision criterion states that a *project should be accepted if its payback period is less than or equal to a specified maximum period. Otherwise, it should be rejected.* Each company should decide what the maximum payback period should be. Thus, if the payback period is 4 years, Project A should be accepted but Project B should be rejected.

Advantages and Disadvantages of the Payback Method The payback method suffers from the following serious disadvantages. First, the payback method gives equal weight to all net cash flows within the payback period, regardless of when they occur during the period. In other words, *the technique ignores the time value of money.*

Table 10.3 Payback Period Calculations

	Project A (NINV = $50,000)			Project B (NINV = $50,000)	
Year (t)	Net Cash Flow	Cumulative Net Cash Flow	Year (t)	Net Cash Flow	Cumulative Net Cash Flow
1	$12,500	$12,500	1	$5,000	$ 5,000
2	12,500	25,000	2	10,000	15,000
3	12,500	37,500	3	15,000	30,000
4	12,500	50,000	4	15,000	45,000
5	12,500	62,500	5	25,000	70,000
6	12,500	75,500	6	30,000	100,000

$$PB = \frac{\text{Net investment}}{\text{Annual net cash flow}} = \frac{50,000}{12,500} = 4 \text{ years}$$

$$PB = \begin{pmatrix}\text{Number of years before full recovery of net investment}\end{pmatrix} + \frac{\text{Unrecovered initial investment at start of year}}{\text{Net cash flow during year}}$$

$$= 4 + \frac{(50,000 - 45,000)}{25,000} = 4.20 \text{ years}$$

Assume, for example, that a firm is considering two projects, E and F, each costing $10,000. Project E is expected to yield net cash flows over a 3-year period of $6,000 during the first year, $4,000 during the second year, and $3,000 during the third year. Project F is expected to yield net cash flows of $4,000 during the first year, $6,000 during the second year, and $3,000 during the third year. Viewed from the payback perspective, these projects are equally attractive, yet the net present value technique (which accounts for the time value of money) clearly indicates that Project E increases the value of the firm more than Project F.

Second, the payback method essentially ignores cash flows occurring after the payback period. Thus, payback figures are biased against long-term projects and can be misleading. For example, suppose a firm is considering two projects, C and D, each costing $10,000. It is expected that Project C will generate net cash flows of $5,000 per year for 3 years and that Project D will generate net cash flows of $4,500 per year forever. The PB period for Project C is 2 years ($10,000/ $5,000), whereas the PB period for Project D is 2.2 years ($10,000/$4,500). If these projects were mutually exclusive, payback would favor C because it has the lower payback period. Yet Project D clearly has a higher net present value than Project C.

Third, payback provides no *objective* criterion for decision making that is consistent with shareholder wealth maximization. The payback method may reject projects with positive net present values. The choice of an acceptable payback period is largely a *subjective* one; different people or firms using essentially identical data may make different accept–reject decisions about a project. The NPV, IRR, and PI, on the other hand, rely on the cost of capital, an objective criterion, as the hurdle rate. Since the cost of capital is the rate of return required by the firm's capital holders, accepting projects that exceed the cost of capital is consistent with maximizing shareholder wealth.

The payback method is sometimes justified on the basis that it provides a measure of the *risk* associated with a project. Although it is true that less risk may be associated with a shorter payback period than with a longer one, risk is thought of best in terms of the *variability* of project returns. Because payback ignores this dimension, it is at best a crude tool for risk analysis.

A more valid justification for the use of the payback method is that it gives some indication of a project's desirability from a *liquidity* perspective because it measures the time required for a firm to recover its initial investment in a project. A company that is very concerned about the early recovery of investment funds—such as one investing overseas in a politically unstable area—might find this method useful. Indeed many multinational businesses that operate in politically unstable areas of the world—such as certain countries in Eastern Europe, Latin America, Asia, and Africa—rely on the payback method as an important supplementary tool to assess the viability of a project. The primary method still would be one of the discounted cash flow models.

The payback method may also be useful in evaluating projects with small outlays that may not merit the time and effort associated with the more sophisticated discounted cash flow models. A company such as General Motors may have an annual capital expenditure of several hundreds of millions of dollars involving hundreds of projects, many of which may be of a routine nature or that involve small sums of money. Buying a forklift truck at a cost of $5,000 for one of General Motors' plants would constitute one such project. It would not be prudent for the plant manager to conduct a full-blown net present value analysis of the project. In such cases a simple payback period approach would suffice. As a matter of policy a company such as General Motors might use a payback criterion of 2 years to approve projects with outlays of less than $25,000.

Table 10.4 Summary of the Capital Budgeting Methods

Model	Project Acceptance Criterion	Strengths	Weakness
Net present value (NPV)	Accept project if project has a positive or zero NPV—if the present value of net cash flows, evaluated at the firm's cost of capital, equals or exceeds the net investment required.	Considers the timing of cash flows. Provides an objective, return-based criterion for acceptance or rejection. Most conceptually correct approach.	Difficulty in working with a dollar return value, rather than percentage returns.
Internal rate of return (IRR)	Accept project if IRR equals or exceeds the firm's cost of capital.	Same benefits as the NPV. Easy to interpret the meaning of IRR.	Multiple rates of return problem. Sometimes gives decision that conflicts with NPV.
Profitability index (PI)	Accept project if PI is greater than or equal to 1.0.	Same benefits as the NPV. Useful to guide decisions in capital rationing problems.	Sometimes gives decision that conflicts with NPV.
Payback (PB)	PB should not be used in deciding whether to accept or reject an investment project.	Easy and inexpensive to use. Provides a crude measure of project risk. Provides a measure of project liquidity.	No objective decision criterion. Fails to consider timing of cash flows.

Table 10.4 presents a summary of the four capital budgeting methods discussed in the chapter.

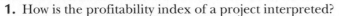

Comprehension Check Questions

1. How is the profitability index of a project interpreted?
2. What are the limitations of the payback method in evaluating capital budgeting projects?

ADJUSTING FOR RISK

In illustrating the concepts in this chapter, we assumed that the firm is investing in a project similar in risk to its existing business. For example, if Ford Motor Company were considering a capital budgeting project involving doubling of capacity at its Romeo, Michigan plant that manufactures the 4.6L-SOHC engines used in Mustang GT and other models, the project would be of similar risk to the firm's existing operations. In a situation like this it would be appropriate to use a discount rate equal to Ford Motor's cost of capital.

However, the firm's cost of capital is not an appropriate discount rate if the project risk is significantly different from the average risk for the firm. If, for instance, Ford Motor Company were to consider investing in a project involving the production of aircraft jet engines, this would take the firm into an industry with risk factors that are considerably different from those in the auto industry.

The Society for Risk Analysis (SRA) provides information on risk assessment, communication, and management, and links to risk-related sites at **http://www.sra.org/**

Consequently, it would be inappropriate to use Ford Motor's cost of capital as a discount rate for the aircraft engine project. Ford Motor's current cost of capital reflects their current business, which is confined to the auto and ancillary industries. Assuming the aircraft engine industry is riskier than the auto industry, the appropriate discount rate should be higher in order to reflect the cost of capital for firms in that industry.

Conversely, if Ford were considering a project that is less risky than their current average risk, it should use a lower discount rate to evaluate that project. For example, if Ford were to implement a new inventory management program that was virtually guaranteed to reduce inventory costs, a discount rate lower than the cost of capital should be used. Thus, the discount rate that should be used is a ***risk-adjusted discount rate*** that reflects the risk of the project. If the project is of similar risk to the firm's current business, the risk-adjusted discount rate used is simply the firm's cost of capital. Firms following the risk-adjusted discount rate approach usually classify their capital budgeting projects into several risk classes: below average, average, above average. Below-average-risk projects, such as straightforward equipment replacement decisions that result in cost savings, might be evaluated at 2 percent *below* the firm's cost of capital (a risk discount). Average-risk projects, such as a moderate increase in existing plant capacity, may be evaluated at the firm's cost of capital; above-average-risk projects, such as introducing a new product line extension, might be assigned a risk premium of 2 percent *above* the firm's cost of capital.

MORE ON PROJECT RISK ANALYSIS

In addition to using the appropriate discount rate to evaluate projects of different risk, a thorough project analysis also requires that we fully understand the nature of a given project's risk. In this section we discuss several tools available to financial analysts and firms to aid them in assessing the risk of a given project.

What-if Analysis or Sensitivity Analysis

How do you analyze cash flow sensitivity? Examine the sensitivity of cash flow in a new business at **http://www.toolkit.cch.com/tools/tools.asp**

Sensitivity analysis, also known as ***What-if analysis,*** is a procedure that calculates the change in net present value given a change in one of the cash flow elements, such as product price. In other words, a decision maker can determine *how sensitive* a project's return is to changes in a particular variable. Sensitivity analysis is usually conducted on what are deemed to be critical variables; for example, the selling price per unit or the price of a critical input to the production process. The decision maker then can ask various "what-if" questions in which the project's net present value (or internal rate of return) is recomputed under various conditions. For example, the best estimate of a product's price might be $10. The net present value of the project could then be computed using this input together with best estimates of all the other variables. The next step would involve asking a question like "What if we cannot charge more than $8 per unit?" The net present value could be recomputed using the $8 price and the best estimates for each of the other input variables to determine the effect of the $8 price on the NPV.

It is often useful to construct *sensitivity curves* to summarize the impact of changes in different variables on the net present value of a project. A sensitivity curve has the project's net present value on the vertical axis and the variable of interest on the horizontal axis. For example, Figure 10.3 shows the sensitivity curves for two variables—sales price and cost of capital for a hypothetical project.

The steep slope of the price–NPV curve in the graph on the left indicates that the net present value is very sensitive to changes in the price for which the product can be sold. If the product price is approximately 10 percent below the base case (or initial analysis) estimate, the net present value of the project drops to $0, and

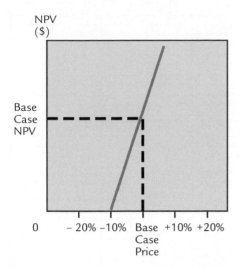
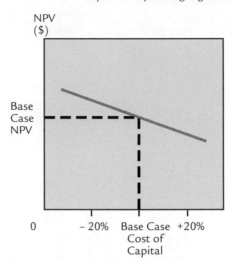

Figure 10.3
Illustrative Sensitivity Curves

the project becomes unacceptable for further price declines. In contrast, the relatively flat cost of capital–NPV curve indicates that the net present value is not very sensitive to changes in the firm's cost of capital. Similar curves could be constructed for project life, salvage value, units sold, operating costs, and other important variables.

Using Spreadsheets for Sensitivity Analysis Spreadsheets, such as Excel, have made the application of sensitivity analysis techniques simple and inexpensive. Once the base case has been modeled and entered into the spreadsheet, it is a very easy task to answer any number of "what-if" questions. For example, assume that revenues from a project are expected to be $20,000 in year 1 and to grow by 10 percent annually over the 5-year life of the project. This assumption would be entered into the spreadsheet along with similar assumptions for all other factors (e.g., operating expenses, taxes, depreciation, etc.) that go into the determination of the annual net cash flows from the project. The net present value of the base case can then be computed.

Let's say you want to now conduct a sensitivity analysis on projected sales. It would be a fairly easy task to recompute the new NPV, assuming revenues grow at 5 percent rather than the originally estimated 10 percent. Only *one change* must be made by the analyst on the spreadsheet (i.e., redefine the growth rate to 5 percent), and it automatically recomputes each period's net cash flows and the net present value of the project. This process can be repeated rapidly—literally hundreds of times—to develop a profile of how sensitive the project is to changes in the individual components of the project's cash flows. This allows the decision maker to focus his or her analysis on the key variables that are critical to the project's success.

An example of how spreadsheets may be used to conduct sensitivity analysis is shown on the next page using the Hole-in-One project data from Chapter 9.

Simulation Analysis

Computers have made it both feasible and relatively inexpensive to apply simulation techniques to capital budgeting decisions. The simulation approach generally is more appropriate for analyzing larger projects. A *simulation* is a financial planning tool that models some event. When simulation is used in capital budgeting, it

	A	B	C	D	E	F	G	H	I	J	K
1	Illustration of Sensitivity Analysis for Hole-in-One Project Using a Spreadsheet										
2	Net investment calculation:										
3			Year 0								
4	New Machine		$275,000								
5	Installation		15000								
6	Increase in NWC		50000								
7	Net Investment (Cash Outflow)		$340,000								
8											
9	The following illustrates what happens to cash flows if sales are only 75% of the original forcast										
10	(Note: Compared to the original spreadsheet (see Chapter 9) a new row was added for revised sales, all other steps are the same)										
11											
12						Years					
13				1	2	3	4	5			
14											
15	Revenue			$250,000	$300,000	$325,000	$300,000	$225,000			
16	Revised sales (75% of orig.)	75%		$187,500	$225,000	$243,750	$225,000	$168,750	Revised revenues at 75% of original. Excel formula: "+H15*$B$16"		
17	-Operating Cost	45%		84,375	101,250	109,688	101,250	75,938			
18	-Depreciation			58,000	58,000	58,000	58,000	58,000			
19	Earnings before taxes			45,125	65,750	76,063	65,750	34,813			
20	-Taxes	40%		18,050	26,300	30,425	26,300	13,925			
21	Earnings after taxes			27,075	39,450	45,638	39,450	20,888			
22	+Depreciation			58,000	58,000	58,000	58,000	58,000			
23	Cash Flow from operations			85,075	97,450	103,638	97,450	78,888			
24	-Increase in NWC			10,000	5,000	-5,000	-15,000	-45,000			
25	+Salvage value							10000			
26	-Tax on salvage value							4,000			
27											
28	Net Cash Flow			$75,075	$92,450	$108,638	$112,450	$129,888			
29											
30	Original cost of capital	15%		This is the NPV one would get if the original or base case cash flows (see Chapter 9) were discounted at 15%.							
31	Original operating expense	45%									
32	Base case NPV	$73,148									
33						Calculated using the NPV formula. Original cost of capital is 15% entered in cell B30. Excel formula: "+NPV($B$30,D28:H28)-C7"					
34	NPV for various "What-if" Scenarios:										
35				NPV							
36						Obtained by replacing value in cell B17 with 55% and assuming revised sales equal to original sales (cell B16 value = 100%) and then recalculating NPV in cell D37.					
37	If forecasted revenues equal	75%		-$4,510							
38	(% of original revenues)										
39											
40	If operating expense equals	55%		$16,669		Obtained by replacing cost of capital in cell B30 with 20% and setting revised sales equal to original sales (cell B16 value = 100%) and then recalculating the NPV in cell D37.					
41											
42	If cost of capital equals	20%		$25,348							

Spreadsheet strategies

requires that estimates be made of the probability distribution of key cash flow element (revenues, expenses, and so on). If, for example, a firm is considering introducing a new product, the elements of a simulation might include the number of units sold, market price, unit production costs, unit selling costs, the purchase price of the machinery needed to produce the new product, and the cost of capital. The probability distributions for these key variables then are entered into the simulation model to compute the project's net present value probability distribution.

Figure 10.4 illustrates just such a simulation model. The starting point to a simulation is specifying the distribution of each of the elements that enter into the calculation of the net present value. In this particular case the elements are: cost of capital, selling price per unit, variable cost per unit, market share, and length of patent protection. Note that the distributions can assume various shapes: discrete (length of patent protection), normal (selling price per unit, cost of capital), right-skewed (variable cost per unit), and uniform distribution (market share). The simulation model then picks a random value for each of the five input variables and calculates the net present value. This is repeated several hundreds of times, yielding a probability distribution for the net present value. In the illustration the resulting net present value distribution is left-skewed. The mean is positive but the left-skewed distribution indicates that there is probability, albeit small, that the project may sustain rather substantial losses to the firm's shareholders. Based on the probability distribution one can calculate the probability of a negative net present value and/or the standard deviation of the net present value.

Step 1: Estimate probability distribution of each input variable:

Figure 10.4
An Illustration of the
Simulation Approach

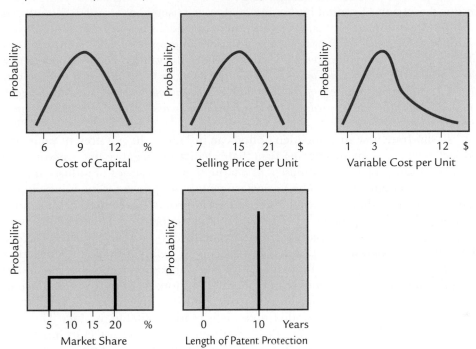

Step 2: Select at random a value from each input variable distribution in step 1.

Step 3: Calculate Net Present Value using random values chosen in step 2.

Step 4: Repeat Steps 2 and 3 several hundred times.

Step 5: Determine the probability distribution of Net Present Values:

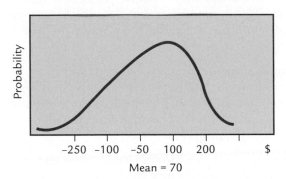

The simulation approach is a powerful tool because it can take into account the uncertainty in several key variables at the same time and analyze its influence on a project's net present value. It provides a complete picture of the expected probability distribution of the net present value. Unfortunately, it can take considerable time and effort to gather the information necessary for each of the input variables and to correctly formulate the model. This limits the feasibility of simulation to very large projects. In addition, the simulation example illustrated assumes that the values of the input variables are independent of one another. If this is not true—if, for example, the price of a product has a large influence on the number sold—then this interaction must be incorporated into the model, introducing even more complexity.

Real Options in Capital Budgeting

In our discussion of capital budgeting analysis we used conventional discounted cash flow techniques; that is, we determined a project's net present value by discounting the expected net cash flows at an applicable cost of capital, minus the net investment. This type of analysis does not consider the value of any **real options** *that may be embedded in the project or the value of any options, or flexibilities, that the firm may choose to incorporate into the project's design. In finance, an option gives its holder the right, but not the obligation, to buy, sell, or otherwise transform an asset at a set price during a specified time period.*

To illustrate how an embedded option can influence the net present value of a project, consider a manufacturing firm that calculates a negative net present value on a proposed project to purchase a new lathe to make a series of industrial parts for a particular application. The project's negative net present value is based on a cash flow analysis that assumes that the lathe will produce the parts for the entire economic life of the project. This cash flow analysis does not take into consideration the option of the company to abandon the project and sell the lathe (before the end of its economic life) in the active secondary market that exists for lathes and other manufacturing equipment. The abandonment option is *embedded* in the project; that's why it is known as an embedded option. Another option the company has is a flexibility option: The company could simply choose to switch from making the specific parts to another potentially more profitable product. The existence of these options can add to the net present value of a project by impacting the potential for future net cash flows and/or reducing the risk of the cash flows.

A partial list of real options occurring in capital budgeting include:

1. Investment Timing Options. Delaying investment in a project, say for a year or so, may allow a firm to evaluate additional information regarding demand for outputs and costs of inputs, for example. Investing in a project today or waiting a year to invest in the same project is an example of two mutually exclusive projects. In this example the firm should select the project with the higher net present value, assuming at least one project has a positive net present value. The "waiting-to-invest" option is a common real option.

2. Abandonment Option. The option to discontinue a project is an important real option in capital budgeting. A project may be discontinued either by shutting it down completely and selling the equipment or by switching its use to an alternative product. Generally, the existence of an abandonment option reduces the downside risk of a project and should be considered in project analysis.

3. Growth Options. A firm may have an opportunity to undertake a research program, build a small manufacturing facility to serve a new market, or make a small strategic acquisition in a new line of business. Each of these examples may be a negative net present value project, but each project can be viewed as having generated a growth option for the company, which, if exercised, may lead ultimately to a large positive net present value project.

To illustrate a growth option, suppose a company is evaluating an Internet investment project consisting of two stages. The first stage (today) is an investment in a Web site and the second stage (1 year from today) is an investment in an electronic commerce venture. The investment in the Web site has an NPV of $-10 million. Setting up the Web site (first stage) gives the company the option, but not the obligation, to invest in the electronic commerce business (second stage) 1 year from today.

FINANCE & The Real World

Boeing Makes a Gutsy Decision

Boeing engineers are designing a new airplane that could move the company past rival Airbus. The 7E7 would bring together the latest manufacturing methods and the newest electronics in a jetliner more efficient than any in the sky.

It's a bold move. Ever since the September 11th terrorist attacks, the airline industry has faced its worst downturn ever. Somehow, Boeing has to look into its crystal ball and decide whether the future cash flows from the new plan justify the huge outlay—estimated at $6 billion to $11 billion. Beyond being a strategic direction for the company, it's a massive capital budgeting decision—a comparison between future cash flows and current investment, where the numbers are in the *billions*.

The company believes that the world's airlines will spend nearly $2 trillion on new airplanes over the next 20 years. The potential market for planes in the 7E7's class is between 2,000 and 3,000 planes, and Boeing thinks it will supply at least half. In addition, the company argues that the 7E7 will have a more efficient engine than current models offer, and that maintenance and spare parts will be cheaper. The icing on the cake: the 250-seat twin-engine jet will help airlines offer long-range point-to-point flights that command premium fares.

While Boeing gears up for the new plane, it has been slashing costs and laying off workers, damaging morale. But by not moving forward, Boeing risks losing market share to the industry's only other major player, Europe's Airbus. The two companies split the market roughly 50–50 for large passenger planes.

Three times in its 86-year history, Boeing has done very well by betting on new jet designs with its 707, 747, and 777 aircraft. But Boeing hasn't introduced a new plane since 1995, preferring to attach high price tags to modified versions of existing models. The last two efforts at building a new aircraft never made it off the drawing board because of cost concerns and faltering demand for new planes. Meanwhile, Airbus launched a new program to develop a 555-seat jumbo aircraft called the A380, which has garnered nearly 100 orders.

The cost of developing the 7E7 is daunting in the current environment. But an overemphasis on short-term profits could cause Boeing to miss its chance to pull ahead of Airbus. And some analysts fear that Boeing could find itself out in the cold like McDonnell Douglas, a company that paid a hefty price for not developing new planes. The result: Boeing swallowed up McDonnell Douglas in a 1997 merger. If Boeing decides to go ahead with the 7E7 jetliner, it has pledged to manufacture it in the United States, despite worries about high production costs.

Source: The Wall Street Journal, April 21, 2003, "Navigating Change: Boeing, Losing Ground to Airbus, Faces Key Choice"; The Boeing Company 2002 Annual Report; The Wall Street Journal, May 16, 2003, "Boeing Says It Will Build New Jetliner at Site in U.S."; The Wall Street Journal, June 23, 2003, "Will Boeing's New Idea Really Fly?"; The Oregonian, July 12, 2003, "Airline Proposal Carries a Lot of Baggage for Boeing."

While the cash flows are highly uncertain, ranging from large losses to substantial profits, the best estimate today is that the electronic commerce business has an NPV of $-60 million. Based on the NPV decision rule, the Internet investment project would be unacceptable since it has an NPV of $-70 million [-$10 million + ($-60 million)]. However, 1 year from today, the company will have more information and be better able to estimate whether the electronic commerce business (second stage) is worth pursuing. At that time, suppose new information about the cash flows of the electronic commerce venture shows that it will be extremely profitable, yielding an overall NPV of $+50 million for the Internet project. Clearly, the project would be worth undertaking at that time.

Investing in the Web site today, even though it has a negative NPV, preserves the company's option to invest in a positive NPV project in the future. By investing only in the Web site initially, the company is able to limit its downside risk ($−10 million NPV) while preserving the upside potential ($+50 million NPV) for the Internet investment project.

4. Designed-in Options. In addition to options that can occur naturally in projects, managers have the opportunity to include options in projects in order to increase net present value. These designed-in options are classified either as input flexibility options, output flexibility options, or expansion options.

a. *Input flexibility options* allow a firm to design into a project the capability of switching between alternative inputs because of input cost differences. To illustrate a designed-in option, consider an electric power plant project that is evaluating whether to use a gas burner or an oil burner to fire the turbines. The designed-in option in this instance would be a flexible dual-fuel boiler that can switch back and forth between gas and oil, depending on which energy source is cheaper to acquire and use. It may be, under certain conditions, that the flexible boiler project has a higher net present value than either of the projects using the gas-fired boiler or the oil-fired boiler, even though the initial cost of the flexible boiler is higher than the cost of either of the two single-fuel boilers. In other words, the value of the designed-in option may be greater than the additional cost of the flexible boiler.

b. *Output flexibility options* allow a firm to design into a project the capability of shifting the product mix of the project if relative product prices dictate such a shift. Oil refineries normally have output flexibility options (e.g., diesel fuel, kerosene, unleaded gasoline of different octane ratings, etc.).

c. *Expansion options* give project managers the ability to add future capacity to a project at a relatively low marginal cost. For example, consider a company that requires at present a manufacturing facility totaling 50,000 square feet. If instead, it builds a facility with 70,000 square feet of space now, the cost to the company to expand by 20,000 square feet in the future may be less than if it has to build a separate 20,000-square-foot facility later. Even if the need for the additional capacity never materializes, the value of the expansion option may justify the cost of the larger initial facility beforehand, particularly if significant uncertainty about future product demand exists.

Using conventional discounted cash flow analyses in capital budgeting without considering real options may result in a downward-biased estimate of the true value of a project's net present value. Some operating options, such as an option to expand, may increase a project's upside potential, while other operating options, such as an option to abandon, may reduce a project's downside risk.

While option valuation in actual capital budgeting projects is complicated, financial managers should recognize the presence of options in projects and should consider including designed-in options when possible in planning projects. A large amount of advanced work on real options is being done.

INFLATION AND CAPITAL BUDGETING ANALYSIS

It is easy to overlook the effect of inflation in capital budgeting analysis. Specifically, if inflation effects are not taken into account in determining the net cash flows, the resulting evaluation of net cash flows may result in the wrong decision. It is important to note that the discount rate or the cost of capital used in evaluating project net cash flows incorporates an inflation premium, thus not adjusting the cash flows for inflation may lead to an incorrect decision. To illustrate, assume that Project Z requires a net investment of $2,000 and has the following cash inflows and outflows over its 2-year project life:

Year	Cash Inflows	Cash Outflows
1	$2,150	$1,000
2	$2,150	$1,000

Subtracting the outflows from the inflows yields net cash flows of $1,150 for each of the 2 years. Assuming the discount rate (cost of capital) is 10 percent, the net present value for Project Z is $−4.13. Thus, the project is unacceptable.

The above cash flows do not reflect the effect of inflation. Now assume that if inflation is taken into account, cash outflows in year 2 will be higher by 6 percent. Also, assume that the firm is able to pass on the increased costs to its customers resulting in year 2 revenues being 5 percent higher than shown above. Making the inflation adjustments, the new cash inflows, cash outflows, and net cash flows are:

Year	Cash Inflows	Cash Outflows	Net Cash Flows
1	$2,150	$1,000	$1,150
2	$2,258	$1,060	$1,198

Using the inflation-adjusted net cash flow yields a net present value of $35.54, making the project acceptable. Thus, not adjusting for inflation in the cash flows can result in the wrong decision with respect to the acceptability of the project.

Comprehension Check Questions

1. How should you adjust for differences in risk when evaluating projects?
2. How are sensitivity analysis and simulation analysis useful in improving capital budgeting decisions?
3. What are real options?
4. How is inflation incorporated into capital budgeting analysis?

Summary

➤ The net present value is calculated by subtracting a project's net investment from the expected net cash flows discounted at the firm's cost of capital. It represents the contribution of the investment to the value of the firm and, accordingly, to the wealth of shareholders.

➤ The internal rate of return of a project is the discount rate that gives the project a net present value equal to zero.

➤ The profitability index is the ratio of the present value of net cash flows to the net investment. It gives a measure of the relative present value return per dollar of initial investment. The profitability index is useful when choosing among projects in a capital rationing situation.

➢ The payback period is the number of years required for the cumulative net cash flows from a project to equal the net investment. The payback method has several weaknesses: It fails to account for the time value of money, it fails to consider cash flows after the payback period, and it does not rely on an objective criterion that is consistent with shareholder wealth maximization.

➢ The net present value and internal rate of return approaches normally yield the same accept–reject decisions for a particular project. However, conflicts may arise when dealing with mutually exclusive projects. The reinvestment rate assumption embodied in the net present value approach—namely, that cash flows from a project are reinvested at the cost of capital—generally is more realistic than that underlying the internal rate of return method. For this reason, the net present value method is preferred to the internal rate of return method.

➢ The cost of capital is the appropriate discount rate to use for projects that are of similar risk to the firm's existing business. For projects that are more or less risky than the current operations of the firm an appropriately revised discount rate must be employed.

➢ Sensitivity analysis is a useful project risk analysis tool that shows the sensitivity of NPV to changes in specific variables.

➢ Simulation analysis is useful in determining the probability distribution of a project's NPV. It is generated by selecting random values for various input variables (e.g., selling price, market share, cost of raw materials) and then calculating the NPV.

➢ Real options analysis involves looking at the flexibilities either inherent in or that can be built into a project in addition to traditional NPV analysis of a project.

➢ It is important to ensure that project cash inflows and outflows reflect the impact of inflation. Not doing so may result in an incorrect evaluation of the project.

Questions and Topics for Discussion

1. How does the net present value model complement the objective of maximizing shareholder wealth?

2. When is it possible for the net present value and the internal rate of return approaches to give conflicting rankings of mutually exclusive investment projects?

3. When are multiple rates of return likely to occur in an internal rate of return computation? What should be done when a multiple rate of return problem arises?

4. Under what circumstance is the PI a useful capital budgeting evaluation technique?

5. What are the primary strengths and weaknesses of the payback approach in capital budgeting?

6. Is the firm's cost of capital the appropriate discount rate for all capital budgeting cases? Explain.

7. Explain how sensitivity analysis and simulation analysis help to provide a better assessment of project risk.

8. What are real options? How would taking into account real options impact traditional capital budgeting analysis as discussed in this chapter?

9. Why is it important to adjust project cash flows for inflation effects?

Self-Test Problems

ST1. Calculate the net present value of a project with a net investment of $20,000 for equipment and net working capital investment of $5,000 at time 0. The project is expected to generate net cash flows of $7,000 per year over a 10-year estimated economic life. In addition, the net working capital will be recovered at the end of the project. The required return on the project is 11 percent. What is the meaning of the computed net present value figure?

ST2. Calculate the internal rate of return and profitability index for a project that is expected to generate 8 years of annual net cash flows of $75,000. The project has a net investment of $360,000 and the required return on the project is 12 percent.

ST3. Two mutually exclusive projects have the following expected cash flows:

Year	G	H
0	−$10,000	−$10,000
1	5,000	0
2	5,000	0
3	5,000	17,000

a. Calculate the internal rate of return for each project.

b. Calculate the net present value for each project, assuming the firm's weighted cost of capital is 12 percent.

c. Which project should be adopted? Why?

Problems

1. Calculate the net present value and profitability index of a project with a net investment of $20,000 and expected net cash flows of $3,000 a year for 10 years if the project's required return is 12 percent. Is the project acceptable? **BASIC**

2. A firm wishes to bid on a contract that is expected to yield the following after-tax net cash flows at the end of each year: **INTERMEDIATE**

Year	Net Cash Flow
1	$5,000
2	8,000
3	9,000
4	8,000
5	8,000
6	5,000
7	3,000
8	$−1,500

To secure the contract, the firm must spend $30,000 to retool its plant. This retooling will have no salvage value at the end of the 8 years. Comparable investment alternatives are available to the firm that earn 12 percent compounded annually. The depreciation tax benefit from the retooling is reflected in the net cash flows in the table.

a. Compute the project's net present value.

b. Should the project be adopted?

c. What is the meaning of the computed net present value figure?

BASIC **3.** A machine that costs $8,000 is expected to operate for 10 years. The estimated salvage value at the end of 10 years is $0. The machine is expected to save the company $1,554 per year before taxes and depreciation. The company depreciates its assets on a straight-line basis and has a marginal tax rate of 40 percent. What is the internal rate of return on this investment?

INTERMEDIATE **4.** Jefferson Products, Inc., is considering purchasing a new automatic press brake, which costs $300,000 including installation and shipping. The machine is expected to generate net cash flows of $80,000 per year for 10 years. At the end of 10 years, the book value of the machine will be $0, and it is anticipated that the machine will be sold for $100,000. If the press brake project is undertaken, Jefferson will have to increase its net working capital by $75,000. When the project is terminated in 10 years, there no longer will be a need for this incremental working capital, and it can be liquidated and made available to Jefferson for other uses. Jefferson requires a 12 percent annual return on this type of project and its marginal tax rate is 40 percent.

a. Calculate the press brake's net present value.

b. Is the project acceptable?

c. What is the meaning of the computed net present value figure?

d. What is the project's internal rate of return?

e. For the press brake project, at what annual rates of return do the net present value and internal rate of return methods assume that the net cash inflows are being reinvested?

BASIC **5.** An acre planted with walnut trees is estimated to be worth $12,000 in 25 years. If you want to realize a 15 percent rate of return on your investment, how much can you afford to invest per acre? (Ignore all taxes and assume that annual cash outlays to maintain your stand of walnut trees are nil.)

INTERMEDIATE **6.** Two mutually exclusive investment projects have the following forecasted cash flows:

Year	A	B
0	−$20,000	−$20,000
1	10,000	0
2	10,000	0
3	10,000	0
4	10,000	60,000

a. Compute the internal rate of return for each project.

b. Compute the net present value for each project if the firm has a 10 percent cost of capital.

c. Which project should be adopted? Why?

INTERMEDIATE **7.** Commercial Hydronics is considering replacing one of its larger control devices. A new unit sells for $29,000 (delivered). An additional $3,000 will be needed to install the device. The new device has an estimated 20-year service life. The estimated salvage value at the end of 20 years will be $2,000. The new control device will be depreciated over 20 years on a straight-line basis to $0. The existing control device (original cost = $15,000) has been in use for 12 years, and it has been fully depreciated (that is, its book value equals zero). Its scrap value now is estimated to be $1,000. The existing device could be used indefinitely, assuming the firm is willing to pay for its very high maintenance costs. The firm's marginal tax rate is 40 percent. The new control device requires lower maintenance costs and frees up personnel who normally would have to monitor the system. Estimated annual cash savings from the new device will be $9,000. The firm's cost of capital is 12 percent.

Evaluate the relative merits of replacing the old control device using the net present value approach.

8. A $1,230 investment has the following expected cash returns:

Year	Net Cash Flow
1	$800
2	200
3	400

Compute the internal rate of return for this project. Under what circumstances would this project be acceptable?

9. A junior executive is fed up with the operating policies of his boss. Before leaving the office of his angered superior, the young man suggests that a well-trained monkey could handle the trivia assigned to him. Pausing a moment to consider the import of this closing statement, the boss is seized by the thought that this must have been in the back of her own mind ever since she hired the junior executive. She decides to consider replacing the executive with a bright young baboon. She figures that she could argue strongly to the board that such "capital deepening" is necessary for the cost-conscious firm. Two days later, a feasibility study is completed, and the following data are presented to the president:

It would cost $12,000 to purchase and train a reasonably alert baboon with a life expectancy of 20 years.
Annual expenses of feeding and housing the baboon would be $4,000.
The junior executive's annual salary is $7,000 (a potential saving if the baboon is hired).
The baboon will be depreciated on a straight-line basis over 20 years to a zero balance.
The firm's marginal tax rate is 40 percent.
The firm's current cost of capital is estimated to be 11 percent.
On the basis of the net present value criterion, should the monkey be hired (and the junior executive fired)?

10. The L–S Mining Company is planning to open a new strip mine in western Pennsylvania. The net investment required to open the mine is $10 million. Net cash flows are expected to be +$20 million at the end of year 1 and +$5 million at the end of year 2. At the end of year 3, L–S will have a net cash *outflow* of $17 million to cover the cost of closing the mine and reclaiming the land.

a. Calculate the net present value of the strip mine if the cost of capital is 5, 10, 15, 30, 71, and 80 percent.
b. What is unique about this project?
c. Should the project be accepted if L–S's cost of capital is 10 percent? 20 percent?

CHALLENGE **11.** Fred and Frieda have always wanted to enter the blueberry business. They locate a 50-acre piece of hillside in Maine that is covered with blueberry bushes. They figure that the annual yield from the bushes will be 200 crates. Each crate is estimated to sell for $400 for the next 10 years. This price is expected to rise to $500 per crate for all sales from years 11 through 20.

In order to get started, Fred and Frieda must pay $150,000 for the land plus $20,000 for packing equipment. The packing equipment will be depreciated on a straight-line basis to a zero estimated salvage value at the end of 20 years. Fred and Frieda believe that at the end of 20 years, they will want to retire to Florida and sell their property.

Annual operating expenses, including salaries to Fred and Frieda and exclusive of depreciation, are estimated to be $50,000 per year for the first 10 years and $60,000 thereafter. The land is expected to appreciate in value at a rate of 5 percent per year. The couple's marginal tax rate is 30 percent for both ordinary income and capital gains and losses.

a. If the couple requires at least a 13 percent return on their investment, should they enter the blueberry business?

b. Assume that the land can be sold for only $50,000 at the end of 20 years (a capital loss of $100,000). Should the couple invest in the land and blueberry business? (Assume that the couple may claim the full amount of their capital loss in the year it occurs—year 20).

CHALLENGE **12.** The Sisneros Company is considering building a chili-processing plant in Hatch, New Mexico. The plant is expected to produce 50,000 pounds of processed chili peppers each year for the next 10 years. During the first year, Sisneros expects to sell the processed peppers for $2 per pound. The price is expected to increase at a 7 percent rate per year over the 10-year economic life of the plant. The costs of operating the plant, exclusive of depreciation, including the cost of fresh peppers, are estimated to be $50,000 during the first year. These costs are expected to increase at an 8 percent rate per year over the next 10 years.

The plant will cost $80,000 to build. It will be depreciated over 8 years to a zero salvage value. The estimated salvage at the end of 10 years is zero. The firm's marginal tax rate is 40 percent.

a. Calculate the net investment required to build the plant.

b. Calculate the annual net cash flows from the project.

c. If Sisneros uses a 20 percent cost of capital to evaluate projects of this type, should the plant be built?

d. Calculate the payback period for this project.

e. How many internal rates of return does this project have? Why?

INTERMEDIATE **13.** Note the following information on the annual cash flows of two mutually exclusive projects under consideration by Wang Food Markets, Inc.

Year	A	B
0	−$30,000	−$60,000
1	10,000	20,000
2	10,000	20,000
3	10,000	20,000
4	10,000	20,000
5	10,000	20,000

Wang requires a 14 percent rate of return on projects of this nature.

   a. Compute the NPV of both projects.

   b. Compute the internal rate of return on both projects.

   c. Compute the profitability index of both projects.

   d. Compute the payback period on both projects.

   e. Which of the two projects, if either, should Wang accept? Why?

14. Channel Tunnel, Inc., plans to build a new 23-mile-long tunnel under the English Channel for added train service. The cost (NINV) of the tunnel is expected to be $3.3 billion. Net cash flows are expected to equal $651 million per year. How many years must the firm generate this cash flow stream for investors to earn their required 11 percent rate of return? **INTERMEDIATE**

15. The Taylor Mountain Uranium Company currently has annual cash revenues of $1.2 million and annual cash expenses of $700,000. Depreciation amounts to $200,000 per year. These figures are expected to remain constant for the foreseeable future (at least 15 years). The firm's marginal tax rate is 40 percent. **INTERMEDIATE**

   A new high-speed processing unit costing $1.2 million is being considered as a potential investment designed to increase the firm's output capacity. This new piece of equipment will have an estimated usable life of 10 years and a $0 estimated salvage value. If the processing unit is bought, Taylor's annual revenues are expected to increase to $1.6 million and annual expenses (exclusive of depreciation) will increase to $900,000. Annual depreciation will increase to $320,000. Assume that no increase in net working capital will be required as a result of this project. (Note: This problem is the same as problem #3 in Chapter 9, except for the following questions.)

   a. Calculate the processing unit's net present value, using a 12 percent required rate of return.

   b. Should Taylor accept the project?

   c. Calculate the processing unit's internal rate of return.

16. Benford, Inc. is planning to open a new sporting goods store in a suburban mall. Benford will lease the needed space in the mall. Equipment and fixtures for the store will cost $200,000 and be depreciated over a 5-year period on a straight-line basis to $0. The new store will require Benford to increase its net working capital by $200,000 at time 0; thereafter, net working capital balances are expected to equal 20 percent of the following year's sales. First-year sales are expected to be $1 million and to increase at an annual rate of 8 percent over the expected 10-year life of the store. Operating expenses (including lease payments and excluding depreciation) are projected to equal 70 percent of sales. The salvage value of the store's equipment and fixtures is anticipated to be $10,000 at the end of 10 years. Benford's marginal tax rate is 40 percent. (Note: This problem is the same as problem #8 in Chapter 9, except for the following questions.) **CHALLENGE**

   a. Calculate the store's net present value, using an 18 percent required return.

   b. Should Benford accept the project?

   c. Calculate the store's internal rate of return.

   d. Calculate the store's profitability index.

CAPITAL STRUCTURE AND DIVIDEND POLICY

PART FOUR

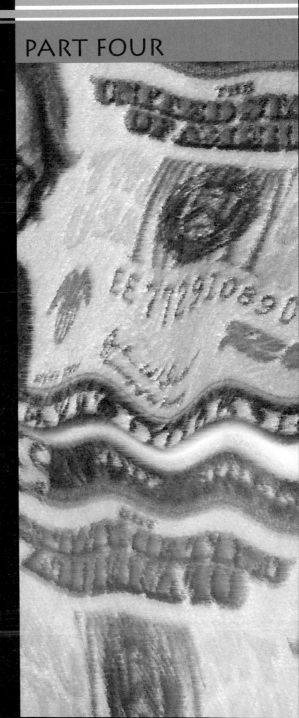

This section of the book examines the cost of capital of the firm and how it is impacted by the capital structure of the firm. The dividend policy decision of the firm is also examined. Chapter 11 illustrates the principles of measuring a firm's cost of capital. The cost of funds to a firm is an important input in the capital budgeting process. Chapter 12 addresses the relationship of a firm's capital structure to its cost of capital. Chapter 13 illustrates tools and techniques that can help a firm determine the best capital structure to employ. Chapter 14 discusses the factors that influence the choice of a dividend policy and the impact of various dividend policies on the value of a firm.

CHAPTER
11 The Cost of Capital

Knowledge of the cost of capital is important for several reasons, including capital budgeting analysis, capital structure choice, and performance assessment. From the preceding chapters on capital budgeting, we know that the cost of capital serves as a critical input to capital budgeting decision analysis. Businesses exist to provide a valuable service or product. To do so requires that firms invest in new plant and equipment, research and development, training, etc. These investments are financed by various sources of capital including debt, preferred stock, and common equity. This is illustrated in Figure 11.1:

The left-hand side of the diagram shows funds flowing from various capital sources (debt, preferred stock, and common equity) to the firm. The firm (management), in turn, invests the funds in various projects (Project 1, Project 2, Project 3, etc.) that may include new plant and equipment, research and development, acquisitions, etc. The capital holders willingly part from their money in the expectation that they will earn a positive rate of return on their investment. For example, if you, as an investor, choose to invest $75 in a share of preferred stock of DaimlerChrysler Corporation, you are doing so with the expectation of getting back more than the $75 that you invested. Similarly, each of the different classes of capital holders has their own expectation for a required rate of return. Debt holders, for instance, require a rate of return of k_d while preferred and common equity holders have required rates of return of k_p and k_e, respectively. Taken together, these costs result in a weighted average cost of capital (or simply cost of capital) to the firm of k_a.

The diagram shows that the returns generated from the various projects (r_1, r_2, r_3) flow back to the various capital holders. The returns generated by the projects are used to compensate the capital holders (k_d for debt, k_p for preferred stock, and k_e for common equity; or an average of k_a across all sources of capital). *In order to meet the cost of capital requirements of various capital holders, the firm's investments must generate sufficient returns to compensate the capital providers.* This is one of the most sig-

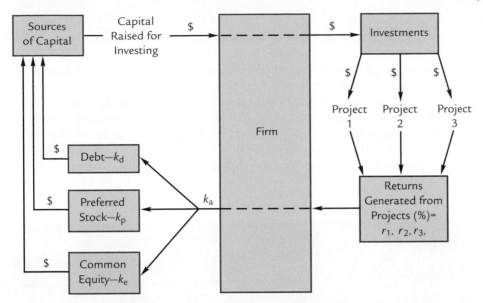

**Figure 11.1
Overview of Cost
of Capital**

nificant reasons why knowledge of the ***cost of capital*** is important: *The firm must make appropriate decisions on which projects to invest in and which ones to reject.* Thus, the cost of capital serves as a *hurdle* rate in the evaluation of capital budgeting proposals. Projects with returns (internal rate or return) that equal or exceed the cost of capital (k_a) should be accepted while others with returns less than k_a should be rejected.

Knowledge of the cost of capital is important for two other reasons. Figure 11.1 shows that the cost of capital is a function of the component costs of capital—that is, it depends on the costs of the various individual sources of capital such as debt, preferred stock, and common stock. This implies that the cost of capital may be influenced by the *relative mix* of the various sources of capital utilized by the firm. *In order to maximize firm value, firms should select the mix of capital that will yield the least overall cost of capital to the firm.* Just as individuals shop around for the cheapest source of loans in buying a car or a house, firms also strive to minimize their cost of capital, which will, in turn, increase overall shareholder wealth. The choice of appropriate capital structure is the subject of the next two chapters.

Finally, knowledge of the cost of capital is useful in evaluating management performance. From Figure 11.1 it should be evident that *good management is one that consistently produces a return on capital that exceeds the firm's cost of capital, thereby adding to shareholder wealth.* On the other hand, poor management is characterized by returns that are consistently less than the cost of capital, ultimately destroying shareholder wealth. In Chapter 4 we learned about the ***EVA®*** measure of performance (produced by Stern Stewart & Co.). Recall that EVA is measured as

Finance in the News

Click on this button at **http://finance.swlearning.com** *for synopses of recent articles on the cost of capital and capital structure.*

$$\text{EVA} = (\text{EBIT})(1 - T) - k_a \times \text{Invested Capital} \tag{11.1}$$

where EBIT is the earnings before interest and taxes, T is the tax rate, k_a is the average cost of capital and *Invested capital* refers to the sum total of all capital contributed by each of the different sources of capital. Multiplying and dividing the right-hand side of the equation by invested capital yields

$$\text{EVA} = \left[\frac{(\text{EBIT})(1 - T)}{\text{Invested Capital}} - k_a \right] \times \text{Invested Capital} \tag{11.2}$$

Replacing the first term inside the square bracket with r, which stands for the return on Invested capital, results in an alternate expression for EVA:

(11.3) $\text{EVA} = [\text{Return on total capital } (r) - \text{Cost of Capital } (k_a)] \times \text{Invested Capital}$

Recall that EVA is a dollar figure that shows how much additional shareholder value is created in a given year. From Equation 11.3 it is evident that EVA is positive whenever the return on capital (r) generated exceeds the cost of capital (k_a). Table 11.1 shows the 1999 EVA values for firms listed on Dow Jones 30 Index. Microsoft's management was one of the best with an increase in shareholder wealth of $5.796 billion. This wealth creation can be attributed to the firm's return on capital of 51.78 percent compared to a cost of capital of 12.62 percent. In contrast, AT&T did very poorly with a return on capital of only 4.39 percent compared to a cost of capital of 9.22 percent. As a consequence, AT&T shareholders lost $6.379 billion in value.

CHAPTER OBJECTIVES

Upon completion of this chapter, you should have mastered the following:

1. Calculate the cost of debt

2. Calculate the cost of preferred stock

3. Calculate the cost of common equity

4. Calculate the weighted average cost of capital

5. Understand the difference between historical and marginal cost of capital

6. Understand the difference between book value weights and market value weights in calculating the cost of capital

SUMMARY OF NOTATION

Before proceeding with the discussion of the cost of capital, it is helpful to summarize some of the notation used in this chapter.

k_d = pretax cost of debt
k_i = after-tax cost of debt
k_p = cost of preferred stock
k_e = cost of common equity
k_a = weighted average (marginal) cost of capital
P_0 = current market price of a security
B = market value of a firm's debt in its capital structure
P_f = market value of a firm's preferred stock in its capital structure
E = market value of a firm's common equity in its capital structure
r_f = riskless (risk-free) rate of return
r_m = expected return on the market portfolio
β = beta (systematic risk) of a company's stock

THE WEIGHTED AVERAGE COST OF CAPITAL CONCEPT

As the introduction to this chapter demonstrated, the *weighted average cost of capital* is an extremely important component of the capital budgeting decision process. It also has important implications in the choice of an appropriate capital structure and for management performance evaluation. Conceptually, determining the cost

Table 11.1 Economic Value Added (EVA®) from Stern Stewart & Co. for Firms on the Dow Jones 30 Index for 1999

	Company Name	EVA ($ million)	Return on Capital (r) (%)	Cost of Capital (k_a) (%)
1	3M	839	15.41	8.54
2	Alcoa	−189	8.38	9.54
3	Altria Group Inc.	6,454	21.73	7.96
4	American Express Company	1,042	23.16	11.69
5	AT & T	−6,379	4.39	9.22
6	Boeing	−830	7.2	9.29
7	Caterpillar	321	12.09	9.36
8	Citigroup	1,003	14.32	12.82
9	Coca-Cola	1,562	21.8	12.31
10	DuPont	1,623	13.21	8.64
11	Eastman Kodak	529	9.78	6.71
12	ExxonMobil	4,440	11.67	8.16
13	General Electric	3,499	17.2	12.47
14	General Motors Corp.	172	7.99	7.81
15	Hewlett-Packard	−195	10.72	11.42
16	Home Depot	884	16.6	10.49
17	Honeywell	371	11.65	10.04
18	IBM	1,349	13.33	11.4
19	Intel	4,695	30.55	12.19
20	International Paper	−1,198	4.2	8.71
21	J.P. Morgan & Company	868	20.33	10.9
22	Johnson & Johnson	1,555	16.24	10.39
23	McDonald's	329	10.23	8.83
24	Merck	3,449	23.09	10.72
25	Microsoft	5,796	51.78	12.62
26	Procter & Gamble	1,782	15.52	9.72
27	SBC Communications	−30	8.59	8.62
28	United Technologies	11	11.26	11.2
29	Wal-Mart Stores	1,528	14.31	10.99
30	Walt Disney	-1,383	5.6	9.28

Source: Data taken from Stern Stewart & Co.'s Web site, http://www.sternstewart.com

of capital is fairly simple. The general expression for calculating the weighted average cost of capital, k_a, is as follows:

$$k_a = \begin{pmatrix} \text{Proportion of} \\ \text{debt in capital} \\ \text{structure} \end{pmatrix} \begin{pmatrix} \text{Marginal} \\ \text{cost of debt} \end{pmatrix} + \begin{pmatrix} \text{Proportion of} \\ \text{preferred stock} \\ \text{in capital} \\ \text{structure} \end{pmatrix} \begin{pmatrix} \text{Marginal} \\ \text{cost of} \\ \text{preferred} \\ \text{stock} \end{pmatrix} \quad (11.4)$$

$$+ \begin{pmatrix} \text{Proportion of} \\ \text{common equity} \\ \text{in capital} \\ \text{structure} \end{pmatrix} \begin{pmatrix} \text{Marginal} \\ \text{cost of} \\ \text{common} \\ \text{equity} \end{pmatrix}$$

$$k_a = \left(\frac{B}{B + P_f + E}\right)k_d(1 - T) + \left(\frac{P_f}{B + P_f + E}\right)k_p + \left(\frac{E}{B + P_f + E}\right)k_e$$

where B is debt, P_f is preferred stock, E is common equity in the capital structure, k_d is the pretax marginal cost of debt, k_p is the marginal cost of preferred stock, k_e is the marginal cost of common equity, and T is the marginal tax rate of the firm.

e-Lecture

It is evident from Equation 11.4 that in order to calculate the weighted average cost of capital we need estimates of the individual costs of the various sources of capital and their proportions in the firm's capital structure. Accordingly, in the next section we discuss how the component costs of capital are estimated. Then we show how the component costs can be combined with the weights of the various sources of capital to arrive at an estimate of the weighted (marginal) average cost of capital to the firm, k_a.

Comprehension Check Questions

1. Why is determining the cost of capital important?

2. Describe the general expression for the cost of capital.

COMPUTING THE COMPONENT COSTS OF CAPITAL

This section develops and applies methods a firm can use to compute the cost of its three major component sources of capital: debt, preferred stock, and common equity.

Marginal Costs

As mentioned in the beginning of the chapter, one important use of the cost of capital is to determine a discount rate to use in evaluating proposed capital expenditure projects. Recall that the purpose of capital expenditure analysis is to determine which proposed projects the firm should actually undertake. Therefore, it is logical that the capital whose cost is measured and compared with the expected benefits from the proposed projects should be the additional or **marginal capital** the firm raises. The *marginal cost of capital* is the *cost incurred by the firm to raise the next increment of capital.* The marginal cost of capital contrasts with the *historical* cost of capital, which is the *cost of funds incurred by the firm currently or in the past.*

From a capital budgeting evaluation perspective, *the historical costs are not relevant.* For example, assume that IBM is currently paying 6.5 percent on its existing loan and that the firm is contemplating financing a new plant in order to build high-end servers. The cost of debt financing for the new project may or may not equal 6.5 percent—the cost on the existing loan. It will depend on the prevailing market conditions, the condition of the firm, and the characteristics of the issue at the time the new debt is raised. For example, if inflation is expected to increase in the future, the marginal bond investor will require a higher rate of return than the 6.5 percent on the existing loan. Thus, the relevant marginal cost of debt would be the new higher rate. A similar logic would apply to the marginal cost of preferred stock and the marginal cost of common equity.

When computing the marginal cost of the various component capital sources, companies typically estimate the component costs they anticipate encountering (paying) during the coming year. If capital costs change significantly during the year, it may be necessary to recompute the new capital costs and use the new estimates when evaluating projects from that time forward. Under most circumstances, a semiannual or annual computation of marginal capital costs is sufficient.

Cost of Debt

The *cost of debt* (pretax) to the firm is the *rate of return required by a firm's creditors.* It is the discount rate, k_d, that equates the present value of all expected future outflows the firm is obligated to make—interest, I, and principal repayment, M—with the price that the marginal creditor is willing to pay for the security:

$$P_0 = \sum_{t=1}^{n} \frac{I_t}{(1 + k_d)^t} + \frac{M}{(1 + k_d)^n} \tag{11.5}$$

or

$$P_0 = I(\text{PVIFA}_{k_d, n}) + M(\text{PVIF}_{k_d, n}) \tag{11.6}$$

Note that solving for the pretax cost of debt, k_d, in the above equations is identical to solving for the yield to maturity in Chapter 7. In reality Equations 11.5 and 11.6 should be modified slightly: P_0 on the left-hand side should be replaced by the price the marginal creditor is willing to pay for the security *less* the **flotation costs** (per unit of debt or bond) that would be incurred in issuing the debt. The flotation expenses consist of commissions to investment bankers, cost of registering the issue with the Securities and Exchange Commission, printing expenses, etc. In other words the relevant figure on the left-hand side of Equation 11.5 and 11.6 is the *net proceeds* the firm receives from issuing the debt security. For the sake of simplicity and also because of the relatively minor impact on the resulting cost of debt, we have chosen to ignore flotation expenses in our calculations.

From the firm's perspective, interest payments made to creditors are deductible from taxable income. Therefore, the after-tax cost of debt, k_i, is computed by multiplying the pretax cost of debt by one minus the firm's marginal tax rate, T:

$$k_i = k_d (1 - T) \tag{11.7}$$

To illustrate the cost of debt calculation let's assume Krispy Treats Mfg. Co. sells $50 million of 20-year 7.8 percent coupon rate bonds. The bonds, which have a $1,000 face value each, sell for $980 per bond. To compute the pretax cost, k_d, of this debt offering, the relationship in Equation 11.6 can be used as follows

$$\$980 = \$78(\text{PVIFA}_{k_d, 20}) + \$1,000(\text{PVIF}_{k_d, 20})$$

The calculation of k_d in the above equation can be solved by trial and error using Tables II and IV on the insert with this book. By trial error, try 8 percent:

$$\$980 = \$78(9.818) + \$1,000(0.215)$$
$$\approx \$980$$

Therefore, the pretax cost of debt is 8 percent. Alternately, we can solve for k_d using the financial calculator.

Enter:	20	−980	78	1,000
	N	**PV**	**PMT**	**FV**

Calculator

Compute:	**I/Y**	= 8.00		

Solution

Assuming a 40 percent marginal tax rate, the after-tax cost of debt is computed using Equation 11.7:

$$k_i = k_d (1 - T)$$
$$= 8\% (1 - .4)$$
$$= 4.8\%$$

The above calculation for the after-tax cost of debt presumes that the firm is making profits. For a firm losing money, the tax rate in Equation 11.7 is *zero*, and the after-tax cost, k_i, is the same as the pretax cost, k_d.

The procedure outlined above to calculate the cost of debt works well when a firm is in the process of selling, or has just sold, bonds at the time that the cost of capital is being computed. However, in most instances, trips to the capital markets are sporadic. How can the marginal cost of debt be computed in these cases? That is, how can one determine what it would cost a firm to sell debt today (at the time of the cost of capital calculation)? This problem has two solutions:

1. If a firm has bonds that are currently outstanding and that are being traded in the marketplace, the firm can observe the current market price for those bonds. Given a current price, the maturity of the bonds, and the coupon rate of interest, the yield to maturity on the bond can be computed. This yield to maturity may be used as an estimate of the marginal pretax cost of debt, k_d, for the firm.

2. If a firm's outstanding bonds are not traded frequently or are privately held, then the best estimate of the marginal pretax cost of debt can be derived by looking at the pretax cost of debt recently sold by other firms having risk similar to the firm under consideration. For these purposes, having similar risk is normally interpreted to mean that firms in question have equivalent bond ratings (according to Moody's or Standard and Poor's).

Cost of Preferred Stock

The **cost of preferred stock** to the firm is the *rate of return required by investors on preferred stock issued by the company*. In the case of conventional preferred stock with a perpetual dividend, it is possible to use the simplified preferred stock valuation model developed in Chapter 8 to estimate the cost of preferred stock:

(11.8)
$$P_0 = \frac{D_p}{k_p}$$

where P_0 is the preferred stock price, D_p the annual preferred dividend, and k_p the investors' required rate of return. The cost of preferred stock, k_p, is given by the following equation:

(11.9)
$$k_p = \frac{D_p}{P_0}$$

As in the case of cost of debt, the above calculation ignores the flotation expenses associated with preferred stock issuance.

To illustrate, assume Krispy Treats Mfg. Co. is ready to issue 100,000 shares of preferred stock that pays an annual dividend of $3.90 per share. The preferred stock has been priced to sell to the public at $48 per share. The marginal cost of preferred stock is:

$$k_p = \frac{\$3.90}{\$48}$$
$$= 0.081 \text{ or } 8.1\%$$

Because payments by the firm to preferred stockholders are in the form of dividends, they are not tax deductible; therefore, the after-tax cost of preferred stock is equal to the pretax rate.

Comprehension Check Questions

1. What is the difference between marginal and historical cost of capital, and which is more relevant?
2. How is the marginal cost of debt determined?
3. Explain the difference between the pretax and after-tax cost of debt.
4. How is the marginal cost of preferred stock calculated?

Cost of Common Equity Capital

Firms raise common equity in two primary ways:

➢ *Internally*, through retained earnings
➢ *Externally*, through sale of new common stock

Some analysts and managers incorrectly assume that the cost of internal equity is zero. The **opportunity cost** concept makes it clear that this is an erroneous assumption. When funds are generated through the earnings of the firm, managers can either pay out these funds as dividends to common stockholders or the funds can be retained and reinvested in the firm. If the funds were paid out to stockholders, they could reinvest the funds elsewhere to earn an appropriate return, given the risk of the investment. Therefore, if managers decide to retain earnings and reinvest them in the firm, there must be investment opportunities in the firm that offer a return equivalent to the returns available to common stockholders (on a risk-adjusted basis) had they decided to invest the funds from the dividends elsewhere. *In other words, the appropriate way to view retained earnings is to think of it as earnings that were disbursed to shareholders, which they chose to reinvest back in the firm.* Consequently, the opportunity cost of retained earnings should be the same as if the firm raised additional common equity through a stock offering with one difference: A new stock offering will require that the firm incur flotation expenses, whereas with retained earnings no such expenses are incurred. *Thus, the cost of internal common equity is somewhat cheaper than the cost of external common equity.*

In determining the cost of common equity, we will ignore the cost of external equity and assume that all of the equity comes from internal sources—that is, retained earnings. We do this for two reasons: (1) Most firms, after the initial issue of common stock, rarely go back to the market to issue additional common stock; (2) the primary source of additional common equity for firms is retained earnings, which is normally preferred to the option of issuing new common stock because it is cheaper (due to the issuance expenses incurred when selling new shares of stock).

Like the cost of debt and preferred stock, the cost of common equity to the firm is the equilibrium rate of return required by the firm's common stock investors. It can be developed using several different approaches. We will consider two approaches, the first based on the *constant growth dividend valuation model* and the second on the *Capital Asset Pricing Model.*

Constant Growth Dividend Model As shown in Chapter 8, if the firm's future per-share dividends are expected to grow each period perpetually at a constant rate, *g*, the dividend valuation model can be written as follows:

$$P_0 = \frac{D_1}{(k_e - g)} \tag{11.10}$$

FINANCE & The Real World

Verizon's Big Gamble

Verizon Communications, the largest telephone company in America, has decided that its traditional network of switches and copper lines that lead to the nation's homes needs a massive upgrade. The company is going to spend billions of dollars to make sure every customer has a blazing fast connection, one that is many times faster than the typical broadband connection through cable modems or digital subscriber lines.

Where is Verizon going to get the money? The company ended 2002 with $45 billion in long-term debt, so it's likely that a new bond issue would carry a credit risk premium in the form of higher interest payments. In mid-2003, issuing new shares of stock looked more promising as the war with Iraq had ended and the stock market began a sharp rally, although that would dilute the investment of other shareholders. Another strategy is to finance the venture internally. Indeed, the company is seeking concessions from organized labor to lower costs for the upcoming broadband project. In addition, the company is making significant shifts in spending away from traditional voice technology and towards broadband.

The company stands to benefit from plummeting prices of high-speed technology, which sell at just 25 cents on the dollar, compared to the higher prices of the 1990s. In addition, high-speed wireless technologies have become cheaper and better. The company is betting on a combination of fiber and wireless to reach every customer.

The market is forcing Verizon's hand. Customers are downloading movies, swapping music files, and working at home with increasing frequency. By bundling voice, video, and data, cable-TV operators have already captured 2 percent of the U.S. phone market. UBS PaineWebber analyst John Hodulik estimates that cable operators held two-thirds of the market for high-speed Internet subscriptions at the end of 2002.

Federal regulations are easing, which ultimately improves the potential return on Verizon's investment. The Federal Communications Commission ruled recently that the telephone companies won't have to share next-generation networks with competitors at low government-established rates. Regulators have also released Verizon from final restrictions on its ability to offer long-distance telephone service.

Will the investment pay off? The company is betting that it will generate strong returns on its invested billions. But its foray into the next generation of communications probably isn't a choice. It's a must, if the company is to remain competitive over the next decade.

Source: Business Week online, March 31, 2003, "Verizon's Mega-Makeover"; Barron's online, March 24, 2003, "Verizon's 100-Megabit Challenge."

where $D_1 = D_0(1 + g)$, and D_0 is the current period dividend ($t = 0$). Equation 11.10 can be rearranged to obtain an expression for calculating the cost of equity:

(11.11)
$$k_e = \frac{D_1}{P_0} + g$$

To illustrate the use of Equation 11.11, suppose Krispy Treats Mfg. Co. common stock is currently selling for $20 a share. Its present dividend, D_0, is $0.96 a share, and the expected long-term dividend growth rate is 7 percent. The cost of common equity, k_e, is calculated as follows

$$k_e = \frac{\$0.96(1 + 0.07)}{\$20} + 0.07$$
$$= 0.121 \text{ or } 12.1\%$$

Thus, the constant dividend growth model provides an effective approach to determining the cost of equity for dividend paying firms that are expected to grow their dividends at a steady rate.

The key element in Equation 11.11 is the growth rate in dividends. How can one estimate this growth rate? There are basically two approaches. The first and easier approach is to use *historical data*. For instance, in the case of Krispy Treats, we can use the growth rate in dividends per share in the preceding 10 years as an estimate for the future growth rate. This is easy to do as it is available from past annual reports and other external sources such as the *Value Line Investment Survey*. The one problem with historical data is that past dividend payment patterns may not necessarily hold in the future because of changed circumstances.

The second, and theoretically superior, approach is to use *forecast data*. Forecasts of earnings (and, hence dividends, given a fixed payout ratio over time) are available from a number of sources. They can be obtained from individual brokerage houses and investment advisory services, such as Merrill Lynch, Goldman Sachs, and Value Line.

In addition, recall from Chapter 8, one can also use *consensus analysts' forecasts* (defined as the average forecasts of several reporting analysts following a stock). These are now widely available through a number of Internet sources (e.g., http://www.yahoo.com; clicking on Research from the individual stock quote page will provide detailed consensus earnings forecast information).

http://www.zacks.com
http://www1.firstcall.com/index.shtml

Capital Asset Pricing Model Approach The Capital Asset Pricing Model (CAPM), discussed in Chapter 8, provides an alternate approach to computing the cost of common equity. The dividend valuation approach discussed above is limited to firms that pay dividends and whose dividends are expected to grow at a constant rate, *g*; the CAPM on the other hand does not suffer from a similar limitation. Compared to the dividend approach, CAPM also has the advantage that risk is explicitly taken into account in the model. Recall from Chapter 8 that the CAPM formally describes the risk required rate of return trade-off for securities where risk is defined as market or systematic risk. This relationship is captured by the equation of the *security market line (SML)* as shown below:

$$k_j = r_f + \beta_j \, (r_m - r_f) \tag{11.12}$$

where k_j = the required rate of return on any security j, r_f = the expected risk-free rate, β_j = the beta (systematic risk) measure for security j, r_m = the expected return on the market portfolio. The value $(r_m - r_f)$ equals the market risk premium, or the risk premium applicable to a stock of average (beta = 1.0) risk. According to the CAPM, the cost of common equity is affected by the systematic risk of the stock (as captured by the beta), current interest rates (the risk-free rate of return), and the market's degree of risk aversion (market risk premium). These input values are determined as follows:

➢ *The risk-free rate* (r_f). The value for r_f that is most frequently used in computing the required return for a security is the current 3- or 6-month U.S. Treasury bill rate. (Some practitioners prefer to use a long-term government bond rate instead.)

➢ *The expected market risk premium* ($r_m - r_f$). The expected market risk premium is the difference between the return on the market portfolio and the risk-free rate. It is difficult to obtain expected values for this measure, so analysts often use estimates based on historical data. Recall from Chapter 6 that the average holding period return for large-company stocks during the time period from

1926 to 2002 was about 12.2 percent per year. These actual returns have varied substantially, depending on the holding periods assumed. In Chapter 6 we also observed that the average *market risk premium measured relative to Treasury bill rates* has been 8.4 percent over the 77-year period from 1926 to 2002. The average *market risk premium measured relative to long-term government bond yields* has been 6.4 percent over the same period. These risk premiums may be used to represent the market risk premium ($r_m - r_f$) in Equation 11.12. (Remember that if risk-free rate (first term in Equation 11.12) is proxied by a short-term T-bill rate then the 8.4 percent market risk premium should be used. If the risk-free rate used is the long-term government bond rate, such as the yield on 20-year U.S. government bonds, then the appropriate market risk premium is 6.4 percent.)

➤ The firm's **beta**, β_j. Beta normally is estimated by using historic values of the relationship between a security's returns and the market returns. In Chapter 6, we illustrated the computation of the beta for Delta Air Lines stock. The *Value Line Investment Survey* and brokerage firms such as Merrill Lynch regularly compute and provide betas.

To illustrate the application of the CAPM approach, assume Krispy Treats' beta is 0.8. If short-term Treasury bills are yielding 3.3 percent, Krispy Treats' cost of equity capital may be computed using the short-term SML as follows:

$$\begin{aligned} k_j &= r_f + \beta_j (r_m - r_f) \\ &= 3.3\% + 0.8(8.4\%) \\ &= 10.0\% \end{aligned}$$

If the longer-term version of the SML is used and the yield on long-term U.S. Treasury bonds is 5.5 percent, Krispy Treats' cost of equity capital may be computed as:

$$\begin{aligned} k_j &= r_f + \beta_j (r_m - r_f) \\ &= 5.5\% + 0.8(6.4\%) \\ &= 10.6\% \end{aligned}$$

The SML concept is one more tool that may be used in computing the firm's cost of equity capital, k_e. If all the parameters required of the model are correctly estimated (r_f, $r_m - r_f$, and β_j), the model should give a reasonably accurate estimate of k_e. Many analysts find it useful to compute k_e in more than one way to arrive at a consensus about the rate of return investors require on a security.

Recall from Chapter 6 that the beta measure of risk considers only the systematic risk or market risk of a stock. Poorly diversified investors may be more interested in total risk than in systematic risk. For such investors, the CAPM may understate returns required by those investors.

Table 11.2 summarizes the cost of capital formulas developed in the preceding sections.

Comprehension Check Questions

1. What are the two sources of common equity and are their costs the same?
2. What are the limitations of the dividend valuation approach to estimating the cost of common equity?
3. Describe the CAPM approach to calculating the cost of common equity.

Table 11.2 Formulas for Computing Component Costs of Capital

Cost of Debt	$k_i = k_d (1 - T)$ where: k_d = pretax cost of debt, which is equal to the yield to maturity on a new bond issued by the firm.
Cost of Preferred Stock	$k_p = \dfrac{D_p}{P_0}$ Where D_p is the annual dividend on the preferred stock and P_0 is price at which the new preferred issue is sold.
Cost of Common Equity	1. Constant growth dividend capitalization model approach, used when dividends grow at a perpetual constant rate: $k_e = \dfrac{D_1}{P_0} + g$ Where D_1 is the dividend next period, g is constant growth rate of dividends, and P_0 is the current price of the firm's common stock. 2. Capital Asset Pricing Model approach: $k_e = r_f + \beta_j (r_m - r_f)$ Where r_f is the risk-free rate of return, β_j is the beta of the stock, $r_m - r_f$ is the market risk premium

COMPUTING THE WEIGHTED AVERAGE COST OF CAPITAL

Now that we have computed the component costs of capital, all that remains to be done is to multiply the individual costs of capital by their respective weights to arrive at the weighted average cost of capital, k_a, as was shown in Equation 11.4 and repeated here:

$$k_a = \left(\begin{array}{c} \textit{Proportion of} \\ \textit{debt in capital} \\ \textit{structure} \end{array} \right) \left(\begin{array}{c} \textit{Marginal} \\ \textit{cost of debt} \end{array} \right) + \left(\begin{array}{c} \textit{Proportion of} \\ \textit{preferred stock} \\ \textit{in capital} \\ \textit{structure} \end{array} \right) \left(\begin{array}{c} \textit{Marginal} \\ \textit{cost of} \\ \textit{preferred} \\ \textit{stock} \end{array} \right)$$

$$+ \left(\begin{array}{c} \textit{Proportion of} \\ \textit{common equity} \\ \textit{in capital} \\ \textit{structure} \end{array} \right) \left(\begin{array}{c} \textit{Marginal} \\ \textit{cost of} \\ \textit{common} \\ \textit{equity} \end{array} \right)$$

$$k_a = \left(\frac{B}{B + P_f + E} \right) k_d (1 - T) + \left(\frac{P_f}{B + P_f + E} \right) k_p + \left(\frac{E}{B + P_f + E} \right) k_e$$

There are two ways to determine the weights: (1) *book value weights* and (2) *market value weights*. Book value weights are, as the phrase denotes, based on the *book values of the different sources of capital as reported in the balance sheet*. Market value weights, on the other hand, are determined from the *market capitalization values of the different securities*. These two approaches are illustrated next.

http:
Pick a search engine and do a search for weighted average cost of capital.
http://www.google.com
http://www.yahoo.com

Table 11.3 Krispy Treats' Book Value of Capital

Debt		
(110,000 bonds)		$110,000,000
Preferred Stock		
(280,000 preferred shares)		$ 14,000,000
Common Equity		
Common stock at par value		
(18,000,000 shares outstanding at		
a par value of $2.00 per share)	$36,000,000	
Capital in excess of par value	$48,000,000	
Retained earnings	$74,000,000	
		$ 158,000,000
Total capital		**$282,000,000**

Book Value Proportions

Table 11.3 shows book values for the different securities for Krispy Treats taken from the firm's balance sheet. The debt (B) consists of $110,000,000 of long-term debt as reported in the balance sheet. The preferred stock (P_f) consists of $14,000,000 reported in the balance sheet. The common equity (E) comprises the sum of the common stock at par value, capital in excess of par value, and retained earnings, which total $158,000,000. Thus, according to the book value based approach Krispy Treats' total capital adds up to $282,000,000. The proportion of debt, preferred stock, and common equity to total capital is determined as:

Proportion of debt in capital structure $= B/(B + P_f + E)$
$$= \$110,000,000 / \$282,000,000$$
$$= 0.39 \text{ or } 39\%$$

Proportion of preferred stock in capital structure $= P_f / (B + P_f + E)$
$$= \$14,000,000 / \$282,000,000$$
$$= .05 \text{ or } 5\%$$

Proportion of common equity in capital structure $= E / (B + P_f + E)$
$$= \$158,000,000 / \$282,000,000$$
$$= .56 \text{ or } 56\%$$

Combining this with the previously computed after-tax cost of debt (4.8%), cost of preferred stock (8.1%), and cost of common equity (12.1%, based on the constant growth model), the weighted average cost of capital for Krispy Treats is determined as:

$$k_a = 0.39 \times 4.8\% + 0.05 \times 8.1\% + 0.56 \times 12.1\%$$
$$= 9.1\%$$

Market Value Proportions

Market value weights are determined from market capitalization values of the different sources of capital. Assume that Krispy Treats' debt consists of just *one issue* of debt in the form of public offered bonds. This debt issue consists of 110,000 outstanding bonds with market price per bond of $980. As in the case of debt, assume Krispy Treats has one type of preferred stock outstanding. The total number of preferred shares outstanding is 280,000 with each preferred share selling for $48. Finally, assume that Krispy Treats has a total of 18,000,000 shares of common stock outstanding with a market price per share of $20. The market capitalization value

---

Table 11.4 Krispy Treats' Market Value of Capital

Debt
   110,000 bonds outstanding × $980 market price per bond $107,800,000
Preferred Stock
   280,000 shares outstanding × $48 market price per share $ 13,440,000
Common Equity
   18,000,000 shares × $20 market price per share $360,000,000
Total market capitalization   **$481,240,000**

---

for *each* security is determined as: number of shares or bonds outstanding times market price per share or bond. The market capitalization values for Krispy Treats are shown in Table 11.4. Note that these values are different from the book values shown in Table 11.3: *The book values are based on security values reflected in the balance sheet, while market values are based on security values reflected in market prices.* Using market values, Krispy Treats has a total market capitalization of $481,240,000. The corresponding proportions of debt, preferred stock, and common equity may be determined as follows:

Proportion of debt in capital structure $= B/(B + P_f + E)$
$$= \$107{,}800{,}000 \,/\, \$481{,}240{,}000$$
$$= 22.4\,\%$$

Proportion of preferred stock in capital structure $= P_f \,/\, (B + P_f + E)$
$$= \$13{,}440{,}000 \,/\, \$481{,}240{,}000$$
$$= 2.8\%$$

Proportion of common equity in capital structure $= E \,/\, (B + P_f + E)$
$$= \$360{,}000{,}000 \,/\, \$481{,}240{,}000$$
$$= 74.8\%$$

The weighted average cost of capital using the market-based proportions and the previously determined cost of debt (4.8%), cost of preferred stock (8.1%), and cost of common equity (12.1%, based on the constant growth model) is given by:

$$k_a = 0.224 \times 4.8\% + 0.028 \times 8.1\% + 0.748 \times 12.1\%$$
$$k_a = 10.4\%$$

Note that this value is considerably different from that using the book value–based proportions. Using book value–based proportions, projects with *IRRs* equal to or exceeding 9.1 percent would be deemed acceptable. Using market value–based proportions, only projects with *IRRs* exceeding or equal to 10.4 percent would be acceptable. The question is which one is right? *Theoretically, the market value–based proportions should be used. This is so because the market values capture the marginal investor's opportunity cost.*

    This is best illustrated by looking at the problem from the perspective of the marginal common stock investor. From the common stock investor's perspective, his or her investment in the firm is $20 (market price of stock) and the investor's expected rate of return is 12.1 percent (cost of common equity using the constant growth model) on this investment. This is exactly the viewpoint adopted when market–based proportions are used to calculate the weighted average cost of capital. However, when book value–based proportions are used, we are assuming that the marginal common stock investor is satisfied with a 12.1 percent return on a book value per share of $8.78 (total book value of common equity divided by shares outstanding = ($36,000,000 + $48,000,000 + $74,000,000) / 18,000,000 shares). Clearly this is incorrect since the appropriate value of the marginal investor's investment is the market price per share of $20 rather than the book value per share of $8.78.

Consequently, one has to be careful to use market values rather than book values in calculating the weighted average cost of capital, especially when the book values and market values diverge significantly. However, we present calculations using both book and market value weights for several reasons. Some firms prefer to use book values since market values change daily and it is impractical to calculate a new cost of capital on a daily basis. In the case of privately held firms book values may have to be used because market prices are not available. Many practitioners blend both approaches by combining book values of debt and preferred stock with market value of common equity. This occurs because most firms have several different issues of debt and preferred stock, not all of which are publicly held or traded; consequently market prices are often unavailable for these securities, and book values have to be substituted.

Comprehension Check Questions

1. Once component costs of capital are determined, how is the weighted average cost of capital calculated?

2. How are book value– and market value–based proportions determined?

3. Why are market value–based proportions superior to book value–based proportions?

ESTIMATING THE COST OF CAPITAL FOR ELI LILLY AND COMPANY—AN ILLUSTRATION

The cost of capital for a publicly traded company may be estimated using widely available information. This is illustrated using Eli Lilly and Company, a large publicly held corporation in the pharmaceutical industry. Most of the data is taken from the *Value Line Investment Survey, The Wall Street Journal,* and Internet sources. For purposes of this illustration we assume it is now May 1, 2003.

The first step is to calculate the component costs of capital. The next step is to determine the weights for the different sources of capital. Finally, we combine the results of the preceding two steps to obtain the weighted average cost of capital.

Component Costs of Capital

Figure 11.2 provides a copy of the *Value Line Investment Survey* information on Eli Lilly and Company. The capital structure box (along the left-hand margin and approximately in the middle) reveals that Lilly has (1) $4,358.2 million in book value of long-term debt, (2) no preferred stock, and (3) approximately 1,122.4 million shares of common stock outstanding. Since there is no preferred stock outstanding, only the cost of debt and cost of common equity need to be estimated.

Cost of Debt

The $4,358.2 million of long-term debt of Lilly is made up of several issues of debt, each with its own specific cost and maturity. This can be seen from the Lilly's annual report (not shown). In order to estimate the cost of debt properly, the cost of each of the individual sources of debt should be estimated separately. However, this is not always possible since rarely are prices available for all of the debt issues of a

LILLY (ELI) AND CO. NYSE-LLY

RECENT PRICE	59.07	P/E RATIO	23.3 (Trailing: 23.6 Median: 27.0)	RELATIVE P/E RATIO	1.51	DIV'D YLD	2.3%	VALUE LINE	1268

| | | | High: | 21.9 | 15.5 | 16.6 | 28.5 | 40.2 | 70.4 | 91.3 | 97.8 | 109.0 | 95.0 | 81.1 | 68.8 | | Target Price Range 2006 | 2007 | 2008 |
| TIMELINESS | 3 | Raised 10/4/02 | Low: | 14.4 | 10.9 | 11.8 | 15.6 | 24.7 | 35.6 | 57.7 | 60.6 | 54.0 | 70.0 | 43.8 | 52.8 | | | | |

LEGENDS
— 17.0 x "Cash Flow" p sh
· · · · Relative Price Strength
2-for-1 split 12/95
2-for-1 split 10/97
Options: Yes
Shaded area indicates recession

SAFETY 2 Raised 4/30/99
TECHNICAL 3 Lowered 4/4/03
BETA .85 (1.00 = Market)

2006-08 PROJECTIONS

	Price	Gain	Ann'l Total Return
High	100	(+70%)	16%
Low	70	(+20%)	7%

Insider Decisions

	J J A S O N D J F
to Buy	0 0 0 0 0 0 0 0 0
Options	1 1 1 0 0 0 0 1 1
to Sell	0 0 1 0 0 0 0 0 0

Institutional Decisions

	2Q2002	3Q2002	4Q2002
to Buy	316	304	358
to Sell	466	409	370
Hld's(000)	732522	743556	747343

| Percent shares traded | 9 6 3 |

% TOT. RETURN 3/03

	THIS STOCK	VL ARITH. INDEX
1 yr.	-23.4	-25.3
3 yr.	-3.1	-10.0
5 yr.	4.4	-1.8

1987	1988	1989	1990	1991	1992	1993	1994	1995	1996	1997	1998	1999	2000	2001	2002	2003	2004	© VALUE LINE PUB., INC.	06-08
3.27	3.71	3.74	4.86	4.89	5.27	5.51	4.87	6.14	6.64	7.67	8.42	9.18	9.65	10.28	9.87	10.55	11.75	Sales per sh A	15.95
.73	.88	1.05	1.29	1.38	1.50	1.49	1.45	1.69	1.81	2.02	2.43	2.72	2.97	3.08	2.85	2.95	3.40	"Cash Flow" per sh	4.75
.54	.67	.80	.98	1.13	1.22	1.15	1.10	1.15	1.33	1.57	1.94	2.28	2.65	2.76	2.55	2.55	3.00	Earnings per sh B	4.25
.25	.29	.34	.41	.50	.55	.61	.63	.66	.69	.74	.80	.92	1.04	1.12	1.24	1.34	1.42	Div'ds Decl'd per sh C	1.74
.31	.34	.34	.94	.98	.78	.54	.49	.50	.40	.33	.38	.48	.60	.79	1.01	1.00	1.00	Cap'l Spending per sh	1.10
2.73	2.94	3.37	3.25	4.24	4.18	3.90	4.57	4.93	5.52	4.18	4.04	4.60	5.37	6.32	7.37	8.40	9.35	Book Value per sh	13.85
1114.9	1097.0	1115.3	1068.6	1170.5	1170.7	1171.0	1171.7	1101.5	1105.6	1096.4	1090.2	1125.6	1123.3	1122.4	1120.0	1120.0	1110.0	Common Shs Outst'g D	1080.0
20.5	15.6	17.7	18.4	17.3	14.0	11.3	12.9	17.5	23.7	33.7	36.9	33.1	29.7	28.8	26.0	Bold figures are		Avg Ann'l P/E Ratio	20.0
1.37	1.30	1.34	1.37	1.11	.85	.67	.85	1.17	1.48	1.94	1.92	1.89	1.93	1.48	1.42	Value Line estimates		Relative P/E Ratio	1.35
2.3%	2.8%	2.4%	2.3%	2.6%	3.2%	4.7%	4.4%	3.3%	2.2%	1.4%	1.1%	1.2%	1.3%	1.4%	1.9%			Avg Ann'l Div'd Yield	2.1%

CAPITAL STRUCTURE as of 12/31/02
Total Debt $4903.6 mill. Due in 5 Yrs $1730 mill.
LT Debt $4358.2 mill. LT Interest $295.1 mill.
(35% of Cap'l)

Leases, Uncapitalized Annual rentals $107.0 mill.

Pension Assets-12/02 $3.16 bill. Oblig. $3.94 bill.

Pfd Stock None

Common Stock 1,122,443,115 shs.

MARKET CAP: $66 billion (Large Cap)

6452.4	5711.6	6763.8	7346.6	8517.6	9236.8	10003	10862	11543	11078	11815	13045	Sales ($mill) A	17200
34.5%	39.0%	37.5%	35.3%	34.8%	35.9%	38.0%	36.8%	36.3%	33.7%	32.5%	33.0%	Operating Margin	34.5%
398.3	432.2	553.7	543.5	509.8	490.4	439.7	435.8	454.9	493.0	530	560	Depreciation ($mill)	650
1347.1	1269.0	1306.6	1457.9	1729.0	2174.8	2524.6	2904.1	3009.1	2707.9	2760	3240	Net Profit ($mill)	4460
28.1%	30.4%	26.0%	25.0%	26.3%	22.1%	21.5%	20.3%	22.1%	21.7%	22.0%	22.0%	Income Tax Rate	22.0%
20.9%	22.2%	19.3%	19.8%	20.3%	23.5%	25.2%	26.7%	26.1%	24.4%	23.4%	24.8%	Net Profit Margin	25.9%
769.1	d1707	d828.4	d330.9	1129.1	799.6	3120.1	2982.3	1735.9	2740.6	2850	2995	Working Cap'l ($mill)	3650
835.2	2126.8	2502.9	2516.5	2326.1	2185.5	2811.9	2633.7	3132.1	4358.2	4000	3800	Long-Term Debt ($mill)	3400
4568.8	5355.6	5432.6	6100.1	4645.6	4429.6	5013.0	6045.9	7104.0	8273.6	9415	10400	Shr. Equity ($mill)	14935
25.4%	17.4%	17.3%	17.9%	26.2%	34.0%	33.3%	34.4%	30.1%	21.7%	20.0%	21.0%	Return on Total Cap'l	21.5%
29.5%	23.7%	24.1%	23.9%	37.2%	49.1%	50.4%	48.0%	42.4%	32.7%	29.5%	31.0%	Return on Shr. Equity	30.0%
14.0%	10.2%	10.3%	11.6%	19.6%	29.3%	30.4%	29.4%	25.4%	16.6%	14.5%	17.0%	Retained to Com Eq	18.0%
53%	57%	57%	52%	47%	40%	40%	39%	40%	49%	53%	47%	All Div'ds to Net Prof	41%

CURRENT POSITION

(SMILL)	2000	2001	12/31/02
Cash Assets	4618.2	3731.0	3654.7
Receivables	1630.7	1406.2	1670.0
Inventory (LIFO)	883.1	1060.2	1495.4
Other	811.0	741.5	983.7
Current Assets	7943.0	6938.9	7804.1
Accts Payable	661.9	624.1	676.9
Debt Due	184.3	286.3	545.4
Other	4114.5	4292.6	3841.2
Current Liab.	4960.7	5203.0	5063.5

ANNUAL RATES

of change (per sh)	Past 10 Yrs.	Past 5 Yrs.	Est'd '00-'02 to '06-'08
Sales	7.0%	8.0%	8.0%
"Cash Flow"	8.0%	10.0%	8.0%
Earnings	9.0%	14.5%	8.5%
Dividends	9.0%	10.5%	7.5%
Book Value	5.0%	5.5%	14.0%

QUARTERLY SALES ($ mill.) A

Cal-endar	Mar.31	Jun.30	Sep.30	Dec.31	Full Year
2000	2451	2621	2811	2977	10862
2001	2806	3033	2875	2829	11543
2002	2561	2775	2786	2956	11078
2003	2650	2925	3040	3200	11815
2004	3000	3200	3345	3200	13045

EARNINGS PER SHARE B

Cal-endar	Mar.31	Jun.30	Sep.30	Dec.31	Full Year
2000	.63	.61	.71	.70	2.65
2001	.74	.76	.66	.60	2.76
2002	.58	.61	.68	.68	2.55
2003	.58	.60	.67	.70	2.55
2004	.70	.73	.77	.80	3.00

QUARTERLY DIVIDENDS PAID C

Cal-endar	Mar.31	Jun.30	Sep.30	Dec.31	Full Year
1999	.23	.23	.23	.23	.92
2000	.26	.26	.26	.26	1.04
2001	.28	.28	.28	.28	1.12
2002	.31	.31	.31	.31	1.24
2003	.335				

BUSINESS: Lilly (Eli) and Co. develops, manufactures, and markets pharmaceuticals and animal health products. The company markets its products in more than 120 countries. Brand names include *Prozac* (antidepressant); *Axid* (anti-ulcer); *Kefzol, Ceclor, Lorabid* (antibiotics); *Zyprexa* (schizophrenia); *Humatrope* (human growth hormone); *Humulin* (human insulin); *Reopro* (angioplasty); *Evista* (osteoporosis). Acquired PCS 11/94. Guidant split off 10/95. Int'l business, 41% of sales; R & D, 19.4%. '02 deprec. rate: 5.9%. Estimated plant age: 17 yrs. Has 43,700 employees, 59,190 stockholders. Lilly Found. owns 14.6% of the stock; FMR, 5.9% (3/03 proxy). Chrmn, CEO, and Pres.: Sidney Taurel. Inc.: Indiana. Addr.: Lilly Corporate Center, Indianapolis, IN 46285. Tel.: 317-276-2000.

Eli Lilly's bottom line isn't likely to deviate much in 2003 from the trajectory established at the beginning of the current decade. The company closed out 2002 with a solid year-over-year quarterly improvement in per-share profits, but earnings were down for the full year. Both comparisons reflect the timing of the incursion of generic competition for *Prozac*, which had long been Lilly's workhorse. The absence of the *Prozac* drag facilitates revenue matchups this year. Share net will likely be little changed from last year's tally, however, as management has indicated that it would spend as much as necessary to launch several new drugs. *Forteo* (for treating osteoporosis) was introduced last December, and sales of *Strattera* (attention deficit-hyperactive disorder) commenced in January. The commercialization of *Cymbalta* (depression) and *Cialis* (erectile dysfunction) are also likely to begin this year, but there are complications, which are discussed below. **Myriad uncertainties temper our enthusiasm for the company's stock.** The timing of *Cymbalta's* (and *Zyprexa IM's*) launch remains subject to the resolution of long-standing manufacturing issues with the Food & Drug Administration. The FDA, meantime, has requested additional data on *Cialis*, which also has to contend with a Pfizer patent lawsuit. Significantly, too, Lilly's current flagship, *Zyprexa*, faces patent challenges from at least three makers of generic drugs. The company appears to have a strong case, but legal clouds may well hover over its stock through next year's second half. Also of concern are the high expectations that Wall Street has for the new products. The conventional wisdom for several years has been that Lilly had the best new-drug pipeline in the industry. We would note, however, that its best prospect, *Xigris*, launched in late 2001 to predictions of multibillion-dollar sales, is proving to be a huge flop, with 2002 sales below $100 million. We would note, too, that its other new drugs face well-entrenched players, like Pfizer's globally popular *Viagra*. **There's probably no urgency to make new commitments here.** Lilly stock isn't timely or inexpensive, and the company faces legal uncertainty on various fronts.
George Rho   April 25, 2003

(A) Excl. Elanco's agri business from '89. (B) Diluted eqs. Primary eqs. prior to '97, except for '92; '93. Excl. nonrec. items: '87, 79¢; '92, d$1.24; '93, d$1.47; '94, d15¢; '96, 6¢; '97, d$1.92; '98, d7¢; '99, 2¢; '00, 20¢; '01, d14¢; '02, d5¢. Excl. discon.: '94, 18¢; '95, 6¢; '99, 16¢. Next eqs. rpt. due late July. (C) Next div'd mtg. about June 15. Next ex date about May (D) In mill., adj. for stock splits. 10. Div'd payment dates: About the 10th of Mar., June, Sept. and Dec. ■ Div'd rein. plan av'ble.

Company's Financial Strength	A++
Stock's Price Stability	70
Price Growth Persistence	100
Earnings Predictability	85

To subscribe call 1-800-833-0046.

Figure 11.2
Value Line Information on Eli Lilly and Company

Source: Value Line Investment Survey, April 25, 2003

firm. Some of the debt may be privately placed and in other instances the debt may consist of commercial bank debt, which do not have secondary market prices. As an *approximation,* we can determine the cost of debt of a *representative bond of the firm* that is traded on an exchange and use that as the estimated cost for *all* debt issued by the firm. This approximation is reasonable since costs are expected to be highly correlated across the debt issues belonging to the same firm. In the case of Lilly, the *Standard & Poor's Bond Guide* shows prices for several of the bonds (Notes) issued by Lilly. These are presented in Table 11.5. We will use the Lilly bond with a coupon rate of $7\frac{1}{8}\%$, maturing in the year 2025. The closing price of this bond on April 30, 2003 was $117.00. Recall that bond prices are quoted per $100 of face value, so the actual closing price of this bond was $1,170.00. Assuming the bond matures on April 30, 2025, the number of years to maturity is 22 years. If the yield on this bond is representative of all debt issued by Lilly we can calculate the pretax cost of debt using Equation 11.6 as:

$$\$1,170 = \$71.25(\text{PVIFA}_{k_d,22}) + \$1,000(\text{PVIF}_{k_d,22})$$

Solving the above equation on the calculator yields a pretax cost of debt of 5.74 percent.

Calculator

Solution

Enter:	22	−1,170	71.25	1,000
	N	**PV**	**PMT**	**FV**
Compute:	**I/Y**		= 5.74	

Assuming a marginal tax rate of 40 percent, the after-tax cost of debt is:

$$k_i = 5.74 \ (1 - 0.40)$$
$$= 3.4\%$$

Cost of Common Equity

The cost of common equity is calculated below using the constant growth dividend valuation approach and also using the CAPM approach.

Table 11.5 Market Data on Eli Lilly and Company Bonds

Bond	Coupon	Maturity Year	S&P Rating	Month-End Price (April 2003)
Notes	5 1/2	2006	AA	109.42
Notes	8 3/8	2006	AA	117.25
Notes	6.57	2016	AA	115.50
Notes	7 1/8	2025	AA	117.00
Notes	6.77	2036	AA	117.74

Source: Standard and Poor's Bond Guide, *May 2003 issue*

Constant Growth Dividend Valuation Approach The constant growth dividend valuation approach (Equation 11.11) requires information on the dividend next period, growth rate in dividends, and the current market price per share. The constant growth rate in dividends is estimated by calculating the compounded growth rate in dividends per share over the preceding 10 years (i.e., from 1992 to 2002 taken from the *Value Line Investment Survey,* Figure 11.2):

$$\$1.24 = \$0.55 \ (\text{FVIF}_{i,\ 10})$$

Solving for *i*, or the growth rate, we obtain 8.5 percent (using the calculator). The dividend next period, D_1, can be estimated as the dividend last period (for our purposes this is assumed to be the 2002 dividend per share of $1.24 taken from Value Line) multiplied by 1 plus the growth rate:

$$
\begin{aligned}
D_1 &= D_0 \ (1 + g) \\
&= \$1.24 \ (1 + 0.085) \\
&= \$1.35
\end{aligned}
$$

The market price per share on April 30, 2002 was $63.82 (you can get this from *The Wall Street Journal* for May 1, 2003 or from an Internet source, such as Yahoo! Finance). Plugging all of the estimated values into the cost of equity equation we have:

$$
\begin{aligned}
k_e &= \frac{\$1.35}{\$63.82} + 0.085 \\
&= 0.106 \text{ or } 10.6\%
\end{aligned}
$$

Thus, the cost of common equity for Lilly using the constant growth dividend valuation approach is 10.6 percent.

Capital Asset Pricing Model Approach The CAPM approach requires estimating Equation 11.12

$$k_j = r_f + \beta_j \ (r_m - r_f)$$

For r_f we use the current (April 30, 2003) 90-day T-bill rate of 1.13 percent. This number was obtained from the Federal Reserve Web site, http://www.federalreserve.gov, but is also available in *The Wall Street Journal* (Markets Diary section). For beta, we use the Value Line reported beta of 0.85 (Figure 11.2). For the market risk premium we can use the historical market risk premium (relative to the short-term government bond rate) of 8.4 percent discussed earlier in the chapter. (As noted earlier, some analysts use the long-term risk-free rate and the market risk premium estimate relative to the long-term risk-free rate.) Plugging the values into the SML equation we have:

$$
\begin{aligned}
&= 1.13\% + 0.85 \ (8.4\%) \\
&= 8.3\%
\end{aligned}
$$

Thus, the cost of common equity for Lilly using the CAPM approach is 8.3 percent, which compares with the 10.6 percent figure using the constant growth dividend valuation approach. This variation across models is normal and highlights the fact that estimates of the cost of common equity are subject to some error. In our further analysis we will use the CAPM derived cost of common equity. Alternatively, we could have averaged the two approaches to yield a blended estimate of the cost of common equity.

Proportions of Debt and Common Equity

The next step is to determine the proportions of debt and common equity to use in the weighted average cost of capital calculations. This requires data on the market value capitalization of debt and common equity for Lilly. Since it is not possible to obtain the market prices of Lilly's different debt issues, we substitute book value of debt for the market value of debt. The market value of common equity is simply the shares outstanding multiplied by the market price per share of Lilly common stock. The estimated market value of various sources of capital for Lilly are provided below:

Market value of debt in millions (substitute book value of debt)	$ 4,358.2
Market value of common equity in millions	
(1,122.4 million shares × $63.82 market price per share)	$71,631.6
Total market capitalization	**$75,989.8**

From the above, the market-based proportions may be determined as follows:

$$\text{Proportion of debt} = B/(B + E)$$
$$= \$4,358.2 / \$75,989.8$$
$$= 0.057 \text{ or } 5.7\%$$

$$\text{Proportion of common equity} = E/(B + E)$$
$$= \$71,631.6 / \$75,989.8$$
$$= 0.943 \text{ or } 94.3\%$$

Weighted Average Cost of Capital

Combining the component costs of capital and the proportions of debt and common equity, the weighted average cost of capital for Lilly is determined as:

$$k_a = (B/(B + E)) \times k_i + (E/(B + E)) \times k_e$$
$$= 0.057 \times 3.4\% + 0.943 \times 8.3$$
$$= 8.0\%$$

Thus, a reasonable estimate for Lilly's weighted average cost of capital is 8.0 percent. This figure, or something reasonably close to this, would be the cost of capital that Lilly would use as a hurdle rate to evaluate capital expenditure proposals of average risk.

Summary

➢ A firm's cost of capital is defined as the weighted average rate the firm has to pay for the debt, preferred stock, and common equity it uses to finance its new investments in assets.

➢ Knowledge of cost of capital is important for several reasons. First, the cost of capital is needed so that capital budgeting proposals may be appropriately evaluated. The cost of capital is the minimum rate of return required on new investments of average risk undertaken by the firm. Second, knowing how to determine the cost of capital will enable firms to select a capital structure that minimizes the cost of capital and, consequently, maximize shareholder value. Finally, the cost of capital is useful in evaluating management performance. Effective management is associated with returns that on average equal or exceed the cost of capital.

➢ The general formula for calculating the weighted cost of capital, k_a, is as follows:

$$k_a = \begin{pmatrix} Proportion \\ of\ debt\ in \\ capital \\ structure \end{pmatrix} \begin{pmatrix} Marginal \\ cost\ of\ debt \end{pmatrix} + \begin{pmatrix} Proportion\ of \\ preferred \\ stock\ in \\ capital \\ structure \end{pmatrix} \begin{pmatrix} Marginal \\ cost\ of \\ preferred \\ stock \end{pmatrix}$$

$$+ \begin{pmatrix} Proportion\ of \\ common\ equity \\ in\ capital \\ structure \end{pmatrix} \begin{pmatrix} Marginal \\ cost\ of \\ common \\ equity \end{pmatrix}$$

➤ Marginal rather than historical costs should be used in estimating the component costs of capital. Marginal costs are relevant as they capture the opportunity cost of various sources of capital to the firm.

➤ The after-tax cost of debt, k_i, is calculated as follows:

$$k_i = k_d (1 - T)$$

where k_d is the pretax cost of debt calculated as the yield to maturity of a new bond issued by the firm and T is the marginal tax rate of the firm. The after-tax cost of debt takes into account the fact that the interest on debt is a tax deductible expense for most firms.

➤ A firm's cost of preferred stock, k_p, is the rate of return required by the preferred stock investors. In the case of perpetual preferred stock, the cost is calculated as follows:

$$k_p = \frac{D_p}{P_0}$$

where D_p is the annual preferred dividend and P_0 is the preferred stock price.

➤ A firm's cost of common equity is defined as the rate of return required by its common stock investors. Equity capital can be raised *internally* through retained earnings and *externally* through the sale of new common stock.

➤ A firm's cost of common equity can be determined by the dividend valuation model, or the Capital Asset Pricing Model (CAPM) using the security market line (SML).

➤ Using the dividend valuation model and assuming that dividends grow perpetually at a rate of g per year, the following equation for calculating the cost of equity capital, k_e, is obtained:

$$k_e = \frac{D_1}{P_0} + g$$

where D_1 is the dividend next period, g is the constant growth rate in dividends, and P_0 is the current stock price.

➤ Using the CAPM, the cost of equity capital can be calculated as follows:

$$k_e = r_f + \beta_j (r_m - r_f)$$

where r_f is the risk-free rate of return, β_j is the beta of the stock, $r_m - r_f$ is the market risk premium.

➤ The weights for the proportions of different sources of capital should be based on the market capitalization of the different sources of capital utilized by the firm. Thus, the proportion of debt is equal to the market value of debt divided by the sum of the market values of debt, preferred stock, and common equity.

The proportion of preferred stock is equal to the market value of preferred stock divided by the sum of the market values of debt, preferred stock, and common equity. The proportion of common equity is equal to the market value of common equity divided by the sum of the market values of debt, preferred stock, and common equity.

Questions and Topics for Discussion

1. Discuss the uses of weighted average cost of capital.

2. What is the difference between historical cost and marginal cost? Which one is relevant for computing the cost of capital? Why?

3. How does internal equity (retained earnings) differ from external equity (new stock issue)?

4. Discuss the pros and cons of various sources of estimates of future earnings and dividend growth rates for a company.

5. What market risk premium should be used when applying the CAPM to compute the cost of equity capital for a firm if

   a. The risk-free rate is the 90-day Treasury bill rate?

   b. The risk-free rate is the 20-year government bond rate?

6. How are book value weights and market value weights estimated in calculating the weighted average cost of capital?

7. Should book value weights or market value weights be used in computing the weighted average cost of capital? Why?

Self-Test Problems

ST1. Scherr Enterprises has a series of 7 percent coupon bonds outstanding with a $1,000 par value. The bonds mature in 10 years and currently sell for $1,068. Scherr's marginal tax rate is 40 percent. What is the marginal after-tax cost of debt for Scherr? (Assume annual interest payments.)

ST2. Clarke Equipment currently pays a common stock dividend of $3.50 per share. The common stock price is $60. Analysts have forecast that earnings and dividends will grow at an average annual rate of 6.8 percent for the foreseeable future. What is the marginal cost of retained earnings?

ST3. Vargo, Inc., has a beta estimated by Value Line of 1.3. The current risk-free rate (long-term) is 3.5 percent and the market risk premium is 6.4 percent. What is the cost of common equity for Vargo?

ST4. Walther Enterprises has a capital structure target of 60 percent common equity, 15 percent preferred stock, and 25 percent long-term debt. Walther's financial analysts have estimated the marginal after-tax cost of debt, preferred stock, and common equity to be 5 percent, 8.5 percent, and 11 percent, respectively. What is the weighted marginal cost of capital for Walther?

Problems

BASIC

1. Calculate the after-tax cost of a $25 million debt issue that Pullman Manufacturing Corporation (40% marginal tax rate) is planning to place privately with a large insurance company. This long-term issue will yield 6.6 percent to the insurance company.

2. Husky Enterprises recently sold an issue of 10-year maturity bonds. The bonds **BASIC** were sold at a deep discount price of $604.50 each. The bonds have a $1,000 maturity value and pay $50 interest at the end of each year. Compute the after-tax cost of debt for these bonds if Husky's marginal tax rate is 40 percent.

3. Calculate the after-tax cost of preferred stock for Bozeman-Western Airlines, **BASIC** Inc., which is planning to sell $10 million of $4.50 cumulative preferred stock to the public at a price of $48 a share. The company has a marginal tax rate of 40 percent.

4. The following financial information is available on Fargo Fabrics, Inc.: **INTERMEDIATE**

   Current per-share market price = $20.25
   Current per-share dividend = $1.12
   Current per-share earnings = $2.48
   Beta = 0.90
   Expected market risk premium = 6.4%
   Risk-free rate (20-year Treasury bonds) = 5.2%
   Past 10 years earnings per share:

20X1	$1.39	20X6	$1.95
20X2	1.48	20X7	2.12
20X3	1.60	20X8	2.26
20X4	1.68	20X9	2.40
20X5	1.79	20Y0	2.48

   This past-earnings growth trend is expected to continue for the foreseeable future. The dividend payout ratio has remained approximately constant over the past 9 years and is expected to remain at current levels for the foreseeable future.

   Calculate the cost of equity capital using the following methods:

   a. The constant growth rate dividend capitalization model approach

   b. The Capital Asset Pricing Model approach

5. The Hartley Hotel Corporation is planning a major expansion. Hartley is fi- **INTERMEDIATE** nanced 100 percent with equity and intends to maintain this capital structure after the expansion. Hartley's beta is 0.9. The expected market return is 16 percent, and the risk-free rate is 10 percent. If the expansion is expected to produce an internal rate of return of 17 percent, should Hartley make the investment?

6. Wentworth Industries is 100 percent equity financed. Its current beta is 0.9. **CHALLENGE** The expected market rate of return is 14 percent, and the risk-free rate is 8 percent.

   a. Calculate Wentworth's cost of equity.

   b. If Wentworth changes its capital structure to 30 percent debt, it estimates that its beta will increase to 1.1. The after-tax cost of debt will be 7 percent. Should Wentworth make the capital structure change?

7. The Ewing Distribution Company is planning a $100 million expansion of its **INTERMEDIATE** chain of discount service stations to several neighboring states. This expansion will be financed, in part, with debt issued with a coupon interest rate of 6.8 percent. The bonds have a 10-year maturity and a $1,000 face value, and they will be sold to net Ewing $990 per bond. Ewing's marginal tax rate is 40 percent.

   Preferred stock will cost Ewing 7.5 percent after taxes. Ewing's common stock pays a dividend of $2 per share. The current market price per share is $35. Ewing's dividends are expected to increase at an annual rate of 5 percent for the foreseeable future. Ewing expects to generate sufficient retained earnings to meet the common equity portion of the funding needed for the expansion.

Ewing's target capital structure is as follows:

Debt = 20%
Preferred stock = 5%
Common equity = 75%

Calculate the weighted cost of capital that is appropriate to use in evaluating this expansion program.

INTERMEDIATE **8.** Pacific Intermountain Utilities Company has a present capital structure (which the company feels is optimal) of 50 percent long-term debt, 10 percent preferred stock, and 40 percent common equity. For the coming year, the company has determined that its optimal capital budget can be externally financed with $140 million of 10 percent first-mortgage bonds sold at par and $28 million of preferred stock costing the company 11 percent. The remainder of the capital budget will be financed with retained earnings. The company's common stock is presently selling at $25 a share, and next year's common dividend, D_1, is expected to be $2 a share. The company has 25 million common shares outstanding. Next year's net income available to common stock (including net income from next year's capital budget) is expected to be $162 million. The company's past annual growth rate in dividends and earnings has been 6 percent. However, a 5 percent annual growth in earnings and dividends is expected for the foreseeable future. The company's marginal tax rate is 40 percent.

Calculate the company's weighted cost of capital for the coming year.

CHALLENGE **9.** Panhandle Industries, Inc., currently pays an annual common stock dividend of $2.20 per share. The company's dividend has grown steadily over the past 9 years from $1.10 to its present level; this growth trend is expected to continue. The company's present dividend payout ratio, also expected to continue, is 40 percent. In addition, the stock presently sells at 8 times current earnings (that is, its P/E multiple is 8).

Panhandle Industries stock has a beta of 1.15, as computed by a leading investment service. The present risk-free rate is 7.0 percent, and the expected return on the stock market is 13.0 percent.

a. Suppose an individual investor feels that 12 percent is an appropriate required rate of return for the level of risk this investor perceives for Panhandle Industries. Using the constant growth dividend capitalization model and the Capital Asset Pricing Model approaches, determine whether this investor should purchase Panhandle Industries stock.

b. Calculate the company's cost of equity capital using both the dividend capitalization model approach and the Capital Asset Pricing Model approach.

BASIC **10.** The Comfort Corporation manufactures sofas and tables for the recreational vehicle market. The firm's capital structure consists of 60 percent common equity, 10 percent preferred stock, and 30 percent long-term debt. This capital structure is believed to be optimal. Comfort will require $120 million to finance expansion plans for the coming year. The firm expects to generate enough internal equity to meet the equity portion of its expansion needs. The cost of retained earnings is 18 percent. The firm can raise preferred stock at a cost of 15 percent. First-mortgage bonds can be sold at a pretax cost of 14 percent. The firm's marginal tax rate is 40 percent.

Calculate the cost of capital for the funds needed to meet the expansion goal.

11. Crispy Cream Corporation is in the process of determining its capital budget for the next fiscal year. The firm's current capital structure as contained in the balance sheet is shown below:

Balance Sheet

Current assets	$ 40,000,000	Accounts Payable	$ 20,000,000
Fixed assets	400,000,000	Other current liabilities	10,000,000
Total assets	$440,000,000	Long-term debt	123,000,000
		Common stock at par	15,500,000
		Paid in capital in excess of par	51,000,000
		Retained earnings	220,500,000
		Total liabilities and stockholders' equity	**$440,000,000**

Through discussions with the firm's investment bankers, lead bank, and financial officers, the following information has been obtained:

➢ The firm considers its current capital structure based on its balance sheet to be appropriate. In other words, management feels book value proportions are appropriate in calculating the firm's weighted average cost of capital.

➢ The marginal cost of debt to the firm is 8 percent on a pretax basis.

➢ The firm currently pays $2.40 per share in dividends (D_0). Dividends have grown at a 5 percent rate in the past. This growth is expected to continue. The firm's common stock currently trades at $34 per share. The firm is expected to generate sufficient funds from retained earnings to meet its equity financing needs in the foreseeable future.

➢ The firm is in the 40 percent marginal tax bracket.

Compute Crispy Cream's marginal cost of capital.

12. Rolodex, Inc., would like to estimate its average cost of capital for the coming year. The capital budgeting plans call for funds totaling $200 million for the coming year. These funds will be raised from long-term debt, preferred stock and common equity in the same proportions as their *book values* in the firm's balance sheet shown below:

Rolodex, Inc. Balance Sheet (in millions of dollars)

Current assets	$110	Accounts payable	$ 30
Fixed assets	260	Other current liabilities	20
Total assets	**$370**	Long-term debt	128
		Preferred stock	32
		Common stock (20 million shares at par)	20
		Contributed capital in excess of par	30
		Retained earnings	110
		Total liabilities and equity	**$370**

Discussions between the firm's financial officers and the firm's investment and commercial bankers have yielded the following information:

➢ Rolodex's maximum borrowing is $80 million from its bank at a pretax cost of 13 percent.

➢ Preferred stock can be issued at a pretax cost of 16.5 percent.

➢ Rolodex expects to generate $140 million in net income. Any earnings remaining after meeting the equity portion of the $200 million capital expenditure budget will be paid out as dividends.

➤ The risk-free rate of return is 5.5 percent. The market risk premium is assumed to equal 10 percent and Rolodex's beta is estimated to be 1.2.

➤ Rolodex's marginal tax rate is 40 percent.

Compute Rolodex's weighted average cost of capital for the coming year.

CHALLENGE **13.** Jenkins Resources, Inc., has the following market capitalization based capital structure:

Financing Source	Proportion of Capital Structure
Debentures (9% coupon, $1,000 par value, 12-year maturity)	27%
Preferred stock ($2 dividend, $25 par value)	8
Common equity	65
Total	100%

Jenkins expects to raise future capital in the proportions currently indicated above. New debentures with the same features as the existing outstanding debt can be sold for $1,055 per bond. New preferred stock with features similar to the existing preferred stock would sell for $19 per share. The common equity portion of the capital needed will come from expected retained earnings. The current market price for Jenkins common stock is $40. The stock pays a current (D_0) dividend of $3. This dividend is expected to grow at an annual rate of 7 percent. What is the weighted (marginal) cost of capital for Jenkins Resources? The firm's marginal tax rate is 40 percent.

■ THOMSON ONE—Business School Edition

Go to the text Web site at http://moyer.swlearning.com, select your book, and click on the Thomson ONE button. Enter Thomson ONE—Business School Edition by using the username and password you created when you registered the serial number on your access card. One of the key inputs needed in the determination of the cost of equity of common stocks is an estimate of near-term and long-term earnings and dividend growth rates. Use the "Estimates" tab from the Thomson ONE database to determine the expected long-term earnings growth rates (LTG) for Wal-Mart Stores (WMT), Tyco International (TYC), DaimlerChrysler (DCX), Dow Chemicals (DOW), Lowe's Companies (LOW), and J.P. Morgan Chase (JPM). What factors do you think account for the differences you observe among these companies?

CHAPTER
12 Capital Structure Policy: Foundation Concepts

O ne of the most important financial decisions that the top management of any firm has to undertake is to determine what kind of *capital structure* policy to adopt. Capital structure policy simply refers to the mix of various sources of long-term capital a firm uses to finance its business. For simplicity we consider only debt and common equity in our discussion of capital structure policy. The other sources of long-term capital—including preferred stock, convertible securities, and leasing—can be thought of as being similar to debt or common equity to varying degrees. Thus, the basic question that confronts every business organization is what proportion of debt and common equity to adopt in its capital structure.

This and the next chapter deal with this question. This chapter focuses on developing an understanding of several foundation concepts that are needed in order to understand the capital structure issue. These concepts include *business risk, financial risk, operating leverage* and *financial leverage*. In addition, the chapter also covers the concept of operating *breakeven analysis,* a concept that is closely related to operating leverage and business risk. Chapter 13 provides an understanding of the various theories and their implications for the choice of appropriate capital structure policy and also examines the practical considerations in setting capital structure policy.

Chapter Objectives

After reading this chapter, you should have developed an understanding of the following:

1. Business risk, financial risk, and the factors that contribute to business and financial risk

2. Meaning and measurement of operating, financial, and combined leverage

3. Operating breakeven analysis and its relation to operating leverage and business risk

BUSINESS AND FINANCIAL RISK

Two elements of risk are primary considerations in the capital structure decision: the **business risk** and the **financial risk** of a firm. Before we define these, look first at the stylized income statement shown in Table 12.1. Contrasted to the standard income statements seen in annual reports, the income statement shown in Table 12.1 shows operating expenses that are classified as *variable* or *fixed*. **Variable operating costs** are expenses that vary directly with sales, such as sales commissions, raw materials used in the production process, and labor that goes into the production process. **Fixed operating costs** on the other hand are expenses that, by definition, are incurred regardless of the level of sales and production. Examples of fixed operating costs include the salary of the CEO, office utility expenses, accounting staff, and other overhead expenses. This dichotomous classification is a simplistic view of how actual expenses behave since in actuality many expenses may be considered to be semivariable. For example, accounting staff salaries may be fixed over a fairly wide range of sales but beyond some level additional staff may have to be added.

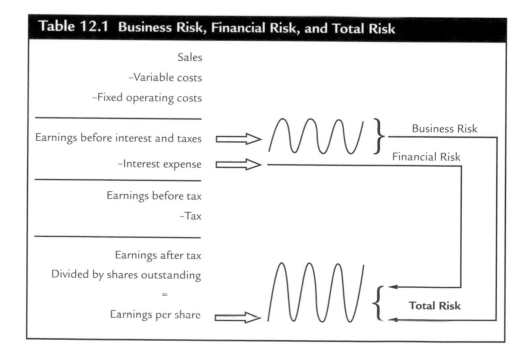

Table 12.1 Business Risk, Financial Risk, and Total Risk

However, the simpler dichotomous classification of all expenses into variable and fixed costs is helpful in explaining the concept of business risk.

Recall from Chapter 8 that common shareholders, as residual claimants, are entitled to earnings of the firm that remain after paying all expenses. Consequently, from a shareholder's perspective, the volatility in earnings per share is of primary concern as it captures *total risk* to shareholders (broken down into *business risk* and *financial risk*). With reference to the income statement in Table 12.1, *business risk is defined as the variability or uncertainty in a firm's operating income (EBIT or earnings before interest and taxes).* It is evident from the income statement that variability in earnings per share is affected by business risk or variability in EBIT. Very simply, business risk is the risk inherent in the business, or the *risk resulting from the asset side of the balance sheet.* The specific factors that contribute to business risk will be discussed shortly. *Financial risk is the additional risk to shareholders resulting from the financing mix adopted by the firm—that is, the liabilities and equity side of the balance sheet.* With reference to the income statement in Table 12.1, financial risk refers to the additional variability in earnings per share (over and above the variability attributed to business risk) as a result of the fixed financial costs (interest expenses) incurred by the firm.

http:

To get access to extensive financial information about virtually any company, explore **http://finance.yahoo.com**

Business Risk

Many factors influence the business risk of a firm.

1. The Variability of Sales Volumes Over the Business Cycle. Firms, such as Delta Air Lines, whose sales tend to fluctuate greatly over the business cycle, have more business risk than firms such as Altria (formerly Philip Morris), which is engaged primarily in the tobacco industry. For example, during the recession of 2001–2002, financial analysts were forecasting that Altria would have record-high sales and earnings. In contrast, analysts were expecting Delta Air Lines to have lower sales and losses during 2001–2002.

2. The Variability of Selling Prices. In some industries, prices are quite stable from year to year, or the firms involved may be able to increase prices regularly over time. This is true for many consumer products, such as brand name prepared-food items (e.g., Kraft cheese, Nabisco cookies). In contrast, price stability is much less certain in other industries. For example, over the past two decades, the oil companies, such as ExxonMobil, Shell Oil, and Chevron, have learned important lessons about the instability of prices as the price of crude oil declined from more than $30 a barrel to less than $10 a barrel during the 1990s, only to recently return to the $30 a barrel range. Generally, the more price-competitive an industry is, the greater is the business risk for firms in that industry.

3. The Variability of Costs. The more variability there is in the cost of the inputs used to produce a firm's output, the greater is the business risk of that firm. For example, airline companies such as Delta, American, and United, have been affected significantly by the volatility in the price of jet fuel.

4. Existence of Market Power. Firms that have greater market power (such as Microsoft), because of their size or the structure of the industries in which they compete, often have a greater ability to control their costs and the price of their outputs than firms operating in a more competitive market environment. Therefore, the greater a firm's market power, the less its business risk.

5. The Extent of Product Diversification. All other things held constant, the more diversified a firm's product line, the less variable its operating income is likely to be. For example, IBM offers a broad spectrum of products and services. IBM's extensive product lineup ranges from personal computers to large mainframe computers and semiconductor chips. IBM also generates substantial revenues from the sale of packaged software, client-specific customized software, and services such as maintenance and consulting projects. When demand for one of IBM's business lines falters, this can be somewhat offset by sales in its other lines. In contrast, EMC primarily concentrates on the manufacture of computer storage devices. Consequently, it has experienced greater volatility in operating earnings over time as demand and prices for its narrow product line have fluctuated.

6. The Degree of Operating Leverage (DOL). Operating leverage involves the use of assets having fixed costs. The more a firm makes use of operating leverage, the more sensitive EBIT will be to changes in sales. The *degree of operating leverage* refers to the multiplier effect that results from a firm's use of fixed operating costs. *The DOL is defined as the percentage change in EBIT resulting from (divided by) a given percentage change in sales (output).* Thus, if a firm is subject to considerable sales volatility over the course of the business cycle, the variability of EBIT (business risk) can be reduced by limiting the use of assets having fixed costs in the production process. Similarly, if a firm's sales tend to be stable over the business cycle, using a high percentage of fixed-cost assets in the production process will have comparatively little impact on the variability of EBIT. The financial implications of operating leverage and its measurement will be discussed more completely in the next section.

Financial Risk

Financial risk refers to the *additional variability of earnings per share and the increased probability of insolvency that arises when a firm uses fixed-cost sources of funds, such as debt and preferred stock, in its capital structure.* (Insolvency occurs when a firm is unable to meet contractual financial obligations—such as interest and principal payments on debt, payments on accounts payable, and income taxes—as they come due.) Fixed financial costs represent contractual obligations that a company must meet regardless of the EBIT level (i.e., they are independent of sales and operating earnings). The use of increasing amounts of debt and preferred stock raises the firm's fixed financial costs; this, in turn, increases the level of EBIT that the firm must earn in order to meet its financial obligations and remain in business. The reason that a firm accepts the risk of fixed-cost financing is that in doing so they hope to increase the possible returns to stockholders.

Whenever a firm uses fixed-cost financing sources it is said to be using *financial leverage* (discussed in Chapter 4). Financial leverage causes a firm's earnings per share (EPS) to change at a rate greater than the change in operating income (EBIT). For example, if a firm is 100 percent equity financed and EBIT increases (decreases) by 10 percent, EPS also will increase (decrease) by 10 percent. When financial leverage, such as long-term debt, is used, a 10 percent change in EBIT will result in a greater than 10 percent change in EPS. The notion of financial leverage is explored in detail in the next section following the discussion of operating leverage.

Comprehension Check Questions

1. How is business risk defined?
2. Name the factors that contribute to business risk.
3. How is financial risk defined?

FINANCE & The Real World

Optimal Capital Structure in the Airline Industry: US Airways versus Southwest Airlines

The commercial air transport industry has historically been a highly risky business from the perspective of investors. The industry is extremely competitive, with many new carriers entering the business, often with a plan to offer low-cost service and attract customers from the larger airlines. Price wars are common and profits suffer. The bankruptcy rate among airlines is one of the highest of any industry.

In addition to the aggressive price competition in the industry, airline companies also have huge fixed costs and very low variable costs. In finance, this characteristic is called *high operating leverage.* It costs nearly the same to fly a plane half empty as it does to fly it full. Hence, very small changes in the load factor (percentage of seats filled on each flight) have a huge impact on profitability. As seen i this and the next chapter, when a company has a high degree of business risk (due to volatility in prices, quantities sold, and operating costs, and to high operating leverage), it is prudent to use a capital structure with a low degree of financial leverage. *Low financial leverage* means that the firm uses relatively small amounts of debt to finance the assets of the firm.

Because of the high business risk of the airline industry, we would expect to see the best firms in the industry use relatively small amounts of debt to finance their assets. Arguably the best firm in the airline industry is Southwest Airlines. It has the lowest cost of operation per passenger mile

of any of the major airlines. It has made a profit every year since it was founded. In 1990, Southwest's capital structure (based on book values of debt and equity) consisted of approximately 65 percent equity and 35 percent long-term debt. By 2002, the equity proportion of the capital structure increased to 74 percent and the long-term debt proportion declined to 26 percent. Value Line projects that during the 2006–2008 period Southwest's capital structure will consist of about 87 percent equity and 13 percent long-term debt. As can be seen from the trends in capital structure for Southwest, the company has steadily moved in the direction of using less financial leverage to offset the high business risk of the airline industry.

In contrast, US Airways has struggled over the years to achieve profitability. In 1990 its capital structure consisted of 34 percent equity and 66 percent long-term debt. By 1995, after a period of sustained losses, the capital structure had slipped to barely 2 percent common equity and 98 percent long-term debt. By the end of 2001, the company had a *negative* shareholders' equity (i.e., the book value of its liabilities exceeded the book value of its assets) of $2,615 million, while long-term debt was $3,515 million. US Airways declared bankruptcy on August 11, 2002. With the bankruptcy, the creditors essentially wound up owning the firm.

Although US Airways never planned to become bankrupt, one has to wonder whether the outcome would have been different if the firm had adopted a more conservative capital structure similar to that of Southwest Airlines.

OPERATING AND FINANCIAL LEVERAGE

As discussed in the preceding section, operating and financial leverage are important components of a firm's business risk and financial risk, respectively. In the jargon of corporate finance, **leverage** refers to the *existence of fixed costs.* **Operating leverage** *exists when a firm incurs fixed operating costs, while financial leverage is present whenever a firm incurs fixed financial costs.* Leverage is a term that has been borrowed from physics. You may remember from basic physics that leverage is used to multiply the effect of a given amount of effort. Figure 12.1 shows that through the principle of leverage, a

 **Finance in the News**

Click on this button at **http://finance. swlearning.com** *for synopses of recent articles on financial leverage and capital structure.*

**Figure 12.1
Illustration of
Leverage**

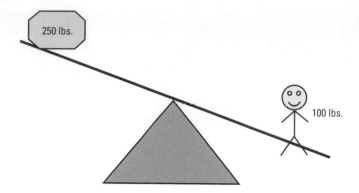

small boy can "lift" a boulder heavier than himself. So too in corporate finance can firms employ leverage to *amplify* the effect of their actions on earnings. *The use of operating leverage causes a given change in sales to have a multiplicative effect on operating profit (EBIT). On the other hand, the use of financial leverage amplifies the effect of a given change in operating profit on earnings per share.*

It is important to note that the effect of leverage is a double-edged sword. If sales increase, the existence of operating leverage will cause EBIT to increase by an even greater percentage; on the other hand a decrease in sales will result in a larger drop in operating profit. Similarly, the presence of financial leverage will cause earnings per share to increase by a larger percentage than the change in operating profit if the change is positive but will cause it to decrease by a similarly large percentage if operating profit declines. Thus, leverage magnifies shareholders' potential losses as well as potential gains. We will now look more closely at the financial implications of operating and financial leverage.

Operating Leverage

We have said that operating leverage arises whenever a firm incurs fixed operating costs. Fixed operating costs do not vary with sales or output levels. Examples are depreciation on property, plant, and equipment; rent; insurance; lighting and heating bills; and salaries of management. Such expenses are incurred regardless of how much the firm sells or produces.

The effects of operating leverage will be illustrated using two hypothetical firms: firm LO, which has low operating leverage, and firm HO, which has high operating leverage. These two firms are identical in every respect except for their operating cost structures. Both firms sell the exact same product, for the same price, and have identical sales levels. The only difference between the two firms lies in their operating expenses. Firm LO has lower fixed operating costs but higher variable costs, while firm HO has higher fixed operating costs but lower variable costs. This cost difference stems from differences in the level of technology used in the production process. Firm LO employs a more labor-intensive production process, resulting in lower fixed operating costs but a higher variable cost per unit. Firm HO on the other hand is more capital intensive (e.g., more automated) with higher fixed operating costs but a lower variable cost per unit. The characteristics of these two firms are described in Table 12.2. Firm LO has a variable cost per unit of $1.50 and annual fixed operating costs of $20,000. Firm HO has a variable cost per unit of $1.00 but annual fixed operating costs of $50,000. Both firms sell the finished product for the same per unit price of $2.00.

Table 12.2 Operating Characteristics of Firm LO and Firm HO

	Firm LO	Firm HO
Extent of operating leverage	Low	High
Selling price per unit	$ 2.00	$ 2.00
Fixed operating cost	$20,000	$50,000
Variable cost per unit	$ 1.50	$ 1.00

To illustrate the financial effects of operating leverage, we examine the impact of a change in sales on the operating profit (EBIT) of the two firms. Initially, we assume that both firms sell 60,000 units (base sales level). Table 12.3 shows the resulting operating profit for the two firms. At a volume of sales of 60,000 units, firm LO has total dollar sales of $120,000 ($2.00 selling price per unit × 60,000 units sold), fixed operating costs of $20,000, and total variable costs of $90,000 ($1.50 variable cost per unit × 60,000 units sold). This yields an EBIT of $10,000 for firm LO. For firm HO the total sales also equal $120,000, but the fixed operating costs are $50,000 and the total variable costs are $60,000 ($1.00 variable cost per unit × 60,000 units sold). The resulting EBIT for firm HO is also $10,000.

Now assume that sales for both companies increase by 10 percent from 60,000 units to 66,000. What is the resulting impact on EBIT for the two firms? Following

Table 12.3 Operating Leverage Effects for Firm LO and Firm HO

Firm LO

	Base Sales Level	10% Increase in Sales	10% Decrease in Sales
Sales volume (units)	60,000	66,000	54,000
Sales (selling price per unit × units sold)	$120,000	$132,000	$108,000
Fixed operating costs	−$ 20,000	−$ 20,000	−$ 20,000
Total variable costs (variable cost per unit × units sold)	−$ 90,000	−$ 99,000	−$ 81,000
EBIT	$ 10,000	$ 13,000	$ 7,000

Firm HO

	Base Sales Level	10% Increase in Sales	10% Decrease in Sales
Sales volume (units)	60,000	66,000	54,000
Sales (selling price per unit × units sold)	$120,000	$132,000	$108,000
Fixed operating costs	−$ 50,000	−$ 50,000	−$ 50,000
Total variable costs (variable cost per unit × units sold)	−$ 60,000	−$ 66,000	−$ 54,000
EBIT	$ 10,000	$ 16,000	$ 4,000

the same procedure as above, we find that the EBIT for firm LO is $13,000 whereas its value is $16,000 for firm HO. The percentage increases in EBIT for firms LO and HO are, respectively:

$$\text{Percentage change in EBIT for firm LO} = \frac{(\$13,000 - \$10,000)}{\$10,000} \times 100\%$$
$$= 30\%$$
$$\text{Percentage change in EBIT for firm HO} = \frac{(\$16,000 - \$10,000)}{\$10,000} \times 100\%$$
$$= 60\%$$

Why did firm HO experience a larger percentage change in operating profits than firm LO did? As one could guess, this effect is seen because firm HO's operating expenses did not go up as much as firm LO's did. The operating expenses did not rise at the same rate since firm HO has comparatively more fixed operating costs, which, by definition, do not vary with sales. On the other hand, firm LO has comparatively greater variable costs which *are* tied closely to sales. Next, we examine what happens to the two firms' EBIT when sales decline by 10 percent, from the initial level of 60,000 units to 54,000 units. Table 12.3 shows that at this level of sales, EBIT for firm LO is $7,000, while for firm HO it is $4,000. Note that on the downside the EBIT for firm HO has dropped considerably more than for firm LO. This sensitivity again occurs because firm HO has comparatively greater fixed operating costs that are incurred regardless of the sales level. On the other hand, firm LO has comparatively greater variable costs, which are simply scaled back when output is reduced. It is evident from this exercise that operating leverage has a magnifying effect on operating profits. On the upside, if sales increase, the high operating leverage firm will *increase its operating profit more* than the low operating leverage firm will. On the downside, if sales decline, the high operating leverage firm will experience a *larger drop in operating profit* than the low operating leverage firm will. *Higher fixed operating costs therefore cause a change in sales revenue to be magnified into an even greater change in earnings before interest and taxes. Consequently firms with higher operating fixed costs are associated with greater volatility or risk in their operating earnings (EBIT).*

The multiplier effect resulting from the use of fixed operating costs is known as the *degree of operating leverage.* Next, we will show how the degree of operating leverage can be measured.

Degree of Operating Leverage A firm's degree of operating leverage (DOL) is defined as *the multiplier effect resulting from the firm's use of fixed operating costs.* More specifically, *DOL can be computed as the percentage change in earnings before interest and taxes (EBIT) resulting from a given percentage change in sales (output):*

$$\text{DOL at sales level X} = \frac{\text{Percentage change in EBIT}}{\text{Percentage change in Sales}}$$

This can be rewritten as follows:

(12.1)
$$\text{DOL at sales level X} = \frac{\frac{\Delta \text{EBIT}}{\text{EBIT}}}{\frac{\Delta \text{Sales}}{\text{Sales}}}$$

where ΔEBIT and ΔSales are the changes in the firm's EBIT and sales, respectively. Because a firm's DOL differs at each sales (output) level, it is necessary to indicate the *sales level X* (units of output or dollar sales), at which operating leverage is measured.

The calculation of the DOL can be illustrated using the two hypothetical firms—LO and HO—discussed earlier. The DOL is calculated for both firms at a sales level of 60,000 units, or $120,000. The DOL for firm LO is calculated first. To apply Equation 12.1 we need the EBIT at the given or base level of sales of $120,000, which we previously determined to be $10,000 (from Table 12.3). We also need to know the EBIT at another level of sales since we want to measure the *sensitivity of EBIT to a given percentage change in sales*. From Table 12.3 we can use either the sales level of $132,000 or the $108,000. For illustrative purposes, we take the $132,000 level of sales, which resulted in an EBIT of $13,000. Plugging this information into Equation 12.1, the DOL for firm LO at a level of sales of $120,000 is calculated as:

$$\text{DOL for firm LO at \$120,000 sales} = \frac{\dfrac{(\$13{,}000 - \$10{,}000)}{(\$10{,}000)}}{\dfrac{(\$132{,}000 - \$120{,}000)}{\$120{,}000}}$$

$$= \frac{0.30}{0.10}$$

$$= 3.0$$

A DOL of 3.0 is interpreted to mean that *each 1 percent change in sales* from a base sales level of $120,000 results in a *3 percent change in EBIT* in the same direction as the change in sales. In other words, a sales increase of 10 percent results in a $10\% \times 3 = 30\%$ increase in EBIT. Similarly, a 10 percent decrease in sales produces a $10\% \times 3 = 30\%$ decrease in EBIT.

Using an identical procedure, the DOL for firm HO is determined to be:

$$\text{DOL for firm HO at \$120,000 sales} = \frac{\dfrac{(\$16{,}000 - \$10{,}000)}{(\$10{,}000)}}{\dfrac{(\$132{,}000 - \$120{,}000)}{\$120{,}000}}$$

$$= \frac{0.60}{0.10}$$

$$= 6.0$$

The DOL of 6.0 for firm HO means that a 1 percent change in sales results in a 6 percent change in EBIT in the same direction as the change in sales. The higher DOL for firm HO compared to firm LO indicates a greater magnification of sales changes into EBIT changes.

Equation 12.1 requires the use of two different values for sales and EBIT for each firm. Another equation that can be used to compute a firm's DOL more easily and does not require two sets of statements is as follows:

$$\text{DOL at sales level } X = \frac{(\text{Sales} - \text{Variable costs})}{\text{EBIT}} \tag{12.2}$$

Inserting data from Table 12.3 for firm LO gives the following:

$$\text{DOL for firm LO at \$120,000 sales} = \frac{(\$120{,}000 - \$90{,}000)}{\$10{,}000}$$

$$= \frac{\$30{,}000}{\$10{,}000}$$

$$= 3.0$$

Note that this is the same answer we got using Equation 12.1. Similarly, computing the DOL for firm HO, we get

$$\text{DOL for firm HO at \$120,000 sales} = \frac{(\$120,000 - \$60,000)}{\$10,000}$$

$$= \frac{\$60,000}{\$10,000}$$

$$= 6.0$$

Once again, the answer we get is identical to that from Equation 12.1.

In summary, firms that have high fixed operating costs will have high degrees of operating leverage, causing them to experience greater multiplicative effects on their EBIT for a given change in sales. A firm's DOL is a function of the nature of its production process. If the firm employs large amounts of labor-saving equipment in its operations, it tends to have relatively high fixed operating costs and relatively low variable operating costs. Such a cost structure yields a high DOL, which results in large operating profits (positive EBIT) when sales are high and large operating losses (negative EBIT) should sales be depressed.

Now that we have examined the effects of fixed operating costs, let us examine the impact of fixed financial costs.

Financial Leverage

Fixed financial costs are incurred whenever a firm uses sources of financing that obligate it to make fixed contractual payments on a periodic basis. Examples of such obligations are interest payments on debt and dividend payments on preferred stock. Similar to operating leverage, the use of financial leverage results in a *multiplier effect* on profits to shareholders. To illustrate the impact of fixed financial costs, let us take two hypothetical firms—ZERO and FIFTY. Firm ZERO has no debt, preferring instead to finance all of its assets with common equity. Firm FIFTY, on the other hand, uses a mix of 50 percent debt and 50 percent common equity to finance its assets. Except for the difference in capital structure, the two firms are identical in all respects. Specifically, this means that the two firms have identical products, selling prices, and operating cost structures. Since their business risks and assets are identical, the EBIT for the two firms will be the same for any given level of sales. This also means that in studying the effects of the financial leverage on the two firms we can hold EBIT constant between the firms and examine the effect of financial leverage on the resulting earnings per share.

Table 12.4 presents the characteristics of firms ZERO and FIFTY. Both firms have the same asset structure with each having $50,000 in total assets; they each have the same selling price, variable cost, and fixed operating costs. Note that the operating cost structure of these two firms is identical to that of firm HO used in illustrating the concept of operating leverage. With regard to the financial structure, firm ZERO's assets are financed entirely with common equity comprised of 10,000 shares at $5 per share, while firm FIFTY's assets are financed with 50 percent debt and 50 percent common equity consisting of a $25,000 loan at 8 percent interest per year and 5,000 common shares at $5 per share. Thus, firm ZERO does not incur any fixed financial cost whereas firm FIFTY has to pay interest expense of $2,000 per year ($25,000 × 0.08). The interest expense is a *contractual obligation* that firm FIFTY has to pay regardless of the level of operating earnings (EBIT).

To illustrate the effect of financial leverage, we examine the impact of a change in EBIT on the earnings per share (EPS) of the two firms. We begin with the assumption that the base level EBIT for the two firms is $10,000. Table 12.5 shows the resulting EPS for firm ZERO and firm FIFTY. Since firm ZERO has no fixed financial costs (i.e., no interest expense), the earnings before tax is the same as the EBIT. Assuming a tax rate of 40 percent, the earnings after taxes are equal to

Table 12.4 Characteristics of Firm ZERO and Firm FIFTY

	Firm ZERO	Firm FIFTY
Total assets	$50,000	$50,000
Selling price per unit	$2.00	$2.00
Variable cost per unit	$1.00	$1.00
Fixed operating costs	$50,000	$50,000
Capital structure	100% common equity ($50,000)	50% debt ($25,000)
		50% common equity ($25,000)
		cost of debt: 8%
Shares outstanding	10,000 shares @ $5/share	5,000 shares @ $5/share

$6,000. Given the 10,000 shares outstanding for firm ZERO, the EPS is equal to $0.60 (earnings after taxes divided by common shares outstanding = $6,000 / 10,000). For firm FIFTY we begin with the same EBIT level of $10,000 but subtract interest expense of $2,000, which yields earnings before taxes of $8,000. Subtracting taxes at the assumed 40 percent tax rate, the resulting earnings after taxes is equal to $4,800. Dividing the earnings after tax by the 5,000 common shares outstanding for firm FIFTY, we get an EPS of $0.96.

Next we assume a change in EBIT from $10,000 to $12,000—a 20 percent increase from the base level. The resulting earnings per share effect on the two firms are shown in Table 12.5. For firm ZERO the EPS is now equal to $0.72, while for firm FIFTY it is $1.20. The percentage increases in EPS for the two firms are calculated as:

$$\text{Percentage change in EPS for firm ZERO} = \frac{(\$0.72 - \$0.60)}{(\$0.60)} \times 100\%$$
$$= 20\%$$

$$\text{Percentage change in EPS for firm FIFTY} = \frac{(\$1.20 - \$0.96)}{(\$0.96)} \times 100\%$$
$$= 25\%$$

Firm FIFTY experiences a higher percentage change in EPS than firm ZERO does. Notice, too, that the percentage change in EPS for firm ZERO is equal to the percentage change in EBIT. This should not be surprising since firm ZERO has no financial leverage. Consequently, the percentage change in EPS always mirrors the percentage change in EBIT. Firm FIFTY registers a greater percentage increase in its EPS because interest expenses are fixed—debtholders do not receive increased interest payments simply because the firm did better (i.e., had a higher EBIT)—leaving shareholders with a larger share of the EBIT. The resulting higher net income for firm FIFTY is spread over fewer shares, yielding a greater percentage change in EPS compared to that seen for firm ZERO. Now let's see what happens on the downside, that is, when EBIT declines.

Table 12.5 shows that when EBIT declines by 20 percent from $10,000 to $8,000, the EPS for firm ZERO drops to $0.48 while for firm FIFTY it drops to $0.72. On a percentage basis the decline for firm ZERO is 20 percent while for firm FIFTY it is 25 percent. The larger percentage drop in EPS for firm FIFTY occurs because interest costs are fixed and have to be paid regardless of the firm's operating performance. As in the case of operating leverage, we find that financial leverage is a double-edged sword. An increase in EBIT translates to a bigger gain in EPS for

Table 12.5 Financial Leverage Effects for Firm ZERO and Firm FIFTY

Firm ZERO

	Base EBIT Level	20% Increase in EBIT	20% Decrease in EBIT
EBIT	$10,000	$12,000	$8,000
Interest expense (Interest rate × debt)	—	—	—
Earnings before taxes	$10,000	$12,000	$8,000
Taxes (40%)	−$ 4,000	−$ 4,800	−$3,200
Earnings after taxes	$ 6,000	$ 7,200	$4,800
EPS (Earnings after taxes divided by shares outstanding)	$ 0.60	$ 0.72	$ 0.48

Firm FIFTY

	Base EBIT Level	20% Increase in EBIT	20% Decrease in EBIT
EBIT	$10,000	$12,000	$8,000
Interest expense (Interest rate × debt)	−$ 2,000	−$ 2,000	−$2,000
Earnings before taxes	$ 8,000	$10,000	$6,000
Taxes (40%)	−$ 3,200	−$ 4,000	−$2,400
Earnings after taxes	$ 4,800	$ 6,000	$3,600
EPS (Earnings after taxes divided by shares outstanding)	$ 0.96	$ 1.20	$ 0.72

the more financially leveraged firm but by the same token a reduction in EBIT results in a bigger decline in EPS for the more financially leveraged firm. *Financial leverage amplifies the effects of changes in EBIT on earnings per share. Consequently, fixed financial costs result in greater volatility in EPS.*

The multiplier effect resulting from fixed financial costs is known as the ***degree of financial leverage.*** Next, we show how the degree of financial leverage can be measured.

Degree of Financial Leverage A firm's degree of financial leverage (DFL) is computed as the *percentage change in earnings per share (EPS) resulting from a given percentage change in earnings before interest and taxes (EBIT):*

$$\text{DFL at EBIT level X} = \frac{\text{Percentage change in EPS}}{\text{Percentage change in EBIT}}$$

This can be rewritten as follows:

(12.3)
$$\text{DFL at EBIT level X} = \frac{\dfrac{\Delta \text{EPS}}{\text{EPS}}}{\dfrac{\Delta \text{EBIT}}{\text{EBIT}}}$$

where ΔEPS and ΔEBIT are the changes in EPS and EBIT, respectively. Because a firm's DFL is different at each EBIT level, it is necessary to indicate the EBIT level, *X*, at which financial leverage is being measured.

Let's apply Equation 12.3 to firm ZERO and firm FIFTY using the data contained in Table 12.5. The formula requires known values for the EPS at the base level of EBIT ($10,000 in this case) and for one other level of EBIT. For illustrative purposes, we can take $12,000 as the second level of EBIT. Plugging in the values for firm ZERO into Equation 12.3, we have:

$$
\text{DFL for firm ZERO at \$10,000 EBIT} = \frac{\dfrac{(\$0.72 - \$0.60)}{(\$0.60)}}{\dfrac{(\$12,000 - \$10,000)}{\$10,000}}
$$

$$
= \frac{0.20}{0.20}
$$

$$
= 1.0
$$

The DFL for firm ZERO is 1.00. This means *every 1 percent change in EBIT* of firm ZERO from a base EBIT level of $10,000 results in *1 percent change in EPS* in the same direction as the EBIT change. Since firm ZERO by assumption has no fixed financial costs the percentage change in EBIT *does not* get magnified into a larger change in earnings per share.

Using Equation 12.3, the DFL for firm FIFTY is:

$$
\text{DFL for firm FIFTY at \$10,000 EBIT} = \frac{\dfrac{(\$1.20 - \$0.96)}{(\$0.96)}}{\dfrac{(\$12,000 - \$10,000)}{\$10,000}}
$$

$$
= \frac{0.25}{0.20}
$$

$$
= 1.25
$$

This indicates that for firm FIFTY each *1 percent change in EBIT* from a base EBIT level of $10,000 produces a *1.25 percent change in EPS* in the same direction as the change in EBIT. A 10 percent increase in EBIT for firm FIFTY results in a 10% × 1.25 = 12.5% increase in EPS. On the other hand, a 10 percent decrease in EBIT produces a 12.5 percent decrease in EPS.

Measuring a firm's DFL using Equation 12.3 is somewhat cumbersome because it necessitates using two EBIT and EPS estimates. An alternative formula that requires data only for the base level of EBIT is:

$$
\text{DFL at EBIT level X} = \frac{\text{EBIT}}{\text{EBIT} - I} \tag{12.4}
$$

where *I* is the firm's interest payment. Substituting the appropriate values for firm ZERO and firm FIFTY yields the following degrees of financial leverage for the two firms:

$$
\text{DFL for firm FIFTY at \$10,000 EBIT} = \frac{\$10,000}{\$10,000 - 0}
$$

$$
= 1.0
$$

$$
\text{DFL for firm FIFTY at \$10,000 EBIT} = \frac{\$10,000}{\$10,000 - \$2,000}
$$

$$
= 1.25
$$

These values are identical to those obtained by using Equation 12.3.

Equation 12.4 assumes that the only fixed financial costs are from interest expenses. The formula can be easily modified to take into account preferred stock financing, which entails fixed preferred dividend payments:

(12.5)
$$\text{DFL at EBIT level X} = \frac{\text{EBIT}}{\text{EBIT} - I - \dfrac{D_p}{(1 - T)}}$$

where D_p is the firm's fixed preferred dividend payments and T the firm's marginal income tax rate. Unlike interest payments, preferred dividend payments are not tax deductible. Therefore, on a comparable basis, a dollar of preferred dividends costs the firm more than a dollar of interest payments. Dividing preferred dividends in Equation 12.5 by $(1 - T)$ puts interest and preferred dividends on an equivalent, pretax basis.

In summary, higher fixed financial costs lead to a higher DFL, which causes changes in EBIT to have a multiplicative effect on earnings per share. Just as a firm can change its DOL by raising or lowering fixed operating costs, it also can change its DFL by increasing or decreasing fixed financial or capital costs. The amount of fixed capital costs incurred by a firm depends primarily on the mix of debt, preferred stock, and common stock equity in the firm's capital structure. Thus, a firm that has a relatively large proportion of debt and preferred stock in its capital structure will have relatively large fixed capital costs and a high DFL.

Combined Leverage

Combined leverage occurs whenever a firm has both fixed operating and financial costs. It represents the magnification of sales increases (or decreases) into relatively larger EPS increases (decreases), resulting from the firm's use of both types of leverage. The joint multiplier effect is known as the ***degree of combined leverage.***

Degree of Combined Leverage A firm's degree of combined leverage (DCL) is computed as the *percentage change in earnings per share resulting from a given percentage change in sales:*

$$\text{DCL at sales level X} = \frac{\text{Percentage change in EPS}}{\text{Percentage change in sales}}$$

This can be rewritten as follows:

(12.6)
$$\text{DCL at sales level X} = \frac{\dfrac{\Delta \text{EPS}}{\text{EPS}}}{\dfrac{\Delta \text{Sales}}{\text{Sales}}}$$

where ΔEPS and ΔSales are the changes in a firm's EPS and sales, respectively, and X represents the level of sales at which the firm's combined leverage is measured. *The degree of combined leverage is also equal to the product of the degree of operating leverage and the degree of financial leverage.*

(12.7)
$$\text{DCL at sales level X} = \text{DOL} \times \text{DFL}$$

To simplify matters, Equations 12.2 and 12.4 can be substituted into Equation 12.7 to obtain a new formula for determining the DCL in terms of basic income statement quantities:

$$\text{DCL at sales level X} = \frac{\text{Sales} - \text{Variable costs}}{\text{EBIT}} \times \frac{\text{EBIT}}{\text{EBIT} - I}$$

or

$$\text{DCL at sales level X} = \frac{\text{Sales} - \text{Variable costs}}{\text{EBIT} - I} \qquad (12.8)$$

If capital sources include preferred stock, the above formula is modified to include preferred dividend payments on a pretax basis in the denominator:

$$\text{DCL at sales level X} = \frac{\text{Sales} - \text{Variable costs}}{\text{EBIT} - I - \dfrac{D_p}{(1 - T)}} \qquad (12.9)$$

The implementation of the above formulas for DCL can be illustrated using the data for firm FIFTY shown in Table 12.6. The table shows EBIT and EPS calculations for firm FIFTY at the base sales level of 60,000 units or $120,000 and also at 66,000 units or $132,000. Inputting the appropriate values into Equation 12.6, the DCL is determined to be

$$\text{DCL for firm FIFTY at } \$120,000 \text{ sales} = \frac{\dfrac{\$1.68 - \$0.96}{\$0.96}}{\dfrac{\$132,000 - \$120,000}{\$120,000}}$$

$$= \frac{0.75}{0.10}$$

$$= 7.5$$

For firm FIFTY this DCL of 7.5 is interpreted as follows: *a 1 percent change in sales* from the base level results in *a 7.5 percent change in EPS* in the same direction as the change in sales. If sales increase by 10 percent, the EPS increases by $10\% \times 7.5 = 75\%$. On the other hand a sales decrease of 10 percent produces a 75% drop in earnings per share.

The second equation for DCL (Equation 12.7) can be used if DOL and DFL for the firm are known. For firm FIFTY the DFL was previously calculated as 1.25.

Table 12.6 Combined Leverage Effects for Firm FIFTY

	Base Sales Level	10% Increase in Sales
Sales volume (units)	60,000	66,000
Sales		
(selling price per unit × units sold)	$120,000	$132,000
Fixed operating costs	−$ 50,000	−$ 50,000
Total variable costs	−$ 60,000	−$ 66,000
(variable cost per unit × units sold)		
EBIT	$ 10,000	$ 16,000
Interest expense (Interest rate × debt)	−$ 2,000	−$ 2,000
Earnings before taxes	$ 8,000	$ 14,000
Taxes (40%)	−$ 3,200	−$ 5,600
Earnings after taxes	$ 4,800	$ 8,400
EPS (Earnings after taxes divided		
by shares outstanding)	$ 0.96	$ 1.68

Recall that operating leverage characteristics of firm FIFTY are identical to that of firm HO discussed in connection with operating leverage, which had a DOL of 6.0. Given the DOL and DFL values, the DCL is calculated using Equation 12.7 as:

$$\text{DCL for firm FIFTY at } \$120,000 \text{ Sales} = 6.0 \times 1.25$$
$$= 7.5$$

This value is identical to the answer obtained using Equation 12.6. Using Equation 12.8 or 12.9, the DCL is:

$$\text{DCL for firm FIFTY at } \$120,000 \text{ Sales} = \frac{\$120,000 - \$60,000}{\$10,000 - \$2,000}$$
$$= 7.5$$

All three formulas yield identical answers. The choice of which formula to use depends on the information provided.

The degree of combined leverage used by a firm is *a measure of overall variability of earnings per share due to fixed operating and capital costs as sales levels vary*. Fixed operating and capital costs can be combined in many different ways to achieve a desired DCL. In other words, a number of possible trade-offs can be made between operating and financial leverage. Equation 12.7 is particularly insightful in this regard. For example, a target DCL of 6.0 can be achieved several different ways: a DOL of 6.0 and a DFL of 1.0, a DOL of 3.0 and DFL of 2.0, a DOL of 2.0 and a DFL of 3.0, etc. However, it is important to keep in mind that DOL is largely determined by the nature of the industry; that is, the choice of DOL is not entirely at management's discretion. Assuming DOL is for the most part not a discretionary variable, Equation 12.7 highlights the role of capital structure in managing total risk of the firm. If a firm has relatively high DOL, for example, and wishes to maintain a moderate level of DCL, it can offset the high DOL with a lower DFL (use less debt financing and therefore incur lower interest expenses). Alternatively, a firm that has a low DOL can afford to have a high DFL and still maintain DCL at a "reasonable" level. This trade-off will become an important consideration when we discuss determinants of optimal capital structure policy in the next chapter.

Comprehension Check Questions

1. Define operating, financial, and combined leverage.
2. What are the formulas for degrees of operating, financial, and combined leverage?
3. What implication does DOL, DFL, and DCL have for the selection of an appropriate capital structure?

OPERATING BREAKEVEN ANALYSIS

Operating breakeven analysis is closely related to the concept of operating leverage discussed earlier in the chapter. A knowledge of breakeven analysis is useful in further understanding the role that operating leverage plays in determining business risk. **Breakeven analysis** (also known as *cost-volume-profit analysis*) considers the relationships among a firm's sales, fixed and variable operating costs, and EBIT (operating income) at various output levels.

Graphic Breakeven Analysis

Breakeven analysis can be developed graphically, algebraically, or as a combination of the two. Figure 12.2 is an example of a basic linear breakeven analysis chart.

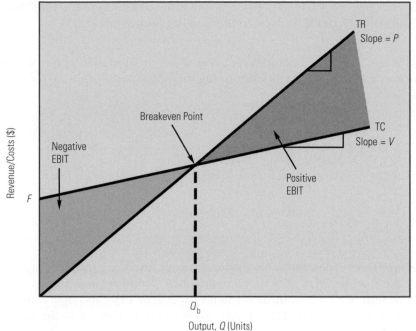

Figure 12.2
Linear Breakeven
Analysis Chart

Costs and revenues (measured in dollars) are plotted on the vertical axis, and output (measured in units) is plotted on the horizontal axis. The *total revenue* function, TR, represents the total revenue the firm will realize at each output level, given that the firm charges a constant selling price, P, per unit of output. Similarly, the *total (operating) cost function*, TC, represents the total cost the firm will incur at each output level. Total cost is computed as the sum of the firm's fixed operating costs, F, which are independent of the output level, plus the variable costs, which increase at the constant rate, V, per unit of output.

The assumptions of a constant selling price per unit, P, and a constant variable cost per unit, V, yield *linear* relationships for the total revenue and total cost functions. The breakeven point occurs at point Q_b in Figure 12.2, where the total revenue and the total cost functions intersect. If a firm's output level is below this breakeven point—that is, if TR < TC—it incurs *operating losses (negative EBIT)*. If the firm's output level is above this breakeven point—that is, if TR > TC—it realizes *operating profits (positive EBIT)*.

Determining a firm's breakeven point graphically involves three steps:

1. Drawing a line through the origin with a slope of P to represent the TR function.
2. Drawing a line that intersects the vertical axis at F and has a slope of V to represent the TC function.
3. Determining the point where the TR and TC lines intersect, dropping a perpendicular line to the horizontal axis, and noting the resulting value of Q_b.

Algebraic Breakeven Analysis

To determine a firm's breakeven point algebraically, it is necessary to set the total revenue and total (operating) cost functions equal to each other and solve the resulting equation for the breakeven volume.

Total revenue is equal to the selling price per unit times the output quantity:

$$TR = P \times Q \qquad (12.10)$$

Total (operating) cost is equal to fixed plus variable costs, where the variable cost is the product of the variable cost per unit times the output quantity:

(12.11)
$$TC = F + (V \times Q)$$

Setting the total revenue and total cost expressions equal to each other (that is, setting EBIT = TR − TC = 0) and substituting the breakeven output Q_b for Q results in the following:

$$TR = TC$$

or

(12.12)
$$PQ_b = F + VQ_b$$

Finally, solving Equation 12.12 for the breakeven output Q_b yields the following:

$$PQ_b - VQ_b = F$$
$$(P - V)Q_b = F$$

(12.13)
$$Q_b = \frac{F}{P - V}$$

The difference between the selling price per unit and the variable cost per unit, $P - V$, sometimes is referred to as the **contribution margin per unit.** It measures how much each unit of output contributes to meeting fixed costs and operating profits. Therefore, it also can be said that the breakeven output is equal to the fixed costs divided by the contribution margin per unit.

Breakeven analysis can also be performed in terms of dollar sales, rather than units of output. The breakeven dollar sales volume, S_b, can be determined by the following expression:

(12.14)
$$S_b = \frac{F}{\left(1 - \frac{V}{P}\right)}$$

where $\frac{V}{P}$ is the variable cost ratio (that is, the variable cost per dollar of sales).

Applying Breakeven Analysis

Consider the case of firm LO discussed earlier in the chapter in connection with the concept of operating leverage. Recall firm LO had a selling price per unit, P, of $2.00; fixed operating costs, F, of $20,000; and a variable cost per unit, V, of $1.50. Substituting these values into Equation 12.13 yields the following:

$$Q_b = \frac{\$20,000}{(\$2.00 - \$1.50)}$$
$$Q_b = 40,000 \text{ units}$$

Thus, firm LO must sell 40,000 units just to cover its fixed costs—that is, EBIT = 0. Sales in excess of the 40,000 units will result in firm LO realizing operating profits. Firm LO's breakeven output also can be determined graphically, as shown in Figure 12.3. The breakeven dollar sales volume for firm LO is given by Equation 12.14:

$$S_b = \frac{\$20,000}{\left(1 - \frac{\$1.50}{\$2.00}\right)}$$
$$S_b = \$80,000$$

Alternatively, we could have simply multiplied the breakeven output, Q_b, by the selling price per unit, P:

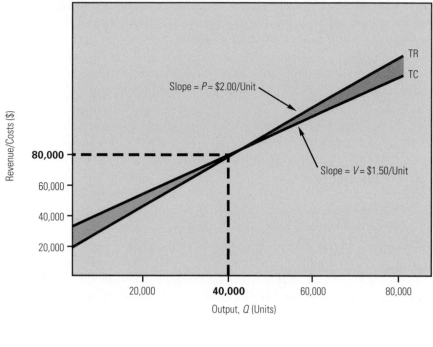

Figure 12.3
Linear Breakeven
Analysis Chart for
Firm LO

$$= 40,000 \times \$2.00$$
$$= \$80,000$$

Relation to Operating Leverage

From an examination of the breakeven output formula, Equation 12.13, it should be evident that breakeven volume increases as operating leverage (fixed operating costs) increases. Recall from earlier in the chapter that firm HO had higher fixed operating costs compared to firm LO. Plugging in firm HO values into Equation 12.13 yields the following breakeven output:

$$Q_b = \frac{\$50,000}{(\$2.00 - \$1.00)}$$
$$Q_b = 50,000 \text{ units}$$

This contrasts with a lower breakeven output of 40,000 units for firm LO. In calculating the DOL we found that firm LO also had a lower DOL of 3.00 compared to a DOL of 6.00 for firm HO (at a base sales level of 60,000 units). *Thus, higher operating leverage (holding everything else constant) results in a higher breakeven output and a higher degree of operating leverage.* The higher breakeven output for firm HO suggests a higher business risk for the firm compared to firm LO.

Summary

➢ Capital structure refers to the relative amount of long-term debt and common equity used to finance a firm.

➢ The business risk of a firm refers to the variability of the firm's operating income (EBIT). It is influenced by the variability of sales volumes, prices, and costs over the business cycle. Business risk is also influenced by a firm's market power and its use of operating leverage.

➤ The financial risk of a firm is the additional variability of earnings per share and the increased probability of insolvency that arises when a firm uses fixed-cost sources of funds, such as debt and preferred stock, in its capital structure.

➤ Leverage refers to a firm's use of assets and liabilities having fixed costs. A firm uses leverage in an attempt to earn returns in excess of the fixed costs of these assets and liabilities, thus increasing the returns to common stockholders.

➤ Operating leverage occurs when a firm uses assets having fixed operating costs. The degree of operating leverage (DOL) measures the percentage change in a firm's EBIT resulting from a 1 percent change in sales (or units of output). As a firm's fixed operating costs rise, its DOL increases.

➤ Financial leverage occurs when a firm makes use of funds (primarily from debt and preferred stock) having fixed capital costs. The degree of financial leverage (DFL) measures the percentage change in the firm's EPS resulting from a 1 percent change in EBIT. As a firm's fixed capital costs rise, its DFL increases.

➤ The combined leverage of a firm is equal to the product of the degrees of operating and financial leverage. These two types of leverage can be combined in many different ways to achieve a given degree of combined leverage (DCL). The total variability of the firm's EPS is a combination of business risk and financial risk.

➤ Breakeven analysis (also known as cost-volume-profit analysis) considers the relationships among a firm's sales, fixed and variable operating costs, and EBIT (operating income) at various output levels.

➤ Operating breakeven volume is the quantity of output that just covers the fixed operating costs, that is, the volume of output that yields an EBIT=0. Algebraically, the breakeven quantity of output is equal to the fixed operating costs divided by the difference between the price per unit and the variable cost per unit.

➤ A higher degree of operating leverage, holding everything else constant, is associated with a higher breakeven volume.

Questions and Topics for Discussion

1. Define leverage as it is used in finance.

2. Define and give examples of the following:
   a. Fixed costs
   b. Variable costs

3. Define the following:
   a. Operating leverage
   b. Financial leverage

4. How is a firm's degree of combined leverage (DCL) related to its degrees of operating and financial leverage?

5. Is it possible for a firm to have a high degree of operating leverage and a low level of business risk? Explain.

6. Explain the difference between business risk and financial risk.

7. What other factors besides operating leverage can affect a firm's business risk?

8. How are the degrees of operating leverage and financial leverage determined?

9. Explain how a linear breakeven chart is constructed when a firm's selling price, variable cost per unit, and fixed costs are known.

10. What is the relation between breakeven volume and degree of operating leverage?

11. Assuming that all other factors remain unchanged, determine how a firm's breakeven point is affected by each of the following:

 a. The firm finds it necessary to reduce the price per unit because of competitive conditions in the market.

 b. The firm's direct labor costs increase as a result of a new labor contract.

 c. The Occupational Safety and Health Administration requires the firm to install new ventilating equipment in its plant. (Assume that this action has no effect on worker productivity.)

Self-Test Problems

ST1. Pinches Salt Company has the following income statement for 20X1:

Sales	$5,000,000
Variable operating costs	1,000,000
Fixed operating costs	2,000,000
EBIT	$2,000,000
Interest expense	500,000
EBT	$1,500,000
Tax (at 40%)	600,000
EAT	$ 900,000
Preferred dividends	100,000
Earnings available to common stockholders	$ 800,000
Shares outstanding	400,000

 a. Compute Pinches' DOL, DFL, and DCL.

 b. If sales increase to $5,500,000, what is your forecast of EPS?

ST2. The OK Tractor Company is attempting to develop and market a new garden tractor. Fixed costs to develop and produce the new tractor are estimated to be $10,000,000 per year. The variable cost to make each tractor has been estimated at $2,000. The marketing research department has recommended a price of $4,000 per tractor.

 a. What is the breakeven level of output for the new tractor?

 b. If management expects to generate a profit target (EBIT) of $2,000,000 from the tractor each year, how many tractors must be sold?

Problems

1. The Hurricane Lamp Company forecasts that next year's sales will be $6 million. Fixed operating costs are estimated to be $800,000, and the variable cost ratio (that is, variable costs as a fraction of sales) is estimated to be 0.75. The firm has a $600,000 loan at 10 percent interest. It has 60,000 shares of common stock outstanding. Hurricane Lamp is in the 40 percent corporate income tax bracket.

 a. Forecast Hurricane Lamp's earnings per share (EPS) for next year. Develop a complete income statement using the format illustrated in Table 12.1. Then determine what Hurricane Lamp's EPS would be if sales were 10 percent above the projected $6 million level.

INTERMEDIATE

b. Calculate Hurricane Lamp's degree of operating leverage (DOL) at a sales level of $6 million using the following:

　　i. Equation 12.1

　　ii. Equation 12.2

　　iii. What is the economic interpretation of this value?

c. Calculate Hurricane Lamp's degree of financial leverage (DFL) at the EBIT level corresponding to sales of $6 million using the following:

　　i. Equation 12.3

　　ii. Equation 12.4

　　iii. What is the economic interpretation of this value?

d. Calculate Hurricane Lamp's degree of combined leverage (DCL) using the following:

　　i. Equation 12.6

　　ii. Equation 12.9

　　iii. The degree of operating and financial leverage calculated in (b) and (c).

　　iv. What is the economic interpretation of this value?

2. The Alexander Company reported the following income statement for 20X1:

Sales		$15,000,000
Less Operating expenses		
Wages, salaries, benefits	$ 6,000,000	
Raw materials	3,000,000	
Depreciation	1,500,000	
General, administrative, and selling expenses	1,500,000	
Total operating expenses		12,000,000
Earnings before interest and taxes (EBIT)		$ 3,000,000
Less Interest expense		750,000
Earnings before taxes		$ 2,250,000
Less Income taxes		1,000,000
Earnings after taxes		$ 1,250,000
Less Preferred dividends		250,000
Earnings available to common stockholders		$ 1,000,000
Earnings per share—250,000 shares outstanding		$　　4.00

Assume that all depreciation and 75 percent of the firm's general, administrative, and selling expenses are *fixed costs* and that the remainder of the firm's operating expenses are *variable costs*.

a. Determine Alexander's fixed costs, variable costs, and variable cost ratio.

b. Based on its 20X1 sales, calculate the following:

　　i. The firm's DOL

　　ii. The firm's DFL

　　iii. The firm's DCL

c. Assuming that next year's sales increase by 15 percent, fixed operating and financial costs remain constant, and the variable cost ratio and tax rate also remain constant, use the leverage figures just calculated to forecast next year's EPS.

d. Show the validity of this forecast by constructing Alexander's income statement for next year according to the format in Table 12.1.

3. Gibson Company sales for the year 20X1 were $3 million. The firm's variable operating cost ratio was 0.50, and fixed costs (that is, overhead and depreciation) were $900,000. Its average (and marginal) income tax rate is 40 percent. Currently, the firm has $2.4 million of long-term bank loans outstanding at an average interest rate of 12.5 percent. The remainder of the firm's capital structure consists of common stock (100,000 shares outstanding at the present time).

CHALLENGE

a. Calculate Gibson's degree of combined leverage for 20X1.

b. Gibson is forecasting a 10 percent increase in sales for next year (20X2). Furthermore, the firm is planning to purchase additional labor-saving equipment, which will increase fixed costs by $150,000 and reduce the variable cost ratio to 0.475. Financing this equipment with debt will require additional bank loans of $500,000 at an interest rate of 12.5 percent. Calculate Gibson's expected degree of combined leverage for 20X2.

c. Determine how much Gibson must reduce its debt in 20X2 (for example, through the sale of common stock) to maintain its DCL at the 20X1 level.

4. Albatross Airline's fixed operating costs are $5.8 million, and its variable cost ratio is 0.20. The firm has $2 million in bonds outstanding with a coupon interest rate of 8 percent. Albatross has 30,000 shares of preferred stock outstanding, which pays a $2 annual dividend. There are 100,000 shares of common stock outstanding. Revenues for the firm are $8 million, and the firm is in the 40 percent corporate income tax bracket.

BASIC

a. Compute Albatross' degree of operating leverage.

b. Compute its degree of financial leverage.

c. Compute its degree of combined leverage and interpret this value.

5. Given the following information for Computech, compute the firm's degree of combined leverage (dollars are in thousands except EPS):

BASIC

	20X1	20X2
Sales	$500,000	$570,000
Fixed costs	120,000	120,000
Variable costs	300,000	342,000
Earnings before interest and taxes	80,000	108,000
Interest	30,000	30,000
Earnings per share (EPS)	**$1.00**	**$1.56**

6. McGee Corporation has fixed operating costs of $10 million and a variable cost ratio of 0.65. The firm has a $20 million, 10 percent bank loan and a $6 million, 12 percent bond issue outstanding. The firm has 1 million shares of $5 (dividend) preferred stock and 2 million shares of common stock ($1 par). McGee's marginal tax rate is 40 percent. Sales are expected to be $80 million.

INTERMEDIATE

a. Compute McGee's degree of operating leverage at an $80 million sales level.

b. Compute McGee's degree of financial leverage at an $80 million sales level.

c. If sales decline to $76 million, forecast McGee's earnings per share.

7. A firm has earnings per share of $2.60 at a sales level of $5 million. If the firm has a degree of operating leverage of 3.0 and a degree of financial leverage of 5.5 (both at a sales level of $5 million), forecast earnings per share for a 2 percent sales decline.

BASIC

INTERMEDIATE

8. A firm has sales of $10 million, variable costs of $5 million, EBIT of $2 million, and a degree of combined leverage of 3.0.

   a. If the firm has no preferred stock, what are its annual interest charges?

   b. If the firm wishes to lower its degree of combined leverage to 2.5 by reducing interest charges, what will be the new level of annual interest charges?

BASIC

9. Fastron, Inc. expects sales of silicon chips to be $60 million this year. Because this is a very capital-intensive business, fixed operating costs are $20 million. The variable cost ratio is 40 percent. The firm's debt obligations consist of a $4 million, 10 percent bank loan and a $20 million bond issue with a 11 percent coupon rate. Fastron has 1 million shares of common stock outstanding and its marginal tax rate is 40 percent.

   a. Compute Fastron's degree of operating leverage.

   b. Compute Fastron's degree of financial leverage.

   c. Compute Fastron's degree of combined leverage.

   d. Compute Fastron's EPS if sales decline by 5 percent.

INTERMEDIATE

10. McFrugal, Inc. has expected sales of $20 million. Fixed operating costs are $2.5 million, and the variable cost ratio is 65 percent. McFrugal has outstanding a $12 million, 8 percent bank loan. The firm also has outstanding 1 million shares of common stock ($1 par value). McFrugal's tax rate is 40 percent.

   a. What is McFrugal's degree of operating leverage at a sales level of $20 million?

   b. What is McFrugal's current degree of financial leverage?

   c. Forecast McFrugal's EPS if sales drop to $15 million.

INTERMEDIATE

11. Earnings per share (EPS) for Valcor, Inc. are $3 at a sales level of $2 million. If Valcor's degree of operating leverage is 2.0 and its degree of combined leverage is 8.0, what will happen to EPS if operating income increases by 3 percent?

INTERMEDIATE

12. East Publishing Company is doing an analysis of a proposed new finance text. Using the following data, answer (a) through (d).

Fixed Costs per Edition:	
Development (reviews, class testing, and so on)	$18,000
Copyediting	5,000
Selling and promotion	7,000
Typesetting	40,000
Total	$70,000

Variable Costs per Copy:	
Printing and binding	$4.20
Administrative costs	1.60
Salespeople's commission (2% of selling price)	.60
Author's royalties (12% of selling price)	3.60
Bookstore discounts (20% of selling price)	6.00
Total	$16.00
Projected Selling Price	$30.00

The company's marginal tax rate is 40 percent.

   a. Determine the company's breakeven volume for this book:

     i. In units.

     ii. In dollar sales.

b. Develop a breakeven chart for the text.

c. Determine the number of copies East must sell in order to earn an (operating) profit of $21,000 on this text.

d. Suppose East feels that $30.00 is too high a price to charge for the new finance text. It has examined the competitive market and determined that $24.00 would be a better selling price. What would the breakeven volume be at this new selling price?

13. Logue Lock Company expects its fixed costs next year to be $750,000. The selling price for its lock is $40. Logue is considering the purchase of some new equipment that is expected to reduce unit variable costs from a current level of $25 to a new level of $20. How large could the additional fixed costs from the new equipment be without impacting the breakeven point? **INTERMEDIATE**

14. Euro Bicycles has current fixed costs of $500,000. The firm produces bicycles for the serious bike enthusiast. The bikes sell for $1,500 per unit. Variable operating costs per unit are $500. Euro Bicycles plans to buy a machining tool that will produce a more precise fit between the various components used to build the frame of the bicycle. The machine tool will add $50,000 in annual fixed costs. Variable operating costs are not expected to change as a result of the new tool. If Euro Bicycles wishes to leave its breakeven point unchanged, what action must it take? **CHALLENGE**

15. Rodney Rogers, a recent business school graduate, plans to open a wholesale dairy products firm. Rogers expects first year sales to total $5,500,000. He desires to earn a target pretax profit of $1,000,000 during his first year of operation. Variable costs are 40 percent of sales. **INTERMEDIATE**

a. How large can Rogers' fixed costs be if he is to meet his profit target?

b. What is Rogers' breakeven level of sales at the level of fixed costs determined in (a)?

CHAPTER

13

Capital Structure Policy: Theory and Practice

Chapter 12 demonstrated that one of the most important financial decisions that the top management of any firm has to undertake is deciding on its capital structure policy—the relative proportion of debt and equity to total capital employed by the firm. Table 13.1 shows the proportion of long-term debt to total capital for selected industries in the United States. From the numbers, it is evident that there is quite a variation between industries. At one extreme, the entertainment technology, e-commerce, and computer software and services industries seem to dislike debt; at the other extreme, natural gas, hotel, and auto and truck manufacturing industries seem to have an affinity for debt financing. Most industries, such as apparel manufacturing, retail stores, and drug manufacturers, appear to favor a middle ground with moderate amounts of debt in their capital structures. Table 13.2 shows the proportion of long-term debt to total capital for selected firms within the pharmaceutical drug industry. Notice the wide variation in corporate **debt ratios** within the industry. The average debt to total capital ratio for the drug industry is about 21 percent (from Table 13.1), but Table 13.2 reveals that Pfizer, Novartis, and Schering-Plough have little or no long-term debt while Wyeth, Cephalon, and IDEC Pharamceuticals have debt structures that are considerably higher than the industry average.

In the preceding chapter we learned about some of the foundation concepts that will aid us in understanding the capital structure issue. In this chapter, we examine from a theoretical and practical perspective the factors that influence the choice of an appropriate capital structure. In addition we will study the EBIT–EPS framework as a potential tool for analyzing alternate capital structure policies.

Chapter Objectives

After reading this chapter, you should have developed an understanding of the following:

1. The different theories of capital structure policy and their implications for optimal capital structure choice

2. The practical considerations in determining an appropriate capital structure for a given firm

3. The EBIT–EPS framework for analyzing capital structure policy

Table 13.1 Debt Ratios (Long-term debt to total capital) for Selected Industries for Year 2002

Industry	Number of Firms	Debt Ratio (%)*
Entertainment Technology	13	1.5
E-Commerce	19	11.4
Computer Software & Services	54	15.7
Retail Special Lines	69	19.5
Drug	46	21.1
Electronics	27	24.9
Entertainment Industry	15	26.1
Telecom Services	23	27.5
Apparel and Textile	18	31.8
Retail Store	21	34.5
Electric Utilities (eastern U.S.)	24	35.1
Electric Utilities (central U.S.)	24	35.1
Electric Utilities (western U.S.)	15	35.9
Chemical Diversified	16	36.1
Tobacco	6	43.5
Food Processing Industry	35	45.6
Paper	16	46.6
Machinery	48	46.9
Food Processing Industry	36	47.4
Chemical Specialty	33	48.2
Beverage (Alcoholic) Industry	7	48.9
Steel (Integrated)	5	51.1
Bank	31	56.1
Hotel	17	57.4
Natural Gas (Diversified)	21	59.4
Auto & Truck	9	67.7
Air Transport	15	75.5

*Debt ratio is defined as the percentage of industry composite long-term debt to the sum of the industry composite long-term debt and stockholders' equity.
Source: Calculated from data taken from various issues of the Value Line Investment Survey, *first quarter, 2003.*

Table 13.2 Debt Ratios (Long-term debt to total capital) for Selected Firms in the Pharmaceutical Industry for Year 2002

Firm	Debt Ratio (%)*
Abbott Laboratories	28.7
Abgenix, Inc.	25.0
Albany Molecular	0.0
Andrx Group	0.0
Aventis	19.8
Barr Labs	5.4
Biovail Corp.	32.9
Bristol-Myers Squibb	36.4
Celgene Corp.	0.0
Cephalon, Inc.	64.7
Chiron	16.2
Covance, Inc.	0.0
Enzon, Inc.	67.7
Forrest Labs.	0.0
Genzyme General	19.1
GlaxoSmithKline	31.2
ICN Pharmaceuticals	37.8
IDEC Pharmaceuticals	46.0
Ivax Corp.	56.3
King Pharmaceuticals	14.4
Lilly (Eli) & Co.	28.3
Medarex, Inc.	33.4
Medicis Pharmaceuticals	48.2
Medimmune, Inc.	11.5
Merck & Co.	20.4
Mylan Labs.	1.4
Nektar Therapeutics	60.1
Neurocrine Biosci.	2.0
Novartis AG	5.3
Perrigo Co.	0.0
Pfizer Inc.	11.7
Pharma Products	1.6
Pharmacia Corp.	24.4
Protein Design	1.8
Quintiles Trans.	1.3
Schering-Plough	0.0
Watson Pharmaceuticals	16.3
Wyeth	52.8

*Debt ratio is defined as the percentage of long-term debt to the sum of the long-term debt and stockholders' equity.

Source: Calculated from data taken from the Value Line Investment Survey, *January 24, 2003.*

CAPITAL STRUCTURE THEORY

Now that we have a basic understanding of financial leverage from Chapter 12, we are ready to tackle the issue of whether **capital structure** matters from a theoretical perspective. We know from the preceding chapter that the more debt a firm chooses to have the greater the potential for higher returns to shareholders, but the greater, too, is the volatility of returns to shareholders.

The question that we pose here is: What effect does increasing debt relative to common equity have on firm value? Alternatively, one could ask what effect does increasing debt relative to common equity have on the firm's cost of capital? To prove that the two questions really are equivalent, recall that according to the principles of *valuation* the value of an asset is simply the discounted value of the cash flows from the asset. *In the case of a firm its value is simply the discounted value of all future cash flows to the firm.* If we assume that there are no taxes and that the firm is a no-growth firm—that it pays out all of its earnings as dividends and reinvests an amount exactly equal to the depreciation for the upkeep of the assets—then the cash flows to the firm can be considered a perpetuity equal to the EBIT. To arrive at firm value, *V*, the EBIT is discounted at the average cost of capital, k_a, since the EBIT is allocated to (belongs to) debt and common stockholders,

$$V = \frac{\text{EBIT}}{k_a}$$

(13.1)

As evident from the formula above, if EBIT is held constant, an increase in *V* means a decrease in k_a. Consequently, *maximizing V is equivalent to minimizing k_a.*

The capital structure theory is concerned with the question of whether the choice of capital structure—that is, proportion of debt to total assets or, alternatively, the proportion of debt to equity—affects firm value or the average cost of capital. If it is determined that the debt ratio has no bearing on firm value or on the cost of capital, then the question of capital structure choice is *irrelevant*—one capital structure is as good as another. In this case, firms need not concern themselves with what debt ratio to adopt; they can choose a debt ratio at random and it will be as good as any. On the other hand, if it is determined that the debt ratio has an effect on firm value or on the cost of capital, it would be in the firm's interest to find out which specific capital structure would maximize firm value or minimize the cost of capital.

There are several theoretical models that help to shed light on this question. Our primary focus will be on:

The Modigliani-Miller model with no corporate income taxes

The Modigliani-Miller model with corporate income taxes

The tax shield-bankruptcy cost trade-off model.

We will also cover a few additional models, but in much less detail; such models include the *agency conflict theory,* the *personal and corporate tax model,* the *information-signaling model,* and the *pecking order theory.*

Modigliani-Miller Model without Corporate Income Taxes

In 1958, two prominent financial researchers, Franco Modigliani and Merton Miller (MM), showed that under certain assumptions, firm value and average cost of capital are independent of the firm's capital structure.[1] They were the first to undertake a formal analysis of the capital structure question using a scientific approach. Basically what they did was to compare the value and cost of capital of two firms identical in every respect except for one feature: one firm had no financial leverage while the other had some debt in its capital structure. In developing their theoretical model, MM listed several assumptions:

1. No corporate income taxes
2. Business risk is constant
3. No growth in cash flows

---

[1] To read their complete paper see Franco Modigliani and Merton Miller, "The Cost of Capital, Corporation Finance, and the Theory of Investment," *American Economic Review* 48 (June 1958): 261–296.

4. Perfect capital market conditions:

There are no transactions costs for buying and selling securities.

All investors have the same information about the firm and this information is available readily at no cost.

No single investor can have significant influence on security prices.

All investors can borrow and lend at the same rate.

5. No bankruptcy costs

Based on these assumptions, MM go on to prove that *capital structure has no impact on firm value or upon the average cost of capital.* The assumptions MM make appear to be far-fetched from reality but remember that this type of research was the first undertaking of its kind at the time. The MM findings are nonetheless insightful in that they show what *did not* affect firm value or cost of capital. Before exploring the MM findings in detail, let us review some of the assumptions MM make. The first assumption of no corporate income taxes was relaxed by MM in a revision published in 1963. (We will examine that revised work in the section dealing with corporate income taxes.)

The second assumption of constant business risk was included in order to control for risk factors other than financial leverage. By holding constant business risk between the leveraged and unleveraged firms, we can focus on the potential firm value or cost of capital differences that can *only be attributed to capital structure differences* and not to differences in business risk. The analytical process MM used was akin to that of a scientific experiment where one controls all other elements except the one being studied. For example, to study the effect of temperature on plant growth one would hold other things constant such as soil nutrients, amount of light, humidity, etc., and vary just the temperature levels.

MM's third assumption of no growth is mostly for convenience. It makes the math easier since zero growth reduces the cash flows to a simple perpetuity, and the **present value** of a **perpetuity**, if you recall from Chapter 5, is simply the annuity amount divided by the appropriate discount rate. The perfect capital market assumptions are a set of assumptions that are commonly invoked in many financial theories.

The last assumption of no **bankruptcy** costs is a significant one. It basically means that if a firm goes bankrupt, unable to discharge its obligations to its bondholders, it can still restructure its assets or liquidate its assets at fair value. The practical implication of the no bankruptcy cost assumption is that bondholders do not sustain any losses in the event of a bankruptcy. As a result bondholders do not require a premium for bankruptcy and the firm is thus able to raise as much debt as it pleases at a constant rate. (This assumption is relaxed by other researchers; we will explore this later.)

Given the above assumptions, MM prove that the values of the levered firm (V_l) and unlevered firm (V_u) are equal. This is their well-known *Proposition I:*

(13.2)
$$V_\mathrm{l} = V_\mathrm{u}$$

This proposition is illustrated in Figure 13.1. The *x*-axis (horizontal) represents the financial leverage of the firm defined as the ratio of debt to equity; *B/E*. The *y*-axis (vertical) represents the value of the firm. According to MM Proposition I (Equation 13.2) the value of the firm is invariant to the financial leverage assumed by the firm. Regardless of how little or how much debt the firm chooses to have, that act alone cannot affect the value of the firm. *MM argue that firm value stems from the earnings generated from the assets owned. Since changing the capital structure (debt-equity ratio)*

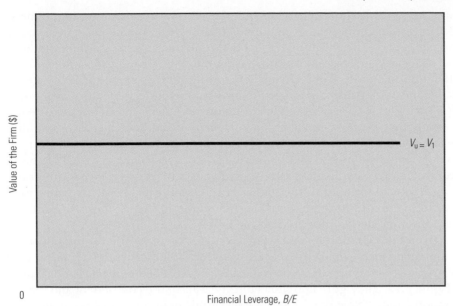

**Figure 13.1
Graphic Representation of MM Theory with No Corporate Income Tax: Effect on Firm Value**

does not affect the asset structure of the firm, the earnings are unaffected; consequently, firm value is unaffected. In other words, capital structure does not affect the asset side of the balance sheet, which is what ultimately determines the earnings power of the firm. All that capital structure determines is how the earnings generated by the assets (EBIT) are allocated between the various capital holders. This concept is illustrated in Figure 13.2: If you think of a pie as representing the earnings of the firm, Figure 13.2 shows that in the case of the unlevered firm the entire pie goes to common equity holders. In the case of the levered firm, the pie is still the same size since the assets are identical; however the pie now has to be shared between debt holders and common equity holders. *MM argue that since the overall size of the earnings pie is the same, the actual value has to be identical for both the levered and the unlevered firm.*

MM support their view by arguing that a process of **arbitrage** will prevent otherwise equivalent firms from having different market values simply because of capital structure differences. *Arbitrage is the process of simultaneously buying and selling the same or equivalent securities to take advantage of price differences and making a profit without taking on any additional risk.* Applying this to the MM theory, suppose there are two unlevered firms with identical business risk—firm A and firm B. If firm A replaced some of its common equity with debt (became leveraged) and the MM theory did

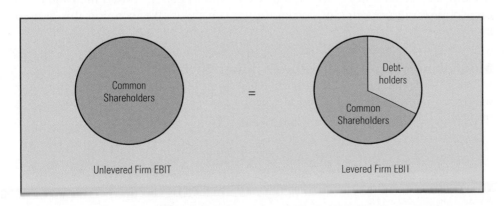

**Figure 13.2
Comparison of Levered and Unlevered Firm Earnings**

not hold, its value should increase and, therefore, its stock price should increase. MM suggest that under these circumstances, investors would engage in an arbitrage transaction. Specifically, in this case, MM argue that investors would sell the over-priced stock of the levered firm (firm A) and use the proceeds from the sale along with additional funds from personal borrowing (at the same rate as a corporation would, one of the MM assumptions) to invest in the undervalued firm's shares (firm B). This arbitrage process results in an additional return without any increase in risk.

Note that in the arbitrage process detailed by MM, the investor has substituted his or her own personal leverage (MM refer to this as *homemade leverage*) for corporate leverage. By doing so the total leverage (corporate leverage plus the personal leverage) and, by extension, risk are held constant. MM argue that this arbitrage process will continue until the selling of the levered firm's stock drives down its price to the point where it is equal to the unlevered firm's stock price, which has been driven up due to increased buying by investors.

From the valuation formula, Equation 13.1, we know that if the values of two firms that are identical in all respects except for capital structure are the same, then the average cost of capital for the two firms also must be identical. This is illustrated in Figure 13.3. The figure also shows the behavior of the cost of debt and the cost of common equity. The cost of debt is a constant throughout the entire range of feasible debt ratios. The cost of equity is increasing with the debt ratio, which is to be expected. With increasing debt comes increasing degrees of financial leverage for which shareholders are going to demand a higher required rate of return for the additional volatility incurred from the leverage. What is most significant about the graph is the shape of the k_a curve: It is horizontal. *The cost of capital for any levered firm is equal to the cost of capital for the unlevered firm.* The horizontal line for k_a is consistent with the invariance of firm value with financial leverage depicted in Figure 13.1. Figure 13.3 shows that as we move to the right and substitute cheaper debt for common equity, the marginal cost of the remaining common equity is increasing just enough to offset the cheaper cost of debt, ultimately resulting in a flat k_a curve. This is simply a restatement of the equal-pie diagram (Figure 13.2): All that leverage does is to reallocate the earnings of the firm between shareholders and debt holders.

The broad implication of the MM model *without* corporate income taxes is that firms may choose whatever capital structure they desire. The choice simply does not matter! *By merely altering the capital structure, firms cannot increase firm value or reduce the average cost of capital.* The original MM results were striking, creating a shock wave through the financial community. But no one could disprove their results; the results simply followed from the assumptions. Researchers and financial practitioners, though, had a big problem with the MM assumption of no corporate income tax and zero bankruptcy costs. MM, in a subsequent paper, revised their model to incorporate the presence of corporate income taxes. We examine this revised model next.

Modigliani-Miller Model with Corporate Income Taxes

In 1963 Modigliani and Miller published a revision of their original paper, this time incorporating the effect of corporate income taxes.[2] With corporate income taxes in place, MM find that the *value of the levered firm is equal to that of an otherwise equivalent unlevered firm plus the **tax shield** benefit from debt,*

(13.3)
$$V_l = V_u + TB$$

---

[2]Franco Modigliani and Merton Miller, "Corporate Income Taxes and the Cost of Capital," *American Economic Review* (June 1963): 433–443.

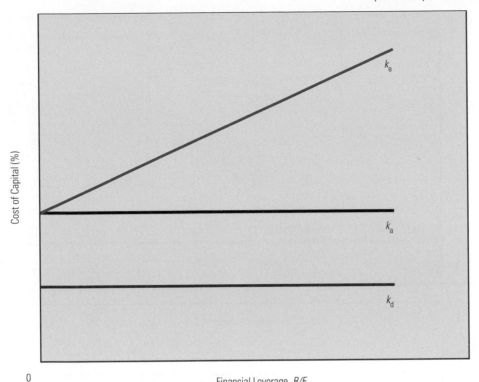

Figure 13.3
Graphic Representation of MM Theory with No Corporate Income Tax: Effect on Cost of Capital

where T is the corporate income tax rate and B is the amount of debt in the firm's capital structure. *The second term on the right hand side of the above the equation (TB) is the present value of the tax shield benefit from debt. Once corporate income tax is introduced, debt becomes advantageous (relative to common equity) because interest expense is tax deductible whereas dividend payments are not.* Let's look more closely at how the term *TB* is derived. For the levered firm with B dollars of debt and interest rate i, the amount of tax shield benefit annually is

$$\text{Annual tax shield benefit} = T \times (i \times B) \tag{13.4}$$

The term in parenthesis is the annual interest expense. The tax shield benefit is the interest expense multiplied by the corporate income tax rate. If debt is perpetual, as assumed in the MM model, the interest tax shield benefit is a perpetuity whose present value is equal to

$$\text{Present value of tax shield benefit in perpetuity} = \frac{T \times (i \times B)}{i} \tag{13.5}$$

Canceling the i in the numerator and denominator yields

$$\text{Present value of tax shield benefit in perpetuity} = TB \tag{13.6}$$

which, as you can see, is the second term on the right-hand side of Equation 13.3. So, *TB* is simply the *present value of all future tax shield benefit from the debt assumed by the levered firm.*

From Equation 13.3 we can conclude that the value of the firm increases as the amount of debt in the capital structure increases. This is illustrated in Figure 13.4. Figure 13.5 portrays the MM original and revised models in terms of its effect on the firm's various costs of capital. The solid lines represent the MM revised model with corporate income taxes. For comparative purposes the various costs of capital under the original MM model with no corporate taxes are also shown—these are

**Figure 13.4
Graphic Representation of MM Theory with Corporate Income Tax: Effect on Firm Value**

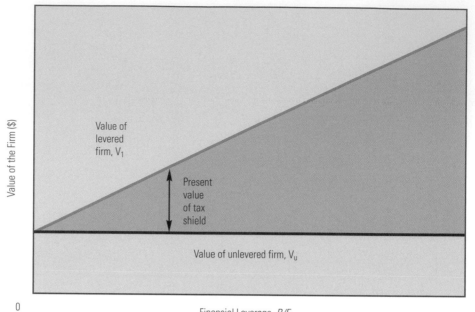

**Figure 13.5
Graphic Representation of MM Theory with Corporate Income Tax: Effect on Cost of Capital**

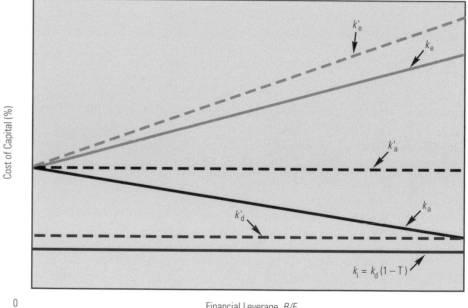

represented by the dashed lines denoted k'_d, k'_e, and k'_a. Previously, we noted that value and cost of capital are mirror images: An increase in firm value is associated with a decrease in cost of capital and vice versa. Consistent with this view, Figure 13.5 shows that under the revised MM model with corporate taxes, the more debt a firm takes on, the lower the average cost of capital to the firm. The figure also shows the cost of debt and cost of common equity. Under the revised model it is clear that both the cost of debt and cost of equity are lower when corporate taxes are factored in. Note that under the MM tax model the effective cost of debt to the firm is only $k_d (1 - T)$ because interest is tax deductible. Also, note that the cost of equity under the MM tax model is less steep than the original MM model because *the tax subsidy benefit of debt accrues to the shareholders* who are therefore willing to accept a lower premium relative to the original no tax model. As a result, the overall cost of capital declines as more debt leverage is used.

The MM model with corporate tax implies that a firm should increase its level of debt to the point where the capital structure consists almost entirely of debt. (We cannot quite say 100 percent debt because at that point the debt holders become, for all intents and purposes, equity holders, and thus the value of the levered firm will then equal the value of the unlevered firm.) In other words, in order to maximize firm value, the capital structure should consist of almost all debt—that is, 99.9 percent debt. This implication is at odds with what we commonly observe in practice. It is rare to find companies with extremely high levels of debt, let alone 99.9 percent debt. Hence, there must be some other factor or factors influencing the choice of an optimal capital structure. One potentially important factor is *bankruptcy cost*. The next section explores the role of bankruptcy cost in determining the optimal capital structure.

Tax Shield and Bankruptcy Cost Trade-off Theory

This theory builds on the Modigliani-Miller corporate tax model with the addition of costly bankruptcy. The MM model assumes zero bankruptcy costs or financial distress costs. Consequently, lenders in the MM world do not demand higher returns as the firm increases its debt leverage. The reality, though, is different from the model. Lenders demand higher interest rates to compensate for the increased financial risk assumed by the firm in order to offset the costs of bankruptcy.

Bankruptcy costs can be broken down into *direct and indirect costs. Direct costs of bankruptcy include legal and administrative costs incurred by a firm subject to bankruptcy proceedings. Indirect costs of bankruptcy, which could be much larger than the direct costs, consist mostly of opportunity costs.* For example, managerial attention in a firm that is subject to bankruptcy is diverted to managing the bankruptcy process instead of running the business and generating revenues. Another example is the loss of sales when suppliers are unwilling to supply goods and services because of potential nonpayment, and customers are unwilling to buy products from financially distressed firms that may not be around much longer to provide services related to such products. For example, just prior to Kmart's declaration of bankruptcy in early 2002, Fleming Cos., a major supplier of groceries to Kmart, withheld supplies due to the uncertainty of getting paid. Another opportunity or indirect cost of bankruptcy is difficulty in attracting labor and managerial talent who might prefer a more stable organization.

The existence of direct and indirect costs of bankruptcy cause debt and equity holders to demand higher premiums to compensate them for potential losses from bankruptcy and financial distress. This premium increases as a firm takes on more debt since bankruptcy potential increases as a firm takes on greater amounts of financial leverage. *In terms of the valuation model, bankruptcy costs serve to act as an offset to the tax shield benefit from debt.* Under this view the market value of the firm with financial leverage can be represented by the following equation:

$$V_l = V_u + \text{Present value of tax shield benefit} - \text{Present value of bankruptcy costs} \quad \textbf{(13.7)}$$

Figure 13.6 illustrates this relationship graphically. Note that firm value *is initially increasing as the present value of the tax shield benefit outweighs the negative effect of bankruptcy costs.* At low levels of debt, the potential for bankruptcy is negligible; as a result the tax shield effect dominates the bankruptcy effect. However, beyond some

Figure 13.6
Graphic Representation of Tax Shield-Bankruptcy Trade-off Theory: Effect on Firm Value

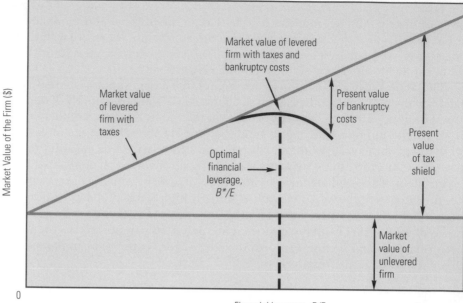

Figure 13.7
Graphic Representation of Tax Shield-Bankruptcy Trade-off Theory: Effect on Cost of Capital

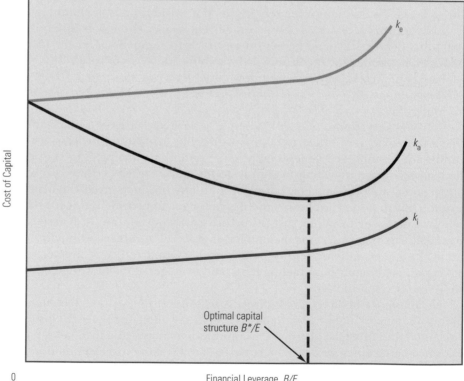

point, B^*/E, the opposite is true—the negative effects of bankruptcy outweigh the positive benefits from the tax shield. *The point B^*/E represents the optimum debt/equity ratio that maximizes firm value.*

Figure 13.7 illustrates the trade-off model using the cost of capital curves. Note that cost of debt is not a constant as in the MM models; rather it is rising with the debt leverage, reflecting the increasing potential for bankruptcy as the firm gets increasingly more leveraged. The cost of debt increases rather slowly for moderate amounts of debt, but there is a point beyond which the capital markets consider any additional debt "excessive" and demand much higher rates of return. The actual region where the cost of debt begins to increase more rapidly varies by firm and industry, depending on the firm's level of business risk. The cost of common equity is also rising with increases in financial leverage. As in the MM models, the cost of equity is increasing due to variability in shareholders' return arising from the increasing degree of financial leverage. However, it is also rising because of additional losses common equity holders suffer due to bankruptcy costs. The cost of common equity increases much more rapidly beyond moderate levels of debt when the threat of bankruptcy becomes significant. As in the debt illustration, the region where k_e increases rapidly varies by firm and industry.

The average cost of capital, k_a, in Figure 13.7 is initially declining, then bottoms out before rising. *The region where k_a is declining represents the area where the present value of the tax shield benefit of debt outweighs the present value of the bankruptcy cost of debt. At the optimal point, B*/E, the tax shield benefit exactly offsets the bankruptcy cost. To the right of the optimal point, the bankruptcy cost dominates the tax shield effect resulting in the positive slope for the cost of capital curve.* Exactly where the optimal leverage ratio occurs depends on the specific nature of the cost of debt and common equity curves, which may vary from firm to firm and industry to industry. As a practical matter it is difficult to pinpoint precisely where the optimal point occurs because of the difficulty in specifying the exact nature of k_d and k_e for firms. Most firms, however, have an idea of the "range" where the optimal debt ratio is located.

The IRS has rulings, notices, and regulations on what corporations cannot do. Click on Abusive Tax Shelters and Transactions when you go to **http://www.irs.gov/businesses/corporations/index.html**

Comprehension Check Questions

1. What are the implications of the MM no corporate tax, MM corporate tax, and the tax shield benefit–bankruptcy cost trade-off models to optimal capital structure?

2. Why do MM argue that with no corporate income taxes capital structure is irrelevant?

3. Under the MM corporate tax model, what is the source of benefit from debt financing?

4. What are bankruptcy costs and what is its relevance to the question of optimal capital structure choice?

Agency Costs and Capital Structure

Jensen and Meckling are largely responsible for developing a theoretical framework for analyzing the role of agency conflicts in capital structure policy.[3] Recall from Chapter 1 that *principal-agent* or *agency conflicts* arise when managers (agents) are not shareholders (principals) of the firm. Managers, for example, may engage in excessive *perquisite (or perk) consumption*. One example of perk consumption is membership in exclusive country clubs paid for by the corporation with personal benefits accruing to the managers. While shareholders may reap some benefit because business relationships and deals are often facilitated in such venues, it is questionable to what extent such memberships add directly to shareholder wealth. Other examples of perk consumption include having expensive and ornate office

---

[3]For their original work see, Michael Jensen and William Meckling, "Theory of the Firm: Managerial Behavior, Agency Costs, and Ownership Structure," *Journal of Financial Economics* (October 1976): 304–360.

furniture, corporate jets, and staff larger than necessary. *In addition to excessive perk consumption there are other more subtle forms of agency problems between managers and shareholders.* Managers, in order to protect their jobs, may invest in projects that may reduce bankruptcy risk but are not necessarily wealth-maximizing for shareholders. Alternately, managers in the pursuit of "empire building" may acquire companies that make the firm larger but do not add value to shareholders. For example, in the 1980s Frank Lorenzo, the CEO of Texas Air, cobbled together several airlines including People Express, Frontier Airlines, Continental, and Eastern Airlines, but it appears to have been motivated by his personal ambition of wanting to manage the largest airline in the country. These acquisitions destroyed significant amounts of shareholder value rather than adding to it.

One way to resolve management–shareholder conflicts is to give managers an ownership stake in the firm. However, as Jensen and Meckling point out, unless managers own 100 percent of the shares there will always be potential for management–shareholder conflicts. Assume that management owns 5 percent of the shares and outside shareholders own the remaining 95 percent. If a firm buys a corporate jet for $1,000,000, management, through its proportional ownership in the stock, bears 5 percent of the cost of the jet—or only $50,000. However, managers reap the primary benefit from the corporate jet. Thus, managers incur only 5 percent of the cost but derive virtually *all* the benefit from the use of the jet.

Jensen and Meckling suggest that one way to reduce the managerial–shareholder agency conflict is through the use of debt. The use of financial leverage does two things:

> ➢ Debt reduces the need for external equity, thereby increasing the concentration of managerial ownership. The greater concentration of managerial stock ownership reduces the agency problem between managers and outside shareholders.
> ➢ The reliance on debt introduces a *disciplining* mechanism. Since debt is a contractual obligation, managers will have less cash flow to "mess" with. Consequently, managers are less likely to misuse the cash flow: Doing so increases the chance of bankruptcy and potential loss of their jobs.

Furthermore, debt is also associated with greater *monitoring*. Monitoring may occur through a number of ways. Debt holders may have a seat on the board so that they can observe firsthand how management is performing. Debtholders can also monitor through requiring regular submission of financial statements. Finally, debt holders may place constraints on management discretion through restrictive covenants.

By now it should be evident that debt can play a useful role in reducing management–shareholder conflicts. However, as the firm takes on more debt, the *agency problems of debt* increase. When debt is used in the capital structure of a firm, common stockholders—or managers acting on behalf of stockholders—have incentives to undertake actions that may be detrimental to the interest of the debt holders. An extreme example would be a case where the firm raises a substantial sum of money through debt and disburses it to the shareholders. Assuming the firm has relatively little or worthless assets, the debt holders would be left with assets of little or no value while the original shareholders would have cashed out. This example is an egregious case of the agency problem of debt. However, a more common problem involves what is known as the *asset substitution problem*. In an asset substitution problem, the firm raises money from debt holders, promising to invest the funds in a certain project, but turns around and invests in a *much riskier* project. The riskier project either generates a lot of money or loses a lot of money. Assuming the firm is already in bad shape, further losses do not really matter to share-holders; on the other hand, if the project pays off big, the shareholders will do very well, but the debt holders still receive only the contracted interest rate. Thus, debt holders bear most of the risk but reap only a small share of the benefit in such a situation.

The asset substitution problem need not necessarily involve an actual switch in the projects: The firm could raise debt at attractive terms by characterizing the project as being of a certain level of risk when in fact it is at a considerably higher level. This leads to a transfer of wealth from debt holders to shareholders as the debt holders agree to a lower interest rate than they might if correctly informed of the true nature of the project. Jensen and Meckling argue that the agency problems of debt are especially severe when a firm has substantial debt or is in financial distress. Consequently *the agency costs of debt increase with the financial leverage of the firm.* Not surprisingly, bondholders will want to take actions that reduce the prospect of this wealth transfer to stockholders. Agency theory argues that expected ***agency costs*** will be borne by the agent. Therefore, debt holders can be expected to demand a higher interest rate on the bonds they purchase in order to compensate them for the expected wealth losses.

In summary, at low levels of debt, the disciplining role of debt acts to minimize management–shareholder conflicts, thereby increasing firm value or, alternatively, reducing the weighted average cost of capital to the firm. Thus in the agency framework, debt, at least initially, is associated with an increase in firm value or, alternately, a decline in the cost of capital. However, as the amount of debt increases as a proportion of the total capital structure, bondholders find themselves subject to increased risk that managers (acting on behalf of stockholders) may make investments or take financing actions that could harm the current bondholders. Accordingly, the cost of debt increases. This increase in the cost of debt has the effect of reducing the total value of the firm's securities, resulting in an optimal debt structure that is less than 100 percent of total firm value.

Personal Taxes and Optimal Capital Structure

The MM model with corporate income taxes led to the implication that a firm should attempt to minimize its taxes by employing the maximum amount of debt. The MM tax case did not consider the effect of personal income taxes, however. Miller extended the MM tax model to include both corporate and personal income taxes in a later work.[4] Miller argued that although a firm can save taxes by increasing its debt ratio, individual investors would pay greater taxes on their returns from the firm if these returns were predominantly interest, rather than dividends and capital appreciation on common stock. Historically, the tax code has favored capital gains income from stock over interest income; capital gains generally have been taxed at a lower rate than ordinary income (including interest income) and taxes on capital gains are deferred until the capital gain is realized (that is, when the stock is sold).

Miller concluded that when both personal and corporate income taxes are considered, there is no optimal debt ratio for an individual firm, although there is an optimal amount of total debt in the marketplace, reflecting the difference in corporate and personal tax rates.

---

[4]See M.H. Miller, "Debt and Taxes," *Journal of Finance* 32 (May 1977): 261–276.

Signaling Theory of Capital Structure

The theories discussed to this point assume that all investors have access to relevant information concerning a firm's future earnings prospects. However, this assumption may not be valid in many cases. Instead one can argue that the officers and managers of a company, as insiders, have access to information about the expected future earnings and cash flows of the firm that is not available to outside investors. This situation is referred to as *asymmetric information.* Under asymmetric information, share prices may not be correctly valued. Assume, for example, that there are two firms in the same industry, firm G and firm P. Firm G is worth $20 per share while firm P is worth $10 per share. However, because of severe information asymmetry investors do not know that firm G is worth $20 and that firm P is worth $10 per share. Investors only know that one of the firms has good prospects and the other has poor prospects and that the good firm is worth $20 per share and the poor firm is worth $10 per share. Given that the market is unable to discriminate which of the two firms is good and which is poor, the market will assign an average price of $15 to each of the two firms. If you were the manager of either of the two firms, how would you react to the market's assessment of your firm's share price? Clearly, if you were the manager of firm G you would be unhappy with this outcome, especially if your compensation depended on the firm's share price. On the other hand, if you were the manager of firm P, you would be perfectly happy with the $15 valuation given that the stock is only worth $10!

As manager of firm G it would be in your interest to take some action to correct the market's perception of your firm's true value. One thing you can do is to send a *signal* to the market of the firm's true worth. However the signal should be *credible*. Generally speaking, for the signal to be credible it should be *costly*. In other words, the consequence of sending a false signal should be severe. Firm G, for example, could take out a billboard ad proclaiming itself to have good prospects. However this is not a costly signal because firm P could do the same with little or no negative consequence if the signal turns out to be false. So, the market is unlikely to put much credence into such a signal.

Ross argued that capital structure is one example of a costly signal.[5] In his model, the good firm, G, would adopt a higher debt ratio than the poor firm, P. You might ask: What is to prevent firm P manager from adopting a higher debt ratio? Firm P manager could adopt the same debt ratio as firm G but the consequence of sending such a false signal could be severe. Given the poor prospects of firm P, taking on a higher debt ratio would result in increased potential for bankruptcy. Because the manager of firm P is unlikely to subject herself to the higher risk of bankruptcy and potential job loss, her preferred choice for the debt ratio will be less than that of firm G. Firm G manager on the other hand would willingly adopt a higher debt ratio because of the inside knowledge that the firm's prospects are good and that the firm can safely service the higher debt amount.

The Pecking Order Theory

The final theory we examine is known as the *pecking order theory.* It is not so much a theory to explain observed debt ratios as a theory to explain *changes* in debt ratios over time. While the pecking order theory has been around for several decades, formal presentation of the model in a theoretical framework is attributed to Myers.[6] According to the pecking order theory, as developed by Myers, a firm

---

[5]Stephen Ross, "The Determination of Financial Structure: The Incentive-Signaling Approach," *Bell Journal of Economics* 8 (1977): 23–40.

[6]See Stewart Myers, "The Capital Structure Puzzle," *Journal of Finance* 39 (July 1984): 575–592.

may not have a particular target or optimal capital structure. Instead, a company's capital structure changes when an imbalance between internal cash flows net of cash dividend payments and acceptable (i.e., NPV > 0) investment opportunities occurs. Firms whose investment opportunities exceed internally generated funds tend to issue more debt securities and hence have higher debt ratios. Conversely, highly profitable firms with limited needs for investment funds will tend to have lower debt ratios. In this situation, the firm builds up *financial slack* in the form of highly liquid assets (i.e., cash and marketable securities) and unused debt capacity. Financial slack allows a firm to take advantage of any attractive investment opportunities that may occur in the future.

The pecking order theory indicates that firms prefer internal financing (retained earnings) to external financing (e.g., debt, preferred, or additional common stock). This preference for internal financing is based on two considerations. First, because of flotation costs of new security issues, internal financing is less costly than external financing. Second, according to Myers, because of information asymmetry, managers are likely to issue external securities when they are overvalued, thereby transferring the gains to existing shareholders whom managers are assumed to favor. Also, according to the pecking order theory, dividends are "sticky," that is, many firms are reluctant to make major changes in dividend payments and only gradually adjust dividend payout ratios to reflect their investment opportunities and thereby avoid the issuance of new securities.

If external financing is required, the "safest" securities—namely debt—are issued first. The information asymmetry problem noted earlier is less severe with debt than it is with external equity. This is because debt holders have a senior claim on earnings and assets, debt is collaterizable (i.e., debt can be secured by assets), and debt holders can impose covenant restrictions on the bonds to protect themselves. External equity is the least preferred as managers are assumed to resort to common stock issues if it is overvalued. Knowing this to be the case, the new common shareholders will buy the stock only if it is offered at a steep discount. This would in turn mean that the new equity holders would have a disproportionate share of any gains from new investment relative to existing shareholders. If managers act on behalf of existing shareholders they are unlikely to want to issue new shares at such a steep discount.

Comprehension Check Questions

1. Why do management–shareholder agency conflicts exist? What are some examples of management–shareholder agency conflicts?

2. What is the role of debt in reducing agency conflicts of equity?

3. What is meant by asymmetric information?

4. How can capital structure reduce information asymmetry, according to Ross?

5. Describe the pecking order hypothesis of capital structure.

EBIT-EPS ANALYSIS

EBIT-EPS analysis is a technique frequently used in practice to aid firms in deciding between alternative capital structures. The objective of the EBIT-EPS framework is to select the capital structure that maximizes EPS (earnings per share).

> ### Table 13.3 Proposed Capital Structures for Yuma Corporation
>
> **Current capital structure:**
>   100% common equity consisting of 35 million shares, stock price per share = $20
>   Total capital = $700 million (35 million shares × $20 per share)
> **Proposed capital structure alternatives:**
>   **Plan I (Equity financing)**
>   Sell an additional 15 million shares @ $20/share to raise $300,000,000 for
>   expansion project.
>
>   *Resulting capital structure:*
>   100% common equity consisting of 50 million shares
>   (35 million old + 15 million new shares)
>   Total capital = $1,000 million (50 million shares × $20 per share)
>   **Plan II (Debt financing)**
>   Sell $300 million of 10% long-term debt.
>
>   *Resulting capital structure:*
>   30% debt consisting of $300 million in long-term debt
>   70% common equity consisting of $700 million in existing equity
>   (35 million shares × $20 per share)
>   Total capital = $1,000 million

Consider Yuma Corporation with a present capital structure consisting only of common stock (35 million shares) valued at $20 per share. Assume that Yuma is considering an expansion and evaluating two alternative financing plans. The expansion plan requires additional funding in the amount of $300 million. These plans and the resulting capital structures are shown in Table 13.3.

The first step in EBIT-EPS analysis is to draw the EBIT-EPS curves for the two alternatives. These curves simply plot the EPS at various levels of EBIT for the alternative debt structures. Usually, EBIT is plotted on the horizontal or *x*-axis and EPS on the vertical or *y*-axis. The EBIT-EPS relationship is a linear one, so we need just two points to plot the curves. Let us arbitrarily choose an EBIT level of $125 million as one of the points at which to calculate the EPS. Table 13.4 shows the EPS calculations. For the other point, let's take the *financial breakeven point*, defined as the level of EBIT that results in an EPS equal to zero. For EPS to be equal to zero, net income to common shareholders should equal zero. The corresponding financial breakeven EBIT can be obtained as follows:

(13.8)
$$\text{Net income to common shareholders} = (\text{EBIT} - I)(1 - T) - D_p$$

where I is the interest payable on debt, T is the corporate tax rate, and D_p is the dividend payable on preferred stock. Setting the left-hand side to zero,

$$0 = (\text{EBIT} - I)(1 - T) - D_p$$

and then dividing both sides of the above equation by $(1 - T)$ and solving for EBIT, we get:

(13.9)
$$\text{EBIT} = I + \frac{D_p}{(1 - T)}$$

If there is no preferred stock this is simply equal to

(13.10)
$$\text{EBIT} = I$$

Thus, when the EBIT is equal to interest, the EPS will equal zero. For plan I, the all-equity plan, the financial breakeven point is zero (interest is zero). For plan II, the

Table 13.4 EPS for Yuma Corporation under Alternative Capital Structures

Plan 1 (Equity financing)

EBIT	$125,000,000
Interest expense (Interest rate × Debt)	—
Earnings before taxes	$125,000,000
Taxes (40%)	−$ 50,000,000
Earnings after taxes	$ 75,000,000
Shares outstanding	50,000,000
EPS (Earnings after taxes divided by shares outstanding)	$1.50

Plan 2 (Debt financing)

EBIT	$125,000,000
Interest expense (Interest rate × Debt)	−$ 30,000,000
Earnings before taxes	$ 95,000,000
Taxes (40%)	−$ 38,000,000
Earnings after taxes	$ 57,000,000
Shares outstanding	35,000,000
EPS (Earnings after taxes divided by shares outstanding)	$1.63

financial breakeven point is $30 million, or the amount of the annual interest expense (amount of debt × interest rate = $300 million × .10).

The EBIT-EPS curves for Yuma Corporation are shown in Figure 13.8. Notice that the two curves intersect; this point is known as the ***EBIT-EPS indifference point*** because the EPS for the two alternatives are identical. To the right of the indifference point, Plan I (the debt alternative) dominates Plan II (the equity plan) as it yields the higher EPS. On the other hand, to the left of the indifference point, the equity plan is found to be superior as it has the higher EPS. The indifference point can be solved mathematically. By definition, the EPS for the debt and equity financing alternatives are equal at the EBIT-EPS indifference point:

$$\text{EPS (debt financing)} = \text{EPS (equity financing)} \qquad \textbf{(13.11)}$$

Substituting the formulas for the respective earnings per share:

$$\frac{(\text{EBIT} - I_d)(1 - T) - D_p}{N_d} = \frac{(\text{EBIT} - I_e)(1 - T) - D_p}{N_e} \qquad \textbf{(13.12)}$$

where EBIT is earnings before interest and taxes; I_d is the firm's total interest payments if the debt alternative is chosen; I_e is the firm's total interest payments if the equity alternative is chosen; and N_d and N_e represent the number of common shares outstanding for the debt and equity alternatives, respectively. The firm's effective tax rate is T, while D_p is the amount of preferred dividends for the firm. This equation may be used to calculate directly the EBIT level at which earnings per share for the two alternatives are equal. For Yuma Corporation, the EBIT-EPS indifference point is calculated as follows:

**Figure 13.8
EBIT-EPS Analysis,
Yuma Corporation**

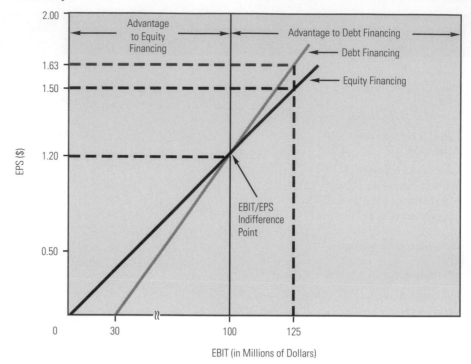

$$\frac{(\text{EBIT} - \$30)(1 - 0.4) - \$0}{35} = \frac{(\text{EBIT} - \$0)(1 - 0.4) - \$0}{50}$$
$$50(0.6\ \text{EBIT} - \$18) = 35(0.6\ \text{EBIT})$$
$$30\ \text{EBIT} - \$900 = 21\ \text{EBIT}$$
$$9\ \text{EBIT} = \$900$$
$$\text{EBIT} = \$100\ (\text{million})$$

The EPS at the indifference point can be calculated by substituting the EBIT indifference level into either side of Equation 13.12. Substituting $100 million for the indifference EBIT level in the right-hand side of Equation 13.12 we have:

$$\text{EPS} = \frac{(\$100 - \$0)(1 - 0.4) - \$0}{50}$$
$$= \frac{\$60}{50}$$
$$= \$1.20$$

Based on the EBIT-EPS analysis, the choice of which capital structure to select depends on our projection of the EBIT level for the firm and our confidence in those projections. If we are reasonably sure that the EBIT level will exceed $100 million, the debt alternative should be recommended—as that yields the higher EPS. However, if there is greater likelihood of EBIT below $100 million the firm is better off selecting the equity alternative, as it yields the higher EPS in this case.

EBIT-EPS Analysis and Stock Price

One limitation of the EBIT-EPS analytical framework is its focus on EPS. Maximizing EPS is not necessarily the same as maximizing stock price. This fact can be easily shown by extending the previous example to include risk. Suppose the expected EBIT for the Yuma Corp. is $125 million. Also, assume that Yuma is a no-growth firm that pays out all of its earnings as dividends. From Table 13.4 we know that given an EBIT level of $125 million, the debt alternative generates an EPS of $1.63 while the equity alternative yields an EPS of $1.50. If all earnings are paid out as dividends and the firm is a no-growth firm, the value of the stock is simply the discounted value of the perpetual EPS stream:

$$V = \frac{\text{EPS}}{k_e} \tag{13.13}$$

Now assume that k_e under the equity alternative is 9 percent and that under the debt alternative it is higher at 11 percent due to the financial risk from the debt leverage. The value of the stock under the two alternatives are given as follows:

$$V \text{ (Debt financing)} = \frac{\$1.63}{0.11}$$
$$= \$14.82$$
$$V \text{ (Equity financing)} = \frac{\$1.50}{0.09}$$
$$= \$16.67$$

Earlier we determined the indifference EBIT level to be $100 million. If the focus were solely on EPS maximization then at a likely EBIT level of $125 million, the debt alternative would be preferred. But as the illustration above shows, once risk is taken into account (via the discount rate) the equity alternative is preferred as it generates a higher stock price. So, as one can see, *maximizing EPS does not necessarily maximize stock price.* Thus the EBIT-EPS framework does not necessarily yield decisions that are consistent with shareholder wealth maximization: The framework's objective is to maximize earnings per share. On the other hand, examining the potential impact of a capital structure on stock price takes into account not just the earnings effect of the decision but the effect on risk as well.

DETERMINANTS OF CAPITAL STRUCTURE IN PRACTICE

In this section we explore from a practical perspective some of the factors firms look at in setting their target capital structure:

Business Risk. Perhaps the most important determinant of capital structure is business risk. Earlier in the chapter business risk was defined as volatility in operating profits (EBIT). Recall that factors affecting business risk include sales variability, variability in selling prices and costs, product diversification, market power, and degree of operating leverage. We know that, for any given level of debt, bankruptcy risk increases with business risk; the probability of nonpayment of debt obligations increases with increasing business risk. Consequently, firms in a high-business-risk environment tend to favor low or moderate proportions of debt in their capital structure.

The consequences of not following this principle can be severe. One example is Eastern Airlines, which assumed a significant amount of debt in the late seventies and early eighties in order to finance an aggressive expansion plan. The expansion plan coincided with the deregulation of the industry, an event that significantly increased business risk to airlines. This, coupled with the recession of the early eighties, put Eastern Airlines on the path to financial distress from which it ultimately never recovered. So, it is important that firms consider their business risk when deciding on an appropriate capital structure for the firm.

Tax Shields. According to the MM tax model and the trade-off theories, a significant source of benefit from debt leverage is the tax shield from interest deductibility of

Part 4 · Capital Structure and Dividend Policy

debt. Many firms take on debt in order to avail themselves of this benefit, which, as we noted from the theory discussion, accrues to shareholders—resulting in higher stock prices. It is important to remember that interest deductibility is not the only source of tax shield benefit to a firm. A major source of tax shield benefit is depreciation. If a firm can generate sufficient tax shield benefits from depreciation, then taking on debt to generate additional tax shield that cannot be used is of no value. Another consideration is the tax rate. Not all firms have the same marginal tax rate. The higher the marginal tax rate of the firm, the greater the tax shield benefit from debt and the higher the likelihood the firm will resort to debt in its capital structure.

Industry Standards. There is considerable evidence that the capital structure of an average firm varies significantly from industry to industry. For example, from Table 13.1 we note that the average long-term debt ratio in the natural gas industry is 59 percent. This ratio is 51 percent for steel manufacturers, 21 percent for the pharmaceutical drug firms, 11 percent for E-commerce firms, and 20 percent for specialty retail stores. Although there are exceptions, firms generally tend to cluster around the industry debt ratio, probably reflecting the fact that the business risk facing a firm largely is industry determined. A firm adopting a capital structure that differs significantly from industry norms will have to convince the financial markets that its business risk is sufficiently different from the risk facing the average firm in the industry to warrant this divergent capital structure.

Asset Structure. The type of assets a firm owns has a bearing on the capital structure of the firm. Firms that are capital intensive usually have an easier time acquiring debt in contrast to firms that are service oriented with few if any fixed assets. From Table 13.1, it is evident that capital-intensive industries such as the steel, paper, and auto and truck manufacturing rely on greater proportions of debt in their capital structure compared to less capital-intensive industries such as computer software and entertainment.

Lender and Bond-Rater Requirements. Lenders and bond rating agencies often impose restrictions on a firm's capital structure choices as a condition for extending credit or maintaining a bond or preferred stock rating. Table 13.5, for example, shows Standard and Poor's bond ratings and the long-term debt ratio for selected pharmaceutical firms. It is evident that higher ratings are generally associated with lower proportions of long-term debt to total capital. Although rating agencies admit that debt ratios are only one of many criteria used to arrive at bond ratings, it is evident from Table 13.5 that firms desirous of maintaining or improving bond ratings should pay attention to the proportion of debt used in the capital structure.

Managerial Attitude. Management's willingness to assume risk often has a major impact on the capital structure chosen by the firm, although the relative risk aversion of management does not influence the firm's optimal capital structure from a theoretical perspective. Some managers adopt unusually high-risk or unusually low-risk capital structures. When a suboptimal capital structure is chosen, the financial marketplace normally will penalize a firm for this action.

For example, because of an extremely conservative owner-management financing philosophy, Adolph Coors (the third largest U.S. brewer) did not have any long-term debt in its capital structure until 1990, when the company issued its first long-term debt securities. Even after the issuance of these securities, Coors' long-term debt ratio was still well below the industry average. Most financial analysts agree that Coors could safely add a significant amount of debt to its capital structure and

Table 13.5 Bond Ratings and Debt Ratios (Long-term debt to total capital) for Selected Pharmaceutical Firms

Firm	Standard and Poor's Bond Rating	Debt Ratio (%)
Novartis AG	AAA	5.3
Pfizer Inc.	AAA	11.7
Lilly (Eli) & Co.	AA	28.3
Abbott Labs	AA	28.7
GlaxoSmithKline PLC	AA	31.2
Wyeth	A	52.8
IDEC Pharmaceuticals	BB	46.0
Cephalon, Inc.	B+	64.7

Source: Ratings are taken from http://www.standardandpoors.com, July 3, 2003. The debt ratio is defined as long term debt to total capital calculated from data taken from Value Line Investment Survey, January 24, 2003.

thereby lower its overall cost of capital and increase the market value of the firm. Coors has been able to sustain this capital structure because the Coors family controls 100 percent of the company's voting shares. If this owner-management control did not exist, it is very likely that Coors would be acquired by new owners, who would then significantly modify the company's capital structure.

Retention of Control. Some firms use debt or preferred stock financing rather than common stock financing to avoid selling new shares of common stock. When new voting common stock is sold, the relative control position of existing stockholders is diluted.

Comprehension Check Questions

1. What is the objective of the EBIT-EPS analysis?
2. What is a primary limitation of the EBIT-EPS framework?
3. What factors do managers look at in setting the firm's capital structure policy?

Summary

➤ Capital structure is defined as the relative amount of long-term debt and common equity used to finance a firm. The capital structure decision is important to the firm because there exists in practice a capital structure at which the cost of capital is minimized. This minimum-cost capital structure is the optimal capital structure, because the value of the firm is maximized at this point.

➤ Modigliani and Miller show that the value of the firm is independent of capital structure given perfect capital markets and no corporate income taxes. MM also show that the optimal capital structure consists almost entirely of debt if corporate income taxes exist.

➤ Given a corporate income tax and the existence of bankruptcy costs, an optimal capital structure consisting of both debt and equity is shown to exist.

Determination of the optimal capital structure involves balancing the present value of the tax shield accruing from debt financing against the present value of the expected bankruptcy costs from debt financing.

➤ Given that managers have access to better information about a firm's future prospects than do outside investors (asymmetric information), capital structure can be used to signal to investors important information about a firm's future prospects.

➤ Debt can be useful in controlling agency conflicts between managers and shareholders. Debt serves as a disciplining mechanism and provides additional monitoring to ensure management does not misuse funds under its control. Excessive use of debt, however, can lead to agency conflicts of debt. With increasing use of debt, managers acting on behalf of shareholders have an incentive to transfer wealth from debt holders to shareholders through asset (risk) substitution.

➤ According to the pecking order theory, there is no particular optimal capital structure for a firm. Companies prefer internal financing to external financing and, given that external financing is necessary, they prefer to issue debt securities first and then equity securities only as a last resort.

➤ EBIT-EPS analysis is a technique that can be used to help determine the circumstances under which a firm should employ financial leverage. Basically, it involves calculating earnings per share at different levels of EBIT for debt and equity financing plans. This information then may be used to graph earnings per share versus EBIT to determine the EBIT levels at which financial leverage is advantageous to the firm.

➤ The indifference point in EBIT-EPS analysis is that level of EBIT where earnings per share are the same, regardless of which of two alternative capital structures is used. At EBIT levels greater than the indifference level, a more financially levered capital structure will produce a higher level of earnings per share; at EBIT levels less than the indifference point, a less financially levered capital structure will produce a higher level of earnings per share.

➤ The financial breakeven point in EBIT-EPS analysis refers to the level of EBIT where EPS is equal to zero.

➤ A limitation of the EBIT-EPS analytical framework is that it assumes that firms maximize EPS. It is important to remember that maximizing EPS will not necessarily maximize stock price. Stock price takes into account both earnings / cash flows as well as risk. A particular capital structure may thus maximize EPS but the same capital structure may not necessarily maximize stock price.

➤ In setting debt policy in practice, firms examine several criteria including business risk, tax shield benefits, industry standards, lender and bond rater requirements, asset structure, managerial attitude, and retention of control.

Questions and Topics for Discussion

1. Explain the Modigliani and Miller models of capital structure both with and without corporate income taxes. Specifically, explain the relationship between debt leverage and the value of the firm and between debt leverage and the cost of capital.

2. What is arbitrage? How is it used by Modigliani and Miller in deriving their proposition that the value of a firm is independent of its capital structure?

3. How does the existence of bankruptcy costs affect capital structure policy?

4. Provide a definition for asymmetric information. According to Ross how can capital structure be used to alleviate asymmetric information?

5. According to the pecking order theory, if additional external financing is required, what type of securities should a firm issue first? Last?

6. What is the underlying objective of EBIT-EPS analysis?

7. What is a primary limitation of EBIT-EPS analysis as a technique to determine the optimal capital structure?

8. In practice what are the factors managers consider in setting a firm's target capital structure?

Self-Test Problems

ST1. Ogden Optical Company has estimated the following costs of debt and equity capital (with bankruptcy costs) for various proportions of debt in its capital structure:

Proportion of Debt	Cost of Debt, k_i	Cost of Equity, k_e
0.00	—	10.0%
0.10	4.0%	10.1
0.20	4.2	10.3
0.30	4.4	10.8
0.40	4.8	11.4
0.50	5.5	12.5
0.60	6.6	14.5
0.70	8.0	18.0

Determine the firm's optimal capital structure. (*Hint:* Using the above data calculate the weighted average cost of capital for each of the debt proportions. The optimal capital structure is the one with the minimum cost of capital.)

ST2. The Euclid Corporation has a present capital structure consisting of 100 million shares of common stock. Euclid is considering an expansion program. Two alternative financing plans are under consideration:

Plan 1 (Equity financing). Sale of 10 million additional shares of common stock at $15 per share.

Plan 2 (Debt financing). Sale of $150 million of 12 percent long-term debt.

The firm's marginal tax rate is 40 percent.

a. Determine the indifference level of EBIT between the two financing plans.

b. Suppose that Euclid's EBIT is likely to be $250 million. Which alternative would you recommend assuming you wanted to maximize EPS?

Problems

1. Geriatric Foods Corporation has no debt and is currently valued at $1,200,000. **BASIC** The firm is planning on altering its capital structure by issuing debt and using the proceeds to buy back some of its common stock. Thus, the firm will go from a zero debt proportion to some positive proportion of debt. Management has

arranged with First Lenders Bank to borrow $400,000 for this purpose. The cost of this debt is 6 percent on a pretax basis. The firm is in the 40 percent corporate tax bracket. Assume all the assumptions of the Modigliani-Miller model with corporate income taxes hold.

a. What is the annual tax shield benefit from the issuance of debt?

b. What is the present value of all future tax shield benefits?

c. What is the new firm value for Geriatric Foods after the change in leverage?

INTERMEDIATE

2. Jersey Computer Company has estimated the costs of debt and equity capital (with bankruptcy costs) for various proportions of debt in its capital structure:

Proportion of Debt	Cost of Debt, k_i	Cost of Equity, k_e
0.00	—	12.0%
0.10	4.7%	12.1
0.20	4.9	12.5
0.30	5.1	13.0
0.40	5.5	13.9
0.50	6.1	15.0
0.60	7.5	17.0

a. Determine the firm's optimal capital structure. (*Hint:* Using the above data calculate the weighted average cost of capital for each of the debt proportions. The optimal capital structure is the one with the minimum cost of capital.)

b. Suppose that the firm's current capital structure consists of 30 percent debt (and 70 percent equity). How much higher is its weighted cost of capital than at the optimal capital structure?

INTERMEDIATE

3. You are provided with the following cost of debt and cost of common equity estimates for various debt proportions for Nick's Media Group.

Proportion of Debt	Cost of Debt, k_i	Cost of Equity, k_e
0.00	—	12.00%
0.10	5%	12.77
0.20	5	13.75
0.30	5	15.00
0.40	5	16.67
0.50	5	19.00
0.60	5	22.50

a. What is the optimal capital structure for Nick's Media Group?

b. Which of the theories discussed in the chapter best describes your finding in (a)?

CHALLENGE

4. Emco Products has a present capital structure consisting only of common stock (10 million shares). The company is planning a major expansion. At this time, the company is undecided between the following two financing plans (assume a 40 percent marginal tax rate):

Plan 1 (Equity financing). Under this plan, an additional 5 million shares of common stock will be sold at $10 each.

Plan 2 (Debt financing). Under this plan, $50 million of 10 percent long-term debt will be sold.

One piece of information the company desires for its decision analysis is an EBIT-EPS analysis.

a. Calculate the EBIT-EPS indifference point.

b. Graphically determine the EBIT-EPS indifference point.

Hint: Use EBIT = $10 million and $25 million.

c. What happens to the indifference point if the interest rate on debt increases and the common stock sales price remains constant?

d. What happens to the indifference point if the interest rate on debt remains constant and the common stock sales price increases?

5. Morton Industries is considering opening a new subsidiary in Boston, to be operated as a separate company. The company's financial analysts expect the new facility's average EBIT level to be $6 million per year. At this time, the company is considering the following two financing plans (use a 40 percent marginal tax rate in your analysis):

Plan 1 (Equity financing). Under this plan, 2 million common shares will be sold at $10 each.

Plan 2 (Debt equity financing). Under this plan, $10 million of 12 percent long-term debt and 1 million common shares at $10 each will be sold.

a. Calculate the EBIT-EPS indifference point.

b. Calculate the expected EPS for both financing plans.

c. What factors should the company consider in deciding which financing plan to adopt?

d. Which plan do you recommend the company adopt?

e. Suppose Morton adopts Plan 2, and the Boston facility initially operates at an annual EBIT level of $6 million. What is the times interest earned ratio?

6. Messrs. Moon and Chittenden are considering a new Internet venture to sell used textbooks. The project requires $300,000 in financing. Two alternatives have been proposed:

Plan 1 (Common equity financing). Sell 30,000 shares of stock at a net price of $10 per share.

Plan 2 (Debt equity financing). Sell a combination of 15,000 shares of stock at a net price of $10 per share and $150,000 of long-term debt at a pretax interest rate of 12 percent.

Assume the corporate tax rate is 40 percent.

a. Compute the indifference level of EBIT between these two alternatives.

b. If the firm's EBIT next year has an expected value of $25,000 which plan would you recommend assuming maximizing EPS is a valid objective?

7. Visit the Yahoo! Finance Web site (http://www.yahoo.com) and calculate the debt ratio of a major auto manufacturer, such as General Motors. Then calculate the debt ratio of a service company, such as Saatchi and Saatchi, a major advertising company. Based on what you learned about leverage in this chapter, what would account for the difference in their debt ratios?

THOMSON ONE—Business School Edition

Go to the text Web site at http://moyer.swlearning.com, select your book, and click on the Thomson ONE button. Enter Thomson ONE—Business School Edition by using the username and password you created when you registered the serial number on your access card. Use the "Financials" tab, "Worldscope Growth Ratios" option, and the "Balance Sheet Ratios" sub-option to compare total debt as a percentage of assets for Anheuser-Busch, Cisco Systems (@CSCO), and Walt Disney Company (DIS). Using the knowledge about the determinants of an optimal capital structure that you have gained in this and the previous chapter, discuss the choice of capital structure of each of these three companies.

CHAPTER
14 Dividend Policy

D
ividend policy impacts investor perceptions of risk and expected future returns, and hence can impact indirectly its cost of capital and valuation. Dividend policy determines how the earnings of a company are distributed: Earnings either are retained and reinvested in the company or they are paid out to shareholders. Two ways in which firms disburse cash to their stockholders is through cash dividends and stock repurchases. Figure 14.1 contains examples of cash dividend and stock repurchase announcements.

Table 14.1 shows clearly that there are systematic differences between industries. At one extreme the electric utility and natural gas industries tend to have the highest *payout ratios;* these industries pay out an average of over 60 percent of their earnings as cash dividends. At the other extreme, high-tech related industries (computer software and services, electronics, E-commerce, and Internet) pay out little to none of their earnings as cash dividends. Others, such as paper mills, food processing and auto and truck manufacturing industries appear to have moderate dividend payout ratios.

The industry ratios can be deceptive, however: Often there can be quite a variation within the industry. Table 14.1 shows that the dividend payout ratio for the pharmaceutical (drug) industry is 43 percent. Table 14.2 shows the dividend payout ratios for selected firms within the pharmaceutical industry. As can be seen, some of the larger pharmaceutical companies including Abbott, Merck, and Lilly pay out in excess of 40 percent of their earnings as dividends. On the other hand, relatively younger and faster growing companies such as Celgene, Ivax, and Medimmune appear to follow a 100 percent earnings retention policy.

In this chapter we examine the theoretical and practical considerations in deciding the dividend policy of a firm. We also examine stock repurchases, which have become extremely popular in recent years, as an alternate means for firms to disburse cash to its shareholders.

Some firms issue stock dividends, which are simply dividends in the form of additional shares of stock. The impact of stock dividends—along with the related concept of stock splits—is explored as well in this chapter.

Figure 14.1
Examples of Dividend and Stock Repurchase Announcements

DIVIDEND ANNOUNCEMENTS

Omnicare Holds Annual Stockholders' Meeting; Declares Quarterly Cash Dividend
05/20/2002
PR Newswire
(Copyright © 2002, PR Newswire)

COVINGTON, Ky., May 20 /PRNewswire-FirstCall/ The board of directors of Omnicare, Inc. (NYSE: OCR) declared today a quarterly cash dividend of 2.25 cents per share on its common stock. The dividend is payable June 12, 2002, to stockholders of record May 31, 2002.

Friday May 31, 1:13 pm Eastern Time
Press Release
SOURCE: FedEx Corp.
FedEx Corp. Declares First Dividend in Its History
Additional 5 Million Share Stock Repurchase Authorized

MEMPHIS, Tenn.—(BUSINESS WIRE)—May 31, 2002—FedEx Corporation (NYSE: FDX—News) today announced that its Board of Directors declared an initial quarterly dividend of $0.05 per share on FedEx Corporation common stock. The dividend is payable July 8, 2002, to shareholders of record at the close of business on June 17, 2002.

"This dividend declaration signals the Board's confidence in the company's future growth and financial prospects and its unique role in the global economy," said Frederick W. Smith, chairman, president and chief executive officer. "The company has reached a significant milestone as it expects to produce positive free cash flow in fiscal year 2002 and in future years. FedEx today is less capital intensive than in the past, and we are now in a better position to realize the benefits of our network investments."

The company's Board also authorized the repurchase of up to 5 million shares of the company's common stock, augmenting the 1.65 million shares remaining under the existing repurchase authorization. Purchases may be made in the open market and in negotiated or block transactions. FedEx currently has 298 million shares outstanding.

NBC Capital Corporation Increases Cash Dividend
05/23/2002
PR Newswire
(Copyright © 2002, PR Newswire)

STARKVILLE, Miss., May 23 /PRNewswire-FirstCall/—NBC Capital Corporation (Amex: NBY), the holding company for National Bank of Commerce, today announced that the Board of Directors declared a regular quarterly cash dividend of $0.29 per share, a 3.6% increase from the previous cash dividend of $0.28 per share. The dividend is payable July 1, 2002, to shareholders of record as of June 14, 2002.

"The increase in the cash dividend represents the 27th consecutive year of increased cash dividends for NBC," stated Lewis F. Mallory, Jr., chairman and chief executive officer of NBC Capital Corporation. "Our Board of Directors is committing to building shareholder value through our cash dividend program and this increase highlights our improved financial performance and strong capital position."

Tuesday June 4, 10:48 am Eastern Time
Qwest Eliminates 2002 Dividend
By: Shawn Young, of THE WALL STREET JOURNAL

DUBLIN, Ohio—(Dow Jones)—Qwest Communications International Inc. will eliminate its dividend this year and apply the cost savings to a debt reduction of about $25 billion, the company announced at its annual meeting here. The Denver telecommunications firm last year paid a dividend of 5 cents a share, spending $83 million.

Qwest also will not increase pension benefits this year.
The company's shares have fallen more than 75% this year amid a slump in the telecommunications industry and problems at the company itself, which include a Securities and Exchange Commission investigation of its finances and the downgrade of its debt to "junk" status. Qwest is working to reduce debt and expects to have a deal in place soon to sell its Yellow Pages business, which is expected to fetch at least $8 billion.

Qwest's NYSE-listed stock recently traded at $5.10 a share, unchanged from Monday's close. The stock hit a trading high of $37.15 a share on June 4, 2001 and a low of $4.35 in late April.

REPURCHASE ANNOUNCEMENT

**Figure 14.1
(Continued)**

Kreisler Manufacturing Corporation Announces Stock Repurchase Program

05/15/2002
PR Newswire
(Copyright © 2002, PR Newswire)

ST. PETERSBURG, Fla., May 15/ PRNewswire- FirstCall /—Kreisler Manufacturing Corporation (Nasdaq: KRSL) today announced that its Board of Directors has unanimously authorized the expenditure of up to $2,000,000 to repurchase part of the company's outstanding common stock. "Based on current market conditions, we believe that our stock may become undervalued and that the repurchase program is a good investment of available finds," said Edward L. Stern President, CEO. Any purchases under Kreisler's stock repurchase program may be made, from time-to-time, in the open market and in negotiated transactions, including through block transactions or otherwise, at the discretion of company's management. Depending on market conditions and other factors, these purchases may be commenced or suspended at any time or from time-to-time without prior notice. As of May 14, 2002 Kreisler has approximately 1,970,125 shares outstanding.

Table 14.1 Average Dividend Payout Ratio for Selected Industries for 2002

Industry	Number of Firms	Dividend Payout Ratio (%)*
Entertainment technology	13	0
Internet industry	16	0
E-commerce	19	0
Hotel	17	1
Computer software & services	54	5
Air Transport	15	5
Electronics	27	5
Retail special lines	69	7
Entertainment industry	15	13
Apparel and textile	18	14
Paper	16	16
Packaging	16	16
Retail store	21	17
Precision instrument	28	28
Medical supplies	58	30
Beverage (alcoholic) industry	7	32
Food processing	35	38
Auto & truck	9	40
Chemical (specialty)	33	40
Drug	46	43
Petroleum (integrated)	21	45
Cosmetics	10	45
Chemical (diversified)	16	48
Banks	31	51
Tobacco	6	54
Machinery	48	55
Natural gas (distribution)	18	65
Electric utilities (Western region)	15	68
Electric utilities (Eastern region)	24	68
Electric utilities (Central region)	24	68
Natural gas (diversified)	21	80

*Calculated as industry consolidated dividends divided by consolidated total net profit times 100.

Source: Various issues of Value Line Investment Survey, first quarter 2003.

Table 14.2 Dividend Payout Ratio for Selected Firms in the Drug Industry for 2002

Company	Dividend Payout Ratio (%)*
Abbott Laboratories	44.0
Abgenix, Inc.	0
Aventis	22.0
Barr Labs	0
Biovail Corp.	0
Bristol-Myers Squibb	107.0
Celgene Corp.	0
Cephalon, Inc.	0
Chiron	0
Enzon, Inc.	0
Forest Labs	0
Genzyme General	0
GlaxoSmithKline	57.6
Icn Pharmaceutical	34.4
Idec Pharmaceutical	0
Imclone Systems	0
Ivax Corp.	0
King Pharmaceutical	0
Lilly (Eli) & Co.	48.6
Medarex, Inc.	0
Medicis Pharmaceutical	0
Medimmune, Inc.	0
Merck & Co.	44.9
Mylan Labs	9.6
Novartis AG	28.9
Novo Nordisk	24.5
Perrigo Co.	0
Pfizer Inc.	32.9
Pharma Products	0
Pharmacia Corp.	34.8
Quintiles Trans	0
Schering-Plough	47.5
Sepracor, Inc.	0
Watson Pharmaceutical	0
Wyeth	41.8

*Calculated as dividends per share as a percentage of earnings per share. Data taken from Value Line Investment Survey, January 24, 2003.

Chapter Objectives

After reading the chapter, you should have an understanding of the following:

1. The theoretical implications of dividend policy

2. The practical determinants of dividend policy

3. The dividend declaration and payment procedure

4. Stock dividends and stock splits and why they are declared

5. Stock repurchases and their impact on the firm

THEORETICAL IMPLICATIONS OF DIVIDEND POLICY

Scholars have long wrestled with the question of whether dividend policy is relevant. Specifically, the question they pose is: Does paying a dividend have an effect on stock price? As we shall find out, the answer is not necessarily obvious. There are basically two schools of thought. Merton Miller and Franco Modigliani in the 1960s proved that dividends are irrelevant: They have no effect on firm value, under certain perfect market assumptions. Others believe dividends have a significant impact on firm value and therefore *are* relevant. Scholars have proposed several different scenarios under which the relevance hypothesis holds. We will explore all of these different viewpoints.

Miller and Modigliani and the Irrelevance of Dividends

Miller and Modigliani (MM) proved that under perfect market assumptions, the value of the firm is unaffected by the particular dividend policy implemented by the firm.[1] They invoke the following assumptions:

Finance in the News

Click on this button at **http://finance. swlearning.com** *for synopses of articles on capital structure and dividend policy.*

1. **No taxes.** Under this assumption, investors are indifferent about whether they receive either dividend income or capital gains income since neither is taxed.
2. **No transaction costs.** This assumption implies that investors in the securities of firms paying small or no dividends can sell at no cost any number of shares they wish in order to convert capital gains into current income.
3. **No issuance costs.** This assumption implies that the cost of new common stock is identical to the cost of retained earnings. Thus firms that pay dividends (and therefore are more likely to issue additional common stock to raise needed equity capital for new investments) will not incur any additional cost (issuance or flotation costs) compared to low- or no-dividend-paying firms that are able to meet their investment needs from retained earnings.

The dividend irrelevance argument can be illustrated using the following example. Assume that firm A is all equity financed with annual earnings of $1,000 and a required rate of return on equity of 10 percent. Furthermore, assume that all earnings are paid out as dividends. Thus, the time line of cash flows to equity holders is given by:

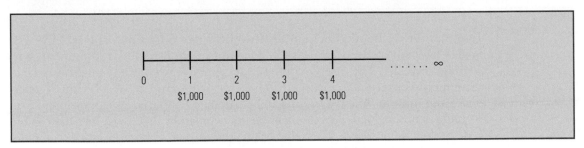

Since this is a perpetuity the total shareholder value at time 0 is:

$$V_0 = \frac{\$1,000}{0.10}$$
$$= \$10,000$$

Now assume that at time 0 you were the sole owner of shares in the firm and that you expect to sell it at the end of year 1 after receipt of the dividends. Your expected return (r) over this 1-year holding period is given by:

---

[1]See Merton Miller and Franco Modigliani, "Dividend Policy, Growth and the Valuation of Shares," *Journal of Business* 34 (October 1961): 411–433.

(14.1)

$$r = \frac{V_1 - V_0 + D_1}{V_0}$$

where V_1 is the value of the shares at end of year 1, V_0 is the value at time 0, and D_1 is the dividend received in year 1. Note from the above formula that the return consists of a capital gain or price appreciation ($V_1 - V_0$) and dividend income (D_1). The value at end of year 1 (V_1) is simply the discounted value of the perpetual stream of $1,000 to be received in year 2 and beyond:

$$V_1 = \frac{\$1,000}{0.10}$$
$$= \$10,000$$

The return over the 1-year holding period, using Equation 14.1, is therefore equal to:

$$r = \frac{\$10,000 - \$10,000 + \$1,000}{\$10,000}$$
$$= .10 \text{ or } 10\%$$

Thus, the entire return of 10 percent consists of *dividend income and no capital gain.* Now take another firm, B, that also has annual earnings of $1,000 but in year 1 the firm *retains* the $1,000 and reinvests it at the cost of capital of 10 percent. This means in subsequent years the firm will earn an additional $100 (.10 × $1,000) on top of the $1,000. Furthermore, let us assume that after year 1 the firm pays out *all* of its earnings as dividends. The time line of cash flows to equity holders is given by:

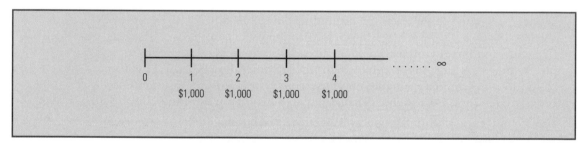

Note that the dividend policies of the two firms are different—at least in year 1. Firm A pays out of all its earnings as dividends; firm B retains 100 percent of its earnings in year 1. The question we are interested in is whether the difference in dividend policy results in divergent values for firm A and B. We previously determined the value at time 0 of firm A to be $10,000. Similarly, we can estimate firm B's value at time 0. Firm B's value may be determined by first finding its discounted value at the end of year 1. The value at the end of year 1 is simply equal to the discounted value of the $1,100 perpetuity to be received in year 2 and beyond:

$$V_1 = \frac{\$1,100}{0.10}$$
$$= \$11,000$$

Discounting this back to year 0, yields:

$$V_0 = \frac{\$11,000}{(1 + 0.10)^1}$$
$$= \$10,000$$

which is the exact same value as firm A! Now assume that at time 0 you were the sole owner of firm B, your expected 1-year return, using Equation 14.1, is:

$$r = \frac{\$11,000 - \$10,000 + \$0}{\$10,000}$$
$$= .10 \text{ or } 10\%$$

This return is identical to that of firm A with one difference: For firm A the return consists *entirely of dividend income* while for firm B it consists *entirely of capital gains.* By retaining the earnings, firm B simply converted the dividend income into a capital gain income. So changing the dividend policy *does not affect share value,* all it does is *exchange one form of income to another—dividend income to capital gains income or vice versa.* This is the essence of the MM argument: Dividends are irrelevant. *Investors only care about the rate of return.* It doesn't matter where the return comes from—dividend income or capital gains income—so long as the expected return is commensurate with the expected risk.

There is one problem with the above illustration. The astute student will note that investment was not held constant between the two firms. Firm B invested $1,000 at the end of year 1 while firm A did not. Unlike in the above illustration, the original MM derivation holds investment fixed. But as a reading of the original MM work will point out, firm A could also invest $1,000 at the end of year 1, but not from year 1 earnings; these are assumed to be paid to the shareholders. Firm A would have to *raise* the $1,000 through a new stock offering. These new shareowners would be entitled to a proportional share of the future earnings, which would equal $100 per year in perpetuity. The net result is that the original time 0 shareholders still would just receive the cash flows shown in the original time line ($1,000 per year) and the stock value at time 0 would remain at $10,000.

Arguments for the Relevance of Dividends

Scholars have presented a number of arguments for the relevance of dividends. Most of these arguments depend on relaxing the assumptions made by MM.

Risk Aversion Myron Gordon, who took exception to MM's views, asserts that shareholders who are risk averse prefer dividends over the promise of future capital gains because dividends are regular, certain returns, whereas future capital gains are less certain.[2] This is the well-known "Bird in hand (dividends) is worth two in the bush (capital gains)" argument. According to Gordon, dividends reduce investors' uncertainty, causing them to discount a firm's future earnings at a lower rate, thereby increasing the firm's value. In contrast, failure to pay dividends increases investors' uncertainty, which raises the discount rate and lowers share prices. The problem with this view, as some scholars—including MM—have noted, is that if this is indeed the case, then firms would invest in projects only if they compensate for this additional uncertainty. In the final analysis share value would still remain unaffected.

Informational Content and Signaling Effect of Dividends Currently, the most popular explanation for the relevance of dividends is based on the notion that dividends signal information about the firm to the market. There is considerable empirical evidence to indicate that changes in dividends influence stock prices. An *increase*

FinanceLinks Online

Click on this button at **http://finance. swlearning.com** *and select Data for links to data and information on stock repurchases, stock splits, share repurchases, and dividends.*

[2]See Myron Gordon, "The Savings, Investment and Valuation of a Corporation," *Review of Economics and Statistics* (February 1962): 37–51.

in dividends is generally viewed as conveying *favorable information* to the shareholders, such as an expectation of higher future earnings. Similarly, a *cut in dividends* may be viewed as conveying *unfavorable information* about the firm's earnings prospects.

Proponents of the signaling theory of dividends argue that the informational content of dividend policy could influence share prices. In effect, changes in dividend payments represent a **signal** to investors concerning management's assessment of the future earnings and cash flows of the company. As explained in Chapter 13 (in connection with capital structure policy), the signaling theory holds management, as an insider entity, to have more complete information about future profitability than is available to investors outside the company.

Transactions Costs   In proving the irrelevance of dividends, one of the assumptions made by MM was the insignificance of transactions costs; that is, no costs are incurred in buying and selling shares. If the assumption of no transaction costs for investors is removed, then investors do care whether they are paid cash dividends or receive capital gains. In the MM world, investors who own stock that pay low or no dividends could periodically sell a portion of their holdings to satisfy current income requirements. In actuality, however, brokerage charges make such liquidations expensive and imperfect substitutes for regular dividend payments.

Taxes   Removal of the no-tax assumption also makes a significant difference to shareholders. Until recently (2002 tax code) the marginal capital gains tax rate for individuals in the United States was much less (a maximum of 20%) than the marginal tax rate on ordinary income (a maximum of 38.6%), implying that investors should have a preference for capital gains over dividend income. President Bush signed into law on May 28, 2003 a new tax code as part of the Jobs & Growth Tax Relief Reconciliation Act of 2003. It provides for a maximum tax rate on dividend income *and* capital gains of 15 percent, effectively making the two rates equal (as written into law the equal tax rates for dividend income and capital gains income expire at the end of 2008). Scholars and practitioners have noted that even if the two rates are the same, capital gains may still be preferred because they are not taxed until the stock is sold while dividends are taxed in the year they are received.

Thus the tax system (especially if dividends are taxed at a rate higher than capital gains) appears to favor a policy of lower dividends and higher retention of earnings that may be converted to capital gains. However, not all researchers buy into this tax argument. Several researchers suggest that firms set their dividend payout policy to suit their shareholder clientele. Specifically, *high payout firms attract investor clientele that desire high payouts presumably because they are in the low or even zero tax bracket.* These investors may be individuals in the lowest marginal tax brackets or institutions that do not pay taxes, such as pension funds or endowment funds. On the other hand, *firms following a low payout or zero payout policy will appeal to individuals and institutions in the high tax brackets that prefer lower taxed capital gains income to higher taxed dividend income.* The clientele argument implies that there is no optimal payout policy at the firm level; altering the payout policy will alter the dividend clientele for the stock but will have no bearing on the stock price.

Issuance (Flotation) Costs   The existence of issuance costs on new equity sales also tends to make earnings retention more desirable. Given a firm's investment policy, the payout of earnings the firm needs for investments may require it to raise external equity. External equity is more expensive, however, because of issuance costs. Therefore, the use of external equity will raise the firm's cost of capital and reduce the value of the firm. In addition, the cost of selling small issues of equity to meet investment needs is likely to be prohibitively high for most firms. Therefore, firms that have sufficient investment opportunities to profitably utilize their retained funds tend to favor retention.

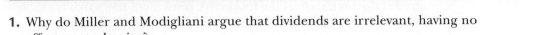

Comprehension Check Questions

1. Why do Miller and Modigliani argue that dividends are irrelevant, having no effect on stock price?
2. Describe the information content and signaling effect of dividend explanation for dividend relevance.
3. How do transactions costs, issuance costs and taxes influence the relevance of dividends?

DETERMINANTS OF DIVIDEND POLICY IN PRACTICE

The previous section provided theoretical insight into the dividend question. Specifically, we observed that under perfect market conditions, dividend policy has no impact on stock price. However, when some of the perfect market assumptions are relaxed, it was determined that dividend policy can affect stock price. This section examines the dividend policy issue from a practical perspective. You will find that in practice several of the determinants of dividend policy are similar to those covered under theoretical considerations. This mutual reinforcement adds to the credibility of the theoretical considerations and the soundness of observed practices. The factors elaborated below also are useful in explaining the differences in dividend policy observed across industries and within industries such as those shown in Table 14.1 and 14.2.

e-Lecture

Legal Constraints

Most states have laws that regulate the dividend payments a firm chartered in that state can make. These laws may be characterized as the *capital impairment restriction,* the *net earnings restriction,* and the *insolvency restriction.*

In general these restrictions are designed to protect the creditors of the firm. It is conceivable that a firm could liquidate its assets, disburse the proceeds to its shareholders in the form of dividends, and leave the creditors holding an "empty bag." Legal restrictions exist to protect creditors from such wealth transfers occurring.

The capital impairment restriction says that *dividends cannot be paid if it reduces the "permanent" capital of the firm.* In some states, capital is defined as including only the par value of common stock; in others, capital is more broadly defined to also include the contributed capital in excess of par (sometimes called capital surplus). For example, consider the following capital accounts on the balance sheet of Johnson Tool and Die Company:

Common stock ($5 par; 100,000 shares)	$ 500,000
Contributed capital in excess of par	400,000
Retained earnings	200,000
Total common stockholders' equity	**$1,100,000**

If the company is chartered in a state that defines capital as the par value of common stock, then it can pay out a total of $600,000 ($1,100,000 − $500,000 par value) in dividends. If, however, the company's home state restricts dividend payments to retained earnings alone, then Johnson Tool and Die could only pay dividends up to $200,000. Regardless of the dividend laws, however, it should be realized that dividends are *paid from a firm's cash account with an offsetting entry to the retained earnings account.*

The second restriction, called the net earnings restriction, requires that a firm *have generated earnings before it is permitted to pay any cash dividends.* This prevents the equity owners from withdrawing their initial investment in the firm and impairing the security position of any of the firm's creditors.

The third restriction, termed the insolvency restriction, states that *an insolvent company may not pay cash dividends.* When a company is **insolvent,** its liabilities exceed its assets. Payment of dividends would interfere with the creditors' prior claims on the firm's assets and therefore is prohibited.

These three restrictions affect different types of companies in different ways. New firms, or small firms with a minimum of accumulated retained earnings, are most likely to feel the weight of these legal constraints when determining their dividend policies, whereas well-established companies with histories of profitable performance and large retained earnings accounts are less likely to be influenced by them.

Restrictive Covenants

Restrictive covenants generally have more of an impact on dividend policy than the legal constraints just discussed. Like the legal constraints, they are there to protect the creditors. These covenants are contained in bond indentures, term loans, short-term borrowing agreements, lease contracts, and preferred stock agreements.

These restrictions limit the total amount of dividends a firm can pay. Sometimes they may state that dividends cannot be paid at all until a firm's earnings have reached a specified level. For example, the 3.75 percent adjustable rate preferred stock issue (Series B) of Dayton Power & Light limits the amount of common stock dividends that can be paid if the company's income falls below a certain level. In a dividend policy study of 80 troubled firms that cut dividends researchers found that more than half of the firms apparently faced binding debt covenants in the years managers reduced dividends.

Tax Considerations

As mentioned earlier, under the 2002 U.S. tax code, the top personal marginal tax rate on dividend income was 38.6 percent, which was considerably higher than the maximum tax rate on long-term capital gains of 20 percent. This served as an incentive for corporations to keep dividends low so that shareholders could receive a greater proportion of their pretax returns in the form of capital gains and thereby increased after-tax returns.

Even though the new U.S. tax code for 2003 equalizes the tax treatment for dividends and capital gains with a maximum marginal rate of 15 percent for both, dividends are still tax-disadvantaged relative to capital gains: Dividend income is taxed immediately (in the year it is received), but capital gains income (and corresponding taxes) can be deferred into the future. If a corporation decides to retain its earnings in anticipation of providing growth and future capital appreciation for its investors, the investors are not taxed until their shares are sold. Consequently, for most investors, the present value of taxes on future capital gains income is less than the taxes on an equivalent amount of current dividend income. The deferral of taxes on capital gains can be viewed as an interest-free loan to the investor from the government.

Whereas the factors just explained tend to encourage corporations to retain their earnings, the IRS Code prohibits corporations from retaining an excessive amount of earnings to protect stockholders from paying taxes on dividends received. If the IRS rules that a corporation has accumulated excess earnings in order to protect its stockholders from having to pay personal income taxes on dividends, the firm has to pay a heavy penalty tax on those earnings. (It is the responsibility of the IRS to prove this allegation, however.)

Liquidity and Cash Flow Considerations

Since dividend payments represent cash outflows, the more liquid a firm is, the more able it is to pay dividends. Even if a firm has a past record of high earnings that have been reinvested, resulting in a large retained earnings balance, it may not be able to pay dividends unless it has sufficient liquid assets, primarily cash. For example, in mid-2002 Qwest Corporation, a major telecommunications firm, suspended cash dividend payments because of cash flow concerns attributable to overexpansion and a heavy debt load. (See the fourth dividend announcement in Figure 14.1, page 396.) Liquidity is likely to be a problem during a long business downturn, when both earnings and cash flows often decline. Rapidly growing firms with many profitable investment opportunities also often find it difficult to maintain adequate liquidity and pay dividends at the same time.

Borrowing Capacity and Access to the Capital Markets

Liquidity is desirable for a number of reasons. Specifically, it provides protection in the event of a financial crisis. It also provides the flexibility needed to take advantage of unusual financial and investment opportunities. There are other ways of achieving this flexibility and security, however. For example, companies frequently establish lines of credit and revolving credit agreements with banks, allowing them to borrow on short notice. Large well-established firms usually are able to go directly to credit markets with either a bond issue or a sale of commercial paper. The more access a firm has to these external sources of funds, the better able it will be to make dividend payments.

A small firm whose stock is closely held and infrequently traded often finds it difficult (or undesirable) to sell new equity shares in the markets. As a result, retained earnings are the only available source of new equity. When a firm of this type is faced with desirable investment opportunities, the payment of dividends is often inconsistent with the objective of maximizing the value of the firm.

Earnings Stability

Most large widely held firms are reluctant to lower their dividend payments, even in times of financial stress. Therefore, a firm with a history of stable earnings is usually more willing to pay a higher dividend than a firm with erratic earnings. A firm whose cash flows have been more or less constant over the years can be fairly confident about its future and frequently reflects this confidence in higher dividend payments.

Information Signaling

Signaling was previously shown to be a theoretically important determinant of dividend changes. From a practice perspective, it is widely perceived that dividends are an important mechanism to convey information to the markets. Empirical research has documented that announcement of changes in dividends are associated with significant stock price reactions in the same direction as the change in the dividends. This is viewed as an indication that the stock markets react to the information content of dividend change announcements. Theoretical work as well as survey results suggest that the information being conveyed by dividend change announcements pertains to the earnings of the firm. Whether information content of dividend changes pertains to future earnings or current or past earnings is still a much-debated issue. It may be all three; there is evidence that changes in dividends are associated with future and current as well as past earnings. Thus, dividends may be viewed as leading, lagging, or coincident indicators of the firm's earnings performance. The dividend increase announcement by NBC Capital Corporation shown in Figure 14.1 appears to be motivated by signaling considerations. It is evident the firm takes pride in the number of consecutive dividend increases it has made over the past three decades.

Growth Prospects

A rapidly growing firm usually has a substantial need for funds to finance the abundance of attractive investment opportunities. Instead of paying large dividends and then attempting to sell new shares to raise the equity investment capital it needs, this type of firm usually retains larger portions of its earnings and avoids the expense and inconvenience of public stock offerings. Table 14.3 illustrates the rela-

Table 14.3 Recent Dividend Payout Ratios and Growth Rates for Selected Companies

Company	2002 Dividend Payout Ratio (%)*	5-Year EPS Growth Rate**
IDEXX Laboratories (Medical supply)	0	76
Cheesecake Factory (Restaurant)	0	29.9
Krispy Kreme (Restaurant)	0	49
Qualcomm Inc. (Wireless communications mfg.)	0	40.3
Dell Computer (Personal computers)	0	20.1
Liz Claiborne (Apparel)	10.4	10.8
Borg Warner Inc. (Auto parts)	11.4	5.2
Target Corp. (Department stores)	13.2	17.2
Wal-Mart (Department stores)	16.6	18.3
Medtronic (Medical)	17.9	17.3
General Dynamics (Defense)	23.2	15.7
Tribune Co. (Publishing—newspapers)	23.5	10.2
Maytag (Consumer durables—appliances)	24.6	9.4
Anheuser-Busch (Beverages—beer)	34.1	13.3
Mc-Graw Hill (Publishing—textbook, business)	34.4	15.2
Avon Products (Cosmetics)	36	12.7
Suntrust Banks (Banking)	36.5	8.5
Washington Federal, Inc. (Banking)	40	8.4
Procter & Gamble (Consumer products)	42.3	9.5
Sara Lee (Conglomerate—bakery, apparel, etc.)	44.1	5.9
Coca-Cola Company (Beverages—soft drinks)	48.2	0.2
SBC Communications (Telecommunications)	49.5	3.3
FPL Group (Utility)	57.7	2.4
Clorox Co. (Consumer products)	61.3	2.5
General Mills (Food processing, cereals)	64.7	2.5
Southern Company (Utility)	73.5	3.2
International Paper (Paper)	89.3	1.7

*Calculated as dividends per share as a percentage of earnings per share.

**EPS growth rate is the 5-year compound growth rate of earnings per share (1997–2002).

Source: Various annual reports.

tionship between earnings growth rates and dividend payout ratios for selected companies. Note that the companies with the highest dividend payout ratios tend to have the lowest growth rates and vice versa.

Shareholder Preferences

In a closely held corporation with relatively few stockholders, management may be able to set dividends according to the preferences of its stockholders. For example, assume that the majority of a firm's stockholders are in high marginal tax brackets. They probably favor a policy of high earnings retention, resulting in eventual price appreciation, over a high payout dividend policy. However, high earnings retention implies that the firm has enough acceptable capital investment opportunities to justify the low payout dividend policy. In addition, recall that the IRS does not permit corporations to retain excessive earnings if they have no legitimate investment opportunities. Also, a policy of high retention when investment opportunities are not available is inconsistent with the objective of maximizing shareholder wealth.

In a large corporation whose shares are widely held, it is nearly impossible for a financial manager to take individual shareholders' preferences into account when setting dividend policy. Some wealthy stockholders who are in high marginal income tax brackets may prefer that a company reinvest its earnings (i.e., low payout ratio) to generate long-term capital gains. Other shareholders, such as retired individuals and those living on fixed incomes, may prefer a high dividend rate. These shareholders may be willing to pay a premium for common stock in a company that provides a higher dividend yield. Large institutional investors that are in a zero income tax bracket, such as pension funds, university endowment funds, philanthropic organizations (e.g., Ford Foundation), and trust funds, may prefer a high dividend yield for reasons different from those of private individual stockholders. First, endowment and trust funds sometimes are prohibited from spending the principal and must limit expenditures to the dividend (and/or interest) income generated by their investments. Second, pension and trust funds have a legal obligation to follow conservative investment strategies, which have been interpreted by the courts to mean that they should invest in companies that have a record of regular dividend payments.

It has been argued that firms tend to develop their own clientele of investors. This *clientele effect,* originally articulated by Miller and Modigliani, indicates that *investors will tend to be attracted to companies that have dividend policies consistent with the investors' objectives.* Some companies, such as public utilities, that pay out a large percentage (typically 70% or more) of their earnings as dividends traditionally have attracted investors who desire a high dividend yield. In contrast, growth-oriented companies, which pay no (or very low) dividends, have tended to attract investors who prefer earnings retention and greater price appreciation. Empirical studies generally support the existence of such a dividend clientele effect.

DIVIDEND POLICIES

This section describes several different types of dividend policies followed by firms.

Passive Residual Policy

The *passive residual policy* suggests that a firm should retain its earnings as long as it has investment opportunities that promise higher rates of return than the required rate. For example, assume a firm's shareholders could invest their dividends in stocks of similar risk with an expected rate of return (dividends plus capital gains) of 18 percent. This 10 percent figure, then, would constitute the required rate of return on the firm's retained earnings. As long as the firm can invest these earnings

FINANCE & The Real World

FedEx Finally Pays a Dividend

After 25 years as a public company, FedEx finally decided to pay its shareholders a dividend of 5 cents per share on June 17, 2002. The dividend payout cost the company $60 million, half its third quarter net profit. The question is, why now, after all these years?

Usually, companies in a growth mode do not pay dividends. They would rather reinvest profits so that they can grow even faster. But FedEx indicated that it is no longer in a rapid growth mode. For one thing, the U.S. economy was mired in a recession, and the months after the September 11th terrorist attacks were among the worst in history for the aviation industry. In addition, the company's chief financial officer was quoted as saying that it is not spending massive amounts of money building up the company. Of course, the company's competitors, United Parcel Service and Airborne, had paid dividends for some time. FedEx wanted to follow suit, so it wouldn't risk alienating its shareholders.

To be sure, offering shareholders a 5-cent per quarter dividend isn't all that generous. That's 20 cents per year per share. In mid-2003, FedEx shares were selling at about $65, which means a dividend yield of .20/$65, or less than 0.3%. In contrast, the average stock in the Standard & Poor's 500 Index pays about 1.6%.

Prior to June 2002, the company's shares had split 2:1 on five occasions. That means that an investor with 100 shares and a stock selling at, say, $50, would have 200 shares of a $25 stock after the split. Unlike dividends, stock splits don't offer anything of real value to shareholders, although there is a psychological boost that often is credited with the stock rising after a split takes place. On other occasions, the company had repurchased shares from investors. There is a tax benefit from share repurchases because the source of value to shareholders is an expected increase in the value of the remaining shares, which have a greater proportionate claim on the company's assets and earnings after the repurchase. Because this capital gain can be deferred until the shares are sold, many investors prefer share repurchases to dividends. Whereas share repurchases are one-time events, dividend payments are viewed as being more of a permanent distribution of cash to investors because of the extreme reluctance to cut dividends. Hence, dividends signal confidence in the cash flow generating ability of the company.

True, there is some debate over whether dividends are good for investors in the long run. After all, the company must first generate profits. Those profits are taxed at the corporate level. After-tax profits are paid out to individual shareholders, who, in turn, must pay tax on the dividend income. This so-called "double" taxation wouldn't take place if the company simply reinvested the money and generated even more profits. Shareholders would benefit because the stock price usually rises when profits increase. However, in 2003, the tax law changed and reduced the maximum tax on dividends from nearly 40% to 15%, making the "double" taxation a bit more palatable.

Source: FedEx corporate Web site; *Traffic World,* June 10, 2002, p. 33, "Payback Time: FedEx Outgrows 'Go Go Growthy' Name; Announces 5 Cents per Share Dividend."

to earn this required rate or more, it should not pay dividends (according to the passive residual policy), because such payments would require either that the firm forgo some acceptable investment opportunities or raise necessary equity capital in the more expensive external capital markets to meet the investment needs of the firm.

Interpreted literally, the residual theory implies that dividend payments will vary from year to year, depending on available investment opportunities. In periods with substantial capital expenditures dividends may be curtailed or even omitted, while in times of limited investment opportunities dividends may be substantial. There is strong evidence, however, that most firms try to maintain a rather stable dividend payment record over time. Of course, this does not mean that firms ignore the principles of the residual theory in making their dividend decisions, because dividends can be smoothed out from year to year in two ways. First, a firm can choose to retain a larger percentage of earnings during years when funding needs are large. If the firm continues to grow, it can manage to do this without reducing the dollar amount of the dividend. Second, a firm can borrow the funds it needs, temporarily raise its debt-to-equity ratio, and avoid a dividend cut in this way. Because issue costs are lower for large offerings of long-term debt, long-term debt capital tends to be raised in large, lumpy sums. If many good investment opportunities are available to a firm during a particular year, this type of borrowing is preferable to cutting back on dividends. The firm will then need to retain earnings in future years to bring its debt-to-equity ratio back in line. A firm that has many good investment opportunities for a number of years eventually may be forced to cut its dividend and/or sell new equity shares to meet financing requirements and maintain an optimal capital structure.

From a broader perspective, residual theory suggests that growth firms normally will have lower dividend payout ratios than firms in mature, low-growth industries. As shown earlier in Table 14.3, companies with low growth rates (e.g., International Paper, FPL Group, General Cereals) tend to have rather high payout ratios, whereas firms with high growth rates (e.g., Dell Computer, IDEXX Laboratories, Target Corporation) tend to have low or even zero payout ratios.

Stable Dollar Dividend Policy

Evidence indicates that most firms and stockholders prefer reasonably stable dividend policies. This stability is characterized by a rather strong reluctance to reduce the dollar amount of dividends from one period to the next. Similarly, increases in the dollar dividend rate normally are not made until the firm's management is satisfied that future earnings will be high enough to justify the larger dividend. Thus, although dividend rates tend to follow increases in earnings, they also tend to lag behind earnings to a certain degree.

Figure 14.2 shows the dividend and earnings history of Kerr-McGee Corporation. Although there has been an upward trend in dividends over time, dividend increases tend to lag earnings increases. Annual dividend payments are also more stable than earnings figures. Note, for instance, that despite the dramatic growth in earnings in 1996, dividends were increased by only $0.09 per share. Despite a significant earnings drop in 1992, the dividend rate was actually increased by $0.04 per share. More recently, note that in 2001 and 2002 Kerr-McGee experienced sharp declines in earnings, yet dividends remained stable.

Investors prefer stable dividends for a variety of reasons. Many investors feel that dividend changes possess informational content; they equate changes in a firm's dividend levels with profitability. A cut in dividends may be interpreted as a signal that the firm's long-run profit potential has declined. Similarly, a dividend increase is seen as a verification of the expectation that future profits will increase.

In addition, many shareholders need and depend on a constant stream of dividends for their cash income requirements. Although they can sell off some of their shares as an alternative source of current income, associated transaction costs make this an imperfect substitute for steady dividend income.

Some managers feel that a stable and growing dividend policy tends to reduce investor uncertainty concerning future dividend streams. They believe investors will pay a higher price for the stock of a firm that pays stable dividends, thereby reducing the firm's cost of equity.

Figure 14.2
Dividends and Earnings per Share for Kerr-McGee Corporation: 1986–2002

Source: Value Line Investment Survey 2003

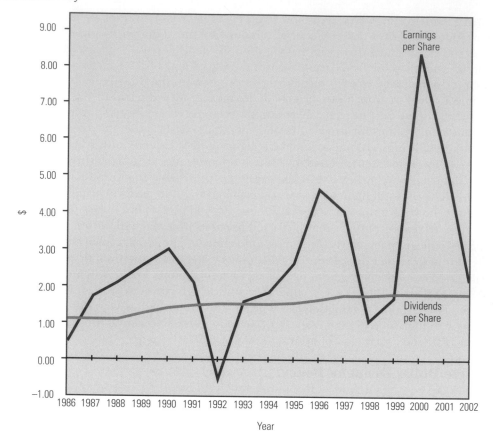

And, finally, stable dividends are legally desirable. Many regulated financial institutions such as bank trust departments, pension funds, and insurance companies are limited as to the types of common stock they are allowed to own. To qualify for inclusion in these legal lists, a firm must have a record of continuous and stable dividends. The failure to pay a dividend—or the reduction of a dividend amount—can result in removal from these lists. This, in turn, reduces the potential market for the firm's shares and may lead to price declines. As shown in Figure 14.2, Kerr-McGee maintained its per share dividend during the 1998–1999 period, even though its earnings per share were less than this amount in each of those years.

Other Dividend Payment Policies

Some firms have adopted a constant payout ratio dividend policy. A firm that uses this approach pays out a certain percentage of each year's earnings—for example, 40 percent of earnings. If the firm's earnings vary substantially from year to year, dividends also will fluctuate. The problem with this approach is that dividends can become very erratic, mirroring the volatility of the firm's earnings.

Other firms choose to pay a small quarterly dividend plus year-end extras. This policy is especially well suited for a firm with a volatile earnings record, volatile year-to-year cash needs, or both. Even when earnings are low, the firm's investors can count on their regular dividend payments. When earnings are high and no immediate need for these excess funds exists, the firm declares a year-end extra dividend. This policy gives management the flexibility to retain funds as needed and still satisfy investors who desire to receive some guaranteed level of dividend pay-

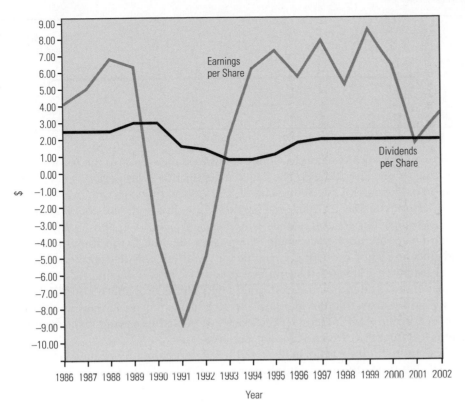

**Figure 14.3
Dividends and Earn-
ings per Share for
GM: 1986–2002**

Source: Value Line Investment
Survey 2003

ments. U.S. Steel, DuPont, and General Motors have all followed this policy from time to time. Figure 14.3 shows how this policy has affected General Motors. Although actual dividend payments have varied dramatically from year to year (compare this figure, for example, with Figure 14.2, which shows Kerr-McGee's earnings and dividends), only in 1993, after 3 years of huge losses, were dividends cut below $1.20, the regular rate in effect since 1975.

HOW DIVIDENDS ARE PAID

In most firms, the board of directors holds quarterly meetings to evaluate the firm's past performance and decide the level of dividends to be paid during the next period. Changes in the amount of dividends paid tend to be made rather infrequently, especially in firms that follow a stable dividend policy, and only after there is clear evidence that the firm's future earnings are likely to be either permanently higher or permanently lower than previously reported levels.

Most firms follow a dividend declaration and payment procedure similar to that outlined below. This procedure usually revolves around a *declaration date,* an *ex-dividend date,* a *record date,* and a *payment date.*

Figure 14.4 is a time line that illustrates Omnicare's dividend payment procedure (the original announcement can be found in Figure 14.1). The board of directors typically declares dividends following one of their regular board meetings where they consider corporate matters. Omnicare's board of directors met and declared a dividend of 2.25 cents per share on Monday, May 20, 2002. The dividends will be payable to shareholders of record on the record date, Friday, May 31, 2002. On that date, the firm makes a list from its stock transfer books of those shareholders who are eligible to receive the declared dividend.

**Figure 14.4
Key Dates in the
Dividend Payment
Procedure for
Omnicare**

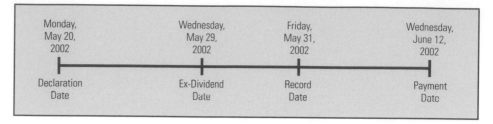

The major stock exchanges require 2 business days prior to the record date for recording ownership changes. The day that begins this 2-day period is called the ex-dividend date (in this case, Wednesday, May 29, 2002). Investors who purchase Omnicare stock prior to May 29, 2002 are eligible for the dividend; investors who purchase stock *on or after May 29, 2002 are not entitled to the dividend.* On May 29, 2002, the ex-dividend date, the stock price would be *expected* to decline by the amount of the dividend since the stock is no longer eligible for the previously declared dividend. Empirical evidence indicates that, on average, stock prices decline by *less* than the amount of the dividend on the ex-dividend day. This is probably because the market adjusts for the taxes that the marginal investor has to pay on the dividends; the net amount the marginal investor of the stock receives after paying taxes on the dividend is less than the dividend amount declared.

The payment date is normally 2 to 4 weeks after the record date (in this case, June 12, 2002). On this date, Omnicare makes dividend payments to the holders of record.

DIVIDEND REINVESTMENT PLANS

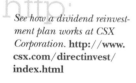

See how a dividend reinvestment plan works at CSX Corporation. **http://www.csx.com/directinvest/index.html**

In recent years, many firms have established dividend reinvestment plans. Under these plans, shareholders can have their dividends automatically reinvested in additional shares of the company's common stock. There are two types of dividend reinvestment plans: one involves the purchase of existing stock and the other involves the purchase of newly issued stock. The first type of plan is executed through a bank that, acting as a trustee, purchases the stock on the open market and then allocates it on a pro rata basis to the participating shareholders. In the second type of plan, the cash dividends of the participants are used to purchase, often at a small discount (up to 5%) from the market price, newly issued shares of stock.

This second type of plan enables the firm to raise substantial amounts of new equity capital over time as well as reduce the cash outflows required by dividend payments. To shareholders the advantage of a dividend reinvestment plan is that it represents a convenient method of purchasing additional shares of the company's common stock while saving on brokerage commissions. The primary disadvantage is that shareholders must pay taxes on the cash dividends reinvested in the company, even though they never receive any cash.

The Internet provides a number of directories that list firms providing dividend reinvestment plans. These directories also provide information on plan particulars, such as the minimum investment required, discounts, fees, etc. One source of information on the Internet is http://www.netstockdirect.com.

Comprehension Check Questions

1. What are some of the determinants of dividend policy in practice?
2. Describe the passive residual, stable dollar, and constant payout dividend policies.

3. Define each of the following dates: declaration date, ex-dividend date, record date, and payment date.

STOCK DIVIDENDS AND STOCK SPLITS

Some firms declare *stock dividends* rather than cash dividends. However, there are firms that declare both stock dividends *and* cash dividends at the same time.

A stock dividend is the *payment of additional shares of stock to common stockholders.* From an accounting perspective it involves making a transfer from the retained earnings account to the other stockholders' equity accounts.

For example, the Colonial Copies Company has the following common stockholders' equity:

Pre–Stock Dividend Common Stockholders' Equity	
Common stock ($5 par, 100,000 shares)	$ 500,000
Contributed capital in excess of par	1,000,000
Retained earnings	5,000,000
Total common stockholders' equity	**$6,500,000**

Suppose the firm declares a 10 percent stock dividend and existing shareholders receive 10,000 (10% × 100,000) new shares. Because stock dividend accounting usually is based on the pre-dividend market price, a total of $200,000 (10,000 shares × an assumed pre-dividend market price of $20 per share) is transferred from the firm's retained earnings account to the other stockholders' equity accounts. Of this $200,000, $50,000 ($5 par × 10,000 shares) is added to the common stock account and the remaining $150,000 is added to the contributed capital in excess of par account. After the stock dividend, Colonial has the following common stockholders' equity:

Post–Stock Dividend Common Stockholders' Equity	
Common stock ($5 par, 110,000 shares)	$ 550,000
Contributed capital in excess of par	1,150,000
Retained earnings	4,800,000
Total common stockholders' equity	**$6,500,000**

The net effect of this transaction is to increase the number of outstanding shares and to redistribute funds among the firm's capital accounts.

Up to now we have examined the accounting transactions associated with a stock dividend declaration. We now discuss the impact of stock dividends from a finance perspective. In other words, do stock dividends affect shareholder wealth? Note from the illustration above that the firm's total stockholders' equity remains unchanged, and each shareholder's *proportionate claim to the firm's earnings remains constant.* For example, if Colonial Copies Company has 100,000 shares outstanding prior to a 10 percent stock dividend and its total earnings are $200,000 ($2 per share), a stockholder who owns 100 shares has a claim on $200 of the firm's earnings. Following the 10 percent stock dividend, earnings per share decline to $1.82 ($200,000/110,000 shares). The stockholder who originally owned 100 shares now has 110 shares but continues to have a claim on only $200 (110 shares × $1.82 per share) of the firm's earnings.

Because each shareholder's proportionate claim on a firm's net worth *and* earnings remains unchanged in a stock dividend, the market price of each share of stock should decline in proportion to the number of new shares issued. This relationship can be expressed as follows:

$$\text{Post–stock dividend price} = \frac{\text{Pre–stock dividend price}}{(1 + \text{Percentage stock dividend rate})} \qquad (14.2)$$

In the Colonial Copies example, a $20 pre–stock dividend price should result in a post–stock dividend price of

$$\text{Post–stock dividend price} = \frac{\$20.00}{(1 + 0.10)}$$

$$= \$18.18$$

If a stockholder's wealth prior to the dividend is $2,000 (100 shares × $20 per share), post-dividend wealth should also remain at $2,000 (110 shares × $18.18 per share). In essence, all a stock dividend does is increase the number of pieces of paper in the stockholders' hands; the stock dividend does not affect the overall wealth of the shareholder.

Nevertheless, there are a number of reasons why firms declare stock dividends. First, a stock dividend may have the effect of broadening the ownership of a firm's shares, because existing shareholders often sell their stock dividends. Second, the declaration of stock dividends effectively lowers the per-share price of a stock, thereby possibly broadening its investment appeal. Investors seem to prefer stocks selling in approximately the $15 to $70 price range, because more of them will be financially able to purchase 100-share round lots. Round lots of 100 shares are more desirable for investors to own because lower transactions costs are associated with their purchase and sale. Third, in the case of a firm that already pays a cash dividend, a stock dividend results in an effective increase in cash dividends, provided that the per-share dividend rate is not reduced. (It is rare for a firm to declare a stock dividend and reduce its cash dividend rate at the same time.) Finally, stock dividends may be used by management to *signal* the firm's future prospects to the market. Stock dividends are usually issued by firms with significant growth opportunities; consequently, it may be viewed as a mechanism for management to inform the market of continued future growth opportunities for the firm.

Stock splits are similar to stock dividends in that they have the effect of increasing the number of shares of stock outstanding and reducing the price of each outstanding share. From an accounting standpoint, *stock splits are accomplished by reducing the par value of existing shares of stock and increasing the number of shares outstanding.* For example, in a two-for-one stock split, the number of shares would be doubled and the par value per share halved. Note that the dollar balances in the various stockholders' equity accounts are unaffected. Thus, unlike in the case of stock dividends, the balances for retained earnings, par value of common stock, and the capital in excess of par value are unchanged.

Although stock splits have an impact similar to stock dividends, they normally are not considered an element of a firm's dividend policy. Stock splits generally are motivated by management's desire to bring the trading price of the stock down to an optimal range. As noted before, some stock dividends are motivated by a similar reason. In the case of a stock split, the post–stock split is given by:

(14.3)
$$\text{Post–stock split price} = \frac{\text{Pre–stock split price}}{\text{Stock split ratio}}$$

For example, Computer Associates' pre–stock split price is $60.00 and the firm declares a three-for-two split: for every two shares you own, the firm gives you an additional share. According to Equation 14.3, Computer Associates' post-split price should drop to:

$$\text{Post–stock split price} = \frac{\$60.00}{\dfrac{3}{2}}$$

$$= \$40.00$$

Computer Associates' management may feel that at this price range ($40.00), the firm will attract a wider following of shareholders. As with stock dividends, often the post-split price may not fall to the level indicated by Equation 14.3. Stock splits are generally associated with growth stocks and thus investors may view stock split declarations as signals of future growth opportunities resulting in a net gain to shareholder wealth.

SHARE REPURCHASES

Share repurchases—the buying back of a company's own shares—have become increasingly popular since the 1980s. The volume of announced share repurchases rose to record levels in the 1990s. A recent study found that aggregate spending on repurchases amounted to 26 percent of corporate earnings over the 1983–1997 period. This compares to only 3 percent during the 1973–1977 period. In this section we will examine the equivalence between share repurchases and cash dividends from a theoretical perspective and then explore some of the motivations for repurchases in practice.

Share Repurchases versus Cash Dividends

As noted in the beginning of the chapter, firms can disburse cash to shareholders in one of two ways: they can pay a cash dividend or they can repurchase stock. In the next few paragraphs we contrast the effects of a stock repurchase and an otherwise similar cash dividend.

Suppose that the Tasty Bite Company plans to distribute to its shareholders $75 million in the form of either a one-time extra cash dividend or a share repurchase. The company has expected earnings of $62.5 million during the coming year and approximately 25 million shares currently outstanding. The current (ex-dividend) market price of Tasty Bite stock is $50 per share. The company can pay a one-time extra cash dividend of $3 per share ($75 million divided by 25 million shares). Alternatively, it can make an offer to its shareholders to buy back shares at $53 per share for 1,415,094 shares ($75 million divided by $53 per share).

If Tasty Bite decides to declare a one-time extra cash dividend of $3 per share, shareholder wealth would be $53 per share, consisting of the $50 (ex-dividend) share price plus the $3 dividend. The effect on shareholder wealth before and after the stock repurchase is shown in Table 14.4, assuming that the price–earnings (P/E) ratio remains the same at 20 ($50 stock price per share divided by $2.50 earnings per share). Recall from Chapter 4 that the P/E ratio is equal to the price per share divided by the earnings per share.) For example, if a stock sells for $40 per share and earns $8

Table 14.4 Tasty Bite Company Share Repurchase

	Before Repurchase	After Repurchase
Expected net earnings	$62,500,000	62,500,000
Shares outstanding	25,000,000	23,584,906
Expected earnings per share	$2.50	$2.65
Price–earnings (P/E) ratio	20x	20x
Expected share price (ex-dividend)	$50	$53
Expected dividend	$3	$0

per share, its P/E multiple is 5 times (40/8). The P/E multiple indicates the value placed by investors on a dollar of a firm's earnings. It is influenced by a number of factors, including earnings prospects and investors' perceptions regarding a firm's risk.

If Tasty Bite repurchases $75 million worth of its common stock (at $53 per share), then shareholder wealth is $53 per share, with $3 of this value representing price appreciation. Note that the pretax returns to shareholders are the same under each alternative.

The illustration above shows that *ignoring taxes, transaction costs, and other market imperfections, shareholders should be indifferent between equivalent returns from cash dividends and share repurchases.* In other words, the value of the firm should not be affected by the manner in which returns (cash dividends versus capital gains) are paid to shareholders. However, empirical studies suggest that share repurchases do increase stock prices (i.e., value of the firm). Some reasons why this occurs are:

1. Some companies engage in large stock buyback programs as a way to return excess cash flow back to shareholders. Typically, these firms have an insufficient number of positive NPV (net present value) investments in which to invest. For example, Quaker Oats (acquired by PepsiCo in 2001) repurchased 20 million shares during the 1980s and early 1990s and was planning the repurchase of an additional 5 million shares. Quaker Oats treasurer at the time, Janet K. Cooper said in reference to the buyback, "We spend on new products, we make acquisitions, and we raise the dividend, and we still can't soak up all the cash."

2. There are firms that buy back stocks as a takeover defense. Firms that are under threat of a hostile takeover sometimes announce large share repurchase programs designed to drain *excess* cash from the firm, thereby making it a less desirable takeover target. Such actions also have the effect of increasing the concentration of ownership by management in the firm, thus decreasing the chance that a hostile party will obtain control of the firm.

3. Many firms announce buyback programs as a signal of their confidence in the firm's future prospects. For example, in the aftermath of the 1987 stock market crash, over 900 firms announced stock repurchase programs in the 2 weeks following Black Monday. The announcement by Kreisler Manufacturing in Figure 14.1 is a specific example of stock repurchase motivated by management's belief that the stock is undervalued.

4. Firms may engage in stock buyback programs to have sufficient common stock to meet the needs of employee stock option plans and convertible securities. If the firm does not buy back stocks for these needs, it will have to issue new stock resulting in a *dilution* effect. That is, the earnings have to be spread over a larger number of shares outstanding thereby depressing earnings per share and even stock prices.

5. Some firms buy their own stock back as an alternative to paying out cash dividends. This has two advantages to the investor. First, participating in a stock repurchase program subjects the investor to the lower capital gains tax rate instead of the higher rate on dividend income (this assumes the tax rate on dividends is higher than on capital gains). Also as noted before, even if the tax rates on dividends and capital gains are the same, because taxes on capital gains can be deferred into the future they may still be preferred.

   Second, in a stock buyback program the investor is free to decide whether or not to participate in the program. In the case of dividends, all stockholders will receive the dividend. It is possible for the investor who does not need the cash to buy additional shares of the stock, but this entails the payment of commissions. Further, the investor has to pay tax on the dividend income.

Although a stock repurchase program seems like a desirable way of distributing a firm's earnings, repurchases may be deterred by the IRS. Specifically, the IRS will not permit a firm to follow a policy of regular stock repurchases as an alternative to cash dividends, because repurchase plans convert cash dividends to capital gains. The IRS looks upon regular repurchases as essentially equivalent to cash dividends, thus requiring that they be taxed accordingly.

Procedures for Repurchasing Shares

Firms carry out share repurchase programs in a number of ways. For example, a company may buy directly from its stockholders in what is termed a ***tender offer;*** it may purchase the stock in the *open market,* or it may *privately negotiate* purchases from large holders, such as institutions. In a tender offer, the firm stipulates a fixed price at which it will buy back a certain number of shares within a specified period of time, usually 2 months. Usually the premium is about 15 to 25 percent of the pre-announcement price of the stock. A variant of the fixed price tender offer called the *Dutch auction tender offer* has become popular in recent years. In the Dutch auction tender offer, the firm, instead of specifying a single price, sets a range of prices it is willing to accept. Investors then would tender their shares and also indicate the price within the specified range at which they are tendering. The firm would then start from the lowest price and work its way up till it has purchased the necessary number of shares. The advantage of the Dutch auction method is that it results in a lower overall premium that the firm has to pay in order to buy back the shares. In an open market purchase the firm buys back the shares at the prevailing market prices spread over a period of several months. In a negotiated purchase the firm offers to buy back from certain large holders at a privately negotiated price. This is usually done for defensive takeover reasons.

Comprehension Check Questions

1. How are stock dividends and stock splits different from each other?
2. What impact will a stock dividend or stock split have on stock price?
3. What are some reasons why stock repurchases are undertaken?
4. Contrast the tax impact of stock repurchases and cash dividends from a stock investor's perspective.

Summary

> Dividend policy determines the ultimate distribution of a firm's earnings between retention (reinvestment) and cash dividend payments to stockholders. Retained earnings provide investors with a source of potential future earnings growth, whereas dividends provide them with a current distribution.

> From a theoretical perspective, Miller and Modigliani show that under perfect market assumptions—including no taxes, no transactions costs, and no issuance costs—dividend policy has no effect on stock price. They show that the stock price and returns to the shareholder are identical regardless of the dividend policy that is followed. The only difference is that stockholders in firms

with higher dividend payout ratios will have more of the return in the form of dividends (and relatively less from capital gains), while stockholders in firms with lower dividend payout ratios will obtain more of the return in the form of capital gains (and relatively less from dividend income). So long as investors are indifferent to the source of the return it does not matter whether the return is in the form of dividends or capital gains.

➤ Proponents of dividend relevance argue that risk aversion, information content and the signaling effect of dividends, transactions costs, taxes, and issuance costs make dividends relevant.

➤ From a practical perspective, a number of factors influence a firm's choice of dividend policy. These include the following:

1. Legal constraints prohibiting dividends that impair capital
2. Restrictive covenants in bond indentures and other financing agreements
3. Tax considerations
4. The need for liquidity
5. Borrowing capacity and access to the capital markets
6. Earnings stability
7. Information signaling
8. Capital expansion (growth) opportunities
9. Shareholder preference

➤ A firm may employ any one of a number of alternative dividend policies, including the following:

1. The passive residual approach
2. The stable dollar dividend approach
3. The constant payout ratio approach
4. The policy of paying a small, regular dividend plus year-end extras

➤ Ample evidence indicates that many firms favor a stable dollar dividend policy.

➤ Stock dividends, in contrast to cash dividends, involve the distribution of additional shares as a dividend rather than cash. The net effect of stock dividends is to leave the total book value of the firm unchanged while increasing the number of shares outstanding and lowering the price per share. Stock dividends are issued to broaden the ownership base of the firm and to signal future growth prospects of the firm.

➤ Stock splits are similar to stock dividends and may be thought of as "large" stock dividends, however, the accounting treatment for stock splits and stock dividends are different. Stock splits are accompanied by a change in the par value per share and the total shares outstanding, but the aggregate common stock par value is unaffected. In the case of stock dividends a transfer is made from the retained earnings account to the common stock and contributed capital in excess of par accounts.

➤ Some firms employ share repurchase plans as an alternative way to disburse cash. Stock buyback programs are implemented for a variety of reasons including: to return excess cash flow to shareholders, to thwart takeovers, to signal confidence in the firm's future prospects, and to meet needs of employee stock option plans and convertible securities.

➤ Stock repurchases may also be used as a tax-favored alternative to cash dividends. Stock repurchases convert shareholder benefits from ordinary income (dividends) to capital gains income. Theoretically, ignoring taxes, transaction costs, and other market imperfections, share repurchases should have the same effect on shareholder wealth as the payment of cash dividends. However, possibly due to tax considerations and signaling effects, share repurchases (via tender offers) are observed to have a more positive effect on shareholder wealth.

Questions and Topics for Discussion

1. What legal constraints limit the amount of cash dividends that may be paid by a firm?
2. What aspects of U.S. tax laws tend to (a) encourage and (b) discourage large dividend payments by corporations? Explain how.
3. Explain what is meant by the clientele effect.
4. Explain what is meant by the signaling effect of dividend policy.
5. In the theoretical world of Miller and Modigliani, what role does dividend policy play in the determination of share values?
6. Why do many managers prefer a stable dollar dividend policy to a policy of paying out a constant percentage of each year's earnings as dividends?
7. Under what circumstances would it make sense for a firm to borrow money to make its dividend payments?
8. Some people have suggested that it is irrational for a firm to pay dividends and sell new stock in the same year because the cost of newly issued equity is greater than the cost of retained earnings. Do you agree? Why or why not?
9. What is the ex dividend date?
10. Why do many firms choose to issue stock dividends? What is the value of a stock dividend to a shareholder?
11. What are the motivations for stock repurchases?

Self-Test Problems

ST1. The board of directors of Complex Computers has decided to declare a 20 percent stock dividend. The company's common stockholders' equity is as follows:

Pre–Stock Dividend Common Stockholders' Equity

Common stock ($1 par, 100,000 shares)	$ 100,000
Contributed capital in excess of par	900,000
Retained earnings	5,000,000
Total common stockholders' equity	**$6,000,000**

The common stock of Complex Computers currently is trading at $80 a share.

The company is growing rapidly and has never paid a cash dividend.

a. Show the company's common stockholders' equity after the stock dividend.
b. Calculate the post–stock dividend price of Complex Computers stock, assuming no other changes occur.

ST2. Sanchez Supermarkets, Inc. currently has annual earnings before interest and taxes of $1,000,000. Its interest expenses are $200,000 a year, and it pays $100,000 in annual dividends to its stockholders. The firm has 50,000 common shares outstanding. The company's tax rate is 40 percent, and its common stock's current dividend yield is 2.0 percent (dividend per share/stock price).

    a. Calculate the company's earnings per share.

    b. Calculate the company's dividend payout ratio.

    c. Calculate the company's current common stock price.

    d. If Sanchez declares and pays a 100 percent stock dividend and then pays an annual cash dividend of $1.10 per share, what is the effective rate by which the dividend has been increased?

ST3. The board of directors of Total Freight Corporation declared a quarterly dividend of $0.10 per share on May 30, 2003 (Friday). The dividends are payable on July 7, 2003 (Monday) to holders of record on June 16, 2003 (Monday). What is the last date you can buy shares of Total Freight and still receive the dividend of $0.10 per share?

Problems

BASIC

1. Jacobs Corporation earned $2 million after tax. The firm has 1.6 million shares of common stock outstanding.

    a. Compute the earnings per share of Jacobs.

    b. If Jacobs' dividend policy calls for a 40 percent payout ratio, what are the dividends per share?

INTERMEDIATE

2. Drew Financial Associates currently pays a quarterly dividend of 50 cents per share. This quarter's dividend will be paid to stockholders of record on Friday, February 22, 20X1. Drew has 200,000 common shares outstanding. The retained earnings account has a balance of $15 million before the dividend, and Drew holds $2.5 million in cash.

    a. What is the ex-dividend date for this quarter?

    b. Drew's stock traded for $22 per share the day prior to the ex-dividend date. What would you expect the stock price to open at on the ex-dividend date? Give some reasons why this might not occur.

    c. What is the effect of the dividend payment on Drew's cash, retained earnings, and total assets?

BASIC

3. Winkie Baking has just announced a 100 percent stock dividend. The annual cash dividend per share was $2.40 before the stock dividend. Winkie intends to pay $1.40 per share on each of the new shares. Compute the percentage increase in the cash dividend rate that will accompany the stock dividend.

INTERMEDIATE

4. Wolverine Corporation plans to pay a $3 dividend per share on each of its 300,000 shares next year. Wolverine anticipates earnings of $6.25 per share over the year. If the company has a capital budget requiring an investment of $4 million over the year and it desires to maintain its present debt to total assets (debt ratio) of 0.40, how much external equity must it raise? Assume Wolverine's capital structure includes only common equity and debt, and that debt and equity will be the only sources of funds to finance capital projects over the year.

5. Tulia Dairy pays a $2.50 cash dividend and earns $5 per share. The cash dividend has recently been increased to $2.65 per share, *and* a 3 percent stock dividend has been declared. What is the effective rate of increase in the dividends for Tulia as a result of this action?

INTERMEDIATE

6. The Mori Egg Noodle Company has the following equity accounts on its balance sheet:

INTERMEDIATE

Common stock ($10 par, 300,000 shares)	$ 3,000,000
Contributed capital in excess of par	1,500,000
Retained earnings	6,000,000
Total common stockholders' equity	**$10,500,000**

a. What is the maximum amount of dividends that may be paid by the Mori Company if the capital impairment provisions of state law are limited to the following?

  i. The par value of common stock.

  ii. The par value and the capital in excess of par accounts.

b. What other factors may limit Mori's ability to pay dividends?

7. Champoux Hair Factory, Inc. has earnings before interest and taxes of $200,000. Annual interest amounts to $80,000, and annual depreciation is $80,000. Taxes are computed at a 40 percent rate. Existing bond obligations require the payment of $40,000 per year into a sinking fund.

CHALLENGE

Champoux wishes to pay a $2 per-share dividend on the existing 20,000 shares. The firm's bond indenture prohibits the payment of dividends unless the cash flow (before dividends and sinking fund payments) is greater than the total of dividends, interest, and sinking fund obligations.

a. Can Champoux pay the proposed dividend?

b. What is the maximum dividend per share that may be paid?

8. Lenberg Lens Company believes in the "dividends as a residual" philosophy of dividend policy. This year's earnings are expected to total $10 million. A very conservative company, Lenberg is financed solely with common stock. The required rate of return on retained earnings is 12 percent, whereas the cost of newly raised capital is 14 percent because of issuance costs.

INTERMEDIATE

a. If Lenberg has $6 million of investment projects having expected returns greater than 12 percent, what total amount of dividends should Lenberg pay?

b. If Lenberg has $12 million of investment projects having expected returns greater than 14 percent, what total amount of dividends should Lenberg pay?

c. What factors, other than its belief in the residual theory of dividends, should Lenberg consider in setting its dividend policy in (b)?

9. Phoenix Tool Company and Denver Tool Company have had a very similar record of earnings performance over the past 8 years. Both firms are in the same industry and, in fact, compete directly with each other. The two firms have nearly identical capital structures. Phoenix has a policy of paying a constant 50 percent of each year's earnings as dividends, whereas Denver has sought to maintain a stable dollar dividend policy, with changes in the dollar dividend payment occurring infrequently. The record of the two companies follows:

CHALLENGE

	Phoenix			Denver		
Year	EPS	Dividend	Average Market Price	EPS	Dividend	Average Market Price
20X1	$2.00	$1.00	$20	$2.10	$0.75	$18
20X2	2.50	1.25	24	2.40	0.75	22
20X3	2.50	1.25	15	1.60	0.75	17
20X4	1.00	0.50	10	0.90	0.75	14
20X5	0.50	0.25	8	0.50	0.50	10
20X6	−1.25	nil	8	−1.10	0.50	10
20X7	1.00	0.50	10	1.10	0.75	14
20X8	1.50	0.75	14	1.45	0.75	17

The president of Phoenix wonders what accounts for Denver's current (20X8) higher stock price, in spite of the fact that Phoenix currently earns more per share than Denver and frequently has paid a higher dividend.

a. What factors can you cite that might account for this phenomenon?

b. What do you suggest as an optimal dividend policy for both Phoenix and Denver that might lead to increases in both of their share prices? What are the limitations of your suggestions?

CHALLENGE **10.** The Emco Steel Company has experienced a slow (3% per year) but steady increase in earnings per share. The firm consistently has paid out an average of 75 percent of each year's earnings as dividends. The stock market evaluates Emco primarily on the basis of its dividend payout because growth prospects are modest.

Emco's management presents a proposal to the board of directors that would require the outlay of $50 million to build a new plant in the rapidly expanding Florida market. The expected annual return on the investment in this plant is estimated to be in excess of 30 percent, more than twice the current company average. To finance this investment, a number of alternatives are being considered. They include the following:

a. Finance the expansion with externally raised equity.

b. Finance the expansion with 50 percent externally generated equity and 50 percent internally generated equity. This alternative would necessitate a dividend cut for this year only.

c. Finance the expansion with a mix of debt and equity similar to their current relative proportions in the capital structure. Under this alternative, dividends would not be cut. Rather, any equity needs in excess of that which could be provided internally would be raised through a sale of new common stock.

Evaluate these various financing alternatives with reference to their effects on the dividend policy and common stock values of the company.

INTERMEDIATE **11.** The Sweet Times Candy Company has the following equity accounts on its balance sheet:

Common stock ($1 par, 500,000 shares)	$ 500,000
Contributed capital in excess of par	2,000,000
Retained earnings	13,000,000
Total common stockholders' equity	**$15,500,000**

The current market price of the firm's shares is $50.

a. If the firm declares a 10 percent stock dividend, what will be the impact on the firm's equity accounts?

b. If the firm currently pays no cash dividend, what is the impact of a 10 percent stock dividend on the wealth position of the firm's existing stockholders?

c. If the firm currently pays a cash dividend of $1 per share and this per-share dividend rate does not change after the 10 percent stock dividend, what impact would you expect the stock dividend to have on the wealth position of existing shareholders?

12. Concave Systems presently has earnings before interest and taxes of $3,000,000. Its interest expenses are $500,000 a year, and it pays $600,000 in annual dividends to its shareholders. Concave has 300,000 common shares outstanding, and its tax rate is 40 percent. Its annual capital expenditures are $900,000. Concave's present price–earnings ratio is 12.   **INTERMEDIATE**

a. Calculate the company's earnings per share.

b. Calculate the company's dividend payout ratio.

c. Calculate the company's dividend yield.

13. On Friday, August 6, the Board of Directors of Cisco Industries declares a $0.22 quarterly dividend payable on September 15 to stockholders of record on Tuesday, August 24. When is the ex-dividend date? If you purchase the stock on this date are you entitled to receive the dividend?   **BASIC**

14. Clynne Resources expects earnings this year to be $2 per share. Clynne plans to pay a dividend of $0.70 per share for the year. During the year Clynne expects to borrow $10 million in addition to its already outstanding loan balances. Clynne has 10 million shares of common stock outstanding   **CHALLENGE**

a. If all capital outlays are funded from retained earnings and new borrowings and if Clynne follows a residual dividend policy, what capital outlays are planned for the coming year?

b. What is Clynne's target capital structure given these assumptions?

15. Using the Internet to access the financial statements of Pfizer and Genentech, compute the two firms' dividend payout ratios for the preceding year. Provide an explanation for the differences in the payout policies of the two firms.   **INTERMEDIATE**

16. Go to http://www.moneypaper.com and see if Intel Corporation participates in the dividend reinvestment plan.

THOMSON ONE—Business School Edition

Go to the text Web site at http://moyer.swlearning.com, select your book, and click on the Thomson ONE button. Enter Thomson ONE—Business School Edition by using the username and password you created when you registered the serial number on your access card. Use either the "Prices" tab or the "Financials" tab to compare the dividend policy of American Express (AXP), Cisco Systems (@CSCO), Exxon Mobil (XOM), Office Depot (ODP), and Nucor (NUE). What factors do you believe account for the differences observed in dividend payout policies and the dividend yields of these stocks?

FINANCIAL PLANNING, WORKING CAPITAL MANAGEMENT, AND INTERNATIONAL FINANCE

PART FIVE

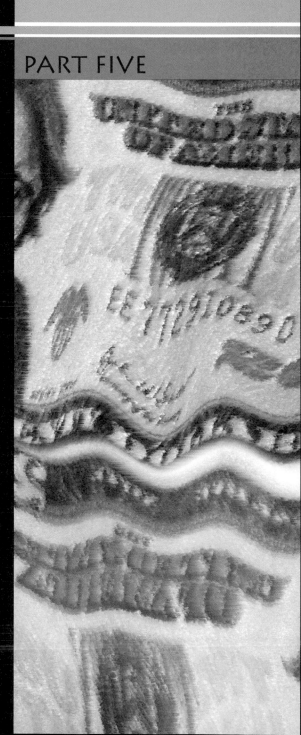

Chapter 15 deals with short-term and long-term financial planning. Chapter 16 begins with a discussion of working capital management including the risk-return trade-offs of alternative working capital policies. The chapter then focuses on effective management of the current assets of the firm including cash, marketable securities, accounts receivable and inventory. Chapter 17 deals with management of current liabilities including a discussion of the sources and costs of various short-term sources of borrowing. Chapter 18, the final chapter of the text, discusses aspects of international finance relevant to financial management of the firm.

CHAPTER
15 Long-term and Short-term Planning

Many firms that fail, especially the smaller ones, do so because of inadequate planning. In order to grow and survive, firms have to conduct two types of planning exercises: *strategic planning* and—a subset—*operational planning.* This chapter considers the important area of financial planning, a critical component of the operational planning process. Chapters 16 and 17 consider the important role played by the management of working capital assets and liabilities in the financial planning process.

Strategic planning is long range in nature and deals with the overall direction of the firm. It is largely concerned with anticipating significant new developments and changes that will have a major impact on the industry and the firm. For example, few would have anticipated 10 years ago that E-commerce would become as big as it has. Companies that did not anticipate this major development in how people buy and transact business are trying to play catch-up to small but agile start-ups that have responded to this new way of merchandising. Take for instance, Barnes & Noble, the largest bookstore chain in the world. A few years ago, when the Internet was still in its nascent stages, Barnes & Noble did not think trading via this medium was going to be a significant factor. For one thing, they felt the experience of going to a bookstore and browsing through the aisles could not be duplicated. As Barnes & Noble found out, this idea couldn't be further from the truth. Among all E-commerce ventures, buying books via the Internet is one of the most dominant businesses. Amazon.com, a firm that began operations only in July 1995, caught the Internet wave and now commands a majority share of all books purchased over the Internet. Barnes & Noble did ultimately start selling its books through the Internet but remains a distant second to Amazon.com. With a proper strategic planning process, Barnes & Noble probably could have positioned itself to better take advantage of the opportunities presented by the Internet medium.

While strategic planning focuses more on the overall direction of the business and the industry, *operational planning, as the phrase denotes, is designed to be a blueprint detailing where the firm wants to be at some future point in time and what resources are needed to get it there.* Operational plans are generally conducted at two levels—long-term and short-term. Long-term plans are typically done over a 5-year planning horizon while short-term plans are conducted over a 12- to 18-month window. This chapter focuses on the operational rather than strategic plan of the firm (and especially on its financial aspect). The operational plan begins with a series of *operational objectives* that define *where the firm wants to be at the end of the planning period.* These objectives are very specific. Some examples are:

➢ Raise market share from 12.5 percent to 17 percent in 12 months.

➢ Develop a new color PDA/wireless phone for sale in less than 6 months at a price point less than $100.

➢ Reduce debt to total capital ratio from 65 percent to 40 percent in 2 years.

➢ Raise operating profit margin from 8 percent to 9.5 percent in 1 year.

➢ Reduce the development phase of new product introduction from an average of 28 months to 12 months.

➢ Decrease dependence on sales to the defense industry from 60 percent to under 40 percent in 2 years.

To address these objectives, the firm must develop an operational plan, which consists of a *marketing plan,* a *production plan,* a *human resource plan,* and a *financial plan.* The marketing plan lays out the marketing resources needed to meet the operational objectives and includes such things as advertising strategy, marketing promotions, channels of distribution and distribution incentives, and assignment of sales territory. The production plan consists of facilities needed to achieve the operational objectives including the number of shifts, plant refurbishment and expansions, vendor and supplier arrangements, inventory control, etc. The human resource plan is concerned with the personnel aspect of the objectives. It looks at the managerial and labor pool that is needed to attain the objectives.

The financial plan, our focus in this chapter, *lays out the financial resources that are needed to achieve the operational (including the financial) objectives of the firm.* Operational planning is crucial to a firm's survival in the short and long run. The lack of adequate operational planning has doomed many a firm, both small and large.

Figure 15.1 presents an overview of the corporate planning process as described above. The strategic plan is determined by the long-term goals of the firm, but it also affects the operational objectives of the firm. The operational objectives in turn are implemented via the operational plan, which consists of marketing, production, human resource, and financial plans. The dashed line from the operational plan to operational objectives and back to the operational plan indicates that the operational plan should be continually monitored to see if the objectives are being met or not. If the objectives are not met, then the operational plan needs to be adjusted so that it is in alignment with the objectives. Thus, the operational plan is not only a *planning* device; it is also a *monitoring* device.

An integral part of the operational plan and the financial plan are the **financial forecasts.** This chapter discusses various techniques for forecasting a company's future need for funds and cash flows. These include *pro forma financial statements* and *cash budgets.* Other techniques, such as computerized financial forecasting and planning models, also are briefly outlined. *The financial forecasts primarily are concerned with whether the firm has sufficient internal resources to meet its operational objectives.* If internal resources are not sufficient, it means the firm needs to either modify its operational objectives or make arrangements to ensure adequate resources are available.

Figure 15.1
An Overview of the
Corporate Planning
Process

Chapter Objectives

After reading this chapter, you should have an understanding of the following:

1. How to prepare pro forma balance sheets and income statements using the percentage of sales method

2. The limitations of the percentage of sales method to forecast external funds requirement

3. How to forecast cash needs by preparing a cash budget

4. The limitations of projected cash budgets

PRO FORMA STATEMENTS

e-Lecture

Pro forma (or forecasted) *financial statements* are an important part of the financial forecasting process. Firms often construct pro forma statements for the income statement, the balance sheet, and the statement of cash flows. Pro forma statements are especially important for long-range planning purposes; firms develop pro forma annual statements for up to 10 years. Firms also may construct short-run pro forma statements on a quarterly basis for a 12- to 18-month horizon. For illustrative purposes we focus on annual projections of balance sheet and income statements. Our intent is to show what the balance sheet and income statement would look like in the future if certain *assumed* events were to occur. They are very useful in identifying future funds needs and projecting future performance.

One method of forecasting pro forma statements is using the simple, yet useful, *percentage of sales forcasting method.* This method is useful in forecasting the amount of external financing a firm will need for a projected increase in sales. As the phrase implies, the method assumes that most variables in the balance sheet and income statement are a *fixed proportion of sales and therefore vary directly with sales.* The use of this method is illustrated with the following example of the Weed Wacker Corporation (WWC).

The present (2003) balance sheet and income statement for Weed Wacker are shown in Tables 15.1 and 15.2, respectively. Management forecasts that sales will increase next year (2004) by 25 percent or $4,000,000 to $20,000,000.

The 25 percent growth represents a significant increase over previous years. Management attributes this to a weed invasion that has swept the nation from neighboring countries. One of management's primary concerns is the amount of funds needed to finance this sales growth. Management is concerned that inter-

Table 15.1 Weed Wacker Corporation Balance Sheet as of December 31, 2003

Cash	$ 500,000	Accounts payable	$1,500,000
Accounts receivable	2,000,000	Accrued expenses	500,000
Inventory	4,000,000	Total current liabilities	$2,000,000
Total current assets	$6,500,000		
		Long-term debt	1,000,000
Net fixed assets	1,000,000		
		Stockholders' equity	
		Common stock at par	$1,000,000
		Capital in excess of par	1,500,000
		Retained earnings	2,000,000
		Total stockholders' equity	$4,500,000
Total assets	**$7,500,000**	**Total liabilities and equity**	**$7,500,000**

Table 15.2 Weed Wacker Corporation Income Statement for the Year Ended December 31, 2003

Sales	$16,000,000
Cost of goods sold	9,780,000
Gross profit	$ 6,220,000
General, sales, and administrative expenses	4,890,000
Operating earnings	$ 1,330,000
Interest expenses	80,000
Earnings before taxes	$ 1,250,000
Taxes	500,000
Earnings after taxes	$ 750,000
Dividends paid	$ 250,000

nally generated funds may not be sufficient to finance the resources needed to support a 25 percent increase in sales. The company would like to construct a pro forma balance sheet and income statement for next year to help plan for additional funds that might be needed. Normally, firms would project the statements out to 3–5 years for planning purposes, however, for illustrative purposes we confine our projections to just 1 year.

To determine the amount of additional financing necessary to reach the expected $20,000,000 annual sales level, the WWC management has made the following observations about the company's income and balance sheet statements:

1. **Cost of goods sold.** Management believes the cost of goods sold as a percentage of sales will remain the same as in the current year.
2. **General, sales, and administrative expenses.** The proportion of general, selling, and administrative expenses to sales is expected to be the same next year as in the current year.
3. **Interest expense.** The interest expense incurred in 2003 was on a long-term loan the firm had taken several years ago. The loan is not due for another 5 years and because it is a fixed interest rate loan, the interest expense next year will be unchanged from this year's expense.

4. **Taxes.** The firm's tax rate this year at 40 percent is expected to remain constant for next year.

5. **Dividends.** This year the firm paid out $250,000 in cash dividends based on a dividend per share of $0.50. The firm currently has 500,000 shares outstanding. The firm anticipates increasing the dividend to $0.60 per share next year.

6. **Cash.** Management feels the company's cash balances are generally adequate for the present sales level and would have to increase proportionately as sales increase.

7. **Accounts receivable.** The company's present average collection period is 45.625 days. Management feels the company's present credit policies are appropriate for its type of business. As a result, they feel that the average collection period will remain approximately constant and that accounts receivable will remain a constant proportion of sales next year.

8. **Inventory.** Management feels the company's inventory is properly managed at present. Therefore, they feel inventory would have to increase proportionately in order to support the sales increase.

9. **Fixed assets.** Because the company's fixed assets are being utilized at nearly full capacity, management feels fixed assets will have to increase as sales grow. For financial planning purposes, management is willing to assume that the net fixed asset figure on the balance sheet will increase proportionately as sales increase.

10. **Accounts payable.** The company now maintains good relations with its suppliers. As the company purchases more inventory, its accounts payable balance will increase proportionately as sales increase.

11. **Accrued expenses.** The accrued expenses are expected to maintain their proportionality with sales.

12. **Long-term debt.** The current long-term debt of $1,000,000 is not due for another 5 years, so this amount is expected to remain outstanding at the end of next year. The annual interest rate on the loan is 8 percent.

From the above assumptions we note that a number of variables in the income and balance sheet statements are expected to vary directly with sales. For these variables we calculate their proportional relationship to sales based on the 2003 historical statements. This is shown in Table 15.3.

We are now ready to forecast the income statement for 2004, shown in Table 15.4. We begin with the projected sales for 2004 estimated to be $20,000,000. The

---

Table 15.3 Selected Balance Sheet and Income Statement Variables as a Percentage of Sales for Weed Wacker Corporation for 2003

Balance Sheet	
Cash/Sales	3.125%
Accounts receivable/Sales	12.5%
Inventory/Sales	25.0%
Net fixed assets/Sales	6.25%
Accounts payable/Sales	9.375%
Accrued expenses/Sales	3.125%
Income Statement	
Cost of goods sold/Sales	61.125%
General, sales, and administrative expenses/ Sales	30.5625%

Table 15.4 Weed Wacker Corporation Pro Forma Income Statement for Year Ending December 31, 2004		
Sales	$20,000,000	
Cost of goods sold	12,225,000	61.125% of sales
Gross profit	$ 7,775,000	
General, sales, and administrative expenses	6,112,500	30.5625% of sales
Operating earnings	$ 1,662,500	
Interest expenses	80,000	held constant
Earnings before taxes	$ 1,582,500	
Taxes (40%)	633,000	
Earnings after taxes	$ 949,500	
Dividends paid	$ 300,000	$0.60 per share × 500,000 shares outstanding
Addition to retained earnings	$ 649,500	

cost of goods sold and general, sales, and administrative expenses are forecast for 2004 using the same percentage to sales relationship as in 2003 (cost of goods sold = 0.61125 × $20,000,000; general, sales, and administrative expense = 0.305625 × $20,000,000). For interest expense we assume that the firm will incur the same expense as in 2003 since the loan balance next year will remain at the current level. Taxes are computed at the assumed 40 percent rate. From the resulting earnings after-taxes figure of $949,500 we deduct estimated dividend payments. Management has forecast dividends to increase to $0.60 per share, yielding estimated dividends of $300,000 ($0.60 × 500,000 shares outstanding). Subtracting the dividends from the forecasted net income gives projected addition to retained earnings of $649,500.

The next step is to forecast Weed Wacker's year 2004 balance sheet as shown in Table 15.5. Cash and accounts receivable are projected to equal 3.125 and 12.5 percent of sales, respectively, based on their historical relationship for 2003. This yields a projected cash balance of $625,000 (0.03125 × $20,000,000) and accounts receivable balance of $2,500,000 (0.125 × $20,000,000) for 2004. Inventory, likewise, is expected to maintain its current proportional relationship to sales yielding a projected balance of $5,000,000 (0.25 × $20,000,000). Based on the percentage of sales assumption, net fixed assets for 2004 is estimated to be $1,250,000 (0.0625 × $20,000,000). Summing the various asset accounts, total assets are projected to grow from the current $7,500,000 in 2003 to $9,375,000 in 2004. This increase is attributable to the projected growth in sales.

Recall that our objective is to find out whether the firm will have sufficient internal financing to provide for the projected growth in the asset base. Projecting the liabilities and shareholders' equity side of the balance sheet should tell us if any additional financing is needed. In making the projections we initially assume that *no* new debt or additional equity will be issued. Our focus is on finding how much *external funding* is needed to meet the objectives of the firm; the choice of how to fund this need—debt or additional stock issue—is dealt with in Chapters 12 and 13.

Let's begin with the current liabilities section of the liabilities and shareholders' equity side of the balance sheet. As previously stated, accounts payable and accrued

Learn how to put together a good business plan for a new venture, including cash flow forecasts and pro formas. Click on "Small Business Guides" at **http://www. smallbusinessbc.ca**

Table 15.5 Weed Wacker Corporation Pro Forma Balance Sheet as of December 31, 2004		
Cash	$ 625,000	⇒ 3.125% of Sales
Accounts receivable	2,500,000	⇒ 12.5% of Sales
Inventory	5,000,000	⇒ 25% of Sales
Total current assets	$8,125,000	
Net fixed assets	1,250,000	⇒ 6.25% of Sales
Total assets	$9,375,000	
Accounts payable	$1,875,000	⇒ 9.375% of Sales
Accrued expenses	625,000	⇒ 3.125% of Sales
Total current liabilities	$2,500,000	
Long-term debt	1,000,000	⇒ Held constant
Additional financing needed	725,500	⇒ 'Plug' figure
Stockholders' equity		
Common stock at par	$1,000,000	⇒ Held constant
Capital in excess of par	1,500,000	⇒ Held constant
Retained earnings	2,649,500	⇒ Last year's retained earnings plus earnings retained this year
Total stockholders' equity	$5,149,500	
Total liabilities and equity	$9,375,000	

expenses are expected to maintain their proportional relationship to sales. In 2003 accounts payable and accrued expenses accounted for 9.375 and 3.125 percent of sales, respectively. Using these percentages, the projected accounts payable for 2004 is $1,875,000, while accrued expenses are estimated to equal $625,000. Long-term debt is held constant from 2003. The common stock at par value and capital in excess of par value accounts are also held constant from 2003, following the assumption that no additional equity will be issued for now. Note that the retained earnings balance has gone up from the 2003 figure of $2,000,000 to $2,649,500, or an increase of $649,500. This difference is the additional amount retained from 2004 *projected earnings* after payment of *projected dividends* in 2004 (see Table 15.4). Summing up the current liabilities, long-term debt and stockholders' equity yields $8,649,500 ($2,500,000 + $1,000,000 + $5,149,500), which is *less* than the projected total assets. The shortfall, or difference, is $725,500. *This is the amount of additional external funding the firm will need for 2004 if it wants to pursue its sales growth target.* On the pro forma balance sheet in Table 15.5, the shortfall is shown as *additional financing needed*. The additional financing needed may be thought of as the **"plug" figure** used to balance the two sides of the balance sheet.

The additional funds needed can be solved algebraically as well. Recall that we assumed *each* of the asset accounts and *each* of the current liabilities accounts increases proportionately with sales. Consequently, rather than forecasting individual asset and current liability values, we can simply forecast the total assets and current liabilities. This difference is equal to the total financing the company will need. In equation form, this can be expressed as follows:

$$\begin{array}{lll} \text{Total} & \text{Forecasted} & \text{Forecasted} \\ \text{financing} = \text{asset} & - & \text{current liability} \\ \text{needed} & \text{increase} & \text{increase} \end{array} \qquad (15.1)$$

$$= \frac{A}{S}(\Delta S) - \frac{CL}{S}(\Delta S)$$

where A is the company's present level of assets that vary proportionately with sales, S is the company's present sales, CL is the company's present level of current liabilities that vary proportionately with sales, and ΔS is the forecasted sales increase. A portion of the total financing needed can be generated internally from increased retained earnings. Specifically, the increased retained earnings generated during the time period when sales increase from S to S + ΔS can be expressed in equation form as follows:

$$\begin{array}{ll} \text{Increased} & \text{Forecasted} \\ \text{retained} = \text{earnings after} - \text{Dividends} \\ \text{earnings} & \text{taxes} \end{array} \qquad (15.2)$$

$$= \text{EAT} - \text{D}$$

The additional financing needed can then be calculated by subtracting the increased retained earnings (Equation 15.2) from the total financing needed (Equation 15.1):

$$\begin{array}{lll} \text{Additional} & \text{Total} & \text{Increased} \\ \text{financing} = \text{financing} & - & \text{retained} \\ \text{needed} & \text{needed} & \text{earnings} \end{array} \qquad (15.3)$$

$$= \left[\frac{A}{S}(\Delta S) - \frac{CL}{S}(\Delta S) \right] - [\text{EAT} - \text{D}]$$

Referring back to the WWC example, the additional financing needed to support a sales increase of $4,000,000 to the $20,000,000 level can now be calculated using Equation 15.3. Plugging in the 2003 historical values for A, CL, and S (from Tables 15.1 and 15.2), the forecasted change in sales (ΔS) of $4,000,000, the forecasted earnings after taxes of $949,500, and the forecasted dividends of $300,000 (from Table 15.4) yields

$$\begin{array}{l} \text{Additional} \\ \text{financing} \\ \text{needed} \end{array} = \left[\frac{\$7,500,000}{\$16,000,000} (\$4,000,000) - \frac{\$2,000,000}{\$16,000,000} (\$4,000,000) \right]$$

$$- (\$949,500 - \$300,000) = \$725,500$$

This is, of course, the same answer we got from projecting the balance sheet in Table 15.5. The next question to tackle is: How should the shortfall of $725,500 be financed? WWC has several options to consider. WWC has to decide whether to: (1) borrow the funds, (2) sell additional common stock, or (3) cut dividends. The factors that influence the debt versus equity decision are discussed in Chapter 13 and the factors that influence the dividend decision are discussed in Chapter 14. As this example illustrates, the investment, financing, and dividend decisions of the firm are interdependent.

Raising the entire $725,500 of additional financing from debt would depend upon whether the firm has sufficient **debt capacity**. If debt is used, the new debt ratio is 45.1 percent determined as follows:

$$\begin{array}{l} \text{Debt ratio} = \text{Total debt/Total assets} \\ = (\$2,500,000 + \$1,000,0000 + \$725,500) \,/\, \$9,375,000 \\ = 0.451 \text{ or } 45.1\,\% \end{array}$$

where total debt is the sum of current liabilities ($2,500,000), existing long-term debt ($1,000,000), and the new debt ($725,500). This debt ratio compares to the 2003 debt ratio of 40.0 percent (($2,000,000 + $1,000,000)/$7,500,000). If the new 45.1 percent debt ratio takes the firm *beyond its optimal or target debt ratio* the firm may not consider it prudent to raise its debt level. Instead the firm should consider the option of selling additional common stock. In the event the $725,500 is raised entirely from an additional stock issue, the new debt ratio will equal:

$$= (\$2,500,000 + \$1,000,000) / \$9,375,000$$
$$= 0.373 \text{ or } 37.3 \%$$

Cutting dividends is also an option, but in the case of WWC even completely eliminating dividends will generate only $300,000, whereas the funds shortfall is $725,500. Thus WWC still has to raise $425,500 ($725,500 − $300,000) either through a debt issue or additional stock issue. Furthermore, recall from Chapter 14 that omitting dividends could send a negative signal to the market that the firm is distressed. Weed Wacker management would have to weigh the advantages and disadvantages of the various options in determining how to obtain the $725,500 of additional financing needed.

The percentage of sales forecasting method for calculating financing needs is a useful and convenient forecasting technique. However, as with all analytical techniques, the application of this method should be supplemented by any additional factors that are unique to the particular situation.

One such factor is *economies of scale*. Economies of scale may result in nonlinear relationships between sales and certain types of assets. In other words, the relationships may not be strictly proportional, as assumed in the model. For example, a 10 percent increase in sales may only require a 5 percent increase in fixed assets or inventories. Another factor in some industries is that capacity can be added only in discrete or *lumpy* increments. Once output reaches the capacity of an existing production facility, expansion requires building another facility. This causes fixed assets to increase in a stepwise manner as sales are increased, rather than increasing proportionately.

Projecting financial statements manually can be very tedious, as you might have observed from the Weed Wacker example. Spreadsheet software lends itself very naturally to forecasting of financial statements. Rather than entering individual values for the variables we can express the variable in terms of mathematical relationships, for example, accounts receivable may be entered as a certain proportion of sales. Thus, it would be easy to forecast statements for several years without having to manually compute projected values for different variables for each year. Spreadsheets also have the advantage of allowing us to conduct *sensitivity analysis* very efficiently. If an analyst wanted to find the effect of a lower sales growth rate on the financing required it would be a simple matter of replacing the original growth rate with the new one.

The illustration on the next page shows you how to forecast Weed Wacker's financial statements using spreadsheets.

Comprehension Check Questions

1. What is the difference between the strategic plan and the operational plan?
2. What is the purpose of a financial plan?
3. Describe how the percentage of sales method is used to forecast the pro forma balance sheet and the income statement.
4. What are some limitations of the percentage of sales method?

	A	B	C	D	E	F
1	Weed Wacker Corporation Pro Forma Income Statement					
2						
3		2003	2004		25 percent increase from 2003. Formula: "+B5*(1+$B$22)"	
4		(Historical)	(Projected)			
5	Sales	$16,000,000	$20,000,000			
6	Cost of goods sold	9,780,000	12,225,000		Same percent of sales as 2003. Formula: "+($B$23)*C5"	
7	Gross profit	$6,220,000	$7,775,000			
8						
9	General Selling and Administrative expenses	4,890,000	6,112,500		Same percent of sales as 2003. Formula: "+($B$24)*C5"	
10	Operating earnings	$1,330,000	$1,662,500			
11						
12	Interest expense	80,000	80,000		Held constant.	
13	Earnings before taxes	1,250,000	1,582,500			
14					40 percent tax rate. Formula: "+$B$25*C13"	
15	Taxes	500,000	633,000			
16	Earnings after taxes	$750,000	$949,500			
17						
18	Dividends paid	$250,000	$300,000		Increased from $0.50 per share to $0.60 per share for 500,000 outstanding shares. Formula: "500000*$B$26"	
19						
20	==========================					
21	Input variables used in pro forma financial statements					
22	Anticipated sales increase	25.0000%				
23	COGS (constant % of sales as for the year 2001)	61.1250%				
24	GSA (constant % of sales as for the year 2001)	30.5625%				
25	Tax rate =	40.0000%				
26	Dividends=	$0.60				
27	Accounts receivable (constant % of sales)	12.5000%				
28	Inventory (constant % of sales)	25.0000%				
29	Net fixed assets (constant % of sales)	6.2500%				
30	Accounts payable (constant % of sales)	9.3750%				
31	Accrued expense (constant % of sales)	3.1250%				
32	Cash (constant % of sales)	3.1250%				
33						
34						
35						
36	Weed Wacker Corporation Pro Forma Balance Sheet					
37						
38		2003	2004		Same percent of sales as 2003. Formula: "$B$32*C5"	
39		(Historical)	(Projected)			
40						
41					Same percent of sales as 2003. Formula: "$B$27*C5"	
42						
43	Cash	$500,000	$625,000			
44	Accounts Receivable	2,000,000	$2,500,000		Same percent of sales as 2003. Formula: "$B$28*C5"	
45	Inventory	4,000,000	$5,000,000			
46	Total current assets	$6,500,000	$8,125,000			
47					Same percent of sales as 2003. Formula: "$B$29*C5"	
48	Net Fixed assets	1,000,000	$1,250,000			
49						
50						
51	Total assets	$7,500,000	$9,375,000		Same percent of sales for 2003. Formula: "$B$30*C5"	
52						
53						
54	Accounts payable	$1,500,000	$1,875,000		Same percent of sales for 2003. Formula: "$B$31*C5"	
55	Accrued expense	500,000	$625,000			
56						
57	Total current liabilities	$2,000,000	$2,500,000		Held constant.	
58						
59	Long term debt	1,000,000	1,000,000		Comment: "plug" figure. The difference in the estimated total assets and estimated total liabilities and equity. Formula: "C51-C72"	
60						
61	Additional funds needed		725,500			
62						
63						
64					Held constant.	
65						
66	Stockholder's equity					
67	Common stock at par (500,000 shares)	1,000,000	1,000,000		Retained earnings for 2003 plus addition to retained earnings in 2004. Formula: "$B$69+(C16-C18)"	
68	Capital in excess of par	1,500,000	1,500,000			
69	Retained earnings	2,000,000	2,649,500			
70	Total stockholder's equity	$4,500,000	$5,149,500			
71					Formula: "+SUM(C57,C59,C70)"	
72	Total liabilities and equity	$7,500,000	$8,649,500			
73						
74						

CASH BUDGETING

Even though the percentage of sales forecasting method is a useful tool that can provide insights regarding financing needs associated with projected sales increases, *cash budgets* can be used to estimate more precisely both the amount of financing needed by a firm and the timing of those financing needs. Generally speaking, firms may want to use the percentage of sales forecasting method for planning funds needs on an annual basis for several years. Cash budgeting, however, is useful for short-range planning extending up to a year or two.

The cash budget is part of the operational budget of the firm. Once a firm has made financial plans, it refers to the budgets when coordinating its overall activities.

For example, the purchasing department examines the budgets when deciding how best to integrate purchasing activities with monthly production requirements to ensure the availability of sufficient raw materials. The production and marketing departments then work together to guarantee that sufficient finished goods inventories are on hand. Finally, the finance department coordinates the company's need for funds with the requirements of the purchasing, production, and marketing departments.

The projected figures in a firm's budgets are also used as a control device against which actual figures are compared; this ensures that the various departments and divisions are functioning properly and working together toward the objectives developed in the planning phase.

Firms generally would prepare monthly cash budgets to forecast cash flows over a 12- to 18-month horizon. For very short-term planning purposes firms prepare weekly and even daily cash budgets. Cash budgeting plays an important role in the firm's financial forecasting process. Effective cash budgeting can help management identify potential cash flow problems. Usually, cash flow problems are easier to solve when they are anticipated.

The cash budget is a pro forma financial statement that details the firm's financial forecasts. It shows how the company's cash will be spent on labor, materials, and capital goods and indicates how cash will be obtained.

Cash budgets are useful in determining the amount of short-term funds the firm may need to borrow to cover any projected cash shortages. Short-term borrowed funds are almost always easier to obtain when the need for them is anticipated. In addition to planning for any cash shortages, the cash budget also indicates the periods when the firm may have cash surpluses. This information is helpful in managing the firm's marketable securities investments. Thus, the cash budget is one of the most important short-range financial forecasting tools.

To explore actual cash budgeting procedures, the Midwestern Manufacturing Company Central Division will be examined. Table 15.6 illustrates a cash budget *worksheet* for that division for the first quarter of 2004. Table 15.7 is an *actual* cash budget for the time period. The cash flow worksheet shows details of how some of the figures in the cash budget are derived.

The worksheet in Table 15.6 shows how cash receipts and payments for purchases are derived. One of the first steps in cash budget preparation is the estimation of cash receipts, which results directly from the sales forecast. As noted in Table 15.6, Midwestern has found that, on the average, about 10 percent of total sales in any given month are cash sales. The remaining 90 percent are credit sales. Further we assume that 30 percent of the company's credit sales are collected during the month in which the sale is made, and all of the remaining 70 percent are collected during the following month. Thus, the total accounts receivable the company can expect to collect during January are equal to 70 percent of the forecasted December credit sales plus 30 percent of the forecasted January credit sales.

$$(0.70 \times \$486,000) + (0.30 \times \$450,000) = \$340,200 + \$135,000$$
$$= \$475,200$$

The forecasted cash receipts for February and March are calculated the same way. The next step in cash budgeting is the scheduling of disbursements, or payments the firm must make to others. Many of these items remain relatively constant from month to month and thus are relatively easy to budget. Others, however, such as the payment of accounts payable for purchases of merchandise, raw materials, and supplies, are more complicated. The key determinants of a firm's schedule of payables are the level of purchases per period and the terms given by suppliers.

Table 15.6 Cash Budget Worksheet for Midwestern Manufacturing Company—Central Division

MIDWESTERN MANUFACURING COMPANY— CENTRAL DIVISION CASH BUDGET WORKSHEET FIRST QUARTER, 2004

	December	January	February	March
Budget of Receipts from Sales				
Estimated sales	$540,000	$500,000	$550,000	$620,000
Estimated credit sales[1]	486,000	450,000	495,000	558,000
Estimated receipts:				
Cash sales[2]		50,000	55,000	62,000
Collections of accounts receivable:				
70% of last month's credit sales		$340,200	$315,000	346,500
30% of current month's credit sales		135,000	148,500	167,400
Total accounts receivable collections		$475,200	$463,500	$513,900
Budget of Payments for Purchases				
Estimated purchases[3]	$275,000	$302,500	$341,000	
Estimated payments of accounts payable[4]		$275,000	$302,500	$341,000

[1] Credit sales are 90 percent of estimated sales for the month.
[2] Cash sales are 10 percent of estimated sales for the month.
[3] Purchases are estimated at 55 percent of next month's sales.
[4] Payments are estimated to lag purchases by one month.

Table 15.7 Projected Cash Budget for Midwestern Manufacturing Company—Central Division

MIDWESTERN MANUFACTURING COMPANY—CENTRAL DIVISION CASH BUDGET* FIRST QUARTER, 2004

	December	January	February	March
Sales	$540,000	$500,000	$550,000	$620,000
Projected cash balance, beginning of month		$ 61,000	$ 50,700	$ 50,000
Receipts				
Cash sales		50,000	55,000	62,000
Collection of accounts receivable		475,200	463,500	513,900
Total cash available		$586,200	$569,200	$625,900
Disbursements:				
Payment of accounts payable		$275,000	$302,500	$341,000
Wages and salaries		158,000	154,500	145,500
Rent		17,000	17,000	17,000
Other expenses		4,500	7,000	8,000
Taxes		81,000	—	—
Dividends on common stock		—	—	30,000
Purchase of new equipment (capital budget)		—	70,000	—
Total disbursements		$535,500	$551,000	$541,500
Excess of available cash over disbursements		$ 50,700	$ 18,200	$ 84,400
Cash loans needed to maintain balance of $50,000		—	31,800	—
Loan repayment		—	—	(31,800)
Projected cash balance, end of month		$ 50,700	$ 50,000	$ 52,600

*Prepared December 15, 2003

Frequently, accounts payable become due before goods are sold and cash is received; this can lead to temporary cash shortages. In fact, many companies experience cash difficulties immediately after a good sales period. Inventories are depleted and must be replenished, but cash is low because collections from the good sales period have not yet been received. Midwestern's purchases generally are estimated to be 55 percent of next month's sales. This percentage is based on the company's past experience and can vary considerably among industries and companies. The actual payments on purchases are made with a 1-month lag: The payments are made in the month after the purchase. The payment schedule is shown in the worksheet for purchases in Table 15.6.

The cash budget in Table 15.7 pulls together the various cash receipts and cash disbursements. Note that depreciation does not appear as a disbursement in the cash budget, because it is a noncash charge.

After cash receipts and disbursements have been estimated, the next step in the cash budgeting process is the determination of a desired cash balance at the beginning of each month. This minimum cash balance figure is usually a function of several factors, including the nature of the business, tax laws, and bank requirements. Table 15.7 lists Midwestern's projected cash balances for the beginning of January, February, and March. In this example, $50,000 is assumed to be the most appropriate minimum cash balance for the first quarter of 2004.

Table 15.7 shows that Midwestern expects to need a short-term loan of $31,800 in February to maintain a minimum cash balance of $50,000, because the company expects a decrease in the collection of accounts receivable in February, brought about by slightly lower than normal sales expected in January. In addition, the company plans to purchase new equipment in February, which will cost $70,000; this also contributes to the expected need for a short-term loan.

If the company planned to spend much more money than this on new equipment, it might decide to secure longer-term financing at this time, instead of the short-term loan. The proceeds from longer-term financing could be budgeted as a separate cash receipt in February, permitting the company to separate short-term and long-term cash needs.

After projecting the need for a short-term loan in February, the cash budget in Table 15.7 shows that the loan probably can be paid at the end of March, because the available cash balance of $84,400 will still be above $50,000 even after the repayment of $31,800. The company has indicated the repayment on the cash budget by adding another side caption: *Loan repayment.*

Most companies follow this same general format for cash budgeting, yet few companies use exactly the same format. A company's actual cash budgeting system will depend on its business and its accounting procedures.

As in the case of forecasting financial statements, spreadsheets are a powerful tool that can help in projecting cash budgets. We show how to use spreadsheets to forecast Midwestern Manufacturing Company Central Division's cash budget on the next page.

RISK ANALYSIS AND FINANCIAL PLANNING

Risk analysis should be an integral part of any planning exercise. In forecasting the pro forma income statement, balance sheet, and cash budget above, it was apparent that the projections were critically dependent on the assumptions made. We had to make a number of assumptions including sales, relationship of various asset classes to sales, relationship of various liabilities to sales, cost of goods sold as a percent of sales, average collection period, labor costs, inventory turnover, etc.

	A	B	C	D	E	F	Annotations (G–K)
2	Cash Budget Worksheet for Midwestern Manufacturing Company Central Division						
3	First Quarter 2002						
5			December	January	February	March	90% of estimated sales. Excel formula: "+$B$7*F6"
6	Estimated sales		$540,000	$500,000	$550,000	$620,000	
7	Estimated credit sales	90%	486,000	450,000	495,000	558,000	
8	Estimated receipts						10% of estimated sales. Excel formula: "+$B$9*F6"
9	Cash sales	10%		50,000	55,000	62,000	
11							70% of last month's credit sales. Excel formula: "+$B$13*F7"
12	Collections of accounts receivables						
13	From last month's credit sales	70%		$340,200	$315,000	$346,500	
14	From current month's credit sales	30%		135,000	148,500	167,400	30% of last month's credit sales. Excel formula: "+$B$13*F7"
15	Total accounts receivable collections			$475,200	$463,500	$513,900	
17	Budget of Payments for Purchases						55% of next month's sales. Excel formula: "+$B$18*F6"
18	Estimated purchases	55%	$275,000	$302,500	$341,000		
19	Estimated payments of accounts payable			$275,000	$302,500	$341,000	
21							Payment for purchases—one month lag. Excel formula: "+E18"
27	Projected Cash Budget Midwestern Manufacturing Company Central Division						
28	First Quarter 2002						
29							From cashbudget worksheet. Excel formula: F9
30			December	January	February	March	
31	Projected cash balance, beginning of month			$61,000	$50,700	$50,000	
32	Receipts:						From cashbudget worksheet. Excel formula: F15
33	Cash sales			50,000	55,000	62,000	
34	Collection of accounts receivable			475,200	463,500	513,900	Excel formula: "+SUM(F31:F34)"
35	Total cash available			$586,200	$569,200	$625,900	
37	Disbursements:						From cashbudget worksheet. Excel formula: F19
38	Payments of accounts payable			$275,000	$302,500	341,000	
39	Wages and salaries			158,000	154,500	145,000	
40	Rent			17,000	17,000	17,000	Excel formula: "+SUM(F38:F44)"
41	Other expenses			4,500	7,000	8,000	
42	Taxes			81,000			
43	Dividends on common stock					30,000	
44	Purchase of new equipment				70,000		
45	Total disbursements			$535,500	$551,000	$541,000	Difference in total cash available and total disbursements of the respective months. Excel formula: "+SUM(F35-F45)"
47	Excess of available cash over disbursements			$50,700	$18,200	$84,900	
48							Excel formula: "+IF(F47>$B$49,0,ABS(F47-$B$49))"
49	Cash loan needed to maintain a balance of	$50,000		0	31800	0	
50	Loan repayment					31800	Excel formula: "+(C49)"
51	projected cash balance, end of month			$50,700	$50,000	$53,100	
54							Excel formula: "+SUM(F47,F49-F50)."

Spreadsheet strategies

Some of the assumptions are based on historical relationships (e.g., estimation of cash receipts in cash budgeting), while others are a result of informed judgment by experts (e.g., projected sales volume provided by the marketing department). There is nothing sacred about these assumptions. No one can predict with any degree of accuracy whether these assumptions will be realized. For example, it may turn out that the sales projections are way out of line with what was initially forecast. Actual sales may turn out to be much higher, or dramatically lower, than expected. The potential uncertainty surrounding the outcome of the assumptions introduces risk into the forecasts. That is, because our assumptions may be incorrect the forecasts could differ from the actual results. This could present a potentially severe problem to the firm. For instance, if in the pro forma cash budget we assumed an average collection period of 40 days and in actuality it is 60 days, this could result in a serious liquidity problem.

For effective planning we should allow for errors in forecast assumptions. Firms can accomplish this in two ways. Good planning should include *sensitivity analysis* and/or *scenario analysis.* The object of sensitivity analysis is to see how sensitive forecasts are to changes in a given variable. Usually, sensitivity analysis is conducted on variables that are likely to have a significant impact on the forecasts. For example, in forecasting the balance sheet and income statement one could look at how sensitive additional financing needed is to a change in the sales growth rate. Management may be interested in knowing how much additional funds are needed if the sales grow at a rate 10 percent higher than was originally forecast. Or, management may want to know the effect on cash receipts (in forecasting the cash budget) if the average collection period is 10 days longer than originally forecast. Sensitivity analysis also is known as *"what-if" analysis* because you are posing a series of "what-if" questions with respect to certain variables.

Scenario analysis also is used to help ensure adequate financial planning. Unlike sensitivity analysis, in scenario analysis several variables are modified at the same time, and their combined effect on the projected financial statements is examined. Often, in preparing pro forma statements, managers consider optimistic, most likely, and pessimistic scenarios. The *optimistic scenario* consists, obviously, of optimistic values for the various assumptions; at the other extreme the *pessimistic scenario* is developed using "worst case" assumptions. Developing a worst-case scenario analysis is especially important so that management can be adequately prepared for that eventuality. For instance, auto companies such as General Motors and Ford Motor Corporation often maintain a hoard of cash that is well in excess of the normal needs of the company. One reason they do this is so the firm can weather even a severe economic downturn.

COMPUTERIZED FINANCIAL FORECASTING AND PLANNING MODELS

In recent years, many companies have spent considerable amounts of time and money developing models to represent various aspects of their financial planning process, as well as cash flow forecasting. Today, these representations usually are computerized and generally are called *financial planning models.* A detailed discussion of these models is beyond the scope of this text, because it requires familiarity with a number of quantitative techniques, such as regression analysis and linear programming—topics not covered here. However, a brief general introduction to the topic is provided for informational purposes.

Financial planning models are often classified according to whether they are *deterministic* or *probabilistic* and whether they attempt to optimize (that is, achieve the most desirable level of) the value of some objective function, such as net income or stock price.

A *deterministic model* *gives a single-number forecast of a financial variable or variables without stating anything about its probability of occurrence.* An example of a deterministic model is a computerized representation of a firm's operating budget, or a budget simulator. Companies that employ budget simulators enter estimated future revenues and expenses into the computer and receive as output an estimate of various financial variables, such as net income and earnings per share. The model tells the company nothing about the chances of achieving these estimates, nor does it indicate whether the company will be able to manage its resources in such a way as to attain higher levels of these variables.

The main advantage of deterministic models is that they allow the user to perform sensitivity analyses quickly and easily. A sensitivity analysis, as noted earlier, essentially consists of rerunning the model to determine the effect on the output variables of changes in a given input variable. For example, a company may want to know what its net income will be if it discontinues some product line.

Some companies prepare different budgets to reflect different assumptions about the type of year they expect to have. For instance, a company may compile three separate budgets to reflect pessimistic, realistic, and optimistic assumptions about the coming year. Whereas these scenario analysis models are essentially deterministic, they represent a first step toward the use of probabilistic models.

Probabilistic models are becoming increasingly popular, because they often provide financial decision makers with more useful information than other models.

Whereas deterministic models yield single-point estimates, probabilistic models yield more general probability distributions. To illustrate, suppose a company is planning to build a new plant. Instead of estimating a single sales figure, the company's planners might estimate a 25 percent chance that the firm's sales will be $2 million, a 50 percent chance that they will be $3 million, and a 25 percent chance that they will be $4 million. *The use of a probabilistic planning model yields output in the form of a probability distribution,* which gives the company's planners more useful information than a deterministic model. In the case of complex probabilistic models, more input data is necessary.

Optimization models determine the values of financial decision variables that optimize (that is, maximize or minimize) some objective function such as profits (or costs). For example, consider an oil refinery whose capacity and production costs are known. By combining these known figures with estimates of the sales prices for gasoline and heating fuel, it is possible, with the use of an optimization model, to specify what output product mix will achieve an optimal level of operating income. Optimization models are not used widely in finance, even though various applications have been proposed in the financial literature.

Comprehension Check Questions

1. How do pro forma cash budgets aid in financial planning?

2. Describe the role of sensitivity analysis and scenario analysis in proper financial planning.

Summary

> For growth and survival firms have to conduct two types of planning exercises:

>> The strategic plan is long range in nature and deals with the overall direction of the firm.

>> The operational plan addresses the operational objectives of the firm. It serves as blueprint detailing where the firm wants to be at some future point in time and what resources are needed to get it there. Operational plans are generally conducted at two levels—long-term and short-term.

> The operational plan consists of a marketing plan, production plan, human resource plan, and a financial plan. The marketing plan lays out the marketing resources needed to meet the operational objectives and includes such things as advertising strategy, marketing promotions, channels of distribution and distribution incentives, and assignment of sales territory. The production plan consists of facilities needed to meet the operational objectives including the number of shifts, plant refurbishment and expansions, vendor and supplier arrangements, inventory control, etc. The human resource plan is concerned with the personnel aspect of the objectives. The financial plan lays out the financial resources that are needed to achieve the operational objectives of the firm including the financial objectives of the firm.

> An integral part of the financial planning process is the projection of financial statements. Pro forma balance sheets, income statements, and cash budgets are useful in identifying future funds needs in order to meet operational objectives of the firm.

➤ The percentage of sales method is a simple technique used in preparing the pro forma balance sheet and income statement. It can be used to estimate the amount of additional financing that will be needed to support a given future sales level. In the percentage of sales method, most of the balance sheet and income statement items are forecasted based on their historical relationships to sales.

➤ Budgets are pro forma financial statements that detail a company's future plans regarding the acquisition and spending of funds. Budgets are used for planning, coordinating, and controlling the operations of the firm.

➤ Cash budgets are projections of cash receipts and disbursements over some future time period. The steps involved in preparing a cash budget include the following:

1. Estimating cash receipts based on historical information about the collection of accounts receivable.
2. Scheduling disbursements.
3. Determining a minimum cash balance.
4. Calculating the amount of loans required to cover any cash shortages.

➤ Sensitivity analysis and scenario analysis are useful techniques to assess the risk inherent in financial plans. The object of sensitivity analysis is to see how sensitive forecasts are to changes in a given variable. Sensitivity analysis is conducted on variables that are likely to have a significant impact on the forecasts. Sensitivity analysis also is known as "what-if" analysis because you are posing a series of "what-if" questions with respect to certain variables.

➤ Scenario analysis also is used to help ensure adequate financial planning. Unlike sensitivity analysis, in scenario analysis several variables are modified at the same time and their combined effect on the projected financial statements is examined.

➤ Computerized financial models also are available to aid in financial forecasting. These financial models usually are classified according to whether they are deterministic or probabilistic and whether they seek to optimize the value of some objective function.

Questions and Topics for Discussion

1. What is the difference between strategic and operational plans?
2. What is the purpose of financial plans?
3. What are the components of an operational plan?
4. What are pro forma financial statements?
5. What is the percentage of sales forecasting method? What are some of the limitations financial analysts should be aware of in applying this method?
6. What is a cash budget? What are the usual steps involved in preparing a cash budget?
7. Explain the difference between deterministic and probabilistic financial planning models.

Self-Test Problems

ST1. Use the percentage of sales forecasting method to compute the additional financing needed by Lambrechts Specialty Shops, Inc. (LSS), if sales are expected to increase from a current level of $20 million to a new level of $25 million over the coming year. LSS expects earnings after taxes to equal $1 million over the next year (20X3). LSS intends to pay a $300,000 dividend next year. The current year balance sheet for LSS is as follows:

Lambrechts Specialty Shops, Inc.
Balance Sheet as of December 31, 20X2

Cash	$ 1,000,000	Accounts payable	$ 3,000,000
Accounts receivable	1,500,000	Notes payable	3,000,000
Inventories	6,000,000	Long-term debt	2,000,000
Net fixed assets	3,000,000	Stockholders' equity	3,500,000
Total assets	**$11,500,000**	**Total liabilities and equity**	**$11,500,000**

All assets, except "cash," are expected to vary proportionately with sales. Of total liabilities and equity, only "accounts payable" is expected to vary proportionately with sales.

ST2. Prepare a cash budget for Focus Eyewear Inc. for the first quarter of 2004, based on the following information. As the Treasurer of the company you received the following from the marketing department:

	Total Sales
December 2003	$825,000
January 2004	730,000
February 2004	840,000
March 2004	920,000
April 2004	700,000

All sales are for cash. The company estimates its purchases at 60 percent of sales 2 months later, and payments are made the month after purchase. Other estimated disbursements for the firm consist of the following:

	January	**February**	**March**
Wages and salaries	$270,000	$270,000	$270,000
Rent	32,000	32,000	32,000
Other expenses	10,000	12,000	14,000

In addition, a tax payment of $135,000 is due on January 15. Also, the company has to make a down payment on a retail property it agreed to purchase. The down payment is $85,000 due in February.

The company's projected cash balance at the beginning of January is $100,000, and the company desires to maintain a balance of $100,000 at the end of each month.

Problems

CHALLENGE

1. Baldwin Products Company anticipates reaching a sales level of $6 million in one year. The company expects earnings after taxes during the next year to equal $400,000. During the past several years, the company has been paying $50,000 in dividends to its stockholders. The company expects to continue this policy for at least the next year. The actual balance sheet and income statement for Baldwin during 20X8 follow.

Baldwin Products Company
Balance Sheet as of December 31, 20X8

Cash	$ 200,000	Accounts payable	$ 600,000
Accounts receivable	400,000	Notes payable	500,000
Inventories	1,200,000	Current liabilities	$1,100,000
Current assets	$1,800,000	Long-term debt	200,000
Fixed assets, net	500,000	Stockholders' equity	1,000,000
Total assets	**$2,300,000**	**Total liabilities and equity**	**$2,300,000**

Income Statement for the Year Ending December 31, 20X8

Sales	$4,000,000
Expenses, including interest and taxes	$3,700,000
Earnings after taxes	$ 300,000

a. Using the percentage of sales method, calculate the additional financing Baldwin Products will need over the next year at the $6 million sales level. Show the pro forma balance sheet for the company as of December 31, 20X9, assuming a sales level of $6 million is reached. Assume that all assets vary proportionally with sales. Accounts payable is the only liability that varies proportionally with sales. Assume that the additional financing needed is obtained in the form of additional notes payable (in other words, assume that notes payable is the "plug" figure).

b. Suppose that the Baldwin Products' management feels that the average collection period on its additional sales—that is, sales over $4 million—will be 60 days, instead of the current level. By what amount will this increase in the average collection period increase the financing needed by the company over the next year?

c. If the Baldwin Products' banker requires the company to maintain a current ratio equal to 1.6 or greater, what is the maximum amount of additional financing that can be in the form of bank borrowings (notes payable)? What other potential sources of financing are available to the company?

CHALLENGE

2. In the Weed Wacker Corporation example in the text (Table 15.1) it was assumed that the company's fixed assets were being used at nearly full capacity and that net fixed assets would have to increase proportionately as sales increased. Alternatively, suppose that the company has excess fixed assets and that *no increase* in net fixed assets is required as sales are increased. Assume that the company plans to maintain its dividend payments at the same level in 2004 as in 2003. Determine the amount of additional financing needed for 2004 under each of the following conditions:

Increase in Sales	Increase in Expenses (cost of goods sold plus general, selling, and administrative expenses)
a. $3,750,000	$3,750,000
b. $3,000,000	$2,800,000
c. $4,500,000	$4,000,000

3. Prepare a cash budget for Atlas Products, Inc. for the first quarter of 20X2, based on the following information. **CHALLENGE**

The budgeting section of the corporate finance department of Atlas Products has received the following sales estimates from the marketing department:

	Total Sales	Credit Sales
December 20X1	$825,000	$770,000
January 20X2	730,000	690,000
February 20X2	840,000	780,000
March 20X2	920,000	855,000

The company has found that, on average, about 25 percent of its credit sales are collected during the month when the sale is made, and the remaining 75 percent of credit sales are collected during the month following the sale. As a result, the company uses these figures for budgeting.

The company estimates its purchases at 60 percent of next month's sales, and payments for those purchases are budgeted to lag the purchases by 1 month.

Various disbursements have been estimated as follows:

	January	February	March
Wages and salaries	$250,000	$290,000	$290,000
Rent	27,000	27,000	27,000
Other expenses	10,000	12,000	14,000

In addition, a tax payment of $105,000 is due on January 15, and $40,000 in dividends will be declared in January and paid in March. Also, the company has ordered a $75,000 piece of equipment. Delivery is scheduled for early January, and payment will be due in February.

The company's projected cash balance at the beginning of January is $100,000, and the company desires to maintain a balance of $100,000 at the end of each month.

4. Prepare a cash budget for Elmwood Manufacturing Company for the first 3 months of 20X7 based on the following information: **CHALLENGE**

Month	Estimated Sales	Estimated Factory Overhead	Estimated Selling and Administrative Expenses
December	$ 4,600,000	$640,000	$1,250,000
January	6,400,000	650,000	1,275,000
February	11,200,000	670,000	1,285,000
March	8,400,000	670,000	1,310,000
April	7,000,000	680,000	1,300,000

The company has found that approximately 40 percent of sales are collected during the month the sale is made and the remaining 60 percent are collected during the month following the sale. Material purchases are 30 percent of next month's estimated sales, and payments lag these purchases by 1 month. Labor costs are 35 percent of next month's sales and are paid during the month incurred. Factory overhead and selling and administrative expenses are paid during the month incurred. In addition, a payment for new equipment of $1.5 million is due in February. Also, a tax payment of $1.6 million and a dividend payment of $650,000 are due in March.

The company's projected cash balance at the beginning of January is $1.5 million. Furthermore, Elmwood desires to maintain a $750,000 cash balance at the end of each month.

INTERMEDIATE **5.** You have been asked to prepare a cash budget for Solo Bicycles Inc. Assume today is the last day of August 20X3. You are provided with the following estimated sales:

	September	October	November	December	January
Estimated sales	$340,000	$500,000	$650,000	$820,000	$400,000

Solo sells all its merchandise for cash; there are no credit sales. Purchases are 60 percent of sales and are made 2 months before the month of sale but payments are made 1 month after the purchase. In addition to the purchases, Solo expects to incur the following disbursements:

Wages and salaries = $180,000 per month

Year-end bonus = $45,000 to be paid in December

Estimated taxes = $54,000 in September, $85,000 in December

Rent and utilities = $16,000 per month

Marketing expenses = $3,000/month in September and October, $6,000/month in November and December

Capital expenditure = $100,000 due in November

Solo has a current cash balance of $60,000, which is also its target cash balance.

a. Prepare a cash budget for Solo Bicycles for the months of September through December.

b. If December sales turn out to be no different from November sales, what impact would this have on the cash balance in December? Assume all other figures are the same as in part (a), including the purchases.

CHALLENGE **6.** Coast-to-Coast Transport Corporation (CTC) is planning a $75 million capital expenditure program for the coming year. Assume that net fixed assets for next year increase by the amount of the planned capital expenditure. Next year, CTC expects to report earnings of $40 million after interest and taxes. The company presently has 20 million shares of common stock issued and outstanding. Dividend payments are expected to increase from the present level of $10 million to $12 million. The company expects its current asset needs to increase from a current level of $25 million to $30 million. Current liabilities, excluding short-term bank borrowings, are expected to increase from $15 million to $17 million. Interest payments are $5 million next year, and long-term debt retirement obligations are $8 million next year. How much external financing is required by CTC for the coming year?

INTERMEDIATE **7.** Appalachian Registers, Inc. (ARI) has current sales of $50 million. Sales are expected to grow to $75 million next year. ARI currently has accounts receivable of $10 million, inventories of $15 million, and net fixed assets of $20 million. These assets are expected to grow at the same rate as sales over the next year. Accounts payable are expected to increase from their current level of $10 million to a new level of $13 million next year. ARI wants to increase its cash balance at the end of next year by $2 million over its current cash balances, which average $4 million. Earnings after taxes next year are forecasted to be $10 million. Next year, ARI plans to pay dividends of $1 million, up from $500,000 this year. ARI's marginal tax rate is 34 percent. How much external financing is required by ARI next year?

CHAPTER
16 Working Capital Policy and Management of Current Assets

This chapter is concerned with the overall working capital policy of the firm and the management of current assets. Working capital policy is an important elements of the financial planning process. Working capital policy involves decisions about a company's current assets and current liabilities—what they consist of, how they are used, and how their mix affects the risk versus return characteristics of the company. Both the terms *working capital* and *net working capital* normally denote the *difference between the company's current assets and current liabilities.* The two terms are often used interchangeably.

Working capital policies, through their effect on the firm's expected future returns and the risk associated with these returns, ultimately have an impact on shareholder wealth. Effective working capital policies are crucial to a firm's long-run growth and survival. If, for example, a company lacks the working capital needed to expand production and sales, it may lose revenues and profits. A firm needs to maintain high enough working capital levels so that it remains liquid; that is, it can meet its cash obligations as they come due. Otherwise, it may incur the costs associated with a deteriorating credit rating, a potential forced liquidation of assets, and possible bankruptcy.

Working capital management is a continuing process that involves a number of day-to-day decisions that determine the following:

➢ The firm's level of current assets
➢ The level of investment in each type of current asset
➢ The proportions of short-term and long-term debt the firm will use to finance its current assets
➢ The specific sources and mix of short-term credit (current liabilities) the firm should employ

In addition to discussing the overall working capital policy of the firm, the chapter also covers the management of various current assets including *cash, marketable securities, accounts receivable,* and *inventory.* We will discuss factors that influence the levels of each of these current asset accounts and how to efficiently manage these accounts.

The chapter begins with a discussion of a firm's operating cycle, which, in the case of a manufacturing firm, is the length of time from the purchase of raw materials to the collection of proceeds from the sale of the finished product. The concept of operating cycle is important to an understanding of working capital policy and management.

Chapter Objectives

After reading this chapter, you should have an understanding of the following:

1. The meaning of the term operating cycle and its role in determining an appropriate working capital policy

2. The factors that affect working capital policy and the risk–return trade-offs of various working capital policies

3. The role of cash and marketable securities in working capital management

4. The meaning of credit terms and its impact on accounts receivable management

5. The purpose of inventory and an overview of effective inventory management policy

OPERATING CYCLE ANALYSIS

An understanding of **operating cycle** is crucial to an understanding of working capital management. *The operating cycle traces the activities / events that a firm engages in from the time raw materials are purchased to the time the cash is collected from the sale of the finished product.* A company's operating cycle typically consists of three primary activities:

Purchasing resources
Producing the product
Distributing (selling) the product

These activities create cash flows that are both unsynchronized and uncertain. They are *unsynchronized* because cash disbursements (for example, payments for resource purchases) usually take place before cash receipts (for example, collection of receivables). They are *uncertain* because future sales and costs, which generate the respective receipts and disbursements, cannot be forecasted with complete accuracy. If the firm is to maintain liquidity and function properly, it has to invest funds in various short-term assets during this cycle. It has to maintain a cash balance to pay the bills as they come due. In addition, the company must invest in inventories to fill customer orders promptly. And, finally, the company invests in accounts receivable in order to extend credit to its customers.

Figure 16.1 illustrates the operating cycle of a typical firm. *The operating cycle is equal to the length of the inventory and receivables conversion periods:*

Operating cycle = Inventory conversion period + Receivables conversion period **(16.1)**

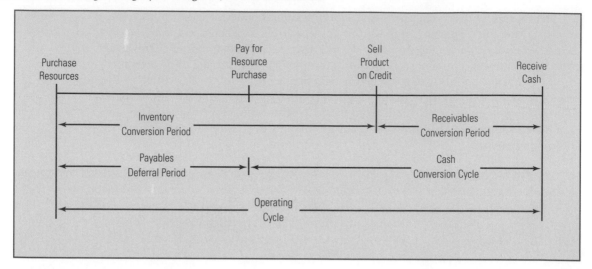

Figure 16.1
Operating Cycle of a Typical Company

The *inventory conversion period* is the *length of time required to produce and sell the product.* It is computed as follows:

(16.2)
$$\text{Inventory conversion period} = \frac{\text{Inventory}}{\dfrac{\text{Cost of sales}}{365}}$$

The *receivables conversion period*, or average collection period, represents the *length of time required to collect the sales receipts.* It is calculated as follows:

(16.3)
$$\text{Receivables conversion period} = \frac{\text{Accounts receivable}}{\dfrac{\text{Annual credit sales}}{365}}$$

The length of the operating cycle is a major determinant of the size of the current asset balance a firm has to maintain. Generally, the longer the operating cycle, the larger the current asset balance of the firm.

Just as a fixed asset investment by a firm must be financed through some source(s) of capital, the current asset investment by a firm must likewise be financed through some combination of capital sources. Fixed asset purchases are typically financed through external sources of capital such as loans and equity capital. In the case of current assets, not all of the investment is financed through external capital sources. Typically a significant part of the current assets are financed through deferment of payables (this type of financing is also sometimes known as a *spontaneous* source of financing). The *payables deferral period* is the *length of time the firm is able to defer payment on its various resource purchases* (for example, materials, salaries and wages, and advertising). The following equation is used to calculate the payables deferral period:

(16.4) Payables deferral period =

$$\frac{\text{Accounts payable} + \text{Salaries and wages payable} + \text{Payables for other resource inputs}}{\dfrac{(\text{Cost of sales} + \text{Selling, general and administrative expenses})}{365}}$$

The difference between the operating cycle and the payables deferral period is defined as the cash conversion cycle. The *cash conversion cycle* represents the *net time interval between the collection of cash receipts from product sales and the cash payments for the company's various resource purchases.* It is calculated as follows:

$$\text{Cash conversion cycle} = \text{Operating cycle} - \text{Payables deferral period} \qquad \textbf{(16.5)}$$

The cash conversion cycle shows the time interval over which additional nonspontaneous sources of working capital financing must be obtained to carry out the firm's activities. Longer cash conversion cycles imply a larger (net) working capital requirement. An increase in the length of the operating cycle, without a corresponding increase in the payables deferral period, lengthens the cash conversion cycle and creates further working capital financing needs for the company.

Table 16.1 shows an actual cash conversion cycle analysis for Caterpillar, Inc., a large manufacturer in the construction and agricultural machinery industry. Pertinent data from the balance sheet and income statements for 2002 and 2001 are shown in the table. Also shown are the calculations for the operating and cash conversion cycles. Caterpillar's 2002 inventory conversion period using Equation 16.2 may be determined as follows:

$$\text{Inventory conversion period} = \frac{\$2{,}763}{\dfrac{\$14{,}709}{365}}$$

$$= \frac{\$2{,}763}{\$40.2986}$$

$$= 68.6 \text{ days}$$

The receivables conversion period using Equation 16.3 is:

$$\text{Receivables conversion period} = \frac{\$9{,}586}{\dfrac{\$20{,}152}{365}}$$

$$= \frac{\$9{,}586}{\$55.211}$$

$$= 173.6 \text{ days}$$

The payables deferral period using Equation 16.4 is:

$$\text{Payables deferral period} = \frac{\$2{,}269 + \$1{,}178 + \$1{,}620}{\dfrac{\$14{,}709 + \$2{,}531}{365}}$$

$$= \frac{\$5{,}067}{\$47.2329}$$

$$= 107.3 \text{ days}$$

This yields a cash conversion cycle, using Equation 16.5, of:

$$\text{Cash conversion cycle} = 68.6 \text{ days} + 173.6 \text{ days} - 107.3 \text{ days}$$
$$= 134.9 \text{ days}$$

Similar calculations are used to derive corresponding figures for 2001, as shown in Table 16.1. The table shows that Caterpillar's cash conversion cycle increased from 121.2 days in 2001 to 134.9 days in 2002. The increase in the cash conversion cycle for Caterpillar appears to be due to the increase in the accounts receivable conversion period. The longer receivables conversion period in 2002 compared to 2001 may be due to the slowing economy in 2002 and/or due to industry competitive factors that necessitated the extension of longer credit periods to customers. An increase in the cash conversion cycle is normally associated with an increase in the net working capital. In the case of Caterpillar the net working capital increased

Table 16.1 Cash Conversion Cycle Analysis for Caterpillar, Inc. (in millions of dollars)

	2002	2001
Balance sheet data:		
Current assets	$14,628	$13,400
Accounts receivables	9,586	8,441
Inventories	2,763	2,925
Current liabilities	11,344	10,276
Accounts payable	2,269	2,123
Salaries and wages payable	1,178	1,292
Other payables	1,620	1,419
Income statement data:		
Net sales	$20,152	$20,450
Cost of sales	14,709	14,752
Selling, general, and administrative expenses	2,531	2,567
Cash conversion cycle calculations:		
Inventory conversion period	68.6 days	72.4 days
Accounts receivable conversion period	173.6 days	150.7 days
Payables deferral period	107.3 days	101.9 days
Cash conversion cycle	134.9 days	121.2 days
Net working capital	$3,284	$3,124

Source: Balance Sheet and Income Statement data taken from Caterpillar's 2002 annual report.

from $3,124 million to $3,284 million (see Table 16.1). The incremental investment in net working capital of $161 million ($3,284 million − $3,124 million) was financed through long-term capital sources.

IMPORTANCE OF WORKING CAPITAL

Inc. Magazine *maintains an "archives" link at its home page enabling you to search back issues for articles about a particular topic. Select from the list of articles by topic to see what Inc. Magazine *advises about your choices.*
http://www.inc.com

In many industries, working capital investment (current assets) constitutes a relatively large percentage of total assets. In the manufacturing sector, for example, current assets comprise about 40 percent of the total assets of all U.S. manufacturing corporations. Among the wholesaling and retailing sectors, the percentages are even higher—in the 50 to 60 percent range.

Table 16.2 shows the distribution of aggregate assets for several large companies. For the five companies shown, current assets as a percentage of total assets range from 25.1 percent to over 43 percent. ExxonMobil, with its relatively high percentage of fixed assets (62.2%), has a relatively low percentage of current assets (25.1%). In contrast, IBM with a relatively low proportion of fixed assets (15.0%) has a very large proportion of current assets (43.3%). Target and 3M have a substantial portion of their current assets tied up in inventories. Target is a diversified retailer that operates the Target, Mervyn's, and Marshall Field's chain of department stores, while 3M is a diversified chemicals manufacturer known for its "Scotch" tape and "Post-It" brand names. The single largest current asset account for IBM and 3M is accounts receivable. In the case of IBM, their investment in accounts receivable exceeds the book value of net fixed assets! Because current assets constitute a relatively high percentage of total assets in most businesses, it is important to have effective working capital policies.

A firm's net working capital (current assets − current liabilities) position is not only important from an internal standpoint; it is also widely used as one mea-

Table 16.2 Distribution of Aggregate Assets in Selected Companies (2002)

	Target	ExxonMobil	IBM	Merck	3M
Cash and marketable securities	2.6%	4.7%	6.2%	10.4%	4.0%
Receivables—net	19.5	13.9	31.1	11.4	16.5
Inventories—net	16.6	5.3	3.3	7.2	12.6
All other current assets	3.0	1.2	2.7	2.2	6.4
Total current assets	41.7%	25.1%	43.3%	31.2%	39.5%
Fixed assets—net	53.5	62.2	15	29.8	36.7
All other noncurrent assets	4.8	12.7	41.7	39.0	23.8
Total assets	**100.00%**	**100.00%**	**100.00%**	**100.00%**	**100.00%**

Source: Calculated from 10-K annual reports available on http://www.sec.gov

sure of the firm's risk. Risk, as used in this context, deals with the probability that a firm will encounter financial difficulties, such as the inability to pay bills on time. All other things being equal, the more net working capital a firm has, the more likely it will be able to meet current financial obligations. Because net working capital is one measure of risk, a company's net working capital position affects its ability to obtain debt financing. Many loan agreements with commercial banks and other lending institutions contain a provision requiring the firm to maintain a minimum net working capital position. Likewise, bond indentures also often contain such provisions.

Levels of Working Capital Investment

Overall working capital policy considers *both a firm's level of working capital investment and its financing.* In practice, the firm has to determine the joint impact of these two decisions upon its profitability and risk. However, to permit a better understanding of working capital policy, the working capital investment decision is discussed in this section while the working capital financing decision is discussed in the following section. The two decisions will then be considered together.

The size and nature of a firm's investment in current assets is a function of a number of different factors, including the following:

- ➤ The type of products manufactured
- ➤ The length of the operating cycle
- ➤ The sales level (because higher sales require more investment in inventories and receivables)
- ➤ Inventory policies. If the firm's policy is to maintain substantial inventory to meet unanticipated sales or delays in obtaining raw materials, this would raise inventory levels
- ➤ Credit policies. The accounts receivable balance depends on the credit policies of the firm—that is, the length of time customers are given to pay their account and cash discounts, if any, that are provided
- ➤ How efficiently the firm manages its current assets. The more effectively management economizes on cash, marketable securities, receivables, and inventories employed, the smaller the working capital requirements

For the purposes of discussion and analysis, these factors are held constant for the remainder of this chapter. Instead of focusing on these factors, this section examines the risk–return trade-offs associated with alternative levels of working capital investment.

FINANCE & The Real World

Microsoft has more cash on its balance sheet than any other company in America—some $46 billion as of mid-2003. That's more than three times its current liabilities. For most companies, having such a strong working capital position would be applauded by the investment community. But investors in Microsoft think the company is simply hoarding cash—and withholding money from shareholders.

True, the company did initiate a dividend program early in 2003 amounting to 8 cents per share, a payout of less than $1 billion per year. And it has repurchased $24 billion worth of stock over the past four years, an action that is similar in impact to a dividend but does not commit the firm to making distributions every year as does a dividend.

Microsoft argues that it needs the money to meet business challenges, but the company's competitive position is secure with its Windows operating systems for personal computers and its Office suite of PC software. The federal government antitrust case against the company is essentially over, so the money won't be needed to pay legal fees and potential settlement costs.

But with growth opportunities and cash demands leveling off, Microsoft's critics say it should return cash to its investors through a much higher dividend—say 50 cents. That would raise the dividend yield (dividend divided by stock price) from negligible to about 2%, roughly the stock market average. There's an added push to do so now that the maximum tax on dividend income is 15%, down from nearly 40% prior to the 2003 tax law changes. Some investors even think that the company should take $25 billion in cash and pay it out as a one-time dividend. Established growth companies such as General Electric, Coca Cola, and Merck have rewarded shareholders with substantial dividends, so why should Microsoft be any different?

Technology companies have traditionally paid little dividends. They argue that they need the cash to reinvest in growth. By raising its dividend, Microsoft might encourage other technology companies such as Intel and IBM to increase their dividends, and companies such as Cisco Systems and Oracle to begin paying dividends.

Source: Microsoft Web site; Barrons, June 30, 2003; cover story: "Share the Wealth."

Profitability versus Risk Trade-off for Alternative Levels of Working Capital Investment Before deciding on an appropriate level of working capital investment, a firm's management has to evaluate the trade-off between expected profitability and the risk that it may be unable to meet its financial obligations.

Figure 16.2 illustrates three alternative working capital policies with regard to the level of working capital investment. Each curve represents the level of total assets. Note that the fixed asset level is a constant; what varies is the amount of current assets across the three alternative working capital policies.

Policy C represents a conservative approach to working capital management. Under this policy, the company holds a relatively large proportion of its total assets in the form of current assets. Because the rate of return on current assets normally is assumed to be less than the rate of return on fixed assets, this policy results in a *lower expected profitability* as measured by the rate of return on the company's total assets. Assuming that current liabilities remain constant, this type of policy also increases the company's net working capital position, resulting in a *lower risk* that the firm will encounter financial difficulties. Policy C's high current asset balance relative to current liabilities implies that the firm will almost always have sufficient current assets to meet its current liability obligations as they come due.

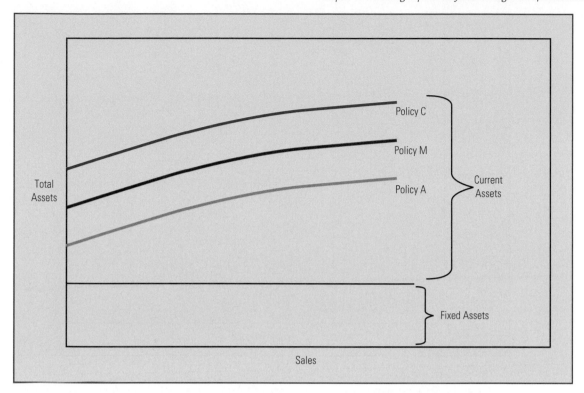

Figure 16.2
Three Alternative
Working Capital
Investment Policies

In contrast to Policy C, Policy A represents an aggressive approach. Under this policy, the company holds a relatively small proportion of its total assets in the form of lower-yielding current assets—hence a lower level of net working capital. As a result, this policy yields a *higher expected profitability* as well as a *higher risk* that the company will encounter financial difficulties. The higher risk follows from the fact that the firm has fewer current assets that can be converted into cash to meet current liabilities as they come due. Finally, Policy M represents a moderate approach. With this policy, expected profitability and risk levels fall between those of Policy C and Policy A. Figure 16.3 summarizes the profitability–risk trade-offs of the alternative working capital financing policies.

The important question is: Which of the three policies is optimal? The optimal level of working capital investment is the level expected to maximize shareholder wealth. However, this is not always easy to determine. It is a function of several factors, including the variability of sales and cash flows and the degree of operating and financial leverage employed by the firm. Therefore, no single working capital investment policy is necessarily optimal for all firms.

Working Capital Financing: Proportion of Short-term versus Long-term Financing

Not only does a firm have to be concerned about the level of current assets; it also has to determine the proportions of short- and long-term debt to use in financing these assets. This decision also involves trade-offs between profitability and risk.

Sources of debt financing are classified according to their maturities. Specifically, they can be categorized as being either short-term or long-term, with short-term sources having maturities of 1 year or less and long-term sources having maturities of greater than 1 year.

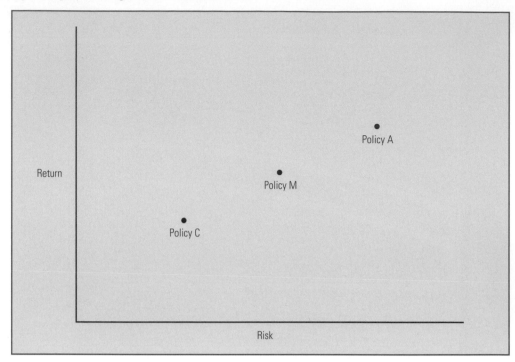

Figure 16.3
Risk–Return Trade-off for Alternative Working Capital Investment Policies

Cost of Short-term versus Long-term Debt Historically, long-term interest rates have exceeded short-term rates. Also, because of the reduced flexibility of long-term borrowing relative to short-term borrowing, the effective cost of long-term debt may be higher than the cost of short-term debt, even when short-term interest rates are equal to or greater than long-term rates. With long-term debt, a firm incurs the interest expense even during times when it has no immediate need for the funds, such as during seasonal or cyclical downturns. With short-term debt, in contrast, the firm can avoid the interest costs on unneeded funds by paying off (or not renewing) the debt. In summary, the cost of long-term debt is generally higher than the cost of short-term debt.

Risk of Long-term versus Short-term Debt The attitudes of borrowing companies toward the relative risk of long-term versus short-term debt differ from those of lenders. Whereas lenders normally feel that risk increases with maturity, borrowers feel that there is more risk associated with short-term debt. The reasons for this are twofold.

First, there is always the chance that a firm will not be able to refinance its short-term debt. When a firm's debt matures, it either pays off the debt as part of a debt-reduction program or arranges new financing. At the time of maturity, however, the firm could be faced with financial problems resulting from such events as strikes, natural disasters, or recessions that cause sales and cash inflows to decline. Under these circumstances the firm may find it very difficult or even impossible to obtain the needed funds. This could lead to operating and financial difficulties. The more frequently a firm must refinance debt, the greater is the risk of its not being able to obtain the necessary financing. Several companies in early 2002 had problems refinancing maturing short-term obligations including Tyco, Ford Motor Company, and Qwest Corporation. Qwest Corporation, for example, was unable to refinance nearly $1 billion of maturing commercial paper obligations, forcing the

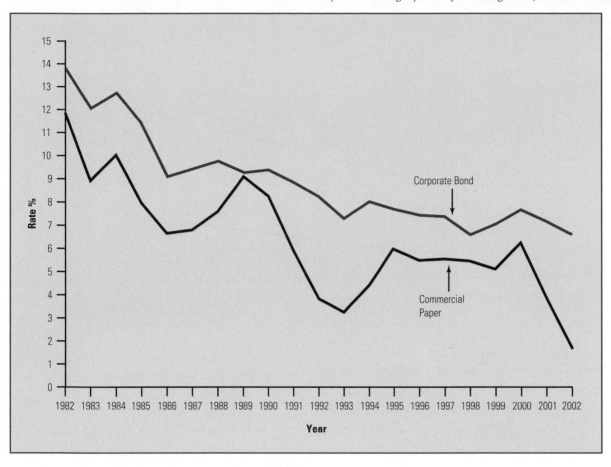

Figure 16.4
Yearly Corporate Bond and Commercial Paper Rates

Note: The corporate bond rate is the rate for Moody's AAA rated corporate bonds. The commercial paper rate is for Moody's AA rated commercial paper issued by nonfinancial companies. Interest rates interpolated from data on certain commercial paper trades settled by The Depository Trust Company.
Source: http://www.federalreserve. gov/releases/H15/data/a/cp1m.txt
http://www.federalreserve.gov/ releases/H15/data/a/aaa.txt

company to tap into its backup line of credit (discussed in Chapter 17) to pay off the maturing obligations.

Second, short-term interest rates tend to fluctuate more over time than long-term interest rates do. As a result, a firm's interest expenses and expected earnings after interest and taxes are subject to more variation over time with short-term debt than with long-term debt. This is evident from Figure 16.4, which shows the yearly average rates from 1982 to 2002 for Moody's AAA corporate bond rate (long-term debt) and the Moody's AA 30-day commercial paper rate for nonfinancial companies (short-term rate). The commercial paper rate, which is very highly correlated with other forms of short-term debt used by corporations, exhibits much *greater volatility* over time and within each year than the long-term rate for high-quality corporate bonds.

Profitability versus Risk Trade-off for Alternative Financing Plans A company's need for financing is equal to the sum of its fixed and current assets. Current assets can be divided into the following categories:

➤ Permanent current assets
➤ Fluctuating current assets

Fluctuating current assets are those affected by the seasonal or cyclical nature of company sales. For example, a firm must make larger investments in inventories and receivables during peak selling periods than during other periods of the year.

**Figure 16.5
Financing Needs
Over Time**

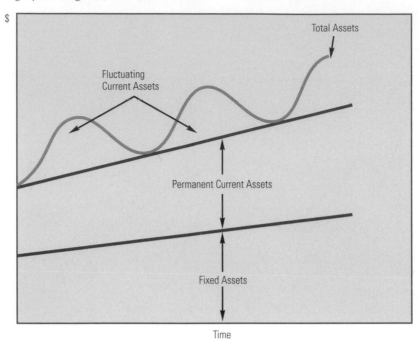

Permanent current assets are those held to meet the company's minimum long-term needs (for example, *safety stocks* of cash and inventories). Figure 16.5 illustrates a typical firm's financing needs over time. The fixed assets and permanent current assets lines are upward sloping, indicating that the investment in these assets and, by extension, financing needs tend to increase over time for a firm whose sales are increasing.

One way a firm can meet its financing needs is by using a ***matching approach*** in which the maturity structure of the firm's liabilities are made to correspond exactly to the life of its assets. The maturity-matching concept is illustrated in Figure 16.6. Fixed and permanent current assets are financed with long-term debt and equity funds, whereas fluctuating current assets are financed with short-term debt. Application of this approach is not as simple as it appears, however. In practice, the uncertainty associated with the lives of individual assets makes the matching approach difficult to implement.

Figures 16.7 and 16.8 illustrate two other financing plans. Figure 16.7 shows a *conservative* approach, which uses a relatively high proportion of long-term debt. The relatively low proportion of short-term debt in this approach reduces the risk that the company will be unable to refund its debt, and it also reduces the risk associated with interest rate fluctuations. At the same time, however, this approach cuts down on the expected returns available to stockholders, because the cost of long-term debt is generally greater than the cost of short-term debt.

Figure 16.8 illustrates an *aggressive* approach, which uses a relatively high proportion of short-term debt. A firm that uses this particular approach must refinance debt more frequently, thus increasing the risk that it will be unable to obtain new financing as needed. In addition, the greater possible fluctuations in interest expenses associated with this financing plan add to the firm's risk. These higher risks are offset by the higher expected after-tax earnings that result from the normally lower costs of short-term debt.

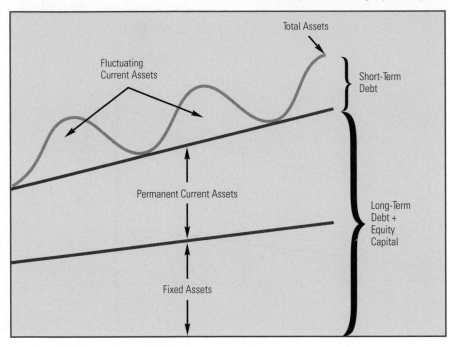

**Figure 16.6
Matching Approach
to Asset Financing**

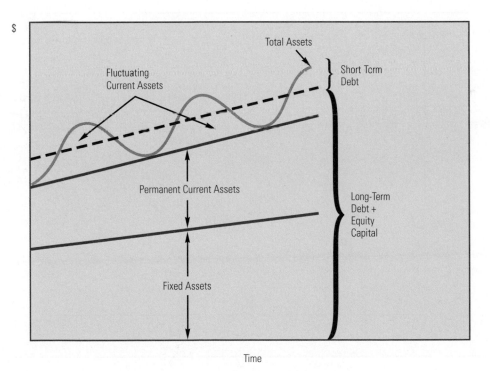

**Figure 16.7
Conservative
Approach to Asset
Financing**

Figure 16.9 summarizes the profitability–risk trade-offs of the alternative working capital financing policies.

Table 16.3 presents actual working capital data for the retailer Target Corporation during fiscal year 2002. The company's total current assets and inventories fluctuate during the year, peaking during autumn (third quarter) as the holiday shopping season approaches. Its current liabilities also fluctuate and peak in autumn.

**Figure 16.8
Aggressive Approach
to Asset Financing**

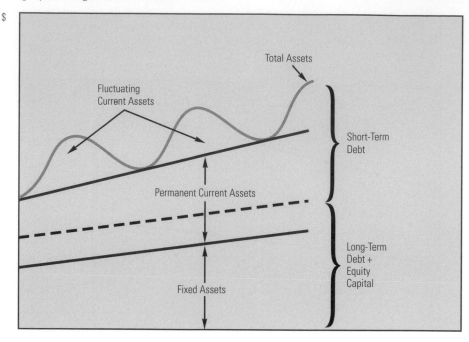

**Figure 16.9
Risk–Return
Trade-off for
Alternative
Working Capital
Financing
Policies**

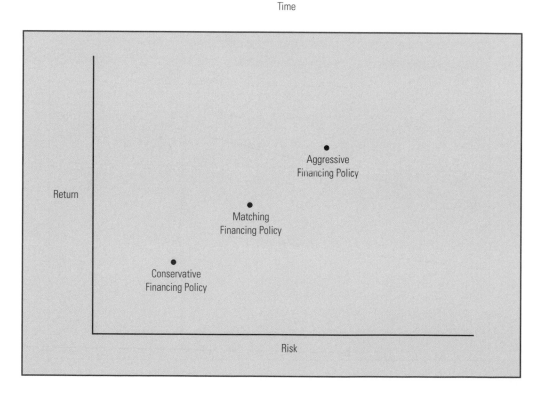

This suggests that Target is using a more or less matching approach to finance its fluctuating current assets.

Optimal Proportions of Short-term and Long-term Debt As is the case with working capital investment policy, no single combination of short- and long-term debt is necessarily optimal for all firms. In choosing a financing policy that maximizes shareholder wealth, a firm's financial manager must also take into account

Table 16.3 Working Capital Data for Target Corporation, Fiscal Year 2002 (in millions of dollars)

QUARTER (Date)	1st (May 4, 2002)	2nd (Aug. 3, 2002)	3rd (Nov. 2, 2002)	4th (Feb. 1, 2003)
Cash and marketable securities	$ 445	$ 1,755	$ 834	$ 758
Accounts receivable	3,949	4,304	4,882	5,565
Inventories	4,565	4,549	5,612	4,760
Other	1,236	1,112	1,147	852
Total current assets	$10,195	$11,720	$12,475	$11,935
Notes payable	1,370	1,583	1,374	975
Accounts payable	3,685	4,187	4,927	6,548
Other	1,796	2,031	1,836	
Total current liabilities	$ 6,851	$ 7,801	$ 8,137	$ 7,523
Net working capital	**$ 3,344**	**$ 3,919**	**$ 4,338**	**$ 4,412**

Source: Calculated from annual and quarterly balance sheet data for Target Corporation available through http://www.sec.gov

various other factors, such as the variability of sales and cash flows that affect the valuation of the firm.

Overall Working Capital Policy

Until now, we have considered the level of working capital investment and financing decisions separately—to illustrate the profitability versus risk trade-offs associated with each. As noted, working capital management requires making decisions on *both* the level and the financing of working capital, thus entailing a consideration of the joint impact of these decisions on the firm's profitability and risk.

However, it should be evident from earlier discussion that the most *conservative policy would be to maintain a high level of current asset investment where most of the current assets are financed using long-term capital.* Although this policy would have the lowest risk, it is likely to be accompanied by the lowest returns. At the other extreme, the *most aggressive policy would be to maintain low current asset balances that are financed mostly by short-term debt.* This would result in the highest returns and also the highest risk. Most firms in practice adopt a working capital policy that lies somewhere between these two extremes.

Comprehension Check Questions

1. Define and identify the components of
   ➤ Operating cycle
   ➤ Cash conversion cycle
2. What is the impact of longer cash conversion cycles on a firm's working capital needs?
3. Explain the profitability–risk trade-off of alternative levels of working capital balances.
4. Explain the profitability–risk trade-off of alternative methods of financing a given working capital investment.

MANAGEMENT OF CURRENT ASSETS

As seen earlier in Table 16.2, current assets make up a large proportion of a firm's total assets in a variety of industries. In this part of the chapter we examine the factors that influence the level of each of the current assets accounts including cash, marketable securities, accounts receivable, and inventory. We will examine the management practices that result in efficient utilization of these assets. This is especially important since current assets do not generate returns directly or, if they do, the returns tend to be fairly low. For example, accounts receivable may have an indirect impact on sales: Easy credit terms may generate higher sales and potentially greater profits. In similar fashion maintaining raw material and finished goods inventory balances ensures the firm will not experience stockouts but by itself this does not generate any returns. Marketable securities and cash accounts may generate returns in the form of interest but these returns tend to be fairly low compared to returns generated from investments in fixed assets.

CASH AND MARKETABLE SECURITIES

Cash and marketable securities are the most liquid of a company's assets. Cash is the sum of the currency a company has on hand and the funds on deposit in bank checking accounts. Cash is the medium of exchange that permits management to carry on the various functions of the business organization. In fact, the survival of a company can depend on the availability of cash to meet financial obligations on time. Marketable securities consist of short-term investments that a firm makes with its temporarily idle cash. Marketable securities can be sold quickly and converted into cash when needed. Unlike cash, however, marketable securities provide a firm with interest income.

As shown in Figure 16.10, the firm's cash balance is affected by every transaction that involves either a cash inflow or a cash outflow. *Cash inflows, or receipts,* occur when customers pay for their purchases, when a firm obtains bank loans, when it sells new issues of debt and equity securities, and when it sells (or collects interest on) marketable securities. *Cash outflows, or disbursements,* occur when a firm makes payments to suppliers, when a firm pays wages to employees, taxes to governments, interest and principal to bondholders, cash dividends to shareholders, and when a

**Figure 16.10
Cash Flows Within
a Typical Firm***

*Arrows indicate direction
of cash flows.

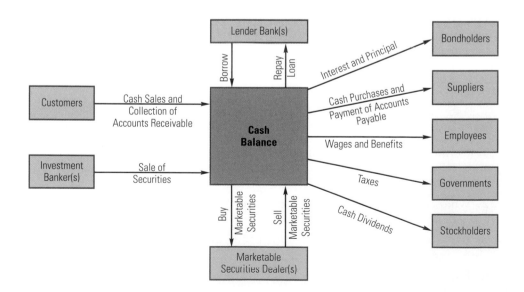

firm repays bank loans and purchases marketable securities. Therefore, the cash balance at the end of any given period is the result of many interrelated activities.

Cash flows differ with respect to their degree of certainty. In general, *future outflows are more certain than future inflows.* Most expenditures (outflows) are directly controllable by a firm and, as a result, can be forecasted more easily. For example, outflows for such items as raw materials, labor, dividends, debt repayments, and capital equipment are determined primarily by management decisions and are usually known in advance of their occurrence. Inflows, in contrast, occur partly as a result of decisions made outside a firm and thus are usually more difficult to control and forecast. For example, cash inflows from sales depend primarily on the buying decisions of customers, as well as on when they make their payments.

Many firms hold significant cash and marketable securities balances. For example, at the end of 2002, IBM's cash balances equaled $6 billion; General Electric's cash balances exceeded $8.9 billion; ExxonMobil had $7.2 billion; and Merck had nearly $5 billion. These cash balances give the firm a cushion to handle economic downturns and the ability to make investments in other firms and assets when the price is attractive.

Firms hold liquid asset balances (cash and marketable securities) for a number of reasons, including:

➤ Transactions motive. Liquid asset balances serve as a buffer between cash inflows and cash outflows that are not perfectly synchronized. For example, if cash outflows occur mostly in the beginning of the month and inflows occur largely towards the end of the month, a policy of maintaining an appropriate cash balance would help ease the liquidity pressure in the beginning of the month.
➤ Precautionary motive. Liquid balances are necessary to meet unexpected requirements for cash. For example, there might be an unexpected labor strike or fire, placing additional liquidity demands on the firm.
➤ Planned future funds needs. Liquid asset balances may be needed to meet planned future outlays including capital expenditures, quarterly dividend payments, loan repayments, and tax payments.
➤ Speculative reasons. Some firms build up cash balances to meet speculative needs such as for an acquisition. For example, several years ago Ford Motor Company built up its liquid asset balances to over $9 billion. Security analysts expected Ford to make major future acquisitions, particularly if it could identify one or more attractively priced firms to acquire. In fact, this is just what Ford did when it acquired Jaguar for $2.5 billion. The large cash balances gave Ford timing flexibility in pursuing acquisitions.

Optimal Liquid Asset Balance

When a firm holds liquid asset balances, whether in the form of currency, bank demand deposits, or marketable securities, it in effect is investing these funds. To determine the optimal investment in liquid assets, a firm must weigh the benefits and costs of holding these various balances. The determination of an optimal liquid asset balance reflects the classic risk versus return trade-off facing financial managers. Because liquid assets earn relatively low rates of return, a firm can increase its profitability in relation to its asset base by minimizing liquid asset balances. However, low liquid asset balances expose a firm to the risk of not being able to meet its obligations as they come due. Effective cash management calls for a careful balancing of the risk and return aspects of cash management.

When a firm holds liquid assets, it incurs an ***opportunity cost.*** The opportunity cost of liquid assets, held in the form of bank deposits, is the return the firm could earn on these funds in their next best use, such as in the expansion of other current or fixed assets. The opportunity cost of liquid asset balances, held in the form of marketable securities, is the income that could be earned on these funds in their next best alternative use less the interest income received on the marketable securities.

Given the opportunity cost of holding liquid asset balances, why would a firm ever maintain a liquid asset balance in the form of cash and/or marketable securities? The answer is that these balances help the firm avoid the *shortage* costs associated with inadequate liquid asset balances. Shortage costs can take many different forms, including:

➤ Foregone cash discounts
➤ Deterioration of the firm's credit rating
➤ Higher interest expenses
➤ Possible financial insolvency

Many suppliers offer customers a cash discount for prompt payment. Having to forgo this cash discount can be quite costly to a firm. In addition, the creditworthiness of a firm is determined at least partially by the current and quick ratios—both of which can be affected by an inadequate liquid asset balance. This, in turn, can cause a firm's credit rating to deteriorate and make loans on favorable terms more difficult to secure in the future. The credit rating also can fall if a firm fails to pay bills on time because of inadequate cash reserves. This can make future credit difficult to obtain from suppliers. If a firm has inadequate liquid asset reserves, it may have to meet unforeseen needs for cash by short-term borrowing. In such a scenario, it may be unable to negotiate for the best terms—including the lowest possible interest rate—if its credit rating is questionable. Inadequate liquid asset balances may cause a firm to incur high transactions costs when converting illiquid assets to cash. Finally, an inadequate liquid asset balance increases a firm's risk of insolvency, because a serious recession or natural disaster would be more likely to reduce the firm's cash inflows to the point where it could not meet contractual financial obligations.

e-Lecture

An inverse relationship exists between a firm's liquid asset balance and these shortage costs: The larger a firm's liquid asset balance, the smaller its associated shortage costs. The opportunity holding costs, in contrast, increase as a firm's liquid asset balance is increased. As shown in Figure 16.11, the optimal liquid asset balance occurs at the point where the sum of the opportunity holding costs and the shortage costs is minimized. Admittedly, many of these shortage costs are difficult to measure. Nevertheless, a firm should attempt to evaluate the trade-offs among these costs in order to economize on cash holdings.

The Practice of Liquidity Management

In practice, a wide variety of liquidity policies are found to exist among firms. Table 16.4 offers a sample of the liquidity policies practiced by different firms in several industries. As the table shows, liquidity practices, as measured by the ratio of cash and marketable securities to total assets, vary significantly among industries and among firms within an industry. Utility firms appear to hold the least proportion of cash and marketable securities to total assets. This may be due to the stable and generally predictable nature of the business. Cash businesses such as retailing and restaurant industries also appear to hold a small proportion of total assets as liquid balances. The auto companies and, especially, computer manufacturers appear to carry significantly more liquid balances as a percentage of total assets. The auto industry is known to be subject to severe recessions and significant liquid balances are needed to tide the firm over until the economy expands again. The computer

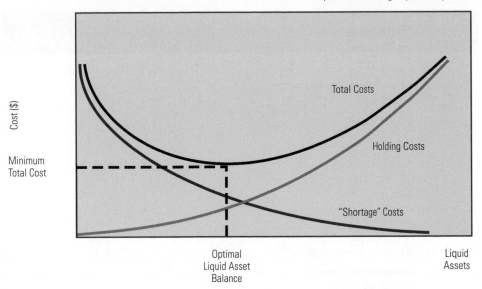

**Figure 16.11
Optimal Liquid
Asset Balance**

industry, especially firms involved in the manufacture of personal computers, is subject to significant business risk, which may explain why these firms tend to have large liquid balances. Although this table does not provide data on small- to medium-sized firms, in general it can be observed that larger firms tend to hold lower liquid asset balances (relative to total assets) than smaller firms. This is because larger firms tend to have better access to *backup* short-term financing should they need it from commercial banks or the ability to sell commercial paper. Because smaller firms have more limited credit access, they tend to hold greater liquid asset balances as a cushion against the unexpected.

Controlling the Collection and Disbursement of Cash

The cash collection and disbursement processes provide a firm with two areas in which it can economize on cash holdings. For example, assume the sales of Briggs & Stratton Corporation average about $5 million per business day. If the company can speed up collections by only one day, the cash balance will increase by $5 million, and these released funds can be invested in other current assets or in fixed assets. If this additional cash can be invested to yield a 5 percent return, it will generate added income of $250,000 per year (5% × $5 million). Cash collection and disbursement policies are designed to reduce a firm's liquid asset balances (cash and marketable securities) by exploiting imperfections in the collection and payment process. The objective is to speed up collections and slow down disbursements.

The primary objective of cash collection involves *expediting collections by reducing the lag between the time customers pay their bills and the time the checks are collected.* In contrast, the primary objective of cash disbursement is to *slow payments so that the firm can keep the funds invested or in the bank as long as possible.* Expediting collections and slowing disbursements help increase a firm's cash balance and provide it with funds to use for other profitable investments. Policies designed to control collections and disbursements take advantage of the *float* present in the payment and disbursement system.

Float A firm's cash balance as shown on the bank's books generally differs from that shown on the firm's own books. This difference is known as *float* and represents the net effect of the delays in the payment of checks a firm writes and the collection

Table 16.4 Ratio of Cash and Marketable Securities to Total Assets (2002)

Firm	Ratio (%)
Aerospace-defense industry:	
Boeing	6.9
General Dynamics	2.80
Lockheed Martin	10.63
Northrop Grumman	3.34
Automotive industry:	
DaimlerChrysler	4.87
Ford	10.55
General Motors	10.32
Honda Motor	8.78
PACCAR Inc.	15.03
Navistar International	8.9
Computer industry:	
Apple Computer	68.86
Dell	29.98
Gateway	42.51
Hewlett-Packard	16.16
IBM	8.11
Sun Microsystems	17.46
Electric utility industry:	
First Energy Corp.	0.6
Duke Energy	4.92
Great Plains Energy	1.86
Consolidated Edison	2.16
Southern Companies	0.86
Restaurant industry:	
Applebee's	2.77
Darden Restaurants	6.43
McDonald's	1.38
Papa John's Int'l, Inc.	3.70
Wendy's	2.60
Retailing industry:	
Family Dollar	12.55
Kohls	8.96
JCPenney	13.85
Target	2.65
Wal-Mart	2.91

Source: Calculated from data taken from 10-K annual reports.

of checks a firm receives. Checks written by a firm result in *disbursement (or positive) float;* that is, an excess of bank net collected balances over the balances shown on a firm's books. In contrast, *collection (or negative) float* arises from the delay between the time a customer writes a check to a supplier or other payee and the time the payee actually receives these funds as collected balances (which are spendable). There are three primary components, or sources, of float:

1. *Mail float* is the delay between the time a payment is sent to the payee through the mail and the time that payment arrives at the payee's office.

2. *Processing float* represents the delay between receipt of payment from a payer and the deposit of that receipt in the payee's account.
3. *Check-clearing float* is the delay between the time a check is deposited in the payee's account and the time the funds are available to be spent. Checks processed through the Federal Reserve System are *cleared* in 2 days or less, although the depositor's bank may not make the funds available quite that fast.

Expediting Collections Figure 16.12 illustrates the main steps in the cash collection process. The total time involved in this process is a combination of mailing (float) time, company processing (float) time, and check-clearing (float) time, each of which may vary depending on where the firm's customers and their respective banks are located. Some methods available for reducing the collection float are discussed below.

Decentralized Collection Centers and Concentration Banks. Cash collection systems can be either *centralized* or *decentralized*. In the centralized system, customers are instructed to send their payments to the firm's headquarters. In the decentralized system, customers mail their payments to a nearby collection center, which is strategically located to minimize mail delay. The collection center then deposits the checks in a local bank and reports this information to the firm's headquarters. Because most of the checks are drawn on banks located in the same geographical area as the collection center, check-clearing float is reduced. Each business day, funds in excess of the amount necessary to compensate the local bank for its services are transferred to an account in a concentration bank, where the firm maintains a disbursement account upon which checks are written.

e-Lecture

Lockboxes. Figure 16.13 illustrates a *lockbox* collection system. A lockbox is a post office box maintained by a local bank for the purpose of receiving a firm's remittances. Customers mail payments to this post office box, which is usually no more than a few hundred miles away. The bank empties the box several times each working day, deposits the payments in the firm's account, puts the checks into the clearing system, and sends the firm a list of the payments received each day. Not only does the lockbox reduce mailing time, it also eliminates company processing time, because the checks are deposited and begin the clearing process before the company's accounting department processes the payments received, rather than after

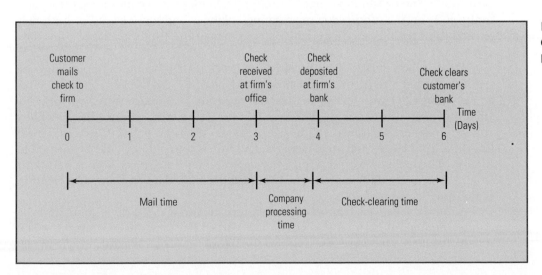

Figure 16.12 Cash Collection Process

Figure 16.13
Lockbox Arrangement

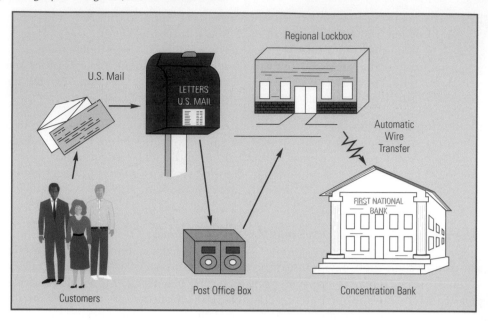

processing them. The bank normally charges a fee for this service, requires a ***compensating balance,*** or both. Funds in excess of the bank's compensating balance requirement are transferred each day to a master collection account in a concentration bank.

The decision to establish a lockbox collection system requires a comparison of the associated benefits and costs of adopting such a system. If the earnings on the funds released by the acceleration of collections exceed the forgone returns on the required compensating balances, the service fees charged by the lockbox bank, or both, the establishment of a lockbox collection system is profitable.

If the number of checks handled is small and the dollar amount of each check is large, a lockbox arrangement is very beneficial to the firm. Under these conditions the bank's workload is light, and the associated service fees, compensating balances, or both, are small. However, when large numbers of checks with small dollar amounts are involved—for example, in the case of oil company credit cards—a lockbox system may not be profitable. Under these conditions, the opportunity costs on the required compensating balances, the service fees, or both may exceed the earnings the firm realizes from having the funds available a few days earlier.

The lockbox decision can be illustrated with the following example. Suppose that the Mutual Life Insurance Company of New York (MONY) currently receives and processes all customer payments at its corporate headquarters in New York City (that is, a centralized system). The firm is considering establishing a bank lockbox collection system for seven southeastern states—Florida, North Carolina, South Carolina, Tennessee, Alabama, Georgia, and Mississippi—that would be located in Atlanta. The lockbox would reduce average mailing time for customer payments from 3 days to 1.5 days, check-processing time from 2 days to 1 day, and clearing time from 3 days to 1.5 days.

Annual collections from the southeastern region are $91.25 million, and the average number of payments received total 550 per day (assume 365 days per year). A bank in Atlanta has agreed to process the payments for an annual fee of $15,000

Table 16.5 Mutual Life Insurance Company of New York's (MONY) Analysis of the Decision to Establish a Lockbox Collection System for the Southeastern Region

Step A: Reduction in collection time = Reduction in mailing time + Reduction in processing time + Reduction in check-clearing time

$$= (3-1.5) + (2-1) + (3-1.5)$$
$$= 4 \text{ days}$$

Average daily collections = Annual collection ÷ 365
$$= \$91,250,000 \div 365$$
$$= \$250,000$$

Amount of funds released = Average daily collections × Reduction in collection time
$$= \$250,000 \times 4 \text{ days}$$
$$= \$1,000,000$$

Step B: Annual (pretax) earnings on released funds = Amount of funds released × Interest rate
$$= \$1,000,000 \times 0.08$$
$$= \$80,000$$

Step C: Annual bank processing fee = Fixed cost + Number of payments per year × Variable cost per payment
$$= \$15,000 + (550 \times 365) \times \$0.10$$
$$= \$15,000 + \$20,075$$
$$= \$35,075$$

Step D: Net (pretax) benefits = Annual (pretax) earnings on released funds − Annual bank processing fee
$$= \$80,000 - \$35,075$$
$$= \$44,925$$

---

plus $0.10 per payment received. Assuming an 8 percent opportunity cost for released funds, should MONY use the lockbox collection system?

Table 16.5 shows an analysis of this decision. In Step A, the amount of funds released ($1 million) is found by multiplying average daily collections ($250,000) by the reduction in collection time (4 days). The annual (pretax) earnings on the released funds ($80,000) are found in Step B by multiplying the amount of funds released ($1 million) by the opportunity cost of funds (0.08). The annual bank processing fee ($35,075) is computed in Step C as the sum of fixed costs ($15,000) and variable costs ($20,075). Finally, in Step D, the net (pretax) benefits of establishing a lockbox system ($44,925) are computed by deducting the annual bank processing fee ($35,075) from the earnings on the released funds ($80,000). Because the net (pretax) benefits are positive, MONY should employ the lockbox collection system.

Wire Transfers and Depository Transfer Checks. Once deposits enter the firm's banking network, the objective is to transfer surplus funds from its local (collection) bank accounts to its concentration (disbursement) bank account or accounts. Two methods used to perform this task are wire transfers and depository transfer checks.

With a *wire transfer*, funds are sent from a local bank to a concentration bank electronically through the Federal Reserve System or a private bank wire system. Wire transfers are the fastest way of moving funds between banks, because the transfer takes only a few minutes and the funds become immediately available (that is, they can be withdrawn) by the firm upon receipt of the wire notice at the concentration bank. Wire transfers eliminate the mailing and check-clearing times associated with other funds-transfer methods. Some firms leave standing instructions with their local (collection) banks to automatically wire surplus funds on a periodic basis (for example, daily, twice a week, and so on) to their concentration bank. Also, some firms specify in their sales contracts that customers must wire their payments on the due dates.

Wire transfer of funds is available to member banks of the Federal Reserve System and to nonmember banks through their correspondent banks. The cost to corporate customers to send a wire transfer at most banks ranges from $10 to $25. A similar charge is made to receive and process a domestic wire transfer. For a firm with multiple collection centers that use wire transfers on a daily basis, the annual costs can be substantial. Consequently, this method of transferring funds should be used only when the incremental value of having the funds immediately available exceeds the additional cost, relative to alternatives, such as depository transfer checks.

A mail *depository transfer check (DTC)* is an unsigned, nonnegotiable check drawn on the local collection bank and payable to the concentration bank. As it deposits customer checks in the local bank each day, the collection center mails a depository transfer check to the concentration bank authorizing it to withdraw the deposited funds from the local bank. Upon receipt of the depository transfer check, the firm's account at the concentration bank is credited for the designated amount. Depository transfer checks are processed through the usual check-clearing process. Although the use of depository transfer checks does not eliminate mailing and check-clearing time, it does ensure the movement of funds from the local collection center banks to the concentration bank in a timely manner. Also, the cost of this method of transferring funds is low; often the only cost involved is postage.

An *electronic depository transfer check (EDTC)* can also be used to move funds from a local bank to a concentration bank. The process of transmitting deposit information to a concentration bank is similar to that for mail DTCs just described, except that the information is sent electronically through an automated clearinghouse, such as the Automated Clearing House (ACH) system of the Federal Reserve (Fedwire) or the Clearing House Interbank Payments System (CHIPS). These systems eliminate the mail float in moving funds from the local bank to a concentration bank. Funds transferred through an automated system are available for use by the firm in 1 day (or less).

Special Handling of Large Remittances. Firms that receive individual remittances in the multimillion-dollar range may find it more profitable to use special courier services to pick up these checks from customers (rather than having their customers mail the checks) and present them for collection to the banks upon which they are drawn.

Use of Preauthorized Checks. A *preauthorized check (PAC)* resembles an ordinary check except that it does not require the signature of the person (or firm) on whose account it is being drawn. This system is especially useful for firms that receive a large volume of payments of a fixed amount each period. Insurance companies, savings and loans, charitable institutions, and leasing firms make extensive use of this collection procedure. When preauthorized checks are used, the payer agrees to allow the payee (the firm that is owed the money) to write a check on the payer's account and deposit that check immediately for collection at an agreed-upon time. Preauthorized checks have the advantages of completely eliminating the mail float, reducing billing and collecting expenses, and making the cash flows

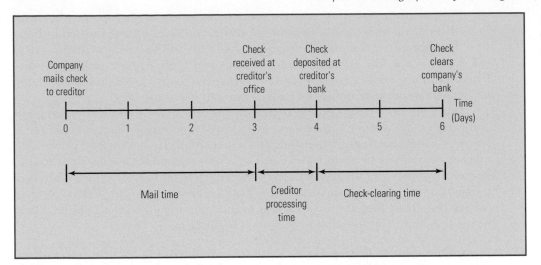

**Figure 16.14
Cash Disbursement Process**

for both parties highly predictable. Many payers like preauthorized check systems because they do not have to bother to write a check each month.

Slowing Disbursements Figure 16.14 illustrates the principal steps involved in the cash disbursement process. Several ways in which a firm can slow disbursements and keep funds in the bank for longer periods of time are discussed below.

Scheduling and Centralizing Payments. A firm should pay bills on time—not before or after they are due. There is no significant benefit to be received by paying bills before they are actually due unless there exists a cash discount for early payment. Payments made ahead of time lower the firm's average cash balance, whereas late payments can impair the firm's credit rating.

Centralizing payments from disbursement accounts maintained at a concentration bank helps minimize the amount of idle funds a firm must keep in local field offices and divisional bank accounts. A number of firms have set up *zero-balance systems* to use disbursement float more effectively. In a zero-balance system, a master, or concentration, account is set up to receive all deposits coming into the zero-balance system. As checks clear through the zero-balance accounts on which they are issued, funds are transferred to these accounts from the master account. These disbursement accounts are called zero-balance accounts because exactly enough funds are transferred into them daily to cover the checks that have cleared, leaving a zero balance at the end of the day. In general, all disbursements for accounts payable, payroll, and whatever other purposes the firm desires are issued from these zero-balance accounts. For a zero-balance system to operate effectively, a firm must have a well-developed network for reporting deposits and disbursements, as well as a close working relationship with its bank.

Drafts. A *draft* is similar to a check, except that it is not payable on demand. Instead, when a draft is transmitted to a firm's bank for collection, the bank must present the draft to the firm for acceptance before making payment. In practice, individual drafts are considered to be legally paid automatically by the bank on the business day following the day of presentation to the firm, unless the firm returns a draft and explicitly requests that it not be paid. Once the draft has been presented, the firm must immediately deposit the necessary funds to cover the payment.

The use of drafts rather than checks permits a firm to keep smaller balances in its disbursement accounts, because funds do not have to be deposited in them until the drafts are presented for payment. Normally, drafts are more expensive to use than checks. The lower account balances and higher processing costs cause banks to impose service charges on firms using drafts; such costs must be included in the analysis of the benefits and costs of using drafts to pay bills.

Drafts are now used primarily to provide for centralized control over payments authorized in field offices, rather than as a means of slowing disbursements. For example, a claims agent for Nationwide Insurance might issue a draft to provide for quick settlement of an insurance claim. The claims agent does not have the authority to write a check against Nationwide's checking accounts. By issuing a draft, centralized control can be maintained over these disbursements. The Federal Reserve System requires a firm to transfer funds to the bank through which payment is to be made as soon as the drafts are presented to the firm.

Maximizing Check-Clearing Float. Some firms make payments to suppliers from checking accounts located a long distance from the supplier. For example, an east coast supplier might be paid with checks drawn on a west coast bank; this increases the time required for the check to clear through the banking system. Some firms maintain an intricate network of disbursing accounts. In such systems, checks are issued from the account most distant from the payee, thereby maximizing check-clearing float.

Electronic Funds Transfer

The previous discussion of methods to speed up collections and slow disbursements assumes that virtually all transactions involve the transfer of paper (checks) between the payer and the payee. These methods to control collections and disbursements are designed to reduce the float involved in financial transactions. In a sense, the total float in the financial system can be viewed as a measure of inefficiency in the financial system. In an idealized world, the total float would be reduced to zero. Payments would be made and received as usable funds instantaneously. Although the financial system has a long way to go before this ideal is realized, in recent years tremendous progress has been made.

Many consumers now have automatic teller cards that give them access to cash 24 hours a day, 7 days a week. In addition, banking customers can use automatic tellers to transfer funds between accounts. Special credit cards, called *debit cards*, are used by some consumers. When a debit card is used, funds are transferred from the consumer's bank account electronically to the account of the retailer. The retailer no longer must be concerned whether a check will be good when it is deposited. Increasingly, small and large businesses are using microcomputer links to manipulate funds between their interest-bearing and noninterest-bearing disbursement accounts.

Large payments can be made by wire transfers or through an automated clearinghouse. Automated clearing house (ACH) systems are computer-based alternatives to the paper-check collection and clearing system. The ACH sorts check-like electronic images and exchanges electronic records of payment and receipt. Although acceptance of electronic checking was initially slow, growth has increased dramatically in recent years. Electronic funds transfer (EFT) systems account for less than 1 percent of the number of all payments in the United States, but they account for more than 80 percent in terms of the value of payments.

EFT mechanisms are profoundly changing the nature of the cash management function. Although paper checks, with their associated mail and processing float, will not disappear completely for some time (if ever), the importance of developing elaborate mechanisms to manage float will be reduced greatly as increased volumes of payments are made electronically. Increased reliance on EFT as the mechanism for payment will free up some of the cash invested in accounts receivable for more productive uses. Contemporary financial managers will be challenged in the years ahead to stay current with a fast-changing, high-technology system of receiving payments and making disbursements.

Comprehension Check Questions

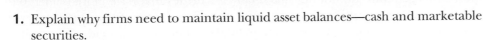

1. Explain why firms need to maintain liquid asset balances—cash and marketable securities.
2. What is float?
3. What are some of the ways in which collections can be expedited?
4. What are some of the ways in which disbursements can be slowed?

Investing in Marketable Securities

The marketable securities account can be thought of as a parking place for cash that is not immediately needed. Rather than letting their cash reserves build up in excess of daily cash requirements, many firms invest in short-term marketable securities that generate at least some interest income.

Choosing Marketable Securities. A firm may choose among many different types of securities when deciding where to invest excess cash reserves. In determining which securities to include in its portfolio, the firm should consider a number of criteria, including:

➢ Default risk
➢ Marketability
➢ Maturity date
➢ Rate of return

Default Risk. Most firms invest only in marketable securities that have little or no *default risk* (the risk that a borrower will fail to make interest and/or principal payments on a loan). U.S. Treasury securities have the lowest default risk, followed by securities of other U.S. government agencies and, finally, by corporate and municipal securities. Various financial reporting agencies, including Moody's Investors Service and Standard and Poor's, compile and publish information concerning the safety ratings of the various corporate and municipal securities. Given the positive relationship between a security's expected return and risk and the desire to select marketable securities having minimal default risk, a firm has to be willing to accept relatively low expected yields on its marketable securities investments.

Marketability. A firm usually buys marketable securities that can be sold on short notice without a significant price concession. Thus, there are two dimensions to a security's marketability: the time required to sell the security and the price realized from the sale relative to the last quoted price. If a long period of time, a high transaction cost, or a significant price concession is required to dispose of a security, the security has poor marketability and generally is not considered suitable for inclusion in a marketable securities portfolio. Naturally, a trade-off is involved here between risk and return. Generally, a highly marketable security has a small degree of risk that the investor will incur a loss, and consequently, it usually has a lower expected yield than one with limited marketability.

Maturity Date. Firms usually limit their marketable securities purchases to issues that have relatively short maturities. Recall that prices of debt securities decrease when interest rates rise and increase when interest rates fall. For a given change in interest rates, prices of long-term securities fluctuate more widely than prices of short-term securities with equal default risk. Thus, an investor who holds long-term securities is exposed to a greater risk of loss if the securities have to be sold prior to maturity. Recall from Chapter 7 that this is called ***interest rate risk.*** For this reason, most firms generally do not buy marketable securities that have more than 180 to 270 days remaining until maturity; many firms restrict most of their temporary investments to those maturing in less than 90 days. Because the yields on securities with short maturities are often lower than the yields on securities with longer maturities, a firm has to be willing to sacrifice yield to avoid interest rate risk.

Rate of Return. Although the ***rate of return,*** or yield, is given consideration in selecting securities for inclusion in a firm's portfolio, it is less important than the other three criteria just described. The desire to invest in securities that have minimum default and interest rate risk and that are readily marketable usually limits the selection to those having relatively low yields.

Types of Marketable Securities. Firms normally confine their marketable securities investments to ***money market*** instruments—those high-grade (low-default-risk), short-term debt instruments having original maturities of 1 year or less. Money market instruments that are suitable for inclusion in a firm's marketable securities portfolio include U.S. Treasury issues, other federal agency issues, municipal securities, negotiable certificates of deposit, commercial paper, Eurodollar deposits, auction rate preferred stocks, money market mutual funds, and bank money market accounts.

Table 16.6 lists the characteristics and yields of various money market instruments. As can be seen in the last three columns of the table, yields on these securities vary considerably over time. Yields are a function of a number of factors, including the state of the economy, the rate of inflation, and government monetary and fiscal policies.

U.S. Treasury Issues. U.S. Treasury bills are the most popular marketable securities. They are sold at weekly auctions through Federal Reserve Banks and their branches and have standard maturities of 91 days, 182 days, and 1 year. Treasury bills are issued at a discount and then redeemed for the full face amount at maturity. Once they are issued, Treasury bills can be bought and sold in the secondary markets through approximately 40 government securities dealers. There is a large and active market for Treasury bills, which means that a firm can easily dispose of them when it needs cash. The smallest denomination of Treasury bills is $10,000 of maturity value.

The advantages of Treasury issues include short maturities, a virtually default-free status, and ready marketability. Their primary disadvantage lies in the fact that their yields normally are the lowest of any marketable security.

The Treasury also issues notes that have original maturities from 2 to 10 years and bonds that have maturities over 10 years. As these securities approach their maturity dates, they become, in effect, short-term instruments that are then suitable for inclusion in a firm's marketable securities portfolio. Treasury bonds and notes pay interest semiannually. Minimum Treasury bond denominations are $1,000.

Table 16.6 Characteristics and Yields of Selected Marketable Securities Instruments

Instrument	Issuers	Denominations	Maturities	Marketability		Yields* (%) Aug. 1981	Oct. 1993	May 2003
U.S. Treasury bills	U.S. Treasury	Various denominations from $10,000 to $1,000,000	91 days, 182 days, 52 weeks	Highly organized secondary market	(3 months) (6 months) (1 year)	15.51 15.52 14.70	3.04 3.13 3.25	1.08 1.09 1.11
Federal agency issues	Agencies of the federal government	Various denominations from $5,000 to $1,000,000	Wide variation in maturities, from several days to more than 10 years	Well-established secondary market for short-term securities of 'big five' agencies		—		
Short-term municipal securities	State and local governments and their agencies	$5,000 to $5,000,000	1 month to 1 year	Not as good as U.S. Treasury and federal agency issues		—		
Negotiable certificates of deposit	Commercial banks	$100,000 to $1,000,000	7 days to 18 months or more	Fairly good secondary market	(1 month) (3 months) (6 months)	17.91 17.96 17.98	3.09 3.24 3.25	3.59 3.48 3.49
Commercial paper	Large corporation and finance companies with strong credit ratings	$100,000 or more	2 or 3 days to 270 days	Weak secondary market	(1 month) (3 months) (6 months)	17.58 17.23 16.62	3.14 3.26 3.27	3.54 3.47 3.42
Auction rate preferred stock	Investment banks	$100,000 to $500,000 depending on issue	—	Salable at auction every 49 days		—		
Money market mutual funds	Securities dealers and mutual fund companies	Minimum of $1,000 is usually required; no standard denominations	Redeemable at any time	Good, because the fund agrees to redeem shares at any time		Yields vary from fund to fund, but usually exceed the yield available on Treasury bills		
Bank money market accounts	Commercial banks	Minimum of $2,500	Normally redeemable at any time (by law, banks reserve the right to require 7 days' written notice for withdrawal)	Excellent		Yields vary from bank to bank, but usually are below Treasury bill yield.		

*Source: Federal Reserve Bulletin, Table 1:35, various issues

Other Federal Agency Issues. A number of federal government–sponsored agencies issue their own securities, including the *big five*: the Federal Home Loan Bank, the Federal Land Banks, the Federal Intermediate Credit Bank, the Bank for Cooperatives, and the Federal National Mortgage Association. Although each of these agencies guarantees its own securities, they do not constitute a legal obligation on the part of the U.S. government. Nevertheless, most investors consider them to be very-low-risk securities, and they sell at yields slightly above U.S. Treasury securities but below other money market instruments. Because these securities are traded in the secondary markets through the same dealers who handle U.S. Treasury securities, they are readily marketable should a firm need to dispose of them before maturity. Minimum denominations generally are $5,000.

Municipal Securities. State and local governments and their agencies issue various types of interest-bearing securities. Short-term issues are suitable for inclusion in a firm's marketable securities portfolio. The yields on these securities vary with the creditworthiness of the issuer. The pretax yields on these securities generally are lower than the yields on Treasury bills because the interest is exempt from federal (and some state) income taxes. The secondary market for municipal issues is not as strong as that for Treasury and other federal agency issues. Municipal (tax-exempt) money market mutual funds also are available.

Negotiable Certificates of Deposit. Commercial banks are permitted to issue certificates of deposit (CDs), which entitle the holder to receive the amount deposited plus accrued interest on a specified date. At the time of issue, maturities on these instruments range from 7 days to 18 months or more. Once issued, CDs become negotiable, meaning they can be bought and sold in the secondary markets. Because CDs of the largest banks are handled by government securities dealers, they are readily marketable and thus are suitable for inclusion in a firm's marketable securities portfolio. Yields on CDs generally are above the rates on federal agency issues having similar maturities.

Commercial Paper. ***Commercial paper*** consists of short-term unsecured promissory notes issued by large, well-known corporations and finance companies. Some finance companies, such as General Motors Acceptance Corporation (GMAC) and C.I.T. Financial Corporation, which issue large amounts of commercial paper regularly, sell it directly to investors. Industrial, utility, and transportation firms and smaller finance companies, which issue commercial paper less frequently and in smaller amounts, sell their commercial paper through commercial paper dealers. Maturities on commercial paper at the time of issue range from 2 or 3 days to 270 days.

The secondary market for commercial paper is weak, although it sometimes is possible to make arrangements with the issuer or commercial paper dealer to repurchase the security prior to maturity. This weak secondary market combined with a somewhat higher default risk results in higher yields on commercial paper than on most other money market instruments.

Auction Rate Preferred Stocks. A number of large investment banks issue, on behalf of their client companies, a type of preferred stock known as ***auction rate preferred stock,*** which is a suitable short-term investment for excess corporate funds. The dividend yield on this type of security is adjusted every 49 days through an auction process, where investors can exchange their stock for cash. As a result, the price of the stock stays near par. Because 70 percent of the dividends received are exempt from corporate income taxes, the after-tax yields often are above the yields on other marketable securities such as CDs or commercial paper. The stock is sold in minimum denominations of $100,000 to $500,000, depending on the issue.

Money Market Mutual Funds. Many of the higher-yielding marketable securities described earlier are available only in relatively large denominations. For example, negotiable CDs usually come in amounts of $100,000 or more. As a result, a smaller firm that has limited funds to invest at any given time is often unable to obtain the higher yields offered on these securities. An alternative is a money market mutual fund that pools the investments of many other small investors and invests in large-denomination money market instruments. By purchasing shares in a money market fund, such as Dreyfus Liquid Assets or Merrill Lynch Ready Assets, a smaller firm can approach the higher yields offered on large-denomination securities. In addition, most of these funds offer check-writing privileges, which provides liquidity and enables firms to earn interest on invested funds until their checks clear.

Bank Money Market Accounts. Banks are permitted to offer checking accounts with yields comparable to those on money market mutual accounts with limited check-writing privileges. These accounts provide yields that are comparable to those on money market mutual funds.

Comprehension Check Questions

1. What is the difference between cash and marketable securities?
2. Why do firms invest in marketable securities?
3. What are the four criteria commonly used to evaluate securities for inclusion in marketable securities?

ACCOUNTS RECEIVABLE MANAGEMENT

Accounts receivable constitute an important investment category for most companies. As we saw earlier in Table 16.2, accounts receivable represent approximately 11 percent to 31 percent of the total assets of firms in a variety of industries. For some firms accounts receivable may represent the single largest investment of all asset accounts. In the case of IBM, accounts receivable amounted to 31.1 percent of total assets in 2002—a proportion that was greater than the firm's investment in net fixed assets!

Visit ACCPAC to see the many ways in which accounts receivable are classified and collected, as well as the many types of reports that AR management requires.
http://www.accpac.com

Accounts receivable consist of the credit a business grants its customers when selling goods or services. They take the form of either *trade credit*, which the company extends to other companies, or *consumer credit*, which the company extends to its ultimate consumers. The effectiveness of a company's credit policies can have a significant impact on its total performance. For example, Monsanto's credit manager has estimated that a reduction of only one day in the average collection period for the company's receivables increases its cash flow by $10 million and improves pretax profits by $1 million.

For a business to grant credit to its customers, it has to do the following:

➢ Establish credit and collection policies
➢ Evaluate individual credit applicants

Shareholder Wealth and Accounts Receivable Management

When a company decides to extend credit to customers, it is making an investment decision—namely, an investment in accounts receivable, a current asset. As with the decision to invest in long-term assets, the primary goal is the maximization of shareholder wealth. Recall from the discussion of capital budgeting analysis in Chapter 10 that accepting all projects whose returns exceed or at least equal the cost of capital maximizes shareholder wealth. Following similar reasoning, *a company will maximize shareholder wealth by investing in accounts receivable as long as the expected marginal returns obtained from each additional dollar of receivables investment exceeds the associated expected marginal costs of the investment,* including the cost of the funds invested.

The establishment of an optimal credit extension policy requires the company to examine and to attempt to measure the marginal costs and marginal returns (benefits) associated with alternative policies. What are the marginal returns and costs associated with a more liberal extension of credit to a company's customers? With respect to returns, a more liberal extension presumably stimulates sales and leads to increased gross profits, assuming that all other factors (such as economic conditions, prices, production costs, and advertising expenses) remain constant. Offsetting these increased returns are several types of credit-related marginal costs, including the opportunity costs of the additional capital funds employed to support the higher level of receivables. Checking new credit accounts and collecting the higher level of receivables also results in additional costs. And finally, a more liberal credit policy frequently results in increased bad-debt expenses, because a certain number of new accounts are likely to fail to repay the credit extended to them.

Credit Policy

In determining an optimal credit extension policy, a company's financial managers must consider a number of major controllable variables that can be used to alter the level of receivables, including:

➤ Credit standards
➤ Credit terms
➤ Collection effort

We will discuss each of these aspects of credit policy.

Credit Standards *Credit standards* are the criteria a company uses to screen credit applicants in order to determine which of its customers should be offered credit and how much. The process of setting credit standards allows the firm to exercise a degree of control over the *quality* of accounts accepted. By quality we are referring to how long the customer takes to repay the credit granted *and* the probability of default—that is, the likelihood that the customer will be unable to pay at all. The first characteristic may be measured by the average collection period, a measure of the promptness with which the customer discharges its credit obligations. The second or default risk characteristic may be measured by the **bad-debt loss ratio,** which is the proportion of accounts receivable that is uncollected.

For purposes of illustration potential customers can be classified into credit risk groups. This is shown in Table 16.7. Customers in the lowest credit risk group (credit risk group 1) are the best customers with the shortest average collection period and no bad-debt loss ratio. Customers in the second group have a comparatively longer average collection period and some bad-debt losses. As we go down the credit risk groups, note that the average collection period lengthens, and the

Table 16.7 Sales by Credit Risk Groups

Credit Risk Group	Credit Sales ($)	Average Collection Period (Days)	Bad-Debt Loss Ratio (%)
1	900,000	25	—
2	1,100,000	30	0.5
3	400,000	45	3
4	300,000	60	7
5	100,000	90	13

bad-debt loss ratio increases. The relevant question that each company has to ask is: To which credit risk group(s) should the company extend credit to?

On the surface it would appear that we should extend credit only to the most worthy group—credit risk group 1. However, by doing so the company's sales reach may be unduly restrictive. There may be very few customers that fall into credit risk group 1; therefore, confining the extension of credit to such a select group of customers may limit the firm's overall sales level. The firm may be turning away potential customers from higher credit risk groups who may prefer to do business with a competitor that is willing to extend them credit. At the other extreme, it also may not make sense to extend credit to customers in the worst credit risk group (credit risk group 5). The opportunity cost of tying up accounts receivable for a very long time and the high bad-debt loss ratios associated with this group may completely wipe out any *incremental* profits generated from selling to this group.

The question of which credit risk group to extend credit to ultimately depends on a *marginal benefit–marginal cost analysis.* Marginal benefit refers to the additional benefit to be gained from extending credit to a new group of customers, while marginal cost refers to the additional costs incurred in extending credit to this group. Management would then have to weigh the benefit of extending credit to a given credit risk group against the marginal costs of extending credit to that group. The marginal benefit would consist primarily of the profit generated from the additional sales to a riskier group of customers. The marginal costs, on the other hand, include the opportunity cost of tying up additional funds in accounts receivable for an extended period of time, bad-debt losses from extending credit to riskier customers, and cost of additional resources expended in collection effort.

Credit Terms   A company's credit terms, or terms of sale, specify the conditions under which the customer is required to pay for the credit extended to it. These conditions include the length of the credit period and the cash discount (if any) given for prompt payment plus any special terms, such as seasonal datings. For example, credit terms of *net 30* mean that the customer has 30 days from the invoice date within which to pay the bill and that no discount is offered for early payment.

Credit Period.   The length of a company's *credit period* (the amount of time a credit customer has to pay the account in full) varies since it is frequently determined by industry customs. The credit period may be as short as 7 days or as long as 6 months. Variation appears to be positively related to the length of time the merchandise is in the purchaser's inventory. For example, manufacturers of goods having relatively low inventory-turnover periods, such as jewelry, tend to offer retailers longer credit periods than distributors of goods having higher inventory-turnover periods, such as food products.

A company's credit terms can affect its sales. For example, if the demand for a particular product depends in part on its credit terms, the company may consider lengthening the credit period to stimulate sales. For example, IBM apparently tried to stimulate declining sales of its PCjr home computer in the 1980s by extending the length of the credit period in which dealers had to pay for the computers. In making this type of decision, however, a company also must consider its closest competitors. If they lengthen their credit periods, too, every company in the industry may end up having about the same level of sales, a much higher level of receivables investments and costs, and a lower rate of return.

Analyzing the possible effects of an increase in a company's credit period involves comparing the profitability of the increased sales that are expected to occur with the required rate of return on the additional investment in receivables and inventories.

Additional bad-debt losses must also be considered. If a company continues to accept the same quality of accounts under its lengthened credit terms, no significant change in the bad-debt loss ratio should occur.

Cash Discounts. A *cash discount* is offered on the condition that the customer will repay the credit extended within a specified period of time. It is normally expressed as a percentage discount on the net amount of the cost of goods purchased (usually excluding freight and taxes). The length of the discount period is also specified when discount terms are offered. For example, credit terms of *2/10, net 30* mean that the customer can deduct 2 percent of the invoice amount if payment is made within 10 days from the invoice date. If payment is not made by this time, the full invoice amount is due within 30 days from the invoice date. (In some cases, the discount period may begin with the date of shipment or the date of receipt by the customer.) Like the length of the credit period, the cash discount varies among different lines of business.

Cash discounts are offered (or increased) to speed up the collection of accounts receivable and, by extension, reduce a company's level of receivables investment and associated costs. Offsetting these savings or benefits is the cost of the discounts that are taken, which is equal to the lost dollar revenues from the existing unit sales volume.

Collection Effort The collection effort consists of the methods a business employs in attempting to collect payment on past-due accounts. Some commonly used methods include:

➤ Sending notices or letters informing the customer of the past-due status of the account and requesting payment
➤ Telephoning and/or visiting the customer in an effort to obtain payment
➤ Employing a collection agency
➤ Taking legal action against the customer

Although the objectives of the collection effort are to speed up past-due payments and reduce bad-debt losses, a company also must avoid antagonizing normally creditworthy customers who may be past due for some good reason—temporary liquidity problems, for example. A collection effort that is too aggressive may reduce future sales and profits if customers begin buying from other businesses whose collection policies are more lenient.

Monitoring Accounts Receivable

For a company to effectively control its receivables investment, the credit manager must monitor the status and composition of these accounts. An *aging of accounts* is a useful monitoring technique. In an aging analysis, a company's accounts are classified into different categories based on the number of days they are past due. These classifications show both the aggregate amount of receivables and the percentage of the total receivables outstanding in each category. Aging of accounts receivable provides more information than such summary ratios as, for example, the average collection period. Comparing aging schedules at successive points in time (for example, monthly, quarterly, or semiannually) can help the credit manager monitor any changes in the *quality* of the company's accounts.

Evaluating Individual Credit Applicants

Once a company has established its credit and collection policies, it can use them as a basis for evaluating individual credit applicants. In general, the credit evaluation process consists of these main steps:

1. Gathering relevant information on the credit applicant
2. Using the information to evaluate applicant's creditworthiness
3. Deciding on whether or not to extend credit and how much

Gathering Information on the Credit Applicant Information for evaluating the creditworthiness of a customer is available from a variety of sources, including:

Financial Statements. A company can ask a credit applicant to supply various kinds of financial information, such as income statements and balance sheets (preferably audited ones), and possibly even a forecasted budget. This information can be used to evaluate the applicant's financial strength and the applicant's ability to repay credit obligations. If the credit applicant is a company that has publicly held securities, the firm must file periodic financial statements with the Securities and Exchange Commission. These documents are available freely to anyone and do not require the permission of the credit applicant. If the applicant is a privately held company, obtaining financial statements without the applicant's cooperation may be more difficult.

Credit-Reporting Organizations. A number of national and local organizations collect information on the financial position and credit standing of businesses. Other companies and lending institutions that are considering extending credit to a company may obtain information about it from these organizations, usually for a fee.

The most widely known credit-reporting organization is Dun and Bradstreet Credit Services, which provides its subscribers with a credit reference book and written credit reports on individual businesses. D&B's reference book is published bimonthly and contains the names and credit ratings of over three million businesses located in the United States, including manufacturers, wholesalers, retailers, business services, and other types of businesses.

A D&B credit report provides far more detailed information about a company's financial position than the reference book does. A typical report contains a summary of trade credit payments to existing suppliers, which can be extremely valuable to companies that are considering extending credit to a particular company. Also included in a typical report are financial data from the firm's balance sheet and income statement, a review of its banking relationships, historical information about the owners, and a description of its operations, including the location of facilities and the kinds of products sold.

The National Association of Credit Management also fills requests for information on the repayment patterns of specific companies. In addition, a number of other organizations collect and disseminate credit information within given industries, such as the toy and furniture industries, as well as within given geographical areas, such as Chicago and New York.

Banks. Many banks will assist their business customers in obtaining information on the creditworthiness of other businesses. Through its contacts with other banks, a customer's bank often can obtain detailed information on the payment patterns and financial status of the company under investigation and pass this information on to a customer.

Prior Experience with the Customer. A company's experience with a credit customer can be extremely useful when deciding whether to continue extending credit, increase the amount of credit it currently grants to the customer, or both. If, for example, the customer tends to remit payments well beyond the due date and/or if the company must employ expensive collection methods in obtaining payments, the credit analyst should weigh this unfavorable information in making future credit extension decisions.

Analyzing Creditworthiness and Making the Credit Decision Credit analysts ideally should obtain information about an applicant from as many sources as possible, but they also should consider the time and costs involved. Specifically, analysts should weigh the expected returns to be derived from any additional information against the cost involved in obtaining it.

A good way to structure information collection is to proceed sequentially, beginning with the least costly and least time-consuming sources. If the results of this initial check indicate that more information is needed, the analyst can proceed to additional sources. For example, the analyst may begin by consulting the customer's past credit history with the company. If further information is needed, the analyst then can check the D&B reference book and/or ask the applicant to supply financial statements and a list of companies that have extended trade credit to it in the past. Finally, if still more information is needed, the credit analyst can request a D&B credit report on the applicant and/or request credit checks through banks and the applicant's trade creditors.

Because a great deal of information is usually available about a credit applicant, the credit manager must be able to sort through this information and extract the key elements that will enable a reliable overall assessment of the applicant's creditworthiness to be made. There are no magic formulas for making unerring credit decisions, but there are some basic guidelines that one should follow. These are often known as the "five Cs of credit":

➢ *Character* refers to the applicant's willingness or desire to meet credit obligations. Past payment patterns are useful in gauging this aspect of creditworthiness.
➢ *Capacity* refers to the applicant's ability to meet financial obligations. A reasonable estimate of capacity can be obtained by examining the applicant's liquidity position.
➢ *Capital* refers to the applicant's financial strength, particularly with respect to net worth. Evidence about a company's capital can be obtained by examining the balance sheet.
➢ *Collateral* refers to the assets that the applicant may pledge as security for the credit extended to it. Collateral, however, is not a critical consideration for the company offering credit since the objective is to ensure timely repayment of credit, not foreclosing on the pledged assets.
➢ *Conditions* refer to the general economic climate and its effect on the applicant's ability to pay. A good credit risk prospect in prosperous times may be unable to make payments during a recession.

Many credit analysts feel that the first two Cs, character and capacity, are the most important insofar as they help to ensure that the firm considering extending credit will not leave anything important out of the analysis.

Numerical credit scoring systems have been found useful in the area of consumer credit. These allow the credit-granting business to quantitatively rate various financial and personal characteristics of the applicant, such as the length of the time in business, its D&B credit rating, and its current ratio. The total credit score then can be computed based on the characteristics thought to be related to creditworthiness. The applicant's credit score next is compared with those of other applicants, or with a minimally acceptable cutoff score. Although numerical credit scoring systems can be beneficial in credit screening, they can be difficult and expensive to install. Furthermore, the ability to make sound credit decisions ultimately depends on the decision maker's experience and judgment in evaluating the available information.

Comprehension Check Questions

1. Why is the measurement of marginal costs and marginal benefits associated with accounts receivable policy decisions important?

2. What are the marginal benefits and costs of a more liberal credit extension policy—that is, extending to more risky credit customers?

3. Define credit standards, credit terms, and collection effort.

4. What are the "five Cs of credit"?

INVENTORY MANAGEMENT

Like any other asset, the holding of inventories constitutes an investment of funds. Determining the optimal level of inventory investment requires that the benefits and costs (including the opportunity cost of the funds invested) associated with alternative levels be measured and compared. In the next few paragraphs we provide an overview of the role of inventory in a firm's operations and the considerations that go into determining an appropriate inventory management policy.

http:
For more on inventory management topics, visit **http://www.inventoryops. com**

Types of Inventory

Manufacturing firms generally hold three types of inventories:

➤ Raw materials inventory
➤ Work-in-process inventory
➤ Finished goods inventory

Raw Materials Inventory Raw materials inventory consists of items a business purchases for use in its production process. It may consist of basic materials (for example, iron ore for a steel-making operation), manufactured goods (for example, memory chips for a computer assembly operation), or both. Maintaining adequate raw materials inventories provides a company with advantages in both purchasing and production. Specifically, the purchasing department benefits by being able to buy needed items in large quantities and thus take advantage of quantity discounts offered by suppliers. In addition, if rising prices, shortages of specific items, or both are forecasted for the future, maintaining a large stock of raw materials ensures that the company will have adequate supplies at reasonable costs.

Knowing that adequate stocks of raw materials will be available when needed permits the production department to meet production schedules and make the most efficient use of its personnel and facilities. Therefore, there are a number of valid reasons why a company's purchasing and production departments will want to maintain large inventories of raw materials. However, as we shall learn in the next few paragraphs, there are also costs associated with maintaining larger inventories of raw materials.

Work-in-Process Inventory Work-in-process inventory consists of all items that presently are in the production cycle at some intermediate stage of completion. For example, they currently may be undergoing some type of operation (such as assembly or painting); they may be in transit between operations; or they may be stored somewhere, awaiting the next step in the production cycle.

Finished Goods Inventory Finished goods inventory consists of those items that have completed the production cycle and are available for sale. With the exception of large-scale, specialized types of equipment—such as industrial machinery, military armaments, jet airplanes, and nuclear reactors, which normally are contracted for before they are produced—most consumer and industrial products are manufactured and stored in inventory to meet forecasted future sales.

Keeping enough finished goods inventories on hand provides significant benefits for both the marketing and the production departments. From marketing's perspective, large finished goods inventories enable it to fill orders promptly, minimize lost sales, and avoid shipment delays due to stockouts. From production's standpoint, maintaining a large finished goods inventory permits items to be manufactured in large production runs, which helps keep unit production costs low by spreading fixed setup expenses over large volumes of output.

Optimal Inventory Management Policy

Proper inventory management policy requires that due consideration be given to costs associated with maintaining an inventory balance. Some of these costs increase with the inventory level while other costs decline with the inventory level. These costs include:

- ➢ Ordering costs
- ➢ Carrying costs
- ➢ Stockout costs

Ordering Costs *Ordering costs* represent all the costs of placing and receiving an order. When a company is ordering from an external source, these include the costs of preparing the purchase requisition, expediting the order (for example, long-distance calls and follow-up letters), receiving and inspecting the shipment, and handling payment. Such factors as an item's price and engineering complexity also affect its ordering costs. The more frequently an item is ordered, the greater the ordering costs that are incurred. Thus, holding everything else constant, maintaining lower levels of inventory for a particular item would mean that the item would have to be replenished more frequently, resulting in greater ordering costs.

Carrying Costs *Carrying costs* constitute all the costs of holding items in inventory for a given period of time. Components of this cost include:

- ➢ Storage and handling costs
- ➢ Obsolescence and deterioration costs
- ➢ The opportunity cost of funds invested in inventories

Storage and handling costs include the cost of warehouse space, such as the rent paid for the space. Storage and handling costs also include depreciation on the inventory handling equipment, such as conveyors and forklift trucks, and the wages and salaries paid to warehouse workers and supervisors.

Inventories are valuable only if they can be sold. Obsolescence costs represent the decline in inventory value caused by technological or style changes that make the existing product less salable. Most personal computer manufacturers, for example, maintain very low levels of raw materials (e.g., processor chips) because of the very high cost of obsolescence. Deterioration costs represent the decline in value caused by changes in the physical quality of the inventory, such as spoilage and breakage.

The opportunity cost of funds invested in inventories is measured by the required rate of return on these funds. Because inventory investments are likely to be of *average risk*, the overall weighted cost of capital should be used to measure the cost of these funds. If it is felt that inventories constitute an investment with either an above-average or below-average risk, some adjustment in the weighted cost of capital may be necessary to account for this difference in risk.

In sum the higher the inventory balances maintained by a firm, the higher are the carrying costs.

Stockout Costs *Stockout costs* are incurred whenever a business is unable to fill orders because the demand for an item is greater than the amount currently available in inventory. When a stockout in raw materials occurs, for example, stockout costs include the expenses of placing special orders (back ordering) and expediting incoming orders, in addition to the costs of any resulting production delays. A stockout in finished goods inventory may result in the immediate loss of profits if customers decide to purchase the product from a competitor, and in potential long-term losses if customers decide to order from other companies in the future. Stockout costs therefore decrease with higher inventory balances as the probability of their occurrence drops.

In summary, stockout costs and ordering costs decline as larger inventory balances are maintained. On the other hand, carrying costs increase with larger inventory balances. Thus maintaining an optimal inventory management policy requires that the firm minimize the sum total of the ordering, carrying, and stockout costs.

Quantitative approaches to identifying the optimal inventory policy are covered in courses in production management/operations management and supply chain management.

Just-in-Time Inventory Management Systems One of the most significant strides in the practice of inventory management in the last decade has been the adoption of *just-in-time (JIT) inventory management systems.* JIT inventory management techniques are part of a manufacturing approach that seeks to reduce the company's operating cycle and associated costs by eliminating wasteful procedures. JIT inventory systems are based on the idea that all required inventory items should be supplied to the production process at *exactly the right time and in exactly the right quantities.* This approach was first developed by the Toyota Motor Company in the 1950s. However it was only with the advent of the Internet and associated improvements in computer software and telecommunications system that the adoption of JIT methods become pervasive. The use of a JIT inventory system requires close coordination between a company and its suppliers, because any disruption in the flow of parts and materials from the supplier can result in costly production delays and lost sales.

Dell Computer Corporation is regarded as one of the best examples of JIT inventory management in practice. In 2002, for example, Dell's inventory was equal to just 3 days' worth of sales. Dell also benefits from the fact that they follow a build-to-order marketing model. That is, computers are built only in response to an order; consequently, the firm does not maintain any finished goods inventory. The combination of JIT inventory practices and a build-to-order business model has meant that Dell can operate with a minimum of raw materials and finished goods inventory. The automotive industry, too, has benefited from developments in the adoption of JIT methods. General Motors' inventory in 2002 amounted to 23.7 days worth of sales compared to 32.7 days in 1992. Much of the decline can be attributed to increased implementation of JIT methods.

Comprehension Check Questions

1. Why is it necessary to hold inventory?
2. What are ordering, carrying, and stockout costs of inventory?
3. Explain the benefits of just-in-time inventory management systems.

Summary

- A firm's operating cycle is equal to the sum of its inventory and receivables conversion periods. The cash conversion cycle is equal to the operating cycle minus the payables deferral period. Generally, the longer the cash conversion cycle the larger the investment in the working capital.

- Working capital (or net working capital) is the difference between current assets and current liabilities. Working capital policy is concerned with determining the aggregate amount and composition of a firm's current assets and current liabilities.

- Working capital decisions affect both the expected profitability and the risk of a firm. In this context, risk refers to the probability that the firm will encounter financial difficulties, such as the inability to meet current financial obligations.

- When the level of working capital is increased, both the expected profitability and the risk are lowered. Similarly, when the level of working capital is decreased, both the expected profitability and the risk are increased.

- When the proportion of short-term debt used is increased, both the expected profitability and the risk are increased. Similarly, when the proportion of short-term debt used is decreased, both the expected profitability and the risk are decreased.

- Effective working capital policy requires that the working capital investment and financing decisions be analyzed simultaneously so that their joint impact on the firm's expected profitability and risk can be evaluated.

- A firm holds liquid asset balances for the following primary reasons:

  To conduct transactions
  For precautionary purposes
  To meet future requirements
  For speculative reasons

- A firm's optimal liquid asset balance reflects risk and return trade-offs and depends on both the opportunity cost of holding excess balances and the "shortage" costs associated with not having enough needed cash available.

- The primary objective in controlling cash collections is to reduce the delay between the time when the customer mails the payment and when it becomes a collected balance. Methods for reducing collection time include decentralized collection centers and concentration banks, lockboxes, wire transfers, depository transfer checks, special handling of large remittances, and the use of preauthorized checks.

- The primary objective in controlling cash disbursements is to slow payments and keep the firm's funds in the bank as long as possible. Techniques for slowing disbursements include scheduling and centralizing payments (zero-balance systems), using drafts rather than checks, and maximizing check-clearing float.

- Cash reserves that are not immediately needed are invested in marketable securities. The primary criteria a firm should use in selecting marketable securities include default risk, marketability (or liquidity), maturity date, and rate of return.

- Accounts receivable arise whenever a firm extends credit to its customers.

- Decisions on accounts receivable policy are associated with marginal benefits and marginal costs. A more liberal credit policy normally leads to marginal benefits in the form of additional profits from increased sales. However, there are also marginal costs associated with a more liberal credit policy. These costs consist of the opportunity cost of investing additional funds in accounts receivable and inventory, any additional credit checking and collection costs, and increased bad-debt expenses. Thus, any change in accounts receivable policy must be based on a careful analysis of marginal benefits and marginal costs of undertaking the policy change. Only if marginal benefits exceed the marginal costs should the change be made.

➤ Accounts receivable management involves decisions on three credit policy variables:

   1. Credit standards. Credit standards are the criteria a business uses to screen its credit applicants.

   2. Credit terms. Credit terms are the conditions under which customers are required to repay the credit extended to them. Credit terms specify the length of the credit period and the cash discount (if any) given for early payment.

   3. Collection effort. The collection effort represents the methods used in attempting to collect payment from past-due customers.

➤ The five Cs of credit are Character, Capacity, Capital, Collateral, and Conditions. These criteria are useful credit-screening guidelines in deciding who to extend credit to and how much.

➤ Firms maintain three types of inventory: raw materials, work-in-process, and finished goods.

➤ Inventory-related costs include ordering costs, carrying costs, and stockout costs. Ordering costs include all the costs of placing and receiving an order. Carrying costs include the various costs of holding items in inventory, including the opportunity cost of funds invested in inventory. Stockout costs are the costs incurred when demand exceeds available inventory, such as lost profits.

➤ High inventory balances reduce ordering costs and stockout costs but are associated with high carrying costs. Optimal inventory policy requires that the sum total of these costs be minimized.

➤ Just-in-time inventory models are based on the concept that required inventory items are supplied exactly as needed by production. Successful implementation of just-in-time models can reduce substantially inventory investment.

Questions and Topics for Discussion

1. Why does the typical firm need to make investments in working capital?

2. Define and describe the difference between the operating cycle and cash conversion cycle for a typical manufacturing company.

3. Discuss the profitability versus risk trade-offs associated with alternative levels of working capital investment.

4. Describe the difference between permanent current assets and fluctuating current assets.

5. Describe the matching approach for meeting the financing needs of a company. What is the primary difficulty in implementing this approach?

6. Discuss the profitability versus risk trade-offs associated with alternative combinations of short-term and long-term debt used in financing a company's assets.

7. a. Which of the following working capital financing policies subjects the firm to a greater risk?

   i. Financing permanent current assets with short-term debt

   ii. Financing fluctuating current assets with long-term debt

   b. Which policy will produce the higher expected profitability?

8. Define the following terms:
   a. Disbursement float
   b. Collection float
   c. Lockbox
   d. Wire transfer
   e. Depository transfer check.
9. What are the primary reasons a firm holds a liquid asset balance?
10. Define float and describe the difference between disbursement float and collection float.
11. Describe the methods available to a firm for expediting the collection of cash.
12. Describe the techniques available to a firm for slowing disbursements.
13. What are the primary criteria in selecting marketable securities for inclusion in a firm's portfolio?
14. What are the marginal returns and costs associated with a more liberal extension of credit to a firm's customers?
15. What are the major credit policy variables a firm can use to control its level of receivables investment?
16. Describe the five *C*s of credit used in evaluating the creditworthiness of a credit applicant.
17. Describe the three types of inventory held by manufacturing companies.
18. What are ordering, carrying, and stockout costs?
19. Describe the just-in-time inventory management system.

Self-Test Problems

Note: When converting from annual data to daily data or vice versa, assume there are 365 days per year.

ST1. The Stowe Manufacturing Company's balance sheet and income statement for last year are as follows:

Balance Sheet (in Millions of Dollars)

Assets		Liabilities and Equity	
Cash and marketable securities	$ 887	Accounts payable	$ 724
Accounts receivable	2,075	Accrued liabilities	
Inventories*	2,120	(salaries and benefits)	332
Other current assets	300	Other current liabilities	1,665
Total current assets	$5,382	Total current liabilities	2,721
Plant and equipment (net)	3,707	Long-term debt and other	
Other assets	687	liabilities	1,677
Total assets	$9,776	Common stock	296
		Retained earnings	5,082
		Total stockholders' equity	$5,378
		Total liabilities and equity	**$9,776**

*Assume that average inventory over the year was $2,120 million, that is, the same as ending inventory.

Income Statement (in Millions of Dollars)

Net sales*	$11,990
Cost of sales	6,946
Selling, general, and administrative expenses	2,394
Other expenses	581
Total expenses	$ 9,921
Earnings before taxes	2,069
Taxes	825
Earnings after taxes (net income)	$ 1,244

All sales are credit sales.

Determine the length of Stowe's

a. Inventory conversion period

b. Receivables conversion period

c. Operating cycle

d. Payables deferral period

e. Cash conversion cycle

ST2. The White Oak Company's annual sales are $219 million. An average of 9 days elapses between when a customer mails its payment and when the funds become usable by the firm.

a. If the company could speed up the collection of funds by 2 days, what would be the increase in the firm's average cash balance?

b. Assuming that these additional funds can be invested in marketable securities that yield 7 percent per year, determine the increase in White Oak's annual (pretax) earnings.

ST3. Builders Circle, a hardware and building supplies company, processes all its customer credit card payments at its Atlanta headquarters. A Boston bank has offered to process the payments from Builders Circle customers located in the New England region for $50,000 per year plus $0.20 per payment. No compensating balance will be required. Under this lockbox arrangement, the average mailing time for payments would be reduced from 3 days to 1.5 days. Check processing and clearing time would be reduced from 5 days to 2. Annual collections from the New England region are $292 million. The total number of payments received annually is 600,000 (an average of 50,000 credit cardholders × 12 payments per year). Assume that any funds released by this lockbox arrangement can be invested by Builders Circle to earn 10 percent per year before taxes. The establishment of a lockbox system for the New England region will reduce payment processing costs at its Atlanta headquarters by $40,000 per year. Using this information, determine

a. The amount of funds released by this lockbox arrangement

b. The annual (pretax) earnings on the released funds

c. The annual fee that Builders Circle must pay the Boston bank for processing the payments

d. The annual *net* (pretax) benefits Builders Circle will receive by establishing this lockbox arrangement with the Boston bank

Problems

Note: When converting annual data to daily data or vice versa in these problems, assume there are 365 days per year.

BASIC

1. The Fisher Apparel Company balance sheet for the year ended 20X6 is as follows:

December 31, 20X6 (in Thousands of Dollars)

Assets

Cash		$ 3,810
Marketable securities		2,700
Accounts receivable		27,480
Inventories		41,295
Plant and equipment	$64,650	
Less Accumulated depreciation	17,100	
Net plant and equipment		47,550
Total assets		**$122,835**

Liabilities and Stockholders' Equity

Accounts payable	$ 14,582
Current portion of long-term debt	3,000
Accrued wage	1,200
Accrued taxes	3,600
Other current liabilities	2,200
Long-term debt	33,000
Common stock ($10 par)	19,500
Capital contributed in excess of par	15,000
Retained earnings	30,753
Total liabilities and stockholders' equity	**$122,835**

a. What is Fisher's investment in current assets?

b. Determine Fisher's working capital investment.

c. Determine Fisher's current ratio.

d. Determine Fisher's return on stockholders' equity if its 20X6 earnings after tax are $10,000(000).

INTERMEDIATE

2. The Garcia Industries balance sheet and income statement for the year ended 20X5 are as follows:

Balance Sheet (in Millions of Dollars)

Assets		Liabilities and Stockholders' Equity	
Cash	$ 6.0	Accounts payable	$10.0
Accounts receivable	14.0	Salaries, benefits, and payroll taxes payable	2.0
Inventories*	12.0	Other current liabilities	10.0
Fixed assets, net	40.0	Long-term debt	12.0
	$72.0	Stockholders' equity	38.0
			$72.0

*The average inventory over the past 2 years also equals $12.0 million.

Income Statement (in Millions of Dollars)

Net sales	$100.0
Cost of sales	60.0
Selling, general, and administrative expenses	20.0
Other expenses	15.0
Earnings after tax	$ 5.0

a. Determine the length of the inventory conversion period.

b. Determine the length of the receivables conversion period.

c. Determine the length of the operating cycle.

d. Determine the length of the payables deferral period.

e. Determine the length of the cash conversion cycle.

f. What is the meaning of the number you calculated in (e)?

3. Wilson Electric Company, a manufacturer of various types of electrical equipment, is examining its working capital investment policy for next year. Projected fixed assets and current liabilities are $20 million and $18 million, respectively. Sales and EBIT are partially a function of the company's investment in working capital—particularly its investment in inventories and receivables. Wilson is considering the following three different working capital investment policies:

Working Capital Investment Policy	Investment in Current Assets (in Millions of Dollars)	Projected Sales (in Millions of Dollars)	EBIT (in Millions of Dollars)
Aggressive (small investment in current assets)	$28	$59	$5.9
Moderate (moderate investment in current assets)	30	60	6.0
Conservative (large investment in current assets)	32	61	6.1

a. Determine the following for each of the working capital investment policies:

   i. Rate of return on total assets (that is, EBIT/total assets)

   ii. Net working capital position

   iii. Current ratio

b. Describe the profitability versus risk trade-offs of these three policies.

4. Reynolds Equipment Company is investigating the use of various combinations of short-term and long-term debt in financing its assets. Assume that the company has decided to employ $30 million in current assets, along with $35 million in fixed assets, in its operations next year. Given this level of current assets, anticipated sales and EBIT, for next year are $60 million and $6 million, respectively. The company's income tax rate is 40 percent. Stockholders' equity will be used to finance $40 million of its assets, with the remainder being financed by short-term and long-term debt. Reynolds is considering implementing one of the following financing policies:

Financing Policy	Amount of Short-Term Debt (in Millions of Dollars)	Interest Rate LTD (%)	Interest Rate STD (%)
Aggressive (large amount of short-term debt)	$24	8.5	5.5
Moderate (moderate amount of short-term debt)	18	8.0	5.0
Conservative (small amount of short-term debt)	12	7.5	4.5

a. Determine the following for each of the financing policies:

    i. Expected rate of return on stockholders' equity.

    ii. Net working capital position.

    iii. Current ratio.

b. Evaluate the profitability versus risk trade-offs of these three policies.

INTERMEDIATE

5. Superior Brands, Inc. wishes to analyze the *joint impact* of its working capital investment and financing policies on shareholder return and risk. The company has $40 million in fixed assets. Also, the firm's financial structure consists of short-term and long-term debt and common equity. Superior wishes to maintain a debt-to-total assets ratio of 50 percent, where debt consists of both short-term and long-term sources. The company's tax rate is 40 percent. The following information was developed for three different policies under consideration:

Working Capital Investment and Financing Policy	Investment in Current Assets (in Millions of Dollars)	Amount of STD (in Millions of Dollars)	Projected Sales (in Millions of Dollars)	EBIT (in Millions of Dollars)	Interest Rate LTD (%)	Interest Rate STD (%)
Aggressive	$56	$48	$118	$11.8	9.5	6.5
Moderate	60	36	120	12.0	9.0	6.0
Conservative	64	24	122	12.2	8.5	5.5

a. Determine the following for each of the three working capital investment and financing policies:

    i. Expected rate of return on stockholders' equity

    ii. Net working capital position

    iii. Current ratio

b. Evaluate the profitability versus risk trade-offs associated with these three policies.

CHALLENGE

6. Nguyen Enterprises is considering two alternative working capital investment and financing policies. Policy A requires the firm to keep its current assets at 65 percent of forecasted sales and to finance 70 percent of its debt requirements with long-term debt (and 30 percent with short-term debt). Policy B, on the other hand, requires the firm to keep its current assets at 40 percent of forecasted sales and to finance 40 percent of its debt requirements with long-term debt (and 60 percent with short-term debt). Forecasted sales for next year are $20 million. Earnings before interest and taxes are projected to be 15 percent of sales. The firm's corporate income tax rate is 40 percent. Its fixed assets total $10 million. The firm desires to maintain its existing financial structure, which consists of 50 percent debt and 50 percent equity. Interest rates on short- and long-term debt are 12 and 15 percent, respectively.

a. Determine the expected rate of return on equity next year for Nguyen under each of the working capital policies.

b. Which policy is riskier? Cite specific evidence to support this contention.

7. The Hopewell Pharmaceutical Company's balance sheet and income state- **INTERMEDIATE** ment for last year are as follows:

Balance Sheet (in Millions of Dollars)

Assets		Liabilities and Equity	
Cash and marketable securities	$1,100	Accounts payable	$ 900
Accounts receivable	1,300	Accrued liabilities	
Inventories*	800	(salaries and benefits)	300
Other current assets	200	Other current liabilities	700
Total current assets	$3,400	Total current liabilities	$1,900
Plant and equipment (net)	2,300	Long-term debt and other	
Other assets	1,000	liabilities	1,000
Total assets	**$6,700**	Common stock	1,800
		Retained earnings	2,000
		Total stockholders' equity	$3,800
		Total liabilities and equity	**$6,700**

Assume that average inventory over the year was $800 million, that is, the same as ending inventory.

Income Statement (in Millions of Dollars)

Net sales	$6,500
Cost of sales	1,500
Selling, general, and administrative expenses	2,500
Other expenses	800
Total expenses	$4,800
Earnings before taxes	1,700
Taxes	680
Earnings after taxes (net income)	$1,020

a. Determine Hopewell's cash conversion cycle.

b. Give an interpretation of the value computed in (a).

8. Brakenridge Industries is considering the following two alternative working **INTERMEDIATE** capital investment and financing policies:

	Policy A	Policy B
Current assets ÷ Sales	50%	40%
Short-term debt ÷ Total debt	40%	50%

Forecasted sales next year are $30 million. EBIT is projected at 25 percent of sales. Fixed assets are $30 million. The firm's income tax rate is 40 percent. Brakenridge desires to maintain its current capital structure, which consists of 50 percent debt and 50 percent equity. Interest rates on the company's short-term and long-term debt are 9 and 12 percent, respectively.

a. Determine the expected rate of return on equity capital under each of the working capital policies.

b. Which working capital policy is riskier? Explain.

INTERMEDIATE   **9.** The Butler-Huron Company's balance sheet and income statement for last year are as follows:

Balance Sheet (in Millions of Dollars)

Assets		Liabilities and Equity	
Cash and marketable securities	$ 103	Accounts payable	$1,166
Accounts receivable*	1,138	Accrued liabilities	
Inventories**	1,827	(salaries and benefits)	536
Other current assets	39	Other current liabilities	493
Total current assets	$3,107	Total current liabilities	$2,195
Plant and equipment (net)	3,523	Long-term debt and other	
Other assets	54	liabilities	2,736
Total assets	**$6,684**	Common stock	105
		Retained earnings	1,648
		Total stockholders' equity	$1,753
		Total liabilities and equity	**$6,684**

*Assume that all sales are credit sales.

**Assume that average inventory over the year was $1,827 million, that is, the same as ending inventory.

Income Statement (in Millions of Dollars)

Net sales	$13,644
Cost of sales	9,890
Selling, general, and administrative expenses	2,264
Other expenses	812
Total expenses	$12,966
Earnings before taxes	678
Taxes	268
Earnings after taxes (net income)	$ 410

a. Determine Butler-Huron's cash conversion cycle.

b. Determine Butler-Huron's cash conversion cycle assuming that 75 percent of annual sales are credit sales (i.e., 25 percent represent cash sales).

c. Determine Butler-Huron's cash conversion cycle assuming that 50 percent of annual sales are credit sales.

BASIC   **10.** Dallas Instrument Company's sales average $3 million per day.

a. If Dallas could reduce the time between customers' mailing their payments and the funds' becoming collected balances by 2.5 days, what would be the increase in the firm's average cash balance?

b. Assuming that these additional funds can be invested in marketable securities to yield 5.5 percent per annum, determine the annual increase in Dallas' (pretax) earnings.

BASIC   **11.** Exman Company performed a study of its billing and collection procedures and found that an average of 8 days elapses between the time when a customer's payment is received and when the funds become usable by the firm. The firm's *annual* sales are $540 million.

a. Assuming that Exman could reduce the time required to process customer payments by 1.5 days, determine the increase in the firm's average cash balance.

b. Assuming that these additional funds could be used to reduce the firm's outstanding bank loans (current interest rate is 8 percent) by an equivalent amount, determine the annual pretax savings in interest expenses.

12. Great Lakes Oil Company currently processes all its credit card payments at its domestic headquarters in Chicago. The firm is considering establishing a lockbox arrangement with a Los Angeles bank to process its payments from 10 western states (California, Nevada, Arizona, Utah, Oregon, Washington, Montana, Wyoming, Colorado, and Idaho). Under the arrangement, the average mailing time for customer payments from the western region would be reduced from 3 days to 1.5 days, whereas check processing and clearing time would be reduced from 6 days to 2.5 days. Annual collections from the western region are $180 million. The total number of payments received annually is 4.8 million (an average of 400,000 credit card customers × 12 payments per year). The Los Angeles bank will process the payments for an annual fee of $75,000 plus $0.05 per payment. No compensating balance will be required. Assume that the funds released by the lockbox arrangement can be invested elsewhere in the firm to yield 10 percent before taxes. The establishment of a lockbox system for the western region will reduce payment-processing costs at the Chicago office by $50,000 per year. Using this information, determine the following:

CHALLENGE

a. The amount of funds released by the lockbox arrangement

b. The annual (pretax) earnings on the released funds

c. The annual fee Great Lakes Oil must pay to the Los Angeles bank for processing the payments

d. The annual net (pretax) benefits Great Lakes Oil will receive by establishing this lockbox arrangement with the Los Angeles bank

Great Lakes Oil also has received a proposal from a Salt Lake City bank to set up a lockbox system for the firm. Average mailing time for checks in the western region would be reduced to 2 days under the proposal from the Salt Lake City bank, and check processing and clearing time would average 2.5 days. The Salt Lake City bank would not charge any fees for processing the payments, but it would require Great Lakes Oil to maintain a $1.5 million average compensating balance with the bank—funds that normally would be invested elsewhere in the firm (yielding 10 percent) and not kept in a noninterest-bearing checking account.

e. Determine the annual *net* (pretax) benefits to Great Lakes Oil of establishing a lockbox system with the Salt Lake City bank.

f. Which of the two lockbox systems (if any) should the firm select?

13. Japanese Motors, a major importer of foreign automobiles, has a subsidiary (Japanese Motor Credit Company, or JMCC) that finances dealer inventories, as well as retail installment purchases of the company's cars. With respect to the financing of retail purchases, JMCC currently employs a centralized billing and collection system. Once a customer's credit has been approved at one of the subsidiary's 50 local branch offices, the information is forwarded to JMCC headquarters (located in Los Angeles), and the customer is issued a book of payment coupons. Each month during the life of the installment contract, the customer mails a coupon stub along with the payment to the Los Angeles office. The average mailing, processing, and check-clearing time with the present collection system is 8 days.

INTERMEDIATE

In an effort to reduce this collection time, JMCC is considering establishing a decentralized collection system. Under this system, customers would be instructed to mail their payments to the nearest local branch office, which would then deposit the checks in a local bank and report this information to JMCC headquarters in Los Angeles. As the checks clear in the local banks, funds would be sent each day to JMCC's central bank in Los Angeles. This decentralized collection system would reduce both mailing time and check-clearing time and reduce the average collection time to 5 days.

JMCC's annual installment collections are $900 million. Implementation of the decentralized collection system is expected to reduce collection costs at the Los Angeles headquarters by $100,000 a year compared with the currently employed centralized collection system. However, branch office collection costs are expected to *rise* by $225,000 if the decentralized system is implemented. JMCC's Los Angeles bank currently requires the firm to maintain a $250,000 balance as compensation for depositing customer payments. Compensating balances at the 50 local banks that JMCC would employ with the decentralized collection system are expected to total $500,000. Any funds released under the decentralized collections system would be used to reduce the firm's debt, which currently carries an interest rate of 7.5 percent.

Using this information, determine the annual *net* pretax benefits JMCC would realize by implementing a decentralized collection system.

INTERMEDIATE **14.** J-Mart, a nationwide department store chain, processes all its credit sales payments at its suburban Detroit headquarters. The firm is considering the implementation of a lockbox collection system with an Atlanta bank to process monthly payments from its southeastern region. Annual credit sales collections from the region are $60 million. The establishment of the lockbox system would reduce mailing, processing, and check-clearing time from 8 days currently to 3.5 days, reduce company processing costs by $25,000 per year, and reduce the compensating balance of its Detroit bank by $200,000. The Atlanta bank would not charge any fee for the lockbox service but would require J-Mart to maintain a $500,000 compensating balance. Funds released by the lockbox arrangement could be invested elsewhere in the firm to earn 15 percent before taxes. Determine the following:

a. The amount of funds released by the lockbox arrangement

b. The annual (pretax) earnings on the released funds

c. The annual net (pretax) benefits to J-Mart of establishing the lockbox system with the Atlanta bank

INTERMEDIATE **15.** Peterson Electronics uses a decentralized collection system whereby customers mail their payments to one of six regional collection centers. The checks are deposited each working day in the collection center's local bank, and a depository transfer check for the amount of the deposit is mailed to the firm's concentration bank in New York. An average of 5 days elapse between the time the checks are deposited in the local bank and the time the funds become collected funds (and available for disbursements) at the concentration bank. Peterson is considering using wire transfers instead of depository transfer checks in moving funds from the six collection centers to its concentration bank. Wire transfers would reduce the elapsed time by 3 days. Depository transfer checks cost $0.50 (including postage), and wire transfers cost $10. Assume there are 250 working days per year. Peterson can earn 7 percent before taxes on any funds that are released through more efficient collection techniques.

Determine the net (pretax) benefit to Peterson of using wire transfers if annual sales are

a. $15 million

b. $75 million

Suppose Peterson is considering using *electronic* depository transfer checks, rather than mail depository transfer checks, to move funds from its six collection centers to its concentration bank. Electronic depository transfer checks would *reduce* collection time by 2 days and would cost $2.50 each. Determine the net (pretax) benefit to Peterson of using electronic depository transfer checks if annual sales are

c. $15 million

d. $75 million

CHAPTER
17 Management of Current Liabilities

In the previous chapter we learned that working capital management is concerned with managing current assets *and* current liabilities. The last chapter examined in detail the management of current assets; now we explore the role of current liabilities in a firm's operations. A primary focus of this chapter is the major sources of *short-term credit*—all of a company's debt obligations that *originally* were scheduled for repayment within 1 year. Short-term credit may be either unsecured or secured. In the case of unsecured short-term debt, a firm obtains credit from the lender without having to pledge any specific assets as collateral, and the lender depends primarily on the cash-generating ability of the firm to repay the debt. If the firm becomes insolvent and declares bankruptcy, the unsecured lender usually stands little chance of recovering all or even a significant portion of the amount owed.

In the case of secured short-term debt, the borrower pledges certain specified assets—such as accounts receivable, inventory, or fixed assets—as collateral. If the borrower defaults on the loan or otherwise fails to honor the terms of the agreement, the lender can seize and sell the collateral to recover the amount owed. Thus, the lender in a secured short-term debt agreement has two potential sources of loan repayment: the firm's cash-generating ability and the collateral value of the pledged assets.

Short-term lenders can be classified as either cash-flow lenders or asset-based lenders, depending upon how they view the two potential sources of loan repayment. *Cash-flow lenders* look upon the borrower's future cash flows as the primary source of loan repayment and the borrower's assets as a secondary source of repayment. *Asset-based lenders* tend to make riskier loans than cash-flow lenders, and as a result, they place much greater emphasis on the value of the borrower's collateral. Generally, large, low-leveraged companies with good expected cash flows are able to borrow from cash-flow lenders, such as commercial banks, at relatively low rates. Smaller, highly leveraged businesses with more uncertain future cash flows often have to borrow on a secured basis from asset-based lenders, such as commercial finance companies, at relatively high rates.

In general, companies prefer to borrow funds on an unsecured basis, because the added administrative costs involved in pledging assets as security raise the cost of the loan to the borrower. In addition, secured borrowing agreements can restrict a company's future borrowing. Many companies, particularly small ones, are not able to obtain unsecured credit, however. For example, a company may be financially weak or too new to justify an unsecured loan, or it may want more credit than the lender is willing to give on an unsecured basis. In any of these circumstances, the company either must provide collateral or it will not receive the loan.

The short-term credit sources available to a company can be either spontaneous or negotiated. Spontaneous sources, which include trade credit, accrued expenses, and deferred income, are discussed in upcoming sections. Later sections of this chapter consider the various negotiated sources, such as bank credit, commercial paper, receivables loans, and inventory loans.

Before studying in detail the sources of short-term financing, we start with a discussion of estimating the cost of short-term funds. Specifically, we show how to calculate the annual financing cost (AFC) and the effective annual percentage rate (EAPR) for various sources of short-term debt.

Chapter Objectives

After reading this chapter, you should have an understanding of the following:

1. Spontaneous and negotiated sources of financing

2. Secured and unsecured sources of short-term borrowing

3. Estimating the costs of various sources of short-term capital

COST OF SHORT-TERM FUNDS

The cost of borrowed funds can be estimated two ways: the *annual financing cost (AFC)* and the effective annual percentage rate (EAPR). AFC is defined as:

$$\text{AFC} = \frac{\text{Interest costs } + \text{ Fees}}{\text{Usable funds}} \times \frac{365}{\text{Maturity (days)}} \tag{17.1}$$

Note that the numerator of the first term on the right-hand side of the equation captures the expenses associated with the loan, and it includes interest expenses as well as fees. Short-term financing sources often involve fees in addition to the interest costs. Also, note that the denominator of the first term is expressed in terms of *usable funds* rather than the total amount of the loan. This is so (as explained later in the chapter) because some of the money from a particular short-term financing source actually may not be available for a company to use. The second term on the right-hand side of the equation, 365/Maturity (days), converts the financing cost to an annual rate.

The annual financing cost calculated using Equation 17.1 is only an approximation to the *effective annual percentage rate*, or *EAPR*, of a loan. Equation 17.1 does

 **Finance in the News**

Click on this button at **http://finance. swlearning.com** *and select Short-term Financial Management for articles on this topic.*

not consider compounding and slightly understates the EAPR. Also, Equation 17.1 is normally used for financing sources of 1 year or less. The following equation gives the EAPR for a short-term financing source:

$$(17.2) \qquad EAPR = \left(1 + \frac{\text{Interest costs} + \text{Fees}}{\text{Usable funds}}\right)^{m} - 1$$

where m is the number of times per year compounding occurs. The EAPR of a loan is the internal rate of return between the funds received and the funds paid back.

To illustrate the use of Equations 17.1 and 17.2, consider a 6-month, $10,000 loan that incurs $500 of interest. If we assume that principal is paid only at maturity and there are 182 days in the 6-month period, the annual financing cost is calculated, using Equation 17.1, as follows:

$$AFC = \frac{\$500}{\$10,000} \times \frac{365}{182}$$
$$= 0.1003 \text{ or } 10.03\%$$

The loan's EAPR is determined as follows, using Equation 17.2:

$$EAPR = \left(1 + \frac{\$500}{\$10,000}\right)^{365/182} - 1$$
$$= 0.1028 \text{ or } 10.28\%$$

The annual financing cost percentage closely approximates the EAPR, unless the number of compounding periods is large.

Equation 17.1 is used throughout this chapter to calculate the annual financing cost of the various short-term financing sources available to a firm.

TRADE CREDIT

Whenever a business receives merchandise ordered from a supplier and then is permitted to wait a specified period of time before having to pay, it is receiving trade credit. In the aggregate, trade credit is the most important source of short-term financing for business firms. Smaller businesses in particular usually rely heavily on trade credit to finance their operations, because they often are unable to obtain funds from banks or other lenders in the financial markets.

Most trade credit is extended on an open account basis. A firm sends a purchase order to a supplier, who then evaluates the firm's creditworthiness using various information sources and decision criteria. If the supplier decides to extend the firm credit, it ships the ordered merchandise to the firm, along with an invoice describing the contents of the shipment, the total amount due, and the terms of sale. When the firm accepts the merchandise shipped by the supplier, it in effect agrees to pay the amount due as specified by the terms of sale on the invoice. Once it has been established, trade credit becomes almost automatic and is subject to only periodic reviews by the supplier. Open account trade credit appears on the buyer's balance sheet as accounts payable and on the seller's balance sheet as accounts receivable.

Credit Terms

Credit terms, or terms of sale, specify the conditions under which a business is required to repay the credit that a supplier has extended to it. These conditions include the length and the beginning date of the credit period, the cash discount (if any) given for prompt repayment, and any special terms, such as seasonal datings.

Cost of Trade Credit

Trade credit is considered a *spontaneous source of financing*, because it normally expands as the volume of a company's purchases increases. For example, suppose a company experiences increased demand for its products. As a result, the company increases purchases from suppliers by 20 percent from an average of $10,000 per day to an average of $12,000 per day. Assuming that these purchases are made on credit terms of *net 30* and that the company waits until the last day of the credit period to make payment, its average accounts payable outstanding (trade credit) automatically will increase by 20 percent from $300,000 ($10,000 × 30) to $360,000 ($12,000 × 30).

Because the use of trade credit is flexible, informal, and relatively easy to obtain, it is an attractive source of financing for virtually all firms, especially new and smaller firms. To make intelligent use of trade credit, however, a firm should consider the associated costs. Unlike other sources of financing, such as bank loans and bonds, which include explicit interest charges, the cost of trade credit is not always readily apparent. It may appear to be *cost-free* because of the lack of interest charges, but this reasoning can lead to incorrect financing decisions.

Obviously, someone has to bear the cost of trade credit. In extending trade credit, the supplier incurs the cost of the funds invested in accounts receivable, plus the cost of any cash discounts that are taken. Normally, the supplier passes on all or part of these costs to its customers implicitly as part of the purchase price of the merchandise, depending on market supply and demand conditions. If a company is in a position to pay cash for purchases, it may consider trying to avoid these implicit costs by negotiating lower prices with suppliers.

If the terms of sale include a cash discount, the firm must decide whether or not to take it. If the firm takes the cash discount, it forgoes the credit offered by the supplier beyond the end of the discount period. Assuming that the firm takes the cash discount and wants to make maximum use of the credit offered by suppliers, it should pay its bills on the last day of the discount period. Under these conditions, trade credit does represent a *cost-free* source of financing to the firm (assuming that no additional discounts are available if the firm pays cash on delivery or cash before delivery).

If a company forgoes the cash discount and pays bills after the end of the discount period, a definite opportunity cost of trade credit is incurred. In calculating the cost of not taking the cash discount, it is assumed that the company will make maximum use of extended trade credit by paying on the last day of the credit period. Paying after the end of the credit period, or *stretching* accounts payable, subjects the company to certain other costs.

The annual financing cost of forgoing a cash discount is calculated using Equation 17.3. In this application, the AFC is equal to the fractional interest cost per period times the number of borrowing periods per year:

$$\text{AFC} = \frac{\text{Percentage discount}}{100 - \text{Percentage discount}} \times \frac{365}{\text{Credit period} - \text{Discount period}} \quad (17.3)$$

For example, suppose the Benson Company has been extended $1,500 of trade credit from a supplier on terms of *2/10, net 30*. As shown in Figure 17.1, the company can either pay the discounted amount ($1,470) by the end of the discount period (day 10) or pay the full amount of the invoice ($1,500) by the end of the credit period (day 30).

By *not* paying on the tenth day—that is, by forgoing the cash discount—the company has the use of $1,470 (98% of the invoice amount) for an additional 20 days and effectively pays $30 in interest. Substituting this information into Equation 17.3 yields the following:

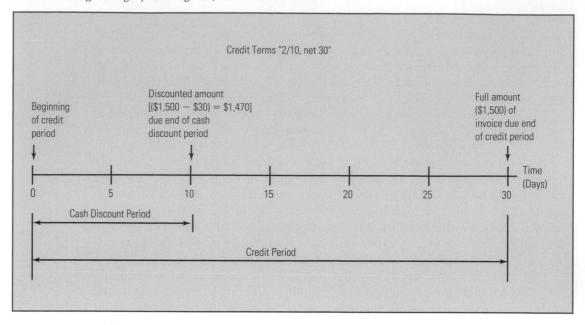

**Figure 17.1
Benson Company's
Cost of Forgoing the
Cash Discount**

$$\text{AFC} = \frac{2}{100-2} \times \frac{365}{30-10}$$

$$= \frac{2}{98} \times \frac{365}{20}$$

$$= 37.24\%$$

As this example shows, the annual cost of forgoing cash discounts can be quite high. Therefore, when making financing decisions, a company should compare this cost to the costs of other sources of credit.

Also, the company that offers credit terms of *2/10, net 30* should consider the annual financing cost of having the use of funds for an additional 20 days. As the preceding calculation illustrates, the annual financing cost of offering cash discounts when the credit terms are *2/10, net 30* is about 37 percent. Accordingly, a company may want to consider other, less expensive methods of encouraging prompt payment of trade credit. However, other benefits may accrue to a company that offers cash discounts. For example, a company may actually increase its sales by offering cash discounts. Or, a company may find that its bad-debt loss ratio is lowered if it offers a discount.

Abuses of cash discounts also exist; for example, a purchaser may deduct the discount amount even when payment is made after the discount period has passed. As a result, the seller has to decide whether simply to accept the lower payment or attempt to collect the unearned cash discount amount. With either alternative, the seller incurs costs.

Stretching Accounts Payable

Rather than pay suppliers within the credit period specified in the terms of sale, a firm can postpone payment of the amount due to beyond the end of the credit period. Stretching payments in this manner generates additional short-term financing for the firm, but this credit is not cost free. Not only does the firm incur the costs of forgoing any cash discounts, but its credit rating also may deteriorate, along with its ability to obtain future credit. Late payment penalties or interest charges also may be added to these costs, depending on specific industry practices. Although occasional stretching of payables—for example, to meet a seasonal need for funds—might be tolerated by suppliers and involve little or no cost to the firm, a firm that persistently stretches accounts payable well beyond their due dates may find its trade credit cut off by suppliers, who may adopt a cash before delivery (CBD) or a cash on delivery (COD) policy when dealing with the firm in the future. Finally, when a firm develops a reputation for being consistently slow in meeting financial obligations, banks and other lenders may refuse to loan funds on reasonable terms.

ACCRUED EXPENSES AND DEFERRED INCOME

Accrued expenses and deferred income are additional spontaneous sources of unsecured short-term credit.

Accrued Expenses

Accrued expenses—such as accrued wages, taxes, and interest—represent liabilities for services rendered to the firm that have not yet been paid for by the firm. As such, they constitute an *interest-free source of financing.*

Accrued wages represent the money a business owes to its employees. Accrued wages build up between paydays and fall to zero again at the end of the pay period, when the employees receive their paychecks. A company can increase the average amount of accrued wages by lengthening the period between paydays. For example, changing from a 2-week pay cycle to a 4-week pay cycle would effectively double a firm's average level of accrued wages. Also, a company can increase accrued expenses by delaying the payment of sales commissions and bonuses. Legal and practical considerations, however, limit the extent to which a company can increase accrued wages in this manner.

The amounts of accrued taxes and interest a firm may accumulate is also determined by the frequency with which these expenses must be paid. For example, corporate income tax payments normally are due quarterly, and a firm can use accrued taxes as a source of funds between these payment dates. Similarly, accrued interest on a bond issue requiring semiannual interest payments can be used as a source of financing for periods as long as 6 months. Of course, a firm has no control over the frequency of these tax and interest payments, so the amount of financing provided by these sources depends solely on the amounts of the payments themselves.

Deferred Income

Deferred income consists of payments received for goods and services that the firm has agreed to deliver at some future date. Because these payments increase the firm's liquidity and assets—namely, cash—they constitute a source of funds.

Advance payments made by customers are the primary sources of deferred income. These payments are common on large, expensive products, such as jet aircraft. Because the firm does not earn these payments until delivery of the goods or services to the customers, they are recognized on the balance sheet as a liability called deferred income.

Comprehension Check Questions

1. What is trade credit?
2. What are credit terms?

3. How is the cost of trade credit determined?

4. Why are accrued expenses and deferred income considered a type of short-term credit?

SHORT-TERM BANK CREDIT

e-Lecture

Commercial banks are an important source of both secured and unsecured short-term credit. In terms of the aggregate amount of short-term financing they provide to business firms, they rank second behind trade credit. Although trade credit is a primary source of spontaneous short-term financing, bank loans represent the major source of negotiated short-term funds.

A major purpose of short-term bank loans is to meet the firm's seasonal needs for funds—such as financing the buildup of inventories and receivables. Bank loans used for this purpose are regarded as *self-liquidating*, because *sale of the inventories and collection of the receivables are expected to generate sufficient cash flows to permit the firm to repay the loan prior to the next seasonal buildup.*

When a firm obtains a short-term bank loan, it normally signs a **promissory note** specifying the amount of the loan, the interest rate being charged, and the due date. The loan agreement may also contain various protective covenants. Short-term bank loans appear on the balance sheet under notes payable.

The interest rate charged on a bank loan is usually related to the **prime rate,** which is the *rate banks historically have charged on loans made to their most creditworthy, or prime, business customers.* The prime rate fluctuates over time with changes in the supply of and demand for loanable funds. Figure 17.2 shows a graph of the average prime rate each year since 1980. The average prime rate in 2002 was 4.7 percent, the lowest in several decades; it was as high as 18.9 percent in 1981. In recent years many large, highly profitable companies have been able to borrow at less than the prime rate. Subprime borrowing is partially the result of increased competition among large banks and other suppliers of short-term financing for especially creditworthy borrowers.

Short-term bank financing is available under three different arrangements:

➤ Single loans (notes)
➤ Lines of credit
➤ Revolving credit agreements

Single Loans (Notes)

Businesses frequently need funds for short time periods to finance a particular undertaking. In such a case, they may request a bank loan. This type of loan is often referred to as a *note*. The length of this type of loan can range from 30 days to 1 year, with most being for 30 to 90 days.

The interest rate a bank charges on an individual loan at a given point in time depends on a number of factors, including the borrower's creditworthiness relative to prime (lowest) credit risks. The interest rate often includes a premium of 1 to 2 or more percentage points above the prime rate, depending on how the bank officer perceives the borrower's overall business and financial risk. If the borrower is in a weak financial position and has overall risk that is thought to be too high, the bank may refuse to make an unsecured loan, regardless of the interest rate. When making the loan decision, the loan officer also considers the size of the checking account balance the company maintains at the bank, the amount of other business it does with the bank, and the rates that competitive banks are charging on similar loans.

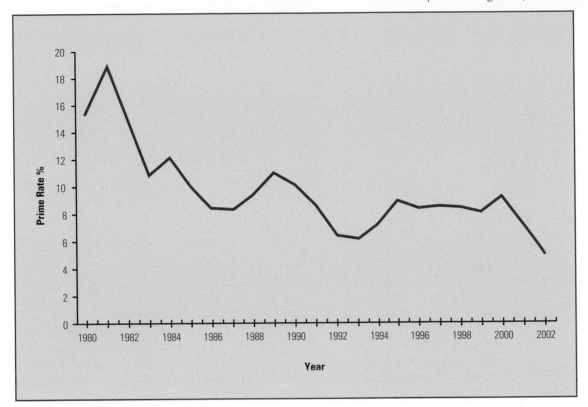

The annual financing cost of a bank note (single loan) is equal to the stated annual interest rate. However, calculating the AFC on a bank loan can get complicated if the bank requires a **compensating balance** as a condition for the loan. *A compensating balance is a certain percentage, usually 5 to 20 percent, of a loan balance that the borrower keeps on deposit with a bank as a requirement of a loan made by the bank.* The compensating balance requirement is stated either in terms of an absolute minimum balance or an average balance over some stipulated period; borrowers prefer average balances to minimum balances. A compensating balance increases the return the bank earns on the loan and also provides the bank with a small measure of protection (*right of offset*) in the event that the borrower defaults. Compensating balances tend to diminish in importance during periods of slack loan demand.

If the required compensating balance is in excess of the amount that normally would be maintained in the company's checking account, the annual financing cost of the loan is greater than the stated interest rate. It can be calculated using Equation 17.1. When a compensating balance is required, the usable funds amount in the denominator is the net amount of the loan that the company can spend after taking into account the amount borrowed, any required compensating balance, and the balance normally maintained in the bank account.

For example, suppose the Butler Company obtains a 6-month (182 days) $200,000 bank loan at 9 percent interest but is required to maintain a 20 percent average compensating balance. In other words, the company must maintain a $40,000 (0.20 × $200,000) average compensating balance to obtain the loan. If Butler currently maintains a $30,000 average balance that can be used to meet the compensating balance requirement, it needs to keep an additional $10,000 in the account, and thus the loan generates $190,000 in usable funds. The interest

**Figure 17.2
Annual Historical
Prime Rate**

Source: Data is taken from the U.S. Federal Reserve Board Web site:
http://www.federalreserve.gov/ releases/H15/data/a/prime.txt

charges on the loan are \$8,975 (\$200,000 × .09 × 182/365). Substituting these values into Equation 17.1 yields the following:

$$AFC = \frac{\$8,975}{\$190,000} \times \frac{365}{182}$$

$$= 9.47\%$$

However, if Butler currently has no balances in its bank account that can be used to meet the average compensating balance requirement, it has to keep \$40,000 of the \$200,000 loan in the checking account, and the amount of usable funds is reduced to \$160,000. In this case, the annual financing cost becomes significantly higher:

$$AFC = \frac{\$8,975}{\$160,000} \times \frac{365}{182}$$

$$= 11.25\%$$

Lines of Credit

A firm that needs funds periodically throughout the year for a variety of purposes may find it useful to negotiate a *line of credit* with its bank. *A line of credit is an agreement that permits the firm to borrow funds up to a predetermined limit at any time during the life of the agreement.* The major advantage of this type of borrowing agreement, as compared with single loans, is that the firm does not have to renegotiate with the bank every time funds are required. Instead, it can obtain funds on short notice with little or no additional justification. Another advantage to establishing a line of credit is that the firm can plan for its future short-term financing requirements without having to anticipate exactly how much it will have to borrow each month.

A line of credit is usually negotiated for a 1-year period, with renewals being subject to renegotiation each year. In determining the size of a credit line, a bank will consider a company's creditworthiness, along with its projected financing needs. As part of the application for a line of credit, the company is normally required to provide the bank with a cash budget for the next year, along with current and projected income statements and balance sheets. The interest rate on a line of credit is usually determined by adding to the prime rate a premium based on the borrower's creditworthiness. Because the prime rate normally fluctuates over time, the interest rate charged varies during the life of the agreement.

To illustrate, suppose the Bellevue Candy Company has a \$500,000 line of credit at 1 percentage point above the bank's prime rate. During the year, the company borrows, or *draws down*, \$200,000 on the line, and no compensating balances are in effect during the year. The bank's prime rate is 8.0 percent from January 1 to March 31, and on April 1, the bank raises its prime rate to 8.25 percent, where it remains for the rest of the year. The annual financing cost is calculated as follows using Equation 17.1:

Interest costs (January 1–March 31):

$$I = \$200,000 \times 0.09 \times \frac{90}{365}$$

$$= \$4,438.36$$

Interest costs (April 1–December 31):

$$I = \$200,000 \times 0.0925 \times \frac{275}{365}$$

$$= \$13,938.36$$

Total interest costs = $4,438.36 + $13,938.36

$$= \$18,376.72$$

$$\text{AFC} = \frac{\$18,376.72}{\$200,000.00} \times \frac{365}{365}$$

$$= 9.19\%$$

A line of credit agreement normally includes certain protective covenants. In addition to possibly including a compensating balance requirement, the loan agreement usually contains an annual *clean-up* provision requiring that the company *have no loans outstanding under the line of credit for a certain period of time each year, usually 30 to 90 days.* This type of policy helps reassure the bank that the company is using the line of credit to finance seasonal needs for funds and not to finance permanent capital requirements. Finally, a line of credit agreement also may contain provisions (similar to covenants in a long-term debt issue) that require the firm to maintain a minimum working capital position, limit total debt and lease financing, and restrict dividend payments.

Revolving Credit Agreements

Although a line of credit agreement does not legally commit the bank to making loans to the firm under any and all conditions, the bank normally will feel morally obligated to honor the line of credit. Some banks, however, have chosen not to provide financing to a firm when the firm's financial position has deteriorated significantly or when the bank lacks sufficient loanable funds to satisfy all its commitments. If the firm desires a guaranteed line of credit, it must negotiate a revolving credit agreement. Under a ***revolving credit agreement,*** or *revolver,* the bank is *legally committed to making loans to a company up to the predetermined credit limit specified in the agreement.* Revolving credit agreements differ from line of credit agreements in that they require the borrower to pay a *commitment fee* on the unused portion of the funds. This fee typically is in the range of 0.25 to 0.50 percent. Revolving credit agreements frequently are made for a period of 2 to 5 years. For example, in 2002, Harley-Davidson Inc. (the motorcycle manufacturer) had revolving credit agreements with various banks that permitted the firm to borrow up to $51.9 million of which $31.9 million was still available at the end of the year.

Calculating the annual financing cost of funds borrowed under a revolving credit agreement is slightly more complex than with either a single loan or a line of credit. In addition to the interest rate, commitment fee, compensating balance, and the firm's normal account balance, the annual financing cost of a revolving credit loan also depends on the amount borrowed and the credit limit of the agreement. The annual financing cost can be calculated based on Equation 17.1, as follows:

$$\text{AFC} = \frac{\text{Interest costs} + \text{Commitment fee}}{\text{Usable funds}} \times \frac{365}{\text{Maturity (days)}} \qquad \textbf{(17.4)}$$

For example, suppose the Keller Company has a $4 million revolving credit agreement with its bank to borrow at the prime rate. The agreement requires the company to maintain a 10 percent average compensating balance on any funds borrowed under the agreement, as well as to pay a 0.5 percent commitment fee on the unused portion of the credit line. The prime rate during the year is expected to be 5 percent. Keller's average borrowing under the agreement during the year is expected to be $2 million. The company maintains an average of $100,000 in its account at the bank, which can be used to meet the compensating balance requirement.

Would you or your business like to apply over the Internet for a line of credit? Using a search engine such as Alta Vista, type in the term "business line of credit" and watch how many thousands (and thousands) of lenders will extend a line of credit to you. **http://www.altavista.com**

To calculate the annual financing cost of the revolving credit agreement, Keller must determine the amount of usable funds generated by the loan, the total interest costs, and the commitment fees. Given average borrowing of $2 million during the year, Keller is required to maintain an average compensating balance of $200,000 (0.10 × $2 million). Because the company currently maintains an average balance of $100,000 in its checking account with the bank, $100,000 of the loan is needed to meet the compensating balance requirement. Therefore, the amount of usable funds is $1.9 million. Interest costs on the average amount borrowed are $100,000 (0.05 × $2 million), and the commitment fee on the unused portion of the credit line is $10,000 [0.005 × ($4 million − $2 million)]. Substituting these figures into Equation 17.4 yields the following annual financing cost of the loan:

$$\text{AFC} = \frac{\$100,000 + \$10,000}{\$1,900,000} \times \frac{365}{365}$$

$$= \frac{\$110,000}{\$1,900,000} \times \frac{365}{365}$$

$$= 5.79\%$$

Thus, the annual financing cost of the revolving credit agreement is higher than the stated interest rate.

Many financially sound companies view revolving credit agreements as a form of financial insurance, and, as a result, these companies frequently have little or no borrowings outstanding against the agreements. For example, in 2002, Boeing Corporation had revolving credit agreements with a group of commercial banks totaling $4.5 billion; however, the company had no loans outstanding under the agreement at the end of 2002.

COMMERCIAL PAPER

As we saw in Chapter 16, **commercial paper** *consists of short-term unsecured promissory notes issued by major corporations.* Only companies with good credit ratings are able to borrow funds through the sale of commercial paper. Purchasers of commercial paper include corporations with excess funds to invest, banks, insurance companies, pension funds, money market mutual funds, and other types of financial institutions.

Large finance companies, such as General Motors Acceptance Corporation (GMAC) and CIT Group, issue sizable amounts of commercial paper on a regular basis, selling it directly to investors like those just mentioned. Large industrial, utility, and transportation firms, as well as smaller finance companies, issue commercial paper less frequently and in smaller amounts; they sell it to dealers who, in turn, sell the commercial paper to investors.

Maturities on commercial paper at the time of issue range from several days to a maximum of 9 months. Companies usually do not issue commercial paper with maturities beyond 9 months, because such issues must be registered with the Securities and Exchange Commission. The size of an issue of commercial paper can range up to several hundred million dollars. It is usually sold to investors in multiples of $100,000 or more. Large issuers of commercial paper normally attempt to tailor the maturity and amounts of an issue to the needs of investors.

Commercial paper represents an attractive financing source for large, financially sound firms, because interest rates on commercial paper issues tend to be below the prime lending rate. For example, in June 2003, the average yield on 30-day commercial paper was 1.06 percent but the prime rate was 4.22 percent. To successfully market commercial paper and get an acceptable rating from rating agencies such as Moody's or Standard and Poor's, however, the company normally must

FINANCE & The Real World

The Commercial Paper Market: Tissue Paper?

In 2001, Eastman Chemical Co., a maker of specialty chemicals, could issue 30-day commercial paper at 2.5 percent. After the paper matured, it had the choice to replace the paper with longer-term debt or roll over the notes every month. For a long time, the decision was simple: take the short-term money and pay the low rates. But with the big-name bankruptcies and accounting scandals from Enron to WorldCom to Kmart, the market changed. There were no takers. Short-term markets became unpredictable as worried investors shunned commercial paper.

After all, who buys commercial paper in the first place? Often, it is money market funds looking for safety and liquidity or other corporations with temporary unused cash balances. They don't want to worry about the uncertainties or major corporate scandals such as Enron, so they temporarily opted out of the market. That leaves fewer "lenders" out there to buy the paper for 30 days and then get their money back. Even under normal circumstances, commercial paper is a risky way to borrow. If questions are suddenly raised about a company's financial health, the company may find it can't reissue those notes. The reason is that the Securities & Exchange Commission requires money market funds to keep at least 95 percent of their assets in the highest-grade commercial paper to protect investors from losses. That paper is constantly being re-rated by Standard & Poor's Corp. and Moody's Investor Services, national credit rating agencies.

As the scandals abated, companies reconsidered the commercial paper market. But then another development took place: interest rates on intermediate-term debt fell dramatically. So companies thought it was better to lock in a low rate—for, say, 5 to 20 years—rather than gamble that interest rates would stay low forever. Another reason the commercial paper market remained slow in 2003 is that companies that hadn't been investing in plant and equipment or new technology found that they were piling up cash. Thus, they really didn't need to borrow money. But even with these fluctuations, the commercial paper market is still huge—$1.33 trillion in June 2003, down from a peak of $1.62 trillion in November 2000.

The good times for the commercial paper market usually come back when the economy starts to sustain business investment in such categories as inventory, which in turn is often financed with commercial paper or other short-term vehicles such as a bank line of credit. Investors in money market funds welcome these issuers with open arms. The reason: blue-chip commercial paper pays a higher yield than the alternative, usually U.S. Treasury bills.

Sources: Dow Jones Newswires, July 15, 2003, "Worst May Be Over for U.S. Commercial Paper Market"; *Business Week,* April 15, 2002, "There Goes the Cheap Money."

---

have unused bank lines of credit equal to the amount of the issue (commercial paper ratings are similar to bond ratings discussed in Chapter 7).

The primary disadvantage of this type of financing is that it is not always a reliable source of funds. The commercial paper market is impersonal. A firm that is suddenly faced with temporary financial difficulties may find that investors are unwilling to purchase new issues of commercial paper to replace maturing issues. This is precisely what happened to Qwest Corporation in early 2002 when the firm was unable to find buyers for an estimated $800 million in commercial paper. The firm was forced to tap into its more expensive line of credit to finance its short-term needs. Another disadvantage of the commercial paper market is that the amount of loanable funds is limited to the amount of excess liquidity of the various purchasers of commercial paper. During tight money periods, enough funds may not be available to meet the aggregate needs of corporate issuers of commercial paper at reasonable rates. As a result, a company should maintain adequate lines of bank credit and recognize the risks of relying too heavily on commercial paper. Finally, a commercial paper issue usually cannot be paid off until maturity. Even if a company no longer needs the funds from a commercial paper issue, it still must pay the interest costs.

Commercial paper is sold on a discount basis; this means that the firm receives less than the stated amount of the note at issue and then pays the investor the full face amount at maturity. The annual financing cost of commercial paper depends on the maturity date of the issue and the prevailing short-term interest rates. In addition to the interest costs, borrowers also must pay a placement fee to the commercial paper dealer for arranging the sale of the issue. The annual financing cost can be computed as follows, based on Equation 17.1:

$$\text{(17.5)} \qquad \text{AFC} = \frac{\text{Interest costs} + \text{Placement fee}}{\text{Usable funds}} \times \frac{365}{\text{Maturity (days)}}$$

The usable funds are equal to the face amount of the issue less the interest costs and placement fee.

For example, suppose Midland Steel Company is considering issuing $10 million of commercial paper. A commercial paper dealer has indicated that Midland could sell a 90-day issue at an annual interest rate of 9.5 percent. The placement fee would be $25,000. Using Equation 17.5, the annual financing cost of this commercial paper issue is calculated as follows:

$$\text{Interest costs} = \$10,000,000 \times 0.095 \times \frac{90}{365}$$

$$= \$234,247$$

$$\text{AFC} = \frac{\$234,247 + \$25,000}{\$10,000,000 - \$234,247 - \$25,000} \times \frac{365}{90}$$

$$= 10.79\%$$

Comprehension Check Questions

1. How does the compensating balance affect the cost of short-term bank credit?
2. What is the difference between a line of credit and a revolving credit agreement?
3. What type of companies issue commercial paper?

ACCOUNTS RECEIVABLE LOANS

Accounts receivable are one of the most commonly used forms of collateral for secured short-term borrowing. From the lender's standpoint, accounts receivable represent a desirable form of collateral, because they are relatively liquid and their value is relatively easy to recover if the borrower becomes insolvent. In addition, accounts receivable involve documents representing customer obligations rather than cumbersome physical assets. Offsetting these advantages, however, are potential difficulties. One disadvantage is that the borrower may attempt to defraud the lender by pledging nonexistent accounts. Also, the recovery process in the event of insolvency may be hampered if the customer who owes the receivables returns the merchandise or files a claim alleging that the merchandise is defective. Finally, the administrative costs of processing the receivables can be high, particularly when a firm has a large number of invoices involving small dollar amounts. Nevertheless, many companies use accounts receivable as collateral for short-term financing by either *pledging* their receivables or *factoring* them.

Pledging Accounts Receivable

The *pledging* process begins with a loan agreement specifying the procedures and terms under which the lender will advance funds to the firm. *When accounts receivable are pledged, the firm retains title to the receivables and continues to carry them on its balance sheet.* However, the pledged status of the firm's receivables should be disclosed in a footnote to the financial statements. A firm that has pledged receivables as collateral is required to repay the loan, even if it is unable to collect the pledged receivables. In other words, the borrower assumes the default risk, and the lender has recourse back to the borrower. Both commercial banks and finance companies make loans secured by accounts receivable.

Finance in the News

Click on this button at **http://finance. swlearning.com** *and select Short-term Financial Management for articles on accounts receivable management.*

Once the pledging agreement has been established, the firm periodically sends the lender a group of invoices along with the loan request. Upon receipt of the customer invoices, the lender investigates the creditworthiness of the accounts to determine which are acceptable as collateral. The percentage of funds that the lender will advance against the collateral depends on the quality of the receivables and the company's financial position. The percentage normally ranges from 50 to 80 percent of the face amount of the receivables pledged. The company then is required to sign a promissory note and a security agreement, after which it receives the funds from the lender.

Most receivables loans are made on a nonnotification basis, which means the customer is not notified that the receivable has been pledged by the firm. The customer continues to make payments directly to the firm. To protect itself against possible fraud, the lender usually requires the firm to forward all customer payments in the form in which they are received. In addition, the borrower is usually subject to a periodic audit to ensure the integrity of its receivables and payments. Receivables that remain unpaid for 60 days or so usually must be replaced by the borrower.

The customer payments are used to reduce the loan balance and eventually repay the loan. Receivables loans can be a continuous source of financing for a company, however, provided that new receivables are pledged to the lender as existing accounts are collected. By periodically sending the lender new receivables, the company can maintain its collateral base and obtain a relatively constant amount of financing.

Receivables loans can be an attractive source of financing for a company that does not have access to unsecured credit. As the company grows and its level of receivables increases, it can normally obtain larger receivables loans fairly easily. And, unlike line of credit agreements, receivables loans usually do not have compensating balance or clean-up provisions.

The annual financing cost of a loan in which receivables are pledged as collateral includes both the interest expense on the unpaid balance of the loan and the service fees charged for processing the receivables. Typically, the interest rate ranges from 2 to 5 percentage points over the prime rate, and service fees are approximately 1 to 2 percent of the amount of the pledged receivables. The services performed by the lender under a pledging agreement can include credit checking,

Table 17.1 Cost of Pledging Receivable for Port City Plastics Corporation

Usable funds $= 0.75 \times$ Pledgeable receivables
$= 0.75 \times \$2,000,000$
$= \$1,500,000$

Interest costs $= \$1,500,000 \times 0.12 \times \dfrac{45}{365}$
$= \$22,192$

Service fee $= \$2,000,000 \times 0.01$
$= \$20,000$

$$AFC = \frac{\$22,192 + \$20,000}{\$1,500,000} \times \frac{365}{45}$$

$= 22.8\%$

keeping records of the pledged accounts and collections, and monitoring the agreement. This type of financing can be quite expensive for the firm.

The following example illustrates the calculation of the annual financing cost of an accounts receivable loan. Port City Plastics Corporation is considering pledging its receivables to finance a needed increase in working capital. Its commercial bank will lend 75 percent of the pledged receivables at 5 percentage points above the prime rate, which is currently 7 percent. In addition, the bank charges a service fee equal to 1 percent of the pledged receivables. Both interest payments and the service fee are payable at the end of each borrowing period. Port City's average collection period is 45 days, and it has receivables totaling $2 million that the bank has indicated are acceptable as collateral. As shown in Table 17.1, the annual financing cost for the pledged receivables is 22.8 percent.

Factoring Accounts Receivable

Factoring receivables involves the outright sale of the firm's receivables to a financial institution known as a factor. A number of so-called old-line factors, in addition to some commercial banks and finance companies (asset-based lenders), are engaged in factoring receivables. When receivables are factored, title to them is transferred to the factor, and the receivables no longer appear on the firm's balance sheet.

Traditionally, the use of factoring was confined primarily to the apparel, furniture, and textile industries. In other industries, the factoring of receivables was considered an indication of poor financial health. Today, factoring seems to be gaining increased acceptance in other industries.

The factoring process begins with an agreement that specifies the procedures for factoring the receivables and the terms under which the factor will advance funds to the firm. Under the normal factoring arrangement, the firm sends the customer order to the factor for credit checking and approval before filling it. The factor maintains a credit department to perform the credit checking and collection functions. Once the factor decides that the customer is an acceptable risk and agrees to purchase the receivable, the firm ships the order to the customer. The customer is usually notified that its account has been sold and is instructed to make payments directly to the factor.

Most factoring of receivables is done on a *nonrecourse basis;* in other words, *the factor assumes the risk of default.* If the factor refuses to purchase a given receivable, the firm still can ship the order to the customer and assume the default risk itself, but this receivable does not provide any collateral for additional credit.

http:

For more information on factoring, read articles at **http://www.factors.com**

In the typical factoring agreement, the firm receives payment from the factor at the normal collection or due date of the factored accounts; this is called *maturity factoring*. If the firm wants to receive the funds prior to this date, it usually can obtain an advance from the factor; this is referred to as *advance factoring*. Therefore, in addition to credit checking, collecting receivables, and bearing default risk, the factor also performs a lending function and assesses specific charges for each service provided. The maximum advance the firm can obtain from the factor is limited to the amount of factored receivables less the factoring commission, interest expense, and reserve that the factor withholds to cover any returns or allowances by customers. The reserve is usually 5 to 10 percent of the factored receivables and is paid to the firm after the factor collects the receivables.

The factor charges a factoring commission, or service fee, of 1 to 3 percent of the factored receivables to cover the costs of credit checking, collection, and bad-debt losses. The rate charged depends on the total volume of the receivables, the size of the individual receivables, and the default risk involved. The factor normally charges an interest rate of 2 to 5 percentage points over the prime rate on advances to the firm. These costs are somewhat offset by a number of internal savings that a business can realize through factoring its receivables. A company that factors all its receivables does not need a credit department and does not have to incur the administrative and clerical costs of credit investigation and collection or the losses on uncollected accounts. In addition, the factor may be able to control losses better than a credit department in a small or medium-sized company due to its greater experience in credit evaluation. Thus, although factoring receivables may be a more costly form of credit than unsecured borrowing, the net cost may be below the stated factoring commission and interest rates because of credit department and bad-debt loss savings.

For example, the Masterson Apparel Company is considering an advance factoring agreement because of its weak financial position and because of the large degree of credit risk inherent in its business. The company primarily sells large quantities of apparel to a relatively small number of retailers, and if even one retailer does not pay, the company could experience severe cash flow problems. By factoring, Masterson transfers the credit risk to the factor, Partners Credit Corporation, an asset-based lender. Partners requires a 10 percent reserve for returns and allowances, charges a 2 percent factoring commission, and will advance Masterson funds at an annual interest rate of 6 percentage points over prime. Assume the prime rate is 8 percent. Factoring receivables will allow the company to eliminate its credit department and save about $2,000 a month in administrative and clerical costs. Factoring also will eliminate bad-debt losses, which average about $6,000 a month. Masterson's average collection period is 60 days, and its average level of receivables is $1 million.

In Table 17.2, the amount of funds Masterson can borrow from the factor and the annual financing cost of these funds are calculated. As the table shows, Masterson can obtain an advance of $859,748, and the annual financing cost is 28.5 percent before considering cost savings and elimination of bad-debt losses. After considering savings and loss eliminations, the annual financing cost drops to 17.2 percent. Masterson can compare the cost of this factoring arrangement with the cost of other sources of funds in deciding whether or not to factor its receivables. This example calculates the factoring cost for a single 60-day period. In practice, if Masterson did enter into a factoring agreement, the agreement most likely would become a continuous procedure.

Table 17.2 Cost of Factoring Receivables for Masterson Apparel Company

Calculation of usable funds:

Average level of receivables		$1,000,000
Less Factoring commission	0.02 × $1,000,000	−20,000
Less Reserve for returns	0.10 × $1,000,000	−100,000
Amount available for advance before interest is deducted		$ 880,000
Less Interest on advance	(0.14 × $880,000 × 60/365)	−20,252
Amount of funds advanced by factor, or *usable funds*		$ 859,748

Interest costs and fees:

Interest costs		$ 20,252
Fee, or factoring commission		20,000
Total		$ 40,252

Calculation of annual financing cost, *before* considering cost savings and bad-debt losses:

$$AFC = \frac{\$40,252}{\$859,748} \times \frac{365}{60}$$
$$= 28.5\%$$

Calculation of annual financing cost, after considering cost savings and bad-debt losses:

Credit department savings, per 60-day period		$ 4,000
Average bad-debt losses, per 60-day period		12,000
Total		$ 16,000

$$AFC = \frac{\$40,252 - \$16,000}{\$859,748} \times \frac{365}{60}$$
$$= 17.2\%$$

INVENTORY LOANS

Inventories are another commonly used form of collateral for secured short-term loans. They represent a flexible source of financing since additional funds can be obtained as the firm's sales and inventories expand. Like receivables, many types of inventories are fairly liquid. Therefore, lenders consider them a desirable form of collateral. When judging whether a firm's inventory would be suitable collateral for a loan, the primary considerations of the lender are the *type, physical characteristics, identifiability, liquidity, and marketability of the inventory.*

Of the three types of inventories (raw materials, work-in-process, and finished goods), normally, only raw materials and finished goods are considered acceptable as security for a loan. The physical characteristic with which lenders are most concerned is the item's perishability. Inventory subject to significant physical deterioration over time is usually not suitable as collateral.

Inventory items also should be easily identifiable by means of serial numbers or inventory control numbers; this helps protect the lender against possible fraud and also aids the lender in establishing a valid title claim to the collateral if the borrower becomes insolvent and defaults on the loan. The ease with which the inventory can be liquidated and the stability of its market price are other important considerations. In the event that the borrower defaults, the lender wants to be able to take possession, sell the collateral, and recover the full amount owed with minimal expense and difficulty.

Both commercial banks and asset-based lenders make inventory loans. The percentage of funds that the lender will advance against the inventory's book value ranges from about 50 to 80 percent and depends on the inventory's characteristics. Advances near the upper end of this range are normally made only for inventories that are standardized, nonperishable, easily identified, and readily marketable. To receive an inventory loan, the borrower must sign both a promissory note and a *security agreement* describing the inventory that will serve as collateral.

In making a loan secured with inventories, the lender can either allow the borrower to hold the collateral or require that it be held by a third party. If the borrower holds the collateral, the loan may be made under a floating lien or trust receipt arrangement. If a third party is employed to hold the collateral, either a terminal warehouse or a field warehouse financing arrangement can be used.

Floating Liens

Under a **floating lien** arrangement, *the lender receives a security interest or general claim on the firm's entire inventory*; this may include both present and future inventory. This type of agreement is often employed when the average value of the inventory items is small, the inventory turns over frequently, or both. Specific items are not identified. Thus, a floating lien does not offer the lender much protection against losses from fraud or bankruptcy. As a result, most lenders will not advance a very high percentage of funds against the book value of the borrower's inventory.

Trust Receipts

A **trust receipt** is a security agreement under which the *firm holds the inventory and proceeds from the sale in trust for the lender*. Whenever a portion of the inventory is sold, the firm is required to immediately forward the proceeds to the lender; these then are used to reduce the loan balance.

Some companies engage in inventory financing on a continuing basis. In these cases, a new security agreement is drawn up periodically, and the lender advances the company additional funds using recently purchased inventories as collateral.

All inventory items under a trust receipt arrangement must be readily identified by serial number or inventory code number. The lender makes periodic, unannounced inspections of the inventory to make sure that the firm has the collateral and has not withheld payment for inventory that has been sold.

Businesses that must have their inventories available for sale on their premises, such as automobile and appliance dealers, frequently engage in trust receipt financing, also known as *floor planning*. Many *captive finance companies* that are subsidiaries of manufacturers, such as General Motors Acceptance Corporation (GMAC), engage in floor planning for their dealers.

Terminal Warehouse and Field Warehouse Financing Arrangements

Under a **terminal warehouse financing arrangement,** the inventory being used as loan collateral is *stored in a bonded warehouse operated by a public warehousing company*. When the inventory is delivered to the warehouse, the warehouse company issues a warehouse receipt listing the specific items received by serial or lot number. The warehouse receipt is forwarded to the lender, who then advances funds to the borrower.

Holding the warehouse receipt gives the lender a security interest in the inventory. Because the warehouse company will release the stored inventory to the firm only when authorized to do so by the holder of the warehouse receipt, the lender is able to exercise control over the collateral. As the firm repays the loan, the lender authorizes the warehouse company to release appropriate amounts of the inventory to the firm.

Under a *field warehouse financing agreement,* the inventory that serves as collateral for a loan is segregated from the firm's other inventory and stored on its

Table 17.3 Advantages and Disadvantages of Various Sources of Short-term Credit

Credit Source	Advantages	Disadvantages
Trade credit	Flexible source of financing—expands as firm's purchases increase Relatively easy to obtain	Opportunity cost of forgoing cash discounts can be quite high
Accrued expenses and deferred income	Interest-free source of financing	Limited by legal, contractual, and practical considerations
Short-term bank credit	Flexible source of financing—credit line can be used to meet seasonal needs for funds	May require compensating balance in excess of firm's normal checking account balance Commitment fees required for guaranteed credit May require clean-up provision and other protective covenants that limit firm's financing activities
Commercial paper	Interest rate is often below bank prime rate	Requires unused bank line of credit to issue commercial paper Not always a reliable source of funds. Tight credit market conditions or temporary financial difficulties may limit firm's access to this source of funds
Accounts receivable loans	Flexible source of financing—additional financing available as sales and accounts receivable increase Possible credit department and bad-debt loss savings Does not require compensating balance or clean-up provisions like line of credit borrowing	Service fees can make this source of financing more expensive than unsecured sources Pledging or selling of accounts receivables may weaken firm's financial strength and limit its access to unsecured credit
Inventory loans	Flexible source of financing—additional financing is available as sales and inventories increase Possible savings in inventory handling and storage costs under field warehouse or terminal warehouse agreement Does not require compensating balance or clean-up provisions like line-of-credit borrowing	Service fees (fixed and variable costs) for a field warehouse or terminal warehouse agreement can make this source of financing more expensive than unsecured sources

premises under the control of a field warehouse company. The field warehouse company issues a warehouse receipt, and the lender advances funds to the firm. The field warehouse releases inventory to the firm only when authorized to do so by the lender.

The fees charged by the warehouse company make this type of financing more expensive than floating lien or trust receipt loans. In a terminal warehouse arrangement, the firm incurs storage charges, in addition to fees for transporting the inventory to and from the public warehouse. In a field warehouse arrangement, the firm normally has to pay an installation charge, a fixed operating charge based on the overall size of the warehousing operation, and a monthly storage charge based on the value of the inventory in the field warehouse.

Overall warehousing fees are generally 1 to 3 percent of the inventory value. The total cost of an inventory loan includes the service fee charged by the lender and the warehousing fee charged by the warehousing company, plus the interest on the funds advanced by the lender. Any internal savings in inventory handling and storage costs that result when a warehouse company holds the inventory are deducted in computing the cost of the loan.

No one source (or combination of sources) of short-term financing is necessarily optimal for all firms. Many other factors, in addition to the cost of financing, need to be considered when choosing the optimal source or sources of short-term financing. Some of these factors include the availability of funds during periods of financial crisis or tight money, restrictive covenants imposed on the firm, and the nature of the firm's operations and funds requirements. The advantages and disadvantages of the various sources of short-term credit are summarized in Table 17.3.

Comprehension Check Questions

1. Explain the difference between pledging and factoring of accounts receivable.

2. What are some types of loans that are secured by inventory?

Summary

> Short-term credit may be either secured or unsecured. In the case of secured credit the borrower pledges certain assets (such as inventory, accounts receivable, or fixed assets) as collateral for the loan. In general, firms prefer to borrow on an unsecured basis, because pledging assets as security generally raises the overall cost of the loan and also can reduce the firm's flexibility by restricting future borrowing.

> Trade credit, accrued expenses, and deferred income are primary sources of spontaneous short-term credit. Bank loans, commercial paper, accounts receivable loans, and inventory loans represent the major sources of negotiated short-term credit.

> The annual financing cost of a loan is calculated as follows:

$$\text{AFC} = \frac{\text{Interest costs } + \text{ Fees}}{\text{Usable funds}} \times \frac{365}{\text{Maturity (days)}}$$

> The effective annual percentage rate of a loan is calculated as follows:

$$\text{EAPR} = \left(1 + \frac{\text{Interest costs } + \text{ Fees}}{\text{Usable funds}}\right)^m - 1$$

where m is the number of times per year compounding occurs.

> Trade credit is extended to a firm when it makes purchases from a supplier and is permitted to wait a specified period of time before paying for them.

> Accrued expenses—such as accrued wages, taxes, and interest—are liabilities for services provided to the firm that have not yet been paid for by the firm.

➤ Deferred income consists of payments received for goods and services a company will deliver at a future date.

➤ Short-term bank credit can be extended to the firm under a single loan, a line of credit, or a revolving credit agreement. A line of credit permits the firm to borrow funds up to a predetermined limit at any time during the life of the agreement. A revolving credit agreement legally commits the bank to provide the funds when the firm requests them.

➤ Commercial paper consists of short-term unsecured promissory notes issued by major corporations with good credit ratings.

➤ Accounts receivable loans can be obtained by either pledging or factoring receivables. In the case of a pledging arrangement, the firm retains title to the receivables, and the lender advances funds to the firm based on the amount and quality of the receivables. With factoring, receivables are sold to a factor, who takes the responsibility for credit checking and collections of the accounts. With pledging, the lender does not assume credit risk and has recourse back to the borrower if payment is not made, whereas factoring is normally a nonrecourse form of financing.

➤ Several types of inventory loans are available. In a floating lien or trust receipt arrangement, the borrower holds the collateral. In a floating lien arrangement, the lender has a general claim on the firm's entire inventory. In a trust receipt arrangement, the inventory being used as collateral is specifically identified by serial or inventory code numbers. In a terminal warehouse and a field warehouse arrangement, a third party holds the collateral; in the case of a terminal warehouse arrangement, collateral is stored in a public warehouse, whereas in a field warehouse arrangement, collateral is stored in a field warehouse located on the borrower's premises.

Questions and Topics for Discussion

1. Define and discuss the function of collateral in short-term credit arrangements.
2. How is the annual financing cost for a short-term financing source calculated? How does the annual financing cost differ from the effective annual percentage rate?
3. Explain the difference between spontaneous and negotiated sources of short-term credit.
4. Under what condition or conditions is trade credit *not* a "cost-free" source of funds to the firm?
5. Define the following:
   a. Accrued expenses
   b. Deferred income
   c. Prime rate
   d. Compensating balance
   e. Commitment fee
6. Explain the differences between a line of credit and a revolving credit agreement.
7. What are some of the disadvantages of relying too heavily on commercial paper as a source of short-term credit?

8. Explain the differences between pledging and factoring receivables.

9. Explain why the annual financing cost of secured credit is frequently higher than that of unsecured credit.

10. Explain why banks normally include a clean-up provision in a line of credit agreement.

11. What savings are realized when accounts receivable are factored rather than pledged?

12. Determine the effect of each of the following conditions on the annual financing cost for a line of credit arrangement (assuming that all other factors remain constant):

    a. The bank raises the prime rate.

    b. The bank lowers its compensating balance requirements.

    c. The firm's average bank balance increases as a result of its instituting more stringent credit and collection policies.

13. Under what condition or conditions, if any, might a firm find it desirable to borrow funds from a bank or other lending institution in order to take a cash discount?

Self-Test Problems

Note: Assume that there are 365 days per year when converting from annual to daily amounts or vice versa.

ST1. Determine the annual financing cost of forgoing the cash discount under each of the following credit terms:

    a. 2/10, net 120

    b. 2/30, net 4 months (assume 122 days)

ST2. Trotter Industries, Inc. has a revolving credit agreement with its bank under which the company can borrow up to $10 million at an interest rate of 1.5 percentage points above the prime rate (currently 5.5 percent). Trotter is required to maintain a 10 percent compensating balance on any funds borrowed under the agreement and to pay a 0.50 percent commitment fee on the unused portion of the credit line. Assume that the company has no funds in its account at the bank that can be used to meet the compensating balance requirement. Determine the annual financing cost of borrowing each of the following amounts under the credit agreement:

    a. $2 million

    b. $7 million

ST3. The Auto Finance Company (AFC) is considering the use of commercial paper to finance a seasonal need for funds. A commercial paper dealer will sell a $25 million issue maturing in 91 days at an annual interest rate of 4.5 percent (deducted in advance). The fee to the dealer for selling the issue is $75,000. Determine AFC's annual financing cost of this commercial paper issue.

ST4. The Banner Furniture Company is considering factoring its receivables. Its average level of receivables is $4 million, and its average collection period is 70 days. Banner's bad-debt losses average $9,000 per month. (Assume 30 days per month.) Factoring receivables will save the company $3,000 per month through the elimination of its credit department. The factor charges a 2 percent commission and requires a 10 percent reserve for returns and allowances. Banner can borrow funds from the factor at 5 percentage points over the prime rate, which is currently 7 percent.

a. Determine the amount of usable funds Banner can obtain by factoring its receivables.

b. Calculate the annual financing cost of this arrangement.

Problems

Note: Assume that there are 365 days per year when converting from annual to daily amounts or vice versa.

BASIC

1. The Milton Company currently purchases an average of $22,000 per day in raw materials on credit terms of "net 30." The company expects sales to increase substantially next year and anticipates that its raw material purchases will increase to an average of $25,000 per day. Milton feels that it may need to finance part of this sales expansion by *stretching* accounts payable.

a. Assuming that Milton currently waits until the end of the credit period to pay its raw material suppliers, what is its current level of trade credit?

b. If Milton stretches its accounts payable an extra 10 days beyond the due date next year, how much *additional* short-term funds (that is, trade credit) will be generated?

INTERMEDIATE

2. Energy Resources, Inc. is considering borrowing $100,000 for 182 days from its bank. Energy Resources will have to pay $3,000 in interest at maturity. The bank also requires a 10 percent compensating balance. The firm currently does not maintain a balance with the bank.

a. Calculate the loan's annual financing cost.

b. Calculate the loan's effective annual percentage rate.

c. What is the reason for the difference in your answers to (a) and (b)?

BASIC

3. Determine the annual financing cost of forgoing the cash discount under each of the following credit terms:

a. 2/10, net 60

b. $1\frac{1}{2}$/10, net 60

c. 2/30, net 60

d. 5/30, net 4 months (assume 122 days)

e. 1/10, net 30

BASIC

4. Calculate the effective annual percentage rate of forgoing the cash discount under each of the following credit terms:

a. 2/10, net 60

b. 2/10, net 30

BASIC

5. Determine the *annual financing cost* of forgoing the cash discount if the credit terms are "1/10, net 30" and the invoice is not paid until it is 20 days past due.

INTERMEDIATE

6. The Pulaski Company has a line of credit with a bank under which it can borrow funds at an 8 percent interest rate. The company plans to borrow $100,000 and is required by the bank to maintain a 15 percent compensating balance. Determine the annual financing cost of the loan under each of the following conditions:

a. The company currently maintains $7,000 in its account at the bank that can be used to meet the compensating balance requirement.

b. The company currently has no funds in its account at the bank that can be used to meet the compensating balance requirement.

7. Pyramid Products Company has a revolving credit agreement with its bank. The company can borrow up to $1 million under the agreement at an annual interest rate of 9 percent. Pyramid is required to maintain a 10 percent compensating balance on any funds borrowed under the agreement and to pay a 0.5 percent commitment fee on the unused portion of the credit line. Assume that Pyramid has no funds in the account at the bank that can be used to meet the compensating balance requirement. Determine the annual financing cost of borrowing each of the following amounts under the credit agreement: **INTERMEDIATE**

   a. $250,000

   b. $500,000

   c. $1,000,000

8. Walters Manufacturing Company has been approached by a commercial paper dealer offering to sell an issue of commercial paper for the firm. The dealer indicates that Walters could sell a $5 million issue maturing in 182 days at an interest rate of 6 percent per annum (deducted in advance). The fee to the dealer for selling the issue would be $8,000. Determine Walters' annual financing cost of this commercial paper financing. **INTERMEDIATE**

9. Becker Company has been approached by two different commercial paper dealers offering to sell an issue of commercial paper for the company. Dealer A offered to market an $8 million issue maturing in 90 days at an interest cost of 8.5 percent per annum (deducted in advance). The fee to Dealer A would be $15,000. Dealer B has offered to sell an $8 million issue maturing in 120 days at an interest rate of 8.75 percent per annum (deducted in advance). The fee to Dealer B would be $12,000. Assuming that Becker wishes to minimize the annual financing cost of issuing commercial paper, which dealer should it choose? **INTERMEDIATE**

10. Wrangler Enterprises is considering pledging its receivables to finance a needed increase in working capital. Its commercial bank will lend 75 percent of the pledged receivables at 1.5 percentage points above the prime rate, which is currently 7 percent. In addition, the bank charges a service fee equal to 1 percent of the pledged receivables. Both interest and the service fee are payable at the end of the borrowing period. Wrangler's average collection period is 50 days, and it has receivables totaling $5 million that the bank has indicated are acceptable as collateral. Calculate the annual financing cost for the pledged receivables. **INTERMEDIATE**

11. Designer Textiles, Inc. is considering factoring its receivables. The company's average collection period is 60 days, and its average level of receivables is $2.5 million. Designer's bad-debt losses average $15,000 a month. If the company factors its receivables, it will save $4,000 a month by eliminating its credit department. The factor has indicated that it requires a 10 percent reserve for returns and allowances and charges a 2.5 percent factoring commission. The factor will advance Designer funds at 4 percentage points over prime, which is currently 8 percent. **CHALLENGE**

   a. Determine the annual financing cost, *before* considering cost savings and bad-debt losses.

b. Determine the annual financing cost, *after* considering cost savings and bad-debt losses.

BASIC **12.** Which of the following credit terms would you prefer as a customer?

  a. 2/10, net 30

  b. 1/10, net 40

  c. 2/10, net 40

  d. 1/10, net 25

  e. Indifferent among all options

  Explain your choice.

INTERMEDIATE **13.** The Odessa Supply Company is considering obtaining a loan from a sales finance company secured by inventories under a field warehousing arrangement. Odessa would be permitted to borrow up to $300,000 under such an arrangement at an annual interest rate of 10 percent. The additional cost of maintaining a field warehouse is $16,000 per year. Determine the annual financing cost of a loan under this arrangement if Odessa borrows the following amounts:

  a. $300,000

  b. $250,000

INTERMEDIATE **14.** The Kittanning Company has a $2 million line of credit with First Interstate Bank under which it can borrow funds at 1.5 percentage points above the prime rate (currently 9 percent). The company plans to borrow $1.5 million and is required by First Interstate to maintain a 10 percent compensating balance. Determine the annual financing cost of the loan under each of the following conditions:

  a. Kittanning currently maintains $100,000 in its account at the bank that can be used to meet the compensating balance requirement.

  b. The company currently has no funds in its account at the bank that can be used to meet the compensating balance requirement.

INTERMEDIATE **15.** The Viceroy Company has a revolving credit agreement with Commerce Bank under which the company can borrow up to $5 million at an annual interest rate of 1 percentage point above the prime rate (currently 4.5 percent). The company is required to maintain a 10 percent compensating balance on any funds borrowed under the agreement and to pay a 0.4 percent commitment fee on the unused portion of the credit line. Assume that Viceroy has no funds in its account at Commerce Bank that can be used to meet the compensating balance requirement. Determine the annual financing cost of borrowing each of the following amounts under the credit agreement:

  a. $1 million

  b. $4 million

INTERMEDIATE **16.** Titusville Petroleum Company is considering pledging its receivables to finance an increase in working capital. Citizens National Bank will lend the company 80 percent of the pledged receivables at 2 percentage points above the prime rate (currently 10 percent). The bank charges a service fee equal to 1.5 percent of the pledged receivables. The interest costs and the service fee are payable at the end of the borrowing period. Titusville has $2 million in receivables that can be pledged as collateral. The average collection period is 45 days. Determine the annual financing cost to Titusville of this receivables-backed loan.

17. Fashion Apparel Company is considering factoring its receivables. The company's average level of receivables is $1.5 million, and its average collection period is 45 days. Fashion's bad-debt losses average $8,000 per month, which it would not incur if it factored its receivables. (Assume 30 days per month.) Also, the company would save $4,000 per month in credit department costs if it factored its receivables. The factor requires a 10 percent reserve for returns and allowances and charges a 2 percent factoring commission. Fashion can borrow funds from the factor at 3 percentage points over the prime rate (currently 6 percent). Determine the *net* annual financing cost of this factoring arrangement.   **CHALLENGE**

18. The Clearfield Company would be permitted to borrow up to $750,000 secured by inventories under a field warehouse arrangement with a sales finance company. The annual interest rate would be 12 percent. The additional cost of establishing a field warehouse would be $35,000 per year. Determine the annual financing cost to Clearfield under this arrangement if Clearfield borrows   **INTERMEDIATE**

   a. $750,000

   b. $500,000

CHAPTER
18 International Financial Management

The importance of understanding the global economy can be seen in the volume of exports and imports in the United States. Table 18.1 shows that merchandise imports totaled $250 billion in 1980 while they were $1,165 billion in 2002. U.S. merchandise exports on the other hand increased from $224 billion to $682 billion over the same period of time. The numbers are indicative of the increasing importance of the international marketplace in a firm's operations.

Business enterprises participate in the global marketplace in a wide variety of ways. Some firms simply export finished goods for sale in another country and/or import raw materials or products from another country for use in their domestic operations. At the other end of the spectrum are multinational enterprises. A *multinational corporation* has direct investments in manufacturing and/or distribution facilities in more than one country. Often, these foreign operations are structured as more or less "free-standing" subsidiaries. Among the largest multinational firms are U.S. firms such as General Motors, ExxonMobil, Ford, IBM, General Electric, and Altria Group (formerly Philip Morris). Large multinational Japanese firms include Toyota, Hitachi, Matsushita, Nissan, and Toshiba. Major European multinationals include Royal Dutch/Shell, DaimlerChrysler, British Petroleum, Siemens, Volkswagen, Fiat, Unilever, and Nestlé.

The rise of the multinational firm has drastically changed the way business is done around the world. The multinational organization makes it relatively easy for firms to transfer the key factors of production—land, labor, and capital—to the location where they can be most productive, which represents a dramatic change from the time when the factors of production were thought to be immobile and only goods and services could be moved easily across borders. As a result, the process of resource allocation and business decision making has become more complex.

At the same time, multinational firms have the opportunity to benefit from imperfections that arise in various national markets for capital and other factors of production. For example, multinational firms can raise capital in countries where it may be cheaper than in their home country. Similarly firms can take advantage of locating their plants in countries that provide the greatest benefit. In making plant location decisions, managers consider wage costs, the quality of the workforce, transportation costs, the cost of raw materials, economic development incentives, exchange rate levels and risks, and political risk (such as the risk of expropriation or the blocking of funds). In addition, firms may decide to locate in multiple countries to gain quicker access to new technologies as they develop.

Some international plant location decisions are designed, at least in part, to avoid political and regulatory barriers. For example, Japanese auto firms, including Toyota, Nissan, and Honda, have built large assembly plants in the United States, partly in response to auto import quotas and to reduce the pressure for greater future import restrictions. As a result it is no longer possible for a U.S. manufacturer, such as Ford Motor Company, to worry just about its domestic competitors. Over the past decade, Japanese and German auto companies have built plants in the United States that directly compete with United States–based companies.

All firms engaged in international business transactions face unique problems and risks not encountered by firms that operate in only one country. First, there are difficulties associated with doing business in different currencies. Financial

Table 18.1 U.S. Merchandise Imports and Exports (U.S. $ million)

Period	Exports	Imports
1980	224,250	249,750
1981	237,044	265,067
1982	211,157	247,642
1983	201,799	268,901
1984	219,926	332,418
1985	215,915	338,088
1986	223,344	368,425
1987	250,208	409,765
1988	320,230	447,189
1989	359,916	477,665
1990	387,401	498,434
1991	414,083	491,020
1992	439,631	536,528
1993	456,943	589,394
1994	502,859	668,690
1995	575,204	749,374
1996	612,113	803,113
1997	678,366	876,485
1998	670,416	917,112
1999	683,965	1,029,987
2000	771,994	1,224,417
2001	718,712	1,145,927
2002	681,874	1,164,746

Source: U.S. Census Bureau, Foreign Trade Division, http://www.census.gov/foreign-trade/statistics/index.html

transactions between U.S. firms and firms (or individuals) in foreign countries normally involve foreign currency that ultimately has to be converted into U.S. dollars. Therefore, firms that do business internationally are concerned with the exchange rate between U.S. dollars and foreign currencies. Second, problems arise because of differing government regulations, tax laws, business practices, and political environments. In this chapter we focus on the exchange rate–related aspects of international financial management.

Chapter Objectives

After reading this chapter, you should gain an understanding of the following:

1. Exchange rates and foreign currency markets

2. Factors that determine exchange rates

3. Various aspects of foreign exchange risk and ways of managing that risk

FOREIGN CURRENCY MARKETS AND EXCHANGE RATES

Whenever a U.S. firm purchases goods or services from a firm in another country, two currencies normally are involved. For example, when a U.S. company purchases materials from a British supplier, the British firm usually prefers payment in British pounds, whereas the U.S. company prefers to make payment in U.S. dollars. If the sales agreement requires that payment be made in pounds, the U.S. company will have to exchange (that is, *sell*) dollars to obtain the required number of pounds. The exact amount of dollars the U.S. company will have to sell depends on the *exchange rate* between the two currencies.

Suppose, for example, that the exchange rate at the time of the transaction is $1.48 per pound, £. Furthermore, assume that the British supplier and the U.S. firm have agreed on a price of £2 million for the materials. Therefore, the U.S. firm will have to exchange $2.96 million (that is, £2,000,000 × $1.48/pound) to obtain the British currency to pay for the purchase.

Foreign currency needed for international financial transactions can be exchanged for domestic currency in most countries either at large commercial banks or at a central bank operated by the government. The volume of foreign currency transactions is very large. For example, the Bank for International Settlements estimates that daily, worldwide foreign currency trading exceeds $1.5 trillion. Of this amount, nearly 60 percent is between international banks; about 25 percent is between banks within a country; and the balance is with foreign currency dealers and other banking customers. The most important foreign currency trading centers are in New York, Tokyo, Hong Kong, Singapore, Bahrain, Frankfurt, Zurich, London, San Francisco, and Los Angeles.

Finance in the News

Click on this button at **http://finance. swlearning.com** *and select International Financial Management for articles on numerous international topics.*

The Eurocurrency Market

A *Eurocurrency* is a currency that is deposited in a bank located outside of the country of origin. Eurocurrencies are created when, for example, a U.S. firm transfers dollars from a bank in the United States to a bank outside of the United States. Also, someone outside of the United States may receive dollars in connection with a business transaction or because of a purchase in the foreign exchange market. When these dollars are deposited in a bank outside of the United States they become *Eurodollars.* The bank may either be a foreign bank, such as Deutsche Bank, or a foreign branch of a U.S. bank, such as J.P. Morgan Chase, located in Frankfurt. Other important Eurocurrencies include Euroyen and Eurosterling (Japanese yen and British pounds), deposited outside of their country of origin. The gross size of the Eurocurrency market is in excess of $8 trillion. About two-thirds of the Eurocurrencies outstanding are U.S. dollar–denominated.

Consider the following example. BMW, the well-known German auto manufacturer, sells a car to an American dealer for $60,000. The American dealer pays BMW with a check for $60,000 drawn on J.P. Morgan Chase. BMW must then decide what to do with this check. BMW could immediately sell the dollars and buy *euros* with it (for a description of the euros, see the next section). However, BMW wants to retain the dollars for use later on (perhaps to pay for goods purchased from U.S. firms), so it buys a Eurodollar deposit by depositing the check in Deutsche Bank in Germany. The typical Eurocurrency deposit is a nonnegotiable time deposit with a fixed term to maturity. Maturities range from overnight to as long as 5 years.

The Eurocurrency market provides an important alternative to domestic sources of funds for multinational firms. For example, in the United States, large, well-established multinational corporations can borrow funds either in the domestic financial market or in the international financial marketplace, such as the Eurocurrency market. If General Motors chooses to borrow in the Eurodollar market it would receive a Eurodollar loan from a foreign bank, such as Barclays Bank in London or Deutsche Bank in Frankfurt. The interest rate in the Eurodollar market is usually related to the ***London interbank offer rate,*** or ***LIBOR***. *LIBOR is the interest rate at which banks in the Eurocurrency market lend to each other.* The cost to borrow in the Eurocurrency market is usually stated as a margin above LIBOR. Typically, Eurodollar borrowing rates are between 0.5 percent and 3 percent over LIBOR, with a median of about 1.5 percent. Eurocurrency loans range in maturity up to 10 years for the best quality borrowers.

The Euro: A Common European Currency

On January 4, 1999, 11 countries of the European Union (EU) turned over control of their monetary policies to a new European Central Bank and the single European currency, the *euro,* was born. During a transition period, the euro was being used only for paperless transactions. But on January 1, 2002, euro bills and coins began circulation, and 6 months later national currencies of these 11 countries ceased to exist. This move toward a single European currency is the logical outgrowth of the development of a single European market, where goods, services, and people flow freely across national borders. The use of a common currency eliminates exchange costs associated with converting from one currency to another within Europe and also eliminates the uncertainty of exchange rate fluctuations among these countries. The euro is sure to become a major international currency, rivaling the dollar in importance. It is likely that other European countries will join the common currency group in future years.

Direct and Indirect Quotes

Exchange rates can be expressed either as ***direct quotes*** or ***indirect quotes.*** *A direct quote is the home currency price of one unit of foreign currency.* For example, from the perspective of a U.S. firm, a quote of $0.7297 per Swiss franc (CHF) would be a direct

Table 18.2 Spot Foreign Exchange Rates

| Country | Currency | Exchange Rate (U.S. Dollars) | |
		July 2, 1999	July 17, 2003
Australia	Dollar	$0.6690	$0.6533
Britain	Pound	$1.5765	$1.5962
Canada	Dollar	$0.6834	$0.7161
India	Rupee	$0.02304	$0.02165
Japan	Yen	$0.008263	$0.008418
South Africa	Rand	$0.1660	$0.1291
Sweden	Krona	$0.1177	$0.1213
Switzerland	Franc	$0.6378	$0.7297
European Union	Euro	$1.0237	$1.1207

Source: The Wall Street Journal, July 6, 1999 and July 18, 2003.

quote. *An indirect quote is the foreign currency price of one unit of the home currency.* A quote of CHF1.3704/$ would be an indirect quote from the perspective of a U.S. firm. Direct quotes and indirect quotes have a reciprocal relationship. Accordingly, the indirect quote was derived by taking the reciprocal (1÷$0.7297/CHF) of the direct quote.

Spot Rates

Foreign exchange actually includes spot contracts, forward contracts, futures, options, swaps, foreign-currency loans/deposits, etc. Visit Global Forex's Web site for a listing of important foreign exchange terminology. **http://www. globalforex.com/ terminology.htm**

Exchange rates between U.S. dollars and the currencies of most countries are reported daily in *The Wall Street Journal*. Table 18.2 lists the (direct quote) exchange rates between U.S. dollars and various currencies as of July 2, 1999 and July 17, 2003. These quotes are for trades made among banks in amounts of $1 million or more. Smaller, retail transactions usually result in fewer units of a foreign currency per dollar. The quotes in Table 18.2 are known as *spot rates. Spot rates represent the rate of exchange for currencies being bought and sold for immediate delivery.* Note from Table 18.2 that exchange rates fluctuate over time. On July 2, 1999 the spot rate for the euro was $1.0237 but on July 17, 2003 it was $1.1207. Thus the U.S. dollar, relative to the euro, had weakened over this time period. Later in the chapter we discuss some factors that account for changes in the exchange rates over time.

Banks profit from their foreign currency transactions by buying currencies at one rate (bid) and selling them at another, higher rate (ask or offer). For example, a bank may quote the Swiss franc at $0.6853 bid, and $0.6865 offer. This quote is

Table 18.3 Forward Foreign Exchange Rates

| Currency | Exchange Rate (U.S. Dollars) July 17, 2003 | | |
	30-day Forward	90-day Forward	180-day Forward
British Pound	$1.5931	$1.5871	$1.5786
Canadian Dollar	$0.7149	$0.7127	$0.7098
Japanese Yen	$0.008426	$0.008442	$0.008466
Swiss Franc	$0.7302	$0.7312	$0.7325

Source: The Wall Street Journal, July 18, 2003.

often written simply as 0.6853–65. The spread between bid and offer for widely traded currencies is likely to be in the range of 0.1 to 0.5 percent.

Forward Rates

In addition to spot transactions, currencies can also be bought and sold today for delivery at some future time, usually 30, 90, or 180 days from today. In these cases, *forward rates* are used, rather than spot rates. Table 18.3 lists some forward exchange rates as of July 17, 2003. A comparison of the spot and forward rates in Tables 18.2 and 18.3 shows that the 30-, 90-, and 180-day forward rates for the British pound and Canadian dollar is below its spot rate, indicating a market expectation that these currencies will *lose* value relative to the U.S. dollar over these time horizons. On the other hand the forward rates for the Japanese yen and the Swiss franc are above the corresponding spot rate, indicating that these currencies will *gain* value relative to the U.S dollar over the time horizons for the forward rates.

The premium or discount between the spot rate, S_0, and a forward rate, F, for a currency (relative to the dollar, for example) can be expressed on an *annualized* percentage basis (using direct quotes) as follows:

$$\text{Annualized forward premium or discount} = \left(\frac{F - S_0}{S_0}\right)\left(\frac{12}{n}\right)(100\%) \tag{18.1}$$

where n is the number of months in the forward contract. A positive value calculated using Equation 18.1 indicates that a currency is trading at a forward premium relative to the dollar, whereas a negative value indicates a forward discount.

Using the exchange rates from Tables 18.2 and 18.3, the following annualized premium for the 180-day forward quote on the Swiss franc (CHF) can be calculated:

$$\text{Annualized forward premium or discount} = \left(\frac{\$0.7325 - \$0.7297}{\$0.7297}\right)\left(\frac{12}{6}\right)(100\%)$$

$$= 0.77\%$$

Thus, we can say that the CHF is trading at a forward premium relative to the dollar (i.e., the dollar is expected to weaken relative to the CHF).

Comprehension Check Questions

1. Define the following:
   - ➢ LIBOR
   - ➢ Direct quote
   - ➢ Indirect quote
   - ➢ Spot rate
2. What is the Eurocurrency market?
3. What is the forward rate?

FACTORS THAT AFFECT EXCHANGE RATES

Exchange rates between currencies vary over time, reflecting supply and demand considerations for each currency. For example, the demand for British pounds comes from a number of sources, which include foreign buyers of British exports who must pay for their purchases in pounds, foreign investors who desire to make investments in physical or financial assets in Britain, and speculators who expect British pounds to increase in value relative to other currencies. The British government may also be a source of demand if it attempts to keep the value of the pound (relative to other currencies) from falling by using its supply of foreign currencies or gold to purchase pounds in the market.

Sources of supply include British importers who need to convert their pounds into foreign currency to pay for purchases, British investors who desire to make investments in foreign countries, and speculators who expect British pounds to decrease in value relative to other currencies.

Exchange rates also are affected by economic and political conditions that influence the supply of, or demand for, a country's currency. Some of these conditions include differential inflation and interest rates among countries, the government's trade policies, and the government's political stability. A high rate of inflation within a country tends to lower the value of its currency with respect to the currencies of other countries experiencing lower rates of inflation. The exchange rate will tend to decline as holders sell or exchange the country's currency for other currencies whose purchasing power is not declining at as high a rate. In contrast, relatively high interest rates within a country tend to increase the exchange rate as foreign investors seek to convert their currencies and purchase these higher-yielding securities.

Government trade policies that limit imports—such as the imposition of tariffs, import quotas, and restrictions on foreign exchange transactions—reduce the supply of the country's currency in the foreign exchange market. This, in turn, tends to increase the value of the country's currency with respect to other currencies and thus to increase exchange rates.

e-Lecture

Finally, the political stability of the government affects the risks perceived by foreign investors and companies doing business in the country. These risks include the possible expropriation of investments or restrictions on the amount of funds (such as returns from investments) that may be taken out of the country.

In the following sections we develop the important relationships among spot rates, forward rates, interest rates, and inflation rates as they impact foreign currency exchange rates.

Covered Interest Arbitrage and Interest Rate Parity

There is a close relationship between the interest rates in two countries and the forward exchange rate premium or discount. Consider a U.S. investor with $1.2 million to invest who notes that the interest rate on 90-day certificates of deposit (CDs) available at Swiss banks is 4 percent for 90 days. At the same time, the 90-day CD rate in the United States is only 2 percent. The spot rate of the Swiss franc (SF) is $0.60/CHF and the 90-day forward rate is also $0.60. As an investor, you know that you can immediately convert $1.2 million into CHF2 million at today's spot rate of $0.60 with no risk. You can also lock in the 4 percent Swiss interest rate for 90 days by purchasing a Swiss CD with your CHF2 million. However, there is risk regarding the exchange rate at which you will be able to convert CHF back to dollars at the end of 90 days. You can guarantee this rate by selling 2 million CHF (plus the interest you will receive on your Swiss CD) in the 90-day forward market at today's forward rate of $0.60. This transaction will guarantee you a risk-free profit. Consider the following steps in this transaction:

1. Convert $1.2 million into CHF2 million at today's spot rate of $0.60/CHF.
2. Buy a 90-day CD at a Swiss bank yielding 4 percent every 90 days.

3. Simultaneously sell CHF2.08 million forward (original CHF2 million plus CHF 80,000 in interest) at $0.60 to net you $1,248,000.

4. This exceeds the $1,224,000 ($1.2 million plus interest at 2 percent) you could have received from investing in a U.S. CD.

This risk-free transaction enabled you to earn an additional return of $24,000 over what would be available by investing in the United States. Because there are virtually no barriers to prevent individuals from engaging in this transaction—called ***covered interest arbitrage***—it can be expected that opportunities to earn risk-free additional returns such as these will not persist very long. The demand by American investors for CHF will put upward pressure on the spot price of CHF, to a price greater than $0.60/CHF. At the same time, as American investors sell CHF forward to cover their position, this will put downward pressure on forward rate of the CHF to a price less than $0.60. Furthermore, as funds leave the United States for Switzerland, the reduced supply of funds will tend to increase U.S. interest rates. The increased supply of funds in Switzerland, on the other hand, will tend to lower Swiss interest rates.

The net effect of these transactions and market pressures will be an equilibrium condition where covered interest arbitrage transactions are not possible. This relationship is called ***interest rate parity (IRP)***. When IRP exists, the forward rate will differ from the spot rate by just enough to offset the interest rate differential between the two currencies. In other words, the forward premium or discount for a currency quoted in terms of another currency is approximately equal to the difference in interest rates prevailing between the two countries. Thus, if interest rates in Switzerland are higher than interest rates in the United States, then the IRP condition indicates that the dollar can be expected to increase in value relative to the CHF. The approximate IRP relationship is given by

$$\text{Approximate IRP:} \quad \frac{F - S_0}{S_0} \approx i_h - i_f \qquad (18.2)$$

where i_h is the home (U.S.) interest rate, i_f is the comparable foreign (Swiss) interest rate, F is the direct quote forward rate, and S_0 is the direct quote spot rate. (Note that the interest rates in Equation 18.2 are for the same period of time as the number of days in the forward price, not necessarily annualized interest rates.) Equation 18.2 indicates that when interest rate parity exists, differences in interest rates between two countries will be (approximately) offset by changes in the relative value of the two currencies.

To illustrate, assume that the 90-day interest rate is 1.5 percent in the United States and 2.5 percent in Switzerland, and the current spot exchange rate between dollars and Swiss francs is $0.60. If IRP holds, what will the 90-day forward rate be? Using Equation 18.2, we find

$$\frac{F - \$0.60}{\$0.60} = 0.015 - 0.025$$
$$F = \$0.60 \,(0.015 - 0.025) + 0.60$$
$$= 0.594$$

In this case, the dollar has increased in value relative to the CHF (i.e., it takes fewer dollars to buy each CHF). Why do you think this should occur?

Purchasing Power Parity

When there are no significant costs or other barriers associated with moving goods or services between markets, then *the price of each product should be the same in each market*. In economics, this is known as the ***law of one price***. When the different markets represent different countries, the law of one price says that prices will be the same in each country after making the appropriate conversion from one currency to another. Alternatively one can say that *exchange rates between two currencies will equal the ratio of the price indexes between the countries.* In international finance and trade, this relationship is known as the absolute version of ***purchasing power parity (PPP)***.

In reality, we know that this relationship does not hold because of the costs of moving goods and services and the existence of tariffs and other trade barriers. For example, *The Economist* newspaper, in a lighthearted look at the law of one price, regularly reports on the price of Big Mac hamburgers in various countries. When the price of a Big Mac was $2.20 in the United States, it cost (after converting currencies) $2.56 in Germany, $1.36 in Yugoslavia, $1.10 in Hong Kong, $6.25 in Russia, and $2.32 in Japan. It is obviously not possible to buy Big Macs in Hong Kong and ship them to New York for sale, for example. Hence the law of one price does not hold for Big Macs. On the other hand, for goods that are standardized and somewhat easier to move and store, such as gold or crude oil, one would expect only minor violations of the law of one price.

A less restrictive form of the law of one price is known as ***relative purchasing power parity.*** The relative PPP principle states that in comparison to a period when exchange rates between two countries are in equilibrium, *changes in the differential rates of inflation between two countries will be offset by equal, but opposite changes in the future spot exchange rate.* For example, if prices in the United States rise by 4 percent per year and prices in Switzerland rise by 6 percent per year, then relative PPP holds if the Swiss franc (CHF) weakens relative to the U.S. dollar by approximately 2 percent.

The approximate relative purchasing power parity relationship is given by

(18.3) $$\text{Approximate relative PPP: } \frac{S_1 - S_0}{S_0} \approx \pi_h - \pi_f$$

where S_1 is the expected future (direct quote) spot rate at time period 1, S_0 is the current (direct quote) spot rate, π_h is the expected home country (U.S.) inflation rate, and π_f is the expected foreign country inflation rate.

Using the previous example, if U.S. prices are expected to rise by 4 percent over the coming year, prices in Switzerland are expected to rise by 6 percent during the same time, and the current spot exchange rate (S_0) is $0.60/CHF, then the expected spot rate in one year (S_1), will be

$$\frac{S_1 - \$0.60}{\$0.60} = 0.04 - 0.06$$
$$S_1 = \$0.60(0.04 - 0.06) + \$0.60$$
$$= -\$0.012 + \$0.60$$
$$= \$0.588$$

The higher Swiss inflation rate can be expected to result in a decline in the *future spot value* of the CHF relative to the dollar by 2 percent.

The market forces that support the relative PPP relationship operate in the following way. If one nation has a higher inflation rate than another, its goods and services will become relatively more expensive, making its exports less price competitive and imports more price competitive. The resulting deficit in foreign trade will place downward pressure on the currency value of the high inflation country until a new, lower equilibrium value is established. The opposite will be true for the country with the lower inflation rate. For example, if the United States has a lower inflation rate than its major trading partners, relative PPP indicates that the value of the dollar can be expected to increase relative to the value of the currencies of these other trading partners.

Tests of relative PPP indicate that the relationship holds up reasonably well over long periods, but it is a less accurate indicator of short-term currency value changes. Also, the relative PPP relationship is stronger for those countries experiencing high rates of inflation. Tests of the strength of the PPP relationship are hampered by the use of noncomparable price indexes between countries and government interference in commodity and currency markets. Nevertheless, the general relationship between inflation rates and currency values is widely accepted, even if it is difficult to measure properly.

Expectations Theory and Forward Exchange Rates

If foreign currency markets are efficient, the forward rate should reflect what market participants expect the future spot rate for a currency to be. For example, if market participants expected the 1-year future spot rate (S_1) for CHF to be $0.58, then what would the 1-year forward rate (F_1), have to be? It would also have to be $0.58. If the forward rate were lower than this amount, market participants would want to buy CHF forward, thereby placing upward price pressure on the CHF until an equilibrium is reached where the forward rate equals the expected future spot rate.

If the expected future spot rate is equivalent to the forward rate, we can say that the forward rate is an *unbiased* estimator of the future spot rate. It is important to recognize that this does not mean that the forward rate will always be equal to the actual future spot rate. Rather it means that the estimates of the future spot rate provided by the forward rate will not systematically overshoot or undershoot the actual future spot rate; it will equal it *on average*.

Evidence regarding the expectations theory of forward exchange rates indicates that, in general, the forward rate is an unbiased estimate of expected future spot rates, if risk in the currency markets is ignored. There is some evidence, however, that when the forward rate implies a large change from the current spot rate, these forecasts tend to overshoot the actual future spot rate.

Forward rates as unbiased estimates of expected future spot rates have important implications for managers. First, managers should not spend the firm's resources to buy forecasts of future exchange rates since unbiased forecasts are provided free in the marketplace. Second, managers will find that hedging their future foreign currency risk by making use of the forward market should be a cost-effective way of limiting this risk exposure.

The International Fisher Effect

The final piece in the international currency market puzzle is the relationship between interest rates and future spot currency rates. Recall from Chapter 7 that the **Fisher Effect** describes the relationship between the nominal (risk-free) interest rate, the real rate, and the expected inflation rate. The approximate Fisher effect is

$$r_f = r'_f + i_n$$

where r_f is the nominal (risk-free) rate, r'_f is the real (risk-free) rate, and i_n is the expected inflation premium.

Fisher argues that in the absence of government interference and holding risk constant, *real rates of return across countries will be equalized through a process of arbitrage.* If real rates of return are higher in the United States than in Japan, for example, capital will flow to the United States from Japan until an equilibrium is reached. The assumption of equal real rates of return across countries ignores differences in risk and attitudes toward risk that may exist in different cultures. Also, to the extent that there are barriers to the movement of capital between countries, real rates of return may be different between countries. In spite of these limitations, the assumption of equal real returns is useful because (1) it is a reasonable representation of reality among the major industrialized countries; and (2) as capital markets become increasingly internationalized and barriers to capital flows fall, differences in real rates of return can be expected to decrease.

If real rates of return tend to be equalized across countries, it follows that differences in observed nominal rates between countries must be due primarily to different inflation expectations. Incorporating the equilibrium condition for real interest rates with relative PPP leads to what has been called the **international Fisher effect (IFE)**. The IFE states that *differences in interest rates between two countries should be offset by equal but opposite changes in the future spot exchange rate.* For example, if 1-year nominal interest rates are 10 percent in the United States and 7 percent in Australia, then IFE predicts that the Australian dollar (A$) should increase in value relative to the U.S. dollar by approximately 3 percent.

The approximate IFE relationship is given by

(18.4)
$$\frac{S_1 - S_0}{S_0} \approx i_h - i_f$$

where S_1 is the expected future (direct quote) spot rate at time period 1, S_0 is the current (direct quote) spot rate, i_h is the home country (U.S.) nominal interest rate, and i_f is the foreign country nominal interest rate.

Using the previous example, if 1-year U.S. nominal interest rates are 10 percent, 1-year Australian nominal interest rates are 7 percent, and the current spot exchange rate, S_0, is \$0.54/A\$, then the expected spot rate in 1 year, S_1, will be

$$\frac{S_1 - \$0.54}{\$0.54} = 0.10 - 0.07$$
$$S_1 = \$0.54 \,(0.10 - 0.07) + \$0.54$$
$$= \$0.5562$$

The lower nominal Australian interest rate results in an expected increase in the value of the A\$ (decrease in the value of the \$) of 3 percent.

An Integrative Look at International Parity Relationships

Figure 18.1 provides an integrative look at international parity relationships. Beginning with the lower box in the figure, suppose one observes that the 1-year nominal interest rate is 10 percent in the United States and 5 percent in Switzerland. This implies, according to the Fisher effect, that the difference in expected inflation rates between the United States and Switzerland is also 5 percent because real rates of return are assumed to be equal between the United States and Switzerland. The 5 percent inflation differential means that the 1-year future spot rate of exchange between dollars and CHF can be expected to change so that the dollar will weaken by 5 percent relative to the CHF. This condition is expected from the purchasing power parity relationship. The 5 percent differential in interest rates also implies that the dollar will sell at a 5 percent discount in the 1-year forward market relative to the CHF. This expectation arises from the interest rate parity relationship. If the forward rate is an unbiased estimator of future spot rates, then the 1-year future spot rate of exchange between dollars and CHF can be expected to change so that the dollar will weaken by 5 percent relative to the CHF.

Finally, the international Fisher effect implies that if 1-year nominal interest rates are 5 percent higher in the United States than in Switzerland, then the 1-year future spot rate of exchange between the dollar and the CHF will change such that the dollar will weaken by 5 percent relative to the CHF.

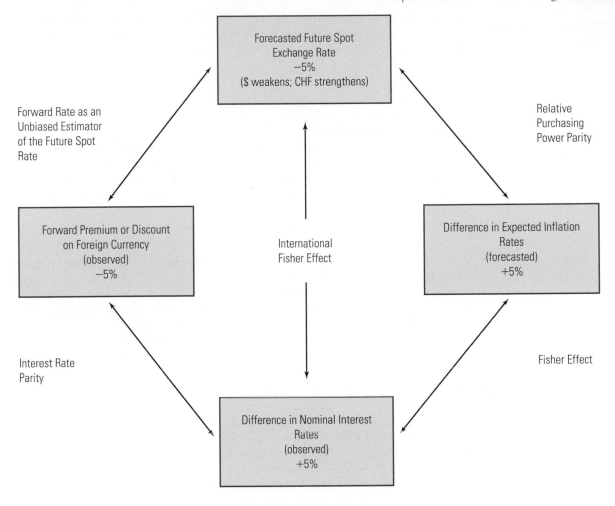

Figure 18.1 International Parity Conditions: An Integrative Look

The figure shows four boxes connected by arrows. Top box: "Forecasted Future Spot Exchange Rate −5% ($ weakens; CHF strengthens)". Left box: "Forward Premium or Discount on Foreign Currency (observed) −5%". Right box: "Difference in Expected Inflation Rates (forecasted) +5%". Bottom box: "Difference in Nominal Interest Rates (observed) +5%". Labels on arrows: "Forward Rate as an Unbiased Estimator of the Future Spot Rate", "Relative Purchasing Power Parity", "International Fisher Effect", "Interest Rate Parity", "Fisher Effect".

Assume: U.S. nominal interest rate = 10%
 Switzerland nominal interest rate = 5%
 Time horizon = 1 year

Comprehension Check Questions

1. What is meant by covered interest arbitrage?
2. Define interest rate parity, purchasing power parity, and relative purchasing power parity.
3. What is the law of one price?
4. Describe the international Fisher effect.

FOREIGN EXCHANGE RISK

Foreign exchange risk is said to exist when a portion of the cash flows expected to be received by a firm are denominated in foreign currencies. As exchange rates

 **Finance in the News**

Click on this button at **http://finance. swlearning.com** *and select Domestic and Global Financial Markets for articles on exchange rates and risk.*

change, there is uncertainty about the amount of domestic currency that will be received from a transaction denominated in a foreign currency. There are three primary categories of foreign exchange risk that multinational firms must consider:

➤ Transaction exposure (short-term)
➤ Economic (operating) exposure (long-term)
➤ Translation (accounting) exposure

Transaction Exposure

Most firms have contracts to buy and sell goods and services, with delivery and payment to occur at some time in the future. If payments under the contract involve the use of foreign currency, additional risk is involved. The potential for change in value of a foreign-currency denominated transaction due to an exchange rate change is called *transaction exposure.*

For example, General Electric is a major producer of locomotives. Suppose that General Electric contracts with the Mexican government to sell 100 locomotives for delivery 1 year from now. General Electric wants to realize $400 million from this sale. The Mexican government has indicated that it will only enter into the contract if the price is stated in Mexican pesos (Ps). The 1-year forward rate is Ps3.11/$. Hence General Electric quotes a price of Ps1,244,000,000. Once the contract has been signed, General Electric faces a significant transaction exposure. Unless General Electric takes actions to guarantee its future dollar proceeds from the sale—that is, unless it *hedges its position,* for example, by selling Ps1,244,000,000 in the 1-year forward market—it stands to lose on the transaction if the value of the peso weakens. Suppose that over the coming year the inflation rate in Mexico rises significantly beyond what was expected at the time the deal was signed. According to relative PPP, the value of the peso can be expected to decline, say to Ps4/$. If this happens, General Electric will receive only $311 million (Ps1,244,000,000/Ps4/$), rather than the $400 million it was expecting.

One well-documented example of the potential consequences of transaction exposure is the case of Laker Airlines. In the late 1970s, in the face of growing demand from British tourists traveling to the United States, Laker purchased several DC-10 aircraft and financed them in U.S. dollars. This transaction ultimately led to Laker's bankruptcy because Laker's primary source of revenue was pounds sterling, whereas its debt costs were denominated in dollars. Over the period from the late 1970s to 1982, when Laker failed, the dollar strengthened relative to the pound sterling. This had a devastating effect because (1) the strong dollar discouraged British travel to the United States, and (2) the pound sterling cost of principal and interest payments on the dollar-denominated debt increased.

Managing Transaction Exposure A number of alternatives are available to a firm faced with transaction exposure. First, the firm may choose to do nothing, and simply accept the risk associated with the transaction. Doing nothing works well for firms with extensive international transactions that may tend to cancel each other out. For example, if General Electric has purchased goods or services from Mexican firms that require the payment in approximately the same number of pesos as it expects to receive from the sale of the locomotives, then it is not necessary to do anything to counter the risk arising from a loss in value of the peso relative to the dollar.

A second alternative is to invoice all transactions in dollars (for a United States–based firm). This avoids any transaction risk for the U.S. firm, but shifts this risk to the other party. For example, in September 1992, in a period of extreme volatility of European currencies, Dow Chemical announced that it would use the

German mark as the common currency for all of its European business transactions. This action shifted currency risks from Dow to its customers who do business in other currencies. When a firm is considering this alternative, it needs to determine whether this strategy is competitively possible, or whether parties on the other side of the transaction may resist or perhaps insist on a lower price if they are forced to bear all of the transaction risk.

A handy currency conversion tool can be found at **http://www.xe.com/ucc/**

Two *hedging* techniques that a U.S. company can use to protect itself against transaction exposure are

> ➢ Execute a contract in the forward exchange market
> ➢ Execute a money market hedge

Consider a situation in which Chemex Corporation purchases materials from a British supplier, Commonwealth Resources, Ltd. Because the amount of the transaction (£2 million) is stated in pounds, Chemex bears the exchange risk. This example of transaction exposure is illustrated in Table 18.4. Assume that Commonwealth Resources extends 90-day trade credit to Chemex and that the value of the pound unexpectedly increases from $1.69/pound on the purchase date to $1.74/pound on the payment date. If Chemex takes the trade credit extended to it, the cost of the purchase effectively increases from $3.38 million to $3.48 million (that is, £2,000,000 × $1.74/pound).

First, Chemex could execute a contract in the forward exchange market to buy £2 million at the *known* 90-day forward rate, rather than at the *uncertain* spot rate prevailing on the payment date. This is referred to as a *forward market hedge.* Assume, for example, that the 90-day forward rate is $1.70/pound. Based on this rate, Chemex effectively would be able to exchange $3.4 million (that is, £2,000,000 × $1.70/pound) 90 days later on the payment date when it is required to pay for the materials. Thus, Chemex would be able to take advantage of the trade credit and, at the same time, hedge against foreign exchange risk.

A second hedging technique, called a *money market hedge,* involves Chemex borrowing funds from its bank, exchanging them for pounds at the spot rate, and investing them in interest-bearing British securities to yield £2 million in 90 days. By investing in securities that mature on the same date the payment is due to Commonwealth Resources (that is, 90 days after the purchase date), Chemex will have the necessary amount of pounds available to pay for the materials. The net cost of this money market hedge to Chemex will depend on the interest rate on the funds it borrows from its bank relative to the interest rate on the funds it invests in securities. If the conditions of interest rate parity are satisfied, these two hedging techniques are equivalent.

For large multinational companies, there will be many international transactions involving many different currencies. Attempting to hedge separately the

Table 18.4 Example of Transaction Exchange Rate Risk: Chemex Corporation

Date	Exchange Rate	Amount of Transaction	
		U.S. Dollars	**British Pounds**
Purchase date	$1.69/pound	$3,380,000	£2,000,000
Payment date	$1.74/pound	$3,480,000	£2,000,000

transaction exposure for each international transaction would be time-consuming and inefficient. For example, consider Sara Lee Corporation, which has operations both in Great Britain and France. The British subsidiary makes purchases in France that require payment in euros. At the same time the French subsidiary makes purchases in Britain that require payments in pounds sterling. To the extent that these transactions offset, no hedge is necessary. Multinational firms often make thousands of overlapping transactions using different currencies. Thus it is a complex matter to keep track of *net* currency exposures and avoid hedging against risks that do not really exist when one takes the consolidated corporate view, rather than the narrow subsidiary view of exchange risk.

Economic Exposure

Economic (or operating) *exposure* refers to changes in a firm's operating cash flows (and hence the firm's value) that come about because of *real* rather than *nominal* changes in exchange rates. Real exchange rate changes occur when there are deviations from purchasing power parity (PPP). Under relative PPP, exchange rates should vary to reflect changes in the price level of goods and services in one country relative to another. For example, if the inflation rate in Mexico is 5 percent higher per year than in the United States, relative PPP says that the value of the Mexican peso can be expected to decline by about 5 percent relative to the dollar. Thus goods purchased in the United States from Mexico will cost the same as they did before the increase in Mexican inflation, after adjusting for the decline in the value of the peso.

Real exchange rate changes can affect the way competing companies in two countries do business and can impact the business conditions in the countries. In April 1995, $1 equaled about ¥83. In July 2003, $1 equaled about ¥118. In relative terms, the dollar was "weak" and the yen was "strong" in April 1995, whereas in July 2003, the dollar was "strong" and the yen was "weak."

The weakening of the dollar and the strengthening of the yen can have a dramatic impact on firms doing business in the United States and Japan. The showcase example of these effects is the relative performance of the Japanese and American automobile industries. In the mid-1980s, Japanese products were generally cheaper (and of better quality) than their American counterparts. The Japanese share of the U.S. auto market was growing, restrained only by voluntary import restrictions agreed to by the Japanese. By 1995, the increased value of the yen relative to the dollar had reversed the fortunes of automakers in both countries. Japanese autos were selling for several thousand dollars more in 1995 than comparable U.S. products. American firms reported significant increases in U.S. market share at the expense of the Japanese. Japanese auto firms were experiencing significant financial difficulties at a time when U.S. auto firms were reporting substantial increases in profit. U.S. firms also had begun exporting vehicles to Japan.

In an attempt to offset the impact of their significant economic exposure in the United States, Japanese firms have aggressively moved to establish manufacturing and assembly operations in the United States and some European countries, so that many of their costs will be denominated in the same currency as their revenues. Also, by locating plants in many different countries, multinational firms have the flexibility to shift production from one location to another, in order to offset unfavorable economic exposure.

Managing Economic Exposure Economic exposure is much more difficult and expensive to manage than the shorter-term transactions exposure already dis-

Numa Financial Systems maintains a comprehensive Web site that tracks the world's major markets (Hong Kong, Tokyo, the United Kingdom, etc.), links to international financial Web sites, and provides guides and calculators.
http://www.numa.com/ index.htm

FINANCE & The Real World

Vying for U.S. Investment

U.S. companies are moving an increasing number of jobs to two destinations: China and India. China, with a population of about 1.3 billion people, has already garnered nearly $50 billion in foreign investment. The country's economy has grown at an annual rate of nearly 10 percent—fueled in part by U.S. dollars—and the poverty rate is relatively low, at 10 percent of the population. India, with a population of 1.1 billion, is relatively new on the international investment scene, with under $10 billion of foreign investment. India has a significantly higher poverty rate, at 25 percent of the population, and less than 5 percent of its population has a telephone.

Nevertheless, when Intel—the giant U.S. semiconductor manufacturer—thinks about expansion, it leans towards India. Intel investments in India involve chip design and software development, and the company can access India's global leadership in software engineering. India is Intel's largest nonmanufacturing site outside the United States, with more than 1,000 professionals engaged at a chip designing center in the city of Bangalore. Intel plans to invest an additional $100 million to expand its staff in India to 3,000 and set up a software development center there. U.S. semiconductor Texas Instruments, Silicon Laboratories and IBM also have facilities in Bangalore, which now contributes a fourth of India's $10 billion in annual software exports. Indeed,

hundreds of thousands of U.S. technology jobs are going overseas, as a wide variety of industries contract major technology work to providers in India and China, saving the companies up to 70 percent in labor costs.

But China isn't letting upstart India win every U.S. contract, as the two countries vie for U.S. investment from companies like Maryland-based Sweetheart Cup Co. The company was looking to outsource the development of a new computer system that would track production at the company's factories, which produce $1 billion worth of disposable plates and utensils for restaurants. The winner was China, offering a package that cost 40 percent less than India's best offer.

Dollars are not the only consideration at play, particularly if the U.S. company is counting on doing business locally. For one thing, there's the question of political stability. China is the last surviving communist power, while India is the world's largest democracy. China has state-controlled media and unelected officials while India has a free press and an open society. So far, on political stability, India wins. With one big exception: every few years, India and neighboring Pakistan threaten each other with war—a business risk that doesn't seem to disturb multinational corporations.

Sources: Online Asia, July 30, 2003, "The Quest for Asia's Outsourcing Crown"; The Wall Street Journal Online, July 24, 2003, "India May Be Primed to Narrow Its Economic Gap with China"; USA Today, June 10, 2003, "Intel Sees India as Place for Investment."

cussed. Strategies to manage the impact of real changes in exchange rates in countries where a multinational firm operates include

1. *Shift production from high-cost (exchange-rate adjusted) plants to lower-cost plants*—for example, moving labor-intensive sewing operations from U.S. textile plants to plants in Mexico
2. *Increase productivity*—adopt labor-saving technologies, implement flexible manufacturing systems, reduce product cycles, make use of benchmarking, that is, copy your strongest competitors
3. *"Outsource" the supply of many of the components needed to produce a product to lower-cost locations*—for example, some U.S. publishing houses' outsourcing typesetting to areas in the Far East with lower labor costs

4. *Increase product differentiation to reduce the price sensitivity in the market*—for example, the Japanese moving more to the luxury car market as the yen has strengthened because of the greater price flexibility the luxury market provides relative to the economy car market

Translation Exposure

When a multinational firm has one or more foreign subsidiaries with assets and liabilities denominated in a foreign currency, it faces ***translation exposure.*** For example, if a United States–based multinational firm operates a subsidiary in Japan, the yen value of the subsidiary's assets and liabilities must be translated into the home (U.S. $) currency when the parent firm prepares its consolidated financial statements. When the translation occurs, there can be gains or losses, which must be recognized in the financial statements of the parent.

Current accounting standards are set forth in *Statement of Financial Accounting Standards Number 52.* The major provisions of this standard are

➤ Current assets, unless covered by forward exchange contracts, and fixed assets are translated into dollars at the rate of exchange prevailing on the date of the balance sheet.
➤ Current and long-term liabilities payable in foreign currency are translated into dollars at the rate of exchange prevailing on the date of the balance sheet.
➤ Income statement items are translated either at the rate on the date of a particular transaction or at a weighted average of the exchange rates for the period of the income statement.
➤ Dividends are translated at the exchange rate on the date the dividend is paid.
➤ Equity accounts, including common stock and contributed capital in excess of par value, are translated at historical rates.
➤ Gains and losses to the parent from translation are not included in the parent's calculation of net income, nor are they included in the parent's retained earnings. Rather they are reported in a separate equity account named "Cumulative foreign currency translation adjustments" or a similar title. Gains or losses in this account are not recognized in the income statement until the parent's investment in the foreign subsidiary is sold or liquidated.

A decline in the value of a foreign currency relative to the U.S. dollar reduces the conversion value of the foreign subsidiary's liabilities, as well as its assets. Therefore, the parent company's risk exposure depends on the foreign subsidiary's net equity position (that is, assets minus liabilities). Thus, on the books of the parent company, the subsidiary's creditors in effect bear part of the decline in the value of the subsidiary's assets.

The impact of a decrease in the exchange rate on the firm's balance sheet can be illustrated with the following example. American Products has a subsidiary, Canadian Products, with total assets of $12 million (Canadian) and total liabilities of $8 million (Canadian). Based on an exchange rate of $0.80 (U.S.) per dollar (Canadian), the net equity position of the Canadian subsidiary on American Products' balance sheet as shown in Table 18.5 is $3.2 million (U.S.). Suppose now that the exchange rate declines to $0.75 (U.S.) per dollar (Canadian) and all other things remain the same. As can be seen in the table, the net equity position of the Canadian subsidiary on American Products' balance sheet declines to $3 million (U.S.), resulting in a $200,000 currency exchange loss.

Managing Translation Exposure In general, when a foreign subsidiary's assets are greater than its liabilities, currency exchange losses will occur when the ex-

Table 18.5 Effect of a Decrease in the Exchange Rate on American Products' Balance Sheet

	$0.80 (U.S.) = $1.00 (Canadian)		$0.75 (U.S.) = $1.00 (Canadian)	
	$(Canadian)	$(U.S.)	$(Canadian)	$(U.S.)
Assets	$12,000,000	$9,600,000	$12,000,000	$9,000,000
Liabilities	8,000,000	6,400,000	8,000,000	6,000,000
Net equity position	$ 4,000,000	$3,200,000	$ 4,000,000	$3,000,000

change rate decreases. The opposite effects are true for increases in the exchange rate. A company can hedge and manage its balance sheet translation exposure by financing its foreign assets with debt denominated in the same currency.

For example, in September 1993, Dow Chemical issued 4.625 percent *Eurobonds.* Instead of being denominated in U.S. dollars, as is usual for securities of U.S. companies, these bonds are denominated in Swiss francs. The Dow Chemical debt issue totaled 150,000,000 Swiss francs, or about $103,000,000, based on the exchange rate between the U.S. dollar and the Swiss franc at the time of issuance.

Dow Chemical's financial managers apparently had a choice between whether to issue Swiss franc–denominated or U.S. dollar–denominated debt. One possible reason for issuing Swiss franc–denominated debt may have been to hedge the company's Swiss assets. For example, if the value of the Swiss franc drops compared to the U.S. dollar value, presumably the U.S. dollar value of Dow Chemical's Swiss assets also decreases. However, if this happens the U.S. dollar amount of both the interest and principal that Dow Chemical has to pay also decreases.

A multinational company can also minimize its exchange rate risk, as well as the risk of expropriation or nationalization of its assets by a foreign government, by developing a *portfolio* of foreign investments. Rather than making all its direct investments in foreign subsidiaries that are located in one particular country, the firm can spread its foreign investments among a number of different countries, thus limiting the risk of incurring large losses within any one country.

Comprehension Check Questions

1. Describe each of the following types of foreign exchange risks:
   - Transaction exposure
   - Economic exposure
   - Translation exposure
2. What are some of the ways in which firms can manage the above three types of foreign exchange risks?

Summary

- A Eurocurrency is a currency deposited in a bank located outside of the country of origin. The Eurocurrency market is an important alternative to domestic sources of financing for multinational firms. The interest rate charged for Eurocurrency loans is tied to LIBOR, the London interbank offer rate.

➤ The exchange rate is the rate at which one currency can be converted into another. The spot rate is the rate of exchange for currencies being bought and sold for immediate delivery today. The forward rate is the rate of exchange between currencies to be delivered at a future point in time—usually 30, 90, and 180 days from today.

➤ The theory of interest rate parity states that the percentage differential between the spot and the forward rate for a currency quoted in terms of another currency is equal to the approximate difference in interest rates in the two countries over the same time horizon.

➤ The theory of relative purchasing power parity states that in comparison to a period when exchange rates between two countries are in equilibrium, changes in differential rates of inflation between two countries will be offset by equal, but opposite changes in the future spot currency rate.

➤ The forward rate is often taken as an unbiased estimator of the future spot currency rate.

➤ The international Fisher effect theory states that differences in interest rates between two countries will be offset by equal but opposite changes in the future spot rate.

➤ Firms that compete in a global economy face three categories of foreign exchange risk:

Transaction or short-term exposure

Economic (operating) or long-term exposure

Translation (accounting) exposure

➤ Many risk-reducing strategies are available to firms facing these risks, including the use of various hedges, such as a forward hedge and a money market hedge.

Questions and Topics for Discussion

1. Define the following terms:
   a. Multinational corporation
   b. Spot exchange rate
   c. Forward exchange rate
   d. Direct quote versus indirect quote
   e. LIBOR
   f. Euro

2. What is the theory of interest rate parity?

3. What is covered interest arbitrage?

4. Describe two techniques that a company can use to hedge against transaction exchange risk.

5. Describe the factors that cause exchange rates to change over time.

6. Describe how the concepts of relative purchasing power parity, interest rate parity, and international Fisher effect are related.

Self-Test Problems

ST1. What is the premium or discount between the spot rate and the 90-day forward rate for the Swiss franc on July 17, 2003? What does this imply about the future spot rate for Swiss francs? (See Tables 18.2 and 18.3.)

ST2. Assume that the annualized discount on forward Canadian dollars is 3 percent. The annualized U.S. interest rate is 8 percent, and the comparable Canadian interest rate is 12 percent. How can a U.S. trader use covered interest arbitrage to take advantage of this situation?

ST3. DaimlerChrysler is planning to sell its new minivan in Japan. Daimler-Chrysler receives $12,000 for each van sold in the United States and wants to get the same net proceeds from its export sales.

   a. If the exchange rate of Japanese yen for U.S. dollars is ¥140 = $1, what price must DaimlerChrysler charge in Japan (in yen)?

   b. What price will DaimlerChrysler have to charge in Japan if the value of the dollar falls to 120 yen?

ST4. The yield on 6-month maturity U.S. government bonds is 4 percent, while the yield on similar maturity Swiss bonds is 5 percent. The current spot exchange rate between the dollar and the Swiss franc (CHF) is $0.68/CHF. What is the expected future spot rate for the CHF in 6 months?

Problems

1. Japanese Motors exports cars and trucks to the U.S. market. On July 2, 1999, its most popular model was selling (wholesale) to U.S. dealers for $15,000. What price must Japanese Motors charge for the same model on July 17, 2003, to realize the same amount (of Japanese yen) as it did in 1999? (Refer to Table 18.2.) — **INTERMEDIATE**

2. Valley Stores, a U.S. department store chain, annually negotiates a contract with Alpine Watch Company, located in Switzerland, to purchase a large shipment of watches. On July 2, 1999, Valley purchased 10,000 watches for a total of 1.26 million Swiss francs. Refer to Table 18.2 and determine the following: — **CHALLENGE**

   a. The total cost and cost per watch in U.S. dollars

   b. The total cost and cost per watch in U.S. dollars of 12,000 watches purchased on July 17, 2003, assuming that Alpine's price per watch (in Swiss francs) remains unchanged

3. Determine the percentage change in the value of the following currencies relative to the U.S. dollar between July 2, 1999 and July 17, 2003 (Refer to Table 18.2). — **INTERMEDIATE**

   a. India

   b. Britain

   c. The Euro

   d. Canada

4. Compute the indirect quote for the rupee, Australian dollar, and yen as of July 2, 1999. (Refer to Table 18.2.) — **BASIC**

5. If the *1-year* U.S. Treasury bill rate is 7.0 percent, the spot rate between U.S. dollars and British pounds is £1 = $1.69, and the *90-day* forward rate is £1 = $1.68, what rate of interest is expected on British Treasury bills, assuming interest rate parity between the dollar and pound exists? (Hint: Convert the — **INTERMEDIATE**

1-year U.S. T-bill yield to a yield for 90 days (3 months), the same period as the forward rate.)

INTERMEDIATE

6. Suppose the British short-term interest rate is 13 percent and the corresponding U.S. rate is 8 percent. Suppose at the same time that the discount on forward pounds is 3 percent per year. Do these conditions present an opportunity for covered interest arbitrage? If so, what steps should a trader in New York take? What annual rate will the trader earn?

INTERMEDIATE

7. Market Mutual Fund of New York has $5 million to invest in certificates of deposit (CDs) for the next 6 months (180 days). It can buy either a Philadelphia National Bank (PNB) CD with an annual yield of 10 percent (5 percent for 6 months) or a Geneva (Switzerland) Bank CD with a yield of 12.5 percent (6.25 percent for 6 months). Assume that the CDs are of comparable default risk. The analysts of the mutual fund are concerned about exchange rate risk. They were quoted the following exchange rates by the international department of a New York City bank:

Switzerland (Swiss Franc, CHF)

Spot	$0.4200
30-day forward	0.4190
90-day forward	0.4170
180-day forward	0.4155

a. If the Geneva Bank CD is purchased and held to maturity, determine the net gain (loss) in U.S. dollars relative to the PNB CD, assuming that the exchange rate in 180 days equals today's spot rate.

b. Suppose the Swiss franc declines in value by 5 percent relative to the U.S. dollar over the next 180 days. Determine the net gain (loss) of the Geneva Bank CD in U.S. dollars relative to the PNB CD for an uncovered position.

c. Determine the net gain (loss) from a covered position.

d. What other factor or factors should be considered in the decision to purchase the Geneva Bank CD?

BASIC

8. Last year, the French marketing subsidiary of International Pharmaceuticals Corporation (IPC), a New Jersey–based drug manufacturer, earned 700,000 euros. This year, partly due to a weaker U.S. dollar, the French subsidiary will earn 900,000 euros. Last year the exchange rate was 1.2 euros per dollar, and this year it is 1.0 euros per dollar. Calculate how many U.S. dollars the French subsidiary contributes to IPC's earnings in each year.

CHALLENGE

9. The Jennette Corporation, a firm based in Mt. Pleasant, South Carolina, has an account payable with a British firm coming due in 180 days. The payable requires Jennette to pay £200,000. Winthrop Jennette, the firm's founder and CEO, is an astute manager. He has asked his CFO, Artis Montgomery, to advise him on the various options for dealing with the exchange risk inherent in this payable. He wishes to know the expected dollar cost of (1) a forward hedge and (2) a money market hedge.

The following information is available to Artis. The spot rate of the pound today is $1.50. The current 180-day forward rate of the pound is $1.47. Interest rates are as follows:

	United Kingdom	United States
180-day deposit rate	4.5%	4.5%
180-day borrowing rate	5.0%	5.0%

a. What is the expected dollar cost of the forward hedge?

b. What is the expected dollar cost of the money market hedge?

c. Which alternative do you recommend? What are the risks associated with this recommendation?

10. The Swiss franc (CHF) is currently trading in the spot market at $0.5800/CHF. The 180-day forward rate is $0.5743/CHF. The U.S. Treasury bill rate for 180 days is 3.1 percent in the United States. What do you expect is the 180-day Switzerland government security rate? Why?   **INTERMEDIATE**

11. The Philippine peso (PHP) is currently trading in the spot market at $0.01851/PHP. The expected spot market price in 6 months is $0.01833/PHP. If the U.S. inflation rate over the next 6 months is expected to be 2 percent what is the implied 6-month inflation rate for the Philippines?   **BASIC**

12. The Indian rupee (INR) is trading in the spot market at $0.02165/INR and the 180-day forward rate is $0.02365/INR. If the forward rate is an unbiased predictor of the spot rate, what is the implied Indian interest rate over the 6-month period, if the U.S. rate for the same period is 1.1 percent?   **BASIC**

13. Using the currency calculator at http://www.bankrate.com, calculate the foreign currency equivalent of $100 (U.S.) in terms of British pounds and Japanese yen. Print out the computer screen with the conversions and turn in your answers to your instructor.   **BASIC**

TABLE I Future Value Interest Factor (FVIF) ($1 at *i*% per period for *n* periods); FVIF = $(1 + i)^n$; $FV_n = PV_0 (FVIF_{i,n})$

Period, n	1%	2%	3%	4%	5%	6%	7%	8%	9%	10%	11%	12%	13%
0	1.000	1.000	1.000	1.000	1.000	1.000	1.000	1.000	1.000	1.000	1.000	1.000	1.000
1	1.010	1.020	1.030	1.040	1.050	1.060	1.070	1.080	1.090	1.100	1.110	1.120	1.130
2	1.020	1.040	1.061	1.082	1.102	1.124	1.145	1.166	1.188	1.210	1.232	1.254	1.277
3	1.030	1.061	1.093	1.125	1.158	1.191	1.225	1.260	1.295	1.331	1.368	1.405	1.443
4	1.041	1.082	1.126	1.170	1.216	1.262	1.311	1.360	1.412	1.464	1.518	1.574	1.630
5	1.051	1.104	1.159	1.217	1.276	1.338	1.403	1.469	1.539	1.611	1.685	1.762	1.842
6	1.062	1.126	1.194	1.265	1.340	1.419	1.501	1.587	1.677	1.772	1.870	1.974	2.082
7	1.072	1.149	1.230	1.316	1.407	1.504	1.606	1.714	1.828	1.949	2.076	2.211	2.353
8	1.083	1.172	1.267	1.369	1.477	1.594	1.718	1.851	1.993	2.144	2.305	2.476	2.658
9	1.094	1.195	1.305	1.423	1.551	1.689	1.838	1.999	2.172	2.358	2.558	2.773	3.004
10	1.105	1.219	1.344	1.480	1.629	1.791	1.967	2.159	2.367	2.594	2.839	3.106	3.395
11	1.116	1.243	1.384	1.539	1.710	1.898	2.105	2.332	2.580	2.853	3.152	3.479	3.836
12	1.127	1.268	1.426	1.601	1.796	2.012	2.252	2.518	2.813	3.138	3.498	3.896	4.335
13	1.138	1.294	1.469	1.665	1.886	2.133	2.410	2.720	3.066	3.452	3.883	4.363	4.898
14	1.149	1.319	1.513	1.732	1.980	2.261	2.579	2.937	3.342	3.797	4.310	4.887	5.535
15	1.161	1.346	1.558	1.801	2.079	2.397	2.759	3.172	3.642	4.177	4.785	5.474	6.254
16	1.173	1.373	1.605	1.873	2.183	2.540	2.952	3.426	3.970	4.595	5.311	6.130	7.067
17	1.184	1.400	1.653	1.948	2.292	2.693	3.159	3.700	4.328	5.054	5.895	6.866	7.986
18	1.196	1.428	1.702	2.026	2.407	2.854	3.380	3.996	4.717	5.560	6.544	7.690	9.024
19	1.208	1.457	1.754	2.107	2.527	3.026	3.617	4.316	5.142	6.116	7.263	8.613	10.197
20	1.220	1.486	1.806	2.191	2.653	3.207	3.870	4.661	5.604	6.728	8.062	9.646	11.523
24	1.270	1.608	2.033	2.563	3.225	4.049	5.072	6.341	7.911	9.850	12.239	15.179	18.790
25	1.282	1.641	2.094	2.666	3.386	4.292	5.427	6.848	8.623	10.835	13.585	17.000	21.231
30	1.348	1.811	2.427	3.243	4.322	5.743	7.612	10.063	13.268	17.449	22.892	29.960	39.116
40	1.489	2.208	3.262	4.801	7.040	10.286	14.974	21.725	31.409	45.259	65.001	93.051	132.782
50	1.645	2.692	4.384	7.107	11.467	18.420	29.457	46.902	74.358	117.391	184.565	289.002	450.736
60	1.817	3.281	5.892	10.520	18.679	32.988	57.946	101.257	176.031	304.482	524.057	897.597	1,530.05

Period, n	14%	15%	16%	17%	18%	19%	20%	24%	28%	32%	36%	40%
0	1.000	1.000	1.000	1.000	1.000	1.000	1.000	1.000	1.000	1.000	1.000	1.000
1	1.140	1.150	1.160	1.170	1.180	1.190	1.200	1.240	1.280	1.320	1.360	1.400
2	1.300	1.322	1.346	1.369	1.392	1.416	1.440	1.538	1.638	1.742	1.850	1.960
3	1.482	1.521	1.561	1.602	1.643	1.685	1.728	1.907	2.067	2.300	2.515	2.744
4	1.689	1.749	1.811	1.874	1.939	2.005	2.074	2.364	2.684	3.036	3.421	3.842
5	1.925	2.011	2.100	2.192	2.288	2.386	2.488	2.932	3.436	4.007	4.653	5.378
6	2.195	2.313	2.436	2.565	2.700	2.840	2.986	3.635	4.398	5.290	6.328	7.530
7	2.502	2.660	2.826	3.001	3.185	3.379	3.583	4.508	5.629	6.983	8.605	10.541
8	2.853	3.059	3.278	3.511	3.759	4.021	4.300	5.590	7.206	9.217	11.703	14.758
9	3.252	3.518	3.803	4.108	4.435	4.785	5.160	6.931	9.223	12.166	15.917	20.661
10	3.707	4.046	4.411	4.807	5.234	5.695	6.192	8.594	11.806	16.060	21.647	28.925
11	4.226	4.652	5.117	5.624	6.176	6.777	7.430	10.657	15.112	21.199	29.439	40.496
12	4.818	5.350	5.926	6.580	7.288	8.064	8.916	13.215	19.343	27.983	40.037	56.694
13	5.492	6.153	6.886	7.699	8.599	9.596	10.699	16.386	24.759	36.937	54.451	79.372
14	6.261	7.076	7.988	9.007	10.147	11.420	12.839	20.319	31.961	48.757	74.053	111.120
15	7.138	8.137	9.266	10.539	11.974	13.590	15.407	25.196	40.565	64.359	100.712	155.568
16	8.137	9.358	10.748	12.330	14.129	16.172	18.488	31.243	51.923	84.954	136.969	217.795
17	9.276	10.761	12.468	14.426	16.672	19.244	22.186	38.741	66.461	112.139	186.278	304.914
18	10.575	12.375	14.463	16.879	19.673	22.901	26.623	48.039	85.071	148.023	253.338	426.879
19	12.056	14.232	16.777	19.748	23.214	27.252	31.948	59.568	108.890	195.391	344.540	597.630
20	13.743	16.367	19.461	23.106	27.393	32.429	38.338	73.864	139.380	257.916	468.574	836.683
24	23.212	28.625	35.236	43.297	53.109	65.032	79.497	174.631	374.144	783.023	1,603.00	3,214.20
25	26.462	32.919	40.874	50.658	62.669	77.388	95.396	216.542	478.905	1,033.59	2,180.08	4,499.88
30	50.950	66.212	85.850	111.065	143.371	184.675	237.376	634.820	1,645.50	4,142.07	10,143.0	24,201.4
40	188.884	267.864	378.721	533.869	750.378	1,051.67	1,469.77	5,455.91	19,426.7	66,520.8	219,562	700,038
50	700.233	1,083.66	1,670.70	2,566.22	3,927.36	5,988.91	9,100.44	46,890.4	229,350	*	*	*
60	2,595.92	4,384.00	7,370.20	12,335.4	20,555.1	34,105.0	56,347.5	402,996	*	*	*	*

*These interest factors exceed 1,000,000

Table II 547

TABLE II Present Value Interest Factor (PVIF) ($1 at $i\%$ per period for n periods);

$$PVIF = \frac{1}{(1 + i)^n} \; ; \; PV_0 = FV_n \, (PVIF_{i,n})$$

Period, n	1%	2%	3%	4%	5%	6%	7%	8%	9%	10%	11%	12%	13%
0	1.000	1.000	1.000	1.000	1.000	1.000	1.000	1.000	1.000	1.000	1.000	1.000	1.000
1	0.990	0.980	0.971	0.962	0.952	0.943	0.935	0.926	0.917	0.909	0.901	0.893	0.885
2	0.980	0.961	0.943	0.925	0.907	0.890	0.873	0.857	0.842	0.826	0.812	0.797	0.783
3	0.971	0.942	0.915	0.889	0.864	0.840	0.816	0.794	0.772	0.751	0.731	0.712	0.693
4	0.961	0.924	0.889	0.855	0.823	0.792	0.763	0.735	0.708	0.683	0.659	0.636	0.613
5	0.951	0.906	0.863	0.822	0.784	0.747	0.713	0.681	0.650	0.621	0.593	0.567	0.543
6	0.942	0.888	0.838	0.790	0.746	0.705	0.666	0.630	0.596	0.564	0.535	0.507	0.480
7	0.933	0.871	0.813	0.760	0.711	0.665	0.623	0.583	0.547	0.513	0.482	0.452	0.425
8	0.923	0.853	0.789	0.731	0.677	0.627	0.582	0.540	0.502	0.467	0.434	0.404	0.376
9	0.914	0.837	0.766	0.703	0.645	0.592	0.544	0.500	0.460	0.424	0.391	0.361	0.333
10	0.905	0.820	0.744	0.676	0.614	0.558	0.508	0.463	0.422	0.386	0.352	0.322	0.295
11	0.896	0.804	0.722	0.650	0.585	0.527	0.475	0.429	0.388	0.350	0.317	0.287	0.261
12	0.887	0.788	0.701	0.625	0.557	0.497	0.444	0.397	0.356	0.319	0.286	0.257	0.231
13	0.879	0.773	0.681	0.601	0.530	0.469	0.415	0.368	0.326	0.290	0.258	0.229	0.204
14	0.870	0.758	0.661	0.577	0.505	0.442	0.388	0.340	0.299	0.263	0.232	0.205	0.181
15	0.861	0.743	0.642	0.555	0.481	0.417	0.362	0.315	0.275	0.239	0.209	0.183	0.160
16	0.853	0.728	0.623	0.534	0.458	0.394	0.339	0.292	0.252	0.218	0.188	0.163	0.141
17	0.844	0.714	0.605	0.513	0.436	0.371	0.317	0.270	0.231	0.198	0.170	0.146	0.125
18	0.836	0.700	0.587	0.494	0.416	0.350	0.296	0.250	0.212	0.180	0.153	0.130	0.111
19	0.828	0.686	0.570	0.475	0.396	0.331	0.276	0.232	0.194	0.164	0.138	0.116	0.098
20	0.820	0.673	0.554	0.456	0.377	0.312	0.258	0.215	0.178	0.149	0.124	0.104	0.087
24	0.788	0.622	0.492	0.390	0.310	0.247	0.197	0.158	0.126	0.102	0.082	0.066	0.053
25	0.780	0.610	0.478	0.375	0.295	0.233	0.184	0.146	0.116	0.092	0.074	0.059	0.047
30	0.742	0.552	0.412	0.308	0.231	0.174	0.131	0.099	0.075	0.057	0.044	0.033	0.026
40	0.672	0.453	0.307	0.208	0.142	0.097	0.067	0.046	0.032	0.022	0.015	0.011	0.008
50	0.608	0.372	0.228	0.141	0.087	0.054	0.034	0.021	0.013	0.009	0.005	0.003	0.002
60	0.550	0.305	0.170	0.095	0.054	0.030	0.017	0.010	0.006	0.003	0.002	0.001	0.001

Period, n	14%	15%	16%	17%	18%	19%	20%	24%	28%	32%	36%	40%
0	1.000	1.000	1.000	1.000	1.000	1.000	1.000	1.000	1.000	1.000	1.000	1.000
1	0.877	0.870	0.862	0.855	0.847	0.840	0.833	0.806	0.781	0.758	0.735	0.714
2	0.769	0.756	0.743	0.731	0.718	0.706	0.694	0.650	0.610	0.574	0.541	0.510
3	0.675	0.658	0.641	0.624	0.609	0.593	0.579	0.524	0.477	0.435	0.398	0.364
4	0.592	0.572	0.552	0.534	0.516	0.499	0.482	0.423	0.373	0.329	0.292	0.260
5	0.519	0.497	0.476	0.456	0.437	0.419	0.402	0.341	0.291	0.250	0.215	0.186
6	0.456	0.432	0.410	0.390	0.370	0.352	0.335	0.275	0.227	0.189	0.158	0.133
7	0.400	0.376	0.354	0.333	0.314	0.296	0.279	0.222	0.178	0.143	0.116	0.095
8	0.351	0.327	0.305	0.285	0.266	0.249	0.233	0.179	0.139	0.108	0.085	0.068
9	0.308	0.284	0.263	0.243	0.225	0.209	0.194	0.144	0.108	0.082	0.063	0.048
10	0.270	0.247	0.227	0.208	0.191	0.176	0.162	0.116	0.085	0.062	0.046	0.035
11	0.237	0.215	0.195	0.178	0.162	0.148	0.135	0.094	0.066	0.047	0.034	0.025
12	0.208	0.187	0.168	0.152	0.137	0.124	0.112	0.076	0.052	0.036	0.025	0.018
13	0.182	0.163	0.145	0.130	0.116	0.104	0.093	0.061	0.040	0.027	0.018	0.013
14	0.160	0.141	0.125	0.111	0.099	0.088	0.078	0.049	0.032	0.021	0.014	0.009
15	0.140	0.123	0.108	0.095	0.084	0.074	0.065	0.040	0.025	0.016	0.010	0.006
16	0.123	0.107	0.093	0.081	0.071	0.062	0.054	0.032	0.019	0.012	0.007	0.005
17	0.108	0.093	0.080	0.069	0.060	0.052	0.045	0.026	0.015	0.009	0.005	0.003
18	0.095	0.081	0.069	0.059	0.051	0.044	0.038	0.021	0.012	0.007	0.004	0.002
19	0.083	0.070	0.060	0.051	0.043	0.037	0.031	0.017	0.009	0.005	0.003	0.002
20	0.073	0.061	0.051	0.043	0.037	0.031	0.026	0.014	0.007	0.004	0.002	0.001
24	0.043	0.035	0.028	0.023	0.019	0.015	0.013	0.006	0.003	0.001	0.001	0.000
25	0.038	0.030	0.024	0.020	0.016	0.013	0.010	0.005	0.002	0.001	0.000	0.000
30	0.020	0.015	0.012	0.009	0.007	0.005	0.004	0.002	0.001	0.000	0.000	0.000
40	0.005	0.004	0.003	0.002	0.001	0.001	0.001	0.000	0.000	0.000	0.000	0.000
50	0.001	0.001	0.001	0.000	0.000	0.000	0.000	0.000	0.000	0.000	0.000	0.000
60	0.000	0.000	0.000	0.000	0.000	0.000	0.000	0.000	0.000	0.000	0.000	0.000

TABLE III — Future Value of an Annuity Interest Factor (FVIFA) ($1 per period at i% per period for n periods); $FVIFA = \dfrac{(1+i)^n - 1}{i}$; $FVAN_n = PMT(FVIFA_{i,n})$

Period, n	1%	2%	3%	4%	5%	6%	7%	8%	9%	10%	11%	12%	13%
1	1.000	1.000	1.000	1.000	1.000	1.000	1.000	1.000	1.000	1.000	1.000	1.000	1.000
2	2.010	2.020	2.030	2.040	2.050	2.060	2.070	2.080	2.090	2.100	2.110	2.120	2.130
3	3.030	3.060	3.091	3.122	3.152	3.184	3.215	3.246	3.278	3.310	3.342	3.374	3.407
4	4.060	4.122	4.184	4.246	4.310	4.375	4.440	4.506	4.573	4.641	4.710	4.779	4.850
5	5.101	5.204	5.309	5.416	5.526	5.637	5.751	5.867	5.985	6.105	6.228	6.353	6.480
6	6.152	6.308	6.468	6.633	6.802	6.975	7.153	7.336	7.523	7.716	7.913	8.115	8.323
7	7.214	7.434	7.662	7.898	8.142	8.394	8.654	8.923	9.200	9.487	9.783	10.089	10.405
8	8.286	8.583	8.892	9.214	9.549	9.897	10.260	10.637	11.028	11.436	11.859	12.300	12.757
9	9.369	9.755	10.159	10.583	11.027	11.491	11.978	12.488	13.021	13.579	14.164	14.776	15.416
10	10.462	10.950	11.464	12.006	12.578	13.181	13.816	14.487	15.193	15.937	16.722	17.549	18.420
11	11.567	12.169	12.808	13.486	14.207	14.972	15.784	16.645	17.560	18.531	19.561	20.655	21.814
12	12.683	13.412	14.192	15.026	15.917	16.870	17.888	18.977	20.141	21.384	22.713	24.133	25.650
13	13.809	14.680	15.618	16.627	17.713	18.882	20.141	21.495	22.953	24.523	26.212	28.029	29.985
14	14.947	15.974	17.086	18.292	19.599	21.051	22.550	24.215	26.019	27.975	30.095	32.393	34.883
15	16.097	17.293	18.599	20.024	21.579	23.276	25.129	27.152	29.361	31.772	34.405	37.280	40.417
16	17.258	18.639	20.157	21.825	23.657	25.673	27.888	30.324	33.003	35.950	39.190	42.753	46.672
17	18.430	20.012	21.762	23.698	25.840	28.213	30.840	33.750	36.974	40.545	44.501	48.884	53.739
18	19.615	21.412	23.414	25.645	28.132	30.906	33.999	37.450	41.301	45.599	50.396	55.750	61.725
19	20.811	22.841	25.117	27.671	30.539	33.760	37.379	41.446	46.018	51.159	56.939	63.440	70.749
20	22.019	24.297	26.870	29.778	33.066	36.786	40.995	45.762	51.160	57.275	64.203	72.052	80.947
24	26.973	30.422	34.426	39.083	44.502	50.816	58.117	66.765	76.790	88.497	102.174	118.155	136.831
25	28.243	32.030	36.459	41.646	47.727	54.865	63.249	73.106	84.701	98.347	114.413	133.334	155.620
30	34.785	40.568	47.575	56.085	66.439	79.058	94.461	113.283	136.308	164.494	199.021	241.333	293.199
40	48.886	60.402	75.401	95.026	120.080	154.762	199.635	259.057	337.882	442.593	581.826	767.091	1,013.70
50	64.463	84.572	112.797	152.667	209.348	290.336	406.529	573.770	815.084	1,163.91	1,668.77	2,400.02	3,459.51
60	81.670	114.052	163.053	237.991	353.584	533.128	813.520	1,253.21	1,944.79	3,034.82	4,755.07	7,471.64	11,761.9

Period, n	14%	15%	16%	17%	18%	19%	20%	24%	28%	32%	36%	40%
1	1.000	1.000	1.000	1.000	1.000	1.000	1.000	1.000	1.000	1.000	1.000	1.000
2	2.140	2.150	2.160	2.170	2.180	2.190	2.200	2.240	2.280	2.320	2.360	2.400
3	3.440	3.473	3.506	3.539	3.572	3.606	3.640	3.778	3.918	4.062	4.210	4.360
4	4.921	4.993	5.066	5.141	5.215	5.291	5.368	5.684	6.016	6.362	6.725	7.104
5	6.610	6.742	6.877	7.014	7.154	7.297	7.442	8.048	8.700	9.398	10.146	10.846
6	8.536	8.754	8.977	9.207	9.442	9.683	9.930	10.980	12.136	13.406	14.799	16.324
7	10.730	11.067	11.414	11.772	12.142	12.523	12.916	14.615	16.534	18.696	21.126	23.853
8	13.233	13.727	14.240	14.773	15.327	15.902	16.499	19.123	22.163	25.678	29.732	34.395
9	16.085	16.786	17.518	18.285	19.086	19.923	20.799	24.712	29.369	34.895	41.435	49.153
10	19.337	20.304	21.321	22.393	23.521	24.709	25.959	31.643	38.592	47.062	57.352	69.814
11	23.044	24.349	25.733	27.200	28.755	30.404	32.150	40.238	50.399	63.122	78.998	98.739
12	27.271	29.002	30.850	32.824	34.931	37.180	39.580	50.985	65.510	84.320	108.437	139.235
13	32.089	34.352	36.786	39.404	42.219	45.244	48.497	64.110	84.853	112.303	148.475	195.929
14	37.581	40.505	43.672	47.103	50.818	54.841	59.196	80.496	109.612	149.240	202.926	275.300
15	43.842	47.580	51.660	56.110	60.965	66.261	72.035	100.815	141.303	197.997	276.979	386.420
16	50.980	55.717	60.925	66.649	72.939	79.850	87.442	126.011	181.868	262.356	377.692	541.988
17	59.118	65.075	71.673	78.979	87.068	96.022	105.931	157.253	233.791	347.310	514.661	759.784
18	68.394	75.836	84.141	93.406	103.740	115.266	128.117	195.994	300.252	459.449	700.939	1,064.70
19	78.969	88.212	98.603	110.285	123.414	138.166	154.740	244.033	385.323	607.472	954.277	1,491.58
20	91.025	102.444	115.380	130.033	146.628	165.418	186.688	303.601	494.213	802.863	1,298.82	2,089.21
24	158.659	184.168	213.978	248.808	289.494	337.010	392.484	723.461	1,322.66	2,443.82	4,450.00	8,033.00
25	181.871	212.793	249.214	292.105	342.603	402.042	471.981	898.092	1,706.80	3,226.84	6,053.00	11,247.2
30	356.787	434.745	530.321	647.439	790.948	966.712	1,181.88	2,640.92	5,873.23	12,940.9	28,172.3	60,501.1
40	1,342.03	1,779.09	2,360.76	3,134.52	4,163.21	5,529.83	7,343.86	22,728.8	69,377.5	207,874	609,890	*
50	4,994.52	7,217.72	10,435.6	15,009.5	21,813.1	31,515.3	45,497.2	195,373	819,103	*	*	*
60	18,535.1	29,220.0	46,057.5	72,555.0	114,190	179,495	281,733	*	*	*	*	*

*These interest factors exceed 1,000,000

Table IV 549

TABLE IV Present Value of an Annuity Interest Factor (PVIFA) ($1 per period at i% per period for n periods); $\text{PVIFA} = \dfrac{1 - \dfrac{1}{(1+i)^n}}{i}$; $\text{PVAN}_0 = PMT\,(\text{PVIFA}_{i,n})$

Period, n	1%	2%	3%	4%	5%	6%	7%	8%	9%	10%	11%	12%	13%
1	0.990	0.980	0.971	0.962	0.952	0.943	0.935	0.926	0.917	0.909	0.901	0.893	0.885
2	1.970	1.942	1.913	1.886	1.859	1.833	1.808	1.783	1.759	1.736	1.713	1.690	1.668
3	2.941	2.884	2.829	2.775	2.723	2.673	2.624	2.577	2.531	2.487	2.444	2.402	2.361
4	3.902	3.808	3.717	3.630	3.546	3.465	3.387	3.312	3.240	3.170	3.102	3.037	2.974
5	4.853	4.713	4.580	4.452	4.329	4.212	4.100	3.993	3.890	3.791	3.696	3.605	3.517
6	5.795	5.601	5.417	5.242	5.076	4.917	4.766	4.623	4.486	4.355	4.231	4.111	3.998
7	6.728	6.472	6.230	6.002	5.786	5.582	5.389	5.206	5.033	4.868	4.712	4.564	4.423
8	7.652	7.325	7.020	6.733	6.463	6.210	5.971	5.747	5.535	5.335	5.146	4.968	4.799
9	8.566	8.162	7.786	7.435	7.108	6.802	6.515	6.247	5.995	5.759	5.537	5.328	5.132
10	9.471	8.983	8.530	8.111	7.722	7.360	7.024	6.710	6.418	6.145	5.889	5.650	5.426
11	10.368	9.787	9.253	8.760	8.306	7.887	7.499	7.139	6.805	6.495	6.207	5.938	5.687
12	11.255	10.575	9.954	9.385	8.863	8.384	7.943	7.536	7.161	6.814	6.492	6.194	5.918
13	12.134	11.348	10.635	9.986	9.394	8.853	8.358	7.904	7.487	7.103	6.750	6.424	6.122
14	13.004	12.106	11.296	10.563	9.899	9.295	8.745	8.244	7.786	7.367	6.982	6.628	6.302
15	13.865	12.849	11.938	11.118	10.380	9.712	9.108	8.559	8.061	7.606	7.191	6.811	6.462
16	14.718	13.578	12.561	11.652	10.838	10.106	9.447	8.851	8.312	7.824	7.379	6.974	6.604
17	15.562	14.292	13.166	12.166	11.274	10.477	9.763	9.122	8.544	8.022	7.549	7.120	6.729
18	16.398	14.992	13.754	12.659	11.690	10.828	10.059	9.372	8.756	8.201	7.702	7.250	6.840
19	17.226	15.678	14.324	13.134	12.085	11.158	10.336	9.604	8.950	8.365	7.839	7.366	6.938
20	18.046	16.351	14.877	13.590	12.462	11.470	10.594	9.818	9.128	8.514	7.963	7.469	7.025
24	21.243	18.914	16.936	15.247	13.799	12.550	11.469	10.529	9.707	8.985	8.348	7.784	7.283
25	22.023	19.523	17.413	15.622	14.094	12.783	11.654	10.675	9.823	9.077	8.422	7.843	7.330
30	25.808	22.397	19.600	17.292	15.373	13.765	12.409	11.258	10.274	9.427	8.694	8.055	7.496
40	32.835	27.355	23.115	19.793	17.159	15.046	13.332	11.925	10.757	9.779	8.951	8.244	7.634
50	39.196	31.424	25.730	21.482	18.256	15.762	13.801	12.233	10.962	9.915	9.042	8.304	7.675
60	44.955	34.761	27.676	22.623	18.929	16.161	14.039	12.377	11.048	9.967	9.074	8.324	7.687

Period, n	14%	15%	16%	17%	18%	19%	20%	24%	28%	32%	36%	40%
1	0.877	0.870	0.862	0.855	0.847	0.840	0.833	0.806	0.781	0.758	0.735	0.714
2	1.647	1.626	1.605	1.585	1.566	1.547	1.528	1.457	1.392	1.332	1.276	1.224
3	2.322	2.283	2.246	2.210	2.174	2.140	2.106	1.981	1.868	1.766	1.674	1.589
4	2.914	2.855	2.798	2.743	2.690	2.639	2.589	2.404	2.241	2.096	1.966	1.849
5	3.433	3.352	3.274	3.199	3.127	3.058	2.991	2.745	2.532	2.345	2.181	2.035
6	3.889	3.784	3.685	3.589	3.498	3.410	3.326	3.020	2.759	2.534	2.399	2.168
7	4.288	4.160	4.039	3.922	3.812	3.706	3.605	3.242	2.937	2.678	2.455	2.263
8	4.639	4.487	4.344	4.207	4.078	3.954	3.837	3.421	3.076	2.786	2.540	2.331
9	4.946	4.772	4.607	4.451	4.303	4.163	4.031	3.566	3.184	2.868	2.603	2.379
10	5.216	5.019	4.833	4.659	4.494	4.339	4.193	3.682	3.269	2.930	2.650	2.414
11	5.453	5.234	5.029	4.836	4.656	4.486	4.327	3.776	3.335	2.978	2.683	2.438
12	5.660	5.421	5.197	4.988	4.793	4.611	4.439	3.851	3.387	3.013	2.708	2.456
13	5.842	5.583	5.342	5.118	4.910	4.715	4.533	3.912	3.427	3.040	2.727	2.469
14	6.002	5.724	5.468	5.229	5.008	4.802	4.611	3.962	3.459	3.061	2.740	2.478
15	6.142	5.847	5.575	5.324	5.092	4.876	4.675	4.001	3.483	3.076	2.750	2.484
16	6.265	5.954	5.669	5.405	5.162	4.938	4.730	4.033	3.503	3.088	2.758	2.489
17	6.373	6.047	5.749	5.475	5.222	4.990	4.775	4.059	3.518	3.097	2.763	2.492
18	6.467	6.128	5.818	5.534	5.273	5.033	4.812	4.080	3.529	3.104	2.767	2.494
19	6.550	6.198	5.877	5.584	5.316	5.070	4.844	4.097	3.539	3.109	2.770	2.496
20	6.623	6.259	5.929	5.628	5.353	5.101	4.870	4.110	3.546	3.113	2.772	2.497
24	6.835	6.434	6.073	5.746	5.451	5.182	4.937	4.143	3.562	3.121	2.776	2.499
25	6.873	6.464	6.097	5.766	5.467	5.195	4.948	4.147	3.564	3.122	2.776	2.499
30	7.003	6.566	6.177	5.829	5.517	5.235	4.979	4.160	3.569	3.124	2.778	2.500
40	7.105	6.642	6.233	5.871	5.548	5.258	4.997	4.166	3.571	3.125	2.778	2.500
50	7.133	6.661	6.246	5.880	5.554	5.262	4.999	4.167	3.571	3.125	2.778	2.500
60	7.140	6.665	6.249	5.882	5.555	5.263	5.000	4.167	3.571	3.125	2.778	2.500

TABLE V   Normal Distribution (Area of the Normal Distribution That Is to the Right of +*z or* the Left of −*z* Standard Deviations from the Mean)

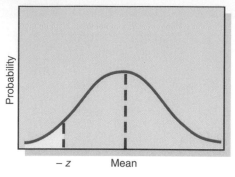 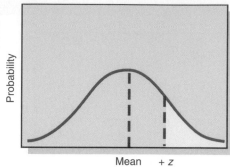

z*	.00	.01	.02	.03	.04	.05	.06	.07	.08	.09
0.0	.5000	.4960	.4920	.4880	.4840	.4801	.4761	.4721	.4681	.4641
.1	.4602	.4562	.4522	.4483	.4443	.4404	.4364	.4325	.4286	.4247
.2	.4207	.4168	.4129	.4090	.4052	.4013	.3974	.3936	.3897	.3859
.3	.3821	.3783	.3745	.3707	.3669	.3632	.3594	.3557	.3520	.3483
.4	.3446	.3409	.3372	.3336	.3300	.3264	.3228	.3192	.3156	.3121
.5	.3085	.3050	.3015	.2981	.2946	.2912	.2877	.2843	.2810	.2776
.6	.2743	.2709	.2676	.2643	.2611	.2578	.2546	.2514	.2483	.2451
.7	.2420	.2389	.2358	.2327	.2296	.2266	.2236	.2206	.2177	.2148
.8	.2119	.2090	.2061	.2033	.2005	.1977	.1949	.1922	.1894	.1867
.9	.1841	.1814	.1788	.1762	.1736	.1711	.1685	.1660	.1635	.1611
1.0	.1587	.1562	.1539	.1515	.1492	.1469	.1446	.1423	.1401	.1379
1.1	.1357	.1335	.1314	.1292	.1271	.1251	.1230	.1210	.1190	.1170
1.2	.1151	.1131	.1112	.1093	.1075	.1056	.1038	.1020	.1003	.0985
1.3	.0968	.0951	.0934	.0918	.0901	.0885	.0869	.0853	.0838	.0823
1.4	.0808	.0793	.0778	.0764	.0749	.0735	.0721	.0708	.0694	.0681
1.5	.0668	.0655	.0643	.0630	.0618	.0606	.0594	.0582	.0571	.0559
1.6	.0548	.0537	.0526	.0516	.0505	.0495	.0485	.0475	.0465	.0455
1.7	.0446	.0436	.0427	.0418	.0409	.0401	.0392	.0384	.0375	.0367
1.8	.0359	.0351	.0344	.0336	.0329	.0322	.0314	.0307	.0301	.0294
1.9	.0287	.0281	.0274	.0268	.0262	.0256	.0250	.0244	.0239	.0233
2.0	.0228	.0222	.0217	.0212	.0207	.0202	.0197	.0192	.0188	.0183
2.1	.0179	.0174	.0170	.0166	.0162	.0158	.0154	.0150	.0146	.0143
2.2	.0139	.0136	.0132	.0129	.0125	.0122	.0119	.0116	.0113	.0110
2.3	.0107	.0104	.0102	.0099	.0096	.0094	.0091	.0089	.0087	.0084
2.4	.0082	.0080	.0078	.0075	.0073	.0071	.0069	.0068	.0066	.0064
2.5	.0062	.0060	.0059	.0057	.0055	.0054	.0052	.0051	.0049	.0048
2.6	.0047	.0045	.0044	.0043	.0041	.0040	.0039	.0038	.0037	.0036
2.7	.0035	.0034	.0033	.0032	.0031	.0030	.0029	.0028	.0027	.0026
2.8	.0026	.0025	.0024	.0023	.0023	.0022	.0021	.0021	.0020	.0019
2.9	.0019	.0018	.0018	.0017	.0016	.0016	.0015	.0015	.0014	.0014
3.0	.0013									
3.05	.0011									
3.10	.0010									
3.25	.0006									
3.50	.00023									
4.00	.00003									
5.00	.0000003									

*Absolute values of z

See the back endsheets for abbreviations used in the text.

Absolute Priority Rule A rule used in bankruptcy proceedings that states that the claims of creditors are satisfied before the claims of stockholders.

Accrual Basis of Accounting System of accounting where revenues and expenses are recognized when they are incurred rather than when the cash is received or paid.

Agency Relationships Occur when one or more individuals (principals) hire another individual (agent) to perform a service on their behalf. Agency relationships often lead to agency problems and costs. Two of the most important agency relationships in finance are the relationship between stockholders (owners) and managers and the relationship between owners and creditors.

Agent The party who acts on behalf of the principal and has a legal responsibility to act in the best interests of the principal in an agency relationship.

Amortization Schedule A schedule of periodic payments of interest and principal owed on a debt obligation.

Annual Financing Cost (AFC) The simple, annual interest rate for a short-term credit source.

Annuity The payment or receipt of a series of equal cash flows per period for a specified amount of time. In an ordinary annuity, payments are made at the end of each period; in an annuity due, payments are made at the beginning of each period.

Arbitrage The process of simultaneously buying and selling the same or equivalent securities in different markets to take advantage of temporary price differences.

Articles of Incorporation Document filed with the state government creating a corporation. It spells out the place of business, purpose of business, and other aspects of the business organization.

Asset Management Ratios Financial ratios that indicate how efficiently a firm is using its assets to generate sales.

Asymmetric Information The assumption that managers of a company, as insiders, have access to information about expected future earnings and cash flows that is not available to outside investors.

Auction Market A market where buyers and sellers come together and present their bids with sellers seeking out the highest bidder to sell to and buyers attempting to acquire from the lowest bidder (e.g. New York Stock Exchange).

Auction Rate Preferred Stock A form of preferred stock where the dividend yield is adjusted every 49 days through an auction process and investors can exchange their stock for cash.

Average Collection Period The average number of days between when a credit sale is made and when the customer's payment is received.

Bad-Debt Loss Ratio The proportion of the total receivables volume that is never collected by a business.

Balance Sheet A financial statement that lists a firm's assets, liabilities, and stockholders' equity at a point in time.

Bank Draft An order to pay, similar to a check, except that it is not payable on demand. Instead, a bank draft is payable when the issuing firm accepts it.

Banker's Acceptance A short-term debt instrument issued by a firm as part of a commercial transaction. Payment is guaranteed by a commercial bank.

Bankruptcy A situation in which a firm is unable to pay its debts and its assets are turned over to the court for administration.

Beta A measure of systematic risk. It indicates the volatility of a security's returns relative to the returns of a broad-based market portfolio of securities.

Bond A long-term debt instrument that promises to pay the lender a series of periodic interest payments in addition to returning the principal at maturity. Most corporate bonds are offered in $1,000 principal amounts (par value).

Bond Rating An evaluation of a bond's probability of default. This is performed by an outside rating agency, such as Standard & Poor's or Moody's.

Bond Refunding The redemption of a callable bond issue and replacement with a lower-interest cost issue.

Book Value The accounting value of an asset or a corporation. The book value per share of common stock is equal to the total book value of the company, or stockholders' equity, divided by the total number of shares of common stock outstanding.

Breakeven Analysis An analysis tool that considers the relationship between sales, fixed costs, variable operating costs, and operating income at various output levels.

Business Risk The variability in a firm's operating earnings (EBIT).

Call Feature A provision that permits an issuer of bonds (and sometimes preferred stock) to retire the obligation prior to its maturity.

Call Option An option to buy an asset at a set price. Also referred to as a call.

Call Premium The difference between a bond's call price and its par value.

Call Price The price at which a bond may be retired, or called, prior to its maturity.

Capital Asset Pricing Model (CAPM) A theory that formally describes the nature of the risk-required rate of return relationship on investments in financial assets (securities) or physical assets.

Capital Budgeting The process of planning for purchases of assets whose cash flows are expected to continue beyond one year.

Capital Expenditure The amount of money spent to purchase a long-term asset, such as a piece of equipment. This cash outlay generally is expected to result in a flow of future cash benefits extending beyond one year in time. (Also called capital investment.)

Capital Gain Profit on the sale of a capital asset.

Capital Gains Yield The expected percentage increase in the price of the stock.

Capital Goods Market Market where long term physical assets are bought and sold, e.g., plant and equpment.

Capital Loss Loss on the sale of a capital asset.

Capital Markets Financial markets in which long-term securities are bought and sold.

Capital Rationing The process of limiting the number of capital expenditure projects because of insufficient funds to finance all projects that otherwise meet the firm's criteria for acceptability or because of a lack of sufficient managerial resources to undertake all otherwise acceptable projects.

Capital Structure Generally refers to the amount of long-term debt, preferred stock, and common equity used to finance a firm.

Capitalization of Cash Flow Valuation Method (also known as the discounted cash flow method) A method of determining the present value of an asset that is expected to produce a stream of future cash flows. This involves discounting the stream of expected cash flows at an appropriate rate.

Carrying Costs All costs associated with holding items in inventory for a given period of time.

Cash Budget A projection of a company's cash receipts and disbursements over some future period of time.

*If you can't find a term, visit the glossary on the text Web site at http://moyer.swlearning.com.

Cash Conversion Cycle The net time interval between the collection of cash receipts from product sales and the cash payments for the company's various resources. The cash conversion cycle is calculated by subtracting the payables deferral period from the operating cycle.

Cash Discount A discount offered for early payment of an invoice.

Cash Equivalents Highly liquid near cash assets such as Treasury bills.

Cash Flow The actual amount of cash collected and paid out by a firm.

Cash Flow Forecasting The projection and estimation of a firm's future cash flows.

Characteristic Line A regression line relating the periodic returns for a specific security to the periodic returns on the market portfolio. The slope of this regression line is an estimate of the beta of the security—a measure of its systematic risk.

Clientele Effect The concept that investors will tend to be attracted to companies that have dividend policies consistent with the investors' objectives.

Coefficient of Variation The ratio of the standard deviation to the expected value. It provides a relative measure of risk.

Commercial Paper Short-term unsecured promissory notes issued by major corporations with good credit ratings.

Common-Size Balance Sheet A balance sheet in which a firm's assets and liabilities are expressed as a percentage of total assets, rather than as dollar amounts.

Common-Size Income Statement An income statement in which a firm's income and expense items are expressed as a percentage of net sales, rather than as dollar amounts.

Common Stock Shares in the ownership of a company. Common stock represents a residual form of ownership in that dividends are paid out only after more senior financial obligations are fulfilled, such as interest on debt.

Comparative Analysis An examination of a firm's performance based on one or more financial ratios, which are compared with the financial ratios of competitive firms or with an industry standard.

Compensating Balance A minimum (absolute or average) balance that a bank requires a customer to keep in its checking account. This balance, which the bank can invest in interest-earning assets, compensates the bank for the services rendered to the customer.

Compound Interest Interest that is paid not only on the principal but also on any interest earned but not withdrawn during earlier periods.

Concentration Banking The use of decentralized collection centers and local banks to collect customer payments. This speeds up a firm's collections.

Contingent Project A project whose acceptance depends on the adoption of one or more other projects.

Contribution Margin per Unit In breakeven analysis, the difference between the selling price per unit and the variable cost per unit.

Conversion Price The effective price an investor pays for common stock when the stock is obtained by converting a convertible security.

Conversion Ratio The number of common shares an investor obtains by converting a convertible security.

Convertible Bond A bond that may be exchanged for common stock at the holder's option.

Convertible Security A fixed-income security that may be exchanged for a firm's common stock at the holder's option. The two most common types of convertible securities are convertible preferred stock and convertible debentures.

Corporation A business organization that is created as a "legal person" separate and distinct from the individual or individuals who own the firm's stock. The primary characteristics and advantages of incorporating include limited liability for the firm's owners, permanency, and flexibility with respect to making changes in ownership.

Correlation A relative statistical measure of the degree to which two series of numbers, such as the returns from two assets, tend to move or vary together.

Cost of Capital The equilibrium rate of return demanded by investors in the securities issued by a firm.

Cost-Volume-Profit Analysis. See Breakeven Analysis

Coupon Rate of Interest The interest rate stated on a bond. The coupon rate of interest times the par, or principal, value of a bond determines the periodic dollar interest payment received by the bondholder.

Covenants Listing of restrictions placed on the firm by the lenders. The firm must satisfy them to keep from defaulting on its obligations.

Covered Interest Arbitrage A risk-free transaction in which short-term funds are moved between two currencies to take advantage of interest rate differentials. Exchange rate risk is eliminated through the use of forward contracts.

Credit Period The length of time a credit customer has to pay the account in full.

Cumulative Dividends A typical feature of preferred stock that requires past-due preferred stock dividends to be paid before any common stock dividends can be paid.

Current Assets Consist of cash and other assets that are likely to be converted to cash in the near term, typically defined as less than one year. The major components of current assets are cash and cash equivalents, accounts receivable, and inventories.

Current Dividend Yield Current annual dividend paid on a share divided by current closing price of the stock.

Current Ratio The ratio of current assets to current liabilities of the firm.

Current Yield (of a Bond) The annual interest payment divided by the current (market) price of a bond.

Debenture A bond that is not secured by a mortgage on any specific asset but instead by the general credit and earning power of the issuing firm.

Debt Capacity The amount of debt contained in a firm's optimal capital structure.

Declaration Date The day on which the directors of a company declare a dividend.

Default Risk The risk that a borrower will fail to make interest payments, principal payments, or both on a loan.

Deferred Tax Asset Deferred tax assets or liabilities occur because of "temporary" differences in the income reported to shareholders and income reported for tax purposes. A deferred tax asset occurs when reported financial income is less than the taxable income.

Degree of Combined Leverage (DCL) The percentage change in a firm's earnings per share (EPS) resulting from a 1 percent change in sales or output. This also is equal to the degree of operating leverage times the degree of financial leverage used by the firm.

Degree of Financial Leverage (DFL) The percentage change in a firm's EPS resulting from a 1 percent change in EBIT.

Degree of Operating Leverage (DOL) The percentage change in a firm's EBIT resulting from a 1 percent change in sales or output.

Depository Transfer Check (DTC) An unsigned nonnegotiable check used to transfer funds from a local collection bank to a concentration bank.

Depreciation The systematic allocation of the cost of an asset over its expected economic life or some other period of time for financial reporting purposes, tax purposes, or both.

Derivative A financial contract that derives its value from some other security or asset, such as stocks, bonds, currencies, commodities, or interest rates. The two broadest categories of derivatives are options and forward-type contracts.

Deterministic Model A financial planning model that projects single number estimates of a financial variable or variables without specifying their probability of occurrence.

Direct Quote The home currency price of one unit of a foreign currency.

Discount Period The length of time a credit customer has to pay the account and still be eligible to take any cash discount offered.

Discount Rate The rate of interest used in the process of finding present values; also called the required rate of return.

Discounted Loan A loan in which the bank deducts the interest in advance at the time the loan is made.

Discrete Distribution Values or outcomes in a distribution assume certain specific values, i.e., are not continuous.

Diversification The act of investing in a set of financial (securities) or physical assets having different risk-return characteristics.

Dividend Reinvestment Plan An option that allows shareholders to have their cash dividends automatically reinvested in additional shares of the company's stock.

Dividend Yield The annual dividend payment divided by the price of the stock.

Double Taxation Case where earnings are taxed twice, for example, a corporation pays taxes on its earnings and dividends paid from those earnings to shareholders are taxed again.

Dow Jones Industrial Average A stock market index made up of 30 large, generally profitable and stable (blue chip) companies.

Draft A financial instrument that is similar to a check except it is not payable on demand. Rather a draft must be presented to the issuer for approval before a payment is made.

DuPont Chart A form of ratio analysis where ratios are decomposed into their constituent elements. For example, return on invesment is a product of net profit margin and total asset turnover.

Dutch Auction Tender Offer A form of tender offer where the firm specifies a range of prices at which it will buy back its stock. Stocks are then bought back from investors starting at the lowest price within the range at which they are willing to sell and going up till the target number of shares is met.

EAT The acronym for earnings after taxes.

EBIT The acronym for earnings before interest and taxes (also called operating earnings).

EBIT-EPS Indifference Point That level of EBIT where the earnings per share of a firm are the same, regardless of which of two alternative capital structures is employed.

Economic Exposure The extent to which changes in real exchange rates lead to a change in the value of a firm's operating cash flows, and hence its value. Also known as operating exposure.

Economic Order Quantity The quantity of an inventory item that should be ordered to minimize total inventory costs.

Economic Value Added See EVA®.

Effective Annual Percentage Rate (EAPR) The true annual interest rate paid on a loan. Also called the effective rate of a loan.

Effective Interest Rate The actual rate of interest paid by the borrower or earned by the lender.

Efficient Capital Market A financial market in which new information is quickly reflected in security prices in an unbiased manner.

EPS The acronym for earnings per share.

Euro The new European single currency that went into circulation in 2002.

Eurobond An international bond issued outside the country in whose currency the bonds are denominated.

Eurocurrency A currency that is deposited in a bank outside of the country of origin.

Eurodollars U.S. dollars deposited in banks outside the United States.

EVA® The acronym for economic value added. This measure of operating performance is equal to the difference between operating profits after tax and the cost of capital and indicates a firm's success in creating MVA.

Ex-ante Return Return expected over a future holding period.

Excess Return Return in excess of what is expected or required given the risk of the asset or security.

Exchange Rate The rate at which a currency can be converted into another currency.

Ex-dividend Date The date on which the right to the most recently declared dividend no longer goes along with the sale of the stock. The ex-dividend date is two business days prior to the record date.

Expected Market Risk Premium Expected market return minus the risk-free rate of return.

Expected Market Return The return investors expect to earn on the market portfolio or on stocks with a beta of 1.0.

Expected Return The benefits (price appreciation and distributions) an individual anticipates receiving from an investment.

Expected Value A statistical measure of the mean or average value of the possible outcomes. Operationally, it is defined as the weighted average of the possible outcomes with the weights being the probability of occurrence.

Ex-post Return Rate of return measured over a historical period.

Face Amount (of a Bond) Principal or par amount of a bond, usually $1,000.

Factoring The sale of a firm's accounts receivable to a financial institution known as a factor.

Field Warehouse Financing Agreement A loan agreement in which the inventory being pledged as collateral is segregated from the company's other inventories and stored on its premises under the control of a field warehouse company.

FIFO The acronym for the first-in, first-out inventory valuation method. The method assumes that firm uses the oldest items in the inventory first. Thus, they are priced out of the inventory based on the oldest inventory acquisition costs rather than the most recent.

Financial Analysis The utilization of a group of analytical techniques, including financial ratio analysis, to determine the strengths, weaknesses, and direction of a company's performance.

Financial Breakeven Point In EBIT/EPS analysis refers to the earnings before interest and taxes that will make the earrnings per share just equal to zero.

Financial Distress Costs The costs incurred to avoid bankruptcy plus the direct and indirect costs incurred if a firm files for bankruptcy protection. Also known as bankruptcy costs.

Financial Forecasts Projection and estimation of a firm's future financial statements.

Financial Intermediary Financial organizations that serve as an indirect channel for transfer of funds between savers and borrowers. Financial intermediaries include commercial banks, thrift institutions, investment companies, pensions funds, insurance companies, and finance companies.

Financial Leverage The extent to which a firm is financed by securities having fixed costs or charges, such as debt and preferred stock.

Financial Leverage Management Ratios Financial ratios that measure the degree to which a firm is financing its assets with fixed-charge sources of funds such as debt, preferred stock, or leases.

Financial Market Where trading in financial assets (e.g., stocks and bonds) takes place.

Financial Planning Model A computerized representation of some aspect of a firm's financial planning process.

Financial Ratio A statistical yardstick that relates two numbers generally taken from a firm's income statement, balance sheet, or both at a specific point in time.

Financial Risk The additional variability of a company's earnings per share and the increased probability of insolvency that result from the use of fixed-cost sources of funds, such as debt and preferred stock. In general, the more financial leverage a firm uses, the greater is its financial risk.

Financial Slack Highly liquid assets (i.e., cash and marketable securities) plus unused debt capacity that allow a firm to take advantage of any attractive investment opportunities.

Financial Structure The amount of current liabilities, long-term debt, preferred stock, and common equity used to finance a firm.

Financing Activities In the statement of cash flows refers to cash flow effects of financing decisions of the firm, including sale of new securities, such as stocks and bonds, repurchase of securities, and payment of dividends.

Fisher Effect A relationship indicating that nominal (and risk-free) interest rates are approximately equal to the sum of the real interest rate and the expected inflation rate.

Fixed Assets Long term assets of a firm, e.g., plant and equipment.

Fixed Charges Periodic fixed financial obligations of a firm such as interest on loans, principal repayments, and lease payments.

Fixed Costs Costs that do not vary as the level of a firm's output changes.

Float The difference between an account balance as shown on the bank's books and as shown on the firm's books. Float represents the net effect of the delays in the payment of checks the firm writes and the collection of checks the firm receives.

Floating Lien An inventory loan in which the lender receives a security interest or general claim on all of a company's inventory.

Floor Planning. See Trust Receipt

Flotation Cost The cost of issuing new securities. This includes both underwriting expenses and other issue expenses, such as printing and legal fees.

Fluctuating Current Assets Current assets affected by the seasonal or cyclical nature of the company's sales.

Forms Financial forms or reports filed with Securities and Exchange Commission.

Forward Rate The rate of exchange between two currencies being bought and sold for delivery at a future date.

Funded Debt Another term for long-term debt.

Future Value (or Terminal Value) The value at some future point in time of a present payment (or a series of payments) evaluated at the appropriate interest (growth) rate.

Futures Contract A contract calling for the delivery of a standardized quantity and quality of some item, such as a foreign currency, crude oil, or government securities, at a future point in time at a price set at the present time.

Generally Accepted Accounting Principles (GAAP) A broad set of accounting rules followed in preparing financial statements.

Going-Concern Value The value of a firm, assuming that the firm's organization and assets remain intact and are used to generate future income and cash flows.

Goodwill An intangible asset equal to the premium over fair market value of the acquired assets that is paid for a company in a merger.

Gross Margin The difference between sales and cost of goods sold.

Hedging A transaction in which a position is taken in another market, such as the forward or futures market, to offset the risk associated with a position in the current cash (spot) market.

Holding Period Return The change in price from holding an asset (security) plus distributions received from the asset divided by the initial price at which the asset was acquired.

Hurdle Rate The minimum acceptable rate of return from an investment project. For projects of average risk, it usually is equal to the firm's cost of capital.

Hybrid Security Security that has features of debt and common stock, e.g., convertible debt.

Income Statement A financial statement that indicates how a firm performed during a period of time.

Indenture The contract between the issuing firm and the lenders in a debt obligation.

Independent Project A project whose acceptance or rejection does not result directly in the elimination of other projects from consideration.

Indirect Quote The foreign currency price of one unit of the home currency.

Informational Content The concept that, for a company following a stable dividend policy, changes in dividend payments convey information (i.e., a signal) to investors concerning management's expectations about the future profitability of the company.

Initial Public Offering (IPO) Common stock sold by the issuing company to the public for the first time.

Insolvency A situation in which either a firm's liabilities exceed its assets or the firm is unable to pay its creditors as required.

Interest The return earned by or the amount paid to an individual who forgoes current consumption or alternative investments and "rents" money to a business, bank, the government, some other form of institution, or another individual.

Interest Rate Parity (IRP) The theory that the percentage differential between the spot and the forward rate for a currency quoted in terms of another currency is equal to the approximate difference in interest rates in the two countries over the same time horizon.

Interest Rate Risk The variation in the market price (and hence in the realized rate of return or yield) of a security that arises from changes in interest rates.

Internal Rate of Return (IRR) The discount rate that equates the present value of net cash flows from a project with the present value of the net investment. It is the discount rate that gives the project a net present value equal to zero. The IRR is used to evaluate, rank, and select from among various investment projects.

International Fisher Effect (IFE) The theory that the difference in interest rates between two countries should be offset by equal but opposite changes in the future spot exchange rate.

Inventory Conversion Period The length of time required to produce and sell the product.

Inventory Cycle The time between placement of successive orders of an item.

Investing Activities In the statement of cash flows refers to cash flow effects from long-term investing activities, such as purchase or sale of plant and equipment.

Investment Bank A financial institution that underwrites and sells new securities. In general, investment banks assist firms in obtaining new financing.

Investment Banker An employee of an investment bank who assists client companies with security offerings, mergers, private placements of securities, and long-range financial planning.

Investment Grade The top four bond rating categories in Moody's and Standard and Poor's industrial bond ratings classification.

Junk Bond A high-yield debt security issued by a company with a low credit rating.

Just-in-Time Inventory Management System An approach to inventory and production management in which required inventory items are supplied exactly as needed by production.

Law of One Price The law in economics which states that when there are no significant costs or other barriers associated with moving goods or services between markets, then the price of each product should be the same in each market.

Leveraged Buyout A transaction in which the buyer of a company borrows a large portion of the purchase price, using the purchased assets as partial collateral for the loans.

LIBOR Acronym for London interbank offer rate.

LIFO The acronym for the last-in, first-out inventory valuation method. The method assumes that a firm uses the most recently acquired items in the inventory first. Thus, they are priced out of the inventory based on the most recent inventory acquisition costs rather than the oldest.

Limited Liability Company (LLC) A form of business organization that has the limited liability feature of a corporation but where earnings are allowed to flow to the owners and taxed at the individual level.

Line of Credit An agreement that permits a firm to borrow funds up to a predetermined limit at any time during the life of the agreement.

Liquidation Value The value of a firm, assuming that it sells all its assets and stops using them to generate future income and cash flows.

Liquidity The ability of a firm to meet its cash obligations as they come due.

Liquidity Ratios Financial ratios that indicate a firm's ability to meet short-term financial obligations.

Listed Security Exchanges Organized secondary security markets that operate at designated places of business. The New York Stock Exchange (NYSE) is an example of a listed security exchange.

Loan Amortization Schedule A schedule of periodic payments of interest and principal owed on a debt obligation.

Lockbox A post office box maintained by a bank to speed up the collection of payments from customers.

London Interbank Offer Rate (LIBOR) The interest rate at which banks in the Eurocurrency market lend to each other.

Making a Market In the over-the-counter market refers to dealers who are willing to buy or sell a security at quoted prices.

Marginal Cost of Capital The weighted after-tax cost of the next dollar of capital the firm expects to raise to finance a new investment project.

Marginal Tax Rate The tax rate on the next dollar of taxable income earned by an individual person or firm.

Market Portfolio The portfolio of securities consisting of all available securities weighted by their respective market values.

Market Risk Premium Return on the market portfolio minus the risk-free rate.

Market Value The price at which a stock trades in the financial marketplace.

Marketability Risk The ability of an investor to buy and sell an asset (security) quickly and without a significant loss of value.

Market-Based Ratios Financial ratios that measure the market's (investors') assessment of the risk and performance of a firm.

Matching Approach A financing plan in which the maturity structure of a firm's liabilities is made to correspond exactly to the life of its assets.

Merger A combination of two or more companies into one surviving company. Mergers also are called acquisitions or consolidations.

Money Markets Financial markets in which short-term securities are bought and sold.

Mortgage Bond A bond secured by a pledge of a specific asset or group of assets.

Multinational Corporation A firm with direct investments in more than one country.

Multiple Internal Rates of Return Two or more internal rates of return from the same project. This situation sometimes arises when the IRR method is being used for project selection. It occurs only with nonnormal projects or with those whose cash flow patterns contain more than one sign change.

Mutually Exclusive Project A project whose acceptance precludes the acceptance of one or more alternative projects.

MVA The acronym for market value added. The difference between the market value of a firm's debt and equity and the capital that has been invested in the firm.

NASDAQ An acronym that stands for National Association of Securities Dealers Automated Quotation. It is an example of an over-the-counter market.

National Market Security A subsection of stocks listed in the NASDAQ that are the most liquid, national in scope, and have a wide following.

Negative Loan Covenant A portion of a loan agreement that outlines actions a firm's management agrees not to take during the term of the loan.

Negotiated Underwriting A process whereby a firm wishing to sell new securities to the public negotiates the terms of the underwriting with the investment banker or bankers.

Net Cash Flow (NCF) In capital budgeting it refers to cash inflows minus cash outflows. It is measured as the change in net operating earnings after taxes plus the change in depreciation minus the change in net working capital requirements associated with a particular investment project. In the terminal year of a project NCF also includes the after tax salvage value, if any.

Net Earnings Another term for Net Income or Earnings After Taxes.

Net Investment The net cash outlay required at the beginning of an investment project.

Net Present Value (NPV) The present value of the stream of net cash flows resulting from a project, discounted at the firm's cost of capital, minus the project's net investment. It is used to evaluate, rank, and select from among various investment projects; the contribution of an investment to shareholder wealth.

Net Working Capital The difference between a firm's current assets and current liabilities. The term net working capital is used interchangeably with working capital.

Nominal Interest Rate The periodic rate of interest that is stated in a loan agreement or security. Frequently, the effective interest rate is greater than the nominal rate because of such factors as the frequency of compounding and the deduction of interest in advance.

Normal Project A project whose cash flow stream requires an initial outlay of funds followed by a series of positive net cash inflows. This is sometimes called a conventional project.

Operating Cycle Includes the three primary activities of purchasing resources, producing the product, and distributing (selling) the product. The operating cycle is calculated by summing the inventory conversion period and the receivables conversion period.

Operating Leverage The extent to which a firm uses assets having fixed costs.

Opportunity Cost (or Rate) The rate of return that can be earned on funds if they are invested in the next best alternative investment.

Optimal Capital Structure The capital structure that minimizes a firm's weighted cost of capital and, therefore, maximizes the value of the firm.

Optimization Model A financial planning model that determines the values of financial decision variables that maximize (or minimize) some objective function such as profits (or costs).

Option A contract (often in the form of a security) that gives its holder the right to buy or sell an asset at a set price during a specified time period.

Ordering Costs All costs associated with placing and receiving an order.

Over-the-Counter (OTC) Securities Markets A network of security dealers connected by a communications system of telephones and computer terminals that provides price quotations on individual securities.

Paid-in Capital The paid-in capital surplus account captures the difference between the actual selling price of the stock when issued and the par value.

Par Value (Bond) Represents the amount of principal borrowed (usually $1,000) and due at maturity.

Par Value (Common Stock) An arbitrary value assigned to common stock by the issuing firm.

Par Value (Preferred Stock) An arbitrary value assigned by the issuing firm.

Partnership A business organization in which two or more persons form a business with the intention of making a profit. In a general partnership, each partner has unlimited liability for the debts of the firm. Limited partnerships allow one or more partners to have limited liability.

Passive Residual Policy A theory of dividend policy that suggests that a company should retain its earnings as long as there are investment opportunities available promising a rate of return higher than the required rate of return.

Payables Deferral Period The length of time a firm is able to deter payment on its resource purchases.

Payback (PB) Period The period of time required for the cumulative cash inflows from a project to equal the initial cash outlay.

Payment Date The actual payment date for dividends on common stock.

Payout Ratio The ratio of dividends paid on common stock to the earnings available to common shareholders.

Pecking Order Theory A capital structure theory indicating that firms prefer internal financing (retained earnings) to external financing (new security issues) and that, if external financing is required, debt is preferred to new common stock.

Percentage of Sales Forecasting Method A method of estimating the additional financing that will be needed to support a given future sales level.

Permanent Current Assets Current assets held to meet the company's long-term minimum needs.

Perpetual Bond A bond that has no maturity date.

Perpetuity A financial instrument that pays an equal cash flow per period into the indefinite future (that is, infinity).

Pledging of Accounts Receivable A short-term borrowing arrangement with a financial institution in which a loan is secured by the borrower's accounts receivable.

Portfolio A collection of two or more financial (securities) or physical assets.

Preauthorized Check (PAC) Similar to an ordinary check except that it does not require the signature of the person (or firm) on whose account it is being drawn. PACs are useful for firms that receive a large volume of payments of a fixed amount each period.

Preemptive Right A provision contained in some corporate charters that gives common stockholders the right to buy on a pro rata basis any new common shares sold by the firm.

Preferred Stock A type of equity with a claim on earnings and assets of a firm—in the form of a (normally) fixed periodic dividend payment—that takes precedence over the claims of common stockholders.

Present Value The value today of a future payment (or a series of future payments) evaluated at the appropriate discount rate.

Price-Earnings Multiple Model Model that mutiplies the earnings per share of the stock by an appropriate price-earnings ratio to determine the value of the stock.

Price-Earnings Ratio Market Price per share of the stock divided by the earnings per share of the stock.

Primary Claims Financial Securities issued by ultimate borrowers in the financial markets, including bonds, stocks, and preferred stocks.

Primary Markets Financial markets in which new securities from an issuing firm are bought and sold for the first time. Investment bankers are active in the primary markets.

Prime Rate The lowest rate normally charged by banks on loans made to their most creditworthy business customers.

Principal 1. An amount of money that has been borrowed or invested. 2. In an agency relationship, the party who employs someone else, the agent, to perform service on behalf of the principal.

Private Placement The sale of an entire security offering to one or more institutional investors rather than the general public. This also is termed a direct placement.

Pro Forma Financial Statements Financial statements that project the results of some assumed event, rather than an actual event.

Probabilistic Model A financial planning model that uses probability distributions as inputs and generates a probability distribution for financial variables as output.

Profitability Index (PI) The ratio of the present value of net cash flows over the life of a project to the net investment. It is used to evaluate, rank, and select from among various investment projects. Frequently it is used in conjunction with resource allocation decisions in capital rationing situations.

Profitability Ratios Financial ratios that measure the total effectiveness of a company's management in generating profits.

Promissory Note A formal short-term credit obligation that states the amount to be paid and the due date.

Prospectus A document that contains information about a company's legal, operational, and financial position. It is prepared for the benefit of prospective investors in a new security issued by the firm.

Proxy Statement Statement filed by corporations with the Securities and Exchange Commission and mailed to shareholders prior to annual shareholder meetings detailing, among other things, matters to be discussed and voted upon.

Public Offering Security sold to the public (as opposed to a private placement).

Purchasing Power Parity (PPP) Relationship in which exchange rates between two currencies will equal the ratio of the price indexes between the countries.

Purchasing Syndicate A group of investment bankers who agree to underwrite a new security issue in order to spread the risk of underwriting.

Put Feature A bond option allowing the bondholder to sell the bond back to the issuer before maturity at a predetermined price. An option to sell an asset at a set price. Also referred to as a put.

Quick Ratio Measure of liqudiity defined as the sum of cash, marketable securities and inventory divided by current liabilities.

Rate of Interest The percentage on the principal that the borrower pays the lender per time period as compensation for forgoing other investment or consumption opportunities.

Rate of Return Return either earned or expected on an investment.

Real Option Managerial opportunities to make decisions that will impact the expected cash flows of a project, their timing, or the future acceptability of the project. Real options include the option to abandon, the option to defer investment, flexibility options, and growth options.

Realized Return Return on an investment earned over some historical period.

Receivables Conversion Period The length of time required to collect sales receipts. Receivables conversion period is another name for the average collection period.

Record Date The date on which a company makes a list from its stock transfer books of those shareholders who are eligible to receive the declared dividend.

Reinvestment Rate The rate of return at which cash flows from an investment project are assumed to be reinvested from year to year. The reinvestment rate may vary, depending on the investment opportunities available to the firm.

Reinvestment Rate Risk Risk that occurs when a bond issue matures (or is called) and because of a decline in interest rates, the owner has to reinvest the principal at a lower coupon rate.

Relative Purchasing Power Parity The theory that the spot exchange rate between two currencies should change by an amount approximately equal to the difference in expected inflation rates in the two countries.

Repurchase Agreement An arrangement with a bank or securities dealer in which an investor acquires certain short-term securities subject to a commitment that the securities will be repurchased by the bank or securities dealer on a specified date.

Required Rate of Return The rate used to value a stream of expected cash flows from an asset (also called the discount rate). The riskier the expected cash flows from the asset, the higher the required rate of return.

Restrictive Loan Covenant A portion of a loan agreement that limits the scope of certain actions a firm may take during the term of the loan.

Revolving Credit Agreement A binding agreement that commits a bank to make loans to a company up to a predetermined credit limit. To obtain this type of commitment from a bank, a company usually pays a commitment fee based on the unused portion of the pledged funds.

Risk The possibility that actual future returns will deviate from expected returns; the variability of returns.

Risk-Adjusted Discount Rate A discount rate that reflects the risk associated with a particular project. In capital budgeting, a higher risk-adjusted rate is used to discount cash flows for riskier projects, whereas a lower risk-adjusted rate is used to discount cash flows for less risky projects.

Risk-free Rate The rate of return on securities that are free of default risk, such as U.S. Treasury bills.

Risk-free Rate of Return The return required by an investor in a security having no risk of default; equal to the sum of the real rate of return and an inflation risk premium.

Risk Premium The difference between the required rate of return on a risky investment and the rate of return on a risk-free asset, such as U.S. Treasury bills. Components include maturity risk, default risk, seniority risk, and marketability risk.

ROI Profitability ratio defined as Net income divided by Total assets.

S Corporation A small business that takes advantage of the corporate form of organization while having its income taxed directly to the stockholders at their individual personal income tax rates.

Scenario Analysis A procedure used to evaluate the change in some objective, such as net present value, to simultaneous changes in several variables influencing that objective, such as price, unit sales volume, and operating costs.

Seasoned Equity Offerings Sale of additional stock by a company that is already publicly held.

Secondary Claims Claims issued by a financial intermediary such as a certificate of deposit issued by a bank, life insurance policy, investment in a mutual fund, and contributions to a pension fund.

Secondary Markets Financial markets in which existing securities are offered for resale. The New York Stock Exchange is a secondary market.

Securities and Exchange Commission (SEC) The government regulatory agency responsible for administering federal securities legislation.

Security Market Line (SML) The relationship between systematic risk and required rates of return for individual securities.

Semistrong-Form Efficiency Markets Are considered to be semistrong efficient if no investor can consistently earn excess returns based on an investment strategy using any publicly available information.

Senior Debt Debt that has a higher claim on a firm's earnings and/or assets than junior debt.

Sensitivity Analysis A method of analysis in which a financial model is rerun to determine the effect on the output variable(s) (for example, profit) of given

changes in the input variable(s) (for example, sales). Sensitivity analysis is sometimes called what-if analysis.

Shareholder Wealth Present value of the expected future returns to the owners (that is, shareholders) of the firm. It is measured by the market value of the shareholders' common stock holdings—that is, the price per share times the number of shares outstanding.

Short Sale Transaction where the investor sells a stock that he or she does not own by "borrowing" it from another investor (done by the stock broker on your behalf). The "borrowed" stock is later replaced by purchasing it, presumably, at a lower price.

Signal Changes in investment, financing, or dividend policies that convey information to outside investors concerning management's assessment of the expected future returns of the company.

Simple Interest Interest paid or earned on the principal only.

Simulation A financial planning tool that models some event, such as the cash flows from an investment project. A computerized simulation is one technique used to assess the risk associated with a particular project.

Sinking Fund An annuity amount that must be invested each period (year) to produce a future value.

Sole Proprietorship A business owned by one person. The owner of a sole proprietorship has unlimited liability for debts incurred by the business.

Specialists Members of the stock exchange who play an important role in maintaining a fair and orderly market in the stocks assigned to them.

Spot Rate The rate of exchange between two currencies being bought and sold for immediate delivery.

Spread In the over the counter market spread refers to the difference between the ask and bid price quoted by a dealer.

Stakeholders The constituent groups in a firm, including stockholders, bondholders, suppliers, customers, employees, community neighbors, and creditors.

Standard Deviation A statistical measure of the dispersion, or variability, of possible outcomes around the expected value, or mean. Operationally, it is defined as the square root of the weighted average squared deviations of possible outcomes from the expected value. The standard deviation provides an absolute measure of risk.

Statement of Cash Flows A financial statement showing the effects of a firm's operating, investing, and financing activities on its cash balance.

Statement of Operations Another term for Income Statement.

Statement of Retained Earnings Statement that reconciles the retained earn-

ings number in the balance sheet with the net income figure from the income statement.

States of Nature Various events or combination of events that determine the outcome of an investment, e.g., return on an investment over a given future period may depend on the particular state of the economy that will transpire—strong, moderate, or poor state of the economy.

Stock Dividend A payment of additional shares of common stock to stockholders.

Stock Repurchase Plan or transaction by the firm to buy back its own stock.

Stock Split The issuance of a number of new shares in exchange for each old share held by a stockholder.

Stockholders' Equity The total of a firm's common stock at par, contributed capital in excess of par, and retained earnings accounts from the balance sheet. It sometimes is called the book value of the firm, owners' equity, shareholders' equity, or net worth.

Stockout Costs The cost of lost sales associated with the inability to fill orders from inventory.

Strong-Form Efficiency Market is strong-form efficient if security prices reflect all information, both public and private.

Subchapter S Corporation A form of corporation with 75 or fewer shareholders that has the limited liability of a corporate form of organization but earnings are taxed similar to a partnership.

Subordinated Debenture A bond with a claim on the issuing firm's assets that is junior to other forms of debt in the event of a liquidation. The claims of subordinated debenture holders can be met only after all the claims of senior creditors have been met.

Sunk Cost Refers to cost or outlay that already has been incurred. In capital budgeting because sunk costs cannot be recovered, they should not be considered in the decision to accept or reject a project.

Syndicate In investment banking refers to a group of investment bankers that get together to underwrite a security issue.

Systematic Risk That portion of the variability of an individual security's returns that is caused by the factors affecting the market as a whole. This also is called nondiversifiable risk.

Target Capital Structure The proportions of long-term debt, preferred stock, and common equity that a firm desires to have in its capital structure.

Tax Deduction An amount subtracted from taxable income. For a corporation with a 35 percent marginal tax rate, a $100 tax deduction reduces taxable income by $100 and reduces taxes owed by $35.

Tax Shield The amount of tax savings from the deductibility of interest payments on debt or depreciation in computing corporate income taxes.

Tender Offer A public announcement by a company or individual indicating that it will pay a price above the current market price for the shares "tendered" of a company it wishes to acquire.

10-K Form Annual financial statement report filed by corporations with the Securities and Exchange Commission.

10-Q Form Quarterly financial statement report filed by corporations with the Securities and Exchange Commission.

Term Structure of Interest Rates The pattern of interest rate yields for debt securities that are similar in all respects except for their length of time to maturity. The term structure of interest rates usually is represented by a graphic plot called a yield curve.

Terminal Warehouse Financing Agreement A loan agreement in which the inventory being pledged as collateral is stored in a bonded warehouse operated by a public warehousing company.

Ticker Unique 1 to 4 letter symbol used to identify a stock listed on an exchange.

Transaction Exposure The potential for a change in the value of a foreign-currency-denominated transaction due to a change in the exchange rate after the transaction is entered into but before it is settled.

Translation Exposure The change in owners' (accounting) equity because of a change in exchange rates that affects the "converted" value of foreign assets and liabilities.

Treasury Stock Common stock that has been reacquired by the issuing company.

Trend Analysis An examination of a firm's performance over time. It is frequently based on one or more financial ratios.

Trust Receipt A security agreement under which the borrower holds the inventory and proceeds from the sale of the inventory in trust for the lender. This is also known as floor planning.

Trustee The bondholder's representative in a public debt offering. The trustee is responsible for monitoring the borrower's compliance with the terms of the indenture.

Underwriting A process whereby a group of investment bankers agrees to purchase a new security issue at a set price and then offers it for sale to investors.

Underwriting Spread The difference between the selling price to the public of a new security offering and the proceeds received by the offering firm. This also is termed an underwriting discount.

Unit A combination of securities sold together, for example, a bond and a warrant sold as a unit.

Unsystematic Risk Risk that is unique to a firm. This is also called diversifiable risk.

Variable Cost Ratio Variable production, administrative, and marketing costs per dollar of sales.

Variable Costs Costs that vary in close relationship with changes in a firm's output level.

Warrant A company-issued long-term option to purchase a specified number of shares of the firm's stock at a particular price during a specified time period.

Weak-Form Efficiency Markets are considered to be weak form efficient if no investor can consistently earn excess or abnormal returns based on an investment strategy using historical stock market information such as past prices, returns, or volume of trading.

Weighted Average Cost of Capital The weighted average of the marginal costs of debt, equity, and preferred stock in proportion to their inclusion in the firm's target capital structure.

What-if Analysis See Sensitivity Analysis

Wilshire 5000 A broad based stock market index consisting of all NYSE, AMEX and the larger more active OTC stocks; in all over 6500 stocks are included.

Wire Transfer The process of electronically sending funds from one bank to another through the Federal Reserve System or private bank wire systems.

Working Capital The difference between a firm's current assets and current liabilities. The term working capital is used interchangeably with net working capital.

Yield to Maturity (YTM) The discount rate that equates the present value of all expected interest payments and the repayment of principal from a bond with the present bond price.

Zero-Balance System A payment system that uses a master disbursing account that services all other disbursing accounts. A zero balance is maintained in all but the master account until payments must be made.

Zero Coupon Bond A bond that pays no coupons. It is sold at a deep discount and the investor receives the face amount at the time of maturity.

SOLUTIONS TO SELF-TEST PROBLEMS

Chapter 2

ST1. The holding period return for TCBY stock is:

$$K_t = \frac{\$8.75 - \$11.00 + \$0.10}{\$11.00}$$

$K_t = -.1955 \; or - 19.55\%$

ST2. The purchase price for the Wal-Mart share is $50.46. One year later the share is assumed to double in price, $100.92 (=2 × $50.46). During the course of the year the expected dividend is $0.30 per share.

$$K_t = \frac{\$100.92 - \$50.46 + \$0.30}{\$50.46}$$

$K_t = 1.0059 \; or \; 100.59\%$

ST3. The holding period return for the AT&T Wireless Services (AWE) bond is:

$$K_t = \frac{\$1,146.50 - \$1,025.00 + \$81.25}{\$1,025.00}$$

$K_t = 0.1978 \; or \; 19.78\%$

Chapter 3

ST1.

Balance Sheet (in thousands of dollars)

Assets		Liabilities & Stockholders' Equity	
Cash	$ 1,500	Accounts payable	$12,500
Marketable securities	2,500	Accrued salaries and wages	12,500
Accounts receivable	15,000	Total current liabilities	$25,000
Inventory	33,000	Long-term debt	22,000
Total current assets	$52,000	Total liabilities	$47,000
Fixed assets (net)	35,000	Stockholders' equity:	
Total assets	$87,000	Common stock (par value)	$ 5,000
		Paid in capital	18,000
		Retained earnings	17,000
		Total stockholders' equity	$40,000
		Total liabilities and stockholders' equity	$87,000

ST2. Income Statement (in thousands of dollars)

Sales	$130,000
Cost of Sales	103,000
Gross Margin	27,000
Operating Expenses	16,000
Earnings before interest and taxes	$ 11,000
Interest Expense	3,000
Earnings before taxes	$ 8,000
Income tax	3,000
Earnings after taxes	$ 5,000

ST3.

	(in thousands of dollars)
Sales	$5,000
Cost of sales	2,800
Selling, general, and administrative expenses	900
Depreciation	400
Interest expense	400
Income before tax	500
Tax	200
Net income	$ 300

Income before tax is determined as follows:

Net income = Income before tax $(1 - \text{Tax rate})$

Income before tax = Net income$/(1 - \text{Tax rate})$

$$= \$300/(1 - .40)$$

$$= \$500$$

The maximum interest expense is $400.

ST4.

	(in thousands of dollars)	
Cash flows from operating activities		
Net income		$(4,500)
Adjustments to reconcile net income to net cash provided by operating activities		
Depreciation	$3,500	
Increase in receivables	(1,400)	
Increase in accounts payable	1,000	
Increase in deferred income tax liability	500	3,600
Net cash provided by operating activities		(900)
Cash flows from investing activities		
Increase in fixed assets	(3,000)	
Net cash provided by investing activities		(3,000)
Cash flows from financing activities		
Issuance of common stock	3,000	
Issuance of long-term debt	1,200	
Net cash provided by financing activities		$4,200
Net increase in cash		300
Cash, January 1, 2001		250
Cash, December 31, 2001		$550

a. The net cash flows provided from operations was negative: ($900). The firm had a net income (loss) of ($4,500). Adjustments of net income to net cash provided by operating activities equaled $3,600 yielding net cash flows from operating activities of ($900).

b. The increase in fixed assets of $3,000 was financed through the issuance of common stock and long-term debt.

c. As a loan officer I probably would not extend the loan of $1,200 since the firm experienced a loss of $4,500.

ST5.

Sales	$3,000,000
Less: Cost of goods sold	1,800,000
Gross profit margin	$1,200,000
Less: Operating expenses	800,000
Operating earnings before interest and taxes	400,000
Less interest expense	200,000
Earnings before tax (taxable income)	200,000

Tax calculation:

Total tax = $22,250 + .39($200,000 − 100,000) = $61,250

The marginal tax rate is 39 percent (34 percent plus 5 percent surcharge). The average tax rate is 30.63 percent ($61,250 divided by $200,000). Note that there are no tax consequences associated with the retirement of maturing debt or the payment of common and preferred stock dividends. None of those outlays is tax deductible.

Chapter 4

ST1. a. Current ratio

$$= \frac{\text{Current assets}}{\text{Current liabilities}} = \frac{\$52,000}{\$25,000} = 2.08$$

b. Quick ratio

$$= \frac{\text{Current assets} - \text{Inventories}}{\text{Current liabilities}} = \frac{\$52,000 - \$33,000}{\$25,000} = 0.76$$

ST2. a. Average collection period

$$= \frac{\text{Accounts receivable}}{\text{Annual credit sales}/365} = \frac{\$15,000}{\$130,000/365} = 42.1 \text{ days}$$

b. Inventory turnover

$$= \frac{\text{Cost of sales}}{\text{Average inventory}} = \frac{\$103,000}{\$33,000} = 3.12$$

c. Fixed asset turnover

$$= \frac{\text{Sales}}{\text{Net fixed assets}} = \frac{\$130,000}{\$35,000} = 3.71$$

d. Total asset turnover

$$= \frac{\text{Sales}}{\text{Total assets}} = \frac{\$130,000}{\$87,000} = 1.49$$

ST3. a. Debt ratio

$$= \frac{\text{Total debt}}{\text{Total assets}} = \frac{\$47,000}{\$87,000} = 0.54$$

b. Debt-to-equity ratio

$$= \frac{\text{Total debt}}{\text{Total equity}} = \frac{\$47,000}{\$40,000} = 1.18$$

c. Times interest earned

$$= \frac{\text{Earnings before interest and taxes (EBIT)}}{\text{Interest charges}} = \frac{\$11,000}{\$3,000} = 3.67$$

d. Fixed charge covered

$$= \frac{\text{EBIT} + \text{lease payments}}{\text{Interest} + \text{lease payments} + \text{preferred}} = \frac{\$11,000 + \$200}{\$3,000 + \$200} = 3.50$$
$$\text{dividends before tax} + \text{before tax sinking fund}$$

ST4. a. Gross profit margin

$$= \frac{\text{Sales} - \text{Cost of sales}}{\text{Sales}} = \frac{\$130,000 - \$103,000}{\$130,000} = 20.8\%$$

b. Net profit margin

$$= \frac{\text{Earnings after tax (EAT)}}{\text{Sales}} = \frac{\$5,000}{\$130,000} = 3.85\%$$

c. Return on investment

$$= \frac{\text{Earnings after tax (EAT)}}{\text{Total assets}} = \frac{\$5,000}{\$87,000} = 5.75\%$$

d. Return on stockholders' equity

$$= \frac{\text{Earnings after tax (EAT)}}{\text{Stockholder's equity}} = \frac{\$5,000}{\$40,000} = 12.5\%$$

ST5. a. Price-to-earnings ratio

$$= \frac{\text{Market price per share}}{\text{Current earnings per share}} = \frac{\$9.50}{\$5,000/5,000} = 9.50$$

b. Market-to-book ratio

$$= \frac{\text{Market price per share}}{\text{Book value per share}} = \frac{\$9.50}{\$8.00} = 1.19$$

ST6. Return on investment:

$$= \text{Net profit margin} \times \text{Total asset turnover}$$

$$= \frac{\$5,000}{\$130,000} \times \frac{\$130,000}{\$87,000} = 5.75\%$$

Return on stockholders' equity:

$$= \text{Net profit margin} \times \text{Total asset turnover} \times \text{Equity multiplier} =$$

$$= \frac{\$5,000}{\$130,000} \times \frac{\$130,000}{\$87,000} \times \frac{\$87,000}{\$40,000} = 12.5\%$$

Chapter 5

ST1. **a.** $FV_n = PV_0(1 + i)^n$ or $PV_0(FVIF_{i, n})$

$FV_5 = \$1,000(1.08)^5 = \$1,000(FVIF_{8, 5}) = \$1,000(1.469)$

$= \$1,469$

The calculator solution is as follows:

Enter: 5 8 −1,000

N	I/Y	PV

Compute: FV = 1,469.33

b. $FV_n = PV_0\left(1 + \dfrac{i}{m}\right)^{mn}$ or $PV_0(FVIF_{i/m, mn})$

$FV_5 = \$1,000(1.02)^{20} = \$1,000(FVIF_{2, 20}) = \$1,000(1.486)$

$= \$1,486$

The calculator solution is as follows:

Enter: 20 2 −1,000

N	I/Y	PV

Compute: FV = 1,485.95

ST2. $PVAN_0 = PMT(PVIFA_{i, n})$

$PVAN_0 = \$1,000\ (PVIFA_{12, 10})$

$= \$1,000(5.650)$

$= \$5,650$

The calculator solution is as follows:

Enter: 10 12 1,000

N	I/Y	PMT

Compute: PV = −5,650.22

ST3. $\text{PVAN}_0 = PMT \, (\text{PVIFA}_{i,n})$

$\quad\quad \text{PVAN}_3 = \$2,000(\text{PVIFA}_{14, 5})$

$\quad\quad\quad\quad = \$2,000(3.433)$

$\quad\quad\quad\quad = \$6,866$

The above step calculates the present value of the 5-year ordinary annuity at the beginning of year 4 (i.e., the end of year 3). Next, PVAN_3 must be discounted to the present:

$\quad\quad \text{PVAN}_0 = \text{PVAN}_3(\text{PVIF}_{14, 3})$

$\quad\quad\quad\quad = \$6,866(0.675)$

$\quad\quad\quad\quad = \$4,635$

The calculator solution is as follows:

Step 1: Calculate the present value of the annuity as of the beginning of year 4 or end of year 3

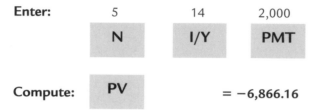

Enter: 5 [N] 14 [I/Y] 2,000 [PMT]

Compute: [PV] = −6,866.16

Step 2: Calculate the present value (year 0) cash flow of the above.

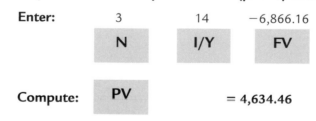

Enter: 3 [N] 14 [I/Y] −6,866.16 [FV]

Compute: [PV] = 4,634.46

ST4. $\quad FV_n = PV_0(\text{FVIF}_{i, n})$

$\quad\quad 1.52 = 0.90(\text{FVIF}_{i, 5})$

$\quad \text{FVIF}_{i, 5} = 1.689$

Using Table I and reading across the 5-year row, 1.685 is found in the 11 percent column. Thus, the growth rate is approximately 11 percent per year.

The calculator solution is as follows:

Enter: 5 [N] −0.90 [PV] 1.52 [FV]

Compute: [I/Y] = 11.05

ST5. $\quad PVAN_0 = \$50,000(PVIF_{10, 20})$

$\qquad\qquad = \$50,000(8.514)$

$\qquad\qquad = \$425,700$ (amount needed in account on 60th birthday)

$\qquad FVAN_{25} = PMT(FVIFA_{10, 25})$

$\qquad \$425,700 = PMT(98.347)$

$\qquad\qquad PMT = \$4,329$

The calculator solution is as follows:

Step 1: Calculate the amount needed on 60th birthday.

Enter:

20	10	50,000
N	I/Y	PMT

Compute: PV $\qquad\qquad = -425,678.19$

Step 2: Calculate the amount to be set aside each year.

Enter:

25	10	425,678.19
N	I/Y	FV

Compute: PMT $\qquad\qquad = -4,328.33$

Chapter 6

ST1. a. The percentage return outcomes for General Motors over the coming year are:

State of Economy	Probability	Return
Recession	0.20	-10%
Normal year	0.60	15%
Boom	0.20	25%

$$\hat{r} = \sum_{j=1}^{n} r_j p_j$$
$$= -10\%(0.20) + 15\%(0.60) + 25\%(0.20)$$
$$= 12\%$$

b. $\sigma = \sqrt{\sum_{j=1}^{n}(r_j - \hat{r})^2 p_j}$

$$= [(-10 - 12)^2(0.20) + (15 - 12)^2(0.60)$$
$$+ (25 - 12)^2(0.20)]^{1/2} = (136)^{1/2}$$
$$= 11.66\ \%$$

ST2. a. $r_p = \sum_{j=1}^{n} w_j r_j$

$r_p = 0.25\,(10.7\%) + 0.25\,(12.5) + 0.25\,(11.9\%) + 0.25\,(11.3)$

$r_p = 11.6\%$

b. $\beta_p = \sum_{j=1}^{n} w_j \beta_j$

$\beta_p = 0.25\,(0.95) + 0.25\,(1.25) + 0.25\,(1.15) + 0.25\,(1.05)$

$\beta_p = 1.1$

ST3. The answers are obtained using the security market line equation:

$$k_j = \hat{r}_f + \beta_j(\hat{r}_m - \hat{r}_f)$$

Note that the market risk premium, $\hat{r}_m - \hat{r}_f$, is 7%.

a. $k_j = 4 + 0.60\,(7)$
$= 8.2\%$

b. $k_j = 6 + 0.60(7)$
$= 10.2\%$

c. $k_j = 4 + 0.60(9)$
$= 9.4\%$

d. $k_j = 4 + 0.85(9)$
$= 11.65\%$

Chapter 7

ST1. $P_0 = I(\text{PVIFA}_{k_d,n}) + M(\text{PVIF}_{k_d,n})$

Try 9 percent:

$$P_0 = \$73.75(\text{PVIFA}_{9,12}) + \$1,000(\text{PVIF}_{9,12})$$
$$= \$73.75(7.161) + \$1,000(0.356)$$
$$= \$884.12$$

Since the present value of future interest and principal payments is approximately equal to the selling price of $884, the yield to maturity of the bond is 9 percent.

The calculator solution is as follows:

Enter:	12	−884	73.75	1,000
	N	PV	PMT	FV

Compute:	I/Y		= 8.99

ST2. $P_0 = I(\text{PVIFA}_{k_d,n}) + M(\text{PVIF}_{k_d,n})$

$\$2,250 = \$5,000(\text{PVIF}_{k_d,11})$, note $I = 0$ since this is a zero coupon bond.

$(\text{PVIF}_{k_d,11}) = 0.450$

Using Table II on the insert and reading across the 11-year row, 0.450 is found between the 7 percent (0.475) and 8 percent (0.429) interest rate columns so the YTM is between 7 and 8 percent. Using the calculator the answer is 7.53 percent:

Enter:

	11	−2,250	0	5,000
	N	PV	PMT	FV

Compute: I/Y $= 7.53$

ST3. $P_0 = I(\text{PVIFA})_{k_d,n} + M(\text{PVIF}_{k_d,n})$

$\qquad = \$90(\text{PVIFA}_{10,\,10}) + \$1,000(\text{PVIF}_{10,\,10})$

$\qquad = \$90(6.145) + \$1,000(0.386)$

$\qquad = \$939.05 \text{ (or } \$939)$

If the investor pays \$939.05, the expected yeld to maturity is 10 percent. If the investor pays more than \$939.05, the expected yield to maturity is less than 10 percent. Therefore, the maximum price the investor should be willing to pay is \$939.05. Note using the calculator the answer is \$938.55:

Enter:

	10	10	90	1,000
	N	I/Y	PMT	FV

Compute: PV $= -938.55$

ST4: The approximate formula for the Fisher effect is given by Equation 7.12:

$$r_f = \hat{r}_f + i_n$$

Expressing this equation in terms of the nominal risk-free rate and substituting the known values we get:

$$\hat{r}_f = 6 - 3.4 = 2.6$$

Therefore, the real risk-free rate is 2.6 percent.

Chapter 8

ST1. $P_0 = \dfrac{\$3.00}{0.12 - .04} = \$37.50$

ST2. $g = k_e - \dfrac{D_1}{P_0} = .12 - \dfrac{\$2.00}{\$24.00} = 0.03667 = 3.67\%$

ST3. $P_0 = \dfrac{D_p}{k_e} = \dfrac{\$25.00 \times .045}{.08} = \dfrac{\$1.125}{.08} = \$14.0625$

Chapter 9

ST1. Net investment (NINV) calculation:

Asset cost	$1,200,000
+ Delivery and installation	100,000
Installed cost	$1,300,000
− Proceeds from sale of old asset	150,000
− Tax savings on loss from sale of old asset ($50,000 (loss) × 0.4)	20,000
NINV	$1,130,000

ST2. a. Net investment (NINV) calculation:

Asset cost	$700,000
+ Delivery and installation	50,000
Installed cost	$750,000
− Proceeds from sale of old asset	275,000
+ Tax on sale of old asset ($275,000 − $250,000)(0.4)	10,000
+ Net working capital	40,000
NINV	$525,000

b. Net cash flow (NCF) calculation:

$$NCF_1 = [\$100,000 - (-\$20,000) - (\$150,000 - \$50,000)]$$
$$(1 - 0.40) + (\$150,000 - \$50,000) - \$10,000$$
$$= \$102,000$$

$$NCF_{2-4} = [\$100,000 - (-\$20,000) - (\$150,000 - \$50,000)]$$
$$(1 - 0.40) + (\$150,000 - \$50,000) - \$0$$
$$= \$112,000 \text{ (Note: in years 2–4 there is no additional investment in net working capital)}$$

$$NCF_5 = NCF_{2-4} + \text{recovery of accumulated net working capital investment} + \text{after-tax cash flow from sale of new unit}$$
$$= \$112,000 + \$50,000 + \$70,000 (1 - 0.4)$$
$$= \$204,000$$

Chapter 10

ST1. $NPV = -(\$20,000 + \$5,000) + \$7,000 (PVIFA_{11,10}) + \$5,000 (PVIF_{11,10})$
$$= \$17,983$$

The value of the firm, and therefore the shareholders' wealth, is increased by $17,983 as a result of undertaking the project. The project is acceptable because its NPV is positive.

ST2. $NPV = PV \text{ net cash flows} - \text{Net investment}$
$$0 = \$75,000 (PVIFA_{r,8}) - \$360,000$$
$$(PVIFA_{r,8}) = 4.80$$
$$r \approx 13\% \text{ (from Table IV)}$$
$$PI = \frac{\$75,000(PVIFA_{12,8})}{\$360,000} = 1.035$$

ST3. a. Project G:

$$\$10,000 = \$5,000 \ (\text{PVIFA}_{r,3})$$
$$(\text{PVIFA}_{r,3}) = 2.0$$
$$r \approx 23.4\% \ (\text{from Table IV})$$

Project H:

$$\$10,000 = \$17,000 \ (\text{PVIFA}_{r,3})$$
$$(\text{PVIFA}_{r,3}) = 0.588$$
$$r \approx 19.3\% \ (\text{from Table II})$$

b. $\text{NPV}_G = -\$10,000 + \$5,000 \ (\text{PVIFA}_{12,3})$
$$= \$2,010$$

$\text{NPV}_H = -\$10,000 + \$17,000 \ (\text{PVIFA}_{12,3})$
$$= \$2,104$$

c. Project H should be adopted because it has the higher NPV. It is assumed that the firm's reinvestment opportunities are represented more accurately by the firm's cost of capital than by the unique internal rate of return of either project.

Chapter 11

ST1. $\$1,068 = \$70(\text{PVIFA}_{k_d,10}) + \$1,000(\text{PVIF}_{k_d,10})$

Using the financial calculator the answer is $k_d = 6.1\%$

Therefore, $k_i = 6.1\%(1 - .4) = 3.7\%$

ST2. $k_e = \dfrac{D_1}{P_0} + g = \dfrac{\$3.50(1 + 0.068)}{\$60} + 0.068 = 0.13 \text{ or } 13\%$

ST3. $k_e = r_f + \beta(r_m - r_f) = 3.5\% + 1.3 \ (6.4\%) = 11.8\%$

ST4. $k_a = 0.25(k_i) + 0.15(k_p) + 0.60(k_e)$
$$= 0.25(5\%) + 0.15(8.5\%) + 0.60(11\%)$$
$$= 9.1\%$$

Chapter 12

ST1. a. DOL at sales level $\$5,000,000 = \dfrac{\text{Sales} - \text{Variable costs}}{\text{EBIT}}$

$$= \dfrac{\$5,000,000 - \$1,000,000}{\$2,000,000}$$

$$= 2.0$$

DFL at EBIT level of $\$2,000,000 = \dfrac{\text{EBIT}}{\text{EBIT} - I - \dfrac{D_p}{(1 - T)}}$

$$= \dfrac{\$2,000,000}{\$2,000,000 - \$500,000 - \dfrac{\$100,000}{(1 - 0.4)}}$$

$$= 1.5$$

$$\text{DCL at sales level of \$5,000,000} = \frac{\text{Sales} - \text{Variable costs}}{\text{EBIT} - I - \dfrac{D_p}{(1-T)}}$$

$$= \frac{\$5,000,000 - \$1,000,000}{\$2,000,000 - \$500,000 - \dfrac{\$100,000}{(1-0.4)}}$$

$$= 3.0$$

Check: DCL = DOL × DFL
$$= 2.0 \times 1.5$$
$$= 3.0$$

b. Current EPS $= \dfrac{\$800,000}{400,000 \text{ shares}} = \$2.00$

A sales increase to $5.5 million represents a 10 percent increase in sales. Hence, EPS should increase by 30 percent (10% × 3.0), to $2.60 ($2.00 + .30 (2.00)).

ST2. a. $Q_b = \dfrac{F}{P-V} = \dfrac{\$10,000,000}{\$4,000 - \$2,000} = 5,000$ units

b. EBIT $= PQ - VQ - F$

$\$2,000,000 \quad = \$4,000\,Q - \$2,000\,Q - \$10,000,000$

$\$12,000,000 = \$2,000\,Q$

$Q = 12,000,000/2,000$

$Q = 6,000$ units per year

Chapter 13

ST1.

Proportion of Debt $\left(\dfrac{B}{B+E}\right)$	Cost of Debt, k_i	Cost of Equity, k_e	Weighted Average Cost of Capital, k_a
0.00	—	10.0%	10.00%
0.10	4.0%	10.1	9.49
0.20	4.2	10.3	9.08
0.30	4.4	10.8	8.88
0.40	4.8	11.4	8.76
0.50	5.5	12.5	9.00
0.60	6.6	14.5	9.76
0.70	8.0	18.0	11.00

Note: $k_a = \left(\dfrac{B}{B+E}\right)k_i + \left(\dfrac{E}{B+E}\right)k_e$

The optimal capital structure consists of 40 percent debt and 60 percent equity since this minimizes the firm's cost of capital.

ST2. a.

$$\frac{(\text{EBIT} - I_d)(1 - T) - D_p}{N_d} = \frac{(\text{EBIT} - I_e)(1 - T) - D_p}{N_e}$$

$$\frac{(\text{EBIT} - \$18)(1 - 0.40)}{100} = \frac{(\text{EBIT} - \$0)(1 - 0.40)}{110}$$

$$\text{EBIT} = \$198\,(\text{million})$$

b. Since $250 million is to the right of the indifference point the more leveraged plan—Plan II or the Debt Plan—should be selected, as it would generate the higher EPS.

Chapter 14

ST1. a. Post–Stock Dividend Common Stockholders' Equity

Common stock ($1 par, 120,000 shares)	$ 120,000
Contributed capital in excess of par	2,480,000
Retained earnings	3,400,000
Total common stockholders' equity	$6,000,000

A total of $1,600,000 (20,000 shares × an assumed market price of $80 per share) is transferred from retained earnings to the other stockholders' equity accounts. Of this $1,600,000, $20,000 ($1 par × 20,000 shares) is added to the common stock account and the remaining $1,580,000 is added to the contributed capital in excess of par account.

b. Post–stock dividend price $= \dfrac{\$80}{1 + 0.20} = \$66.67$

ST2. a.

EBIT	$1,000,000
Interest	200,000
EBT	$ 800,000
Taxes	320,000
EAT	$ 480,000

Earnings per share $= \dfrac{\$480,000}{50,000 \text{ shares}} = \$9.60$

b. Dividends per share $= \dfrac{\$100,000}{50,000 \text{ shares}} = \$2.00$

Dividend payout ratio $= \dfrac{\$2.00}{\$9.60} = 20.8\%$

c. Dividend yield $= \dfrac{\text{Dividend per share}}{\text{Price per share}}$

$$0.02 = \frac{\$2.00}{\text{Price per share}}$$

Price per share $= \$100.00$

d. Equivalent (pre–stock dividend)

Dividend per share: $\dfrac{\$2.00}{2} = \$1.00$

Dividend rate increase $= \dfrac{\$1.10 - \$1.00}{\$1.00} = 0.10 \text{ or } 10\%$

ST3. To receive the dividend, you must purchase the stock the day before it goes ex-dividend. The ex-dividend date is 2 business days prior to the record date. Since the record date is June 16, which is a Monday, the stock goes ex-dividend on June 12, Thursday. To receive the dividend the latest you can buy the stock is on June 11, Wednesday.

Chapter 15

ST1. Forecasted income and retained earnings for 20X3:

Sales	$25,000,000
EAT	$1,000,000
Dividends	$300,000
Forecasted addition to retained earnings	$700,000

Forecasted balance sheet for 20X3:

Cash	$ 1,000,000	Accounts payable	$ 3,750,000
Accounts receivable	1,875,000	Notes payable	3,000,000
Inventories	7,500,000	Long-term debt	2,000,000
Net fixed assets	3,750,000	**Additional financing needed**	**1,175,000**
		Stockholders' equity	4,200,000
Total assets	$14,125,000	**Total liabilities and equity**	**$14,125,000**

Note:
- Cash stays constant.
- Accounts receivable equal 7.5 percent of sales.
- Inventories equal 30 percent of sales.
- Net fixed assets equal 15 percent of sales.
- Accounts payable equal 15 percent of sales.
- Notes payable and long-term debt remain constant.
- Stockholders' equity increases by the amount of forecasted addition to retained earnings of $700,000.

Additional financing needed is $1,175,000. This can also be solved algebraically:

Additional financing needed =

$$\left(\frac{\$10,500,000}{\$20,000,000}(\$5,000,000) - \frac{\$3,000,000}{\$20,000,000}(\$5,000,000) \right) - (\$1,000,000 - \$300,000)$$

$$= \$1,175,000$$

Note: $10,500,000 = Assets that vary with sales
       $ 3,000,000 = Accounts payable (current liability that varies with sales)
       $ 5,000,000 = Sales increase
       $20,000,000 = Current sales

ST2.

Focus Eyewear, Inc.
Cash Budget Worksheet (for Purchases)

	December	January	February	March	April
		First Quarter, 2004			
Estimated sales	$825,000	$730,000	$840,000	$920,000	$700,000
Purchases*	504,000	552,000	420,000		
Payment for purchases**		504,000	552,000	420,000	

*Purchases are estimated at 60% of sales two months later.
**Payments on purchases are made one month after the purchase.

Cash Budget
First Quarter, 2004

	January	February	March
Sales	$730,000	$840,000	$920,000
Projected cash balance beginning of month	$100,000	$100,000	$100,000
Receipts:			
Cash sales	730,000	840,000	920,000
Total cash available	$830,000	940,000	1,020,000
Disbursements:			
Payment of accounts payable	$504,000	$552,000	$420,000
Wages and salaries	270,000	270,000	270,000
Rent	32,000	32,000	32,000
Other expenses	10,000	12,000	14,000
Taxes	135,000	—	—
Purchase of retail property	—	85,000	—
Total disbursements	$951,000	$951,000	$736,000
Excess of available cash over disbursements	($121,000)	($11,000)	$284,000
Cash loans needed to maintain balance			
of $100,000	221,000	111,000	—
Loan repayment	—	—	(184,000)
Projected cash balance, end of month	$100,000	$100,000	$100,000

Based on the pro forma cash budget Focus Eyewear should plan on borrowing $221,000 in January and an additional $111,000 in February. The firm should be able to pay back $184,000 in March. Projections beyond the first quarter of 2004 should be undertaken to see when the firm can completely repay the loans undertaken in January and February.

Chapter 16

ST1. a. Inventory conversion period $= \dfrac{\text{Average inventory}}{\text{Cost of sales}/365}$

$$= \frac{\$2,120}{\$6,946/365} = 111.4 \text{ days}$$

b. Receivables conversion period $= \dfrac{\text{Accounts receivable}}{\text{Annual credit sales}/365}$

$$= \frac{\$2,075}{\$11,990/365} = 63.2 \text{ days}$$

c. Operating cycle = Inventory conversion period
      + Receivables conversion period
      = 111.4 + 63.2 = 174.6 days

d. Payables deferral period =

$$\frac{\text{Accounts payable} + \text{Salaries and benefits payable}}{(\text{Cost of sales} + \text{Selling, general, and admin. expenses})/365}$$

$$= \frac{724 + 332}{(6,946 + 2,394)/365} = 41.3 \text{ days}$$

e. Cash conversion cycle = Operating cycle − Payables deferral period
      = 174.6 − 41.3 = 133.3 days

ST2. a. Increase in average cash balance = Average daily sales × Decrease in payment processing time
$$= (\$219{,}000{,}000/365) \times 2$$
$$= \$1{,}200{,}000$$

b. Increase in (pretax) earnings = Increase in average cash balance × Interest rate
$$= \$1{,}200{,}000 \times 0.07 = \$84{,}000$$

ST3. a. Reduction in collection time = Reduction in mailing time + Reduction in processing and check clearing time = $(3.0 - 1.5) + (5.0 - 2.0) = 4.5$ days

Average daily collections = Annual credit sales/365
$$= \$292{,}000{,}000/365 = \$800{,}000$$

Amount of funds released = Average daily collections × Reduction in collection time
$$= \$800{,}000 \times 4.5 = \$3{,}600{,}000$$

b. Annual (pretax) earnings on released funds = Amount of funds released × interest rate = $\$3{,}600{,}000 \times 0.10 = \$360{,}000$

c. Annual bank processing fee = Fixed cost + Number of payments per year × Variable cost per payment = $\$50{,}000 + (600{,}000 \times \$0.20)$
$$= \$170{,}000$$

d. Net (pretax) benefits = Annual (pretax) earnings on released funds + Reduction in firm's payment processing costs − Annual bank processing fee = $\$360{,}000 + \$40{,}000 - \$170{,}000 = \$230{,}000$

Chapter 17

ST1. a.
$$\text{AFC} = \frac{\text{Percentage discount}}{100 - \text{Percentage discount}} \times \frac{365}{\text{Credit period} - \text{Discount period}}$$
$$= \frac{2}{100 - 2} \times \frac{365}{120 - 10} = 6.77\%$$

b.
$$\text{AFC} = \frac{2}{100 - 2} \times \frac{365}{122 - 30} = 8.10\%$$

ST2. a.
$$\text{AFC} = \frac{\text{Interest cost} + \text{Commitment fee}}{\text{Usable funds}} \times \frac{365}{\text{Maturity (days)}}$$
Interest cost = $0.07\ (\$2{,}000{,}000) = \$140{,}000$
Commitment fee = $0.005\ (\$8{,}000{,}000) = \$40{,}000$
Usable funds = $0.90\ (\$2{,}000{,}000) = \$1{,}800{,}000$
$$\text{AFC} = \frac{\$140{,}000 + \$40{,}000}{\$1{,}800{,}000} \times \frac{365}{365} = 10.0\%$$

b. Interest cost = $0.07\ (\$7{,}000{,}000) = \$490{,}000$
Commitment fee = $0.005\ (\$3{,}000{,}000) = \$15{,}000$
Usable funds = $0.90\ (\$7{,}000{,}000) = \$6{,}300{,}000$
$$\text{AFC} = \frac{\$490{,}000 + \$15{,}000}{\$6{,}300{,}000} \times \frac{365}{365} = 8.02\%$$

ST3. $\text{AFC} = \dfrac{\text{Interest cost} + \text{Placement fee}}{\text{Usable funds}} \times \dfrac{365}{\text{Maturity (days)}}$

Interest costs $= 0.045\,(\$25,000,000)(91/365) = \$280,479$

Usable funds $= \$25,000,000 - \$280,479 - \$75,000 = \$24,644,521$

$\text{AFC} = \dfrac{\$280,479 + \$75,000}{\$24,644,521} \times \dfrac{365}{91} = 5.79\%$

ST4. a.

Average level of receivables		$4,000,000
Less Factoring commission	0.02 × $4,000,000 =	−80,000
Less Reserve for returns	0.10 × $4,000,000 =	−400,000
Amount available for advance before interest is deducted		$3,520,000
Less Interest on advance	0.12 × $3,520,000 × $\frac{70}{365}$ =	−81,008
Amount of funds advanced by factor (Usable funds)		$3,438,992

b.

Interest costs		$ 81,008
Factoring commission		80,000
Total interest and factoring costs		$ 161,008
Less Credit department savings per 70-day period	$3,000 × $\frac{70}{30}$ =	−7,000
Less Average bad-debt losses per 70-day period	$9,000 × $\frac{70}{30}$ =	−21,000
Net financing cost per 70 days		$ 133,008

$\text{AFC} = \dfrac{\$133,008}{\$3,438,992} \times \dfrac{365}{70} = 20.17\%$

Chapter 18

ST1. Annualized forward premium or discount $= \left(\dfrac{F - S_0}{S_0}\right)\left(\dfrac{12}{n}\right)(100\%)$

$= \left(\dfrac{\$0.7312 - \$0.7297}{\$0.7297}\right)\left(\dfrac{12}{3}\right)(100\%)$

$= 0.82\%$

The forward premium implies that the spot rate is expected to increase, that is, the Swiss franc will appreciate relative to the U.S. dollar.

ST2. A U.S. trader could sell U.S. dollars, buy spot Canadian dollars, and invest in Canadian securities to earn 12 percent. Simultaneously, the trader could sell Canadian dollars forward at a 3 percent annual discount. At the end of the forward period, the trader could convert Canadian dollars back to U.S. dollars. The net effect of these transactions is the trader earns 9 percent (12% interest less 3% depreciation in value) compared with the 8 percent return available in the U.S. market.

ST3. a. Yen price = 140 yen/dollar × $12,000 = 1,680,000 yen

b. Yen price = 120 yen/dollar × $12,000 = 1,440,000 yen

A decline in the value of the dollar relative to the yen makes U.S. goods more attractive abroad.

ST4. IFE:

$\dfrac{S_1 - \$0.68}{\$0.68} = 0.04 - 0.05$

$S_1 = \$0.68\,(0.04 - 0.05) + \$0.68$

$= \$0.6732$

INDEX

A	Assets	FV	Future value
AFC	Annual financing cost	FVAN	Future value of an annuity
ATSV	After-tax salvage value	FVAND	Future value of an annuity due
B	(1) Debt in a firm's capital structure	FVIF	Future value interest factor
	(2) Market value of a firm's debt	FVIFA	Future value interest factor of an annuity
β_j	Beta (systematic risk) for security j	g	Expected annual growth rate in earnings, dividends, and/or stock price
CAPM	Capital Asset Pricing Model		
CF	Cash flow	i	Interest rate per time period
CL	Current liabilities	I	Interest payments before taxes
D	Common stock dividends	I	Interest payment on a bond
Dep	Depreciation expense	i_{eff}	Annual effective interest rate
DCL	Degree of combined leverage	i_f	Interest rate in the foreign currency country
DFL	Degree of financial leverage		
DJIA	Dow Jones Industrial Average	IFE	International Fisher effect
DOL	Degree of operating leverage	i_h	Interest rate in the home currency country
D_p	Preferred stock dividends		
E	(1) Common equity in a firm's capital structure	IRP	Interest rate parity
		IRR	Internal rate of return
	(2) Market value of a firm's equity	k	A percentage required return or cost of capital; discount rate
e	Exponential e; value ≈ 2.71828		
EAPR	Effective annual percentage rate	k_a	Weighted (marginal) cost of capital
EAT	Earnings after taxes	k_d	Required return on a bond; pretax cost of debt; yield to maturity on a bond
EBIT	Earnings before interest and taxes		
EBITDA	Earnings before interest, taxes, depreciation, and amortization	k_e	Required return on common stock; cost of internal equity
EBT	Earnings before taxes	k_i	After-tax cost of debt
EPS	Earnings per share	k_j	Required return for security j
EVA	Economic value added	k_p	Required return on preferred stock; Cost of preferred stock financing
F	(1) Forward rate in foreign exchange		
	(2) Fixed costs	k_t	Holding period return for period t
FCF	Free cash flow	LIBOR	London interbank offer rate
FIFO	First-in, first-out inventory valuation	LIFO	Last-in, first-out inventory valuation